About Pearson

Pearson is the world's learning company, with presence across 70 countries worldwide. Our unique insights and world-class expertise come from a long history of working closely with renowned teachers, authors and thought leaders, as a result of which, we have emerged as the preferred choice for millions of teachers and learners across the world.

We believe learning opens up opportunities, creates fulfilling careers and hence better lives. We hence collaborate with the best of minds to deliver you class-leading products, spread across the Higher Education and Test Preparation spectrum.

Superior learning experience and improved outcomes are at the heart of everything we do. This product is the result of one such effort.

Your feedback plays a critical role in the evolution of our products and you can contact us at reachus@pearson.com. *We look forward to it.*

About Pearson

UGC NET

Sociology

2025

THIRD EDITION

Manoj Sonker

Pearson

ISBN 978-93-615-9793-0

First Impression

Published by Pearson India Education Services Pvt. Ltd, CIN: U72200TN2005PTC057128.

Head Office: 1st Floor, Berger Tower, Plot No. C-001A/2, Sector 16B, Noida - 201 301, Uttar Pradesh, India.
Registered Office: Featherlite, 'The Address' 5th Floor, Survey No 203/10B, 200 Ft MMRD Road, Zamin Pallavaram, Chennai – 600 044.
Website: in.pearson.com, Email: companysecretary.india@pearson.com

Compositor: Satish Kumar Shrivastava
Printed in India by Rajkamal Electric Press, Kundli, Haryana-131 028.

Table of Contents

UNIT II: RESEARCH METHODOLOGY AND METHODS

UNIT III: BASIC CONCEPTS AND INSTITUTIONS

UNIT IV: RURAL AND URBAN TRANSFORMATIONS

UNIT V: STATE POLITICS AND DEVELOPMENT

UNIT VI: ECONOMY AND SOCIETY

UNIT VII: ENVIRONMENT AND SOCIETY

UNIT VIII: FAMILY, MARRIAGE, AND KINSHIP

UNIT IX: SCIENCE, TECHNOLOGY, AND SOCIETY

UNIT X: CULTURE AND SYMBOLIC TRANSFORMATION

APPENDIX

MOCK TESTS

Preface

Through this book, my aim is to help every student who dreams to qualify UGC NET/JRF, and specifically to those ones who face difficulties in preparing for the exam due to factors like financial constraints, or remote location. This is my genuine attempt to cover all aspects of the syllabus in detail, which will assist in your journey of qualifying UGC NET/JRF. The curriculum of the University Grants Commission for the National Eligibility Test Sociology– for lectureship has been dynamically evolving over the years. It now encompasses a larger field of human learning, including Economic Sociology, Political Sociology, Sociology of Education, Research and many more. We have made consistent efforts to incorporate each and every topic of the syllabus comprehensively, taking utmost care to provide up-to-date and reliable information. This book will guide the aspirants to qualify one of the difficult competitive examinations in India: National Eligibility Test and Junior Research Fellowship (NET-JRF). We are pleased to publish our book on UGC NET-JRF for Sociology subject with an integrated approach.

The structure of this book was considerably altered following consultation with subject matter experts to match it with the demands of new curriculum and make it compatible with the current teaching techniques. Each volume offers a considerable number of multiple-choice questions to engage students in the learning process. The purpose is to acquaint potential candidates with current trends and question formats.

To enable better usability and to accommodate additional content, the book has been divided into 10 Units as per the syllabus given by UGC.

Key Highlights

- The book has been organized to aid the applicant in learning, comprehending, and retaining knowledge for a longer length of time.
- Important information on the topic of discussion is provided in concise manner. These cutting-edge tit-bits of knowledge make learning more engaging and also enhances the quality of learning.
- Comprehensive coverage of syllabus helps students to grasp the subject knowledge and readily comprehend examination questions.
- These MCQ-based practice questions together with previous year's papers at end of every unit will assist students to gain a deeper understanding of the learned concepts.

I genuinely hope that readers will enjoy and benefit from the book. Any feedback or suggestions for enrichment of the content would be appreciated and will significantly contribute towards making this book an outstanding resource.

Manoj Sonker

Acknowledgement

I would like to take this opportunity to acknowledge everyone who has been a part of preparation of this book. Special gratitude towards my parents, students and friends, who are the constant source of inspiration for my achievements till date.

Manoj Sonker

About The Author

Manoj Sonker, a senior faculty in a prestigious edtech company, holds a Bachelor's degree in Chemical Engineering from MITS, Gwalior and a Master's Degree in Sociology. He has also qualified UGC NET Sociology (Dec. 2021 & June 2022 Merged Session), (Dec. 2020 & June 2021 Merged Session), (June 2020) and (December 2019 Session). He is an Educator, Career Counsellor, and Motivator. He has an experience of 15 years in the field of teaching. He is also the founder of 'The Path to Success' YouTube Channel, a platform for reaching out to students of sociology. Under his valuable guidance hundreds of students have been qualifying NET/JRF every year.

UGC NET Sociology January 2025

1. Which of the following are examples of 'Fallacy of Reification' done by W.I. Thomas 'Four Wishes'?

A. Experiencing new situation
B. Securing the recognition of others
C. Hypothetical participation
D. Retaining feelings of security
E. Eliciting response from others

Choose the correct answer from the options given below:

(a) A, B, D, E only
(b) A, B, C, D only
(c) B, C, D, E only
(d) A, C, D, E only

2. Match the List I with List II

List I	List II
A. Article 51 (g)	I. Collection and disposal of garbage (New Delhi Municipal Corporation)
B. Article 21 read with Article 48 (A)	II. Pollution free water
C. Subhash Kumar vs. State of Bihar	III. To protect and improve the natural environment
D. M.C. Mehta vs. Union of India	IV. Conversion of vehicles to CNG

Choose the correct answer from the options given below:

(a) A-I, B-II, C-III, D-IV
(b) A-II, B-I, C-III, D-IV
(c) A-IV, B-I, C-II, D-III
(d) A-III, B-I, C-II, D-IV

3. Human sexuality freed from the needs of reproduction and moulded by individual choices is called:

(a) Sexuality
(b) Plasticsexuality
(c) Heterosexuality
(d) Homosexuality

4. Match the List I with List II

List I	List II
A. Transsexual Man	I. A man who becomes a women
B. Transsexual Women	II. A women who regularly dresses as a man
C. Transvestite Women	III. A man who regularly dresses as a women
D. Transvestite Man	IV. A women becomes a man

Choose the correct answer from the options given below;

(a) A-III, B-II, C-IV, D-I
(b) A-II, B-III, C-I, D-IV
(c) A-IV, B-I, C-II, D-III
(d) A-I, B-II, C-IV, D-III

5. Which one of the following will be categorized as an achieved status?

(a) Sex
(b) Age
(c) Caste
(d) Marital Status

6. Arrange the village studies of India in chronological order:

A. Kota village of Nilgiri Hills
B. Bisipara and Bolscopa villages in the hills of Odisha
C. Kumbapettao village of Tanjore of Madras state
D. Senapur village of Eastern U.P.
E. Kisangarhi village of U.P.

Choose the correct answer from the options given below:

(a) C, B, A, E, D
(b) E, D, B, A, C
(c) B, C, D, E, A
(d) A, B, E, C, D

7. Match the List I with List II

List I (Authors)	List II (Books)
A. Karl Marx	I. The Elementary Forms of Religious Life
B. Max Weber	II. Course de Philosophie Positive
C. Emile Durkheim	III. The Protestant Ethics and Spirit of Capitalism
D. Auguste Comte	IV. The Economic and Political Manuscript of 1844

Choose the correct answer from the options given below:

(a) A-I, B-IV, C-III, D-II
(b) A-IV, B-III, C-I, D-II
(c) A-III, B-I, C-II, D-IV
(d) A-II, B-I, C-IV, D-III

8. Who rejected the idea that sociologists should study individual psychology?
(a) Talcott Parsons
(b) Max Weber
(c) Emile Durkheim
(d) Vilfredo Pareto

9. The divisions of caste, class, gender and ethnicity combine to produce complex forms of social inequality. The statement is closest to the idea of whom?
(a) R.W. Connell
(b) K.W. Crenshaw
(c) Mannuel Castells
(d) Michel Foucault

10. Arrange the following in order in which penal system tackles with crime:
A. Deterrence
B. Rehabilitation
C. Restoration
D. Incapacitation
E. Retribution

Choose the correct answer from the options given below:

(a) B, C, A, E, D
(b) A, B, C, D, E
(c) A, B, C, E, D
(d) B, A, C, D, E

11. Non-orthodox political action reflects which of the following characteristics?
A. Mass movements
B. Violence
C. Collective attempt
D. Common goals
E. Conventional goals

Choose the correct answer from the options given below:

(a) A, C, D, E only
(b) B, C, D, E only
(c) C, A, D, B only
(d) A, B, C, E only

12. 'The use of communicative power as well as material class struggles as being central to the overthrow of capitalism'. Who associates with this statement?
(a) Karl Marx (b) A. Gramsci
(c) D. Harvey (d) R. Miliband

13. Who among the following did the famous study on Nuer society?
(a) Robin Fox
(b) Evans-Pritchard
(c) G.P. Murdock
(d) Lucy Mair

14. Arrange the publication of Foucault's books in chronological order.
A. Archaeology of Knowledge and Discourse on Language
B. Madness and Civilization
C. The Order of Things: An Archeology of Human Science
D. The Birth of the Clinic: An Archaeology of Medical Perception
E. Discipline and Punish: The Birth of the Prison

Choose the correct answer from the options given below:

(a) B, E, C, D, A
(b) A, C, E, B, D
(c) B, D, C, A, E
(d) A, D, B, E, C

15. J. Habermas emphasizes on three basic types of knowledge that encompass the full range of human reason. These three basic types of knowledge are:
A. Empirical analytic knowledge
B. Desirable knowledge
C. Hermeneutic-historical knowledge
D. Critical knowledge
E. Empirical theoretical knowledge

Choose the correct answer from the options given below:

(a) A, C and D only
(b) B, A and C only
(c) B, C, D and E only
(d) A, B, and D only

16. Match the List I with List II

List I	List II
A. Social Institution	I. Group of people united for a specific purpose or limited number of purposes
B. Mob	II. A collection of individual interacting with each other under recognisable structure
C. Social Group	III. Enduring and acceptable forms of procedure governing the relation between individuals and groups
D. Association	IV. Unruly crowd characterized by instability and disorder

Choose the correct answer from the options given below:

(a) A-IV, B-II, C-I, D-III
(b) A-I, B-II, C-IV, D-III
(c) A-III, B-IV, C-II, D-I
(d) A-II, B-I, C-III, D-IV

17. Who suggested that an interpretation that breaks with common sense?
(a) Talcott Parsons
(b) Emile Durkheim
(c) Robert K. Merton
(d) Max Weber

18. Who is the author of the book 'Society in America'?
(a) Janne Addams (b) Harriet Martineau
(c) Nancy Frazer (d) Tithi Bhattacharya

19. Arrange the history of media in a chronological order:
A. First permanent cinema
B. Publication of 'The Times' for the first time
C. First USA Radio Station
D. Rapid expansion of mobile phones
E. First local British Broadcasting Company in United Kingdom

Choose the correct answer from the options given below:

(a) A, B, C, D, E
(b) A, B, C, E, D
(c) B, A, C, E, D
(d) B, A, C, D, E

20. According to Radha Kamal Mukerjee civilization has a spiritual dimension. How does he explain this phenomena?
A. Human beings are gradually scaling transcendental heights.
B. People's search for unity wholeness and transcendence.
C. People deep involvement in the physical and material condition.
D. Human beings are overcoming the constraints of biogenic and existential levels.
E. People's deep involvement in the endurance of art and myth.

Choose the correct answer from the options given below:

(a) C, B, A, D only
(b) A, B, C, D only
(c) A, D, B, E only
(d) A, C, D, E only

21. The theoretical and philosophical insights provided by Ambedkar includes:
A. Hindu social order with the place of individual
B. Annihilation of caste
C. Encouraging the practice of inter caste marriages
D. Accepting the practice of priesthood by a single caste
E. Accepting the legitimacy of sacred text of the Hindus

Choose the correct answer from the options given below:

(a) B, D, E only
(b) B, C, A only
(c) B, C, D only
(d) B, A, E only

22. According to Max Weber, ideal types can be characterised as:
A. Heuristic devices
B. Devices helpful in doing empirical research
C. Devices helpful in understanding specific aspect of the social world
D. An analytical construct
E. Are the products of the whims and fancies of a social scientist

Choose the correct answer from the options given below:

(a) B, A, E, D only
(b) E, B, D, C only
(c) B, A, D, E only
(d) D, B, A, C only

23. What are the features of New Social Movement theory?
A. Primacy of non-class character
B. Focus on identity and autonomy
C. Focus on capturing state power
D. Focus on grassroot politics
E. Non-hierarchical in character

Choose the correct answer from the options given below:

(a) A, C and D only
(b) A, B, D and E only
(c) B, C, D and E only
(d) C, D, A and B only

24. Max Weber sees objectivity through which one of the following?
(a) Ethnocentrism
(b) Rationalization
(c) Universalism
(d) Regionalization

25. In the domain of interaction which of the following is not associated with Goffman's formulation on interaction?
(a) Actors may want to conceal secret pleasures.
(b) Actors may want to conceal errors that have been made in the preparation of the performance as well as steps that have been taken to correct these errors.
(c) Actors may find it necessary to show only end products and to conceal the process involved in producing of them.
(d) Goffman suggests various forms of dramaturgic loyalty for fastening high in-group loyalty.

26. Methodology-Orientation-Postfactum-Generalization sequencing was given by whom?
(a) Robert Merton
(b) Talcott Parsons
(c) Max Weber
(d) George C. Homans

27. Which among the following is not a component of culture?
(a) Symbols
(b) Language
(c) Value and belief
(d) Cultural conflict

28. Match the List I with List II

List I	List II
A. Robert K. Merton	I. Marxism
B. Fred Davis	II. Ethnomethodology
C. Don H. Zimmerman	III. Symbolic Interactionism
D. Karl Marx	IV. Functionalism

Choose the correct answer from the options given below:
(a) A-III, B-II, C-I, D-IV
(b) A-II, B-I, C-IV, D-III
(c) A-I, B-III, C-IV, D-II
(d) A-IV, B-III, C-II, D-I

29. Which of the following research designs are used in social science research?
A. Ramdomized two group design
B. Four group design
C. Quasi experimental design
D. Time series design
E. Lateral design

Choose the correct answer from the options given below:
(a) A, B, C, D only
(b) A, C, D, E only
(c) C, A, E, B only
(d) A, B, D, E only

30. Collective consciousness has an important place in the social world. It refers to:
A. Totality of people's beliefs and sentiments
B. Independent, determinate and cultural system
C. Individuality of people's beliefs and sentiments
D. Independent, indeterminate and cultural system
E. Primacy of self interest

Choose the correct answer from the options given below:
(a) A, C only
(b) B, C only
(c) C, D only
(d) A, B only

31. Match the List I with List II

List I	List II
A. Konyak Naga	I. Kichuki
B. Angami Naga	II. Ban
C. Oraon	III. Ghotul
D. Gond	IV. Dhumkuria

Choose the correct answer from the options given below:
(a) A-II, B-I, C-IV, D-III
(b) A-I, B-II, C-III, D-IV
(c) A-IV, B-III, C-II, D-I
(d) A-III, B-IV, C-I, D-II

32. Cyber crime are considered as offences under the following act:
A. 66 A
B. 66 B
C. 66 C
D. 66 D
E. 66 E

Choose the correct answer from the options given below:
(a) A. B, C, D only
(b) B, C, D, E only
(c) C, D, E, A only
(d) A, B, E, D only

33. Neil J. Smelser proposed six value added elements which are necessary for a social movement to emerge:
A. Structural strain
B. Structural conduciveness
C. Generalization beliefs and precipitating factors
D. Mobilization for action
E. Charismatic leadership

Choose the correct answer from the options given below:

(a) E, C, B, A only
(b) D, B, A, C only
(c) A, B, D, C only
(d) B, C, D, E only

34. Who has propounded the concept of runway world?
(a) Arjun Appadurai
(b) Anthony Giddens
(c) Saskia Sassin
(d) Mannuel Castells

35. Arrange the sociological studies on caste in India in chronological order:

A. Caste in contemporary India
B. Caste and class in India
C. Caste in modern India and other essays
D. Homo Hierarchieus
E. Caste, class and power

Choose the correct answer from the options given below:

(a) A, B, C, D, E
(b) B, E, D, C, A
(c) E, D, B, A, C
(d) C, A, D, B, E

36. Who is the author of the book 'Culture and Imperialism'?
(a) Gayatri Spivak
(b) Edward Said
(c) Patricia Hill Collins
(d) Judith Butler

37. According to Yogendra Singh which of the following is not a function of law?
(a) As an indicator of change
(b) As an initiator of change
(c) As an integrator of change
(d) As an opponent of change

38. Group the factors influencing educational attainment:
A. Food habits
B. Social class
C. Height of the individual
D. The quality of schools
E. Gender

Choose the correct answer from the options given below:

(a) B, D, E only
(b) A, E, C only
(c) C, A, E only
(d) B, D, C only

39. 'The God of the clan can be nothing but the clan itself' who is associated with this statement?
(a) J.G. Frazer (b) E. Durkheim
(c) W.R. Smith (d) L.H. Lowie

40. Match the List I with List II

List I	List II
A. R. Karsten	I. Magic, Science and Religion
B. R.H. Lowie	II. Primitive Religion
C. B. Malinowski	III. The Threshold of Religion
D. R.R. Marett	IV. The Origins of Religion

Choose the correct answer from the options given below:

(a) A-II, B-I, C-IV, D-III
(b) A-IV, B-II, C-I, D-III
(c) A-I, B-II, C-IV, D-III
(d) A-III, B-IV, C-II, D-I

41. Match the List I with List II

List I	List II
A. M.N. Srinivas	I. Caste and Kinship in Central India
B. E.K. Gough	II. The Hindu Family in its Urban Setting
C. A.C. Mayer	III. Religion and Society among the Coorgs of South India
D. A.D. Ross	IV. Changing Kinship in the Setting of Political and Economic Change among the Nayars of Malabar

Choose the correct answer from the options given below:

(a) A-III, B-IV, C-I, D-II
(b) A-I, B-II, C-IV, D-III
(c) A-II, B-I, C-III, D-IV
(d) A-III, B-IV, C-II, D-I

42. The concept central to the new economic sociology according to Anthony Giddens, that enables sociologist to reformulate economic issues in sociological term is:
(a) Family Capitalism
(b) Social Embeddedness
(c) Managerial Capitalism
(d) Welfare Capitalism

43. Which one of the following term denoting people whose gender identify and/or performance corresponds with that which is assigned gender at birth or according to dominant norms of masculinity and femininity.
(a) Transgender
(b) Bigender
(c) Cisgender
(d) Xenogender

44. Match the List I with List II

List I	List II
A. Disability studies	I. G.S. Ghurye
B. Subaltern studies	II. Anita Ghai
C. Kinship studies	III. Partha Chatterjee
D. Caste studies	IV. A.C. Mayer

Choose the correct answer from the options given below:

(a) A-IV, B-III, C-I, D-II
(b) A-II, B-III, C-IV, D-I
(c) A-III, B-II, C-IV, D-I
(d) A-I, B-II, C-III, D-IV

45. Anthony Giddens developed theoretical perspective on the changes occurring in the present day world on the basis of ________.

A. Social reflexivity
B. Emphasis on customary laws
C. Post modern condition
D. Death of meta narratives
E. Runway world

Choose the correct answer from the options given below:

(a) D and E only
(b) C and A only
(c) A and E only
(d) A and D only

46. Who argues that 'Gender is something that is 'done' or 'performed', then, it is also something that can be 'undone' when it is used by one group to exert power over another'?

(a) Judith Butler
(b) K.W. Crenshaw
(c) Simon de Beauvoir
(d) Martha Nussbaum

47. What are the difficulties in formation of hypothesis in social research?

A. Absence of a clear theoretical framework.
B. Absence of an ability to utilize theoretical framework.
C. Failure to be familiarity with available research techniques.
D. Biasness in formulation of topic.
E. Gender bias in selection of samples.

Choose the correct answer from the options given below:

(a) B, C, D only
(b) A, C, D only
(c) A, B, C only
(d) C, D, E only

48. Cultural process of change in India has been explained with the help of the little and great traditions. Each tradition has its social organization and there is a continual flow of themes, ideas or symbols. This above process is triggered through?

(a) Material and non-material factors
(b) Communal and secular factors
(c) Orthogenetic and heterogenetic factors
(d) Empirical and theoretical factors

49. Who is not associated towards the development of a body of explanatory concept relating to acculturation?

(a) R Linton (b) R. Redfield
(c) M.J. Herskovits (d) B. Malinowski

50. According to Marxist perspective the major function of education is:

(a) Reproduction of labour power
(b) Develop full potential of an individual
(c) Bring cohesion and integration in society
(d) Eliminate inequality in society

51. Arrange the following enactments of social legislations in chronological order.

A. Domestic Violence Act
B. Hindu Marriage Act
C. Right to Property Act
D. Special Marriage Act
E. Hindu Succession Act

Choose the correct answer from the options given below:

(a) D, B, E, C, A
(b) D, E, C, A, B
(c) B, C, A, D, E
(d) B, E, C, A, D

52. What are the basic assumptions of civil society?

A. The civility of civil society
B. Separateness of civil society and the state
C. Intrinsic relationship between civil society and the market
D. Intrinsic relationship between civil society and primordial loyalties
E. Intrinsic relationship between civil society and democracy

Choose the correct answer from the options given below:

(a) A, B, E only
(b) B, C, D only
(c) C, D, E only
(d) D, E, A only

53. Man and the region are not separate but inter-dependent entities, plastic, fluent growing emphasized by whom?

(a) Radha Kamal Mukerjee
(b) D.P. Mukerji
(c) A.K. Saran
(d) D.N. Majumdar

54. Match the List I with List II

List I	List II
A. Power	I. Refers to the degree to which individuals or groups can impose
B. Prestige	II. Social group ranked in terms of ritual purity
C. Wealth	III. Related to the amount of esteem or honour
D. Caste	IV. Refers to material possessions

Choose the correct answer from the options given below:

(a) A-I, B-II, C-IV, D-III
(b) A-II, B-III, C-IV, D-I
(c) A-I, B-III, C-IV, D-II
(d) A-IV, B-III, C-II, D-I

55. March the List I with List II

List I	List II
A. Dalit Movement	I. Birsa Munda
B. Backward Class Movement	II. G.B. Pant
C. Tribal Movement	III. Sharmila Rege
D. Women's Movement	IV. Jyotiba Phule

Choose the correct answer from the options given below:

(a) A-IV, B-II, C-III, D-I
(b) A-III, B-IV, C-II, D-I
(c) A-IV, B-II, C-I, D-III
(d) A-I, B-II, C-IV, D-III

56. Who argues that the migrants are the representatives of rural cosmopolitanism on the basis of their studies?

(a) B.S. Baviskar and others
(b) S.S. Jodhka and others
(c) R. Bhagat and others
(d) Jan Breman and others

57. Group the scholars who contributed to feminist methodology

A. Margaret Mead
B. Sandra Harding
C. Carrol Gilligan
D. Heidi I. Hartmann
E. D. Harvey

Choose the correct answer from the options given below:

(a) B, C and D only
(b) A, B and D only
(c) E, C and A only
(d) C, D, E only

58. Arrange following Indian Laws in chronological order:

A. Oriental Gas Company Act
B. Indian Petroleum Act
C. The Atomic Energy Act
D. The Motor Vehicle Act
E. The Factories Act

Choose the correct answer from the options given below:

(a) A, B, E, D, C
(b) A, B, D, E, C
(c) A, B, D, C, E
(d) B, A, D, C, E

59. Imagined communities refers to:

(a) A socially constructed community one which is imagined by the people who perceived themselves as part of that group
(b) A category of people who share biologically transmitted traits that members of society deem socially significant
(c) A group of people who share common class position in society
(d) A group of people sharing common social status in society

60. Arrange the following patterns of urban life in chronological order:

A. The evolution of early cities
B. The rise of industrial cities
C. The explosive growth of mega cities
D. The recent rise of global cities
E. The endless city

Choose the correct answer from the options given below:

(a) A, B, C, D, E
(b) A, C, B, D, E
(c) A, D, B, E, C
(d) A, B, E, D, C

61. Arrange the logical progression of type of questions placed before to the respondent:

A. Drawn into the interview by awakening interest
B. Brought along from items which are simple to complex
C. Sudden and early request for personal information
D. Smooth transition of frame with no back and forth group
E. Embarrassing without an opportunity to explain

Choose the correct answer from the options given below:

(a) A, B, C, D, E
(b) A, C, B, E, D
(c) A, B, C, E, D
(d) A, D, E, C, B

62. What is the primary characteristics of capitalism according to Karl Marx?

(a) Psychological trait of greed
(b) Emphasis on collective interest
(c) Relentless pursuit of profit
(d) The capitalists are honest and generous people

63. Which theory suggests that the structure and action are necessarily related to each other and are nor opposites?

(a) Structuralism
(b) Structural-functionalism
(c) Structuration
(d) Post-structuralism

64. Arrange the following stages in the development of human communication.

A. The Age of Signs
B. The Age of Electronics
C. The Age of Print
D. The Age of Writing
E. The Information Age

Choose the correct answer from the options given below:

(a) A, D, B, E, C
(b) A, D, C, B, E
(c) A, B, E, D, C
(d) A, B, D, E, C

65. Group the correct argument explaining rational choice theory of religion.

A. It originated from America.
B. It argues that subordination of women is God's will.
C. It assumes that most people are naturally religious.
D. Religion encourages development from the reality of human struggle.
E. It argues that there are rational reasons behind belief in religion.

Choose the correct answer from the options given below:

(a) E, B, C only
(b) A, C, E only
(c) B, A, E only
(d) B, E, C only

66. Who used the metaphor of the theatre in sociological theory?

(a) Harold Garfinkel
(b) Erving Goffman
(c) Alfred Schutz
(d) Peter Berger

67. Match the List I with List II

List I	List II
A. Null Hypothesis	I. Hypothesis that aims to predict the direction of the relationship between two variables
B. Alternate Hypothesis	II. Statement in which there is no relationship between the two variables
C. Directional Hypothesis	III. Hypothesis that predicts a relationship between the two variables. However, the nature or direction of relationship is not defined
D. Non-directional Hypothesis	IV. Statement in which there is some statistical relationship between the variables

Choose the correct answer from the options given below:

(a) A-I, B-II, C-IV, D-III
(b) A-IV, B-III, C-I, D-II
(c) A-II, B-IV, C-I, D-III
(d) A-III, B-I, C-IV, D-II

68. Which of the following is incorrect?

(a) Gender is a socio-cultural and man made notion.
(b) Gender refers to masculine and feminine qualities between patterns, roles and responsibilities.
(c) Gender is a variable.
(d) Gender cannot be changed.

69. Arrange disease pattern and their frequency of occurrence in chronological order:

A. Epidemics
B. Tuberculosis
C. Heart diseases
D. Alzheimer
E. Cancer

Choose the correct answer from the options given below:

(a) A, B, E, C, D
(b) A, B, C, D, E
(c) A, B, D, E, C
(d) A, B, C, E, D

70. Match the List I with List II

List I	List II
A. Structuralism	I. Erving Goffman
B. Feminism	II. Emile Durkheim
C. Functionalism	III. Juliet Mitchell
D. Symbolic Interactionism	IV. Levi Strauss

Choose the correct answer from the options given below;

(a) A-I, B-II, C-IV, D-III
(b) A-II, B-IV, C-I, D-III
(c) A-III, B-II, C-I, D-IV
(d) A-IV, B-III, C-II, D-I

71. Who argues that modernity is an 'incomplete project'. Instead of consigning it to the dustbin of history, we should be extending it, pushing for more democracy, more freedom and more rational policies?

(a) Edward Said
(b) Jurgen Habermas
(c) Manuel Castells
(d) Anthony Giddens

72. Who differentiated city as 'Parasite' (dampens effect on economic growth) and 'Generative' (acts as a center of change and stimulates economic growth?
(a) Park & Burgess
(b) A.G. Frank
(c) Hoselitz
(d) R.K. Mukerjee

73. Merton's role theory reflects:
A. Consumerism
B. Role sets are composed of normative expectations and obligations
C. The actor internalises expectations
D. Gender roles
E. Conspicuous consumption

Choose the correct answer from the options given below:
(a) A and B only
(b) A and E only
(c) B and C only
(d) C and E only

74. What are the models of e-governance?
A. The Broadcasting Model
B. The Critical Flow Model
C. The Lobbying Model
D. The Third Stage
E. The Sixth Stage

Choose the correct answer from the options given below:
(a) B, C, D only
(b) C, D, E only
(c) A, B, C only
(d) B, D, E only

75. Arrange the following backward class movements in India in chronological order:
A. Self Respect Movement
B. Satyasodhak Samaj
C. Mahar Movement
D. Dravidian Movement
E. S.N.D.P Movement

Choose the correct answer from the options given below:
(a) C, B, E, A, D
(b) A, D, B, C, E
(c) B, E, D, C, A
(d) E, D, A, C, B

76. Which of the following is not an impact of 19th century socio-religious reform movements?
(a) The creation of national awakening among the masses.
(b) The revival of Hinduism as a tolerant, and rational religion.
(c) An attack on the hereditary character and rigidity of the caste system.
(d) Improvement of the social status of elderly people.

77. The shift beyond nation-state-based thinking towards analysing the human world as a single community is known as:
(a) Cosmopolitanism
(b) Urbanism
(c) Liberalism
(d) Neo-liberalism

78. Match the List I with List II

List I	List II
A. Liberal Feminism	I. Friedrich Engels
B. Socialist and Marxist Feminism	II. Shulamith Firestone
C. Radical Feminism	III. Bell Hooks
D. Black Feminism	IV. John Stuart Mill

Choose the correct answer from the options given below:
(a) A-I, B-II, C-IV, D-III
(b) A-II, B-III, C-I, D-IV
(c) A-IV, B-I, C-II, D-III
(d) A-I, B-II, C-III, D-IV

79. Arrange the following tribal revolts in India in chronological order.
A. Birsa Munda revolt
B. Santhal revolt
C. Munda revolt
D. Baba Tilka Majhi revolt
E. Tana Bhagat revolt

Choose the correct answer from the options given below:
(a) B, E, D, C, A
(b) A, C, B, D, E
(c) D, B, A, C, E
(d) E, A, C, B, D

80. Ethical principles in social research does not involve which one of the following?
(a) Consent (b) Privacy
(c) Deception (d) Cognition

81. Who defined joint family as 'a group of people who generally live under one roof, who eat food cooked in one kitchen, who hold property in common, participate in common family-worship and are related to one another as some particular type of kindred'?
(a) Iravati Karve
(b) K.M. Kapadia
(c) A.M. Shah
(d) I.P. Desai

82. Who has propounded the term 'neo-tribes' in the context of small grouping of people who voluntarily band together on the basis of shared musical tastes, ideas, consumer preferences and so on?
(a) Martineu (b) Marcuse
(c) Marshall (d) Maffesoli

83. Match the List I with List II

List I	List II
A. Cognates	I. Those who are related to person by marriage
B. Lineal	II. It indicates the side of the kinship group
C. Lateral	III. It refers to the line of the kinship group
D. Affinal	IV. All the people who are related by blood in any way to an individual

Choose the correct answer from the options given below:
(a) A-III, B-IV, C-I, D-II
(b) A-IV, B-III, C-II, D-I
(c) A-II, B-I, C-IV, D-III
(d) A-I, B-II, C-IV, D-III

84. Census method research is _____ percentage enumeration of sample.
(a) 25% (b) 50%
(c) 75% (d) 100%

85. Karl Marx engaged in the process of objectification which meant that:
A. Men produce object like food, clothes and shelters.
B. It reaffirms materialist orientation.
C. It reaffirms his intervention the real world of real actors.
D. It reaffirms that the pleasure from art and culture is important in social world.
E. It is considered as the true arena in which people express their human capacities.

Choose the correct answer from the options given below:
(a) B, C, D, E only
(b) A, C, D, E only
(c) A, B, C, E only
(d) A, B, C, D only

86. Which of the following are the characteristics of traditional societies or civilization?
A. Very large in size some numbering several millions of people.
B. Some cities exist in which trade and manufacture are concentrate.
C. Based largely on industry.
D. Based largely on agriculture.
E. Distinct government apparatus headed by king or emperor.

Choose the correct answer from the options given below:
(a) A, B, D, E only
(b) A, C, D, E only
(c) B, C, D, E only
(d) A, B, C, D, E

87. Group the traits as explained by Saskia Sassen in the 'global city'.
A. They have developed into command posts for the global economy.
B. They are key locations for financial and specialized service firms.
C. They are sites of production and innovation.
D. They are markets in which the products of financial and service industries.
E. They are relatively large forms of human settlement.

Choose the correct answer from the options given below:
(a) A, B, D, C only
(b) A, B, C, D only
(c) A, C, D, E only
(d) A, C, B, E only

88. 'Sociobiology' was first developed by whom?
(a) E.O. Wilson
(b) David Barash
(c) Darwin
(d) George Peter Murdock

89. Social change cannot be perceived by which of the following viewpoint?
(a) Ideational
(b) Value patterns
(c) Cognitive structure
(d) Sojurn

90. Who has given three-fold classification of social movement - charishmatic, organizational and ideological on the basis of his study?
(a) P.N. Mukherji (b) Ghanshyam Shah
(c) D.N. Dhanagare (d) T.K. Oommen

Directions (91–95): Read the following passage carefully and answer the questions:

Globalization is a composite process. It results from the convergence of a series of developments in society which are qualitatively new arrival. These include: contemporary revolution in science and technology of communication, high velocity movements of finance, capital and market, increased social mobility, migration of personnel and the emergence of a global diaspora. Its associated contributory processes are:

intensification of cultural interaction among diverse groups through media exposure, increased incidence of leisure-time activities, growth in tourism, infrastructures of entertainment and marketing of cultural products, personnel and styles. In a segmental approach, analysts have studied 'financial or capital globalization,' 'telecommunication or media globalization' and 'cultural globalization' as separate developments, and then tried to view the impact of the one, for instance, 'financial or capital' globalization upon other segments such as the 'media', 'communication' or 'culture'. This segments such as the 'media', 'communication' or 'culture'. The approach has two weaknesses: first, it fails to help us in comprehending the role of the residual social structural realities and their emergent properties and the way they interact with any one of these three aspects of globalization, be it capital, communication or culture. Consequently, such treatment is unable to explain why some societies, communities or groups resist globalization and reject its institutions and ideology, whereas others accept it, celebrate its arrival. The emergence of a new society inheres a basic structural transformation of economy, polity and culture, and the potential to go beyond the systemic features of a capitalist or a post-capitalist social order. Its unfolding may eventually contribute to the birth of a new social order.

91. Which one of the following is not a consequence of the process of globalization in India?
(a) Increased incidences of leisure time activities
(b) Marketing of cultural products
(c) Increased social values
(d) Infrastructures of entertainment

92. Which one of the following is not a consequence of globalization process?
(a) Emergence of a global diaspora
(b) Ethnocentrism
(c) High velocity movements of finance
(d) Improved technology of communication

93. The emergence of a 'new' society is based on the structural transformation of:
A. Economy and Polity
B. Culture and Economy
C. Culture and Polity
D. Economy, Polity and Culture
E. Beyond post capitalist economic order, polity and culture

Choose the correct answer from the options given below:
(a) A and B only
(b) A and C only
(c) D and E only
(d) E only

94. Segmental approach to the process of globalization includes:
A. Cultural globalization
B. Media globalization
C. Capital globalization
D. Political globalization
E. Environmental globalization

Choose the correct answer from the options given below:
(a) A and B only
(b) A, B and C only
(c) A and C only
(d) C and D only

95. Which one of the following not a weakness of segmental approach to globalization?
(a) Rejection of globalization
(b) Influence of capital on media and culture
(c) Role of the residual structural realities
(d) Historicity of globalization

Directions (96–100): Read the following passage carefully and answer the questions:

There are broadly two different approaches to rural planning in the Third World: the improvement approach, which aims to encourage agricultural development within existing peasant production system, and the transformation approach which attempts to establish new forms of agricultural and social organization, and which makes a radical break with existing system in terms of scale of operation production techniques, and socio-legal structure. The improvement approach was especially characteristic of the development policies pursued by British colonial government in Africa, India and elsewhere. Under colonial rule extension works as often coupled with the enforcement of various administrative ordinances to prevent soil erosion or to encourage the cultivation of certain crops. Hence, general incentives to production were combined with principle of 'persistent persuasion'. The cases of non-observance were reported to authorities for court action. Various government encouraged the marketing of these crops through state agencies or cooperative societies composed of basically small farmers for selling their produce. Thus, the colonial governments were willing to assist in developing an infrastructure concerned with distribution as well as production.

96. The strategy of improvement was implemented by whom?
(a) French government
(b) British government
(c) Spanish government
(d) American government

97. The extension work during colonial rule was done through:
- (a) Using coercive power
- (b) Freedom given to peasants
- (c) Continuous persuations
- (d) Radical changes in organization of agricultural activities

98. How was soil erosion prevented during colonial period?
- (a) Launching government projects by the government department
- (b) By voluntary organization of the area
- (c) By enforcement of administrative orders
- (d) By making appeal to peasants

99. In what ways the transformation approach to development was different from improvement approach?
- (a) It emphasized on the principle of persistence persuation.
- (b) It attempts to establish new forms of agricultured and social organization.
- (c) It was interested in continuation of existing system of agriculture.
- (d) It operates at a small scale in agriculture sector.

100. What was the aim of improvement approach in colonial period?
- (a) To encourage the farmers to adopt non-agricultural occupations.
- (b) To encourage the farmers to grow only certain specific crops.
- (c) To encourage the farmers to grow any type of cash crops.
- (d) To encourage the farmers to grow indigenous crops only.

Answer Key

1. (a)	**16.** (c)	**31.** (a)	**46.** (a)	**61.** (c)	**76.** (d)	**91.** (c)
2. (d)	**17.** (d)	**32.** (a)[1]	**47.** (c)	**62.** (c)	**77.** (a)	**92.** (b)
3. (b)	**18.** (b)	**33.** (b, c)	**48.** (c)	**63.** (c)	**78.** (c)	**93.** (c)
4. (c)	**19.** (c)	**34.** (b)	**49.** (d)	**64.** (b)	**79.** (c)	**94.** (b)
5. (d)	**20.** (c)	**35.** (*)	**50.** (a)	**65.** (b)	**80.** (d)	**95.** (d)
6. (b)	**21.** (b)	**36.** (b)	**51.** (a)	**66.** (b)	**81.** (a)	**96.** (b)
7. (b)	**22.** (d)	**37.** (d)	**52.** (a)	**67.** (c)	**82.** (d)	**97.** (c)
8. (c)	**23.** (b)	**38.** (a)	**53.** (a)	**68.** (d)	**83.** (b)	**98.** (c)
9. (b)	**24.** (b)	**39.** (b)	**54.** (c)	**69.** (d)	**84.** (d)	**99.** (b)
10. (*)	**25.** (d)	**40.** (b)	**55.** (c)	**70.** (d)	**85.** (c)	**100.** (b)
11. (c)	**26.** (a)	**41.** (a)	**56.** (d)	**71.** (b)	**86.** (a)	
12. (b)	**27.** (d)	**42.** (b)	**57.** (a)	**72.** (c)	**87.** (a, b)	
13. (b)	**28.** (d)	**43.** (c)	**58.** (b)	**73.** (c)	**88.** (a)	
14. (c)	**29.** (a)	**44.** (b)	**59.** (a)	**74.** (c)	**89.** (d)	
15. (a)	**30.** (d)	**45.** (c)	**60.** (a)	**75.** (c)	**90.** (d)	

*Answer keys marked (*) are dropped by the NTA.

[1]The NTA initially listed (b) in the provisional answer key but later changed it to (a) in the final answer key. According to the Author, the correct answer is (b), as per the Supreme Court ruling of 12/October/2022. According to this, no one should be prosecuted under Section 66A of the Information Technology Act 2000, which had been declared unconstitutional by the Court in the Shreya Singhal case.

UGC NET Sociology August 2024

1. K. Manheim states that idea emerge from specific sectors of the social world. Therefore, ideas can be referred as:

(a) inherently limited, one-sided and distorted.
(b) not limited inherently, multi-sided and distorted.
(c) inherently limited, one-sided and not-distorted.
(d) inherently limited, multi-sided and distorted.

2. Arrange the following social revolutions in chronological order of their occurrence.

A. Information Technology Revolution
B. French Revolution
C. Bolshevik Revolution
D. Palace Revolution

Choose the *correct* answer from the option given below:

(a) D, A, B, C
(b) A, B, C, D
(c) B, C, A, D
(d) C, B, D, A

3. Which is not true about 'ecocentric view' to address environmental issues?

A. They see economic growth at odds with environmental objectives.
B. They believed that by adopting scientific and technical solutions, environmental issues can be addressed.
C. They believed that there must be limit to growth.
D. They argued that planet is not just for humans but for all living things.

Choose the *correct* answer from the option given below:

(a) A, B and C only
(b) B, C and D only
(c) A. B and D only
(d) A, C and D only

4. Arrange the following sociological works on modernity in a chronological order of their publication.

A. The consequence of modernity (Anthony Giddens)
B. Liquid modernity (Zygmunt Bauman)
C. Risk Society: Towards a New Modernity (Ulrich Beck)
D. Facing up to Modernity (Peter L. Berger)

Choose the *correct* answer from the option given below:

(a) A, B, C, D
(b) B, C, D, A
(c) D, C, A, B
(d) C, D, B, A

5. In the Tibetan kinship system, there is the existence of Fraternal Polyandry. What are the premises of this system?

A. Several brothers sharing a wife.
B. Age range of the brothers is often large.
C. Eldest brother is in control as much as father is.
D. Regulated sexual access within the 'family'.
E. No regulated sexual access within the 'family'.

Choose the *correct* answer from the option given below:

(a) B, C, D and E only
(b) A, B, C and E only
(c) A, B, C and D only
(d) B, C and E only

6. Which of the following are the characteristics of an ordinal scale?

A. It places events in order.
B. There is an attempt to make the intervals of the scale equal in terms of some roles.
C. Rank orders represent ordinal scale and used in relating to qualitative phenomena.
D. Ordinal scale only permits the ranking of items from highest to lowest.

Choose the *correct* answer from the option given below:

(a) A, B and C only
(b) A, C and D only
(c) A, B, C and D only
(d) B, C and D only

7. A man's lineage fellows are literally and figuratively close to him for they are, after all, the brothers who have separated their fields and hearths but who continue to sustain their fraternal allegiance. This ambivalence takes place because:

A. Ideal of lineage solidarity is not so strongly proclaimed as is fraternal ideal.
B. It is not always clear who should be counted as a full lineage member.
C. Lineage ties lapse after several generations.
D. The member of obligated generations is not specified clearly.
E. A father's brother's son who moves to a distant village is a member for ritual purposes but cannot fully participate in corporate activity.

Choose the *correct* answer from the option given below:

(a) B, C and D only
(b) C, D and E only
(c) A, B, C and D only
(d) A, B, C, D and E only

8. Which among the following are the characteristics of 'social network groups"?

A. They are often called online communities.
B. They do not involve direct face to face communication.
C. They may not be local and bound to a place.
D. They generate their own language, values, rules and norms.
E. They give members a sense of self and esteem.

Choose the *correct* answer from the option given below:

(a) A, B and C only
(b) B, C and D only
(c) A, B, C and D only
(d) A, B, C, D and E only

9. Arrange the following works on "Family and Intimate Relationships" in chronological order

A. A Sociology of Family Life (Deborah Chambers)
B. Rethinking Family Practices (David H.J. Morgan)
C. Families in Today's World (David Cheal)
D. The Changing Experience of Childhood (C. Smart, B. Neale, and A. Wade)

Choose the *correct* answer from the option given below:

(a) C, D, A, B
(b) A, D, B, C
(c) B, C, D, A
(d) D, C, B, A

10. Social constructionist theorists reject biological basis for gender differences. According to these theorists-

(a) Gender identities emerge in relation to perceived sex differences in society and in turn help to shape those societies.
(b) Gender identities partially emerge in relation to overall sex differences in society and in turn help to shape those societies.
(c) Gender identities do not emerge in relation to perceived sex differences in society and in turn help to shape those societies.
(d) Gender identities emerge in relation to perceived sex differences in society but in turn do not help to shape those societies.

11. Match the List I with List II

List I (Goal of Good Governance)	List II (How e-government can help)
A. Increasing Transparency	I. Reduction of cost-associated with travel for citizens to interact with government
B. Improving service Delivery	II. Disclosure of public assets, government budget, procurement information
C. Empowerment of people	III. Putting procedures online so that transactions can easily be monitored
D. Reducing administrative corruption	IV. Providing new channel to marginalized communities to receive government services

Choose the *correct* answer from the options given below:

(a) A-I, B-II, C-III, D-IV
(b) A-IV, B-III, C-II, D-I
(c) A-I, B-IV, C-II, D-III
(d) A-II, B-I, C-IV, D-III

12. If we add 'measurement error' or 'non-sampling error' to 'sampling error", we get

(a) Frame Error
(b) Total Error
(c) Chance Error
(d) Response Error

13. Which among the following is not true about the first generation 'cyber crimes'?

(a) Use of computers to assess traditional type of offending.
(b) Finding information on how to build weapons or bombs may be easier on the internet but there have been and still are, conventional sources available.

(c) First generation cybercrimes were 'hybrid' traditional offences but within a new global network environment.
(d) Drug dealers employ whatever forms of communication exist and, even in the absence of computers, would continue to buy or sell drugs.

14. The distinction between 'culture' and "civilization" can be recognized by distinguishing between 'material' and 'non-material culture'. Who is associated with this?
(a) A. Weber
(b) Arnold Toynbee
(c) R.M. MacIver
(d) Irving Hallowell

15 The term refers to movement away from a residential location either within the same country or to another country.
(a) Immigration
(b) Emigration
(c) Migration
(d) Forced migration

16. The term used to refer to simple counts of the frequencies with which the various categories in each set occur in the data is referred as
(a) cross-tabulation
(b) coding
(c) marginals
(d) totalling

17. Who is the author of the book '*Tribe to Empire*'?
(a) Emile Durkheim
(b) A. Moret and G. Davy
(c) H. Spencer
(d) F. Tönnies

18. Match the List I with List II

List I (System)	List II (Location)
A. Ryotwari	I. Princely States of Rajasthan
B. Mahalwari	II. Madras
C. Jamindari	III. Bengal and Uttar Pradesh
D. Jagirdari	IV. Agra and Audh

Choose the *correct* answer from the options given below:
(a) A-I, B-II, C-III, D-IV
(b) A-II, B-IV, C-III, D-I
(c) A-III, B-IV, C-II, D-I
(d) A-IV, B-III, C-II, D-I

19. Match the List I with List II

List I (Book)	List II (Author)
A. An American Dilemma: The Negro Problem and Modern Democracy	I. Robert and Helen Lynd
B. The American Soldier	II. Gunnar Myrdal
C. Middle Town in Transition	III. Samuel Stouffer
D. Sexual Behaviour of Human Male	IV. Alfred Kinsey

Choose the *correct* answer from the options given below:
(a) A-IV, B-I, C-III, D-II
(b) A-I, B-II, C-IV, D-III
(c) A-II, B-III, C-I, D-IV
(d) A-III, B-IV, C-II, D-I

20. Match the List I with List II

List I (Concept)	List II (Author)
A. Class situation	I. Amartya Sen
B. Capability Approach	II. Max Weber
C. The Stages of Economic Growth	III. Thorstein Veblen
D. Conspicuous Consumption	IV. W.W. Rostow

Choose the *correct* answer from the options given below:
(a) A-III, B-IV, C-II, D-I
(b) A-IV, B-III, C-I, D-II
(c) A-I, B-II, C-III, D-IV
(d) A-II, B-I, C-IV, D-III

21. The simplest possible measure of dispersion which is defined as the difference between the values of the extreme items of a series is called
(a) Mean
(b) Median
(c) Range
(d) Mode

22. Which among the following is not true about Common Property Resources (CPRs)?
(a) These are the resources accessible to the whole community of a village
(b) On these resources some individuals have an exclusive property right
(c) Some of the examples of these resources are village pastures, waste dumping places, community forests, village ponds, tanks, rivers/rivulets
(d) Common Property Resources are declining in India after independence

23. Who argued that urbanism promotes diverse sub cultures rather than submerging everyone within an anonymous mass?
(a) Fischer
(b) David Harvey
(c) Manual Castells
(d) Louis Wirth

24. Match the List I with List II

List I (Books)	List II (Authors)
A. New Rules of Sociological Method	I. Peter Winch
B. Phenomenology of Social World	II. Anthony Giddens
C. Studies in Ethnomethodology	III. Alfred Schutz
D. The Idea of a Social Science	IV. Harold Garfinkel

Choose the *correct* answer from the options given below:

(a) A-IV, B-III, C-I, D-II
(b) A-II, B-III, C-IV, D-I
(c) A-III, B-IV, C-II, D-I
(d) A-III, B-I, C-IV, D-II

25. Match the List I with List II

List I (Author)	List II (Book)
A. Ann Oakley	I. The Second Industrial Divide: Possibilities and Prosperities
B. T Piketty	II. The Borderless World: Power and Strategy in Industrial Economy
C. M. Piore and C.F. Sable	III. The Sociology of Housework
D. K Ohmae	IV. Capital in The Twenty-First Century

Choose the *correct* answer from the options given below:

(a) A-II, B-I, C-III, D-IV
(b) A-IV, B-III, C-II, D-I
(c) A-III, B-IV, C-I, D-II
(d) A-I, B-II, C-IV, D-III

26. Which of the following are the characteristics of a good sample design?

A. It must result in a truly representative sample
B. It must be such which results in a small sampling error.
C. It must be viable in context of funds available for the research study.
D. It must be such so that systematic bias can be controlled in a better way.

Choose the *correct* answer from the option given below:

(a) A, B and C only
(b) A, B, C and D only
(c) A, C and D only
(d) B, C and D only

27. If the purpose of research is to test a hypothesis of a causal relationship between variables, which of the following research design is most suitable for such a research study?

(a) Formulative Research Design
(b) Descriptive Research Design
(c) Experimental Research Design
(d) Diagnostic Research Design

28. Which among the following is not true about Weber's notion of 'Verstehen'?

(a) Verstehen is a rational procedure of study.
(b) Verstehen is simply the use of 'intuition' and sympathetic participation by the researcher.
(c) Verstehen involved doing systematic and rigorous research.
(d) Weber's thoughts on 'Verstehen' were derived from a field known as hermeneutics.

29. Who gave examples of developed systems of administration of justice, particularly among African Negroes?

(a) R.H. Lowie
(b) Max Gluckman
(c) B. Malinowski
(d) Max Weber

30. Who has theorized the triumph of capitalist democracy in the Cold War – and thus the 'end of history'?

(a) M. Foucault
(b) Francis Fukuyama
(c) Daniel Bell
(d) Anthony Giddens

31. Following table presents frequency distribution of weights of 265 male students.

Class Interval (weight)	Frequency
90-99	1
100-109	1
110-119	9
120-129	30
130-139	42
140-149	66
150-159	47
160-169	39
170-179	15
180-189	11
190-199	1
200-209	3
	N = 265

What is the mean ($\overline{X}$) of weight of male students?

(a) 138.5
(b) 148.74
(c) 168.75
(d) 198.75

32. Match the thinkers with their concepts-

List I (Thinkers)	List II (Concepts)
A. Emile Durkheim	I. Fetishism
B. Karl Marx	II. Elementary Structures
C. Claude Levi-Strauss	III. Discourses
D. Michel Foucault	IV. Morality

Choose the *correct* answer from the option given below:

(a) A-IV, B-I, C-II, D-III
(b) A-II, B-I, C-IV, D-III
(c) A-II, B-III, C-IV, D-I
(d) A-III, B-I, C-IV, D-II

33. The origins of hermeneutics philosophy in the modern age are most appropriately attributed to
(a) J.S. Mills
(b) Harold Garfinkel
(c) Schleiermacher
(d) Robert K. Merton

34. According to R.K. Mukherjee, Indian culture is very well blended with various religious texts. He emphasises that the spirit of tolerance of diversities is reflected in-
(a) Rig Veda
(b) Atharva Veda
(c) Arthasastra
(d) Dharmasastra

35. Match the List I with List II

List I (Legal)	List II (Judgement Ruling)
A. Rameshwar Vs. State of Rajasthan 1952	I. Supreme Court held that the testimony of the rape victim should not be rejected unless there are very strong evidences mitigating its veracity.
B. Rafiq Vs. State of UP, 1980	II. Supreme Court held that corroborative evidence of the woman's testimony is not necessary.
C. Harpal Singh and another Vs. State of Himachal Pradesh, 1981	III. Supreme Court held that in case of rape the necessity of corroboration was to be treated only as a 'rule of prudence'.
D. Bharwada Bhogibhai Hirjibhai Vs. State of Gujarat, 1983	IV. Supreme Court held that a woman is used to sexual intercourse is immaterial in a rape trial.

Choose the *correct* answer from the options given below:

(a) A-IV, B-I, C-II, D-III
(b) A-I, B-II, C-III, D-IV
(c) A-II, B-IV, C-I, D-III
(d) A-III, B-I, C-IV, D-II

36. Match the List I with List II

List I (Method / Developer)	List II (Example)
A. Multivariate Analysis	I. Chi-Square Test
B. Test of Significance	II. Coefficient of Skewness
C. Central Tendency	III. Cluster Analysis
D. Karl Pearson	IV. Standard Deviation

Choose the *correct* answer from the options given below:

(a) A-III, B-I. C-IV, D-II
(b) A-IV, B-I, C-III, D-II
(c) A-II, B-III, C-I, D-IV
(d) A-I, B-IV, C-II, D-III

37. According to Manuel Castells, the rise of the new global informational economy is accompanied with emergence of a new 'network enterprise'. Which among the following is not the characteristics of the network enterprise?
(a) A flexible production and new management.
(b) An organization based on horizontal model.
(c) An organization based on vertical model.
(d) The fundamental component of organization is a series of networks.

38. C. Von Furer–Haimendorf studied intensively the family structures and cultural life of Nagas. Which group of Naga did he focus in his study?
(a) The Ao Nagas
(b) The Konyak Nagas
(c) The Tangkhul Nagas
(d) The Angamis

39. A state expressing, in a variable geometry, the aggregate interests of its constituent members is called
(a) Nation-state
(b) Capitalist state
(c) Super nation-state
(d) Estate

40. 'Poverty exists because poor people serve useful functions for society'. Who is associated with this statement?
(a) Herbert Gans
(b) Barbara Ehrenreich
(c) Banfield and Lewis
(d) Oscar Lewis

41. Who is not the spokesman for cultural determinism?
(a) E.B. Tylor
(b) A.L. Kroeber
(c) R.M. MacIver
(d) Leslie Whyte

42. Who coined the term ethnocentrism?
(a) W.G. Sumner
(b) E. Gellner
(c) L. Kuznar
(d) E.B. Tylor

43. The changing material culture is impacted by the:
A. Integrated, global capital identities, which determine global economics and influence global societies.
B. Integrated, global capital network, whose movements and variable logic do not determine economies and influence societies.
C. Integrated, global capital marketing infrastructure, whose functioning impacts on the various economies and influence societies.
D. Integrated, global capital currency system, whose movements and variable logic determine economies and influence societies.
E. Integrated, global capital network, whose movements and variable logic which determine economies and influence societies.

Choose the *correct* answer from the option given below:
(a) A and D only
(b) B only
(c) C and E only
(d) E only

44. Phenomenological approach of Alfred Schutz refers to 'life world" as-
(a) 'taken-for-granted' and not based on 'mundane reality'.
(b) 'taken-for-granted" and based on 'mundane reality'.
(c) not "taken-for-granted' but based on 'mundane reality'.
(d) not 'taken-for-granted' and not based on 'mundane reality'.

45. Which among the following is correct about Parsons' notion of socialization?
A. In the socialization process norms and values of a system are internalized and become part of the actors conscience.
B. Socialization is a conservative process in which need dispositions bind children to the social system.
C. Parsons sees socialization as a lifelong experience.
D. In socialization process, there is little or no room for creativity.

Choose the correct answer from the option given below:
(a) A, B, D only
(b) B, C, D only
(c) A, B, C only
(d) A, B, C and D only

46. Which of the following risks are created by globalization?
A. The spread of weapons of mass destruction
B. Pollution
C. International Financial Crisis
D. Terrorism

Choose the *correct* answer from the option given below:
(a) A, B and C only
(b) A, C and D only
(c) B, C and D only
(d) A, B, C and D only

47. The 'Precariat is a new class in the making, it consists of those who are unable to gain access to the labour markets which offer secure employment and decent wages. Which of the following are included in this class?
A. Older People
B. Unskilled workers
C. Less qualified young people
D. Those who regularly move into and out of work

Choose the correct answer from the option given below:
(a) A, B and C only
(b) B, C and D only
(c) A, B, C and D only
(d) A, C and D only

48. Who has used the term 'polyarchy'?
(a) R.A. Dahl
(b) G. Mc Lennan
(c) J. Tronto
(d) A. Smith

49. 'A social structure that organizes the residence and activities of people in physical space', is known as
(a) group
(b) community
(c) society
(d) association

50. Match the List I with List II

List I (Concept)	List II (Explanation)
A. Gaia hypothesis	I. A theoretical paradigm that explores the relationship of human culture and physical environment.

B. Global Commons	II. A situation in which our relationship to the environment while yielding short term benefits, will have profound negative long term effects.
C. Environmental deficit	III. Resources shared by all members of the International Community.
D. Cultural Ecology	IV. Planet Earth itself should be seen as a living organism, in which humans and other species each have a vital part to play.

Choose the *correct* answer from the options given below:

(a) A-IV, B-III, C-II, D-I
(b) A-I, B-III, C-IV, D-II
(c) A-III, B-II, C-I, D-IV
(d) A-II, B-IV, C-I, D-III

51. 'Capitalism produces wasted population not just the poor and refuges but huge prison populations and other outsiders.' Who is associated with this statement?
(a) Judith Butler
(b) Zygmunt Bauman
(c) Giorgio Agamben
(d) Chrystia Freeland

52. Arrange the following research activities of a research project in a chronological order
A. Writing of the Report
B. Formulation of Research Problem
C. Administering an interview Schedule
D. Selection of the sample
E. Tabulation of Data

Choose the *correct* answer from the option given below:

(a) D, C, E, B, A
(b) D, B, C, E, A
(c) B, C, D, E, A
(d) B, D, C, E, A

53. According to Neil J. Smelser, the social transformations accompany economic development which can be defined as growth of output per head of population. Which of the following processes are necessary for economic development?
A. The commercialization of agriculture
B. Modernization of technology
C. Industrialization process
D. Urbanization

Choose the *correct* answer from the option given below:

(a) A, B and C only
(b) A, C and D only
(c) A, B, C and D only
(d) B, C and D only

54. Arrange the following regulations in the chronological order of their year of enactment
A. Hindu Woman's Separate Residence and Maintenance Act
B. Parsi Marriage and Divorce Act
C. Caste Disabilities Removal Act
D. Indian Divorce Act
E. Hindu Inheritance (Removal of Disabilities) Act

Choose the *correct* answer from the option given below:

(a) C, D, B, E, A
(b) C, B, D, E, A
(c) D, C, E, A, D
(d) B, D, A, C, E

55. According to the Islami Law match definitions of the term given which refer to different forms of property rights

List I	List II
A. Mehr	I. Women have the right to stipulate conditions in the marriage contract.
B. Hedaya	II. Women enter into pre-marriage agreements regarding their individual property and access to husband's income.
C. Nikahnama	III. Mark of respect to the woman which form an essential ingredient of a marriage contract.
D. Kabin nama	IV. Women have the right to refuse cohabitation if the husband does not make prompt payment.

Choose the *correct* answer from the options given below:

(a) A-III, B-IV, C-I, D-II
(b) A-III, B-I, C-II, D-IV
(c) A-III, B-IV, C-II, D-I
(d) A-III, B-II, C-IV, D-I

56. Match List I with List II

List I (Books)	List II (Authors)
A. Magic, Science and Religion	I. Karl Marx

B. The Poverty of Philosophy	II. Bronislaw Malinowski
C. The Structures of Life World	III. G.H. Mead
D. Mind, Self and Society	IV. Alfred Schutz and Thomas Luckmann

Choose the *correct* answer from the option given below:

(a) A-III, B-IV, C-II, D-I
(b) A-II, B-I, C-IV, D-III
(c) A-I, B-II, C-III, D-IV
(d) A-IV, B-I, C-II, D-III

57. Which among the following are correct about virtual communities?

A. These are self-defined electronic network of interactive communities organized around a shared interest.
B. Such communities may be relatively formalized or be spontaneously formed by social network.
C. They have specific rules and dynamics.
D. Like physical personal network most virtual communities are specialized and diversified.

Choose the *correct* answer from the option given below:

(a) A, B and C only
(b) A, C and D only
(c) A, B, C and D
(d) A and D only

58. Match the List I with List II

List I (Book)	List II (Thinker)
A. Virtual Communities	I. Alvin Tofler
B. Surveillance Society	II. Barry Wellman
C. Personal Communities	III. Howard Rheingold
D. Third Wave	IV. David Lyon

Choose the *correct* answer from the options given below:

(a) A-III, B-IV, C-II, D-I
(b) A-II, B-IV, C-III, D-I
(c) A-I, B-IV, C-III, D-II
(d) A-II, B-IV, C-I, D-III

59. Arrange the following sociological works on 'Post Modernism' in chronological order of their publication.

A. The Condition of Postmodernity (D. Harvey)
B. The Postmodern Condition (J.F. Lyotard)
C. Postmodernism, Reason and Religion (E. Gellner)
D. Images of Postmodernism Society (N.K. Dezin)

Choose the *correct* answer from the option given below:

(a) D, B, A, C
(b) C, D, B, A
(c) A, B, C, D
(d) B, A, D, C

60. Match the List I with List II

List I (Concept)	List II (Explanation)
A. Ecological Modernization	I. Emphasizes on the combination of industrialization, capitalism and consumerism have transformed society-environment relations.
B. Sociology of consumption	II. Accepts that 'business as usual' is no longer possible but also rejects radical environmentalist solutions involving deindustrialization.
C. Critical Realism	III. Approach to investigate how some environmental issues come to be seen as significant and in need of urgent action while others are largely ignored.
D. Social constructionism	IV. Approaches environmental issuer m a scientific way, bringing together evidence from across the social and natural sciences to understand why environmental problems occur.

Choose the *correct* answer from the options given below:

(a) A-I, B-II, C-III, D-IV
(b) A-II, B-I, C-IV D-III
(c) A-IV, B-III, C-I, D-II
(d) A-I, B-III, C-II, D-IV

61. Which among the following are correct about genetically modified crops?

A. Genetically modified crops may reduce the genetic diversity.
B. 'Terminator Gene' was planned to be used by Monsanto company in Genetically Modified crops.
C. 'Terminator Gene' ensured that seeds would be sterile after three generations.
D. Genetically modified crops are resistant to commonly used agricultural herbicides and pesticides.

Choose the *correct* answer from the option given below:

(a) A, B and C only
(b) B, C and D only
(c) A, B and D only
(d) A, C and D only

62. G. H. Mead defines 'I' as the:
(a) incalculable, unpredictable and creative aspect of the self.
(b) calculable, predictable and non-creative aspect of the self.
(c) calculable, unpredictable and creative aspect of the self.
(d) incalculable, predictable and creative aspect of the self.

63. Which among the following is not true about the 'International Treaty on Climate Change' - the Kyoto Protocol?
(a) It was signed in 1995.
(b) The developed countries agreed to cut their emissions by an average of 5.2% over 1990 level by the period 2008–12.
(c) It also initiated the Clean Development Mechanism (CDM).
(d) The CDM allowed industrial countries to get credits to put towards their Kyoto targets by funding clean energy projects in developing countries.

64. A Noniya of Banaras, flees from his village and take refuge to his mother's brother or to his wife's brother, when he is in trouble in his home village with the dominant landowners. This is because-
A. They are related through affinal ties.
B. He has a lot of property with them.
C. He does not want to stay in his own village.
D. They are his biological ties.
E. He feels lonely in his own village.

Choose the *correct* answer from the option given below:

(a) C and D only
(b) A only
(c) B only
(d) D and E only

65. Match the List I with List II

List I (Concept)	List II (Explanation)
A. Symbolic dominance	I. The maintenance of power and privilege between social classes from one generation to the next.
B. Social Reproduction	II. The exercise of dominance through culture and its Mystification.
C. Habitus	III. The process by which a society transmits dominant knowledge from one generation to another.
D. Cultural Reproduction	IV. Learned dispositions which lead people to behave in certain ways.

Choose the *correct* answer from the options given below:

(a) A-I, B-II, C-III, D-IV
(b) A-IV, B-III, C-II, D-I
(c) A-III, B-IV, C-I, D-II
(d) A-II, B-I, C-IV, D-III

66. Which among the following is not correct about consumerism?
(a) Mass production must be accompanied by large scale consumption
(b) Consumerism is also a way of thinking, a mentality.
(c) Consumption is independent of economic development.
(d) Consumption patterns can damage the environmental resource base and exacerbate pattern of inequality.

67. "Left-right party divisions reflect the class division in capitalist society". This view is criticized by T.B. Bottomore on which of the following arguments.
A. Parties are alliances between a variety of distinctive groups with divergent interests.
B. These alliances are stable and this results into permanent development of Splinter groups.
C. Political parties are relatively autonomous from their class basis.
D. There is often a gap between local class support for a parry and the capacity of any government to fulfill these aspirations at the state level.

Choose the correct answer from the option given below:

(a) A, B, C and D only
(b) B, C and D only
(c) A, C and D only
(d) A, B and D only

68. Match the List I with List II

List I (Book)	List II (Authors)
A. Nai Talim	I. M.N. Srinivas
B. States and Minorities	II. M.K. Gandhi
C. On Living in a Revolution and Other Essays	III. R.K. Mukherjee
D. The Philosophy of Social Science	IV. B.R. Ambedkar

Choose the *correct* answer from the options given below:

(a) A-III, B-II, C-IV, D-I
(b) A-II, B-IV, C-I, D-III
(c) A-I, B-III, C-II, D-IV
(d) A-IV, B-I, C-III, D-II

69. 'Technology is socially shaped' — which among the following is not correct about this statement?

(a) Technological change is conditioned by social factors.
(b) Technological design and functions are the outcome of social process rather than of internal standards of scientific technological rationality.
(c) Technological change follows a fixed, linear path, which can be explained by references to some inner technological logic.
(d) Technological change involves controversies, disagreements and difficulties that engage relevant social groups in strategies to shape technology.

70. Arrange the following sociological works on social stratification in chronological order of their publication.

A. Social Class and Stratification (P. Saunders)
B. Social Class in America (L. Warner)
C. Political Power and Social Class (N. Poulantzas)
D. Class and Class Conflict in Industrial Society (R. Dahrendorf)

Choose the *correct* answer from the option given below:

(a) A, B, C, D
(b) B, D, C, A
(c) C, B, A, D
(d) D, C, B, A

71. In addition to feeding themselves, peasants use the rest of the produce to create three different funds

A. Ceremonial fund
B. The replacement fund
C. The rent fund
D. The recreational fund

Choose the *correct* answer from the option given below:

(a) A only
(b) A, B and D only
(c) A, B and C only
(d) C and D only

72. Arrange the following regulations in the chronological order of their year of enactment

A. Child Marriage Restraint Act
B. Prohibition of Female Infanticide Act
C. Hindu Gains of Learning Act
D. Age of Consent Act
E. Bengal Sati Regulation Act

Choose the *correct* answer from the option given below:

(a) D, B, E, C, A
(b) D, A, E, B, C
(c) E, D, B, A, C
(d) E, B, D, C, A

73. A social science having as its main focus the study of the social institutions brought into being by the industrial transformations of the past two or three centuries... (it involves) a historical anthropological and critical sensitivity. Who has explained this?

(a) Edward Said
(b) Michel Foucault
(c) Manuel Castells
(d) Anthony Giddens

74. Match the List I with List II

List I (Book)	List II (Author)
A. The Ruling Class	I. Robert Michels
B. Political Parties	II. Vilfredo Pareto
C. Elites and Society	III. Gaetano Mosca
D. The Mind and Society	IV. T.B. Bottomore

Choose the *correct* answer from the options given below:

(a) A-IV, B-III, C-I, D-II
(b) A-III, B-I, C-IV, D-II
(c) A-I, B-II, C-III, D-IV
(d) A-IV, B-III, C-II, D-I

75. In, 'The Elementary Form of Religious Life'. Emile Durkheim refutes:

(a) Comteian epistemology as it is based on idealistic and aprioristic assumption.
(b) Hegelian epistemology as it is based on idealistic and aprioristic assumption.
(c) Weberian epistemology as it is based on idealistic and aprioristic assumption.
(d) Kantian epistemology as it is based on idealistic and aprioristic assumptions.

76. Ethnic differences have a bearing on social conflict. In order to understand the scale and intensity of conflicts between ethnic groups a number of factors should be taken into account. These factors are-

A. Objective differences
B. Economic differences
C. Religious differences
D. Social Awareness
E. Political Organization

Choose the *correct* answer from the option given below:

(a) A, B and C only
(b) A, D and E only
(c) B, C and D only
(d) C, D and E only

77. Match the List I with List II

List I (Authors)	List II (Books)
A. C. Wright Mills	I. The Lonely Crowd
B. David Riesman	II. Who Rules America
C. G. William Domhoff	III. The Robber Barons
D. Matthew Josephson	IV. The Power Elite

Choose the *correct* answer from the options given below:

(a) A-IV, B-I, C-II, D-III
(b) A-I, B-II, C-III, D-IV
(c) A-IV, B-I, C-III, D-II
(d) A-II, B-I, C-III, D-IV

78. Arrange the following in chronological order of their publication

A. Models of Democracy (III Edition) (David Held)
B. Understanding Social Movements (Greg Martin)
C. Political Ideologies: An Introduction (5th Edition) (Andrew Heywood)
D. Power: A Radical View (Stephen Lukes)

Choose the *correct* answer from the option given below:

(a) D, A, C, B
(b) B, D, C, A
(c) C, B, D, A
(d) A, B, C, D

79. Who is associated with the concept of 'humane city'?

(a) Richard Sennett
(b) Manual Castells
(c) John Betjeman
(d) Paul Harrison

80. Who refers to two useful concepts in regard to community power structure namely "power pool" and "power dispersion"?

(a) T.K. Oommen
(b) M.N. Srinivas
(c) S.C. Dube
(d) Rajni Kothari

81. Match the List I with List II

List I (Book/Substance)	List II (Author/Discoverer)
A. Population Bomb	I. Sherwood Rowland & Mario Molina
B. Ozone Layer depleting chemicals	II. Rachel Carson
C. Silent Spring	III. Paul Ehrlich
D. The Waste Makers	IV. Vance Packard

Choose the *correct* answer from the options given below:

(a) A-I, B-II, C-III, D-IV
(b) A-III, B-I, C-II, D-IV
(c) A-IV, B-II, C-III, D-I
(d) A-IV, B-III, C-I, D-II

82. Important characteristics of Estates were

A. Each Estates had a status.
B. The Estates represented a broad division of labour.
C. The Estates were a political group.
D. All Estates had an equal status.

Choose the *correct* answer from the option given below:

(a) A only
(b) A, B and D only
(c) A, B and C only
(d) C and D only

83. Who among the following is not associated with 'The Chicago School"?

(a) Robert Park
(b) Ernest Burgers
(c) Ferdinand Tonies
(d) Louis Wirth

84. Who is the author of the book 'A *Philosophy of* NEFA'.

(a) Virginius Xaxa
(b) Surajit Sinha
(c) M.N. Srinivas
(d) Verrier Elwin

85. Which among the following is not the characteristic feature of indigenous knowledge?

(a) Embeddedness of knowledge in the local cultural milieu.
(b) Boundedness of local knowledge in space and time.
(c) Proper separation between nature and culture.
(d) A non-instrumental approach to nature.

86. Which among the following thinkers saw modernity as an 'unfinished project'?

(a) Anthony Giddens
(b) Manuel Castells
(c) Jurgen Habermas
(d) Michel Foucault

87. Which of the following premises characterize the dramaturgical school of interactionism?

A. Focuses on the ways that actors manipulate gestures to create an impression in a particular social scene.
B. Emphasizes on the process of impression management and not the purposes or goal toward which action is oriented.

C. Focuses on the goal orientation and particular structures which create different forms of interaction.
D. Emphasizes on the form of interaction itself rather than on the structures it creates, sustains or changes.

Choose the *correct* answer from the option given below:

(a) A, B and C only
(b) B and C only
(c) A, C and D only
(d) A, B and D only

88. Arrange the following works on 'gender studies' in chronological order of their publication.
A. Masculinities (Raewyn Connel)
B. Sexual Behaviour in the Human Male (Alfred Kinsey)
C. The Transformation of Intimacy (Anthony Giddens)
D. Paradoxes of Gender (Judith Lorber)

Choose the *correct* answer from the option given below:

(a) B, C, D, A
(b) C, B, A, D
(c) A, B, D, C
(d) D, C, B, A

89. Match the List I with List II

List I (Type of Society)	List II (Features)
A. Hunting and Gathering Societies	I. Distinct inequalities. Ruled by chiefs or warrior kings. Based on domestication and subsistence livelihood.
B. Agrarian Societies	II. Based on agriculture. Distinct government apparatus headed by a king.
C. Pastoral Societies	III. Few inequalities. Differences of rank limited by age and gender.
D. Traditional Societies or Civilization	IV. Stronger Inequalities. Ruled by the chiefs. Based on small rural communities.

Choose the *correct* answer from the options given below:

(a) A-II, B-I, C-IV, D-III
(b) A-II, B-IV, C-III, D-I
(c) A-III, B-IV, C-I, D-II
(d) A-IV, B-I, C-II, D-III

90. Marxian Dialectics is based on the ideas of:
A. Dialectical analysis does not see a simple, one-way, cause and effect relationship among the various parts of the social world.
B. Dialectical analysis is based on social values that are not separate from social facts.
C. Dialectical Analysis focuses on relations within and among various aspects of social world.
D. Dialectical Analysis has relation only with the material world and not the social world.

Choose the *correct* answer from the option given below:

(a) A and E only
(b) B, C and E only
(c) A, B and C only
(d) C and D only

Directions (91–95): Read the following passage carefully and answer the question that follows:

The process of urbanization should not unilaterally be associated with forces of modernization or secularization, even though hi some limited sense, as stated by Milton Singer and R. Redfield, in the metropolitan unban centers as growth occurs from the stage of primary (orthogenetic) to secondary (heterogenetic) urbanization, *traditional literati* may be transformed into professional intelligentsia, whose function in the changed circumstances may be to mediate between tradition and modernity. Urbanization even in the "secondary' phases may strengthen the sinews of the Great tradition because the communication channels which otherwise could be used for transmission of modern values, such as modern means of transport, press, radio, sound amplifiers, etc. are used to further the diffusion of the value system of the Great tradition. Every step in the intensification of communication thus means not only a benefit to modernity but equally, or probably more than equally, a benefit to the cause of the reinforcement of the Great tradition. Cultural renaissance and reformation as processes of change have relevance for Great tradition. Their significance has been both textual and contextual. Sanskritization as a process of cultural change has primarily a contextual significance; it is particularistic in origin and therefore belongs to the little tradition. Sanskritization, above all, describes an empirical process in cultural change and has been most widespread.

91. The notion of modernity is closely associated with
(a) intensification of communication through mass media
(b) performance of rituals in temples
(c) orthogenetic changes
(d) strengthening of Jajmani system

92. What are the characteristics of Sanskritization:
A. It has a contextual significance
B. It belongs to the Great Tradition
C. It is particularistic in origin
D. It has been most wide-spread

Choose the *correct* answer from the options given below:

(a) A, B, C and D
(b) A, B and C only
(c) A, C and D only
(d) B, C and D only

93. As growth occurs from primary urbanization to secondary urbanization, in the metropolitan urban centers the traditional literati are transformed into
(a) Labour class
(b) White collars
(c) Professional intelligentsia
(d) Semi-skilled workers

94. The Great Tradition may become more strong in heterogenetic urbanization as a result of
(a) constructions of more temples
(b) changes in traditional dress code
(c) diffusion of value system through mass media
(d) door to door campaign of religious events

95. The processes of urbanization should not be associated with forces of modernization in metropolitan urban centers-
(a) Unilaterally
(b) Bilaterally
(c) Multilaterally
(d) Unrelated with each other

Directions (96–100): Read the following passage carefully and answer the question that follows:

There are broadly two different approaches to rural planning in the Third World: the improvement approach, which aims to encourage agricultural development within existing peasant production system, and the transformation approach, which attempts to establish new forms of agricultural and social organization, and which makes a radical break with existing system in terms of scale of operation, production techniques, and socio-legal structure. The improvement approach was especially characteristic of the development policies pursued by British colonial government in Africa. India and elsewhere. Under colonial rule extension works as often coupled with the enforcement of various administrative ordinances to prevent soil erosion or to encourage the cultivation of certain crops. Hence, general incentives to production were combined with principle of "persistent persuasion". The cases of non-observance were reported to authorities for court action. Various governments encouraged the marketing of these crops through state agencies or cooperative societies composed of basically small farmers for selling their produce. Thus, the colonial governments were willing to assist in developing an infrastructure concerned with distribution as well as production.

96. By whom the strategy of improvement approach was implemented.
(a) By French Government
(b) By British Government
(c) By Spanish Government
(d) By American Government

97. How was soil erosion prevented during colonial period?
(a) Launching govt projects by the govt. departments
(b) By voluntary organizations of the area
(c) By enforcement of administrative orders
(d) By making appeal to peasants

98. What was the aim of improvement approach in colonial period?
(a) To encourage the farmers to adopt non-agricultural occupations
(b) To encourage them to grow only certain specific crops
(c) To encourage the farmers to grow any type of cash crop
(d) To encourage the farmers to grow indigenous crops only.

99. With what the extension work was coupled during colonial period?
(a) with humble request to farmers
(b) with coercive power
(c) no control over peasants
(d) radical changes in organization of agricultural activities

100. In what ways transformation approach to development was different from improvement approach?
(a) It emphasized on the principle of persistence persuasion.
(b) It attempts to establish new forms of agricultural and social organizations.
(c) It was interested in continuation of existing system of agriculture.
(d) It operates at a small scale in agriculture sector.

Answer Key

1. (a)	**16.** (c)	**31.** (b)	**46.** (d)	**61.** (c)	**76.** (b)	**91.** (a)
2. (*)	**17.** (b)	**32.** (a)	**47.** (c)	**62.** (a)	**77.** (a)	**92.** (c)
3. (*)	**18.** (b)	**33.** (c)	**48.** (a)	**63.** (a)	**78.** (a)	**93.** (c)
4. (c)	**19.** (c)	**34.** (d)	**49.** (b)	**64.** (b)	**79.** (a)	**94.** (c)
5. (c)	**20.** (d)	**35.** (d)	**50.** (a)	**65.** (d)	**80.** (a)	**95.** (a)
6. (b)	**21.** (c)	**36.** (a)	**51.** (b)	**66.** (c)	**81.** (b)	**96.** (b)
7. (d)	**22.** (b)	**37.** (c)	**52.** (d)	**67.** (c)	**82.** (c)	**97.** (c)
8. (d)	**23.** (a)	**38.** (b)	**53.** (c)	**68.** (b)	**83.** (c)	**98.** (b)
9. (d)	**24.** (b)	**39.** (c)	**54.** (b)	**69.** (c)	**84.** (d)	**99.** (b)
10. (a)	**25.** (c)	**40.** (a)	**55.** (a)	**70.** (b)	**85.** (c)	**100.** (b)
11. (d)	**26.** (b)	**41.** (c)	**56.** (b)	**71.** (c)	**86.** (c)	
12. (b)	**27.** (c)	**42.** (a)	**57.** (c)	**72.** (c)	**87.** (d)	
13. (c)	**28.** (b)	**43.** (d)	**58.** (a)	**73.** (d)	**88.** (a)	
14. (a)	**29.** (a)	**44.** (b)	**59.** (d)	**74.** (b)	**89.** (c)	
15. (b)	**30.** (b)	**45.** (d)	**60.** (b)	**75.** (d)	**90.** (c)	

*These questions are dropped by the NTA.

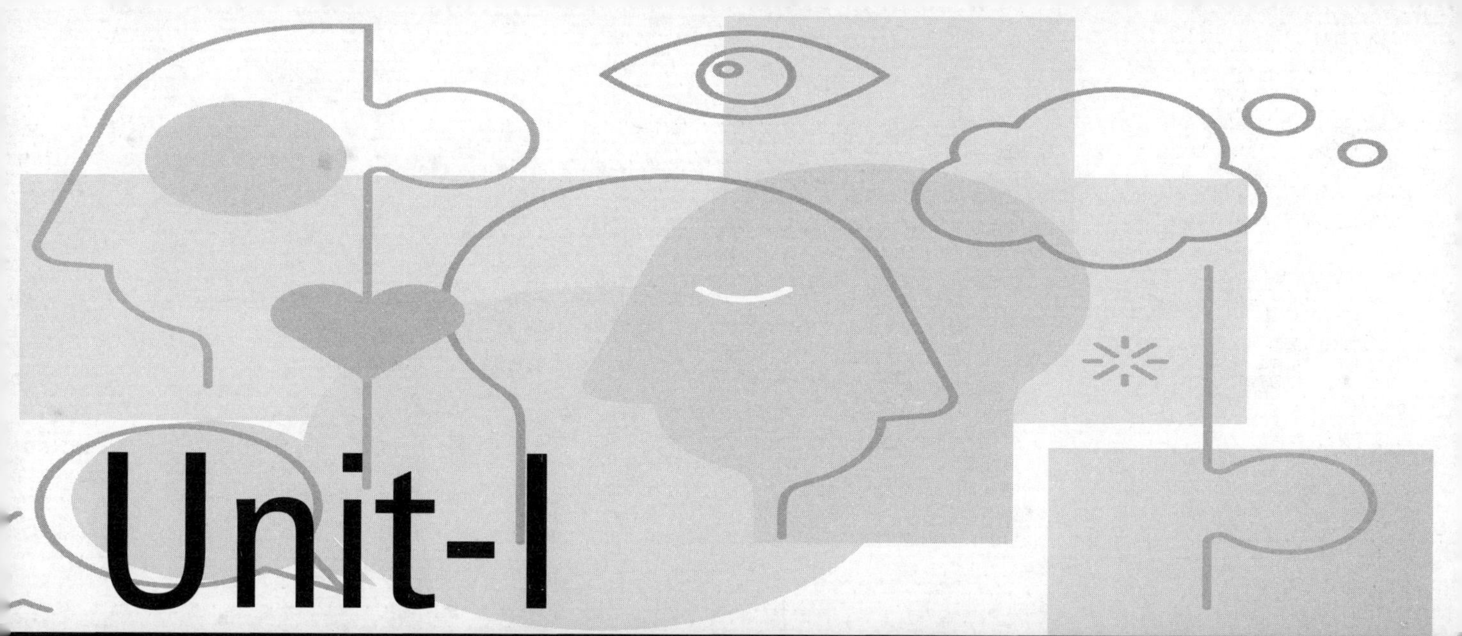

Unit-I

Sociological Theory

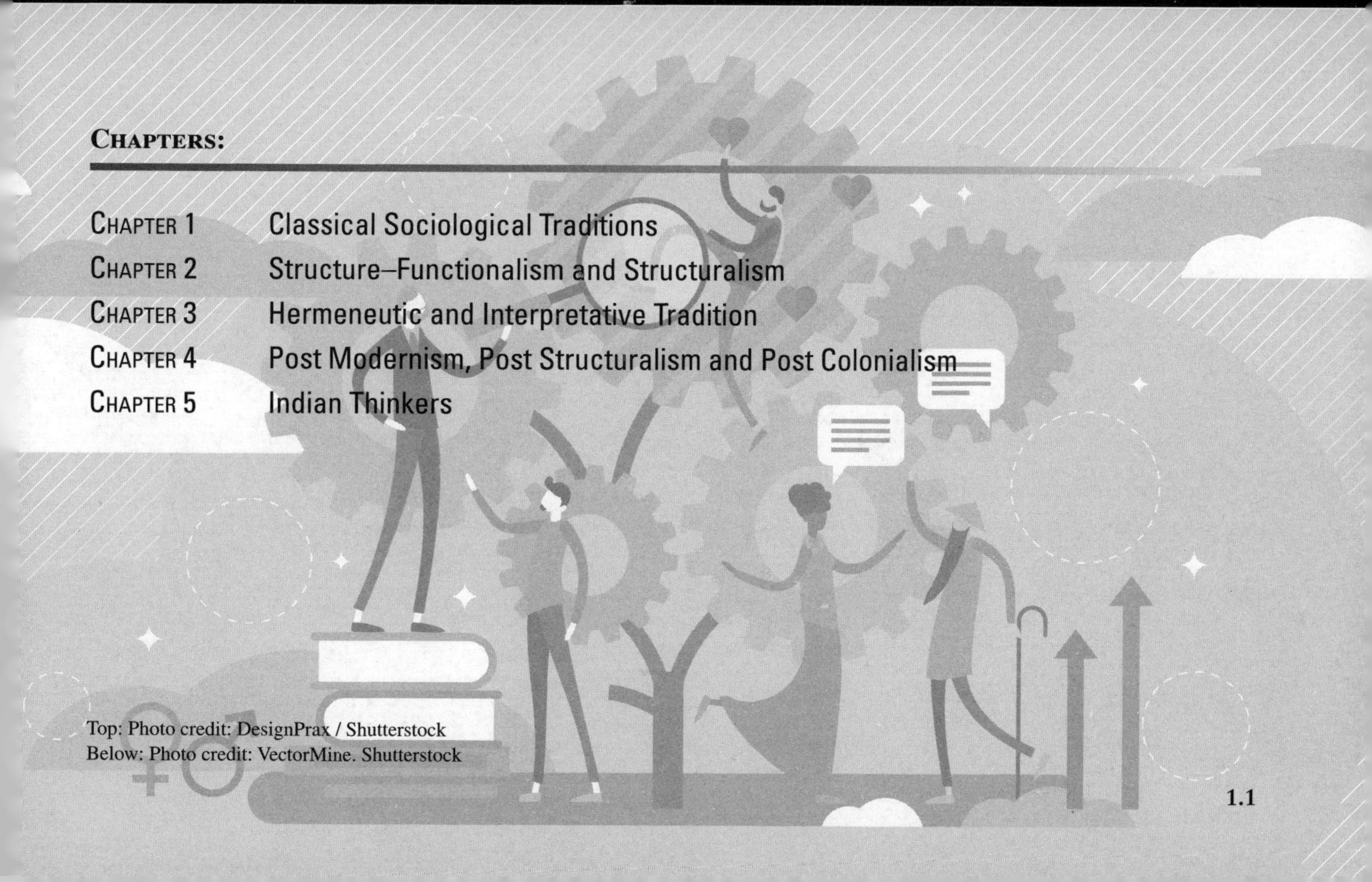

CHAPTERS:

Top: Photo credit: DesignPrax / Shutterstock
Below: Photo credit: VectorMine. Shutterstock

CHAPTER

1 Classical Sociological Traditions

Learning Objectives:

In this chapter, we will discuss the following important topics.

- Emile Durkheim
- Max Weber
- Karl Marx

INTRODUCTION

The emergence of sociology as a scientific discipline can be traced back to the period of the 18th and 19th centuries, which saw tremendous social, political, and economic changes such as those embodied in the French Revolution and the Industrial Revolution, giving thinkers much thought about it. Thus, the field of sociology was initially concerned with the broader historical processes related to these changes. The three major sociological theories that came into existence in this period are the functionalist perspective of Émile Durkheim, the conflict perspective of Karl Marx, and the interactionist perspective of Max Weber. Each of these perspectives has its own way of explaining various aspects of society and human behaviour. These perspectives have been termed classical tradition as they reflect the era of enlightenment and antiquity. In spite of the criticism these perspectives have generated, they are an integral part of Sociology as they present the perspectives of the early sociologists who had envisaged the discipline.

Now, we will take a detailed look at each of them.

EMILE DURKHEIM (1858–1917)

Émile Durkheim was born on 15 April 1858 in Epinal, a small town in eastern France. He grew up in a Jewish family, and his father was a rabbi (i.e., a spiritual leader and religious teacher of the Jewish community).

His doctoral thesis: *At first, he decided to do his thesis on the relationship between individualism and socialism. Later he focused on the relationship between the individual and society. Finally, he defined his subject as the relationship between individual personality and social solidarity.*

Important Books

1. The Division of Labour (1893)
2. The Rules of Sociological Method (1895)
3. Suicide (1897)
4. Primitive Classification (1903)
5. The Elementary Forms of Religious Life (1912)
6. Education and Sociology (1922)
7. Sociology and Philosophy (1924)

Major Theories

Solidarity

Durkheim analyzed economic and social solidarity in The Division of Labour in Society. He was curious to know the forces that govern and control social life. Durkheim recognized that solidarity can be expressed in two different ways which are 'mechanical' and 'organic'.

Mechanical Solidarity In small societies with mechanical solidarity, individual autonomy is minimal and there is a likeness of beliefs in the society. There is no specialization of functions and there is little division of labour. Collective conscience pervades all the individuals in the group.

The links connecting the individual to the social whole are deep and there is complete social integration. In such a society the institution of religion is dominant and the place of the individual in the society is determined by kinship. A system of the penal law that is repressive and punishes crime severely.

Organic Solidarity On the other hand, societies with organic solidarity have a greater division of labour and individuals depend on each other for specific tasks rather than on the society as a whole. Such societies are dense and cover a large geographical area.

Political, legal, and economic institutions are more specialized and the collective conscience exerted over individuals has weakened. There are more individual differences between individuals and integration of individuals when social cohesion is weakened. Restitutive law is operative and aims at restoring the wrongs to their original state.

Social Facts

Durkheim defined social facts as 'ways of acting, thinking and feeling external to the individual, and endowed with the power of coercion by virtue of which they control him'.

Durkheim took social facts as objects. They are real and independent of the will or desire of the individual. They are external to individuals and are capable of exerting pressure on them.

The second social fact refers to the general ways of thinking, behaving, feeling, etc. that are prevalent in society. They are external to an individual i.e., they exist independently of the individual's will or desire and exert pressure on them.

To Durkheim society is a reality subgenres. Society comes into being through the association of individuals. Hence society represents a specific reality that has its own characteristics.

Types of social facts Durkheim made an important distinction between normal and pathological social facts. A social fact is general when it is commonly encountered in a society at a certain stage of its development. Every deviation from this norm is a pathological fact.

For example, some degree of crime is inevitable in any society. Therefore, according to Durkheim crime to that extent is a normal social fact. However, an extraordinary increase in the rate of crime is a pathological social fact.

Main Characteristics of Social Facts The main characteristics of social facts are

- **i.** externality,
- **ii.** constraint,
- **iii.** independence, and
- **vi.** generality.

According to Durkheim, social facts exist outside the individual conscience. Their existence is external to individuals. For example, domestic or civil, or contractual obligations are defined externally in personal laws and customs. Religious beliefs and practices exist outside and prior to the individual.

An individual takes birth in a society and leaves it after birth, although the social facts in the society are already given and continue to exist irrespective of the birth or death of an individual. For example, language continues to function independently of any one individual.

The second characteristic of a social fact is that it exerts constraint (pressure) on individuals. Social fact is recognized because it imposes itself on the individual. For example, the institutions of law, education, faith, etc. are already given to everyone from outside. They are obligatory for all.

A social fact is one that has a more or less general occurrence in society. Also, it is independent of the personal characteristics of individuals or universal characteristics of human nature. The beliefs, feelings, and practices of a group taken collectively are examples of this.

In short, the social fact is specific. It is born of the association of individuals. It represents the collective content of a social group or society. It differs in kind from what occurs in individual consciousness. Social facts can be subjected to categorization and classification. Above all social facts are the subject matter of the science of sociology.

Rules for the Observation of Social Facts While studying social facts as 'things' the following three rules have to be followed in order to be objective.

- **i.** All preconceptions must be eradicated.
- **ii.** Sociologists have to formulate the concepts precisely.
- **iii.** When sociologists undertake the investigation of some order of social facts, they must consider them from an aspect that is independent of their individual manifestations.

Suicide

Durkheim became interested in the study of suicide because of an increase in the number of suicides in Europe with the coming of industrialization in the 1850s.

Due to industrialization, individualism increased in society and social integration decreased.

Durkheim analyzed suicide rates from different sections of society and found:

1. Men have higher suicide rates than women (though married women who remained childless for many years ended up with higher rates of suicide).
2. The suicide rate is higher for those who are unmarried than those involved in sexual relationships.
3. The suicide rate is higher for people without children than for people with children.
4. Protestants have a higher suicide rate than Catholics and Jews.
5. The suicide rate is higher among soldiers than among civilians.
6. The suicide rate is higher in times of peace than in times of war. (War reduced the suicide rate: After war broke out between Austria and Italy in 1866, the suicide rate in both countries dropped by 14 percent.)
7. Suicide rates are high in Scandinavian countries.
8. The higher the level of education, the more likely a person is to choose suicide. However, Durkheim established that there is a greater correlation between a person's religion and suicide rates than a person's education level. Jewish people were generally highly educated but had a low suicide rate.

From the above analysis, Durkheim believed that suicide cannot be explained by individual or psychological factors but must be explained by analyzing the link between social institutions and the individual.

Types of suicides Durkheim explained the different forms of suicide by looking at how individuals are able to develop bonds in society and how individuals are controlled by society.

He gave 4 types of suicide

1. Egoistic Suicide
2. Altruistic Suicide
3. Anomic Suicide
4. Fatalistic Suicide

He described Egoistic and Altruistic suicides, by referring to the level of social integration of individuals.

He examined anomic and fatalistic suicides, citing the level of social regulation(control) of individuals.

Due to the weakening of social bonds, the individual separates himself from society. The individual turns to the self and personal goals take precedence over social goals.

Individuals' bonds with family, religious, and political institutions weaken and they become more dependent on themselves.

Egoistic suicide is the result of the absence of social bonds and the loosening of individuals' attachment to groups in society. Durkheim, for example, recognized that family life creates duties and obligations towards society and a greater relationship with an institution outside of oneself.

The polar opposite of Egoistic suicide is altruistic suicide in which individuals are highly integrated with society and sacrifice their lives for society.

For example, military soldiers on the battlefield lay down their lives for the service of the nation-state. Similarly, in the earlier Hindu society, widows used to commit Sati and sacrifice their lives on the funeral pyre of their husbands. In such cases, individuals are bound to give their lives for society and are socially honoured for doing so.

The third form of suicide that Durkheim analyzed was anomic suicide, which occurs when social regulation weakens. For example, anomic suicide levels may increase in times of economic prosperity or hardship.

Thus, society sets goals and wants for individuals which are unattainable. Individuals may become depressed and this reflects the failure of society to control needs.

This form of suicide occurs when the desires are unbridled and the economy dominates other institutions in society.

The fourth form of suicide is Fatalistic Suicide which occurs when individuals are highly regulated by society. Durkheim explains this type of suicide by citing the case of suicides by slaves.

Religion

Durkheim's last major book, '*Elementary Forms of Religious Life*' (1912), has been considered one of the most profound and most original works on religion. It is considered his best and most mature work. While Suicide focused on a large amount of data from various sources.

To define religion, says Durkheim, we must first free our minds from all preconceived notions of religion. Durkheim rejects the notion that religion is concerned only with 'mystical' or 'supernatural' phenomena, with gods, spirits, and ghosts. He points out that religion has as much to do with the ordinary as it does with the extraordinary aspects of life. He rejected the pre-existing theories i.e., the theory of animism and naturalism

To define religion, he says, the various religious systems of the world must be examined in order to derive elements or characteristics that they have in common.

According to Durkheim, all religions have two basic components, namely religious beliefs, and rituals. Beliefs are collective representations and prescribed modes of action, which are influenced by beliefs.

The religious beliefs studied by Durkheim categorize all things into 'sacred' and 'profane'.

The sacred is that which is set apart, that which is regarded as sacred and respected, or that which is feared and avoided. The sacred is usually of higher status, more valuable than profane things, and its identity and power are protected by social rules. For example, we are suggested to enter the temple after taking bath.

The profane, on the other hand, refers to the mundane, ordinary aspects of day-to-day existence. The sacred and the profane says Durkheim, are kept apart because they are contrasting (separate), antagonistic (in conflict), and distinct (separate).

Keeping these factors in mind, the definition of religion given by Durkheim is as follows. 'A religion is a unified system of beliefs and practices relative to sacred things, that is, separate and forbidden things—beliefs and practices that unite into a single ethical community called a church.'

Durkheim believed that in order to understand more complex religions one must first understand the simpler forms or primary forms. He says that totemism is the simplest form of religion. He chose to study totemism as practiced by the Aborigines of Central Australia.

The totem is associated with the social organization of the clans. Clan members consider themselves descended from some common ancestor - an animal, a plant, or even some inanimate object. The 'common ancestor' is the 'totem object'. This totem is the object that gives the clan its name and identity.

But it is more than just a name, it is a symbol. When it is engraved, carved, or designed on other objects of the clan, even on the body of the members of the clan, that object becomes special. There is purity in them. Many taboos or 'don'ts' are attached to the totemic object. It can neither be killed nor eaten, it should be treated with reverence.

Durkheim states that it is not in fact the animal or the plant that is worshiped or considered sacred, but an anonymous and impersonal force that is present throughout the world and pervades all material things in the world. This force is variously described as 'mana', 'wakan' by Samoans, 'oranda' by Melanesians, and 'oranda' by some North American tribes.

In Durkheim's view, 'God' is nothing but society which has been divined or glorified and given a different shape and form. Why is society worshipped? Durkheim says that it is physically and morally superior to individuals. It is 'sui-generis', it has a reality of its own. Its power is feared, its authority respected. When a soldier sacrifices his life to protect the flag of the country, he is not worshiping the flag itself, but the flag is being worshipped, that is, the nation (collective consciousness).

The worshiping society inculcates a sense of unity, solidarity, and enthusiasm among its members, helping them to participate in the collective life and expression of the society.

Durkheim believes that the origin of scientific thought lies in religious thought. Both religion and science reflect nature, man, and society. Both attempts to classify, relate and explain things.

Education

According to Durkheim, every society has some form of an educational system that it imposes on its people with irresistible general force. It is futile to believe that we can raise our children exactly the way we want to. There are customs that we must follow; If we deviate too much from them, they will take their revenge on our children.

Durkheim focuses on the role of education in the preservation of society and culture (which occurs through the transmission of values, knowledge, beliefs, and skills of culture through the family, kinship group, and school).

For an educational system to exist there must be a generation of adults and a generation of youth, and the latter must be served by the former.

Education preserves and reinforces these homogenous principles of the society in the child from the very beginning. Durkheim writes, "Education is the influence exercised by the adult generation on those who are not yet prepared for social life."

According to Durkheim, specific skills imparted in educational institutions are necessary to maintain the division of labour in society. As societies change from simple to complex, there is a corresponding increase in the complexity of the division of labour and the emergence of more specialized occupations.

MAX WEBER (1864–1920)

Max Weber was born on April 21, 1864, in Erfurt, Germany, into a comparatively affluent Protestant family. He spent most of his early life in Berlin. Weber's father was a bureaucrat who rose to a very high political position. He was a German sociologist and political economist best known for his thesis on the 'Protestant ethic', relating Protestantism to capitalism, and for his ideas on bureaucracy.

Important Works

1. The Protestant Ethics and The Spirit of Capitalism–1905
2. The Religion of India–1916
3. Politics as Vocation–1919
4. Science as Vocation–1919
5. The Sociology of Religion–1920
6. The City–1921
7. Basic Concepts in Sociology–1922
8. Economy and Society–1922
9. The Theory of Social and Economic Organization–1947
10. The Religion of China–1951 (First published in 1915 under the title Konfuzianismus und Taoismus)

Major Theories

Ideal Type

An ideal type is made up of two words i.e., ideal and type. The literal meaning of 'ideal' is 'a concept or a standard in the highest perfection of something'. It refers to a mental image or concept rather than a physical object. This is a model.

The word 'type' means a type, form, class, or group that is distinguished by a particular character. Thus, it is understood that ideal type is a type, category, class, or group of things, things, or persons with particular characteristics which seem to be the best examples of it.

Weber used the ideal type in a specific sense. For him, the ideal type is a mental construct like a model for the investigation and systematic characterization of a concrete situation.

Max Weber was particularly concerned with the problem of objectivity in the social sciences. So, he used the ideal type as a methodological device that looks at reality objectively.

It investigates, classifies, organizes, and defines social reality without subjective bias. Ideal types have nothing to do with values. Its function as a research tool is to classify and compare.

For Weber: 'The ideal specific concept would develop our skill in research. It is not a description of reality, but its purpose is to give such a description a clear means of expression.'

In other words, ideal types are concepts formulated on the basis of carefully and analytically collected facts for empirical research.

Construction of Ideal Types Ideal types are formed by the abstraction and combination of an indefinite number of elements which, although found in reality, are rarely or never discovered in a specific form.

Ideal types do not represent general or average characteristics but focus on specific and essential characteristics.

The ideal type is thus a selection of certain elements, certain traits, or characteristics that are specific and relevant to the study undertaken. However, one thing that must be kept in mind here is that although ideal types are constructed from facts existing in reality, they do not represent or describe the whole of reality, they are pure types in the logical sense.

Features of Ideal Type Ideal types are not normal or average types. That is, they are not defined by characteristics common to all phenomena or objects of study. They are formulated on the basis of certain characteristic features, which are essential for the construction of an ideal type concept.

Ideal types are not representations of total reality or they do not explain everything. They represent a partial conception of the whole.

Ideal types are neither a description of a fixed concept of reality, nor a hypothesis, but they can aid in both description and interpretation. Ideal types differ in scope and usage from descriptive concepts.

They also help in arriving at general propositions and in comparative analysis.

Ideal types guide empirical research and are used in the systematization of data on historical and social reality

Authority

The German word 'Herrschaft', used by Weber, has been variously translated. Some sociologists term it as 'authority', others as 'domination' or 'command'. Herrschaft is a situation in which a 'Herr' or master dominates or commands others.

Raymond Aron defines Herrschaft as the master's ability to obtain the obedience of those who theoretically owe it to him.

But when it comes to Weber, Herrschaft means authority. As Authority refers to legitimized power, hence to understand authority we must the term Power

Power refers to the ability or capacity to control or influence the action of others.

Elements of Authority For a system of authority to exist the following elements must be present.

- **i.** An individual ruler/lord or a group of rulers/lords.
- **ii.** A person/group that is ruled.
- **iii.** The will of the ruler to influence the conduct of the ruled which can be expressed through commands.
- **vi.** Evidence of the influence of rulers in terms of compliance or obedience shown by the rulers.
- **v.** Direct or indirect evidence that shows that the rulers have internally accepted and accepted the fact that the orders of the ruler must be obeyed.

Types of Authority According to Weber, there are three systems of legitimation, each with its respective norms, which justify the power to command. It is such systems of legitimacy that are designated as the following types of authority.

- **i.** Traditional authority
- **ii.** Charismatic authority
- **iii.** Rational-legal authority

Traditional Authority: This system of legitimation flows from traditional action. In other words, it is based on customary law and the sanctity of ancient traditions. It is based on the belief that a certain authority should be respected as it has been in existence since time immemorial.

In traditional authority, rulers enjoy personal authority based on their inherited status. His orders are in accordance with the customs and he also has the authority to make the governed comply.

The monarchy, the classic example of traditional authority, still exists, but in a highly diluted form. The Queen of England is a traditional figure of power but as you know, she doesn't actually exercise her authority. The laws of the country are made in his name, but their content is determined by the legislators, the representatives of the public. The Queen has a parliament, which rules the kingdom, but she does not appoint ministers. She is the nominal head of state.

Charismatic Authority: Charisma means an extraordinary quality possessed by some individuals. This gives such people the unique power to capture the imagination and devotion of the common people.

Charismatic authority is based on extraordinary devotion to a person and to the way of life preached by this person. The validity of such a right depends on the person's belief in supernatural or magical powers.

The charismatic leader 'proves' his power through miracles, military and other victories or the dramatic prosperity of the disciples. Charismatic leaders retain their authority as long as they 'prove' their miraculous powers in the eyes of their disciples.

You may have realized that the type of social action that is related to charismatic authority is effective action. Disciples are in a highly charged emotional state as a result of the teachings and appeals of charismatic leaders. They worship their hero.

Charismatic authority is not dependent on customary beliefs or written rules. It is purely the result of the special qualities of the leader who rules or rules in his personal capacity. Charismatic authority is not organized; Therefore, there is no paid staff or administrative structure.

***Routinization of Charisma*:** As charismatic authority is based on the personal qualities of a person, the problem of succession arises with the death or disappearance of the leader.

The person who takes the position of leader may not have charismatic powers. A type of organization develops to disseminate the core message of the leader.

Original charisma is transformed into either traditional authority or rational-legal authority. Weber calls this the Routinization of Charisma.

If the charismatic figure is followed by a son/daughter or a close relative, traditional authority results. On the other hand, if charismatic qualities are identified and written down, it translates into rational-legal authority, where anyone who possesses these qualities can become a leader. Charismatic authority can thus be described as unstable and temporary.

Rational-Legal Authority: The term refers to a system of authority, both rational and legal. It is vested in a regular administrative staff that functions according to certain written rules and laws.

Those who exercise authority are appointed to do so on the basis of their acquired qualifications, which are prescribed and codified. Those in power consider it a profession and are paid a salary. Thus, it is a rational system. It is legal because it is in accordance with the laws of the land that people recognize and feel bound to follow.

People accept the validity of both the ordinance and the rules and at the same time respect the position or titles of those who enforce the rules. Rational-legal authority is a distinctive feature of modern society. It is a reflection of the process of rationalization.

Recall that Weber regards rationalization as a key feature of Western civilization and a typical product of human thought and deliberation.

KARL MARX (1818–1883)

Marx was born on 5th May 1818 in Trier, Rhineland (Prussia) in a Jewish family. He embraced Christianity during his childhood. He studied History, Law, and Philosophy at Bonn, Berlin, and Jena. In 1841 he received his doctorate (Ph.D. Degree) in Philosophy from the University of Jena for his thesis, entitled, "On the Differences between the Natural Philosophy of Democritus and Epicurus."

After completing his doctorate degree, he began writing for a radical, left-wing paper and became its editor in 1842, following the forced closure of the paper, he was compelled to move from Cologne, Germany to Paris, France. Here he came into the influence of Hegelian ideology and wrote extensively upon Hegelian themes of 'alienation', 'estrangement', and 'loss of being' confronting modern industrial man.

Important Works

1. Economics and Philosophical Manuscripts: 1843
2. Theses on Feuerbach: 1845
3. [A Critique of] German Ideology (Marx and Engels): 1845
4. The Communist Manifesto (Marx and Engels): 1848
5. Wage-Labour and Capital: 1849
6. Preface to A Contribution to the Critique of Political Economy: 1859
7. Das Capital, Volume 3 + 1: 1867–1883, 1872
8. The Civil War in France: 1871
9. Critique of the Gotha Program: 1875

Major Theories

Historical/Dialectical Materialism

During his student days, Marx was attracted to Hegelian Idealism but he soon shifted his interest to Humanism and ultimately to Scientific Socialism.

Marx borrowed his dialectical method from Hegel but modified it in a fundamental way. While Hegel applied his dialectical method to the realm of ideas, Marx applied dialectics to explain the material conditions of life.

The term 'dialectics' refers to a method of intellectual discussion through dialogue. It is a word of logic. According to the Greek philosopher Aristotle (384–322 BC), it referred to the art of refutation by question and answer.

For Hegel, the change in ideas (thesis) affects the development of society. He said that there is a contradiction in the idea (thesis) itself which gives rise to opposing ideas (anti-thesis) and so on:

Thesis + **Anti-Thesis** ⇨ **Synthesis**

Marx denounced the Hegelian philosophy of dialectical idealism and said that it is not due to change in idea affecting the development of society but the change in material condition affecting the structure and development of society.

For Marx, there is a contradiction in the material which led to change in the structure and development of society

Marx pointed out that Hegel's 'dialectic idealism is standing on its head. It must be turned right side up'. This he did by making matter primary and mind secondary.

He derived his own theory of society and history which is called Dialectical Materialism.

Marx holds that the material and the idea are not only different but opposite and constitute a unity in which the material is primary and the mind (idea) is secondary.

This is so because matter can exist without the mind but mind cannot exist without matter because historically it (mind) has developed out of matter.

In his Socialism: Utopian and Scientific Engels defined historical materialism as a theory that holds that the ultimate cause which determines the whole course of human history is the economic development of society.

The whole course of human history is explained in terms of changes occurring in the modes of production and exchange.

Force of Production + Relation of Production = Mode of Production

Starting with primitive communism the mode of production has passed through three stages: slavery, feudalism, and capitalism, and the consequent division of society into distinct classes and the struggle of these classes against one another.

This contradiction between forces of production and relations of production divides society into classes.

Starting with primitive communism the mode of production has passed through three stages: slavery, feudalism, and capitalism, and the consequent division of society into distinct classes and the struggle of these classes against one another.

Stages of Development

Stages	Society	Class
1st Stage	Primitive Communism	Classless Society
2nd Stage	Ancient Society	Master and Slave
3rd Stage	Feudal Society	Feudal lords and Serfs
4th Stage	Capitalist Society	Capitalist and labour

According to Marx, 'Capitalism contained the seeds of its own destruction.'

Alienation

This is contained in his early work Economic and Philosophical Manuscripts which were written in 1843 but were discovered nearly fifty years after his death.

These Manuscripts show that 'early Marx' was mainly interested in the problem of alienation, in order to understand the Marxian Theory of Alienation it is important to understand Hegel's views on alienation. This is so because Marx borrowed his idea of alienation from Hegel, and Feuerbach's, particularly from Hegel.

For Hegel, alienation is the state of consciousness as it acquaints itself with the external world in which objects appear to man as external or alien.

Hegel's discussion of alienation includes a different conception of man and his place in the spiritual world, and of reality.

For Hegel, alienation is needed to raise an average person to a high level of culture. In this sense, it is a moment to attain this level.

Feuerbach's position is just the opposite, for him, man is not a self-alienated God; rather God is the self-alienated man.

God is created by man, but he is above man and is separated from man in all respects. He is estranged from man and Feuerbach calls it alienation.

In Feuerbach's opinion, religion is the best example of estrangement or alienation. He further says that it is peculiar that the religion or God is man's own creation and ultimately, he is separated from it. Naturally, if a man wants to make himself alienation-free, the best way is de-alienation.

God is created by man, but he is above man and is different from man in every way. He is separated from man and Feuerbach calls this alienation.

In Feuerbach's opinion, religion is the best example of alienation. He further says that it is strange that religion or God is man's own creation and ultimately, he is separated from it. Naturally, if a man wants to make himself alienation-free, the best way is de-alienation.

Marx vehemently attacks Hegel for identifying the existence of objects with alienation, which makes the objective world a mere phantasm. Marx does so by distinguishing between objectification and alienation.

Objectification is the material existence of the objects; while alienation is a state of consciousness resulting from a specific type of relationship between men and objects. Such relationships cannot be a fantasy because objects are real.

For Marx alienation is rooted in the historical situation and its consequences. In the capitalist society, the creation of objects (production) does not help man to realize himself, i.e., to realize his potential.

This inability of a man to realize his potential while being engaged in the creation of objects causes alienation. Hence, alienation will be overcome when the production of objects will lead to unfolding of the human potentialities.

In capitalism, production takes place in alienating circumstances and this makes objectification (creation of objects) into dehumanization.

The object produced by the labourer, now stands opposed to him as an alien being as a power independent of him. In essence, labour itself becomes an object.

Now the product of his labour does not belong to the labourer, it is no longer his own. It belongs to someone else: the capitalist.

The greater this product is, the more he is diminished and dehumanised. Thus, you can say that, for Marx, labour becomes a dehumanizing act when it is not a voluntary but a coercive activity.

Alienation as it exists in a capitalist society has many dimensions. It is said that:

(a) Man is alienated from nature,
(b) From himself, that is from his own activity,
(c) From his species-being,
(d) And, finally, he is alienated from his fellow citizens.

Class Struggle

For Marx the most basic unit of human life is production, therefore the sole criterion on the basis of which the class of a person is determined is his ownership (or control) of means of production (land, capital, machines & technology).

Those who own ' or control the means of production constitute the bourgeoisie (exploiters), and those who own only labour power constitute the proletariat (exploited).

It is clear that according to Marx the mode of production or economic structure is the base or foundation of society. Any change in infrastructure (material economy) will cause fundamental changes in the superstructure (idea) and consequently in society.

In Communist Manifesto, Marx-Engels said: "The history of all hitherto existing society is the history of class struggles". They argued that class conflict is the real driving force of human history.

In capitalist societies class differentiation is most clear; class consciousness is more developed and class conflict is most acute.

Here the question arises what is the basis of this antagonism? Marx's answer is that the contradiction between the forces and the relations of production is the basis of this antagonism.

The bourgeoisie is constantly creating more powerful means of production. But the relations of production that is, apparently, both the relations of ownership and the distribution of income are not transferred at the same rate.

This contradiction, according to Marx, will eventually produce a revolutionary crisis. The proletariat, which constitutes and will increasingly constitute the vast majority of the population, will become a class, that is, a social entity aspiring for the seizure of power and transformation of social relations.

At this stage 'class in itself' he said will become 'class for itself'. In 'class in itself' people do not have consciousness of their real situation, whereas in "class for itself" people have full consciousness of their situation.

Marx said that class antagonism and subsequently class conflict in the capitalist system will usher in socialism in place of capitalism through a revolution.

Surplus Value

The key feature of class relations in capitalism, according to Marx, is the expropriation of surplus value by the bourgeoisie from the labour of the proletariat. Marx admits that human labour cannot create value by itself alone.

The capitalist buys the 'labour power' of the labour and applies it to the raw material to produce commodities that have an exchange value. The difference between the exchange value of the commodity and the wages paid to the worker by the capitalist in producing that commodity is surplus value.

In fact, Marx explains the whole process of exploitation with the help of his theory of surplus value. It is a distinct feature of the capitalist mode of production. To put it in simple words, surplus value accrues because the commodity produced by the worker is sold by the capitalist for more than what the worker receives as wages.

This capital has two parts constant capital and variable capital. Constant capita! relates to means of production like raw material, machinery, tools, etc. used for commodity production. The variable capital refers to the wages paid to the worker.

Hence, surplus value is the difference between the value produced by the worker and what he gets in exchange for this value of his labour. This is called variable capital.

Religion

Marx was concerned more with the understanding of capitalist order than with the understanding of religion. But in his general understanding of capitalism, Marx also developed a general theory of society that extended to almost all social institutions, especially politics, and religion.

Marx's model of society had an economic base that controls the superstructure constituted by religion, politics,' arts, etc. According to Marx, society determines man's consciousness.

Hence, religion comes not just from within the individual but from specific exploitative social conditions created by bourgeoisie. His views on religion and its relationship with capitalism have three aspects:

Firstly, religion is an illusion that veils real exploitative conditions in society;

Secondly, religion is a mode of protest albeit in a mild form;

Third, religion can be removed not through criticism of religion, but only by changing the social conditions that give rise to religion.

Religion has a twofold function, first, it serves as the ideology (political thought of a social class) of the ruling elite and second, it serves as an opium for the masses.

Much of Marx's understanding of religion seems to have arisen from his experience of Protestantism in the early nineteenth century in the Kingdom of Prussia.

Marx was critical of the Prussian state which promoted Protestantism, as it helped the state justify economic inequalities.

It can also be said that Protestantism served as the ideology of the new class that emerged on the break of feudalism.

CHAPTER

2 Structure–Functionalism and Structuralism

Learning Objectives:

In this chapter, we will discuss the following important topics.

- Bronislaw Malinowski
- A.R. Radcliffe- Brown
- Talcott Parsons
- Robert K. Merton
- Claude Levi Strauss

INTRODUCTION

In Sociology, structural functionalism addresses social structures both in their entirety and in terms of the essential functions achieved by their constituent elements. Structural functionalism emphasized the formal ordering of parts and their functional interrelationships as contributing to the maintenance needs of an ordered arrangement of parts. The function of any institution is the role it plays in the maintenance of the larger structural totality. This notion attributed social systems to the internal integration of similar parts found in organisms. Structural functionalism places stability and social order as the ultimate goal of society. Other social structures such as religion, family, education, and other government institutions all support this goal with norms and values. In structural functionalism, social change is considered as an adaptive response to some stress within the social system. When some part of an integrated social system changes, tension between this and other parts of the system is created, which will be resolved by the adjustive change of the other parts. The origin of contemporary references to Structural functionalism can be traced to the English philosopher Herbert Spencer, who compared society to the human body. Each part of the body works together with the other parts like how each part of society works with the other parts. They work together to keep each part regulated and functioning.

We will now discuss some of the prominent thinkers of this approach.

BRONISŁAW KASPER MALINOWSKI (1884–1942)

Bronisław Malinowski, born in April 1884 in Kraków, Poland (then Austria), was a brilliant Polish scientist turned anthropologist, who founded the functionalist school in Britain. This marked a turning point in the history of sociology because, under the leadership of Malinowski, functionalism was firmly established in directly observable and scientifically gathered information (also known as empirical reality) about society and its institutions.

Important Books

1. The Trobriand Islands (1915)
2. Argonauts of the Western Pacific (1922)
3. The Sexual Life of Savages in North-Western Melanesia (1929)
4. Coral Gardens and Their Magic: A Study of the Methods of Tilling the Soil and of Agricultural Rites in the Trobriand Islands (1935)
5. The Scientific Theory of Culture (1944)
6. Magic, Science, and Religion (1948)
7. The Dynamics of Culture Change (1945)
8. A Diary in the Strict Sense of the Term (1967)

Major Theories

Culture

Culture for Malinowski is inherited artifacts, goods, technical processes, and habits. It is a balanced system of beliefs, practices, customs, and institutions.

For Malinowski culture was a vast apparatus, partly material, partly human, and partly spiritual by which man is able to cope with concrete specific problems that face him.

These statements show that Malinowski's concept of culture included

- **i. Material Culture**–Material culture includes implements and consumer goods. These were artifacts or physical objects. They were the products of human actions and were instrumental in satisfying human needs.
- **ii. Concrete categories of human activity**–Concrete categories of human activity, is being covered by the term custom, which included elements of social organization.
- **iii. Constitutional charters for social groups, and beliefs**–Constitutional charters for social groups and beliefs, included cultural objects and also some aspects of social organization.

The above description shows that Malinowski treated culture as almost everything that concerned human life and action and that it was not a part of the human organism as a physiological system.

For Malinowski, culture was that form of behaviour that individuals learned and held in common and passed on to other individuals.

Malinowski used the term culture as a functioning whole and developed the idea of studying the 'use' or 'function' of the beliefs, practices, customs, and institutions which together made the 'whole' of a culture.

He viewed different aspects of culture as a scheme for empirical research, which could be verified by observation.

In this sense, we can say that Malinowski became the architect of what is known in anthropology/sociology as the fieldwork method.

Malinowski in a way used 'culture' as equivalent to society or social system.

Malinowski published the results of his painstaking fieldwork in 1922 in his famous monograph, Argonauts of the Western Pacific.

In this, he used the concept of culture as a balanced system of many parts. He explained that the function of a custom or institution was to be understood in the way it helped to maintain the culture as a whole.

Theory of Needs/Imperatives

Malinowski's search for concepts to analyze primitive culture led to a particular approach to the explanation of social facts. This approach is known as his 'theory of needs'.

It was presented in A Scientific Theory of Culture by Malinowski. According to him the 'needs' were two-fold, namely, the needs of the individual and the needs of the society.

Malinowski defined the term need, as follows. By need, he refers to the system of conditions in the human organism, in the cultural setting, and in relation of both to the natural environment, which are sufficient and necessary for the survival of the group and organism.

A need, therefore, is the limiting set of facts. Habits and their motivations, the learned responses, and the foundations of organization, must be so arranged as to allow the basic needs to be satisfied.

These are necessary for the survival of society. They are

- **i.** Basic Needs (F M K)
- **ii.** Derived Needs/secondary needs (economy, education)
- **iii.** Integrative imperatives (religion)

Magic, Religion, and Science

Magic – provides a practical way out of difficulties;
Religion – provides courage and confidence;
Science – the primitive knowledge

Malinowski is mainly concerned with putting some order into the facts, determining 'more precisely the character of the domain of the Sacred and mark it off from that of the profane' and stating the relation between magic and religion.

He begins with the last point and says that a prima facie distinction between magic and religion is that magical rites have a clear-cut aim and refer to their results in terms of subsequent events.

Malinowski rejects Durkheim's sociological theory of religion.

Malinowski basically showed the functional value of religious ceremonies. In brief, he has surveyed the main types of religious rites and concluded that the main types of religious rites have the following functions.

- **i.** Initiation ceremonies give a sacred character to traditional knowledge.
- **ii.** In a primitive society the occurrence of death sets in motion a pattern of religious rites that counteract the forces of fear and destruction.
- **iii.** Rituals involving food, sacrifice, and totemic beliefs put people in direct contact with the forces that provide sustenance.

Kula Ring of Exchange

According to Malinowski, Kula is a ceremonial exchange among the Trobriand Islanders of New Guinea. Kula is also known as kula exchange or kula ring. It is a complex system of visits and exchange of two kinds of ornaments as well as trading of food and other commodities with the people of other (nearby or far-off) islands.

Kula ornaments are of two types. One consists of shell-disc necklaces known as vegan or soluva, which are traded in the north, circling the ring in a clockwise direction and the other consists of shell armbands known as mawali, which are traded in the southern direction, circulating counter-clockwise.

These are exchanged in a ceremonial ambiance purely for the purposes of enhancing mutual trust relationships, securing trade, and enhancing one's social status and prestige.

Malinowski over Marriage and Kinship

Malinowski believed monogamy to be the natural condition among monkeys and apes, humans everywhere having inherited 'individual marriage' and 'the family' from their primate forebears. Malinowski supported Westermarck's view that man was monogamous in primitive times.

Bronisław Malinowski studied matrilineal peoples, like Morgan before him, for whom the role of the father was very different and much less important than in European society. Instead, it was the mother's brother, the adult male who came from the mother's lineage, who represented authority, discipline, and the ideal of adulthood for young men, a fact that led Malinowski to challenge Freud's ideas of Oedipus's complex.

Pointing out that young men in matriarchal societies tend to express their animosity toward their mother's brothers rather than their father's, he contends that competition over the right to claim political authority, rather than sexual tension, within growing boys leads to their resentment felt towards the adult males in the family.

Malinowski's Functionalism

Malinowski was a Polish anthropologist and one of the most famous anthropologists of the 20th century. Malinowski is sometimes referred to as the father of ethnography because of his extensive fieldwork in the Trobriand Islands. He was a strong functionalist. This can be understood in the following two ways.

He believed that all customs and institutions in a society are integrated and interrelated so that if one changes the other would change as well. Each then is a function of the other.

The second strand of Malinowski's Functionalism is known as 'needs functionalism'.

Malinowski (1944) believed that human beings have a set of universal biological needs and various customs and institutions are developed to fulfill those needs. The function of any system is the role it plays in meeting these biological needs such as the need for food, shelter, etc.

Malinowski looked at culture as the needs of the people and thought that the role of culture was to meet the needs of the people. Malinowski identified seven biological needs (nutrition, reproduction, bodily comforts, safety, relaxation, movement, and growth) of individuals. Due to the emphasis on biological needs in Malinowski's approach, his functionalism is also known as Bio-cultural Functionalism.

As Malinowski gave importance to individual needs so his functionalism is also known as 'Psychological Functionalism'.

Culture comprised all those things – material and non-material – that human beings have created right from the time they separated from their simian ancestors, culture has been the instrument that satisfies the biological needs of human beings. It is a need-serving and need-fulfilling system.

A.R. RADCLIFFE BROWN (1881–1955)

Alfred Reginald Radcliffe-Brown was born in 1881 in Birmingham. He belonged to the English lower middle class. With financial support from her brother,

Radcliffe-Brown began her medical studies. But his teachers encouraged him to go to Cambridge and study anthropology. While at Cambridge, Radcliffe-Brown met leading ethnologist W.H.R. and became a disciple of River. He completed his undergraduate degree at Cambridge in 1904 and remained there for postgraduate work. Between 1906 and 1908, Radcliffe-Brown conducted fieldwork on the Andaman Islands in the Indian Ocean as part of her research. He went on to participate in an expedition to Western Australia from 1910 to 1911, where he focused on family organization and kinship. He is often associated with functionalism and is considered by some to be the founder of structural functionalism.

Important Books

The Distribution of Native Tribes in Part of Western Australia: 1912
Three Tribes of Western Australia: 1913
The Andaman Islanders: A study in social anthropology: 1922
Social Organization of Australian Tribes: 1931
On Joking Relationships: 1940
A Natural Science of Society: 1948
Structure and Function in Primitive Society: 1952

Major Theories

Structure and Functions

Émile Durkheim systematically applied the concept of function to the study of social institutions. Both Durkheim and Malinowski spoke of function in terms of the needs of the social organism.

Radcliffe-Brown replaces the idea of 'needs' with 'necessary conditions of existence'. In other words, he holds that human societies must satisfy certain basic conditions in order to exist.

Just as the animal must breathe, eat, excrete, and reproduce, similarly, the social organism must perform certain activities. According to Radcliffe-Brown, the 'necessary conditions for existence' can be discovered by the proper kind of scientific inquiry.

Let us now elaborate on the relationship between structure and function described by Radcliffe-Brown.

For Radcliffe-Brown the life of an organism is conceived as a function of its structure. It is through continuity of functioning that continuity of structure is preserved".

The continuity of the social structure is maintained by the process of social life. Social life involves the activities and interactions of various human beings and the groups of which they are a part.

Social life, in other words, refers to the way in which the social structure functions. The function of any recurrent social activity is the role it plays in maintaining the continuity of the social structure. For example, marriage is a recurring social activity.

Through marriage persons of the opposite sex are brought together and society legitimizes their sexual relations. Children may be born and new members may join the society.

Thus, by providing a socially acceptable outlet for sexual relations and a legitimate method through which society gains new members, marriage contributes to or functions in maintaining the social structure.

In Radcliffe-Brown's own words, 'The concept of function includes the notion of a structure consisting of a set of relationships between unit entities, the continuity of the structure being maintained by a life process made up of the activities of the constituent units'.

According to Radcliffe-Brown, 'Some features of social structure, such as the geographic distribution of individuals and groups, can be directly observed, but most of the social relations that constitute the structure in their totality, such as father and son, buyers and sellers, rulers, and subjects, cannot be seen except in the social activities in which the relations are functioning'.

In other words, for Radcliffe-Brown, 'social morphology' (i.e., the study of types of social structure, their similarities, differences, and classification) and 'social physiology' (the study of how social structures function) are interdependent.

The function of activity refers to the contribution it makes to the functioning of the total social system.

This implies that there is a special kind of unity in the social system, which Radcliffe-Brown calls 'functional unity'. By this, he meant a condition in which all parts of a social system work together in a harmonious, consistent manner i.e., without creating persistent conflicts that cannot be resolved or regulated.

The science of pathology deals with the problem of organic dysfunction, in other words, disease, when some part of the organism fails to adequately perform its function, disease results, which if uncontrolled can lead to death.

In the case of biological structures, we can identify strictly objective criteria that can help us distinguish the disease from health or pathological from normal. For example, we can say that if a person's body temperature rises above 98°F, he or she is ill.

Radcliffe-Brown explains that this is an attempt to apply the notion of health and disease to society and the state. It was built by the Greeks in the fifth century BC.

He distinguished 'Eunomia' (good order, social health) from ' Dyssomnia' (disorder, social malaise).

In the nineteenth century, Durkheim tried to understand social pathology with the help of the concept of 'anomie'.

Radcliffe-Brown also adopts the terms 'Eunomia' and 'Dyssnomia'. He points out that societies 'do not get sick and die in the same sense that animals do,' and acknowledges that it is not possible to have definite, objective criteria for determining the 'health' of society, because the science of human society, according to him, not mature enough to do so.

For Radcliffe-Brown, Eunomia of society refers to the harmonious working together of its parts, or in other words, the functional unity or internal consistency of the system.

On the other hand, Dyssnomia is a state of functional disparity or dissonance. A society is thrown into a state of Dyssnomia rarely dies, but instead struggles for Eunomia or a new state of social health. In the process, it may also change its structural type.

Structural Functionalism

Radcliffe-Brown is more than just a 'functionalist', he is a 'structural functionalist'. By this, we mean that it is not merely concerned with customs and social institutions as a way of satisfying certain needs or conditions of existence. It is also concerned with the relationship between different types of social relations. He never distinguished between social structure and social relationships. His method of structural-functionalism can be best understood through a few examples.

Andamanese ceremonies are marked by ceremonial crying. The Andamanese cry, formally on many occasions, e.g. When friends and relatives are reunited after a long separation, after death, during marriage and initiation ceremonies, peace-making ceremonies, etc.

Radcliffe-Brown concludes that formal crying occurs in situations in which social relations that have been disturbed or disrupted are about to resume.

Totemism

'In totemism, a specific group within a society adopts a ritual attitude towards a natural species or object.' Durkheim argues that totemism is a way in which collective sentiments are expressed and ritualized through symbolism, and this symbolization helps to maintain group solidarity. But Durkheim does not touch upon a crucial question, namely, why are natural objects selected as totems?

This is precisely what Radcliffe-Brown tries to explore. He observes in his Australian field studies that some tribes in New South Wales are divided into two exogamous moieties.

They are named after two birds, the Eagle hawk and the crow. Eagle hawk men marry Crow women and vice versa. Other such dual divisions have been found in Australia, which is also named after pairs of birds or animals.

Myths depict these pairs of birds or animals as opponents in a struggle. Despite this opposition, there is also a kind of fundamental similarity or similarity between them. In the case of Eagle hawks and crows, both are carnivorous birds. Interestingly enough, the relationship between the moieties are also one of alliance and competition; They are in pairs and in opposition at the same time.

Thus, Radcliffe-Brown sees totemism not only as a technique (that is, its function) of maintaining group unity but also as a way in which social antagonism between groups is expressed. (That is, the structure of relations).

Joking and Avoidance Relationship

Radcliffe-Brown sought to study the formation of groups in society and the rules governing their behaviour by employing the concept of social structure. A classic example of this approach was his analysis of the 'joke' and 'avoidance' relationship.

A joking relationship was one where one party was allowed to tease or make fun of the other party, who need not take offense. For example, in Robert Lowie's account of the Crow Indians, a man was allowed to treat his wife's sister with utmost license and she would mock him in a similar fashion.

On the other hand, an avoidant relationship was characterized by mutual respect and the limitation of direct personal contact. For example, older Navaho women traditionally wore small 'mother-in-law bells' designed to warn sons-in-law of their arrival so that men should make themselves absent.

Kinship

Radcliffe-Brown saw great potential in Durkheimian analysis of kinship. The kinship system was understood as an unwritten constitution for social interaction. It was an important institution for the understanding of the social organization in small-scale societies.

Kinship was seen as the engine of a self-sustaining, organically integrated but abstract entity called the social structure. For Radcliffe-Brown the importance of kinship was not its origin but its meaning in contemporary society.

Radcliffe-Brown studied how these primitive societies were integrated and what social structures bound them together as a whole. Radcliffe-Brown put forth two theories of totemism. His first paper on the subject was titled 'The Sociological Theory of Totemism' and was delivered at a conference in Java in 1929.

He explained how Aboriginal Australians classified the world and people as members of different social groups. He agreed with Durkheim that the function of the totem is to express the unity of the clan. For Radcliffe-Brown, totemism was a specific development of the symbolism of nature. One group chose a species to represent them because that species already had ritual significance.

His second essay on totemism, titled 'The Comparative Method in Social Anthropology' was presented as a public lecture in 1951. This second theory was not only about how Aboriginal people classified people as members of social groups, but also about how they classified animals as member species.

For example, the eagle and crow represent moieties in parts of Western Australia. Radcliffe-Brown questions why the eagle and crow were chosen and what the symbolic relationship between the eagle and the crow was.

The moiety system, also called dual organization, is a form of social organization in which society is divided into two complementary parts called "moieties".

TALCOTT PARSONS (1902–1979)

American sociologist who attempted to integrate all the social sciences into a science of human action. He was converted to functionalism under the influence of the anthropologist Bronisław Malinowski. In 'The Social System' 1951, Parsons argued that the important characteristic of societies as biological organisms is homeostasis (maintaining a stable state) and that their parts can only be understood in terms of the whole. Parsons began his career as a biologist and later became interested in economics and sociology. He studied in Heidelberg, Germany. He taught sociology at Harvard from 1931 until his death and founded the Department of Social Relations there. He published more than 150 books and articles. Like the German sociologist Max Weber, whose work he translated, Parsons wanted to describe concrete logical types of social relations applicable to all groups, large or small. His great achievement was the creation of a system or general theory to cover all aspects of social action, drawing on many disciplines and reinterpreting previous theories. His first attempt at this systematization appeared in 'The Structure of Social Action' in 1937, followed by 'Essays in Sociological Theory, Pure, and Applied' in 1942.

Important Books

1. The Structure of Social Action (1937)
2. The Social System (1951)
3. The Evolution of Societies
4. System of Modern Societies (Foundations of Modern Sociology)
5. Social System and The Evolution of Action Theory

Major Theories

Theory of Social Action

Behaviour becomes action when four conditions are present.

- **i.** it is oriented to the attainment of ends or goals or other anticipated affairs,
- **ii.** it occurs in situations
- **iii.** it is regulated by norms and values of society,
- **iv.** it involves an investment of 'energy' or motivation or effort.

Talcott Parsons enumerates the four elements of social action as

- **i.** an actor,
- **ii.** an end, a future state of affairs which the actor's mindsets in motion,
- **iii.** a set of conditions, aspects of the situation over which the actor has no control, and
- **vi.** a set of means, and aspects of the situation over which the actor has control.

Hence the orientation to action can be divided into two components, motivational orientation, and value orientation. Motivational orientation refers to a situation in which actions are taken with needs, external appearances, and plans in mind. Value orientation is based on the ideas of values, aesthetics, ethics, and standards of thinking.

Social System

Social system is defined by Mitchell (1979: 203) as consisting of 'a plurality of actors interacting directly or indirectly with each other in a bounded situation.

There may be physical or territorial boundaries but sociologically the main point of reference is that here individuals are oriented to a common focus or interrelated focus, in a broad sense.

According to this definition, diverse relationships such as families, political parties, kinship groups, and even entire societies can be considered as social systems.

Parsons insisted that both utilitarian and idealistic approaches to the study of social systems and social reality were one-sided. The utilitarian approach regarded social systems as products of the rational impulses of human beings (individuals) to integrate their needs and urges into orderly systems.

These systems are based on the compatibility of interests through contractual reciprocity. An example of contractual reciprocity is the polity (government and state) which represents an organized system of power.

Similarly, in the idealistic practice of social order, democracy is seen as the fulfilment of the spirit of the nation. Idealism places too much emphasis on values and ideas and not enough on social behaviour.

Talcott Parsons was the first to formulate a systematic theory of social systems, which he did as part of his theory of social action and the AGIL paradigm. He defined a social system as only a segment (or a 'subsystem') of what he called action theory.

He defines a social system as a network of interactions between actors. According to Parsons, social systems depend on systems of language, and culture that must exist in a society to qualify as a social system.

According to Parsons (1973), the action does not occur in isolation. It is 'not empirically discrete but occurs in constellations' that constitute the system. These constellations of action from the system. There are three modes of organization in these systems of action, which Parsons describes as

i. personality system,
ii. cultural system and
iii. social system.

Characteristics of Social System: According to Parsons, the social system has the following characteristics.

i. It involves interaction between two or more actors, and the process of interaction is its main focus.
ii. The interaction takes place in a situation that implies other actors or alters. These transformations are the objects of emotions and value judgments and through them, the ends and the means of action are attained.
iii. In a social system there exist collective goal orientations or common values and agreed-upon expectations in the normative and cognitive (intellectual) senses.

There is a mode of organization of action in a social system, which is called a role. It is the basic conceptual unit of a social system and it encompasses the total system of action of the individual actor. It is also an intersection point between the functioning of an individual actor and the social system.

According to Parsons, the primary element of a role is role expectation. It implies reciprocity between the actor and it's alter (other persons), and is governed by a range of motivational and value orientations.

Motivational orientation refers to a situation in which action takes place with individual actors' needs or objectives, external appearances, and plans in mind.

Value orientation refers to the aspects of action like values, aesthetics, ethics, etc. The organization of the entity functions in social systems, therefore involving the objectives and values that link it to the personality system in the first case and to the cultural system in the second case.

AGIL Model

Parsons explored why societies are stable and functioning. His AGIL model represents four basic actions that all social systems must perform in order to survive, they are:

i. **Adaptation:** The problem of getting enough resources. Ex. economic system
ii. **Goal Attainment:** The problem of setting and implementing goals. Ex. political party
iii. **Integration:** The problem of maintaining cohesion or coordination among the subunits of a system. Ex. Religion
vi. **Latency:** The problem of creating, preserving, and transmitting the distinctive culture and values of the society. Ex. family

Pattern Variables

In order to develop concepts that could reflect the properties of all action systems, Parsons developed a set of concepts that could capture the variable properties of these systems. These concepts are called pattern variables.

The role is the most important element of the social system its performance generates forces of tension or stress. The extent of tension depends on the extent to which role expectations are institutionalized in society and also on the extent to which the values of role expectations are internalized by social actors. In the performance of roles, each actor is faced with dilemmas, regarding motivational orientation and value orientation.

These dilemmas arise from tensions in an individual's choices or preferences within a range of orientations related to both needs and values. Although these dilemmas are often viewed as dichotomous, they are in fact placed along a continuum.

All five patterns are variable, with each side representing a polar extreme. These pattern variables are

- **i.** affectivity versus affective neutrality
- **ii.** self-orientation versus collectively orientation
- **iii.** universalism versus particularism
- **vi.** ascription versus achievement
- **v.** specificity versus diffuseness.

Affectiveness versus affective neutrality is related to the dilemma of role performance where evaluation is involved in relation to a situation. To what extent should the situation be assessed from an emotional point of view or with a degree of emotional neutrality? It is a difficult choice in most of the roles we are expected to play in society.

Take for example the mother-child relationship. It has a high degree of emotional orientation, but also requires discipline. So, on many occasions, a mother will have to take on an affectively-neutral role in relation to her child's socialization. But maternal bonding is inevitably affected by efficacy.

The main issue in the self-orientation versus collectivism orientation pattern variable is that of the moral standard in the process of evaluation. The moral standard arises from the fact that the actor has to choose between his own gratification and its delay for the good of a large number of people, a collectivist. Some form of altruism and self-sacrifice is involved.

Universalism versus particularism is a pattern variable that defines role-play situations where the actor's dilemma is between cognitive versus cathartic (or emotional standards) evaluation. A very good example of roles that follow universal standards of human behaviour is role performances that are strictly governed by legal norms and legal sanctions.

It would be an example of the universality of role performance if it followed the rule of law regardless of personal, kinship, or friendship considerations. If one violates legal norms simply because the person involved is a relative or friend, the special consideration would be called particularism.

The actor's dilemma in the ascription versus achievement pattern variable is based on whether the actor defines the objects of his role in terms of quality or performance. A very good example of this pattern variable in India is the role performance governed by the caste system.

In the caste system, the status of individuals is determined not on the basis of their personal achievement or personal skill, or knowledge but on the basis of their birth. The attribution is based on attributing some quality to a person either by birth, age, gender or kinship, or caste. Achievement is based on an individual acquisition of skills and level of performance in society.

Specificity vs Diffusion pattern is related to the scope of the object of variable role performance. In this case, the scope should be understood in the context of the nature of social interaction. Some social interactions, such as those between doctors and patients or between buyers and sellers of goods in a market, have a very specific scope.

The nature of these interactions is defined in terms of a very precise context of the interaction. A doctor does not need to understand the social, financial, or political background of his patients in order to treat them and give them prescriptions. The job of a doctor is very specific.

On the contrary, some role relationships are very general and broad in nature. Such roles involve many aspects of the object of conversation. Some examples of such role relations are friendship, marital relations between husband and wife, and relations between relatives of different degrees.

R K MERTON (1910–2003)

Robert King Merton, an American sociologist, was born on 4 July 1910 in Philadelphia as Meyer Robert Schkolnick into a family of Yiddish-speaking Russian Jews who had immigrated to the United States in 1904. He is considered a founding father of modern sociology and a major contributor to the subfield of criminology. He served as the 47th President of the American Sociological Association. He spent most of his career teaching at Columbia University, where he attained the rank of University Professor. In 1994 he was awarded the National Medal of Science for his contributions to the field and for establishing the sociology of science. Merton's contributions to sociology fall into three areas: (1) the sociology of science; (2) the sociology of crime and deviance; (3) the Sociological theory.

Important Works

1. Social Structure and Anomie (1938)
2. The Normative Structure of Science (1942)
3. Social Theory and Social Structure (1949), revised (1968)
4. The travels and adventures of serendipity (1950)
5. The Sociology of Science (1973)
6. Sociological Ambivalence (1976)
7. On the Shoulders of Giants: A Shandean Postscript (1985)
8. On Social Structure and Science (1996)

Major Theories

Middle Range Theory

According to Merton, the middle-range theory begins its theory with clearly defined aspects of social phenomena rather than with broad, abstract entities such as society in general. Middle-range theory is an approach to sociology that bridges the gap between theory and empirical evidence.

Middle-range theories must be strongly supported by empirical data. These theories must be built up with observed data in order to form theoretical problems and incorporate them into propositions that allow empirical testing.

Middle-range theories apply to limited categories of data, go beyond the explicit description of social phenomena and fill the void between raw empiricism and grand or all-inclusive theory.

Merton criticized strict empiricism, which emphasized solely the collection of data without regard to any theory, and scholastic abstract theory, which attempted to construct a total theoretical system covering all aspects of social life, in other words, 'Grand Theory'.

Function: Latent and Manifest

The function can be explained as the result of one's action. These results may be either latent functions or manifest functions in a social institution. In his book, Social Theory and Social Structure, Robert K. Merton explained the difference between them.

Manifest functions are generally expected from the institutions to be fulfilled. They are intentional, conscious, or deliberate acts of social policies or actions designed for the benefit of society. Whereas latent functions are those functions that are unintended or unrecognized consequences of a social pattern. They are present but not immediately apparent.

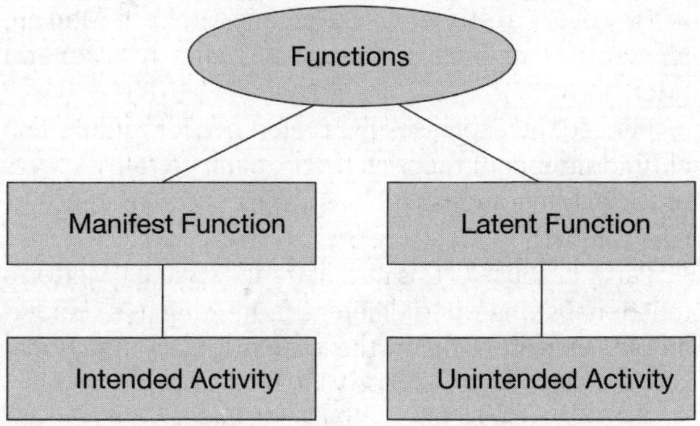

Merton used the Native American (Hopi tribe) tradition of the rain dance as an example to explain these works. The manifest function of the rain dance is to produce rain which is the intended result for all those involved in the dance. Latent functions can be either negative or positive depending on the manifest function. In Merton's example of the Hopi rain dance, the latent function is to enhance the group's identity by performing such a sacred tradition.

Functionalism of Talcott Parsons and Robert K. Merton

Parsons refers to his student, Robert Merton, and himself as 'arch-functionalists'. He explains here why he has abandoned the term 'structural functionalism' which he had at one time used for his approach.

For him, structure refers to 'any set of relationships between the parts of a living system'. He thinks that his original formulation under the title of 'structural functionalism' analyzes society as if it is static, but the new formulation, where the emphasis is on the concept of function rather than structure, in the name of functionalism, is very Takes more account of change and development.

Parsons's functionalism is best known in terms of 'functional imperatives', the necessary conditions required for the sustainable existence of a system.

Also known as the 'AGIL model' (based on the initials of the four functions formulated by Parsons) or the 'four-function paradigm', it was developed by Robert F. developed from Parsons's collaborative work with Bell's experiments on lead in small group.

These four functions help us to explain how a state of equilibrium (i.e., equilibrium) emerges in a system. Parsons explores the role of these four functions in giving rise to equilibrium in a system.

Parsons's theory is popularly referred to as a 'Grand Theory' – an all-encompassing, unifying theory – that is believed to have great explanatory power.

However, a student of Parsons, Robert Merton, is skeptical of such a theory as being too general (Merton, 1957).

Instead, he expresses his preference for middle-level (middle-range) theories that explain certain aspects of social phenomena (such as group, social mobility, or role conflict).

Partly because of this middle-range strategy, Merton's functionalism is quite different from Parsons's. For example, Merton eschews the search for any functional prerequisites that would be valid in all social systems.

He also rejects the earlier functionalists' view that recurring social phenomena should be explained in terms of their benefits to society as a whole. to criticize,

Merton identifies three postulates of the earlier functionalists as given below:

1. Postulate of the functional unity of society.
2. Postulate of universal functionalism.
3. Postulate of indispensability.

Postulates of Functional Analysis (Paradigms for Functional Analysis) Merton refutes the principles of functionalism, the principles of unity, universality, and indispensability, and proposes refreshingly innovative changes, changes that enable him to see that not everything is functional.

Merton proposed three theories drawn from Malinowski and Radcliffe-Brown of functional unity, functional universality; And functional inevitability constitutes the axioms from which the theorems of functional sociology would derive.

- **i.** The postulate of functional unity. Radcliffe-Brown states that a social function has a certain kind of unity and that all parts of a social system work together with a sufficient degree of cohesion or internal consistency.

  Perhaps the postulate of functional unity makes sense and remains valid in a relatively homogeneous, illiterate civilization. But in a modern complex society, as Merton argues, the principle of functional unity needs to be redefined. First, Merton doubts whether all societies are solidly integrated and therefore culturally standardized practice or belief is functional for the whole society.

  Second, Merton wants sociologists to remember that social practices or beliefs may be functional for some groups and dysfunctional for others in the same society.
- **ii.** Postulate of Universal Functionalism. This postulate holds that all social or cultural forms have positive functions. Malinowski takes this to its most extreme, says Merton. As Malinowski puts it, 'In every type of civilization, every custom, material object, idea and belief fulfills some important function.'

  Merton argues that functionalists should focus on a net balance of functional consequences, positive and negative, but, by no means, only positive. East. Cricket
- **iii.** The postulate of indispensability. Malinowski claims that whatever serves some important function, be it a custom, or cultural practice is inevitable in that society. In other words, whatever remains in society is inevitable and it seems that nothing can be changed.

A functional analyst, says Merton, must assume that nothing is really inevitable. Functional substitutes are equivalents or substitutes. Merton notes that neither of these concepts is empirically justified. For example, there is no reason to believe that specialized institutions are the only ones performing the tasks.

Bureaucratic Dysfunction

Merton's analysis outlines the dysfunctions resulting from bureaucratic structures. The negative consequences he identifies are the displacement of goals, trained inefficiency, over-conformity of officers, and depersonalization of the esprit de corps and relationships.

Robert K. Merton (1910–2003), approaches bureaucracy with functional analysis and suggests that Weber's characteristics of bureaucracy simply do not provide positive and efficient results. Merton observes the fostering tendency in bureaucracy e.g., target displacement.

This means that strict adherence and conformity to norms and rules may lead to a situation where these rules become ends in themselves, which may hinder the organization from achieving its goals and lead to adverse consequences. can be the reason. The negative consequences of Merton Weber's theories are called 'latent dysfunction'.

Reference Group

The concept of reference group behaviour in sociology was given by Heyman. Later, Turner, Merton, and Sheriff further elaborated on the concept. According to Heyman, there are certain individuals in society whose standards or values become ideal for other people and are followed by them. Sheriff provided a psychological explanation of reference behaviour. The group to which individuals do not necessarily belong but compare themselves.

Anticipatory Socialization

Adopting the attitudes and values of a group to which one does not belong, serves the dual functions of facilitating entry into that group and easing the process of adjustment once one becomes a member. The concept was popularized by the American sociologist Samuel Stauffer (1900–60) and several co-authors of the monumental study of the US military called The American Soldier (1949).

This suggested that privates in the military who espoused the attitudes and values of officer rank were more likely to be promoted, and was later analyzed in detail in relation to reference groups by the American sociologist Robert King it was done. Merton (1910–2003) in his book Social Theory and Social Structure (1957).

Strain Theory/Theory of Deviance/ Merton's Five Modes of Adaptation

Merton argued that the general stress theory is developed by an obstruction in a person's life that does not allow them to achieve their goals, which inevitably leads to deviant behaviour.

Merton uses progress toward achieving the 'American Dream' as an example. If a person cannot achieve this, it may prove hopeless for the individual and may lead to illegal escape routes or venturing into anger-based crime.

Merton's Paradigm of Deviant Behaviour		
Attitude to Goals	**Attitude to Means**	**Modes of Adaptation**
Accept	Accept	Conformity
Accept	Reject	Innovation
Reject	Accept	Ritualism
Reject	Reject	Retreatism

The Ethos of Modern Science

In 1942, Robert K. Merton introduced 'four sets of institutional imperatives taken to comprise the ethos of modern science are communism, universalism, disinterestedness, and organized scepticism'.

A later part of his book, *The Sociology of Science*, elaborated on these principles at 'the heart of the Mertonian paradigm, the powerful juxtaposition of the normative structure of science with its institutionally distinctive reward system'.

The four Mertonian norms (often abbreviated as the CUDO-norms) can be summarised as:

i. **Communism:** all scientists should have common ownership of scientific objects (intellectual property), to promote collective collaboration; secrecy is the opposite of this norm.
ii. **Universalism:** scientific validity is independent of the socio-political status/personal attributes of its participants.
iii. **Disinterestedness:** scientific institutions act for the benefit of a common scientific enterprise, rather than for the personal gain of individuals within them.
vi. **Organized scepticism:** scientific claims should be exposed to critical scrutiny before being accepted, both in methodology and institutional codes of conduct

CLAUDE LEVI STRAUSS (1908–2009)

Claude Lévi-Strauss was born in Brussels, Belgium in 1908 to a Jewish family, his father was a painter. He grew up in Paris and studied philosophy at the Sorbonne, graduating in 1928 at an exceptionally young age. After completing his studies, he worked as a school teacher in Picardy. He abandoned philosophy and instead became interested in anthropology.

Important Works

1. The Elementary Structures of Kinship (1949)
2. Tristes Tropiques (1955)
3. The Structural Study of Myth (1955)
4. The Savage Mind (1962)
5. The Totemism (1962)
6. Structural Anthropology appeared in (1963)
7. The four-volume Mythologiques series (1964)
8. Myth and Meaning (1978)
9. The Way of the Masks (1975)

Major Theories

Structuralism

Structuralism is the name given to a method of analyzing social relations and cultural products, which came into existence in the 1950s.

Levi-Strauss drew many ideas from structural linguistics, including Ferdinand de Saussure, Roman Jacobson, Emile Durkheim, and Marcel Mauss. Saussure argued that linguists needed to move beyond the recording of paroles (individual speech acts) and come to an understanding of each language's grammar, the langue.

According to Saussure, any language is structured in the sense that its elements are interconnected in non-arbitrary, regular, rule-bound ways; A competent speaker of the language largely follows these rules without being aware of doing so.

Claude Lévi-Strauss, the French structuralist, who is famous for his ingenious cross-cultural analysis of myths and kinship systems. If for functionalism, society is a 'kind of living creature', consisting of parts, which can be 'dissected and distinguished', for structuralism, it is the analogy from language that helps us in conceptualizing society.

In structuralism, the shift is from observable behaviour to structure, from biological analogy to language. Furthermore, structuralism posits that the set of relationships between different parts can be converted into 'something' that appears to be different than it was before.

It is the idea of transformation of one into the other, rather than the quality of relations, that is at the core of structuralism. To make this clear, Edmund Leach has given a good example. A piece of music can be transformed in a variety of ways. It is written, played on the piano, recorded on phonograph records, broadcast on the radio, and finally performed in front of an audience.

In each case, the piece of music undergoes a 'whole series of changes'. It appears 'as printed notes, as patterns of finger movements, as sound waves, as modulation of grooves on a piece of Bakelite, as electromagnetic vibrations, and so on.'

But what all these manifestations of music have in common, different from each other, and each conditioned by its own laws, is their structure. Similarly, while different societies differ, what remains unchanging (and common) to them is their structure.

Lévi-Strauss (1963) aptly showed this in one of his studies where he compared the totemic society of Australian aborigines with the Indian caste system and found that both had similar structures. If for Radcliffe-Brown, the structure is observable, then for Levi Strass, it is an abstract concept. If for Radcliffe-Brown, what persists is the 'structure' of a particular society at a particular time and place, then for Levi-Strauss, what persists is the 'structure of the whole of human society'.

Lévi-Strauss says that social structure is not a field of study; This is not the 'province of inquiry'. We do not study social structure, but it is an explanatory method and can be used in any type of social study.

In opposition to Radcliffe-Brown, Lévi-Strauss states that the term 'social structure' has nothing to do with empirical reality. It refers to models that are constructed from empirical reality. He writes: 'the study of social structure aims at understanding social relations with the help of models'.

Lévi-Strauss makes three distinctions: first, between observation and experiment on models; second, the conscious and unconscious character of the models; and third, between mechanical and statistical models.

Following these facts, there is a need to distinguish observation and building of models of social relations from 'experiments' on the models. By experiment, Lévi-Strauss means a 'controlled comparison' of models of the same or a different type, with the aim of identifying the model that best fits the observed facts.

In structural analysis, the first step is to observe facts without bias, then to describe them in relation to themselves and in relation to the whole. From this, models are built, and in the final analysis, the best model is chosen. This distinction is in the context of the anthropologist who studies society.

Lévi-Strauss notes that many different cultures present similar myths, a fact that does not sit well with the arbitrary nature of myths. While the content varies in myth, both across cultures and times, the structure remains the same and remains the same across different cultures and times. According to Lévi-Strauss, the 'deep structure' of myth should be of interest to anthropologists and the study of myth.

Alliance

In the study of kinship, the alliance principle is also known as the general principle of exchange. It has its roots in the French structuralist Claude Lévi-Strauss and is therefore also known as a structuralist method of studying kinship relations.

The coalition principle was first discussed in Levi-Strauss's monumental book Les Structures élémentaires de la parente (1949). Its English version is known as the Elementary Structure of Kinship.

Alliance theory seeks to inquire about how inter-individual relationships are woven and how they ultimately constitute society. According to Lévi-Strauss alliance theory, incest is based on prohibition, and the prohibition of adultery is universally recognized. It is seen as a fundamental condition of human social life.

A man is not allowed to take as his wife a woman who is his near relative and in fact, he must give her to another man. It is the prohibition of incest that prompted human groups to practice exogamy.

Lévi-Strauss states that this prohibition is beyond any sociological explanation and clearly states the distinction between kinship and affinity as the basis of the kinship system.

For them, the incest prohibition is thus seen as a negative prescription and it is only because of this that men have to move out of the main kinship group or come into it from another group. The theory has much in common with Sigmund Freud's work Totem and Taboo (1913). This process of incest prohibition where a daughter or sister is sent to a different family begins a cycle of exchange of women.

Strauss sees marriage primarily as a process of exchange (between one man and another man, or between a domestic group and others). He follows the positive precepts of marriage from the negative precepts of prohibition. The core assumption of alliance theory is a mutual exchange that produces affinity. It is positive marriage rules that govern this exchange and thus give rise to what Strauss calls 'elementary' structures.

For Lévi-Strauss, there are two models of structure in the study of kinship and exchange in marriage. When women in the ego's group are offered to another group that is eligible for such an exchange, such a situation can be called a primary structure of kinship. Similarly for women, if the set of potential mates is not known and is kept open within the ego set, excluding special kin like the nuclear family, an uncle, an aunt, etc., this is what Strauss refers to as complex structures of kinship.

This is easily seen in western landscapes. Keeping in mind the prohibition of incest in a society, a kinship system is formed by a combination of many characteristics like inheritance, affinity, descent, residence, etc.

Totemism

Totemism refers to an institution, mostly found among the tribal community, where each of its clan members considers themselves to be descendants of some plant, animal, or any other animate or inanimate object, for which they have a special relationship in their mind. There is a feeling of special reverence, which leads to forming a ritualistic relationship with that object.

A plant, animal, or any other object is called a 'totem'. The word 'totem', states Lévi-Strauss, is derived from Ojibwa, an Algonquin language of the region north of the Great Lakes of North America. Members sharing the same totem form a 'totem group'. People have a special reverent attitude towards their totem, they refrain from killing and/or eating it, or they may sacrifice and eat it on ceremonial occasions. The death of the totem may be formally mourned. Some societies have grand ceremonies for the multiplication of the totem, and totems can be approached to bless and bestow long-term well-being.

Lévi-Strauss does not believe in the 'reality' of totemism. He states that totemism was 'invented' and became one of the most favourite anthropological topics to be investigated in the late nineteenth century with Victorian scholars aiming to discover its origins and varieties.

In contrast, Lévi-Strauss's study is not of totemism, it belongs to the totemic phenomenon. In other words, it is an 'attributive study', not a 'substantive study', which means that it is 'the study of phenomena that are totemic' rather than 'what is contained or the substance of a totem'.

Totemic phenomena are nothing but methods of classification. They provide tribal communities with consciously or unconsciously held concepts that guide their social actions. Food taboos, economic exchanges, and kinship relationships can be conceptualized and organized using schemes that are comparable to totemic homology between natural species and social characteristics.

Lévi-Strauss also extends this analysis to understand the relationship between totemism and the caste system. Totemism is the connection between man and nature. Similarities and differences between natural species are used to understand the similarities and differences between humans. Totemism, which is a kind of religion for the people, is a way of understanding the similarities and differences between man and nature.

Binary Opposite

In the 1900s, Lévi Strauss, a French anthropologist, proposed a theory of 'binary opposition', which states that most narratives in media forms such as books and films have opposing main characters.

These binary contrasts help to thicken the plot and propel the narrative forward by introducing contrast. For example, in a superhero film it may be good versus evil, in a horror film it may be human versus supernatural, and in a comedy, it may be young versus old.

One problem with binary oppositions is that they can often perpetuate negative stereotypes. For example, if the binary contrast were male versus female, according to gender stereotypes, the male might be portrayed as 'strong' while the female is the 'damsel in distress'.

Phoneme

Roman Jakobson regarded phoneme as a relational element, a purely differential and meaningless sign. Like in mathematics, where a point is defined by its relation to other points.

Lévi-Strauss uses this relational concept of phonetics as a methodological model for research in mythology. He formulates contextual distinctions between mythological elements and derives the rules that govern their relations.

Just as Jacobson used phonemes to describe the linguistic structure, Lévi-Strauss analyzed the relationships between elements in what he called "mythemes".

Mythemes consist of bundles of relationships that produce meaning. He does not study Mythemes separately, but the relations between them, and by studying the interplay of binary opposites and change laws, he concludes that Mythemes are opposite, relative, and negative entities.

A mytheme, therefore, exists at a higher level than a narrative element and is not tied to any particular story. It is simply defined in opposition to some other mytheme.

CHAPTER

3 Hermeneutic and Interpretative Tradition

LEARNING OBJECTIVES:

In this chapter, we will discuss the following important topics.

- G.H. Mead
- Karl Manheim
- Alfred Schutz
- Harold Garfinkel
- Erving Goffman
- Clifford Geertz

INTRODUCTION

In sociology, hermeneutics is the interpretation and understanding of social events through the analysis of their meanings for human participants in the events. It gained prominence during the 1960s and 1970s and differs from other interpretive schools of sociology in that it emphasizes both the context and the form within any given social practice. The central tenet of sociological hermeneutics is that it is possible to know the meaning of an act or statement in the context of the discourse or worldview from which it originates. Friedrich Schleiermacher, widely regarded as the father of sociological hermeneutics, believed that, for an interpreter to understand another author's work, they must familiarize themselves with the historical context in which the author published his ideas. Wilhelm Dilthey and other social scientists extended the theory of interpretation to sociology, claiming that the goal of hermeneutic tradition in sociology is the understanding of human action based on intention and context.

Let us now discuss some of the major thinkers and their contributions to this approach.

G.H. MEAD (1863–1931)

George Herbert Mead, born February 27, 1863, in South Hadley, Massachusetts, was an American philosopher, sociologist, and psychologist, primarily affiliated with the University of Chicago, where he was one of the most distinguished behaviorists. He is considered one of the founders of symbolic interactionism and what is known as the Chicago sociological tradition.

Important Works

- The philosophy of the present (1932)
- Mind, Self, and Society (1934)
- The Individual and the Social Self (1982)

Major Theories

Development of Self

According to the American sociologist George Herbert Mead (1972), young children begin to develop as social beings by imitating the actions of those near them.

By doing so the child is able to develop the ability to understand the action of the person with whom he is interacting. 'Play' is one of the ways by which children often imitate what adults do.

The play stage begins around the third year during which the child begins to adopt different roles of adults in her/ his life. Mead refers to these others as 'significant others'.

Children's play gradually develops from simple imitation to difficult games where a child of four or five years old will enact the role of an adult.

For example, children are often found imitating the classroom situation where one becomes the teacher, the others become students and they enact a classroom teaching session. Most children locally refer to this play as 'Teacher-Teacher'.

Mead refers to this act of imitation as 'taking the role of the other'. This stage being complex is known as the game stage where children begin to attain maturity and develop a sense of self and others.

Children begin to understand themselves as 'me' by looking at themselves through other people's views and opinions about them.

The "me" is the social self while the 'I' is the response to the 'me'. In simple words, "I" comprises the response of the child to the action of others while "me" is the organized set of reactions of others that the child takes on.

Another stage of self-development occurs around the age of eight or nine. At this stage, children are able to act as members of a group and also understand their role as a member of that group.

Here, Mead introduces the concepts of 'generalized others and 'significant others'. The "generalized other" can be understood as the rules and values of the culture of a particular group in which the child is engaged. By understanding the "generalized other" the child is able to understand what manners are expected as well as valued in any given social setting.

'Significant others' include individuals who are important in a child's life and influence the child's feelings and behaviours as well as his or her sense of self. Mead was one of the first thinkers to understand the role of the "significant other" in the development of the self. According to him, socialization depends on the child understanding the views of others who are important in his life.

Preparatory Stage (1 to 3 Years)

This is the beginning of the child's second year. In this stage, the child starts reacting to the external environment. To an outsider these reactions are meaningless. The behaviour of the child can be understood by the mother or other person in close contact with the child. By the end of the second year, the child begins to speak and has a vocabulary of many words.

Play Stage (3 to 4 Years)

This stage begins with the onset of the third year of age. The following are examples of this.

- **i.** Reaction to significant others. The child assumes the role of a significant another like a mother, father, etc. The child behaves like a significant other while playing with toys.
- **ii.** The child acquires many selves. In this stage, the child acquires several selves at the same time. On the one hand, he unconsciously plays his own role and on the other hand, plays the role of persons belonging to significant others.

Game Stage (4 to 5 years)

The game phase begins in the child's fourth year. The child starts thinking about others as well as he tries to understand a question of what he is and what he is not. At this stage, the child has a role to play and changes behaviour according to the influence of others and different situations.

Popular Quotes

'Self reflects society', i.e., 'society shapes self which shapes social behaviours'.

KARL MANNHEIM (1893–1947)

Karl Mannheim, (born March 27, 1893, in Budapest, Austria-Hungary—died January 9, 1947, in London, England), a sociologist in Germany before the rise of Adolf Hitler and then in the United Kingdom, remembered for his 'sociology' goes. Enlightenment and for his work on the problems of leadership and consensus in modern societies.

Important Works

1. Ideology & Utopia (1929).
2. Essay on Sociology of knowledge (1928).
3. Man, and society in an age of reconstruction (1980).

Major Theories

Sociology of Knowledge

Karl Mannheim is best known for his work on the sociology of knowledge. Basically, the sociology of knowledge involves the systematic study of knowledge, ideas, or intellectual phenomena in general. It was the German sociologist, Max Scheler (1874–1928) who established the term, the sociology of knowledge (Wissenssoziologie) in 1924.

Its core elements were defined as the collective, social nature of knowledge, the sociological distribution of knowledge through specific social institutions such as schools and newspapers, and the creation of different types of knowledge.

Mannheim's theory on the sociology of knowledge is based on some of Immanuel Kant's epistemological discoveries. The sociology of knowledge is characterized as a section of the larger field known as the sociology of culture. The idea of sociology of culture is defined as the relationship between culture and society.

In the 1920s, a series of his essays was published in Germany under the name Essays in the Sociology of Knowledge. These essays focused on the search for meaning behind social reality, the notion of "truth", and the role of empirical intellectuals in the search for these truths.

Another collection of his essays, Essays in the Sociology of Culture, was published posthumously in 1956. This basically served to merge his concern with social reality and democracy.

According to Mannheim, ideology was linked to a perception of reality, meanwhile, culture focused more on the mind of the individual and how it perceives reality, although both "still belong to the role of intellectuals."

According to Mannheim, knowledge is determined by social existence. The sociology of knowledge focuses on the 'social and existential determination of thought'. We don't think in isolation. We think as a social group. What we think or the way we see the world depends on our group experiences, the lives we lead, the struggles we engage in, the interests we seek to uphold, and the hopes we cherish.

Ideology and Utopia.

Mannheim is perhaps best known for his distinction between two thought systems—ideology and utopia. An ideology is a system of thought that attempts to hide and protect the present by interpreting it from the perspective of the past.

Mannheim distinguishes between two types of 'ideology': 'particular' and 'total'. Particular ideologies are the local representations of things in the world that may be coloured by specific interests or attitudes. They are limited to specific domains and ultimately rest with individuals

Total ideology - Every social group has a 'perspective' or 'worldview' which, according to Mannheim, can be considered as the group's 'total ideology'. As a total ideology, it is rooted in concrete socio-historical experiences. It is not to be confused with the 'psychological motive' of a particular person. For example, when we say that capitalists have an ideology, we are not talking about what capitalists are thinking as individuals. Instead, we are interested in finding out how the capitalists as a class are viewing the world.

Utopia 'Utopia'. He begins with a very simple definition of a state of mind incongruous with reality. A utopia, in contrast, is a system of ideas that seeks to transcend the present by focusing on the future.

By Utopia, he meant just the opposite and was supported by the oppressed. The conflict between ideologies and utopias is a constant reality in society. Mannheim states that "today's utopias become tomorrow's reality. 'Utopias are often only crude truths' (Lamartine).

Mannheim explains that if utopianism were to end, it would "bring about a stagnant state in which man himself becomes no more than a thing. Mannheim lists four distinct utopian mindsets, each with a different class base and orientation toward history and time:

i. **Orgiastic chiliasm**–a sudden burst inward, like a revolution
ii. **Liberal Humanistic Utopia**–Gradual, Developmental Progress of Utopia, Not a Sudden Leap
iii. **The conservative idea thought**–oriented towards the past
vi. **Modern Communism**–Strategically Approached

Mannheim and Macro-sociology

Mannheim's work was mostly written through a macro-sociological lens. When writing Ideology and Utopia Mannheim's fundamental question was 'Why do humans behave differently within the framework of different social groups and class structures'. In answer to this question, his intellectual contributions to sociology focused more on social problems than on sociological problems.

The bulk of his work focused on themes such as "social stability, social groups, and mental differences consistent with social status or class cleavages". For Mannheim, the public was essential and fundamental to a democratic society. Therefore, ensuring that one ideology does not dictate the entire population is vital to the preservation of democracy.

Popular Statement

All truths are ideologically biased, all truths ultimately reflect the interest and prejudices of social groups.

ALFRED SCHÜTZ (1899–1959)

Alfred Schütz was born in Austria as an only child to an upper-middle-class Jewish family. He studied at the University of Vienna and lived in New York City from 1939 until his death, where he was a professor of philosophy and sociology at the New School for Social Research.

Important Works

1. Phenomenology of Social World (1967)
2. On Multiple Realities (1945)
3. The Well-Informed Citizens (1946)
4. The Structures of the Life-World (Co-Authored Thomas Luckmann) (1980).

Major Theories

Life World

In the inter-subjective world people interact, communicate, and understand one another through the process of typification: a process that enables people to fix and define one another, and have a shared role expectation.

It is through this process of typification, that a meaningful and stable social order is possible.

The inter-subjective life world, Thomas Luckman, who served as a co-author for the posthumous publication of Schütz's The Structures of the Life-world, developed the sociology of knowledge implications of Schütz's ideas stressed the differences between science and the life world as well as the importance of language, symbolism, and the moral order of society. People depend upon language and a stock of knowledge to enable social interaction.

In an inter-subjective world people interact, communicate, and understand each other through a process of typification. It is only through this process of typification that a meaningful and stable social order is possible.

Typification

Typification is a term coined by Alfred Schütz. The process of abstraction and formalization by which we classify things as 'apples', 'cars', 'plants' etc. is what Schütz calls typification. Thus, typology is the process of making general definitions and is based on general works of the past.

For Schütz the everyday world in which people interact is the paramount reality. It is taken for granted. And that's what makes society possible. But then, there are other realms, such as the realm of dreams, or the realm of scientific theory, in which people experience the world.

All of these finite realms of meaning have their own notions of time and space, and the transition from one realm to another involves a 'shock'. But again, for Schütz, the paramount reality is what matters most, and we all have to come back to it and experience the world as direct/real actors.

For Schütz, sociology must describe and understand how people experience the world. This means that sociology must take descriptions and definitions of people seriously.

Action and Act

Action and Act - Schütz made a distinction between 'action' and 'act'. Action is understood as purposive conduct anticipated by the actor while an act is defined as a completed action.

There are two types of motives for acts, the 'in-order-to' motive and the 'because' motive. The first is explained in terms of the goals and ends of the actor; the second, in terms of his background and disposition.

In popularizing this approach, Schütz used the philosophy of Edmund Husserl to criticize Max Weber's methodology. He does this in order to formulate a fundamental account of the nature of social action. In Schütz's view, Weber failed to provide any real account of the way in which actions can be constructed by drawing on a shared set of social concepts, symbols, and meanings.

Phenomenology

His major philosophical work involved the application of Edmund Husserl's Phenomenology to the problems of social reality, while his major methodological contribution was an attempt to link phenomenological concepts with the sociology of Max Weber.

Phenomenological sociology developed largely from the works of Alfred Schütz, best known for The Phenomenology of the Social World (1967). Schütz suggests that in ordering our own course of action, we employ assumptions about society and how it works and that we use Verstehen in a crude way to predict the actions of others.

Consequently, our actions are 'meaningful', not because we have any particular intention or motive, but because other actors interpret our action as having a symbolic significance. The phenomenological perspective is said to take to the extreme the interpretative approach, which was developed initially by Max Weber and later by other thinkers.

This perspective further states that our reality consists only of meanings; So, the task of the sociologist is to discover the meanings of actions and behaviour and nothing else.

Phenomenological sociology is the study of the formal structures of concrete social existence, as made available through the analytical description of acts of intentional consciousness.

The object of such analysis is the meaningfully lived world of everyday life or the 'life-world'. Bilton suggests that symbolic interactionists accepted shared definitions and emphasized symbolic communication through language.

So, Schütz originally developed this perspective to suggest that, we as individuals only function successfully when everyone shares the same meaning. Thus, in many ways, we can understand this approach as a departure from the traditional model of interpretative sociology.

Like Weber, Schütz believed that social research is distinct from research in the physical sciences and that people engage in understanding the world. In conversation with other comrades, we are trying to make sense of their understanding.

What distinguishes the social sciences is that the social scientist assumes the position of a disinterested observer. He is not involved in the lives of the people observed - their activities are not of any practical interest, but only of cognitive interest. Here, shared meaning and common-sense gain importance, in contrast to the Weberian model, in which only individual subjective experiences were given primary importance.

- Schütz's division of Husserl's lebenswelt (the mundane 'lifeworld') into four distinct sub-worlds
    1. the umwelt ('environment'), the environment defined through the perception and action of agents fellow men,
    2. the world of contemporaries (mitwelt);
    3. the world of predecessors (vorwelt); and
    4. the world of successors (folgewelt).

ERVING GOFFMAN (1922–1982)

Goffman was born on June 11, 1922, in Manville, Alberta, Canada, to Max Goffman and Anne Goffman. He was from a family of Ukrainian Jews who emigrated to Canada at the turn of the century. In 1939 he enrolled at the University of Manitoba, majoring in chemistry. During this, he met the famous North American sociologist Dennis Wrong. Their meeting inspired Goffman to leave the University of Manitoba and enrolled at the University of Toronto, where he studied under C.W. Hart and Ray Birdwhistell, graduating in 1945 with a BA in sociology and anthropology. He later went to the University of Chicago, where he received his MA (1949) and Ph.D. (1953) in sociology. Goffman's doctoral dissertation, titled Communication Conduct in an Island Community (1953), was completed under the supervision of W. Lloyd Warner, Donald Horton, and Anselm Strauss.

Important Works

1. On Face-Work (1955)
2. The Nature of Deference and Demeanor (1956)
3. The Presentation of Self in Everyday Life (1959)
4. Asylums (1961)
5. Encounters (1961)
6. Stigma (1963)
7. Behaviour in Public Places (1963)
8. Interaction Ritual (1967)
9. Strategic Interaction (1969)
10. Relations in Public (1971)
11. Frame Analysis (1974)
12. Forms of Talk (1981)

Major Theories

Total Institution

Goffman highlighted a class of organizations that differ from each other in some respects yet share a common distinguishing feature. Consider hospitals, monasteries, prisons, and boarding schools, these are different from each other in many respects yet share a common feature that is, the participants all live within the organization.

These institutions may be different in many regards such as schools, where entry is voluntary, unlike prisons where entry is forced and involuntary.

Similarly, there may be differences between those total institutions that exist to perform a work task such as army camps, and those that 'treat' people often without their explicit consent. These institutions were termed as total institutions by Goffman (1961).

Their lives in these different areas of life and under different control. Goffman (1961) argued that all these institutions have a similar structure despite differences in the personal characteristics of their participants, which is strikingly different from the basic arrangement of 'normal society'.

He suggests that a 'normal society' is characterised by distinctly defined spheres of work, leisure, and home.

'Total Institutions' are organizations whereby all these functions are localised in the contained space and under one control. Inmates, patients, prisoners, or monks spend their lives in an enclosed formally structured setup and undergo more or less similar experiences. In these 'total institutions', inmates have prescribed 'careers' (work) and a setup with the privileged position that reinforces their conformity to careers/expected behaviour/work and for causing the least inconvenience to those who run these organizations.

The interactions between inmates and administrative staff are individualistic and yet what brings inmates together is a commonality of experiences and a collective opposition to the staff forming a controlling and powerful group.

They argue that inmates in such institutions yearn to be released but miss these places after release. Goffman suggests that when people are living in batches, the institutional arrangements made to structure and administer, their lives are more or less the same.

Role Distance

Role performance (the expression of a role) is how a person expresses their role, describing it as a 'performance'. Role distance is a term coined by E. Goffman that refers to the separation of the performer from the role he or she is performing. This makes an important distinction between the existence of expectations related to role performance and personal commitment to the role.

Basic Requirements for Social Interaction

Goffman argued that a normal person needs four basic skills to interact normally in society. These are the four rules:

i. **Situational Propriety.** Goffman argued that in order to have a normal conversation an individual must have knowledge of how to act and react instinctively in various social situations. They should know how to take appropriate action.

ii. **Involvement.** During the conversation, the people involved have to show that they are fully involved in the conversation. If they project that they are not fully engaged in the conversation, it can prevent the development of a good social relationship. For example, during a conversation, if a person constantly uses a mobile phone and constantly interrupts the conversation, then such behavior shows a lack of participation.

iii. **Civil inattention.** Sometimes during social interaction situations arise in which we need to act in such a way that what we saw/heard/touched is not seen/heard/touched. For example, at a party, a guest accidentally drops a glass of wine and breaks it. In such a situation, the host will behave as if he did not see it, or if he does, he will behave as if it did not matter to him. This act of not paying attention to the event in order to maintain social relations is called 'Civil inattention'. Civil inattention is also used when conversing with strangers.

iv. **Accessible.** To have a good social relationship the people involved in the interaction must be accessible. That means they must not be difficult to contact. If they become difficult to contact and get involved in conversation then there is very little possibility for the development of a good social relationship.

Body Idiom

These comprise bodily appearance and personal acts: dress, bearing, movement and position, sound level, physical gestures such as waving or saluting, facial decorations, and broad emotional expression.

Ordinarily, we think of involvement shields as one means by which the individual can maintain the impression of proper involvement while he is actually delinquent in his situational obligations.

Involvement Shields

There are involvement shields that have the useful attribute of being portable. Thus, while women in European society no longer employ fans, let alone masks, to conceal a blush or a failure to blush, hands are now used to cover closed eyes that are obliged to be open, and newspapers to cover mouths that should not be open in a yawn.

Felicity Condition

'Felicity Condition' is a verbal or bodily gesture or both that makes other people feel that they are not having a conversation with 'strangers' but with a person, they can trust and rely on.

Dramaturgical Model—Front stage, Back Stage, and Off stage

In stage drama, as in everyday interactions, according to Goffman, there are three regions, each with different effects on an individual's performance: front stage, backstage, and off-stage.

The front stage is where the actor formally performs and adheres to conventions that have particular meaning for the audience. The actor knows he or she is being watched and acts accordingly.

When in the backstage region, the actor may behave differently than when in front of the audience on the front stage. This is where the individual truly gets to be herself and get rid of the roles that she plays when she is in front of other people.

Finally, the off-stage region is where individual actors meet the audience members independently of the team performance on the front stage. Specific performances may be given when the audience is segmented as such.

Stigma

Erving Goffman described stigma as a phenomenon whereby an individual with an attribute that is deeply discredited by their society is rejected as a result of the attribute. Goffman saw stigma as a process by which the reaction of others spoils normal identity.

CLIFFORD JAMES GEERTZ (1926–2006)

Geertz was born on August 23, 1926 in San Francisco. He served in the US Navy in World War II from 1943 to 1945. Geertz earned a Bachelor of Arts in Philosophy and a Doctor of Philosophy degree in 1950 from Antioch College in Yellow Springs, Ohio. in Anthropology from Harvard University in 1956 titled '*Religion at Modjokuto: A Study of Ritual Belief in a Complex Society*'.

Important Works

1. The Religion of Java (1960)
2. Peddlers and Princes (1963)
3. Agricultural Involution (1963)
4. Islam Observed (1968)
5. Deep Play (1972)
6. The Interpretation of Cultures (1973)
7. Negara (1980)
8. Local Knowledge (1983)

Major Theories

Symbols

Clifford Geertz's hermeneutic approach emphasizes that human beings require symbolic 'sources of light' to orient themselves to the system of meaning in a particular culture.

Geertz was largely influenced by sociologist Max Weber and concerned himself more with overall cultural operations.

Victor Turner believed that symbols initiate social action, and are "definite influences that spur individuals and groups to action." Turner's influence largely came from *Émile* Durkheim, who cared more about the way symbols functioned within society.

The two different schools of perspective on symbolic anthropology also have their roots in different cultures, with Victor Turner's work traditionally identified as the British idea, while Clifford Geertz's work is seen as the American way.

Geertz's symbol is used for any object, action, phenomenon, quality, or relation that represents an idea. It serves as the 'Vehicle of Conception', which is the meaning of the symbol. The number six is as much a symbol as the cross.

Mood and Motivation–The major difference between mood and motivation is that motivation has 'vectorial properties', whereas moods are 'scalar'.

Objectives have a directional role, they describe a certain overall course, moving towards some definite, usually temporary, end. But moods differ only in intensity: they don't go anywhere.

They arise from certain circumstances but they are responsive to some end. Like fog, they simply settle and rise; Like fragrance, wear and tear. They are holistic when present: if someone is sad then everything and everyone seems sad; If one is gay, everything and everyone seems fantastic.

Thus, although a man may be haughty, brave, strong-willed, and independent at the same time, he cannot very well be fickle and melancholy, or joyful and sad, at the same time.

Furthermore, where motives persist for more or less extended periods, moods only recur with greater or lesser frequency, coming and going for what are often quite unfathomable reasons.

But perhaps the most important difference between moods and motivations, as far as we are concerned, is that motivations are 'made meaningful' in terms of the goals they are conceived to motivate, while moods are 'made meaningful'. goes. The conditions from which they are conceived until spring. We tend to explain motivations in terms of their consumption, but we tend to explain moods in terms of their sources.

We say that a person is hardworking because he wants to be successful; We say that a person is worried because he is aware of the looming threat of a nuclear holocaust. And this is no less the case when interpretations are ultimate.

Coarse description - He followed the concept of 'coarse description' from Gilbert Ryle and the concept of 'family resemblance' from Ludwig Wittgenstein.

Geertz's methods were in response to his criticism of existing anthropological methods that searched for universal truths and principles. He was against broad theories of human behaviour; Rather, he advocated methods that uncover culture from the point of view of how people see and experience life. His 1973 article, '*Thick Description: Towards an Interpretive Theory of Culture*', synthesizes his approach.

In the social sciences and related fields, a rough description is a description of human social action that describes not only physical behaviours but also the context in which they are interpreted by actors so that it is better understood by an outsider. Can go A rough description usually adds a record of the subjective interpretations and meanings provided by those engaged in the practice, which makes the collected data of greater value for study by other social scientists.

Coarse description emphasized a more analytical approach, whereas earlier only observation was the primary approach. According to Geertz, analysis separated observation from explanatory methods.

An analysis is meant to pick out the important structures and established codes. This analysis begins with isolating all the individuals involved and arriving at a unified synthesis that accounts for the actions produced.

The ability of coarse descriptions to reflect the totality of a situation was called a mixture of descriptors to aid an overall understanding of the findings. As Lincoln and Guba (1985) indicate, the findings are not the result of rough description; rather they arise as a result of analyzing materials, concepts, or persons that are 'broadly described'.

Geertz takes issue with the status of anthropological practices in understanding culture. By exposing the reductive nature of ethnography, reducing culture to 'minor observations', Geertz hoped to recast ideas of culture as figurative.

Geertz pushes for the search for a 'web of meaning'. This approach brings its own difficulties. study of communities through large-scale anthropological interpretation will lead to inconsistencies in understanding.

Religion

Clifford Geertz defines religion as

1. a system of symbols that acts to
2. establish powerful, pervasive, and long-lasting moods and motivations in men [and women] by
3. formulating conceptions of a general order of existence and
4. clothing these conceptions with such an aura of factuality that
5. the moods and motivations seem uniquely realistic

Dissatisfied with earlier approaches, Geertz proposes religion as part of the cultural system. His conception of religion rests on the notion that people act basically according to the systems of meanings that they have and the job of an anthropologist is to interpret these meanings and provide for their description.

The system of meanings engages continuous dialogue between the meanings acting upon people and people's actions upon meaning – the cultural system shapes and gets shaped by the people.

He says, 'For an anthropologist, the importance of religion lies in its capacity to serve, for an individual or for a group, as a source of general, yet distinctive, conceptions of the world, the self, and the relations between them, on the one hand—its model of aspect—and of rooted, no less distinctive 'mental' dispositions—its model for aspect—on the other. From these cultural functions flow, in turn, its social and psychological ones'.

The sacred symbols condition the people's thoughts, tone, and tenor of their life, their moral and aesthetic styles, the way in which they construct and order the universe around them, and the meaning they attribute to their existence.

Religious symbols have power derived from some specific metaphysics or philosophy, which also presents to people a specific cosmic (or 'supernatural') order. Religion endeavours to adjust human actions to the cosmic order and the images of the latter are 'projected onto the plane of human experience.'

In many societies, religious symbols are uncritically held (they are held without questioning); they are beyond the pale of any skeptical inquiry. Here, Geertz says that those individuals who do not subscribe to the norms that the symbols formulate are regarded as 'stupid, insensitive, unlearned.'

Giving an example from Java, where he had done his fieldwork, he says that small children, simpletons, boors, and immoral people are regarded as 'not yet Javanese', which actually means 'not yet human'.

Among them, the same word is used for 'science' and 'religion', which advises them to conduct their social life properly as dictated by the set of norms and values.

Culture

Culture is a product of acting social beings trying to make sense of the world in which they find themselves. It is through symbols that people communicate. Symbols operate as vehicles of culture.

They are context—specific, i.e., they derive their meaning in the specific contexts in which they occur. Culture is embodied in public symbols, symbols through which the members of society communicate their worldview, value orientations, ethos, and all the rest to one another, to future generations, and of course, to anthropologists.

Hence, in order to study culture, the ethnographer should be able to situate him/herself in the position from which it was constructed. Thus, while Geertz provides an objective view of culture, at the same time he also provides a hermeneutical orientation.

Culture is, thus, like a text, the meaning of which can be interpreted. The text involves symbolic actions. The cultural texts are not free-floating with inexhaustibly reinterpretable meanings but have a 'convention-laden form, more or less tidily self-enclosed, susceptible to plural but not infinite number of plausible interpretations'.

An ethnographer trying to interpret the text will find the logic of the context of the action seemingly messy. In this endeavour to unravel the meaning, the language of the native interlocutors becomes insightful. This hints at the repository of orientations that are not fixed but flexible.

Ideology as a Cultural System

Geertz divided diagnostic accounts of ideology into the 'interest' theory and the 'strain' theory.

The interest theory goes back to Marx. In the interest theory, 'ideas are weapons' used to promote this or that interested class in a 'universal struggle for advantage'.

The strain theory, on the other hand, developed a psychology that was premised on 'the chronic malintegration of society', where individuals embrace ideology to 'flee anxiety'.

According to the strain theory (according to Geertz), 'In the modern world at least, most men live lives of patterned desperation'. They attempt to fulfill a certain social function, and when they fail to do so, they are led into a state of existential anxiety, and so they turn to reassuring ideology, 'thus ensuring the performance of roles that might otherwise be abandoned in despair or apathy'.

Deep Play

Bentham's concept of "deep play" is found in his The Theory of Legislation. By this he means a game in which the stakes are so high that it is, from his utilitarian point of view, irrational for men to engage in it. If a man who has a fortune of one thousand pounds (or ringgit) wages five hundred of it on an even bet, the marginal utility of the pound he stands to win is clearly less than the marginal disutility of the one he stands to lose.

In a real deep play, it's a matter of both sides. They are both in over their heads. Having come together in search of pleasure they have entered into a relationship that will bring the participants, collectively, pure pain rather than pure joy. Bentham's conclusion was therefore that deep play was immoral from first principles and that a specific move, for that matter, should be legally prevented.

HAROLD GARFINKEL (1917–2011)

Harold Garfinkel was born in Newark, New Jersey. He was an American sociologist and ethnographer who taught at the University of California, Los Angeles. Having developed and established ethnomethodology as a field of inquiry in sociology, he is perhaps best known for Studies in Ethnomethodology (1967), a collection of articles.

Important Works

1. Studies in Ethnomethodology (1967)
2. Toward Sociological Theory of Information (2008)
3. Seeing Sociologically (2005)
4. Ethnomethodology Program (2002)
5. Sociology of Information (2008)

Major Theories

Ethnomethodology

The term ethnomethodology is a combination of ethno and methodology. The term ethno- refers to the cultural context, including language, myths, symbols, and codes of behaviour, and the term methodology refers to the means, arguments, and philosophical beliefs involved in an approach to investigating such phenomena.

The term ethnomethodology was coined by Harold Garfinkel who is best known for the study of his work in Ethnomethodology (1967). He defined Ethnomethodology as 'the study of the body of common-sense knowledge and the range of processes and ideas (methods) through which ordinary members of a society make sense of it, find their way about it, and act upon the circumstances in which they find themselves'. Phenomenological sociologists focus on what people think, ethnomethodologists are more concerned with what people 'actually' do. Thus, ethnomethodologists pay great attention to the detailed study of conversation.

Ethnomethodology emphasizes that social action and social organization are produced by knowledgeable agents who guide their actions using common sense reasoning. Ethnomethodological research was directed at the social processes hidden under that achievement. The resulting research focus on the properties of common-sense knowledge and reasoning represents an aspect of what has been termed the 'cognitive revolution' in the social sciences.

Sociologist Harold Garfinkel studied the customs of people to discover how tacit and often unconscious social rules and norms not only influence behaviour but enable social order to exist (Weber, 2011). Like the symbolic interactionists, they believed that the members of a society together constitute a social system. He said, however, that people often resort to presumed knowledge and unstated consent to do so.

Ethnomethodology is the study of how social order arises in and through processes of social interaction. It generally seeks to provide an alternative to mainstream sociological approaches. In its most radical form, it is a challenge to the social sciences as a whole.

Ethnomethodology is a perspective within sociology that focuses on how people make sense of their everyday world. In this regard, Garfinkel postulates that "Ethnomethodological studies analyze everyday activities as members' methods to make the same activities apparently rational and reportable for all practical purposes".

People are viewed as rational actors, but use pragmatic reasoning rather than formal reasoning to make sense of and act in society. It refers to the analysis of the ways in which we actively understand what others say and do.

Most of our everyday interactions with others take place through informal conversations. Garfinkel analyzed these conversations. He showed how these interactions are based on shared understanding and knowledge.

He refers to these shared understandings and knowledge as 'background expectations'. The theory argues that human societies are completely dependent on these ways of gaining and displaying understanding.

The example of so-called glossing illustrates the type of interpretive process that ethnomethodology is interested in. To gloss over everyday life means to avoid the issue. For ethnographers, all talk is glossed, because the issue cannot be stated directly. In glossing, we apply a variety of rules, such as the 'etc. rule', which adds a clause to every other rule that says 'except in reasonable circumstances'.

Although this approach was developed by Garfinkel, it is based on Schütz's ground-breaking reconstruction of Max Weber's interpretative sociology. As Bilton testifies, ethnomethodologists work from Schütz's claim that the social world is constructed and reproduced by the practical actions of actors, based on given assumptions.

Thus, most importantly, ethnomethodology has its roots in the fusion of symbolic interactionism and phenomenology. Garfinkel's usage is now widely known as 'logger' or 'boarder'. He advocated this technique of de-familiarizing everyday life by challenging certain unstated assumptions as a way of discovering the existence of hidden norms. He called it a 'breaching'.

Accounting

For Garfinkel accounting is the process of describing or explaining social situations or how members make sense of their everyday world. Ethnomethodologists are interested in both the account itself and the method by which the account is made meaningful to the recipient, and place an emphasis on the latter.

Breaching Experiments

According to George Ritzer, a sociologist, breaching experiments are experiments where 'social reality is violated in order to shed light on the ways in which social reality is constructed by people'. In Garfinkel's work, Garfinkel encouraged his students to attempt breaching experiments to provide examples of basic Ethnomethodology.

Breaching experiments involve the conscious exhibition of violations of 'expected' behaviour/social norms, observation of the types of social responses to such environmental violations, and analysis of the social structure that makes these social responses possible. The idea of studying violations of social norms and related reactions has found its way into the disciplines of the social sciences and is used today in both sociology and psychology.

Harold Garfinkel and 'Making Commonplace Scenes Visible'

Garfinkel suggests that each member of society uses 'background expectations' to interpret and decide how to act in a social situation. However, individuals are unable to clearly state what each of these expectations or rules are. One way to help make background expectations more visible is to have a 'stranger to the life as usual character of everyday scenes'.

For example, saying 'hello' at the end of a conversation. Although the term 'breaching experiment' developed as a result of Garfinkel's approach, he cautions that it should not properly be called an experiment, but more accurately, a demonstration meant to produce disorganized interaction in order to highlight how the structures of everyday activities are ordinarily created and maintained.

Cultural Dope

Harold Garfinkel argues that mainstream sociology has generally portrayed man as a 'cultural dope' who follows standardized instructions provided by the culture of his society. By 'cultural dope', Garfinkel means to the sociologist a person in a society who has created stable characteristics of society by acting in compliance with pre-established and legitimate options of action provided by the general culture.

In place of cultural dope, ethnomethodologists portrayed skilled members who are constantly attending to the particular sequential properties of situations, giving them meaning, making them knowable, transmitting this knowledge to others, and maintaining the presence and creating a sense of order. From this perspective, members of a society create and fulfill their own social order rather than being shaped by it.

Indexicality and Reflexivity

The term indexicality means that there is no such thing as a clear, comprehensive definition of any word or concept in a language because meaning comes from the context of other words and from the context in which the words are spoken.

Reflexivity refers to the fact that our sense of order is the result of interactive processes. It is made by talking. Yet we usually think of ourselves as describing the order that already exists around us.

Reflexivity means that individuals shape action in relation to context, while context is constantly being redefined through action. In other words, reflexivity is an important concept in ethnomethodology in that it examines how, 'social systems are not imposed from outside but are created by people in their reflections, and talk about, the social world'. Garfinkel considered sequential expressions as the dominant phenomenon. For example, ordinal words like here, now, and I change their meaning depending on when and where they are used.

A low level of reflexivity will result in a person being shaped largely by their environment (or 'society'). A high degree of social reflexivity would be defined by an individual shaping their own norms, tastes, politics, desires, etc. This is similar to the notion of autonomy.

CHAPTER

4 Post Modernism, Post Structuralism and Post Colonialism

LEARNING OBJECTIVES:

In this chapter, we will discuss the following important topics.

- Edward Said
- Pierre Bourdieu
- Michel Foucault
- Jurgen Habermas
- Anthony Giddens
- Manuel Castells

INTRODUCTION

Poststructuralism, postmodernism, and postcolonial criticism are some of the 'terms' that go into the making of contemporary theory. Postmodernism is an intellectual discourse that is critical of modernism's 'grand narrative', it is a rejection of epistemological certainty or stability of meaning, and its emphasis on ideology as a means of maintaining political power. It rejects the claims of objectivity in social science, drawing attention to the conditional nature of knowledge claims within particular historical, political, and cultural discourses. It rejects the universal validity of binary opposites, static identities, hierarchies, and categorizations.

Post-structuralism is a theoretical practice that builds on and rejects the ideas established by structuralists. Poststructuralists hold that society and the individual are 'linguistically bound' to each other and that the relationship between the two is complex and that 'reality' itself is constructed within the social matrix and tends to reproduce itself over time.

As far as postcolonialism is concerned, it refers to the historical phase in many countries of the world (mainly in Asia and Africa) after the collapse of European empires until the middle of the twentieth century. The postcolonial era began when people from so many Asian, African, and Caribbean countries were left to take stock of their postcolonial culture and take a closer look at the cultural, economic, legal, and linguistic effects of colonial rule, and a new National identity emerged.

Some of the prominent thinkers which are widely known for their contribution to the understanding of postmodernism, post-structuralism, and postcolonialism are discussed below.

EDWARD SAID (1935–2003)

Edward Wadi Said was a Palestinian-American professor of literature at Columbia University, a public intellectual, and a founder of the academic field of postcolonial studies. He was born in Mandatory Palestine, United States.

Important Works

1. Beginnings: Intention and Method (1975)
2. Orientalism (1978)
3. The Question of Palestine (1979)
4. The World, the Text, and the Critic (1983)
5. Musical Elaborations (1991)
6. Culture and Imperialism (1993)
7. The Politics of Dispossession (1994)

Major Theories

Orientalism

Orient for Said is the Style, artifacts, or traits of the people and culture of Asia. He argues that the West's (Occident) view of the East (Orient) came from a belief in cultural superiority and Western imperialism.

By projecting the people of the Orient and especially the Arab world as volatile, irrational, backward, vicious, tyrannical, and threatening, the West has created a false and dangerous stereotype of 'otherness' and this has facilitated and justified western imperialism.

Edward says that with the start of European colonization, the Europeans came in contact with the lesser-developed countries of the east. Europeans found their culture and civilization very exotic and established the science of Orientalism. These Europeans divided the world into two parts the east and the west or the occident and the orient or the civilized and the uncivilized or us and them or theirs and ours.

Orients	Occident
Eastern	Western
Uncivilized	Civilized
Them	Us
Others	Ours
Inferior	Superior

Edward Said in 1978 in Orientalism lays bare both the strategies of cultural domination of the Occident over the Orient and provided the methodology for recognizing and resisting these strategies.

The salient features of Said's argument are that the world is divided into two unequal halves, the 'superior' Occident and the inferior and subordinated Orient, and that thus there occurs an invisible suppressive dimension to it.

In the realm of knowledge, given the historical fact of European colonization with its imperative to maintain power structures, all prior knowledge becomes a construction.

In other words, the Orient is an ideological construct, glorified or debased as the case may be, to prove the superiority of the Europeans and thus to perpetuate and justify the logic of European dominance. This project of the 'producers' of the Orient in the field of culture Siad called Orientalism and aims to label the Orient as Europe's Other - it is not all that.

He shows how this is a false creation, limited at the best of times, driven by the insistence of cultural hegemony that is so important to rule with the consent of the oppressed.

He advocates the urgency of the need to expose the power structures that form the context of cultural production. No narration or description is 'obvious' or 'innocent' anymore. The possibility of 'pure' knowledge does not exist. All knowledge is conceptually generated and is, therefore, conceptually imprinted.

Said uses Gramsci and his idea of cultural hegemony to explain how Orientalism functioned effectively. Antonio Gramsci's analysis of society makes a distinction between civil and political society.

Culture operates within civil society and cultural leadership emerges through a process of some cultures dominating others, which Gramsci calls 'hegemony'. It alludes to the Gramscian notion of the cultural hegemony of the industrial West, to show how Orientalism is produced and maintained within a historical, socio-political context.

Said locates the central idea that defines the culture of Europe as 'the idea of European identity as a superior one compared to all non-European peoples and cultures'.

Orientalism stems from Europe's need to identify the other, on which it can assert its superiority, in a neat binary of 'us' against 'them'. The binary of self/other is not a static one. The power and longevity of Orientalism are founded on its strategy of 'flexible positional superiority'.

This strategy is likely to result in a series of relationships and situations between West and East in which the West always emerges superior. Said points to the historical circumstances that facilitated this claim to cultural superiority, the extraordinary ascent of Europe from the late Renaissance to the present.

The economic and political status of Europe and the Orient allowed diverse peoples to exist in the Orient and speak about it – that is, to construct knowledge about it – with little resistance from the Orient itself. The creation of 'us' and 'them'.

Cultural Identity

On cultural identity, Edward Said said, "No one is completely one thing today. Labels such as Indian, Woman, Muslim, or American, are no more than just a starting points that can be understood if only for a moment in actual experience." If followed, they are quickly left behind.

Imperialism consolidated a mixture of cultures and identities on a global scale. But its worst and most paradoxical gift was to allow people to believe that they were only, primarily, exclusively, white, black, Western, or Oriental.

Yet just as human beings make their own history, they also make their own culture and ethnic identity. One cannot deny the continued continuity of long traditions, permanent habitats, national languages, and cultural geographies, but there seems to be no reason other than fear and prejudice to keep insisting on their separation and distinctiveness, as if that was all human life was about.

Survival in fact is about the connections between things. It is more rewarding - and more difficult - to think concretely and sympathetically, contrapuntally, about others than only about 'us'.

But it also means not trying to rule others, not trying to categorize them or place them in a hierarchy, and above all, not constantly repeating how 'our' culture or country is number one (or not number one, for that matter).

Human Rights–Universal or Western Construct?

Human rights are universal, often claiming that these rights are expressive of Western values, ethos, and norms.

The debate often hinges on the idea that although human rights are said to have universal validity, they originated in the West, reflect Western interests, and are, therefore, weapons of a new form of cultural hegemony or imperialism.

Similarly, others argue that human rights emanate from a European, Judeo-Christian, and/or Enlightenment heritage (usually labeled Western) and cannot be enjoyed by other cultures that are exposed to the conditions and conditions of "Western" societies. Don't follow values.

Edward Said a Pianist

In addition to being a public intellectual, Edward Said was an accomplished pianist, served as a music critic for The Nation magazine, and wrote four books about music: *Musical Elaborations* (1991); *Parallels and Paradoxes: Explorations in Music and Society* (2002), with Daniel Barenboim as co-author; *On Late Style: Music and Literature Against the Grain* (2006); and *Music at the Limits* (2007)), the last book in which he sought to find musical reflections of his literary and historical ideas in bold compositions and strong performances.

PIERRE BOURDIEU (1930–2002)

Pierre Bourdieu, born in 1930, was a French sociologist and public intellectual. Bourdieu's contributions to the sociology of education, the theory of sociology, and the sociology of aesthetics have gained wide influence in many related academic fields (such as anthropology, media and cultural studies, education, popular culture, and the arts). During his academic career he was mainly associated with the School for Advanced Study in the Social Sciences in Paris and the Collège de France.

Important Works

1. Reproduction in Education, Society, and Culture (1970)
2. Distinction and Rules of Art (1979)
3. The logic of practice (1980)
4. Sociology in Question (1992)
5. Practical Reason (1994)
6. The Art of Resistance (1998)
7. Masculine Domination (1998)
8. Science of Science and Reflexivity (2004)

Major Theories

Theory of Practice

Bourdieu's theory of practice, includes the concept of cultural capital, the concepts of habitus (one's worldview or disposition), and field (the context in which social action occurred).

The Forms of Capital

Bourdieu (1986) identified (at least) three broad types of capital. The first is cultural capital, cultural capital being a vehicle through which culture is reproduced. By cultural reproduction, it is meant that the higher status classes reward individuals who demonstrate virtues and hold the knowledge of the upper class, therefore maintaining their power.

The second type of capital is economic capital, which refers to characteristics that are quickly and relatively easily converted into money. This type of capital includes educational attainment, job skills, and job experience because their transformation into money is a well-understood process.

The third type of capital is social capital, which Bourdieu conceptualized as micro-based networks and personal relationships that potentially lead to access to resources.

Cultural capital Cultural capital refers to the collection of symbolic elements such as skills, tastes, posture, clothing, behaviour, material goods, credibility, etc. that are acquired through being part of a particular social class.

The concept was coined by Pierre Bourdieu and Jean-Claude Passeron in "Cultural Reproduction and Social Reproduction" (1977). Bourdieu expanded on this in his essay "The Forms of Capital" (1985) and in his book The State Nobility: Elite Schools in the Field of Power (1996). In the essay, Bourdieu describes cultural capital as a person's education (knowledge and intellectual skills) that provides an advantage in achieving high social status in society.

Pierre Bourdieu, a French sociologist, developed the idea of cultural capital as a way to explain how power in society is transferred and social classes are maintained.

Karl Marx believed that economic capital (wealth and property) determines your position in a social system. Bourdieu believed that cultural capital played an important and subtle role. For both Marx and Bourdieu, the more capital you have, the more powerful you are.

Bourdieu defined cultural capital as 'acquaintance with legitimate culture within a society'; What we can call 'high culture'. He saw families giving their children cultural capital by introducing them to dance and music, taking them to theaters, galleries, and historical sites, and talking about literature and art at the dinner table. Bourdieu identified three sources of cultural capital: objective, embodied, and institutional.

Embodied cultural capital Embodied cultural capital includes knowledge that is consciously acquired and passively inherited through the socialization of culture and tradition.

Unlike property, cultural capital is not transmissible but is acquired over time, as it is influenced by the habit (i.e., character and way of thinking) of the individual, who in turn becomes more receptive to similar cultural influences.

Linguistic cultural capital is the mastery of language and its relations; Embodied cultural capital, which is a means of communication and self-presentation of an individual, is acquired from the national culture.

Objective cultural capital Objectified cultural capital consists of a person's possessions (such as a work of art, scientific equipment, etc.) that can be transmitted for economic gain (buying and selling), and symbolically owning such things constitutes cultural capital.

Nevertheless, while possessing a work of art (objectified cultural capital) one can consume the art (understand its cultural meaning) only with the proper conceptual and historical foundation of prior cultural capital.

As such, cultural capital is not transmitted in the sale of a work of art, except by chance and independent causation, when the seller explains the value of the artwork to the buyer. For example, cultural goods, books, works of art

Institutional cultural capital Institutional cultural capital involves an institution's formal recognition of an individual's cultural capital, usually through academic credentials or professional qualifications.

The greatest social role of institutional cultural capital is in the labor market (a job), in which it allows the expression of an individual's array of cultural capital as qualitative and quantitative measures (which can be compared against measures of other people's cultural capital).Institutional recognition facilitates the transformation of cultural capital into economic capital by acting as a heuristic (practical solution) with which the seller can describe his cultural capital to the buyer. For example, Qualifications, Education Credentials.

Social Inequality

Bourdieu also points out that cultural capital is a major source of social inequality. Some forms of cultural capital are valued more than others and can help or hinder one's social mobility as much as income or wealth.

Habit and Field

Habit: Habit refers to the physical embodiment of cultural capital. We have deep roots, skills, and temperament because of our life experiences.

An individual's cultural capital is linked to his or her place of residence (i.e., embodied dispositions and dispositions) and region (i.e., social status), which are configured as a social-relationship structure.

A person's habit is made up of the intellectual dispositions developed in him or her by the family and the family environment and is manifested according to the person's nature.

As such, the social formation of a person's habitus is influenced by family, objective changes in social class, and by social interactions with other people in daily life moreover, the habitus of a person also changes when he or she changes social positions within the field.

Field: Bourdieu understood the social world as being divided into different areas or "sectors" of practice such as art, education, religion, law, etc., each with its own unique rules, forms of knowledge, and capital.

The territory is that space of social status that is formed by the conflicts that occur when social groups attempt to establish and define cultural capital within a given social space. Therefore, depending on the social sector, a type of cultural capital can be both legitimate and illegitimate at the same time. In this way, the legitimation (social recognition) of a type of cultural capital can be arbitrary and derived from symbolic capital.

Symbolic Capital and Symbolic Violence

Bourdieu saw symbolic capital (things like prestige, honor, and the right to be heard) as an important source of power. Symbolic capital is any species of capital that is regarded through socially developed classification schemes. When a holder of symbolic capital exercises power, it is against an agent who holds less and thereby tries to change their actions, they exercise 'symbolic violence'.

Symbolic violence is basically the imposition of categories of thought and perception on dominated social agents who then perceive the social order as desirable. Symbolic violence is in some sense more powerful than physical violence, in that it is embedded in many ways of functioning and structures of individuals' perception and enforcement of the social order's vision of legitimacy.

MICHEL FOUCAULT (1926–1984)

Paul Michel Foucault was born on 15 October 1926 in Poitiers, France. He was a historian of ideas, writer, political activist, and literary critic. He became established academically during the 1960s, holding a number of positions in French universities, before his election to the prestigious Collège de France in 1969, where he was a Professor of the History of Systems of Thought until his death. An early victim of AIDS, Foucault died in Paris on June 25, 1984.

Important Works

1. Madness and Civilization (1961)
2. 'The Father's No (1961)
3. The Birth of the Clinic (1963)
4. The Order of Things (1966)
5. The Archaeology of Knowledge (1969)
6. Discipline and Punish (1975)
7. The History of Sexuality (1976)
8. Nietzsche, genealogy, history (1971)
9. 'Sexuality and power' (1978)
10. What is Enlightenment?' (1984)
11. What calls for punishment (1984)
12. The Use of Pleasure (1984)
13. Care of the Self (1984)

Major Theories

Power/Knowledge

Foucault rejected the pre-existing theories of power such as the Constant Sum Concept supported by Marx and Weber and the Variable Sum Concept of power supported by Parsons. Foucault is generally critical of 'theories' that try to give absolute answers to 'everything'.

According to Foucault, most people misunderstand power. For this reason, he clarifies that power cannot be described solely as a set of institutions or mechanisms intended for the citizen to obey and delegate to the state, nor as a rule of thumb. Neither as submission nor as a general and oppressive system where one social class or group oppresses another.

He used two complementary methods in his work:

i. The Archeology of Knowledge in Early Works; And

ii. Genealogy of power in later work.

Archeology focuses on a given historical moment, whereas genealogy deals with a historical process. Both of these Foucauldian methods have a continuing and driving force in what is called postmodern Foucault discourse in order to bring to light the surface-level principles that characterize the subject's modes of thinking and acting.

As a set of speech practices carrying values, categorizations, and meanings, discourse simultaneously constitutes a truth about subjects, and subjects constitute the context of this truth regime.

Employing the archaeological method in his early works such as Madness and Civilization and The Order of Things, Foucault brought to light two modernist themes:

i. Foucault rejected the Enlightenment project of humanism (the human self as an independent entity) because of his focus on discourse on the human subject as a practice, rather than an abstraction, as the structuralists do; And

ii. against structuralism and liberal humanism.

He rejected the themes of the history of ideas, such as the origin of ideas, their continuity, and the process of totality, by arguing that discourses were not fixed and closed within a single location, but rather dispersed across a range of sites, times, and activities.

In these transitions from one discourse to another, new forms of authority, power, social subjectivity, and institutional organization were created, as Foucault views discourses as not simply isolated patterns of discourse but principles embedded in wider patterns of social organization and practice.

Therefore, there is no single universal truth and dominance is never absolute and will never be absolute. In his later works, Foucault revised his idea of discourse through genealogical analysis, for example in Punishment and Sexuality, in which he examined the complex and emergent emergence of contemporary systems of social discipline and knowledge.

- He defines truth as a system of ordered processes for the production, distribution, regulation, circulation, and operation of statements. Through this system of truth, power structures are created and enforced.

Here, the discourse was conceived not as an autonomous formation of statements within a specific setting, but as a dynamic meeting point between power and knowledge.

Consequently, there is no objective knowledge as claimed by modernity. Within critical theory, Foucault's work provides a comprehensive analysis of power. Against traditional models of power (that is, Marxist and libertarian approaches), Foucault argues that power is located neither in a single class nor in an individual, but is spread throughout the social structure and exists within and through it.

As he puts it: 'Power is never localized here or there but is planned and exercised through a net-like organization'. His theory of power says that power is exercised only through relations (Foucault analyzed power relations and not power itself), that is, power relations in their different modalities, strategies, tactics, practices, and techniques.

All social relations are relations of power, capable of highlighting the various ways by which human beings are subject in our culture. Power is basically a bottom-up feature of social interaction (micropower).

Power is positive, productive, and constructive rather than negative, prohibitive, and repressive, even if it sometimes takes the form of dominance; that is, it brings into existence the meanings, themes, and social systems, these are its effects rather than its content or its priority.

Power has nothing to do with resistance because resistance always means self-empowerment; One is merely restructuring the relation of power. Knowledge and power are mutually constituted and therefore cannot be separated; Foucault, in fact, preferred terminological power/knowledge.

Power is impersonal and flows through or influences language, knowledge, and institutional practices; and power and freedom are not opposites because there is no subject, and therefore no freedom, outside power.

Thus, he finds the notion of sovereign power to be insufficient to understand the diverse modes of power operating in modern societies. As he puts it: "Political theory, in general, has not ceased to be attached to the person of the sovereign.

He identified three instruments of disciplinary power derived in large part from the military model:

i. Hierarchical observation, or the ability of officials (metaphorically norms of society) to oversee all they control with a single glance;
ii. Ability to make general decisions and punish those who violate norms; And
iii. The use of examination to observe subjects and make general judgments about them.

Thus, Foucault's analysis of power comes in two forms: empirical and theoretical. The empirical analysis concerns itself with historical (and modern) forms of power and how these have emerged from previous forms of power. Foucault describes three types of power in his empirical analysis: universal power, disciplinary power, and biopower. And the fourth type of power is pastoral power which is theoretical.

With 'sovereign power' Foucault alludes to a power structure that is similar to a pyramid, where one person or a group of people (at the top of the pyramid) holds the power, while the 'ordinary' (and oppressed) people are in power. There is a bottom of the pyramid. In the middle of the pyramid are those who implement the orders of the sovereign. A typical example of sovereign power is an absolute monarchy.

The purpose of what Foucault calls 'disciplinary power' is to use the skills of the body as effectively as possible. The more useful the body becomes, the more it has to be obedient. Its purpose is not only to use the skills of the bodies but also to prevent these skills from being used to rebel against authority. Disciplinary power creates a certain type of person by producing new movements, habits, and skills.

With 'biopower' Foucault refers to power over bios (life)—power over the population. Biopower mainly depends on norms that are created internally by people rather than external forces. It encourages, strengthens, controls, supervises, adapts, and organizes the forces beneath it. Foucault sometimes distinguished biopower from disciplinary power, but at other times he described disciplinary power as a manifestation of biopower.

Foucault develops the concept of pastoral power by drawing on the Judeo-Christian tradition of the shepherd caring for the flock. The pastor, unlike a prophet, fortune-teller, or shaman, 'designates a very special form of power'. Foucault notes four unique characteristics of pastoral power: it seeks to liberate the individual; It is ready to sacrifice itself for the life of the herd; It is concerned as much for the one as for the many, for the part and for the whole; It requires knowledge of conscience, inside the mind of the people

Sexuality

Michel Foucault differs from other thinkers due to his path-breaking reading of sexuality as evidenced in some of his most well-known works especially The History of Sexuality, 4 volumes 1976–1984 and posthumously in 2018.

The first volume, *The Will to Knowledge* (*La volonté de savoir*),1976; an English translation appeared in 1978. *The Use of Pleasure* (*L'usage des plaisirs*), and *The Care of the Self* (*Le souci de soi*), 1984. The fourth volume, *Confessions of the Flesh* (*Les aveux de la chair*), was published posthumously in 2018.

Michel Foucault differs from other thinkers due to his path-breaking reading of sexuality as evidenced in some of his most well-known works especially The History of Sexuality, 1976-1984.

Foucault was influenced by the works of George Canguilhem in biology and medicine. Canguilhem argued that the 'abnormal arouses theoretical interest in the normal'.

Foucault analyzed the links between sexuality, subjectivity, and truth. Foucault argues that a new technology of sex emerged at the end of the eighteenth century to become a major site of state-centric interventions. These interventions were carried out to control social bodies and resulted in producing new forms of surveillance.

Repression of sexuality was a part of this process. It is argued that the term 'sexuality', as we now understand it, was absent in the period before the nineteenth century. In this context, it is important to understand Foucault's ideas about knowledge and power since he claims that power can produce knowledge.

He proposes four ways in which knowledge and power are associated with the new practices and technologies of sex.

These are related to Foucault's critique of psychoanalysis and the cultural construction of sexuality. Briefly, the four phenomena can be listed as follows:

- **i.** The 'hysterization of women's bodies': Women's bodies are perceived as being saturated with sexuality. Therefore, women are represented as unstable bodies that can be prone to hysteria, resulting in images of 'nervous women'.
- **ii.** The "pedagogization of children's sex": Children who indulged in sexual activities are viewed as functioning contrary to the law of nature. Parents, doctors, experts, and educationists realized the consequences of the sexual potential of children. Myths of masturbation are related to these perceptions.
- **iii.** The "socialization of procreative behaviour": The regulation of population operated as a means of controlling procreative behaviour in line with the needs of society. Foucault claimed that this process of control is political in nature. For instance, financial support and contraception are embedded in this political discourse.
- **vi.** The "psychiatrization of perverse pleasure": Sexuality comes to be treated as a separate psychical and biological instinct that can be subjected to psychiatry.

According to Foucault, these four phenomena related to knowledge and power result in the creation of four subjects - the hysterical woman, the masturbating child, the Malthusian couple, and the perverse adult.

The above-mentioned four forms of knowledge showed the emergence of a calculated approach to life and mechanisms, which exerted control over people through the establishment of certain structures, as in the four instances mentioned above. Foucault calls this control through structures 'bio-power'.

For Foucault, biopower is a technique of power for the management of human beings in large groups; The distinctive quality of this political technique is that it allows for the control of an entire population. It refers to the control of the human body through social disciplinary institutions through the body-politics of the human body and the bio-politics of the population.

JURGEN HABERMAS (1929)

Habermas was born on 18 June 1929 in Düsseldorf, Rhine Province. He was born with a cleft palate and had corrective surgery twice during his childhood. Habermas argues that his speech disability forced him to think differently about the profound interdependence and importance of communication. Habermas completed his dissertation at the University of Bonn in 1954, writing on the conflict between the Absolute and History in Schelling's view. At least in Germany, he first attracted serious public attention in 1962 with the publication of his book 'Structural Transformation of the Public Sphere.'

Important Works

1. Theory and Practice (1973)
2. Legitimation Crisis (1975)
3. Communication and the Evolution of Society (1979)
4. The Theory of Communicative Action (1984)
5. Structural Transformation of the Public Sphere; English ed., (1989)

Major Theories

Theory of Communicative Action and Strategic Social Action

Communicative action can be understood as a cyclic process in which the actors are two things:

- **i.** an initiator, who masters situations through actions for which he is accountable,
- **ii.** The other is a product of the transitions around him, of the groups whose solidarity is based on the solidarity to which he belongs, and of the processes of socialization in which he is brought up.

In "Communicative action," actors address one another with the aim of practical attitude (mutual understanding) i.e their goals depend upon cooperative behaviour.

In Strategic social action, actors are not so much interested in mutual understanding, the actors achieve their individual goals.

Communicative action is thus an inherently consensual form of social coordination in which actors "mobilize the potential for rationality" and rationally motivated agreement.

He came under the influence of thinkers like Karl Marx, Hegel, and George Lucas. His Theory of Communicative Action (1981), is based on an adaptation of Talcott Parsons AGIL Paradigm.

According to Habermas language is a medium for coordinating action, although not the only such medium. There are three interrelated concerns in the theory of communicative action:

- **i.** to develop a concept of rationality
- **ii.** to construct a two-level concept of society that integrates the lifeworld and systems paradigms
- **iii.** to sketch out, a critical theory of modernity.

Lifeworld (Lebenswelt)

For Habermas, the lifeworld is more or less the 'background' environment of competencies, practices, and attitudes in the context of one's cognitive horizon. Habermas focuses on the lifeworld consisting of socially and culturally embedded linguistic meanings.

It is a vibrant area of informal, culturally based understanding and interaction. The rationalization and colonization of the lifeworld by the mechanistic rationality of bureaucratic and market forces is Habermas' primary concern.

Modernity

Modernity is defined by Habermas as a set of problems related to the issue of time, problems arising from the transformation of European society into what Hegel called the 'principle of subjectivity', the notion of individual autonomy as the essence of man.

This freedom from all forms of external authority, including that of nature as well as tradition, means that the subject ' has to create his ideality by himself'; Because it is free, it cannot accept any value or law that it does not recognize as its own.

Social Action

Habermas distinguishes four types of actions by individuals in society. All four of them are really 'models':

- **i.** Teleological action
- **ii.** Normatively regulated action;
- **iii.** Dramaturgical action;
- **vi.** Communicative action

Teleological Action. The actor makes a 'decision among alternative courses of action, with a view to the realization of an end, guided by maxims, and based on an interpretation of the situation'. In a subset called strategic action, actors anticipate what other actors will do, guided by goals, and a model that lies behind decision theory and game theory.

Normatively Regulated Action. Actors in a social group pursue common values or norms of the group, 'fulfilling a generalized expectation of behavior'. This model of action underlies role theory in sociology. In some places, Habermas suggests that often this action is performed almost automatically, in rote fashion, from second nature, out of deeply entrenched shared habits, and regarded as unproblematic by the actors, rather than in a calculated instrumental way.

Dramaturgical Action. Sometimes an actor is neither solitary nor a member of a social group, but is interacting with people who are 'constituting a public for one another, before whom they present themselves. The actor evokes in his public a certain image, an impression of himself'. He has privileged access to his own intentions, desires, etc. but can monitor or regulate public access to them. There is a 'presentation of self', not spontaneously but stylized, with a view to the audience.

Communicative Action. Here two or more actors establish a relationship and seek to reach an understanding about the action situation and their plans of action in order to coordinate their actions by way of agreement. Habermas credits George Herbert Mead (1934) and Harold Garfinkel (1967) for helping to give paradigmatic importance to the act of communication.

Theory of Knowledge

Habermas' main claim was that the knowledge of scientific and social progress is tacitly guided by three types of 'knowledge constitutive interests'—technical, practical, and emancipatory, that are 'anthropologically deep-seated' in the human species.

Habermas distinguishes three primary general cognitive areas in which human interest generates knowledge. These fields determine the categories related to what we interpret as knowledge.

That is, they are called 'structuring knowledge'– they determine the way knowledge is discovered and determine whether knowledge claims can be verified.

These areas define domains of cognitive interests or learning and are based on different aspects of social existence–work, interaction, and power.

Work Knowledge

Work broadly refers to the way in which the individual controls and manipulates his environment.

It is commonly known as heuristic action -- knowledge based on empirical investigation and governed by technical rules. The test of effective control of reality dictates what is or is not an appropriate action.

Empirical-analytical sciences using hypothetical-deductive principles characterize this domain. Most of what we consider to be 'scientific' research domains–For example, Physics, Chemistry, and Biology are classified by Habermas as belonging to the field of Work.

Practical Knowledge

The Practical domain identifies human social interaction or 'communicative action'. Social knowledge is governed by binding agreed norms, which define mutual expectations about behaviour among individuals. Social norms may be related to empirical or analytical propositions, but their validity is based only on the 'interdisciplinarity of mutual understanding of intentions'.

The criterion of clarification of the conditions for communication and intertextuality (understanding of meaning rather than causation) is used to determine what is the appropriate course of action. Most of the— descriptive social science, history, aesthetics, legal, ethnographic, literary, and so forth, are classified by Habermas as belonging to the realm of the practical.

Emancipatory Knowledge

The Emancipatory domain identifies 'self-knowledge' or self-reflection. This involves 'interest in the way one's history and biography has expressed itself in the way one sees oneself, one's roles, and social expectations. Emancipation is from libidinal, institutional, or environmental forces which limit our options and rational control over our lives but have been taken for granted as beyond human control ('reification').

Insights gained through critical self-awareness are emancipatory in the sense that at least one can recognize the correct reasons for his or her problems.' Knowledge is gained by self-emancipation through reflection leading to a transformed consciousness or 'perspective transformation'. Examples of critical sciences include feminist theory, psychoanalysis, and the critique of ideology.

The Public Sphere

Jürgen Habermas wrote extensively on the concept of the 'public sphere', using accounts of conversations that took place in coffee houses and which promoted Enlightenment ideals of equality, human rights, and justice in eighteenth-century England.

The public sphere was guided by a norm of reasoned argument and critical discussion, in which the strength of one's argument was more important than one's identity.

As a historical formation, the public sphere consisted of a "space" separate from family life, the business world, and the state.

Crisis in Capitalist Society

He has delineated four types of crises:

- **i.** economic crisis
- **ii.** rationality crisis
- **iii.** legitimation crisis
- **iv.** motivation crisis

Legitimation Crisis

A legitimacy crisis refers to a decline in trust in administrative functions, institutions, or leadership.

Habermas argued that a legitimation crisis occurs when citizens experience a democratic deficit: in other words, when people feel themselves to be underrepresented.

An institution or organization does not have the administrative capacity to maintain or establish effective structures in achieving its ultimate goals.

Economic Crisis

Capitalism is always a victim of economic crisis due to its internal contradictions. After the war, after liberal capitalism.

The state, Habermas argues, has come to play a greater role in the management of the economy in order to offset these economic crisis tendencies. The state now monitors inflation and unemployment, combating potentially harmful trends by manipulating the money supply or interest rates, or by making policy changes.

Rational Crisis

This increased role of the state represents a 'functional adaptation' within capitalism: it involves class struggle.

This leaves open the possibility of what Habermas calls the crisis of rationality, or the crisis posed by the philosophy of mediocrity adopted by the state.

Motivation Crisis

The fourth type of crisis is what Habermas calls the crisis of motivation. This can happen when the institutions of primary and secondary socialization fail to produce and reproduce the work ethic.

The weakening of the work ethic can leave citizens, especially the youth, unresponsive or indifferent to the 'essentials to work' that fuel the sub-systems of the economy (directly) and the state (indirectly).

ANTHONY GIDDENS (1938)

Anthony Giddens was born on 18 January 1938 in Edmonton, North London. He graduated from the University of Hull in 1959. Growing up in North London, he supports Tottenham Hotspur, and while doing his Masters at the London School of Economics, he wrote a dissertation on Sport and Society in Contemporary Britain.

Important Works

1. The Nation State and Violence (1998)
2. The Consequences of Modernity (1990)
3. Capitalism and Modern Social Theory (1971)
4. The Constitution of Society (1984)
5. Essentials of Sociology (2001)
6. Reflexive Modernization co-author Ulrich Beck (1994)

Major Theories

Reflexivity

Reflexivity is the idea that both individuals and society are defined not just by themselves, but also in relation to each other. So, they must constantly redefine themselves both in response to others and to new information.

It is the routine use of knowledge that institutions and individuals continually collect and apply to organize and transform society. Corporations conduct market surveys to help them formulate sales strategies. This increased reflexivity has been facilitated by the development of mass communication.

In information societies, he states that information gathering is perceived as a routine process for the greater security of the nation. Information gathering is known as the concept of individuation. Individuality comes about as a result of individuation as people are given more informed choices.

The more information the government has about an individual, the more entitlements are given to the citizens.

The process of gathering information helps the government identify enemies of the state, and isolate individuals who are suspected of plotting activities against the state.

Globalization

Anthony Giddens views globalization as, 'the intensification of worldwide social relations that link distant regions in such a way that local events are shaped by events many miles away and vice versa'.

Giddens defines four dimensions of globalization:

- **i.** The most obvious one is the world capitalist economy.

ii. The nation-state system, is the second dimension of globalization.
iii. "The third dimension is the world military order.
vi. "The fourth dimension of globalization concerns industrial development.

The term has been widely used to include a vast range of characteristics of contemporary life. Five of them can be considered important for its understanding:

i. Stretched Social Relations. Globalization calls for a cultural, economic, and political network of relations spread across the globe, which is denser than in any previous period. Also, they are not limited to specific regions only; they cover the whole world.
ii. Intensification of Flows. Globalization and Liberalization Globalization is manifested in the rapid flow of information, capital, and goods. They result in networks and interactions that transcend any effective monitoring and control by nation-states. They give rise to social interactions that may have little to do with geographic and cultural proximity. Mobile phones, satellite television, and the Internet, which are based on these flows, do not respect the spatial framework that has hitherto bound communication.
iii. Increasing Interpenetration Under globalization, cultures and societies that were hitherto separate come face-to-face with each other and are integrated into others' ways of social life. Differences in language, food habits, dress, and beliefs constitute the social structure.
iv. Global Infrastructure. They are the formal and informal institutional arrangements in the economic, political, and cultural domains that facilitate networking and flows. Their reach transcends the boundaries of the nation-state. They facilitate the functioning of a global market. They embody the codes and regulations that govern transnational interactions. They provide mechanisms of global governance.
v. Reformulation of Social Relations Under globalization relations between social classes are brought sharply to focus on a global scale. In the earlier phases of capitalism class relations were primarily defined within the vortex of the nation-state. Globalization brings about a dense interaction between dominant classes and regions outstripping national cleavages. It throws up new social strata and factions both at the national and global levels. It reformulates inequalities and existing unevenness in economic and power relations.

Characteristics The above five-fold features inform the following characteristics of the globalizing world.

It is an inter-connected world: It is connected on account of modes of simultaneous communication to any part of the world. It is also a connected world on account of the problems that confront humanity as a whole. Problems such as global climatic changes, the depletion of the ozone layer, drugs, terrorism, pollution of the oceans, etc. are beyond the scope of any particular nation-state.

Remote action in one corner of the world has rapid and significant consequences in other parts. For example, the East Asian Crisis of 1997–1998 on the New York Stock Market or Nasdaq on the Bombay Stock Market, etc.

Global social strata sharing some common cultural characteristics have emerged. For example, English Language, Blue Jeans, Sweat Shirts, etc. These features increasingly permeate national cultures and may tend to bring about a level of homogenization of ways of life, thought, and interaction.

Globalization encompasses a whole range of social relations. It affects every aspect of life. However, the pace of these ties may not grow at a uniform pace. Under globalization power relations come to be articulated increasingly at the global level. New organizations come to be established for this purpose.

The development of communication technology undermines the authority of the nation-state and poses a threat to its sovereignty. '

It connects localities with the world bypassing national boundaries.

Sometimes individuals and smaller institutions in control of front-line technology can challenge the power of global organizations by forming alliances. There grows up new entrepreneurship around such knowledge-based industry.

The prevailing pattern of globalization has widened economic inequalities and has worsened a lot of the impoverished. It has threatened the existence of local cultures.

Globalization also brings new opportunities. It widens tremendously the range of choices available to people. It breaks down such geographic barriers as town and countryside and metropolis and periphery to access resources and information. One can live locally while being in tune with the global context.

It involves a struggle to dominate global markets and centralisation of power in a few organizations. The rise of Multinational Corporations (MNCs) and the new role that the International Monetary Fund (IMF), the World Bank, and the World Trade Organization (WTO) have come to play bear witness to it.

The process of Globalization has hitherto been accompanied by a strong dose of Arnericanisation manifest in such symbols as 'Coca-Cola' and 'Macdonald' and has reinforced its influence over the other regions of the world.

Modernity

Giddens is among those who have opposed the equation of modernity with liberalism or modernity with capitalism. Giddens borrows much from Marx and takes his own position in defining modernity.

According to him, modernity is multi-dimensional. It is this emphasis, which sets him apart from other sociologists.

Giddens, therefore, makes an attempt to analyze different dimensions of modernity:

1. Capitalism characterized by commodity production, private ownership of capital, property less wage labour.
2. Industrialism involves the use of inanimate power sources and machinery to produce goods.
3. Coordinated administrative power focused through surveillance.
4. Military power or the control of the means of violence.

According to Giddens, the main features of contemporary civilization are the nation-state, the modern political system, hyper-mechanized and hyper-technological production methods, wage labour, commodification of all relations, including the workforce, and urbanization.

Modern society is much more dynamic than premodern society. The speed, intensity, and scope of change in modern society is high.

The most dynamic aspects of modernity can be grouped into three aspects that run through Giddens' entire analysis of modernity:

1. Time-space separation,
2. Dis-embedding mechanisms, and
3. The reflexive character of modernity.

Giddens states that time has become standardized and globalized in modern society. It enables people to interact with each other and with the world around them without any problems. Not only the concept of time but also the concept of space is changing. Each new technological development significantly expands our space. The fact that we may be in one place, but not the same place is one of the driving forces behind the modern rational organization.

Social institutions such as family, kinship, education, and politics were earlier integral parts of local society. The local society thus survived through the ages with these institutions. But, with the advent of modernization, these institutions were separated from the local society or community.

Reflexivity helps us to explain all human actions. In the context of modernity, there has been the emergence of a modern self, which is characteristic of the contemporary period. Modern society is undergoing a reflexive process that exists at an institutional as well as individual level and which is instrumental in creating and changing modern systems and forms of social organization.

De-traditionalisation

Another major theme in Gidden's work is de-traditionalisation. Giddens argues that 'there is no need for someone who follows a traditional practice to ask questions about alternatives. Tradition provides a framework for action that may be largely unquestioned... Tradition gives stability'. and gives the ability to identify oneself against a static background.

Globalization perpetuates this as local cultures and traditions are exposed to new cultures and ideas, which often means that traditional ways of acting are questioned. As a result of globalization, societies, and cultures undergo a process of de-traditionalisation, where day-to-day life becomes less and less informed by 'tradition for tradition's sake'.

De-traditionalisation and Self-identity

De-traditionalisation also has consequences for self-identity. According to Giddens, 'Where tradition dies out, and lifestyle choice prevails, self-identity must be created and recreated on a more active basis than before'.

Giddens further argues that individuals must engage in an ongoing process of reflecting on their lives and adapting them in light of new knowledge being generated in a rapidly changing, globalizing world. This whole process of reflecting on one's life and changing accordingly is known as reflexivity.

Risk Society

The risk society hypothesis, initially developed by Ulrich Beck and Anthony Giddens, has gained traction in the field of sociology and created a very interesting debate about risk in postmodern society.

Giddens and Beck argued that humans have always been subjected to a level of risk – such as natural disasters which have always been perceived as produced by non-human forces.

But in modern societies, humans are exposed to risks like pollution, newly discovered diseases, and crime, which are the result of the process of modernization. Hence Giddens distinguished two types of risk:

i. External Risks (natural disasters)
ii. Manufactured Risks

Manufactured risks are characterized by a high degree of human agency involved in both creating and mitigating such risks.

Giddens termed it 'late' or 'high' modernity which is reflexive in the sense that they are self-induced.

In late modernity, risks such as the threat of disastrous nuclear reactor incidents are plainly the consequences of human activities (Beck 1986).

According to Giddens, we have little experience dealing with these new threats because they have only existed for the past half-century. He argues that there is a '"new vulnerability to risk"' in that these new technologies could have catastrophic consequences for humanity, yet we do not yet know all the consequences associated with them.

For example, we cannot be sure of the potential impacts that would modify the genetic composition of our basic foods, and we do not know exactly how much global warming is due to human influence.

Structuration

Giddens developed the theory of structuration in his book The Constitution of Society, giving an analysis of agency and structure in which primacy is granted to neither. (Agency is the capacity of individuals to act independently and to make their own free choices; whereas an agent's common interaction with structure, as a system of norms, is described as structuration)

His theory of structuration explores the connection between individuals and social systems.

He argues that in order to understand society, one cannot look only at the actions of individuals or the social forces that maintain the society. Instead, it is both that shape our social reality This process of structures producing and re-producing systems (i.e., 'duality of structure') is called structuration.

Systems here mean to Giddens, 'the situated activities of human agents' and 'the patterning of social relations across space-time'. Structuration is very useful in synthesizing micro and macro issues.

On a micro scale, one of individuals' internal sense of self and identity, for example of a family in which we are increasingly free to choose our own mates. On a macro scale, one of the state and social organizations like multinational capitalist corporations.

The Duality of Structure

Duality of structure refers to the fact that individual behavior is constrained by existing social structures, but at the same time, this behavior constitutes social structures by reifying or challenging the current status.

Giddens uses the 'dualities of structure' (i.e., content/ideology, micro/macro) to emphasize the nature of structure as both medium and result. Structures exist both internally as memory traces within agents that are products of phenomenological and hermeneutic inheritance and externally as expressions of social action.

Similarly, social structures have agents and/or are products of past actions of agents. Giddens holds this duality, along with 'structure' and 'system', in addition to the concept of recursion as the core of structure theory.

The Third Way

The third way, in politics, a proposed alternative between two dominant models, namely left-wing and right-wing political groups.

He argues that the political concepts of "left" and "right" are now breaking down as a result of many factors, but mainly because of the absence of a clear alternative to capitalism.

Anthony Giddens used the term "third way" to describe an alternative to neoliberalism and social democracy in an era of globalization.

The third approach supports the pursuit of greater egalitarianism in society through action to increase the distribution of skills, abilities, and productive endowments while rejecting income redistribution as a means of achieving this. It emphasizes commitment to balanced budgets, and providing equal opportunity which is combined with an emphasis on personal responsibility, the decentralisation of government power to the lowest level possible, encouragement and promotion of public–private partnerships, improving labour supply, investment in human development, preservation of social capital and protection of the environment.

Plastic Sexuality

The concept of plastic sexuality has been developed theoretically by Anthony Giddens (1993). "Plastic" refers to the malleability of erotic expression both in terms of personal choice and within the framework of societal norms. "Flexible sexuality" is argued to emerge in the context of the social changes in late modernity and postmodernity. It stands in contrast to the features associated with modernist sexuality, conceptualized as fixed, by biology or by social norms.

"Fixed sexuality" is associated with the binaries of modernity – either heterosexual or homosexual, either marital (legitimate) or extramarital (illegitimate), either committed or promiscuous, either normal (coital) or perverse (anal, autoerotic, sadomasochistic).

For Giddens, plastic sexuality results in the effective contravention of women's economic and social independence, which "liberates" men from the constraints of traditional gender expectations. Plastic sexuality is one that can be shaped according to individual erotic needs and wants. It can also serve as a marker of individual identity and/or as the means by which to make radical sexual demands.

Thus, the consequence of disengaging sex from reproduction is to increase the emphasis on pleasure and decrease the emphasis on phallic sexuality. Giddens's key claim for plastic sexuality Blackwell said is "autonomous" sexuality.

Thus, the important characteristics of plastic sexuality are as follows.

- Fulfilling physical needs without marriage
- Fulfilling physical needs anywhere, anytime
- Multiple simultaneous partners
- Postponement of marriage
- High risk of spreading HIV/AIDS and other STDs

Cosmopolitanism and Democratization

The positive side of de-traditionalisation is the spread of what Giddens refers to as cosmopolitanism in which the individual is much less constrained by arbitrary tradition than in 'traditional' or pre-global societies.

In a cosmopolitan society, the individual has more freedom to consider pre-existing cultural practices such as those associated with marriage, religion, and politics, and to choose which aspects of these cultural practices are appropriate for him/her.

As a result, culture becomes something that is more fluid, more open to debate, and more open to adaptation by individuals than ever before in human history. According to Giddens, culture becomes more democratic as more people have a say in how the culture will inform their lives.

MANUEL CASTELLS (1942)

Manuel Castells was born on February 9, 1942, in a small town in the La Mancha region of Spain. As a child, he lived in Helin, Albacete, Madrid, Cartagena, Valencia, and Barcelona, where he completed his secondary education. He studied law and economics at the University of Barcelona in 1958–62. As a student activist against Franco's dictatorship, he had to flee to Paris, where he took advantage of a political refugee fellowship, and graduated in 1964 from Sorbonne's Faculty of Law and Economics. He received his Ph.D. in Sociology from the University of Paris. In 1967. He also holds a doctorate d'état in anthropology from the Sorbonne and a doctorate in sociology from the University of Madrid. His University of Paris Ph.D. dissertation was based on a statistical analysis of the location strategies of industrial firms in the Paris region.

Important Works

1. The Rise of the Network Society (1996)
2. Informational City (1989)
3. Communication Power (2009)
4. Networks of Outrage and Hope (2012)
5. The Information Age: Economy, Society, and Culture (1996)
6. Trilogy of books by sociologist Manuel Castells in the age of Information Revolution: 'The Rise of the Network Society (1996), The Power of Identity (1997), and End of Millennium (1998)

Major Theories

The Network Society

Manuel Castells defining the concept of Network Society in his book, *The Rise of the Network Society* (1996). He studied the changes caused by the spread of networked, digital information and communications technologies into the social, political, economic and cultural function of the society.

According to Castells, three processes led to the emergence of this new social structure in the late 20th century:

i. the restructuring of industrial economies to accommodate an open market approach

ii. the freedom-oriented culture, the civil rights movement, the feminist movement, and the environmental movement

iii. the revolution in information and communication technologies

Castells claims that we are passing from the industrial age into the information age. This historical change is brought about by the advent of new information technologies – particularly those for communication and biological technologies.

Society remains capitalist, but the basis of the technological means by which it acts has changed from energy to information.

Networks have become a 'key feature of social morphology' because communication technologies, such as the Internet, allow for the decentralization of operations and focus on control, increasing the effectiveness of networks relative to hierarchical structures.

According to Castells, the power now rests in networks: 'the logic of the network is more powerful than the powers of the network'.

He defined a 'network society' as a society where major social structures and activities are organized around electronically processed information networks. So, it's not just about networks or social networks, because social networks have been very old forms of social organization.

It is about social networks that process and manage information and are using micro-electronic based technologies. For Castells, networks have become the basic units of modern society. He argues that it is not purely technology that defines modern societies, but also cultural, economic, and political factors that create networked societies.

Influences such as religion, cultural upbringing, political organization, and social status all shape networked societies. Society is shaped by these factors in many ways. These influences can either enhance or inhibit these societies.

According to Castells, empowerment is reinforced by social media, including networking (such as Facebook) and social movements connected through the Internet. He sees social media as evidence of trends within globalization that promote cultural diversity, innovation, and some form of freedom.

Space of Flows and Timeless Time

The space of flows plays a central role in Castells' vision of the network society, it is a network of communications, defined by hubs where these networks intersect. Societies are not attached to a specific place but instead to the space of flows. He argues that "while organizations are located in places, the organizational logic is placeless, being fundamentally dependent on the space of flows that characterizes information networks".

Castells developed the notion of timeless time, which he saw as an index of social change. He believed time has become more complicated and sequences of life are becoming scrambled. Space and time are fundamental experiences of social life but are being transcended in social practice, for example, users of 'Skype' can speak to each other in any number of different countries at any one time and all communication is instant.

Flows vs. Places and the Role of the Nation-State

Castells is an urban geographer, so his examination of space is central to his work. One of his key characteristics of the information age is the "space of flow". It is the domain of networks, capital, information, business alliances, etc.

This space of flows challenges the location of castell spaces, including regional communities and nation-states. While "the space of flows can be abstract in social, cultural, and historical terms. The space of places is the condensation of human history, culture, and matter.

There is a conflict between flows and places which have an impact on the nation-state. Sovereignty is assigned to regional and communal groups in the upstream and downstream regions of the flow.

The states are caught in a bind. If they represent the identity of the communities within them, they disconnect themselves from the network. If they follow network logic, they cease to represent their populations; They become nodes in the network and surrender their sovereignty: 'nation-states will survive, but not their sovereignty'.

Theory of Globalization

Castells argues that globalization is a network of production, culture, and power that is constantly shaped by advances in technology, which range from communications technologies to genetic engineering.

Castells suggests that the rules of global capitalism have changed to embrace these new information technologies.

Power now flows not from corporations or states, but through the informational flows and codes that connect those corporations and states to each other and the world. For Castells, the advancement of the Information Age does not necessarily mean that the world has become flat; rather, with technological advance, he argues, come new global forms of exclusion and inclusion, fragmentation, and integration.

Theory of Urban Social Movements

Manuel Castells, In 'The Urban Question' (1972) he presented a model of the dynamics of the urban system with a single mechanism for structural change. He called this mechanism 'urban social movement'".

Castells, in particular, has been involved in the search for a general theory. He was the first to elaborate on the idea that urban movements had a latent function in the class struggle. He stated that urban movements can only be significant for social change if they are linked to the organizations involved in the class struggle in the field of production.

In a later effort, Castells (1983) stated that the local focus of urban movements inhibited the transformation of production, communication, and government. The kind of social change that an urban movement will be able to produce is resistance to domination or, in other words, changing 'urban meaning', resulting in a 'reactive utopia'.

Urban movements could achieve their maximum potential for social change when they were multi-issue, pursuing the following three goals.

i. the realization of collective consumption demands (such as those related to social housing) as use value against commodification within the framework of city promotion.

ii. establishing and strengthening an autonomous cultural identity and promoting communication instead of 'programmed one-way information flows'.

iii. territorially based self-management.

Castells Formulation of Identity

He proposes a distinction between three forms and origins of identity construction:

i. Legitimate identity: introduced by the dominant institutions of society to enhance and rationalize their dominance.

ii. Resistance identity: generated by actors who are in the status/situations devalued and/or stigmatized by the logic of supremacy, thus creating gaps of resistance.

iii. Project identity: When social actors, based on whatever cultural material is available to them, create a new identity that redefines their position in society and, in doing so, seeks to transform the overall social structure.

This is the case, for example, when feminism moves out of the trenches of resistance to women's identity and women's rights, to challenge patriarchy, thus the patriarchal family, and thus the whole of production, reproduction, sexuality, and personhood. The structure on which society is historically based.

CHAPTER

5 Indian Thinkers

Learning Objectives:

In this chapter, we will discuss the following important topics.

- M.K. Gandhi
- B.R. Ambedkar
- Radha Kamal Mukherjee
- G. S. Ghurye
- M.N. Srinivas
- Irawati Karve

INTRODUCTION

In this chapter, we will discuss the contribution of various Indian thinkers, their important works, and major concepts. We will also try to understand how these contributions led to the development of sociology as a subject in the Indian subcontinent.

MOHANDAS KARAMCHAND GANDHI (1869–1948)

Mohandas Karamchand Gandhi was born on 2 October 1869 to a Gujarati Hindu Modh Bania family in the coastal town of Porbandar in the Kathiawar Agency of the British Raj. He was an Indian revolutionary, anti-colonial nationalist, and political ethicist who employed nonviolent resistance to lead the successful campaign for India's independence from British rule and later inspired movements for civil rights and independence around the world Did. The term Mahatma was first used for him in South Africa in 1914, which is now used worldwide.

Important Works

An Autobiography: *The Story of my Experiments with Truth* (1925).

The collective works of Mahatma Gandhi are Panchayati Raj, Satyagraha in South Africa; Sarvodaya and Hind Swaraj.

He edited Young India which he later renamed as Harijan.

Gandhiji was also influenced by many: Tolstoy (What to Do, The Kingdom of God is Within You), Ruskin (Unto This Last), Thoreau (Essay on Civil Disobedience), Swami Vivekananda, Gokhale, and Tilak

Major Theories

Views on Human Nature

Gandhiji's views on man, human nature, and society are consistent with his philosophical outlook and reflect his firm belief in the morality of life and the moral pursuit. At the same time, he was deeply aware of the imperfections of man.

What is important, however, is nature: "There is no one 'without faults', not even men of God. They are men of God not because they are faultless, but because they know their own faults, and are always ready to correct himself".

Since Gandhi was aware of man's weakness as an individual or as a member of a group, he did not think of man as merely an animal. Man, he was convinced, was after all a soul too.

He realized that even the cruelest person could not deny the spiritual element in him, that is, his potential for goodness. He had a lot of faith in human nature even while considering man as imperfect.

'I refuse', he says, 'to doubt human nature. Its will is bound to respond to any noble and friendly action'. In another place, he says, 'there are strings in every human heart. If we only know how to play the right chord, we bring out the music'.

What separates man from the animal is the self-conscious impulse to realize the divinity inherent in him. He writes: 'We were born with brute strength but we were born to feel the God who lives within us'.

It is indeed the prerogative of man and it separates him from the brute creation. He argued that every man and woman have the capacity to transform their lives and to truly be themselves.

'Man as an animal', he says, 'is violent, but as spirit (he) is non-violent. The moment he awakens the spirit within him he cannot remain violent'. Man is naturally sensitive to his self-realization.

In them, moral virtues and social virtues like love, cooperation, and tolerance prevail over violence, selfishness, and cruelty and man continues to work for a higher life. He writes: 'I hold that the sum total of the energies of mankind is not to bring us down but to lift us up and that it is the result of a definite, if unconscious, the action of the law of nature'.

Gandhi believed that human nature, in its essence, is one and that each individual has the potential for the highest possible development: 'The soul is one in all, therefore, its potential is the same for all. It is this undoubted universal possibility that distinguishes the human from the rest of God's creation'.

Concept of Religion

Gandhiji believed in the fundamental truth of all the great religions of the world, that at the lowest level, they were one and all were helpful to each other. According to him, there were as many religions as there were minds. Each mind, he would say, had a different conception of God from the other. Yet they follow the same God.

He insisted that religion should be separated from ethics. The fundamental moral precepts are the same in all religions, although religions may differ from one another with respect to their beliefs and practices. Gandhiji said, 'I believe that fundamental ethics are the same for all religions. By religion I do not mean fundamental ethics, but what is known as sectarianism'.

Dharma enables us to pursue truth and righteousness. Sometimes they distinguished religion in general and religion in a specific sense. One belongs to a specific religion with its beliefs and practices. As one progresses through the path suggested by it, he also transcends its limitations and appreciates the common thread that binds the followers of all religions and truths.

Gandhiji once said, 'Let me explain what I mean by religion. It is not Hinduism that I certainly regard above all other religions, but that religion which is beyond Hinduism, which changes the nature of that which binds one to the truth'.

He felt that communal criminalization of any kind was a violation of human nature and its authentic endeavour. He said, "Religion does not mean sectarianism. It means belief in an orderly moral government of the universe."

It is no less real because it is invisible. This religion is above Hinduism, Islam, Christianity, etc. It does not supersede them. It harmonizes them and gives them a reality. Talking about specific religions, he says, 'Religions are different paths meeting at the same point'.

He said that while the diversity of religions was acceptable, he did not think that any religion could claim itself to be superior to others. In fact, when a religion asserts itself as superior to others, its credibility becomes questionable and it becomes an obstacle in the path of our self-realization. In his Autobiography, Gandhi states that self-realization requires self-purification as a moral foundation.

Gandhiji invoked the five-fold moral principles:

i. truth,
ii. non-violence,
iii. non-stealing,
iv. non-possession and
v. celibacy.

Concept of Hinduism

Gandhi's religious life was mostly influenced by the Bhagavad Gita. He was a firm believer in the Karma theory of Hinduism. And, he preferred to call himself a Sanatan Hindu. He spoke and wrote about Hinduism in different ways on different occasions.

Gandhi believed that the Bhagavad Gita does not support the practice of untouchability. On the contrary, the Bhagavad Gita taught him that all life is one and came from God and therefore must return to God.

According to Gandhi, 'the central principle of Hinduism is salvation. I am always striving for this. All my activities are for salvation'.

He had full faith in the 'Varna system'. He said that I believe that a person gets his caste by birth. "It is certainly necessary that the number of castes should be reduced, and this can be brought about by councils of different castes without harm to Hinduism.

'Now the issue of untouchability remains. No one can trace the origin of this custom, that an untouchable cannot live in our neighbourhood and owe land, that an untouchable shouts at us: 'Please stay away! Don't touch me!' - This is not Hindutva. That is Dyerism – Satanic Activity or dictatorship.'

Gandhi believed that the most important external form of Hinduism was cow protection and that the essence of Hinduism is truth and non-violence. I firmly believe that I am filled with love. I have never felt ill will towards anyone even in my dreams.

Concept of Politics

For Gandhi, politics was just a part of human life. He saw political power as an instrument that enables the people to improve their condition in every department of life.

The political activity of man is closely related to other activities of man and according to Gandhiji, all these activities influence each other. 'Life is one indivisible whole, and all my activities run into each other'.

Therefore, political activity is closely related to other spheres of life and activities. What he hated in politics was the centralization of power and the use of violence associated with political power.

Relationship between Religion and Politics

He formulated a close relationship between politics and religion. Religion cannot be separated from politics. Considering the fundamental purpose of life as self-realization, if politics does not enable religious activities, then it is not meaningful at all.

He bluntly said, 'For me, politics devoid of religion is utter filth, which should be shunned forever'. He wrote, 'The whole gamut of man's activities today forms an indivisible whole. You cannot divide social, economic, political and purely religious pursuits into watertight compartments'.

For Gandhi, politics is a way of discovering a part of the truth of the whole. Political activity helps man to acquire the ability to govern himself, an ability in which he obeys the laws of society without any external force or external imposition.

Religion and politics understood in this way, make a good case for Swaraj. He regards the concentration of power as detrimental to individual liberty.

Gandhiji never considered political power as an end, it was a means to enable people to improve their status in every sphere of life. For him, political power was a means of regulating public life at various levels in accordance with the above principles.

Unity of Ends and Means

That ends and means are related to each other is one of the core principles of Gandhian philosophy. Gandhiji made no distinction between means and ends, implying that one leads to the other and the latter an effect of the former. Such an assertion, to him, presupposes a scientific theory of the relation between cause and effect.

Gandhiji would not like to achieve that noble goal if it has to be achieved through impure means. Refuting those who say 'means are everything', he said, 'means are everything'. As is the means, so is the end. There is no wall of separation between means and ends.

For him, 'impure means result in impure ends, no one can reach the truth from untruth. Only right conduct can reach the truth'. Inspired by the Gita, the ethical principle he supported was self-power. A person does not do his duty expecting the fruits of his action and does it for the sake of duty.

Satya, Satyagraha and Ahimsa

Satya Truth or Satya for Gandhiji is God himself. So, he later in his life changed the statement 'God is Truth' to 'Truth is God' and suggested that this was one of the fundamental discoveries of his life's experiments.

It is Truth, he says, that exists, what does not exist is untruth. Man's life for Gandhiji is a march in search of Truth or God. He believed that only knowledge leads a person toward the truth while ignorance takes a person away from the truth.

Satyagraha Satyagraha means truth or insistence on truth. Satyagraha is not merely an insistence on truth. In fact, it is upholding the truth through ethical and non-violent means. This is not to impose one's will on others, but to attract the opponent's argument. It is not coercion but persuasion.

Gandhiji highlighted several features of Satyagraha, he said;

i. It is a moral weapon and does not take into account ill will towards the adversary,

ii. It is a non-violent tactic and calls upon its user to love their enemy,
iii. It does not weaken the opponent but strengthens him morally,
vi. It is the weapon of the brave and creative in its approach.

For Gandhi, a satyagrahi is always truthful, morally grounded, non-violent, and without malice; He is the one who is devoted to the service of all.

Ahimsa or Non-violence In its positive sense, non-violence means love for others. In its negative sense, it refers to not wanting to hurt others in both words and deeds. Gandhiji spoke of the non-violence of various people:

i. There is the non-violence of the brave: one has the force but he does not use it as a principle,
ii. There is the non-violence of the weak: one does not have faith in non-violence, but he uses it for attaining his objectives;
iii. There is the non-violence of the coward: it is not non-violence, but impotency, more harmful than violence. For Gandhiji, violence was a better option than cowardice.

Through non-violence one appeal to the Truth that dwells in the people and makes the latter feel it in themselves, comes around, and join hands in the common march of truth with those whom they previously regarded as their adversaries.

Looking at the web of means and ends, Gandhi often saw love, truth, God, and nonviolence as interchangeable terms. Truth or God or self-realization is the ultimate goal of man's life, this goal can only be achieved through ahimsa or non-violence.

Concept of Swaraj

'The word 'Swaraj' is a sacred word, a Vedic word, meaning self-rule and self-restraint, not freedom from all restraints, which independence often means. Gandhiji's concept of Swaraj was not limited only to freeing India from British rule. He wanted such freedom but said that he did not want to exchange 'the king log for the king stork'.

Swaraj is not the transfer of political power to Indians. Nor does it mean, as he insisted, mere political self-determination. For him, there was no Swaraj in Europe. For him, the movement to Swaraj primarily consisted of the process of freeing oneself from all the shackles that one is a victim of, both internal and external.

He felt, 'real swaraj would come not from the acquisition of authority by a few, but from the ability by all to oppose the abuse of power'. He used to say that Swaraj is the power of the people to determine their destiny by their own efforts and shape their destiny according to their will.

In other words, 'Swaraj is to be achieved by educating the masses to a sense of their capacity to regulate and control power'. He saw Swaraj as having freedom for all and self-control for all. It is concerned with the inner strength and potential of people that enable them to understand and control their social world.

Our main energy should be focused on achieving reform from within. In Swaraj-based non-violence, people need not know their rights, but it is necessary for them to know their duties. There is no duty that does not create corresponding rights and only those rights which flow from the performance of duty are real rights.

Gandhiji made it very clear that the Swaraj of India does not mean the rule of the majority community i.e., the Hindus. 'Under the Swaraj constitution, every community will be equal to each other.'

Democracy, therefore, is not the exercise of voting power, the holding of public office, or the criticism of the government; Nor does it mean equality, liberty, or security, although they are all important in a democratic setup.

It is when people are able to develop their inner freedom which is people's ability to regulate and control their desired impulses in the light of reason that freedom rises from the individual and strengthens him. Hence his Swaraj had economic, social, political, and international meanings:

i. Economic Swaraj, as he himself says, 'stands for social justice, it promotes goodness equally to all, including the weakest, and is essential to a decent life'.
ii. Social Swaraj focuses on 'equality of status'.
iii. The object of political swaraj is to enable the people to better their condition in every department of life."
vi. In the international arena, Swaraj emphasized interdependence. There is, he says, 'no limit to which we can extend our services to our neighbours beyond state-created borders. God never created those borders'.

On Parliamentary Democracy

Gandhi did not agree with the view that democracy meant rule by the majority, he gave several definitions of democracy on several occasions.

When we put them together, Gandhiji could say, 'Democracy essentially means the art and science of mobilizing the entire physical, economic, and spiritual resources of all different classes of people in the service of the common good of all'.

The golden rule of conduct in a democratic system, he said, is mutual tolerance, noting that we will never all think alike and that we will always see the truth in fragments and from different angles of vision. Gandhi realized that adult suffrage was the only way to protect the interests of all, minorities, the poor, the downtrodden, farmers, and women.

He hoped that voters give importance to the merit of the candidates and not their caste, community, or party affiliation. He wanted people of character to enter the legislatures, even if they commit mistakes, they would never do anything against the interests of the voters. Men and women without character elected by the people will destroy the democratic system.

He put his vision of a free India as follows: 'I will work for an India in which the poorest feel that this is their country and that they have an effective voice in its making, an India in which there will be no upper class and lower class of people, an India in which all communities would live in perfect harmony'.

In such an India there can be no place for the curse of untouchability, or for the curse of intoxicating drinks and drugs. Women will get equal rights as men. Since we will live in peace with the rest of the world, neither exploiting nor being exploited.

We would have the smallest army imaginable. All interests, whether foreign or indigenous, will be sincerely respected without conflicting with the interests of millions of people. He said 'Personally, I hate the distinction between foreign and indigenous. This is the India of my dreams. I will not settle for anything less.'

Gram Swaraj or Development from Below

According to Gandhian thinking, democracy can function smoothly and according to the concept of Swaraj only when it is decentralized. 'Centralization as a system is incompatible with the nonviolent structure of society'. He wanted the center of power to move from the cities to the villages.

The building blocks of democracy should be villages. Gandhiji wanted every village to have an annually elected panchayat to manage the affairs of the village. Each village following the oceanic circle principle would be autonomous yet interdependent.

As Gandhiji argued, 'My 'idea' of village swaraj is that it is a perfect republic, independent of its neighbours for its vital needs, and yet interdependent for many others in which dependence is a Needed'.

Ideas on Economy

Gandhiji's political philosophical views centrally shaped his views on the economy. His economic thought revolves around the following normative ideas:

i. Economic process should work towards equality and non-exploitation,
ii. It must correspond to full employment,
iii. It should provide low-cost consumer goods that satisfy the needs of the people,
vi. All those industries with sophisticated technology should be in the public sector,
v. No mass production without equal distribution.

For Gandhiji, the two major principles in his economic thought are the promotion of social justice as well as equality. The three principles he laid down for this purpose are:

i. Non-possession means pursuing economic policies based on need and not need
ii. Inequality stems from irrational desires to have more than what one person required.
iii. In technologically advanced countries, people do not consume goods in the same proportion as they produce them. Labour-intensive technologies should be preferred to capital-intensive technologies.

Gandhi's economics emphasized equality, social justice, full employment, and harmonious labour-capital relations. Gandhiji opposed capitalism as well as communism. To him, the individual, his freedom, dignity, and a satisfactory life were more important than the mere economic progress that both capitalism and communism promised. Anything that did not liberate man was unacceptable to Gandhi.

Morals and ethics hold a central place in the Gandhian concept of economics. 'True economics never falls short against the highest ethical standard, as should all true ethics worthy of the name. True economics, on the other hand, stands for social justice. It promotes the well-being of all, including the vulnerable equally, and is essential to civilized life'.

In Gandhian economics, the supreme consideration is a man. Every person has the right to live and hence the right to find work to meet his basic needs of food, clothing, housing, education, health, and self-respect.

He felt, 'these should be freely available to all just as air and water should be to God. They should not be made vehicles of transport for the exploitation of others. Their monopoly by any country, nation, or group of persons would be unjust'. He argued that we should use up all human labour before considering employing mechanical power.

'True planning', according to Gandhi, 'consists in the best utilization of all the manpower of India and the distribution of India's raw products among her many villages instead of sending them out and repurchasing the finished goods at fabulous prices'.

Concept of Swadeshi

For Gandhi ji, Swaraj and Swadeshi go hand in hand. Indigenous is 'the feeling in us which restricts us to the use of the services of our immediate surroundings, to the exclusion of those more remote'. Swadeshi will not only strengthen autonomous local units but also build cooperative relationships with others with whom they need to associate.

If we follow the Swadeshi principle, it will be your and my duty to find our neighbours who can meet our needs and teach them to supply them. Then every village in India will be almost self-sufficient and self-supporting. The vested unit exchanges with other villages only such essential commodities as are not produced locally".

Swadeshi and self-reliance go hand in hand. The former is possible only if the latter is accepted as a principle. Every individual, every family, every village, and every region shall be economically self-reliant, 'Self-reliance does not mean narrow-mindedness, being self-reliant does not mean being completely self-sufficient'.

There are two other concepts that go hand in hand with Swadeshi: they are decentralization and collaboration. 'Interdependence is and should be as much man's ideal as is self-sufficiency. Man is a social animal, without interconnection with society he cannot realize his oneness with the universe or suppress his ego'.

For Gandhi, the concept of Swadeshi is comprehensive. In religion, it means being faithful to the religion of one's ancestors. In politics, this means the use of indigenous institutions. In economics, it emphasized the use of goods produced in the immediate neighbourhood, one should give preference to locally produced things, even if they are of relatively inferior quality or expensive.

This does not mean that one should hate foreign products. Gandhiji had a place for foreign manufactured goods, especially drugs, and life-saving drugs when they were not produced in the country.

Sarvodaya: The Rise of All

Gandhi was critical of the way economies, both capitalist and socialist, fostered mass poverty in the midst of abundant wealth in America. He argued, 'America is the most industrialized country in the world, and yet it has not overcome poverty and decline. This is because it ignores universal manpower and concentrates power in the hands of a few who amass wealth at the expense of the many'.

Socialist economies, he felt, put the cart before the horse, 'As I look at Russia where the apotheosis of industrialization has been reached, life there does not appeal to me'. To use the language of the Bible, 'What shall it profit a man if he gains the whole world and loses his soul?

In modern terms, it is beneath human dignity to lose one's individuality and become a mere cog in the machine. I want each person to be a fully developed member of society. 'While he viewed socialism positively, he felt that it was deeply entrenched in violence'. Socialism was not born with the discovery of the abuse of capital by capitalists.

As I have said, the only goal of socialism is material progress. 'I want freedom for the full expression of my personality. Under socialism, there is no personal freedom. You don't own anything, not even your body'.

Against capitalism and socialism, Gandhi proposed the concept of Sarvodaya, which was based on three basic principles:

i. The good of the individual lies in the good of all,
ii. that the work of a lawyer has the same value as that of a barber (all have an equal right to earn their livelihood by their work),
iii. That the life of labour, that is, the life of the tiller and artisan of the soil is a life worth living.

Theory of Trusteeship

One of the most original contributions of Gandhi to the field of economics is the concept of trusteeship. Gandhiji wanted complete equality as far as the basic needs of the people were concerned. The fact is that he wanted the basic needs of everyone, including animals, to be satisfactorily met. But at the same time, he wanted people to have the incentive to be economically active and produce more.

This will naturally lead some people to have more than they need. They will be rich but no one will be poor as everyone's basic needs will be met. To ensure that those who were wealthy did not use their wealth for selfish purposes or to control others, he coined the term "trusteeship".

Explaining the underlying meaning of this word, he said, 'Everything was of God and belonged to God. Therefore, it was for his people as a whole, not for specific individuals. When a person has more than his proportionate share, he becomes the trustee of that share for the people of God.He wished that the idea of trusteeship should be a gift from India to the world.

Then there will be neither exploitation nor reservation. In these differences, he found the seeds of war and conflict. He elaborated extensively on his idea of trusteeship. He suggested, 'As a successor, the trustee in office shall have the right to nominate his successor subject to legal sanction'.

The idea underlying the concept of trusteeship was twofold:

i. All human beings are born equal and therefore have the right to equal opportunities. This means that everyone should have their basic needs fully satisfied.

ii. However, not all human beings are endowed with the same intellectual and physical abilities. Some will have more capacity to produce than others. Such persons should consider themselves as trustees of the product beyond their basic needs.

Violence and force as a method of distribution of products have to be rejected.

B.R. AMBEDKAR (1891–1956)

Babasaheb Ambedkar was born in the untouchable Mahar Caste in Maharashtra on 14 April 1891. He completed his graduation from Bombay University and went on to do his Masters and Ph.D. from Columbia University in the U.S.A. He formed the *Bahishkrit Hitkarini Sabha* (Depressed Classes Welfare Association) in 1924. He led the famous Mahad Satyagraha or Chavdar Tale Satyagraha on 20 March 1927 to allow untouchables to use water in a public tank in Mahad (currently in Raigad district), Maharashtra, India.

The day (20 March) is observed as Social Empowerment Day in India. He started the fortnightly journal *Bahishkrit Bharat* in Marathi and formed two organizations, *SamajSamata Sangh* and *SamataSainik Dal* in 1927 to reinforce the demand for equality of the depressed classes. In 1928, the Depressed Classes Education Society, Bombay was founded. Pandit Nehru rightly described him as the 'symbol of the great revolt against all the oppressive features of Hindu society'.

Important Works

1. His doctoral dissertations on The Problem of the Rupee (1923), and The Evolution of the Provincial Finance in British India (1925),
2. He wrote Annihilation of Caste (1936),
3. Thoughts on Pakistan (1940),
4. What Congress and Gandhi have done to the Untouchables (1945),
5. Who were the Shudras? (1946),
6. The Untouchables: Who were They and Why They became Untouchables? (1948)
7. States and Minorities (1947),
8. Thoughts on Linguistic States (1955)
9. The Buddha and his Dharma (1957)

Major Theories

His Views on Brahmanical Ideology

He was very critical of the Brahmanical ideology which, he felt, has been the dominant ideological expression in India.

It subscribed to the principle of graded inequality in organizing social institutions and relations; defended the principle of birth over the principle of worth; undermined reason and upheld rituals and priest-craft.

It reduced the Shudra and the untouchable to perpetual drudgery and ignominy. It defended inequality and unequal distribution of resources and positions and sanctified such measures by appealing to doctrines such as karma-siddhanta.

It had little sympathy towards the degraded and the marginalized. It left millions of people in their degraded condition, away from civilization, and defended their abominable conditions.

He constructed Brahmanism as totally lacking in any moral values and considerations based on such values.

His Views on Gandhian Philosophy

Ambedkar was a bitter critic of Gandhi and Gandhism. He attacked Gandhi's approach to the abolition of untouchability, an approach that denied its sanction in the shastras and which called upon caste Hindus to voluntarily renounce it and make reparations for the same.

Ambedkar felt that rights and humanity cannot be left to the mercy and prejudices of people who have developed a vested interest in undermining them. He did not demarcate the caste system and varna system, as Gandhi did, but saw both of them as upholding the same principle of graded inequality.

Even if untouchability is abolished through the Gandhian appeal to conscience, which Ambedkar did not think possible, untouchables will continue to occupy the lowest rung of society as a layer of the Shudras.

Ambedkar rejected many central notions as propounded by Gandhi such as Swaraj, nonviolence, decentralization, Khadi, trusteeship, and vegetarianism. He subscribed to a modern polity with the modern economy.

Religion

Ambedkar dwelt extensively on major religions of the world, particularly Hinduism, Islam, Christianity, and Buddhism. He wrote a great deal on Hinduism and Buddhism.

The mainstream trajectory of religious evolution that he traced in early India was the Vedic society getting degenerated into Aryan society, the rise of Buddhism and the social and moral transformation that it brought about, and the counterrevolution manifest in the development of a specific ideological and political expression which he termed Brahmanism.

Ambedkar developed a new interpretation of Buddhism and saw it as socially engaged. It privileged the poor and the downtrodden and concerned itself with the sufferings and joys of this world.

It does not subscribe to the existence of God or the eternity of the soul. It supports reason, affirms the existence of this world, subscribes to an ethical system, and is in line with science. He saw the great values of liberty, equality, and community as central to the Buddha's teachings.

His View on Caste

Ambedkar's understanding of caste and the Caste system underwent certain significant changes over time. Initially, he identified the characteristics of caste as endogamy superimposed on exogamy in a shared cultural milieu.

Once a caste closed its boundaries, other castes too followed suit. The Brahmins closing themselves socially first gave rise to castes.

Ambedkar thought that caste is an essential feature of Hinduism. A few reformers may have denounced it but for the vast majority of Hindus breaking the codes of caste is a clear violation of deeply held beliefs. The principles governing the *varna* system and caste system are one and the same. Both perpetuate graded inequality and support the principle of birth rather than worth.

Ambedkar argued for the annihilation of caste without which wielding community bonds, and upholding freedom and equality becomes impossible.

He suggested inter-caste marriages and inter-caste dining for the purpose of enduring bonds. He further argued that shastras that defend 'varnashramdharma' have to be abandoned as they justify and legitimize graded organization of society.

He also felt that the priesthood in Hinduism should be open to all co-religionists on the basis of certified competence rather than on birth. At the same time, he thought this project is well-nigh impossible to be carried out because what is to be renounced is believed to be religiously ordained.

Untouchability

Ambedkar distinguished the institution of untouchability from that of caste although the former too is stamped by the same principle of graded inequality as the latter.

Untouchability is not only an extreme form of degradation of caste but is qualitatively different as the system kept the untouchable out of the purview and made any social contact with him polluting and deplorable.

He argued that despite differences and crevices all untouchables share the same disadvantages and are treated equally by caste Hindus: they are kept in ghettos on the outskirts of the village, and they are universally despised and kept away from the human association.

He did not agree with the position that the basis of untouchability was caste. He saw it as a social institution protected by the ideology of Brahmanism.

Ambedkar was of the view that there is no easy solution to this malaise. The removal of untouchability required a transformation of the entire society in which respect and rights towards the other person become a way of life rather than just a constitutional mechanism.

Therefore, he felt that the primary burden of emancipating themselves fell on the untouchables themselves. Such self-help required not only struggles but also education and organization. Further, a constitutional democracy with preferences at various levels can help enormously in such an endeavour.

Constitutional Democracy

He was adept in different constitutions of the world, particularly those that provided an expansive notion of democracy. Rule of law as a bond uniting people and according to equal participation of people in collective affairs was quite central to his imagination.

He was deeply sensitive to the interface between law on the one hand and customs and popular beliefs on the other. However, he realized that customs may protect parochial interests and popular beliefs may become deeply entrenched in prejudices and may not uphold fairness.

They cannot conform to the demands of time, morality, and reason. But if the law upholds liberty and democracy, it can be put to the service of the common good.

Such emphasis on democracy and rule of law forced Ambedkar to emphasize the autonomy of the state. The state needs to rise above the narrow interests prevailing in society which often tend to reduce the state as an instrument of their purpose.

Social Justice

Ambedkar was the first major theoretician in India who argued that consideration for the disadvantaged should be the constitutive basis of a state if the state is committed to upholding rights. He developed a complex set of criteria to determine disadvantages. Untouchability was only one of the great social disadvantages, though it was one of the most humiliating and disgusting.

According to BR Ambedkar, social justice is a means to create an ideal or just society. For him, a just society is a casteless society, based on principles of social justice and a combination of three components: liberty, equality, and fraternity. Ambedkar's ideal society is based on two basic principles.

The first is that the individual is an end in itself and the aim and objective of the society is the growth of the individual and the development of his personality. Society is not above the individual and if the individual has to subordinate himself to society, it is because such subordination is for his good and only to the extent necessary. The second imperative is that the conditions of life concerned among the members of society should be governed by ideas based on liberty, equality, and fraternity.

RADHA KAMAL MUKHERJEE (1889–1968)

He was born on 7 December 1889 in a large Bengali Brahmin family in Berhampur (Murshidabad), a small town in West Bengal. He completed his Ph.D. degree in 1920 (University of Calcutta) in his study of 'Socio-Economic Changes in the Indian Rural Community'. He was a highly original philosopher of history and an astute interpreter of culture and civilization and was the recipient of the third highest Indian civilian honour of the Padma Bhushan in 1962.

Important Works

1. The Rural Economy of India (1926)
2. Regional Sociology (1926)
3. The Land Problems of India (1927)
4. Field and Farmers of Oudh (1929)
5. Regional Balance of Man (1938)
6. Man, and his Habitation (1940)
7. Indian Working Class (1945)
8. The Social Structure of Values (1949)
9. Inter-caste Tensions (1951)
10. Dimensions of Human Values (1964)

Major Theories

Indian Culture and Civilization

Mukherjee (1964) writes extensively on Indian art and architecture, history, and culture. He believes that Asian art is aimed at collective development. According to him, harmony is the basic value of life. He adequately portrayed this harmony in the Indian life plan of the past ages. Indian culture has seen men as a responsible members of a community. Man is not isolated.

In this context, Mukherjee writes: Art became the torchbearer of social and spiritual upheaval for millions of people in Asia. Oriental art is most strongly influenced by community spirit and is thus primarily responsible for the historical continuity of Oriental cultures. In contrast, such artistic endeavours in the West were dominated by either individualism or a feeling that art was an end in itself. It was not conducive to social cohesion or spiritual growth.

Indian art is embedded in the social or moral sphere. Mukherjee writes: 'India's innumerable temples, stupas, and viharas bear witness to the link between one and moral, religious, and social values. Art in India is a permanent component of the interaction of people with each other which reflects the aspirations of the people and illustrates the active relationship between artistic creativity and concrete forms.

Indian art is constantly linked to religion. Mukherjee is impressed by the largely non-aggressive nature of Indian religions such as Hinduism, Buddhism, or Jainism. The spirit of tolerance towards diversity is also reflected in the scriptures. These codes are flexible enough to accommodate the ethnic diversities of the communities.

The emphasis on the ultimate truth rather than a particular set of beliefs or rituals has been a consistent feature of Indian religions. It is through the peaceful agency of Dharma that Indian culture and civilization spread beyond the natural geographical boundaries of India to Ceylon (Sri Lanka) and countries in the South East. Therefore, Indian influence spread to many countries not through war or conquest but through friendship and goodwill.

Theory of Society

Radhakamal Mukherjee emphasized an interdisciplinary or inter-disciplinary approach to understanding human life. He sought to develop a general theory of society. To achieve this, first of all, he proposed to break down the barriers between the physical or natural sciences and the sciences concerned with the social and psychological aspects of man.

Secondly, the division of social sciences such as economics, sociology, and psychology should also be avoided. There should be continuous interaction between different social sciences. Mutual exchange of ideas between the physical and natural sciences is necessary to adequately appreciate the diverse dimensions of the human personality and its interaction with the natural environment and the social environment.

Society, according to Radhakamal, is the sum total of structures and functions through which man orients himself to three dimensions or levels of his environment:

- **i.** ecologic,
- **ii.** psycho-social, and
- **iii.** moral.

Thus, the society ' satisfies the basic needs of subsistence status and value fulfillment.

Concept of Universal Civilization

Mukherjee used the term 'civilization' in an inclusive sense; Culture is part of it. He proposes that human civilization should be studied at three interrelated levels.

- **i.** Biological evolution
- **ii.** Universalization
- **iii.** Spiritual dimension

Biological Evolution

The biological evolution of man has facilitated the rise and growth of civilization. They have the ability to change the environment as an active agent. Animals can only adapt to one environment, but humans can adapt to it in various ways. Humans, as biological species, are capable of overcoming competition and conflict and achieving cooperation (symbiosis).

Universalization

In social psychology, people are often portrayed within the framework of race, ethnicity, or nationality. Human beings are seen as prisoners of small selves or egos whose tendencies are narrow or ethnic.

In contrast, man has the capacity to overcome narrow sentiments and achieve universalism, that is, identifying himself as a member of a larger collectivity such as his nation or the universe itself.

For Mukherjee, moral relativism, implying that values differ from society to society, is not helpful in present times. There is a need for moral universalism, which affirms the oneness of mankind.

In the new perspective, men and women become free moral agents capable of recognizing the common aspects that bind humanity. They are no longer determined by division or relativity.

Spiritual Dimension

For him, every civilization has a spiritual dimension. Man is slowly touching transcendental heights. It means that they are moving towards the ladder of spirituality by crossing the barriers of biological and existential levels, that is, physical and material limitations.

In this regard, he lauded the Indian and Chinese civilizations, which had persisted as stable entities since the 6th century BCE. Their strength is derived from their universal myths and values that foster spiritual pursuit.

Personality, Society, and Values

In his book Personality, Radhakamal views the personality of the individual as an agent, who makes decisions and choices, and seeks value-fulfillment. Human beings choose and act in terms of values relating to (i) the self, (ii) others, and (iii) the cosmos.

The individual human being is, of course, subject to two kinds of influences. On the one hand, there are the influences of nature, environment, and biological drives and needs. Add to them the psychological impulses of man. On the other hand, there is pressure from society or collectivity.

Mukherjee defined personality as the sum total of an individual's characteristic modes of adjustment on different dimensions:

- **i.** biological,
- **ii.** social, and
- **iii.** ideal, cosmic, or transcendental.

The human personality deals with the environment as a biological and social being. But it is much more than that. It is a 'psycho-social whole responsive to the cosmic whole'. According to Mukherjee, 'personality is essentially transcendence'. The personality of a man or a woman has a social dimension.

Values

Values are 'socially accepted desires or goals which are internalized through the process of conditioning and socialization. They generate subjective preferences, standards, and aspirations. Values help man to orient his desires and goals in a set pattern We do.

Thus, man resolves internal tensions or conflicts of excessive biological drives. Further, he succeeds in achieving harmonious social roles and orderly relations with his fellow men with the help of proper values.

The concept of value cuts across desires, goals, ideals, and norms. Desires are goals in social action. The ideal is constructed in an imaginary social situation characterized by a conflict of goals. Norms are the mediators of opposition or contradiction of ideals. They express a beyond-human, teleological order of the universe.

Urban Social Problems

Mukherjee envisages an advanced approach to the problems of the working class. Industrialization in India, which has been taking place during the last several decades, has been successful in bringing together people from diverse regions and languages.

But, the living conditions of workers in urban centres like Mumbai, Kanpur, Kolkata, and Chennai were adversely affected by slum life. In the early days of industrialization, urban slums gave rise to evils such as prostitution, gambling, and crime. Therefore, to improve the economic and moral conditions of the workers it was necessary to bring about radical changes in their lives.

Today many private industries and public sector units have been providing social welfare facilities to their workers. In addition, the Central and State Governments have enacted legislative enactments, which are binding on the employers. However, unorganized workers (that is, those who are unemployed, or employed temporarily) continue to live in slums.

Social Ecology

For the harmonious development of man, it is necessary that he should live in harmony with other members of the community as well as with nature, or environment, or ecology. Radhakamal Mukherjee's contribution to the study of what is called 'social ecology' is unique.

Social ecology, as a discipline, requires the cooperation of a member of the sciences, including the social sciences. Geological, geographical, and biological factors work together to form an ecological region. Ecological conditions are also conditioned by social, economic, and political factors. Indeed, human or social ecology is the study of all aspects of the interactions between man and his environment.

Regional Sociology

In his book, *Regional Sociology* (1926), Mukherjee defines the scope of human ecology as 'a concise study of the balance of plant, animal and human communities, which are systems of correlated working parts in the organization of territory'.

Mukherjee argued that ecological relationships among humans are largely similar to those among lower organisms. But, in the case of human beings, cultural norms play a very important role.

Social habits, values, and traditions become very important in the formation of an ecological unit like a 'region'. There is solidarity among persons having the same or similar values. The ecological approach in which the continuous efforts, aspirations, and ideals of human beings coexist quietly with ecological forces and processes. Social ecology always emphasizes the complex transactional relationship between man and the region.

Mukherjee's ideas about social ecology advocated regional development. He stood for a balance between economic development and ecological fitness. Traditional crafts and skills such as weaving or engraving should be redesigned to achieve economic development without causing any major damage to the ecology of a region. Deforestation has created havoc. Mukherjee had warned his countrymen about this long back. He strongly advocated the conservation of forests and the preservation of ecological balance.

Mindless urbanization was also lamented by Mukherjee. He upheld the idea and process of urbanization from an ecological point of view. Urban growth at the cost of rural areas should be kept in check. There should be diversification in agriculture and decentralization of industries.

Mukherjee notices with concern that (i) overgrazing, (ii) haphazard destruction of trees and shrubs, and (iii) faulty method of cultivation bring about serious imbalances in the bio-physical constitution of the entire region. This seriously disrupts the cycle of nature.

Industrial civilization, because of its indiscriminate exploitation of natural resources, faces a 'security threat due to the exhaustion of coal and petroleum' and a dwindling supply of minerals and vitamins, which cannot be manufactured artificially. The importance of ecological values, even in an industrial society, can hardly be over-emphasized.

GOVIND SADASHIV GHURYE (1893–1983)

G S Ghurye was born on 12 December 1893 in a Saraswat Brahmin community in Malvan, Maharashtra. After completing his MA, Ghurye received a scholarship for further studies in England, and in 1922 received his Ph.D. from the University of Cambridge. Ghurye was greatly influenced by WHR Rivers, who was his Ph.D. guide. After the untimely death of Rivers in 1922, he completed his thesis under A.C. Haddon on Caste and Race in India. He is the founder of the Indian Sociological Society and its newsletter, the Sociological Bulletin.

Important Works

1. Caste and Race in India (1932)
2. Caste Class and Occupation (1969)
3. Indian Sadhus (1953)
4. Bharatnatyam and Its Costume (1958)
5. Cities and Civilization (1962)
6. The Scheduled Tribes (1943, 1959, 1963)
7. Religious Consciousness (1965)
8. Indian Costume (1966)
9. Social Tensions in India (1968)
10. Vedic India (1979),
11. The Legacy of Ramayana (1979).

Major Theories

Ghurye Views on Caste and Kinship

In his book *'Caste and Race in India'* (1932), he combined historical, anthropological, and sociological approaches to understand the caste and kinship system in India. Ghurye highlights six structural features of the caste system:

- **i.** Segmental division
- **ii.** Hierarchy
- **iii.** Pollution and purity
- **vi.** Civil and religious disabilities and privileges of different sections
- **v.** Lack of choice of occupation
- **iv.** Restrictions on marriage

According to GS Ghurye, 'the caste is the Brahmanical offspring of the Indo-Aryan culture, which grew up in the lands of the Ganges and the Yamuna and therefore migrated to other parts of the country'.

Each caste was in the past divided into smaller sub-divisions or sub-castes. Each of these sub-castes practiced endogamy. For example, Vaishya (Bania or Mahajan) castes are divided into various sub-castes such as Agrawal, Maheshwari, etc.

Caste is also linked to kinship through endogamy and gotra exogamy. Gotra has come to be regarded as an entirely ostracized entity by Brahmins and later by non-Brahmins.

The basic assumption here is that all the members of a gotra are related to each other through blood, that is, their forefathers are sages. Therefore, marriage between two persons of the same gotra would give rise to an incestuous relationship.

For him caste and sub-caste integrated people into a rank in a category based on criteria of purity-pollution. The rules of endogamy and commensality separated castes from each other.

It was a unifying device that organized them into a totality or collectivity. He regarded the caste system as a unifying force.

Ghurye's View on the Tribe

In his book, *'The Scheduled Tribes'* he explained the historical, administrative, and social dimensions of the Indian tribes. He also wrote about specific tribes like 'Koli' in Maharashtra. He believes that most of the tribes have been Hinduised after prolonged contact with Hindus. He called them 'backward caste Hindus'.

He believed in the integration of tribes into mainstream Hinduism rather than maintaining a separate identity. A fierce debate ensues between G.S. Ghurye and Verrier Elwin. Elwin in his book 'Loss of Nerve' states that the tribals should be allowed to remain isolated, whereas Ghurye argued that the tribals should be assimilated into the Hindu castes.

For Ghurye, the incorporation of Hindu values and norms into tribal life was a positive step in the process of development. Under Hindu influence, the tribes gave up drinking alcohol, gained education, and improved their agriculture.

Ghurye suggests that the economic motivation among tribes to adopt Hinduism is very strong. They can come out of their tribal craft and take up a particular type of occupation that is in demand in society.

His Views on Rural Urbanization (Rur-urbanization)

He is of the view that urbanization in India was not a simple function of industrial development. In India, the process of urbanization, at least until recent years, began from within the rural sector.

He traced Sanskrit texts and documents to show the growth of urban centres from the need for a market area in rural areas.The development of agriculture required more and more markets to exchange the surplus in food grains. As a result, in many rural areas, a market began to function as a part of a larger village.

This led to the formation of a township, which in turn developed administrative, judicial, and other institutions.

He said that in the colonial period, the growth of metropolitan centres transformed Indian life.

Towns and cities were no longer outlets for agricultural produce and handicrafts, but they became major manufacturing centers.

These centres used rural areas to produce raw materials and turned them into a market to sell industrial products. Thus, the metropolitan economy emerged to dominate the rural economy.

His Views on Culture and Civilization

According to Ghurye, culture constitutes the central or basic element to understand society and its development.

In fact, culture is a totality encompassing the entire heritage of mankind.

Ghurye's abiding interest was in analyzing the course of cultural development and the nature of the heritage that mankind has denied in the past.

Culture is related to the realm of values. It is a matter of personal achievement of excellence and creativity.

Ghurye was a firm believer in the power of man to preserve the best of his old culture while building the new culture in his own spirit.

In his view, the process of acculturation is more relevant than the process of diffusion.

Ghurye was fuelled by the belief that there is 'a common heritage of modern civilization' and that civilization is the 'collective effort of humanity'. He believes that behind the rise and fall of civilization there has been a continuous development of culture.

Breaking through the ups and downs of a civilization's development, there are certain values that have been established as final. Ghurye has called these values as the 'foundation of culture'. He delineates five such values or foundations of culture. These:

1. Religious Consciousness
2. Conscience
3. Justice
4. Free pursuit of knowledge and free expression
5. Toleration

His Views on Religion

Religion is fundamental to man. Man becomes conscious of a force beyond his understanding almost at the dawn of civilization. This area has attracted the attention of sociologists such as Weber (The Protestant Ethic and Spirit of Capitalism, 1930) and Durkheim (The Elementary Forms of Religious Life, 1915).

Ghurye believes that religion is central to the entire cultural heritage of man. As mentioned earlier in the description of culture and civilization, he gives five bases of culture, of which 'religious consciousness' is the most important. It moulds and directs the behaviour of man in society.

Ghurye made original contributions to the study of Indian religious beliefs and practices. He wrote six books to highlight the role of religion in society. These are Indian Sages (1953), Gods and Men (1962), Religious Consciousness (1965), Indian Sanchay (1977), Vedic India (1979), and The Legacy of the Ramayana (1979).

All these works reflect Ghurye's interest in the sociology of religion. For example, in Gods and Men, Ghurye discusses the nature of Hindu ideas of divinity and the relationship, if any, between the climate of the era and the type of deity.

Ghurye believes that religion is central to the entire cultural heritage of man. It moulds and directs the behaviour of man in society. Ghurye analyzes the three oldest human civilizations, namely Mesopotamian, Egyptian, and Hindu, in various aspects of mythological beliefs, speculations, cosmology, life after death, the vision of God, temple architecture, etc.

National Unity and Integration

Ghurye's three books, known as his 'trilogy', are *Social Tension in India* (1968), *Where India* (1974), and *India Recreates Democracy* (1978). In these books, he developed a theoretical framework to explain unity at the social or cultural level.

Ghurye holds that although groups play a unifying role in society, this is true only up to a certain extent. In modern society, there are five sources of danger to national unity because they create an excessive attachment to groups:

i. The Scheduled Castes
ii. The Scheduled Tribes
iii. The Backward Classes
iv. The Muslims as religious minority groups
v. The linguistic minorities

He thinks that it is largely the result of Brahmanical effort that cultural unity has been created in India. All the major institutions of Hindu society originated in Brahmins. Ghurye's concept of cultural unity is new and not secular in orientation. He relates India to 'Hindu culture' and uses the terms 'Indian culture' and 'Hindu culture' synonymously.

According to Ghurye, society is not just a set of isolated individuals, but it is a collective life that acts as a bridge between the individual and the society. An individual acquires social characteristics and is socialized through groups. It is the unifying function of the groups in society.

In his view, religious and linguistic minorities are the source of the most potential threat to unity in modern India. Religion and linguistic groups are the major areas that led to the disintegration of the harmony of India.

Ghurye gave great importance to the role of language in the process of nation-building in India. Ghurye is of the view that the regional language has a symbolic unifying value of the nation. Regional languages ensure the unity of the region at the local level and all efforts should be made to improve it.

Indian Sadhus

The Indian Sadhus is an excellent sociology of the various sects and religious centres founded by the great Vedantic philosopher Shankaracharya and other notable religious figures. In this work, Ghurye throws light on the contradictory nature of sacrifice in India. A sadhu or sanyasi is considered to be separate from all castes, norms, social conventions, etc.

He is outside the purview of society. Yet strangely enough, since the time of Shankaracharya, Hindu society has been more or less directed by sadhus. These sages were not the only sages. Most of them belonged to the monastic order, which has distinctive traditions.

The monastic organization in India was a product of Hinduism and Buddhism. The rise of Buddhism and Jainism marked the decline of individual ascetics such as Vishwamitra. Indian sages have acted as arbiters of religious disputes, protected the teachings of the scriptures and sacred learning, and even defended the religion against external attacks.

MYSORE NARSIMHACHARYA SRINIVAS (1916–1999)

The full name of MN Srinivas is Mysore Narasimhachar Srinivas. He was born in Mysore in 1916 and died in Bangalore in 1999. He was one of the best Indian sociologists. His study is prominent in the field of caste and its other classifications, Sanskritization, and many other topics revolving around caste. He received his D.Phil. from Oxford on religion and society among the Coorgs of South India. He was advised by Radcliffe-Brown to analyze the same field data with a different theoretical lens, reflecting the interrelationships between religion and society, rather than choosing a different topic of investigation.

Important Works

1. Social change in Modern India (1966)
2. Religion and Society among Coorgs of South India (1952)
3. Caste in Modern India and Other Essays (1966)
4. The Dominant Caste and Other Essays (1987)
5. India's Villages (1955)
6. India: Social Structure (1980)

Major Theories

His Methodology

As part of his methodological practice, Srinivas strongly advocated ethnographic research based on participant observation, but his concept of fieldwork was bound by the notion of locally confined sites.

Thus, some of his best papers, such as the paper on the dominant caste and on a joint family dispute, were largely inspired by his direct involvement (and as a participant observer) in rural life in South India. He wrote several papers on the topics of national integration, gender issues, new technologies, etc.

Field View and Book View

Religion, varna, caste, family, village, and geographical structure are the major elements, which are known as the basis of Indian society. Knowledge of such elements is obtained from holy texts or books. Srinivasa calls it the Kitabi Nazriya or Bookish Nazriya. Book view is also called Indology, which is not acceptable to Srinivasa and he insisted on field view.

Sanskritization

Srinivas coined the term *Sanskritisation* to describe the social dynamics present in Indian society. According to M.N. Srinivas, '*Sanskritization* is a process of cultural change by which a 'low' Hindu caste, or tribal or other groups, changes its customs, rituals, ideology, and way of life to a higher, and often, a 'twice' born caste. It then claims a higher position in the caste hierarchy.

In his study of a Mysore village, Srinivas found that at some point or the other, every caste tries to change its rank in the hierarchy by giving up its own characteristics and trying to adopt the castes above it. This process of attempting to change one's rank by giving up characteristics that indicate a lower caste and adopting characteristics that indicate higher status is called '*Sanskritisation*'.

This process essentially involves a change in one's dietary habits from non-vegetarian to vegetarian, and a change in one's occupational habits from impure to clean occupation. Caste characteristics form the basis of interaction between castes.

Dominant Caste

The concept of dominant caste has been used for the first time in sociological literature by M.N. Srinivas in his essay Social System of a Mysore Village, which was written after his study of Rampura village. The concept occupies an important place in the process of '*Sanskritisation*'.

The term dominant caste is used to refer to a caste that "executes economic or political power and occupies a fairly high position in the hierarchy." These castes are accorded high status, and status in all spheres of social life. People from other lower castes see them as their 'reference group' and try to imitate their behaviour, ritual patterns, customs, and ideology.

Thus, the dominant caste of a particular area plays an important role in the 'process of cultural transmission' in that area. Srinivasa has defined the following six major characteristics of the dominant caste:

- **i.** Land ownership
- **ii.** Numerical strength
- **iii.** High position in the local hierarchy
- **iv.** Education
- **v.** Job in administration and urban sources of income
- **vi.** Political involvement

Vote Bank

A vote bank is a loyal block of voters from a single community that consistently supports a certain candidate or political formation in democratic elections. Such behavior is often the result of an expectation of real or perceived benefits from political structures at the expense of other communities.

Vote bank politics is the practice of creating and maintaining vote banks through divisive policies. As it encourages voters to vote based on narrow sectarian considerations, often against their better judgment, it is considered detrimental to the principles of representative democracy.

Brahminization

Srinivas' work, *Religion and Society among the Coorgs of South India* (1952) inspired him to formulate the concept of *Brahmanization*. Brahminization represents the process of copying the way of life and ritual practices of Brahmins by lower caste Hindus.

The concept was used as an explanatory device to explain the observed changes in the ritual practices and lifeways of the lower castes through intensive and careful field studies.

In religion and society, Srinivasa was concerned with the spread of Hinduism. He talked about 'cultural Hinduism" and its values. Related to this was the notion of '*Sanskritisation*' which was employed by *Srinivas* 'to describe the process of penetration of cultural values into remote parts of India'. Imitation of the way of life of the highest *dvija* castes was said to be the principal mechanism by which the lower castes tried to raise their social status.

Westernization

Srinivas defines Westernization as 'the changes brought about in Indian society and culture as a result of more than 150 years of British rule, a term that refers to changes at various levels of technology, institutions, ideology, and values'.

Therefore, westernization is a vast, multidimensional, and complex process that impacts different domains through multiple institutions and hence has a significant impact on caste dynamics. It not only changed the existing structure but also opened new avenues and doors for social mobility.

The land became a saleable commodity under British rule and this had far-reaching consequences for mobility. Members of a lower caste who could afford to buy land could now be upwardly mobile and those who lost their rights to land faced downward mobility.

Jajmani system

William H. Wiser was the first to introduce the term *Jajmani* system which clearly describes how different castes interact with each other for agriculture and economic process. According to M.N. Srinivasa, the *Jajmani* system which promoted interdependence among castes acted as one of the major factors promoting vertical solidarity in the caste system.

IRAWATI KARVE (1905–1970)

Irawati Karve was born on 15 December 1905 to a wealthy Chitpawan Brahmin family in Burma, where her father Ganesh Hari Karmakar worked for the Burma Cotton Company. He studied philosophy at Ferguson College, from which he graduated in 1926. She then received a fellowship in 1928 to study master's degree in Sociology and did her thesis on the subject of his caste titled Chitpavan Brahmins – An Ethnic Study under GS Ghurye at Bombay University. She married Dinkar Dhondo Karve, son of Dhondo Keshav Karve, a Bharat Ratna and pioneer of women's education.

Important Works

1. Kinship Organization in India (1953)
2. The Bhils of West Khandesh (1958)
3. Hindu Society: An Interpretation (1961; 1968)
4. Group Relations in Village Community (1963)
5. The Social Dynamics of a Growing Town and Its Surrounding Area (1965)
6. Yuganta: The End of an Epoch (1968)
7. Gangajal (in Marathi) (1972)
8. Samskruti (in Marathi)
9. Karve Irawati: A Survey of the People Displaced through the Koyna Dam.

Major Theories

Society

She draws a parallel between society and a quilt, just as a whole quilt is made up of pieces of different colours and sizes, similarly, society is made up of different people who come together, form relationships with each other, mix with each other and break up. And yet, the thread connecting them to society still remains.

She defined caste as 'an extended kinship'. She has written about the character of great epics like Mahabharata and Ramayana in her book Yugantak.

Kinship Organization in India

For her, three things are absolutely necessary to understand any cultural phenomenon in India. These:

- **i.** configuration of linguistic regions,
- **ii.** institution of caste and
- **iii.** Family organization.

Karve has presented material on Indian kinship dividing the country into four distinct cultural zones according to marriage practices, linguistics, caste, and family organization.

- **i.** Northern,
- **ii.** Central,
- **iii.** Southern,
- **iv.** Eastern.

Kinship in North India This region is situated between the Himalayas in the north and the Vindhya ranges in the south. In this region, most of the people speak languages derived from Sanskrit. Some of these languages are Hindi, Bihari, Sindhi, Punjabi, Bengali, and Assamese.

In North India, kinship is traced through (a) blood ties and (b) marriage ties. Most of the castes in this region have their roots in Indo-Aryan, they are patrilineal, patrilineal, and patriarchal families. A village is an exogamy unit here, thus, there are at least four basic features of kinship in North India:

- **i.** Territoriality,
- **ii.** Genealogy,
- **iii.** Incest taboos, and
- **vi.** Local exogamy.

Here the rule of *sasan* (four gotra rules) means avoidance of father, mother, grandmother and maternal grandmother, which is generally prevalent among brahmins and other upper castes. According to which a person cannot marry in his paternal family and can also avoid marriage with *Sapind* i.e., 7 degrees from father and 5 degrees from mother. In this zone people follow descriptive system of terminology in kinship system.

Kinship in Central India It includes regions like Rajasthan, Gujarat, Kathiawar, Chhattisgarh, Orissa, and Maharashtra, their languages are Rajasthani, Gujarati, Kathiawadi, Oriya, and Marathi. Somehow these languages are related to Sanskrit and are located in the northern region of India. The following points may be noted with respect to the central region:

- **i.** Cross-cousin marriages are prevalent which are not seen in the northern region.
- **ii.** Many castes are divided into exogamous gotras as in the northern region.
- **iii.** In some castes the exogamous clans are arranged in an exogamous hierarchy.

However, none of these features are found uniformly throughout the zone. For example, in Rajasthan, Jats follow village exogamy as well as two-gotra exogamy; Baniyas follow the four gotra rule; And the Rajputs have exogamous gotras, and feudal status is an important consideration in marriage relations.

Rajputs are not a homogeneous caste. They laid great emphasis on the purity and nobility of the lineage. Symbolic marriages (marriage with the sword) were in vogue.

- A mixture of peculiar local customs and northern practices is found in Kathiawar and Gujarat. Some castes permit cross-cousin marriages. The practice of '*Nantra*' (Levirate) exists even today. The Brahmin, Bania, Kunbi, and higher artisan castes follow the northern pattern of kinship organization, but some practices from the southern region are also observed.
- Cross-cousin marriage is quite common among the Kathi, Ahir, Garhwacharan, and Garasia castes.

Both the Kolis and Dheds and Bhils (tribes) allow cross-cousin marriages. Thus, Rajasthan and Gujarat largely follow the northern pattern.

- Tribal peoples in Orissa such as the Gonds, Oraons, and Konds speak Dravidian languages, and their kinship system can be linked to that of Dravidian-speaking peoples. Munda, Ho, and some Saora speak the Mundari language.

Kinship in South India The regions that come under South India are Andhra Pradesh, Karnataka, Tamil Nadu, Kerala, and other regions that have people with different languages. Southern regions are complex to study because they are dominated by patrilineal and patriarchal systems and in some areas matrilineal and matriarchal systems.

The Nairs, Tiyans in the Malabar region, and some Moplas and Bunts in the Kanara district have matrilineal and matrilineal clans and are called *Tharavads*. Tharavad includes a woman, her siblings, her own, and her sister's sons and daughters. There is no matrimonial relationship in Tharavad.

In the southern region, there is a system of caste endogamy and gotra exogamy similar to the northern system. It is called '*Bedagu*' or '*Bedaga*' or 'Bali' in Karnataka. The Kotas of the Nilgiris calls it 'Keri', the Kottai Vellalas call it 'Kilai', the Koyas call it 'Gotta' and the Kurubas call it 'Gunpu'. Some Telugu-speaking people call it 'Inti-Peru', and Malayalees call it 'Ilom'. In Travancore, it is called 'Veli'. The word 'Gotra' is also widely used. The main symbols used for the clans are silver, gold, axe, elephant, snake, jasmine, stone, etc.

If we compare southern and northern kinship then we can say that in southern regions there is no difference between a family of birth and a family of marriage and in the northern part we have a clear difference. Marriages in the southern region are used to strengthen ties between each other. It maintains unity and understanding among the kin.

They follow classificatory types of kinship terminology such as: they have a single word for mother, chachi, mausi, etc called 'ami' and for father, uncle, mausa, fufa, etc called 'apu'.

Kinship in East India The eastern region has no distinct boundaries and is not compact. Northern languages are prominent as well as other languages such as *Monkhmer* and *Mundari*. The communities found here are Khmer, Mon, and Chan. People with Mundari linguistic backgrounds have a patriarchal or patrilineal system.

The Ho and Santhals practice 'cross-cousin marriage', but only as long as the father's sister or mother's brother is alive, marriage with the daughter is not permitted. That's why cross-cousin marriages are rarely seen. For example, the Bondo people do not practice cross-cousin marriages.

The Khasis in Assam speak the Monkhmer language and they follow a matrilineal system like the Nairs but they are not completely identical. The Ho and Munda have separate dormitories for unmarried and young women but premarital relation is common among them. Sometimes these relationships result in marriage, but often the marriage partner is different from the dormitory partner. All these people are divided into exogamous totemistic clans. A person must marry outside the clan and also outside the circle of close relations such as first cousins.

Money is offered for procuring a bride. The service rendered by the future husband in the house of the girl's father is also considered as the bride price. After marriage, the couple sets up a separate house of his own but may keep his younger brother and widowed mother, etc. with him in his newly established house. Thus, Mundari people are different from the rest of India because of not having a joint family.

The Khasis of Assam speak the *Monkhmer* language, and they are a matrilineal people. The Khasis have a joint family with common worship and a common burial ground, but the husband and wife live together in their own small house. After death, the property goes to the mother or the youngest daughter. If there is no female relative, the widow gets half the property if she does not remarry.

ASSESS YOUR LEARNING

PRACTICE QUESTIONS

1. According to Marx which of the following society is characterized by 'Master and Slave'?
(a) Primitive Communism
(b) Ancient Society
(c) Feudal society
(d) Capitalist Society

2. Émile Durkheim's endeavour to establish sociology as a separate academic discipline centred on his efforts to:
(a) Develop an all-encompassing synthesis of major sociological perspectives.
(b) Demonstrate the influence of social forces on people's behaviour.
(c) Show how an understanding of sociological principles could be used to solve social problems.
(d) Chart the evolution of major social institutions.

3. Durkheim's research suggested that
(a) Catholics had much higher suicide rates than Protestants.
(b) There seemed to be higher rates of suicide in times of peace than in times of war and revolution.
(c) civilians were more likely to take their lives than soldiers.
(d) suicide is a solitary act, unrelated to group life.

4. The book '*The Division of Labour*' was written by
(a) Karl Marx
(b) Ralf Dahrendorf
(c) Emile Durkheim
(d) Max Weber

5. Who said that Society is '*a reality sui generis*'?
(a) Emile Durkheim
(b) Talcott Parsons
(c) Max Weber
(d) Spencer

6. Karl Marx was born in:
(a) France
(b) Russia
(c) Germany
(d) Italy

7. The Communist Manifesto was authored by:
(a) Stalin
(b) Karl Marx
(c) Laski
(d) George Bernard Shah

8. According to Marxian theory revolutions come in society because of:
(a) Capitalists desire
(b) The religious exploitation
(c) Class struggle
(d) Educated masses get dissatisfied

9. Karl Marx believed that social change can be brought about by:
(a) Evolutionary means only
(b) Change in means of production
(c) Change in technology
(d) Change in ideas

10. Who pointed out that Hegel's 'dialectic idealism is standing on its head? It must be turned right side up'?
(a) Stalin
(b) Karl Marx
(c) Laski
(d) George Bernard Shah

11. Marx borrowed his idea of alienation from?
(a) Hegel
(b) Feuerbach
(c) Hegel and Feuerbach
(d) Hegel and Lukas

12. Weber discussed his concept of Bureaucracy in his book:
(a) The Protestant Ethics and The Spirit of Capitalism
(b) Economy and Society
(c) Politics as Vocation
(d) The Theory of Social and Economic Organisation

13. Who defined Sociology as 'the science which attempts the interpretative understanding of social actions'?
(a) Emile Durkheim
(b) Karl Marx
(c) Max Weber
(d) Talcott Parsons

14. Which one of the following is not involved in Weber's ideal type of bureaucracy?
(a) Offices are impersonal
(b) Recruitment based on qualification
(c) Political decisions
(d) Fixed tenure

15. Who said that sociology must pay attention to the gap in ideal representations, material social organizations, and their constituent actions?

(a) Max Weber (b) Talcott Parsons
(c) Karl Marx (d) Emile Durkheim

16. Who is the author of the book '*Argonauts of the Western Pacific*'?
(a) A R Radcliffe Brown
(b) Clifford Geertz
(c) Claude Levi Strauss
(d) B Malinowski

17. Who said "that education helps to ensure the continuity of norms and values through transmitting the culture of society to new generations?
(a) Tonnies
(b) Erving Goffman
(c) Talcott Parsons
(d) Karl Mannheim

18. Who has refuted Malinowski's idea of 'functional indispensability' and introduced the concept of 'functional alternatives'?
(a) Kingsley Davis
(b) Talcott Parsons
(c) R.K. Merton
(d) R. Radcliffe Brown

19. A.R. Radcliffe-Brown contributed to
(a) Functionalist
(b) Cultural Materialism
(c) Structural – Functionalism
(d) Structuralism

20. Who developed the concept of anomie on the basis of an imbalance between cultural goals and institutionalized means?
(a) Kingsley Davis
(b) Talcott Parsons
(c) R.K. Merton
(d) R. Radcliffe Brown

21. To Malinowski, which elements are crucial to understanding the functioning of society?
(a) Needs
(b) Structures
(c) Motivations
(d) Both A and C

22. Alliance Theory in Kinship Studies is associated with which of the following scholars?
(a) Kathleen Gough
(b) Pauline Kolenda
(c) C. Levi-Strauss
(d) A. R Radcliffe-Brown

23. Which of the following thinker is associated with the 'theory of needs'?
(a) A R Radcliffe Brown
(b) Clifford Geertz
(c) Claude Levi Strauss
(d) B Malinowski

24. Which of the following theories has a 'Micro' orientation?
(a) Functionalism
(b) Conflict theory
(c) Interactionism
(d) Critical theory

25. Which of the following thinkers borrowed the concept of 'thick description' from Gilbert Ryle and the concept of 'family resemblance' from Ludwig Wittgenstein?
(a) Karl Mannheim
(b) Alfred Schutz
(c) Erving Goffman
(d) Clifford Geertz

26. Who is associated with the variable sum concept of power?
(a) Talcott Parsons (b) Max Weber
(c) Vilfred Pareto (d) G Mosca

27. Who is the author of the books 'The Totemism' and 'The Savage Mind'?
(a) A R Radcliffe Brown
(b) Clifford Geertz
(c) Claude Levi Strauss
(d) Emile Durkheim

28. Who coined the term 'Atom of kinship'?
(a) Radcliffe brown
(b) Murdock
(c) Levi-Strauss
(d) Krober

29. Who introduced the concept of 'functional alternative' and 'functional substitutability'?
(a) B Malinowski
(b) Raymond Firth
(c) Radcliffe Brown
(d) Robert K Merton

30. The concept of 'Anticipatory Socialization' has been developed by
(a) R. K. Merton
(b) K. Marx
(c) P.A. Sorokin
(d) M. Weber

31. Meads contribution towards the development of self can be summed up into three Stages, which of the following is not given by him?
(a) Oral Stage
(b) Preparatory Stage
(c) Play Stage
(d) Game Stage

32. Which of the following thinkers pioneered dramaturgical analysis?
(a) Charlotte Perkins Gilman
(b) Robert Park
(c) Karl Mannheim
(d) Erving Goffman

33. Alfred Schutz is known as a(n) ________ sociologist.
(a) structuralist
(b) neo-Marxian
(c) postmodern
(d) phenomenological

34. Ethnomethodology is known as a(n):
(a) sociology of everyday life.
(b) sociology of culture.
(c) sociology of traditions.
(d) fusion of Marx and Weber.

35. Who has given an extensive analysis of the Balinese cockfight?
(a) Claude Levi Strauss
(b) Clifford Geertz
(c) Karl Mannheim
(d) Alfred Schutz

36. Who said that religion establishes powerful, pervasive, and long-lasting moods and motivations in men by formulating conceptions of a general order of existence?
(a) Claude Levi Strauss
(b) Clifford Geertz
(c) Karl Mannheim
(d) Alfred Schutz

37. Which of the following thinker divided diagnostic accounts of ideology into the 'interest' theory and the 'strain' theory?
(a) Claude Levi Strauss
(b) Clifford Geertz
(c) Karl Mannheim
(d) Alfred Schutz

38. In his book 'Ideology and Utopia' he considers that ideological knowledge or thought is propounded by those benefiting from the status quo whereas utopia is rooted in the thoughts of under privileged. Who is he?
(a) Claude levi Strauss
(b) Clifford Geertz
(c) Karl Mannheim
(d) Alfred Schutz

39. Which of the following book is not authored by Karl Mannheim?
(a) Ideology & Utopia (1929).
(b) Essay on Sociology of knowledge 1928.
(c) Culture & Communication 1976
(d) Man, and society in an age of reconstruction.

40. There are two central ideas in ethnomethodology: indexicality and reflexivity.
1. Reflexivity means that there is no such thing as a clear, extensive definition of any word or concept in a language.
2. Indexicality refers to the fact that our sense of order is a result of conversational processes.

Choose the correct answer from the code given below
(a) Only statement 1 is correct
(b) Only statement 2 is correct
(c) Both statements are correct
(d) Neither 1 nor 2 is correct

41. The term refers to the detachment of the performer from the role he or she is performing is known as?
(a) Role handicapped
(b) Role distance
(c) Role strain
(d) Role taking

42. Who defined Impression management as projecting an 'idealized image' of ourselves, which involves concealing a number of aspects of performance?
(a) Karl Mannheim
(b) Alfred Schutz
(c) Harold Garfinkel
(d) Erving Goffman

43. Goffman (1959) breaks down the regions of performance, which of the following is not among them?
(a) front stage
(b) backstage
(c) off stage
(d) side stage

44. Who said that 'self reflects society', i.e., 'society shapes self which shapes social behaviours'?
(a) G H Mead
(b) Emile Durkheim
(c) Sigmund Freud
(d) C H Cooley

45. Who made a distinction between 'action' and 'act'?
(a) Claude Levi Strauss
(b) Clifford Geertz
(c) Karl Mannheim
(d) Alfred Schutz

46. Who is the author of the book '*Orientalism*'?
(a) Clifford Geerz
(b) Edward Said
(c) Rudolf Ernest
(d) Karl Manheim

47. According to Habermass, there are three kinds of knowledge which is not among them.
(a) Empirical knowledge
(b) Hermeneutics knowledge
(c) Critical knowledge
(d) Subjective knowledge

48. Who said, 'No one today is purely one thing. Labels like Indian, woman, Muslim, or American'?
(a) Clifford Geerz
(b) Edward Said
(c) Michel Foucault
(d) Karl Manheim

49. 'Theory of Practice' was propounded by which of the following thinker?
(a) Pierre Bourdieu
(b) Clifford Geertz
(c) Edward Said
(d) Edward Tylor

50. Who regarded the western form of knowledge as an instrument of domination rather than an instrument of truth?
(a) Antonio Gramsci
(b) Meilasoux
(c) Michel Foucault
(d) Erving Goffman

51. Which combination of the following thinkers is said to be 'the Holy Trinity' of postcolonial, theory?
(a) Edward Said, Anthony Giddens and Manuel Castells
(b) Edward Said, Pierre Bourdieu and Michel Foucault
(c) Edward Said, Gayatri Spivak and Homi Bhabha
(d) Edward Said, Manuel Castells and Homi Bhabha

52. Who said that person's identity is multifaceted and is always evolving?
(a) Edward Tylor
(b) Pierre Bourdieu
(c) Clifford Geertz
(d) Edward Said

53. Choose the incorrect match:

Author	Books
(a) Pierre Bourdieu	Theory and Practice
(b) Jurgen Habermas	The Theory of Communicative Action
(c) Edward Said	Culture and Imperialism
(d) Anthony Giddens	A New Rules of Sociological Methods

54. Jurgen Habermas's theory of Communicative Action (1981), is based on:
(a) Max Weber's social action
(b) Talcott Parson's social action
(c) Max Weber's wertrational action
(d) Talcott Parson's AGIL Paradigm

55. Who believed, 'Society only has form, and that form only has effects on people, insofar as the structure is produced and reproduced in what people do'?
(a) Anthony Giddens
(b) Michel Foucault
(c) Manuel Castells
(d) Jurgen Habermas

56. Which of the following statement does not refers to Pierre Bourdieu's Cultural Capital theory?
(a) Cultural capital refers to the collection of symbolic elements such as skills, tastes, posture, clothing, mannerisms, material belongings, credentials, etc.
(b) Sharing similar forms of cultural capital with others creates a sense of collective identity and group position ('people like us').
(c) Cultural capital is a major source of social inequality
(d) Certain forms of cultural capital promote cultural equality

57. Who defined Globalisation as 'the intensification of worldwide social relationships'?
(a) Anthony Giddens
(b) Michel Foucault
(c) Manuel Castells
(d) Jurgen Habermas

58. Who is the author of the book, '*The Network City*'?
(a) Anthony Giddens
(b) Michel Foucault
(c) Manuel Castells
(d) Barry Wellman

59. The risk society hypothesis, was initially developed by Ulrich Beck and Anthony Giddens. They distinguished two types of risks:
(i) External Risks
(ii) Manufactured Risks
(iii) Internal Risks
(iv) Outer risks

Choose the correct answer from the code given below
(a) i and ii
(b) ii and iii
(c) iii and iv
(d) i and iii

60. Who said 'Society remains capitalist, but the basis of the technological means by which it acts has changed from energy to information'in his book, '*The Rise of the Network Society* (1996)'?
(a) Anthony Giddens
(b) Michel Foucault
(c) Manuel Castells
(d) Barry Wellman

61. Who was the founder of the Independent Labour Party?
(a) Irawati Karve
(b) B R Ambedkar
(c) M K Gandhi
(d) R K Mukherjee

62. Who said, 'means are after all everything, as the mean so the end'?
(a) B.R. Ambedkar
(b) M.K. Gandhi
(c) Irawati Karwe
(d) Rabindranath Tagore

63. Which of the following statements given below is incorrect in relevance to Mahatma Gandhi?
(a) "Man as an animal, 'he says, is violent, but as spirit (he) is non-violent'.
(b) Hinduism lies in holding the actual belief that all life is one, i.e., all life comes from One universal Source.
(c) Politics bereft of religion is absolute dirt.
(d) Swaraj means the rule of the majority community.

64. Gandhiji invoked the five-fold moral principles:
i. truth,
ii. non-violence,
iii. non-stealing,
iv. non-possession
v. right action
vi. right exercise
vii. celibacy.
Chose the correct answer from the codes given below
(a) i, ii, iii, iv, v
(b) i, ii, iii, iv, vi
(c) i, ii, iii, vi, vii
(d) i, ii, iii, iv, vii

65. Who classified values as Intrinsic value and Instrumental value?
(a) Irawati Karve
(b) B R Ambedkar
(c) M K Gandhi
(d) R K Mukherjee

66. Who is the author of the book *Annihilation of Caste* (1936) and *The Untouchables*?
(a) Irawati Karve
(b) B R Ambedkar
(c) M K Gandhi
(d) R K Mukherjee

67. Who advocated the use of direct observation, field study, and field experience in Sociology?
(a) Irawati Karve
(b) M N Srinivas
(c) G S Ghurye
(d) R K Mukherjee

68. The process by which a 'low' caste or tribe or other group takes over the custom, ritual, beliefs, ideology, and style of life of a high and, in particular, a 'twice-born' (dwija) caste is known as:
(a) Westernization
(b) Brahminization
(c) Sanskritization
(d) Dominant Caste

69. Which of the following is not written by Irawati Karve?
(a) Kinship Organisation in India (1953)
(b) Yuganta: The End of an Epoch (1968)
(c) Gangajal (in Marathi) (1972)
(d) Social Tensions in India (1968)

70. Who formed the Bahishkrit Hitkarini Sabha (Depressed Classes Welfare Association)?
(a) Irawati Karve
(b) B R Ambedkar
(c) M K Gandhi
(d) R K Mukherjee

71. Who is the author of the book Religion and Society among the Coorgs of South India (1952)?
(a) M N Srinivas
(b) Irawati Karve
(c) G S Ghurye
(d) R K Mukherjee

72. Irawati Karve has divided the country into four different cultural zones in accordance with the marriage practices, linguistics, caste, and family organization which of the following is not one of them?
(a) Western
(b) Central
(c) Northern
(d) Southern

73. Who said, 'Caste is the Brahminic child of Indo-Aryans culture, cradled in the Land of the Ganga and the Yamuna and hence transferred to the other parts of the country'?
(a) Irawati Karve
(b) B R Ambedkar
(c) M K Gandhi
(d) G S Ghurye

74. Irawati Karve kept Monkhmer and Mundari-speaking people in which kinship zone?
(a) Central
(b) Northern
(c) Southern
(d) Eastern

75. Who called tribes 'Backward Caste Hindus'?
(a) M N Srinivas
(b) Irawati Karve
(c) G S Ghurye
(d) R K Mukherjee

76. Who believes 'Man makes choices and acts in terms of values relating to (i) self, (ii) the other, and (iii) cosmos'?
(a) M N Srinivas
(b) Irawati Karve
(c) G S Ghurye
(d) R K Mukherjee

77. Who is the author of Regional Sociology (1926)?
(a) M N Srinivas
(b) Irawati Karve
(c) G S Ghurye
(d) R K Mukherjee

78. What social forces were responsible for the emergence of sociology in the late 18th and early 19th Century?

(a) French Revolution (the Enlightenment period)
(b) Industrial Revolution
(c) Both A and B
(d) None of the above

79. Sociology had its formal beginning in 1917 in India at
(a) Calcutta University
(b) Bombay University
(c) Madras University
(d) Lucknow University

80. Who was the head of the Department of Economics and Sociology in 1921, at Lucknow University?
(a) Radhakamal Mukherjee
(b) B N Seal
(c) G S Ghurye
(d) Patrick Geddes

81. Which of the following is NOT a characteristic of Weberian Bureaucracy?
(a) Specialization
(b) Hierarchy
(c) Job tenure
(d) Reservation

82. Which of the following works is concerned with a process of development from primitive to modern society?
(a) Division of Labour in Society (E. Durkheim)
(b) Economy and Society (Max Weber)
(c) The Handbook of Economic Sociology (N.J. Smelser)
(d) The Origin of the Family, Private Property and State (F. Engels)

83. In which community did Durkheim examine Totemism?
(a) Red Indian
(b) Trobriand Islanders
(c) Australian Arunta
(d) African Gypsies

84. According to Durkheim, low regulation in society will lead to which type of suicide?
(a) Egoistic
(b) Fatalistic
(c) Altruistic
(d) Anomic

85. Which option is correct about the 'Social fact' according to Durkheim?
A. It is common in a given society
B. It is common in every individual
C. It is like a thing
D. It does not provide any pressure on the individual

Choose the correct option:
(a) A and B (b) C and D
(c) B and C (d) A and C

86. The main works of Karl Marx were:
1. Dictionary of Marxist Thought
2. Power: A Radical View
3. Grundrisse
4. Class and class conflict in Industrial Society
5. A contribution to a critique of political economy

Choose the correct answer from the options given below:
(a) 3 and 5 only
(b) 1 and 4 only
(c) 4 and 5 only
(d) 2 and 4 only

87. Karl Marx regarded the _______ structure as the basic structure of society.
(a) Ideological
(b) Political
(c) Religious
(d) Economic

88. Who has given the idea of rationality which gave impetus to the study of the organizational structure of industries?
(a) E Durkheim
(b) Karl Marx
(c) Georg Simmel
(d) Max Weber

89. According to Durkheim, there are many social facts in a given society but they do not present themselves in crystallized forms. What is the term Durkheim used for them?
(a) Pathological condition
(b) Social currents
(c) Collective conscience
(d) Dynamic density

90. Who among the following denied objective social science and believed that theory is inseparable from socialist practice?
(a) Friedrich Engels
(b) Karl Marx
(c) Louis Althusser
(d) Michel Foucault

91. Who saw incest taboo as a positive injunction to marry outside the group?
(a) Levi Strauss (b) Murdock
(c) Morgan (d) Radcliffe Brown

92. Who has given the '"Functional Fit Theory' in his/her study on the family?
(a) Slyvia Walby
(b) Ann Oakley
(c) George Murdock
(d) Talcott Parsons

93. According to Robert K. Merton, _____ functions in a social structure are intended and obvious.
(a) Latent (b) Relative
(c) Manifest (d) Systematic

94. Select the four sets of institutional imperatives taken to comprise the ethos of modern science, as distinguished by R.K Merton?

1. Communism
2. Universalism
3. Dichotomy
4. Disinterestedness
5. Organized skepticism

Choose the correct option below:

(a) 1, 2, 3, and 4 only
(b) 2, 3, 4, and 5 only
(c) 1, 2, 4, and 5 only
(d) 1, 3, 4, and 5 only

95. Which among the following social actions is NOT classified by Talcott Parsons?

(a) Purposeful Action
(b) Cognitive Action
(c) Cathetic Action
(d) Evaluative Action

96. Who wrote '*On the Shoulders of Giants: A Shandean Postscript*'?

(a) Talcott Parsons
(b) Bronisław Malinowski
(c) A R. Radcliffe-Brown
(d) Robert K. Merton

97. Among the following, who stated that any object that can be subjected to structural-functional analysis must 'represent a standardized (patterned and repetitive) item'?

(a) T. Parsons
(b) R.K. Merton
(c) E Durkheim
(d) Jeffrey C. Alexander

98. Among the following, whose functional theory is based on social, cultural, and personality systems?

(a) Merton (b) Simmel
(c) Alexander (d) Parsons

99. Who has argued that a theoretical science of human society is possible like a natural science?

(a) A R. Radcliffe-Brown
(b) E E Evans-Pritchard
(c) A M. Carr-Saunders
(d) H.A Hodges

100. Who among the following has considered culture as essentially a response to human society?

(a) Redfield
(b) Radcliffe-Brown
(c) Malinowski
(d) Herskovits

Answer Key

1. (b) **2.** (b) **3.** (a) **4.** (c) **5.** (a) **6.** (c) **7.** (b) **8.** (c) **9.** (b) **10.** (b) **11.** (c) **12.** (b) **13.** (c) **14.** (c) **15.** (d)

16. (d) **17.** (c) **18.** (c) **19.** (c) **20.** (c) **21.** (d) **22.** (c) **23.** (d) **24.** (c) **25.** (d) **26.** (a) **27.** (c) **28.** (c) **29.** (d) **30.** (a)

31. (a) **32.** (d) **33.** (d) **34.** (a) **35.** (b) **36.** (b) **37.** (b) **38.** (c) **39.** (c) **40.** (d) **41.** (b) **42.** (d) **43.** (d) **44.** (a) **45.** (d)

46. (b) **47.** (d) **48.** (b) **49.** (a) **50.** (c) **51.** (c) **52.** (d) **53.** (a) **54.** (d) **55.** (a) **56.** (d) **57.** (a) **58.** (d) **59.** (a) **60.** (c)

61. (b) **62.** (b) **63.** (d) **64.** (d) **65.** (d) **66.** (b) **67.** (b) **68.** (c) **69.** (d) **70.** (b) **71.** (a) **72.** (a) **73.** (d) **74.** (d) **75.** (c)

76. (d) **77.** (d) **78.** (c) **79.** (a) **80.** (a) **81.** (d) **82.** (a) **83.** (c) **84.** (d) **85.** (d) **86.** (a) **87.** (d) **88.** (d) **89.** (b) **90.** (b)

91. (a) **92.** (d) **93.** (c) **94.** (c) **95.** (a) **96.** (d) **97.** (b) **98.** (d) **99.** (a) **100.** (c).

PREVIOUS YEARS' QUESTIONS

DECEMBER 2023

1. Ethnomethodology is concerned with

A. The study of ordinary people's method for making sense of and creating order in everyday life.

B. When people talk or act, they are constantly engaged in interpreting what is going on around them.

C. There is an inherent relationship between talk and action.

D. The study of social phenomena by using highly structured interviews of a very large sample size.

Choose the correct answer from the options given below:

(a) A, C and D only
(b) A, B and C only
(c) B, C and D only
(d) A, C and D only

2. Match List I with List II.

List I	List II
A. Historical-comparative method	I. Emile Durkheim
B. Comparative method	II. Karl Marx
C. Dialectical method	III. Max Weber
D. Neo-functionalism	IV J.C. Alexander

Choose the correct answer from the options given below:

(a) A-I, B-II, C-III, D-IV
(b) A-III, B-I, C-II, D-IV
(c) A-IV, B-III, C-I, D-II
(d) A-II, B-IV, C-III, D-I

3. Match List I with List II.

List I	List II
A. The Network Society	I. Zygmunt Bauman
B. Liquid modernity	II. Manuel Castells
C. Late modernity	III. Ulrich Beck
D. Reflexive modernity	IV. Anthony Giddens

Choose the correct answer from the options given below:

(a) A-II, B-I, C-IV, D-III
(b) A-I, B-II, C-III, D-IV
(c) A-III, B-IV, C-II, D-I
(d) A-IV, B-III, C-I, D-II

4. The normative response to disease, according to Talcott Parsons, is for an individual to assume the sick role. What are the characteristics of a sick role?

A. Illness suspends routine responsibilities.

B. A person's illness is not deliberate.

C. A sick person must want to get well soon.

D. A sick person must take care of himself/herself.

E. A sick person must adhere to doctor's advice.

Choose the correct answer from the options given below:

(a) A, B, D and E only
(b) A, B, C, D and E only
(c) A, C, D and E only
(d) A, B, C and E only

5. In which of the following works, did Marx write about 'The commodity form'?

(a) Das Kapital
(b) The German Ideology
(c) The Poverty of Philosophy
(d) The Class Struggle in France

6. Match List I with List II.

List I	List II
A. Sex and Repression in Savage Society	I. Claude Lévi-Strauss
B. The Andaman Islanders	II. B. Malinowski
C. The Savage Mind	III. Alfred R. Radcliff Brown
D. Social Structure and Personality	IV. Talcott Parsons

Choose the correct answer from the options given below:

(a) A-III, B-II, C-I, D-IV
(b) A-II, B-III, C-I, D-IV
(c) A-I, B-II, C-III, D-IV
(d) A-I, B-III, C-IV, D-II

7. In which year did Michael Foucault write his famous book, 'The History of Sexuality'?

(a) 1984
(b) 1993
(c) 1976
(d) 1980

8. Match List I with List II.

List I	List II
A. Freedom and Civilization (1944)	I. Levi-Strauss
B. Folk Culture of Yukatan (1941)	II. Robert Redfield
C. The Elementary Structure of Kinship (1949)	III. A.R. Redcliff-Brown
D. A Natural Science of Society (1948)	IV. Bronislaw Malinowski

Choose the correct answer from the options given below:

(a) A-I, B-II, C-III, D-IV
(b) A-IV, B-III, C-II, D-I
(c) A-III, B-II, C-I, D-IV
(d) A-IV, B-I, C-II, D-III

9. Who among the following sociologists belong to Frankfurt School of critical theory?

A. Anthony Giddens
B. Herbert Marcuse
C. M. Horkheimer
D. Eric Fromm

Choose the correct answer from the options given below:

(a) A, B and C only
(b) B, C and D only
(c) A, C and D only
(d) A, B and D only

10. According to B. Malinowski, which among the following are true about culture?

A. Culture is an instrument which enables man to secure his bio-psychic survival.
B. Culture is a super organic reality.
C. Culture helps mental and intellectual survival of man.
D. Each aspect of a culture is rooted in the needs of the human being.

Choose the most appropriate answer from the options given below:

(a) A, B and C only
(b) B, C and D only
(c) A, C and D only
(d) A and B only

11. 'Every society is divided into groupings and strata with distinctive life styles'. Who said this?

(a) Karl Marx
(b) Emile Durkheim
(c) Max Weber
(d) Thorstein Veblen

12. Match List I with List II.

List I	List II
A. Mythologies	I. B. Malinowski
B. A Scientific Theory of Culture	II. Claude Levi-Strauss
C. Taboo	III. Talcott Parsons
D. The Structure of Social Action	IV. Alfred R. Radcliffe-Brown

Choose the correct answer from the options given below:

(a) A-IV, B-I, C-II, D-III
(b) A-III, B-IV, C-II, D-I
(c) A-II, B-I, C-IV, D-III
(d) A-IV, B-III, C-II, D-I

13. A concept used by Manuel Castells to refer to processes of consumption of common goods promoted by the city, such as transport services and leisure amenities is called

(a) Control consumption.
(b) Collective consumption.
(c) Civil consumption.
(d) Comparative consumption.

14. Who is the author of the book, 'The Rise of the Network Society'?

(a) M. Crossley
(b) A. Mayer and S. L Puller
(c) Georg Simmer
(d) M. Castells

15. The concept of 'Timeless Time' was given by

(a) Scott Lash and John Urry
(b) David Held
(c) Manuel Castells
(d) Ulrich Beck

16. Who among the following sociologists wrote the book 'The Rules of Sociological Method'?

(a) Marx Weber
(b) Emile Durkheim
(c) Karl Marx
(d) August Comte

17. Which among the following are true according to Karl Mannheim about sociology of knowledge?

A. All knowledge and all ideas are bound to a location.
B. It refers to a theory of the social or existential conditioning of thought.
C. Ideas are rooted in different locations in historical time and social structure.
D. At times, a particular group can have full access to the understanding of a social phenomenon than other groups.
E. No group has total access to understanding of a social phenomenon.

Choose the correct answer from the options given below:

(a) B, C, D and E only
(b) A, B, C and D only
(c) A, B and C only
(d) A, B, C, D and E

18. What is the correct chronological sequence of the following books of Anthony Giddens?

A. The Consequences of Modernity
B. Capitalism and Modern Social Theory
C. New Rules of Sociological Method
D. Runaway World: How globalisation is shaping our lives

Choose the correct answer from the options given below:

(a) C, B, D, A
(b) A, C, B, D

(c) B, C, A, D
(d) A, B, C, D

19. What is the correct chronological sequence of Emile Durkheim's writings?
A. The Rules of Sociological Method.
B. The Division of Labour in Society.
C. The Elementary Forms of Religious Life
D. Suicide: A study in Sociology.
Choose the correct answer from the options given below:
(a) A, B, C, D
(b) B, A, D, C
(c) A, C, D, B
(d) D, A, C, B

20. Who gave the concept of 'time-space–distinction' in the context of the globalization and modernity?
(a) Jurgen Habermas
(b) Pierre Bourdieu
(c) Edward Said
(d) Anthony Giddens

21. Which book of Durkheim is devoted to a close and careful analysis of primitive religion?
(a) Moral Education
(b) The Elementary Forms of Religious Life
(c) Suicide
(d) The Division of Labour in Society

22. What is the chronological sequence of the following writings of C Levi-Strauss?
A. Structural Anthropology
B. The Savage Mind
C. The Elementary Structure of kinship
D. Introduction to a Science of Mythology
Choose the correct answer from the options given below:
(a) A, B, C, D
(b) C, A, B, D
(c) B, C, A, D
(d) D, A, C, B

23. Which among the following studies is the best example of comparative method?
(a) Mind, Self and Society (G.H. Mead)
(b) Ideology and Utopia (Karl Mannheim)
(c) Suicide (Emile Durkheim)
(d) The Communist Manifesto (Karl Marx and F. Engels)

JUNE 2023

24. Who among the following have not significantly contributed to the analyses of their contemporary capitalist society?
A. Karl Marx
B. A.R. Radcliffe-Brown
C. Max Weber
D. Claude Levi-Strass
E. Emile Durkheim
Choose the appropriate answer from the options given below:
(a) A, B, and D only
(b) B and D only
(c) A, E, and C only
(d) E and D only

25. Karl Marx identified various forms of divisions of labour as stages of development in history of Europe. Identify the correct sequence of these stages from the following:
A. Tribal
B. Barbarism
C. Ancient
D. Feudal
Choose the appropriate answer from the options given below:
(a) A, B, and C only
(b) B, A, and D only
(c) A, C, and D only
(d) B, C, and D only

26. Who among the following suggested a 'value reference' instead of 'value judgement' as methodology to have the status of sociology as objective science?
(a) Auguste Comte
(b) Vilfredo Pareto
(c) Emile Durkheim
(d) Max Weber

27. Who among the following scholars had used comparative method in their analysis?
A. Emile Durkheim
B. Herbert Spencer
C. Herbert Blumer
D. Max Weber
E. Rene Weber
Choose the appropriate answer from the options given below:
(a) A, D, and E only
(b) B, C, and E only
(c) C, D, and E only
(d) A, B, and D only

28. Match List I with List II

List I (Thinker)	List II (Concepts)
A. Max Weber	I. Rationality
B. George Simmel	II. Sociation
C. Thornstein Veblen	III. Conspicuous consumption
D. Dorothy S. Thomas	IV. Definition of the situation

Choose the correct answer from the options given below:

(a) A - I, B - II, C - III, D - IV
(b) A - II, B -III, C - IV, D - I
(c) A - III, B - IV, C - I, D - II
(d) A - IV, B - I, C - II, D - III

29. The famous book *The Theory of Communicative Action* is authored by

(a) Manuel Castells
(b) Jurgen Habernas
(c) Anthony Giddens
(d) Talcott Parsons

30. Match List I with List II:

List I (Name of social movements)	List II (States)
A. Anthony Giddens	i. One dimensional man
B. Alfred Schtuz	ii Ideal Speech situation
C. Jurgen Habermas	iii. Life world
D. Herbert Marcuse	iv. Juggernaut

Choose the correct answer from the options given below:

(a) A-iv, B- iii, C-ii, D-i
(b) A-iii, B-ii, C-i, D-iv
(c) A- ii, B- l, C-iv, D-iii
(d) A-i, B-iv, C-iii, D-ii

31. Which among the following is not a mode of motivational orientation according to Talcott Parsons?

(a) Cognitive (b) Moral
(c) Cathectic (d) Evaluative

32. Who among the following sociologists wrote the book, *The Religion of India: The Sociology of Hinduism and Buddhism*?

(a) Karl Marx (b) Max Muller
(c) Max Weber (d) B. Malinowski

33. Who of the following social scientists developed the idea of reflexive society?

A. C. W. Mills B. G. M. Mead
C. P. Bourdieu D. A. Giddens
E. E. Goffman

Choose the correct answer from the codes given below:

(a) Only A and B
(b) Only B and C
(c) Only C and D
(d) Only D and E

34. What was a key theoretical promise in Edward Said's discussion on Orientalism?

A. Archeology of knowledge
B. Archeology of residence
C. Archeology of marriage
D. Archeology of power
E. Archeology of relationships

Choose the correct answer from the options given below:

(a) A and B only (b) B and C only
(c) C and D only (d) A and D only

35. According to Marx, the sequence of progression of society was:

A. Capitalism
B. Feudalism
C. Socialism
D. Ancient Society
E. Communism

Choose the correct answer from the options given below:

(a) E, D, C, B, A (b) A, B, C, D, E
(c) D, B, A, C, E (d) E, A, C, D

36. Habermas identified which one of the following types of capitalist societies?

A. Conservative capitalism
B. Liberal capitalism
C. Organized capitalism of western industrial societies
D. Unorganized capitalism of Third World societies
E. Post capitalism of state socialist societies

Choose the appropriate answer from the options given below:

(a) A, B, and C only (b) B, C, and D only
(c) C, E, and D only (d) B, C, and E only

37. Match List I with List II

List I (Authors)	List II (Books)
A. E. Durkheim	I. The Structure of Social Action
B. F. Engels	II. The Rules of Sociological Method
C. R.K. Merton	III. The Origin of the Family, Private Property and the State
D. T. Parsons	IV. Social Theory and Social Structure

Choose the correct answer from the options given below:

(a) A- III, B- IV, C-I, D-II
(b) A- IV, B- I, C-II, D-III
(c) A- I, B-II, C-III, D-IV
(d) A- II, B- III, C-IV, D-I

38. Who among the following argues on the duality of the structure?

(a) A. Giddens
(b) M. Foucault
(c) J. Derrida
(d) F. Lyotard

39. Given below are two statements:

Statement I: Marx, Simmel and Dahrendorf are major theorists of conflict perspective.

Statement II: Max Weber was the first to offer a definitional description of conflict by treating it as a form of social relationship.
In the light of the above statements, choose the most appropriate answer from the options given below
(a) Both Statement I and Statement II are correct
(b) Both statement I and Statement II are incorrect
(c) Statement I is correct and Statement II is incorrect
(d) Statement I is incorrect and Statement II is correct

40. Radha Kamal Mukherjee does not offer an alternative world view of sociology from which one of the following philosophical traditions?
(a) Vedanta
(b) Buddhism
(c) Zorostrian
(d) Taoism

41. The game of Tic-Tac-Toe, as referred by M. Lynch is closely related with which phenomenon?
(a) Queer Theory
(b) Fordism
(c) Breaching experiments
(d) McDonaldization

42. Match List I with List II

List I (Theory/ Contribution)	List II (Theorists)
A. Dramaturgical	I. Alfred Schutz
B. Post modernism	II. Michel Foucault
C. Symbolic interactionism	III. Erving Goffman
D. Phenomenology	IV. Herbert Blumer

Choose the correct answer from the options given below:
(a) A - IV, B - III, C - I, D - II
(b) A - III, B - IV, C - II, D - I
(c) A - II, B - III, C - IV, D - I
(d) A - III, B - II, C - IV, D - I

43. Given below are two statements: one is labelled as Assertion A and the other is labelled as Reason R.
Assertion A: According to Talcott Parsons, an action is an actor's orientation towards a situation.
Reason R: According to Max Black, orientation towards a situation is not exactly action, but an attitude towards a situation.
In the light of the above statements, choose the correct answer from the options given below:
(a) Both A and R are true and R is the correct explanation of A
(b) Both A and R are true but R is Not the correct explanation of A
(c) A is true but R is false
(d) A is false but R is true

44. Who among the following gave the essential idea of explaining individual phenomena by the state of collectivity, and not state of collectivity by individual phenomena?
(a) Karl Marx
(b) Max Weber
(c) Auguste Comte
(d) Emile Durkheim

45. Which of the following basic institutions was not discussed by Anthony Giddens in defining modernity?
(a) Capitalism
(b) Military Power
(c) Education
(d) Industrialism

46. According to Malinowski, while studying diffusion at the field level, one is to focus on which one of the following units of transformation?
(a) Cultural traits
(b) Role sets
(c) Status sets
(d) Organized systems or institutions

47. Who among the following sociologists in India applied the theoretical insights of Claude Levi-Strauss in studying structure and cognition in Hindu society?
(a) M.N. Srinivas
(b) Mckim Marriott
(c) S.C. Dube
(d) Veena Das

48. What causes the change from mechanical solidarity to organic solidarity according to Durkheim?
(a) Dynamic density
(b) Population density
(c) Static density
(d) Fluctuating density

49. Which one of the following forms of authority expounded by Max Weber is not a form of traditional authority?
(a) Patriarchal household
(b) Bureaucracy
(c) Feudalism
(d) Patrimonialism

50. Who among the following established the relationship between power, ideology, and discourse in relation to modern organizations?
(a) M. Foucault
(b) F. Fukoyama
(c) K. Mannheim
(d) M. Castells

51. To Talcott Parsons, the unit act of social system includes:
A. Acts
B. Ends
C. Situations
D. Beliefs
E. Means
Choose the appropriate answer from the options given below:
(a) A and B only
(b) A, B, and C only
(c) B, C, and D only
(d) A, B, C, and E only

52. In the maximum calculation of organic composition of capital, which of the following are calculated?
(a) Constant capital and surplus value
(b) Constant capital and variable capital
(c) Variable capital and profit
(d) Profit and surplus value

53. Who among the following saw the gaze as a kind of language, a language without words?
(a) Randall Collins
(b) Michel Foucault
(c) Pierre Bourdieu
(d) Jurgen Habermas

54. Arrange the concepts associated with classical sociologists in chronological order:
A. Exploitation
B. Rationality
C. Solidarity
D. Positivism
Choose the correct answer from the options given below:
(a) D, A, C, B
(b) C, B, D, A
(c) A, C, D, B
(d) B, D, C, A

55. According to Merton, the unintended and unrecognized functions are called _____
(a) Manifest function
(b) Latent function
(c) Dysfunction
(d) Eufunction

56. Arrange the works of Anthony Giddens in chronological order:
A. The Third Way: The Renewal of Social Democracy
B. The Global Third Way Debate
C. The Constitution of Society
D. The Transformation of Intimacy: Love, Sexuality and Eroticism in Modem Societies
Choose the correct answer from the options given below:
(a) B, C, A, D
(b) D, A, B, C
(c) C, D, A, B
(d) A, B, C, D

57. Whose sociology had outlined a method for the study of ideas as functions of Social involvement?
(a) Karl Mannheim
(b) Karl Marx
(c) Karl Pearson
(d) Gunnar Myrdal

MARCH 2023

58. Arrange the following works chronologically:
A. The Postmodern Condition
B. Economy and Society
C. The Division of Labour in Society
D. The German Ideology
E. The Culture Industry: Enlightenment as Mass Deception
Choose the correct answer from the options given below:
(a) A, D, C, B, E
(b) B, A, E, C, D
(c) D, C, B, E, A
(d) E, D, B, C, A

59. Which of the following statements are correct about Karl Mannheim?
A. Mannheim has sketched the broad contours of the sociology of knowledge.
B. Mannheim's procedure and substantive findings clarify relations between knowledge and social structure.
C. Mannheim argued that Marx created the prototype of the sociology of knowledge.
D. Mannheim has not written the book 'Ideology & Utopia'.
E. According to Mannheim, the sociology of knowledge can lead to the 'Scientific guidance of Political life'.
Choose the correct answer from the options given below:
(a) A, B, C, and D only
(b) A, B, and D only
(c) A, B, C, D, and E
(d) A, B, C, and E only

60. Who wrote the book *The Transformation of Intimacy*?
(a) P. Bourdieu
(b) U. Beck
(c) J. Baudrillard
(d) A. Giddens

61. According to Talcott Parsons, two main functions of family are
A. Primary socialization.
B. Personality stabilization.

C. Religious harmonization.
D. Property mobilization.
E. Conflict neutralization.
Choose the correct answer from the options given below:
(a) A and E only
(b) B and D only
(c) C and D only
(d) A and B only

62. On which of the following set of assumptions is Parsonian view based on?
A. Systems have the property of order and interdependence of parts.
B. Systems tend toward self-maintaining order or equilibrium.
C. The System may be static or involved in an ordered process of change.
D. Systems maintain boundaries with their environments.
E. The nature of one part of the system has an impact on the form that the other parts can take.
Choose the correct answer from the options given below:
(a) A and B only
(b) B, C, and D only
(c) A, B, C, D, and E only
(d) A and C only

63. Which of the following are correct for Labelling theory, which is a dominant paradigm in the explanation of deviance?
A. Labelling theory is used interchangeably with the 'societal reaction theory'.
B. Julia Kristeva is an important contributor to this theory.
C. M.G. Sumner's concept 'folkways' is a central concept in labelling theory.
D. Labelling theory was significantly influenced by the Chicago School.
E. It has also been influenced by radical criminologists.
Choose the correct answer from the options given below:
(a) A only
(b) A and D only
(c) A, B, and C only
(d) B, C, D, and E only

64. Given below are two statements:
Statement I: Ambedkar asserted that for the emancipation of scheduled castes, they should come forward and assert for their own cause.
Statement II: Ambedkar wanted to liberate Dalits by building an egalitarian social order and suggested to them a mantra: educate, organize, and agitate.
In light of the above statements, choose the correct answer from the options given below:
(a) Both Statement I and Statement II are true.
(b) Both Statement I and Statement II are false.
(c) Statement I is true but Statement II is false.
(d) Statement I is false but Statement II is true.

65. Bourdieu developed an idea of socialization through the concept of 'Habitus'.
Habitus includes:
A. Skills and the ways of looking at the world.
B. Human capacities and opportunities embodied in forms of capital.
C. Habitus posits and bestows specific properties.
D. The process of making Habitus does not begin in the family setting.
E. Bourdieu opined that all classes possess the same Habitus.
Choose the correct answer from the options given below:
(a) A, B, and C only
(b) D and E only
(c) A, D, and E only
(d) B and E only

66. Match List I with List II

List I	List II
A. E. Durkheim	I. New Rules of Sociological Method
B. A. Giddens	II. The Rules of Sociological Method
C. M. Foucault	III. The Archaeology of Knowledge
D. N. Fairclough	IV. Critical Discourse Analysis: The Critical Study of Language

Choose the correct answer from the options given below:
(a) A - III, B - II, C - I, D - IV
(b) A - II, B - I, C - IV, D - III
(c) A - II, B - I, C - III, D - IV
(d) A - III, B - II, C - IV, D - I

67. Arrange the following works of Max Weber in sequential order.
A. The Religion of China
B. Ancient Judaism
C. Economy and Society
D. The Protestant Ethic and the Spirit of Capitalism
E. The Religion of India
Choose the correct answer from the options given below.
(a) A, B, C, D, E
(b) A, B, D, E, C
(c) B, A, C, D, E
(d) D, A, E, B, C

68. Emile Durkheim's concept of 'Anomie' predominantly appeared in his works:

A. Suicide.
B. The Rules of Sociological Method.
C. The Elementary Forms of the Religious Life.
D. The Division of Labour in Society.
E. Moral Education.

Choose the correct answer from the options given below:

(a) A, B, and C only
(b) A and D only
(c) B, C, and D only
(d) D and E only

69. Given below are two statements:

Statement I: Critical discourse analysis (CDA) emphasizes the role of language as a power resource that is related to ideology arid socio-cultural change.
Statement II: CDA draws in particular on the theories and approaches of Foucault

In the light of the above statements, choose the most appropriate answer from the options given below:

(a) Both Statement I and Statement II are correct.
(b) Both Statement I and Statement II are incorrect.
(c) Statement I is correct but Statement II is incorrect.
(d) Statement I is incorrect but Statement II is correct.

70. Match List I with List II

List I (Thinkers)	List II (Theories)
A. Pierre Bourdieu	I. Phenomenological approach
B. Anthony Giddens	II. Theory of social capital
C. Erving Goffman	III. Theory of structuration
D. Alfred Schutz	IV. Dramaturgical approach

Choose the correct answer from the options given below:

(a) A - III, B - II, C - I, D - IV
(b) A - IV, B - I, C - II, D - III
(c) A - II, B - III, C - IV, D - I
(d) A - I, B - IV, C - II, D - III

71. Mention the manuscripts of Marx which were published after his death.

A. The Poverty of Philosophy
B. The Communist Manifesto
C. The Economic and Philosophic Manuscripts
D. The Eighteenth Brumaire of Louis Bonaparte
E. Grundrisse

Choose the correct answer from the options given below:

(a) A, B, and C only
(b) C and E only
(c) B and C only
(d) A, C, and D only

72. Who among the following was influenced by Foucault's ideas of Body Self, Society and Power?

(a) Jeremy Bentham
(b) Bryan S. Turner
(c) Ferdinand de Saussure
(d) Theodor Adorno

73. Match List I with List II

List I (Work)	List II (Scholar)
A. Kinship Organization in India	I. M.N. Srinivas
B. Caste, Class and Occupation	II. M.K. Gandhi
C. Caste in Modern India and Other Essays	III. Irawati Karve
D. Hind Swaraj	IV. G.S. Ghurye

Choose the correct answer from the options given below:

(a) A - III, B – IV, C – I, D - II
(b) A - II, B - I, C - IV, D - III
(c) A - IV, B - II, C - III, D - I
(d) A - II, B - IV, C - III, D - I

74. Who has talked about Communicative Action?

(a) Pierre Bourdieu
(b) Manuel Castells
(c) Jurgen Habermas
(d) None of these

75. Who gave the concept of 'I' and 'Me '?

(a) Radcliffe-Brown
(b) Alfred Schutz
(c) Erving Goffman
(d) G. H. Mead

76. 'Indian Sadhus' is an excellent sociography written by:

(a) M.N. Srinivas
(b) B.R. Ambedkar
(c) G.S. Ghurye
(d) Radha Kamal Mukerjee

77. Anthony Giddens has talked about

(a) Neutral space
(b) Time-space distanciation
(c) Placeless space
(d) All of these

78. Alfred Schutz's approach falls in the philosophical tradition of

(a) Ethnomethodology
(b) Phenomenology
(c) Dramaturgical perspective
(d) Symbolic interactionism

79. Malinowski did his anthropological field work among

(a) Trobriand Islanders
(b) Andaman Islanders

(c) Tutuila Islanders
(d) Ionian Islanders

80. Which of the following statement/statements is/are true?
A. Durkheim did not believe that Gods are man-made symbols of society.
B. Durkheim thought that all religions originated in totemism.
C. Durkheim studied the religious practices of African tribes.
D. Durkheim offered a theological explanation of religion.
E. Durkheim did not believe that the tribe (aborigin) he studied represented a stage of evolution that every society should pass.
Choose the correct answer from the options given below:
(a) A only
(b) B only
(c) C and E only
(d) D only

81. The intended and recognized consequences of social action upon other social actors or institutions is
(a) Latent function
(b) Dysfunction
(c) Manifest function
(d) All of the above

Read the following passage carefully and answer the question that follows:

The thinking of early sociologists was dominated by a conception of man and society seen progressing up definite steps of evolution leading through ever greater complexity to some final stage of perfection. The general evolutionary model of society is represented by a large number of specific theories. Comte, for example, delineated three great stages through which all societies must go—those of conquest, defense, and industry. For each, he enunciated a parallel step in the development of man which he conceived as progressing from the theological through the metaphysical to arrive ultimately at the perfection of Comte's own Positive Philosophy. While Spencer's scheme of evolution was much less grandiose, he too took the position that sociology is 'the study of evolution in its most complex form.'

The evolutionary model treated society as if there were an imminence inherent in man's social development which requires that each stage appears in turn to play its role according to 'natural law'. This concept understandably tempted the promulgators of social philosophies to capture the evolutionary theory and use it in support of their political positions. The American sociologist William Graham Sumner, for example, justified the privileges of the advantaged classes over the disadvantaged, on the grounds that such differentiation was a law of nature in keeping with the principle of the survival of the fittest. Sumner, who has been labelled a 'Social Darwinist', used the idea of evolution, as had Spencer, to block efforts at reform and social change, arguing that social evolution must follow its course, dictated by nature. 'That is why', he said, 'it is the greatest folly of which a man can be capable, to sit down with a slate and pencil to plan out a new social world.'

82. For William Graham Sumner, the law of nature based on the survival of the fittest justifies:
(a) Privilege of the disadvantaged over advantaged
(b) Privilege of the advantaged over disadvantaged
(c) Equality between advantaged and disadvantaged
(d) None of the above

83. The thinking of early sociologists was dominated by a conception of man and society seen progressing up definite steps of evolution leading to:
(a) Greater independence and superiority
(b) Greater dependence and complexity
(c) Greater complexity and perfection
(d) None of the above

84. According to whom, sociology is the study of evolution in its most complex form?
(a) Comte
(b) Spencer
(c) Sumner
(d) All of the above

85. Who has been labelled a 'Social Darwinist'?
(a) Sumner
(b) Spencer
(c) Both of the above
(d) None of the above

86. According to which scholar, all societies must go through the stages of conquest, defense, and industry?
(a) Durkheim
(b) Marx
(c) Comte
(d) Weber

DEC 2021 & JUNE 2022

87. The most systematic general theory of cultural reproduction is given by:
(a) Karl Mannheim
(b) Pierre Bourdieu
(c) Auguste Comte
(d) Durkheim

88. Which of the following constitute(s) an important methodological component(s) in Foucault's works?
A. Discipline and Punish
B. The History of Sexuality
C. Madness and Civilisation
D. The Archaeology of Knowledge
E. The Order of Things

Choose the correct answer from the options given below:

(a) A and B only
(b) D only
(c) C, D and E only
(d) D and E only.

89. Match List-I with List-II

List I (Thinkers)	List II (Concepts)
A. Alfred Schutz	I. Stigma
B. Erving Goffman	II. Field
C. Jürgen Habermas	III. Recipe
D. Pierre Bourdieu	IV. Communicative Action

Choose the correct answer from the options given below:

(a) A - I, B - III, C - II, D - IV
(b) A - IV, B - I, C - III, D - II
(c) A - III, B - I, C - IV, D - II
(d) A - II, B - IV, C - III, D – I

90. There are two levels of meanings which are implicit in Sanskritization. These are:
(a) Historical specific and contextual specific
(b) Contextual specific and culture specific
(c) Historical specific and culture specific
(d) None of the above

91. Given below are two statements

Statement I: Karl Marx, Max Weber and Michel Foucault are the most influential figures in an intellectual movement known as post-structuralism.

Statement II: Michel Foucault has had immense influence on social sciences.

In light of the above statements, choose the correct answer from the options given below:

(a) Both Statement I and Statement II are correct
(b) Both Statement I and Statement II are incorrect
(c) Statement I is correct but Statement II is incorrect
(d) Statement I is incorrect but Statement II is correct

92. Who had given the concept of "modes of individual adaptation"?
(a) E. Durkheim (b) T. Parsons
(c) R. K. Merton (d) P. Blau

93. Who is known as the "Bourgeois Marx"?
(a) Emile Durkheim
(b) Max Weber
(c) Talcott Parsons
(d) Georg simmel

94. Who wrote the book, 'Caste and Race in India' ?
(a) A. R. Desai
(b) G. S. Ghurye
(c) Louis Dumont
(d) None of the above

95. Match List-I with List-II:

List I (Thinkers)	List II (Work)
A. G.H. Mead	I. Structuration
B. E. Goffman	II. Governmentality
C. M. Foucault	III. Symbolic interactionism
D. A. Giddens	IV. Total institutions

Choose the correct answer from the options given below:

(a) A - IV, B - I, C - II, D - III
(b) A - III, B - IV, C - I, D - II
(c) A - III, B - IV, C - II, D - I
(d) A - II, B - I, C - IV, D - II

96. Which sociologist coined the concept, "social relationship" to describe patterned human interaction which is intentional, meaningful and symbolic?
(a) C. H. Cooley
(b) Erving Goffman
(c) Max Weber
(d) V. Pareto

97. Chronologically arrange the following schools of thought as they appeared in the history of Sociology.
A. Positivism
B. Symbolic interactionism
C. Postmodernism
D. Functionalism
E. Structuralism

Choose the correct answer from the options given below

(a) A, E, B, D, C
(b) D, A, C, B, E
(c) A, D, E, B, C
(d) D, B, A, C, E

98. Who has classified action into logical and nonlogical action?
(a) Max Weber (b) T. Parsons
(c) V. Pareto (d) None of the above

99. "The generalised elsewhere" has been given by:
(a) G. H. Mead
(b) Alex Inkeles
(c) T. B. Bottomore
(d) Joshua Meyrowitz

JUNE 2021

100. Which one of the following is NOT correct according to Marx?
(a) Political economy conceals the estrangement inherent in the nature of labour by not consid-

ering the direct relationship between the worker (labour) and production.
(b) The direct relationship of labour to its products is the relationship of the worker to the objects of his production.
(c) Labour is external to the worker
(d) Life activity and productive life for labour is to maintain a luxurious life.

101. Distinct economic systems that are characterized by a specific set of relations of production combined with forms of productive forces is called:
(a) Means of production
(b) Instruments of production
(c) Mode of production
(d) Relations of production

102. 'All truths are ideologically biased, all truths ultimately reflect the interest and biases of social groups', whose views are these?
(a) Karl Marx (b) Karl Mannheim
(c) Charles Lemert (d) Clifford Geertz

103. Which book on research methodology was written by Emile Durkheim that is considered one of his first works?
(a) Methods in Social Research
(b) Research Methods in Social Relations
(c) Rules of Sociological Method
(d) Research Methodology in Social Sciences

104. Who emphasized the significance of the dialectical model in studying rural society?
(a) A. B. Mukherji
(b) Ramkrishna Mukherjee
(c) Sudipta Mukherjee/
(d) P. N. Mukherji

105. Which village was studied by Andre Beteille in his work on 'Caste, Class and Power'?
(a) Sripuram
(b) Rampura
(c) Mohana
(d) Kumbapettai

106. Among the earlier industrial sociologists, who has written the book, Social Framework of an Indian Factory?
(a) E. A. Ramaswamy
(b) G. S. Ghurye
(c) N. R. Sheth
(d) Sharat K. Bhaumik

107. Who has written the book 'Urbanization and Family Change' in the Indian context?
(a) S .C. Dube (b) Irawati Karve
(c) M. S. Gore (d) A. M. Shah

108. Levi-Strauss interpreted the sign systems of 'Primitive Culture' examining everything from the ________
(a) Kinship structure
(b) Caste structure
(c) Class structure
(d) Racial system

109. Who is the author of "Myth and Meaning"?
(a) B. Malinowski
(b) Claude Levi-Strauss
(c) S. F. Nadal
(d) A. R. Radcliffe-Brown

110. Who gave the concept of plastic sexuality?
(a) Ulrich Beck
(b) Zygmunt Bauman
(c) Anthony Giddens
(d) David Matthew

111. According to Manuel Castells, Informational Revolution is:
A. A new social order
B. A network society
C. Legitimation crisis
Choose the correct answer from the options given below:
(a) A and B only
(b) C only
(c) B and C only
(d) A and C only

112. Michel Foucault has used which of the following concepts?
A. Governmentality and Bio-politics
B. Bio-politics and Lifeworld
C. Sovereignty and Discipline
D. Archeology of Discourse and Solidarity
Choose the correct answer from the options given below:
(a) A and C only
(b) A and B only
(c) B and C only
(d) A and D only

113. Clifford Geertz's framework of Symbolic Anthropology accepts which of the following?
A. Conception of culture in the non-semiotic form
B. Prime attention to the role of symbols in constructing the public meaning
C. Analysis of culture is on an experimental basis
D. Symbolic forms by which men communicate, perpetuate and develop their knowledge about and attitudes towards life
E. Role of anthropologists to interpret the guiding symbols of each culture
Choose the correct answer from the options given below:
(a) A, B and C only
(b) B, C and D only
(c) B, D and E only
(d) C, D and E only

114. Which of the following characteristics of the caste system were NOT emphasized by G. S. Ghurye?

A. Segmental division
B. Hierarchy
C. Open system
D. Achieved
E. Pollution and purity

Choose the correct answer from the options given below:

(a) A and B only
(b) B and E only
(c) C and D only
(d) A and E only

115. Which among the following are NOT the works of Irawati Karve?

A. Hindu society: An interpretation
B. Hierarchy and Marriage Alliance in South India
C. Religious Consciousness
D. Kinship Organization in India
E. Yuganta: The End of an Epoch

Choose the correct answer from the options given below:

(a) A and D only (b) B and C only
(c) D and E only (d) A and C only

116. Which of the following aspect(s) is/are NOT associated with the works of M. N. Srinivas?

A. Statistical-view of caste
B. Field-view of caste
C. Functional unity of caste

Choose the correct answer from the options given below:

(a) A only
(b) B only
(c) C only
(d) B and C only

117. Match List I with List II

List I (Thinkers)	List II (Works)
A. Radha Kamal Mukherji	I. Buddha and Karl Marx
B. G.S. Ghurye	II. Village, Caste, Gender and Method
C. B.R. Ambedkar	III. The Land Problems of India
D. M.N. Srinivas	IV. Social Tensions in India

Choose the correct answer from the options given below:

(a) A–III, B–IV, C–I, D–II
(b) A–II, B–IV, C–I, D–III
(c) A–I, B–IV, C–III, D–II
(d) A–IV, B–II, C–III, D–I

118. Match List I with List II

List I (Concepts)	List II (Sociologists)
A. Proletariat	I. W. H. Wiser
B. Spirit of Capitalism	II. Emilie Dukheim
C. Division of Labour	III. Karl Marx
D. Exchange (Jajmani system)	IV. Max Weber

Choose the correct answer from the options given below:

(a) A–I, B–II, C–III, D–IV
(b) A–II, B–III, C–IV, D–I
(c) A–III, B–IV, C–II, D–I
(d) A–IV, B–I, C–II, D–III

119. Give the correct chronological sequence of the works of B . R. Ambedkar.

A. Who Were the Shudras?
B. Annihilation of Caste
C. Castes in India: Their Mechanism, Genesis and Development
D. The Untouchables: Who Were They and Why They Became Untouchable

Choose the correct answer from the options given below

(a) D, C, A, B
(b) C, B, A, D
(c) A, B, C, D
(d) B, D, A, C

120. Arrange the following functionalists in chronological order as they have contributed

A. A . R. Radcliffe Brown
B. B . Malinowski
C. E . Durkheim
D. R. K. Merton
E. Talcott Parsons

Choose the correct answer from the options given below

(a) B, C, A, D, E
(b) A, D, B, C, E
(c) C, B, A, E, D
(d) B, A, C, D, E

121. Arrange the writings of Durkheim in chronological order

A. Moral Education
B. The Division of Labour
C. The Rules of Sociological Method
D. Suicide
E. The Elementary Forms of The Religious Life

Choose the correct answer from the options given below

(a) D, E, C, B, A
(b) C, B, E, A, D
(c) B, C, D, E, A
(d) A, C, D, B, E

122. Given below are two statements

Statement I: According to A. Schutz, the world of everyday life is not permeated by the epoch of the natural attitude

Statement II: All the objects of the Social World are constituted within a framework of familiarity and pre-acquaintanceship

In light of the above statements, choose the most appropriate answer from the options given below

(a) Both Statement I and Statement II are correct
(b) Both Statement I and Statement II are incorrect
(c) Statement I is correct but Statement II is incorrect
(d) Statement I is incorrect but Statement II is correct

JUNE 2020

123. Concept of a runaway world is used by
(a) Anthony Giddens
(b) Pierre Bourdieu
(c) Jurgen Habermas
(d) Manuel Castells

124. Who was the first one to use case materials in his comparative studies of different cultures?
(a) William Healey
(b) Fredrick Leplay
(c) Herbert Spencer
(d) August Comte

125. Who has used the term 'Serendipity in sociological research?
(a) R.K. Merton
(b) J. Galtung
(c) Karl Popper
(d) C. Selltiz

126. Who is of the view that incest taboo enables relationships with wider society?
(a) C. Levi-Strauss
(b) H. Spencer
(c) K. Gough
(d) E. Westermarck

127. According to Goffman when passers-by glance at one another quickly and then look away again, it is called
(a) Disengagement
(b) Interaction
(c) Symbolic interaction
(d) Civil inattention

128. Who is regarded as the leading scholar of 'symbolic anthropology?
(a) Clifford Geertz
(b) Alfred Schutz
(c) G.H. Mead
(d) Karl Mannheim

129. Mead delineates three stages in which the concept of self-arises and develops; the stage of imitative acts, the play stage and the
(a) Skill stage
(b) Adult stage
(c) Game stage
(d) Infant stage

130. The transformation of time in, modern society in the form of timelessness was emphasized by which scholar?
(a) Marshall McLuhan
(b) David Harvey
(c) Manuel Castells
(d) Anthony Giddens

131. Who has systematically undertaken the influence of politics on science in his study of the sociology of science?
(a) Emile Durkheim
(b) A.R. Radcliffe-Brown
(c) R.K. Merton
(d) T.B. Bottomore

132. According to R.K. Merton, Manifest functions are:
(a) Partially intended and recognized
(b) Intended and recognized
(c) Not intended and not recognized
(d) Partially intended and partially recognized

133. Malinowski's functionalism is often termed as
(a) Individualistic functionalism
(b) Collective functionalism
(c) Fundamental functionalism
(d) Psychological functionalism

134. Radcliffe-Brown did not distinguish between social structure and
(a) Social system
(b) Social cognition
(c) Social relations
(d) Social conflict

135. The Doctoral thesis of Dr. Ambedkar is entitled as:
(a) Ancient Indian Commerce
(b) State and minorities: Annihilation of caste
(c) Commercial Relations of India
(d) The problem of Rupee: Its origin and its solution

136. Who said that 'tribals should be assimilated into Hindu caste'?
(a) Verrier Elwin
(b) G.S. Ghurye
(c) Surajit Sinha
(d) N.K. Bose

137. Who is the author of '*Yuganta: The End of an Epoch*'?
(a) David G. Mandelbaum
(b) G.S. Ghurye
(c) Irawati Karve
(d) Leela Dube

138. The main works of Karl Marx were:
1. Dictionary of Marxist Thought
2. Power: A Radical View
3. Grundrisse
4. Class and class conflict in Industrial Society
5. A contribution to a critique of political economy

Choose the correct answer from the options given below:
(a) 3 and 5 only
(b) 1 and 4 only
(c) 4 and 5 only
(d) 2 and 4 only

139. Who among the following, has used the comparative method in their studies?
1. Emile Durkheim
2. B. Malinowski
3. A.R. Radcliffe-Brown
4. Max Weber

Choose the most appropriate answer from the options given below:
(a) 1, 2 and 3 only
(b) 2, 3 and 4 only
(c) 1, 3 and 4 only
(d) 2, 3 and 1 only

140. According to R.K. Merton, which of the following constitutes the 'ethos of science'?
1. Organised skeptism
2. Interestedness
3. Universalism
4. Communalism
5. Cognitivism

Choose the most appropriate answer from the options given below:
(a) 1, 2, 3 only
(b) 5, 3, 1 only
(c) 1, 3, 4 only
(d) 3, 4, 5 only

141. The works of P. Bourdieu were
1. The Rules and Network in society
2. The State Nobility
3. Economy and Society
4. Distinction
5. Raw and cooked

Choose the most appropriate answer from the options given below:
(a) 2 and 4 only
(b) 1 and 3 only
(c) 5 and 2 only
(d) 1 and 4 only

142. Match List I with List II:

List I (Social Thinkers)	List II (Concepts)
A. M. Castells	I. Binary Oppositions
B. M. Foucault	II. Networking Logic
C. Levi-Strauss	III. Plastic Sexuality
D. A. Giddens	IV. Panoptical Surveillance

Choose the correct answer from the options given below:

	A	B	C	D
(a)	II	IV	III	I
(b)	II	IV	I	III
(c)	IV	I	II	III
(d)	III	IV	I	II

143. Talcott Parsons has given the following functions of the social system:
1. Integrative Function
2. Adaptation Function
3. Latency Function
4. Goal Attainment Function

Choose the correct sequence from the options given below:
(a) 3, 4, 1, 2
(b) 1, 2, 3, 4
(c) 4, 3, 1, 2
(d) 2, 4, 1, 3

144. Choose the correct chronological sequence of Yogendra Singh's books:
1. Culture change in India: Identity and globalization
2. Essays on Modernization
3. Modernization of Indian Tradition
4. Ideology and theory in Indian Sociology
5. Social Stratification and social change

Choose the correct sequence from the options given below:
(a) 1, 3, 5, 4, 2
(b) 3, 4, 1, 5, 2
(c) 3, 2, 5, 1, 4
(d) 2, 3, 1, 5, 4

145. Arrange the works of G.S. Ghurye chronologically:
1. Two Brahamanical Institutions: Gotra and Charan
2. Religious Consciousness
3. Social Tensions in India
4. Indian Sadhus
5. Mahadev Kolis

Choose the sequence from the options given below:
(a) 4, 1, 2, 3, 5
(b) 1, 5, 3, 2, 4
(c) 5, 4, 2, 3, 1
(d) 3, 5, 1, 2, 4

146. Given below are two statements: One is labelled as Assertion A and the other is labelled as Reason R.

Assertion (A): To Merton, Middle range theory is concerned with a limited range of data.

Reasons (R): In the sociological work of the few past decades there has been much less concern with the construction of all-embracing theories.

In light of the above statements, choose the most appropriate answer from the options given below:

(a) Both (A) and (R) are correct and R is the correct explanation of A
(b) Both (A) and (R) are correct but R is not the correct explanation of A
(c) (A) is correct but (R) is not correct
(d) (A) is not correct but (R) is correct

DECEMBER 2019

147. Any signifier which signifies a concept or meaning the signified, is called
(a) Object (b) Image
(c) Sign (d) Symbol

148. Who has written the book 'Social background of Indian Nationalism'?
(a) T.K. Oommen (b) R.S. Misra
(c) A.R. Desai (d) D.N. Dhanagare

149. From among the classical sociologists, who have used the comparative method but in different ways?
A. Emile Durkheim
B. Karl Marx
C. Max Weber
D. Auguste Comte

Choose the correct option:
(a) B and C (b) C and D
(c) D and A (d) A and C

150. Which two of the following principles explain the Alliance theory?
A. Principle of reciprocity
B. Rules of Exogamy
C. Rules of Endogamy
D. Incest taboos

Choose the correct option:
(a) (A) and (B)
(b) (B) and (C)
(c) (C) and (D)
(d) (A) and (D)

151. Who is the author of the book '*The Religion of Java*'?
(a) Erving Goffman
(b) Manuel Castells
(c) Clifford Geertz
(d) Claude Levi-Strauss

152. Who among the following viewed status as an 'effective claim to social esteem'?
(a) R. Linton (b) H. Maine
(c) M. Weber (d) R.K. Merton

153. Who among the following has said, that the caste system has organic links with the tribal cultur in India?
(a) G.S. Ghurye (b) Verier Elwin
(c) W.V. Gingson (d) T.B. Naik

154. The stages in the development of property according to Marx can broadly be classified as
(a) Classless society, primitive communism, class differentiation, and inequality
(b) Class differentiation and Inequality, classless society, primitive communism
(c) Primitive communism, classless society, class differentiation, and inequality
(d) Primitive communism, class differentiation, and inequality, classless society

155. Match List I with List II

List I (Method)	List II (Sociologist)
A. Indirect experiment	I. A. Schultz
B. Participant observation	II. W. Dilthey
C. Phenomenology	III. Emile Durkheim
D. Evolving typology of culture	IV. B. Malinowski

Choose the correct option:

	A	B	C	D
(a)	I	II	III	IV
(b)	III	IV	I	II
(c)	IV	I	II	III
(d)	II	III	IV	I

156. Who had given the name 'Harijan' to the "Untouchables"?
(a) B.R. Ambedkar
(b) M.K. Gandhi
(c) J.L. Nehru
(d) Madan Mohan Malviya

157. Who among the following holds the view that an 'Indian Tribe' as converted to Indian caste when it loses a territorial meaning and social significance?
(a) Max Weber (b) D.N. Majumdar
(c) T.N. Madan (d) J. Hutton

158. Match List I with List II

List I (Sociologist)	List II (Book)
A. W.F. Ogburn	I. Social Evolution and Social Progress
B. K. Marx	II. Civilization and Culture
C. A. Weber	III. Basic and Superstructure
D. L.T. Hobhouse	IV. Material and Non-material Culture

Choose the correct option:

	A	B	C	D
(a)	II	III	IV	I
(b)	IV	III	II	I
(c)	III	IV	II	I
(d)	I	II	III	IV

159. Match the following authors with their books

Author	Books
A. Pierre Bourdieu	I. Legitimation Crisis
B. Jurgen Habermas	II. The Constitution of Society
C. Edward Said	III. Distinction
D. Anthony Giddens	IV. Orientalism

Choose the correct option:

	A	B	C	D
(a)	III	I	IV	II
(b)	I	II	III	IV
(c)	III	II	I	IV
(d)	II	IV	III	I

160. Who has advocated the scientific method for the study of social phenomena?

A. A. R. Radcliffe Brown
B. Emile Durkheim
C. Max Weber
D. B. Malinowski

Choose the correct option:

(a) A and C (b) A and B
(c) B and C (d) C and D

161. Who said that globalization is the growing reciprocal interdependence and integration of various economies around the globe?

(a) A. Giddens
(b) Meghnad Desai
(c) Henderson Hazel
(d) Martin Knor

162. The symbol deals with

(a) Transmission of a message
(b) Deviation of a message
(c) Restriction of a message
(d) Dilution of a message

163. Which option is correct about the 'Social fact' according to Durkheim?

A. It is common in a given society
B. It is common for every individual
C. It is like a thing
D. It does not provide any pressure on the individual

Choose the correct option

(a) A and B (b) C and D
(c) B and C (d) A and C

164. Who among the following is considered as a practitioner of Theoretical Pluralism'?

(a) A.R. Desai
(b) M.N. Srinivas
(c) G.S. Ghurye
(d) R.K. Mukherjee

165. Who talks about structuration as the structuring of social relations across time and space?

(a) Erving Goffman
(b) Harold Garfinkel
(c) Manuel Castells
(d) Anthony Giddens

166. Who viewed education as the action exercised by the older generation upon those who are not yet ready for social life?

(a) Emile Durkheim (b) T.B. Bottomore
(c) R.H. lowie (d) Lord William Bentick

167. Match List I with List II

List I (Author)	List II (Book)
A. A. Bateson	I. Nature's Economy
B. F. Berkos	II. The Ascent of Man
C. J. Beonowski	III. Sacred Ecology
D. D. Worster	IV. Steps to Ecology

Choose the correct option:

	A	B	C	D
(a)	IV	III	II	I
(b)	II	III	I	IV
(c)	III	IV	II	I
(d)	I	II	III	IV

168. Who saw much in common between theatrical performance and the kind of 'acts'?

(a) Erving Goffman
(b) Alfred Schultz
(c) Harold Garfinkel
(d) G.H. Mead

JUNE 2019

169. According to Durkheim, low regulation in society will lead to which type of suicide?

(a) Egoistic
(b) Fatalistic
(c) Altruistic
(d) Anomic

170. Which one of the following is NOT the work of G. S. Ghurye?

(a) Class, Caste, and Occupation
(b) The Scheduled Community
(c) Caste and Race in India
(d) Indian Sadhus

171. Who has popularized the term 'Total Institution'?
(a) F. Tonnies
(b) Erving Goffman
(c) Talcott Parsons
(d) Karl Mannheim

172. Who held the view that Indian tribals were 'backward Hindus'?
(a) G. S. Ghurye (b) A. R. Desai
(c) N. K. Bose (d) Y. B Damle

173. Who has authored the work, *Distinction* (1981)?
(a) Anthony Giddens
(b) Pierre Bourdieu
(c) C. Geertz
(d) Jurgen Habermas

174. The use of phonemes in relation to the kinship system was done by whom?
(a) C. Levi-Strauss
(b) A. R. Radcliffe-Brown
(c) B. Malinowski
(d) S. F. Nadel

175. Match List-I with List-II

List I (Author)	List II (Contribution)
A. Max Weber	I. Interaction Ritual
B. E. Goffman	II. The Nation State and Violence
C. A. Giddens	III. The Religion of India
D. David Held	IV. Models of Democracy

Chose the correct option from those given below:

	A	B	C	D
(a)	I	IV	III	II
(b)	III	IV	II	I
(c)	III	I	II	IV
(d)	IV	I	II	III

176. The History of Sexuality (3 volumes) was authored by
(a) Paul Rabinow
(b) Michel Foucault
(c) Peter Brown
(d) Saint Augustine

177. Which form of crisis in capitalist societies was NOT discussed by Habermas?
(a) Legitimation
(b) Rationality
(c) Motivation
(d) Emotional

178. Who is considered as the father of the functionalist theory of culture?
(a) R. K. Merton
(b) Malinowski
(c) R. Radcliffe-Brown
(d) H. Spencer

179. Match List-I with List-II

List I (Sociologists)	List II (Sociological Traditions)
A. Emile Durkheim	I. Structuralism
B. Clifford Geertz	II. Post-modernism
C. Claude Levi-Strauss	III. Interpretative
D. Michel Foucault	IV. Functionalism

Chose the correct option from those given below:

	A	B	C	D
(a)	IV	III	I	II
(b)	I	III	IV	II
(c)	I	III	IV	II
(d)	III	I	II	IV

180. Which scholar is associated with the term 'thick description'?
(a) Karl Mannheim
(b) Alfred Schutz
(c) Erving Goffman
(d) Clifford Geertz

181. Who stated 'Magic is sacred and science is profane'?
(a) Malinowski
(b) J. Frazer
(c) Durkheim
(d) B. Tylor

182. Who is associated with the concept of 'Reflexive Modernization'?
(a) Edward Said
(b) J. Habermas
(c) Manuel Castells
(d) Anthony Giddens

183. Which of the following motives of the actor was NOT dealt by T. Parsons?
(a) Cognitive
(b) Evaluative
(c) Numerative
(d) Cathectic

184. Alliance Theory in Kinship Studies is associated with which of the following scholars?
(a) Kathleen Gough
(b) Pauline Kolenda
(c) Levi-Strauss
(d) R Radcliffe-Brown

185. Among the following, who supported the ideal-typical cultural theme of Hinduism?
(a) M.K, Gandhi
(b) B R. Ambedkar
(c) Kabir
(d) Periyar

186. Who said that 'the habitus is the product of past experiences, but it always transmits their experiences in an active creative fashion'?
(a) H. Garfinkel
(b) Giddens
(c) Leach
(d) P. Bourdieu

187. Which of the following authority types is based on unique personality traits?
(a) Traditional
(b) Personal
(c) Charismatic
(d) Rational-legal

188. In Goffman's dramaturgy, which one of the following is NOT included?
(a) Side stage
(b) Mystification
(c) Front stage
(d) Impression management

189. Who coined the term 'Vote Bank' in India?
(a) M. N. Srinivas
(b) Rajni Kothari
(c) Girish Kumar
(d) Dipankar Gupta

190. Which of the following pairs is NOT correct?

(a) Robert Redfield	America
(b) Karl Mannheim	Germany (born in Hungary)
(c) Claude Levi-Strauss	France (born in Belgium)
(d) Anthony Giddens	England

191. Which critical theory has Jurgen Habermas emphasized?
(a) Theory of Neo-colonialism
(b) Theory of exchange
(c) Theory of structuration
(d) Theory of communicative action

192. According to Max Weber, which entities are always struggling for domination?
(a) Class
(b) Parties
(c) Class situation
(d) Status

193. Which of the following works is concerned with a process of development from primitive to modem society?
(a) Division of Labour in Society (E. Durkheim)
(b) Economy and Society (Max Weber)
(c) The Handbook of Economic Sociology (N. J. Smelser)
(d) The Origin of the Family, Private Property and State (F. Engels)

194. Match List-I with List-II:

List I (Concepts)	List II (Authors)
A. Timeless Time	I. David Held
B. Hyperglobalizers	II. Anthony Giddens
C. Late Modernity	III. Immanuel Wallerstein
D. World System Theory	IV. Manuel Castells

Select the correct option from the options given below:

	A	B	C	D
(a)	I	II	III	IV
(b)	II	I	IV	III
(c)	IV	I	II	III
(d)	III	IV	I	II

195. In which community did Durkheim examine Totemism?
(a) Red Indian
(b) Trobriand Islanders
(c) Australian Arunta
(d) African Gypsies

Answer Key

1. (b)
2. (b)
3. (a)
4. (d)
5. (a)
6. (b)
7. (c)
8. NA
9. (b)
10. (c)
11. (c)
12. (c)
13. (b)
14. (d)
15. (c)
16. (b)
17. (d)
18. (c)
19. (b)
20. (d)
21. (b)
22. (b)
23. (c)
24. (b)
25. (c)
26. (d)
27. (d)
28. (a)
29. (b)
30. (a)
31. (b)
32. (c)
33. (c)
34. (d)
35. (c)
36. (d)
37. (d)
38. (a)
39. (a)
40. (c)
41. (c)
42. (d)
43. (b)
44. (d)
45. (c)
46. (d)
47. (d)
48. (a)
49. (b)
50. (a)
51. (d)
52. (b)
53. (b)
54. (a)
55. (b)
56. (c)
57. (a)
58. (c)
59. (d)
60. (d)
61. (d)
62. (c)
63. (b)
64. (a)
65. (a)
66. (c)
67. (d)
68. (b)
69. (a)
70. (c)
71. (b)
72. (b)
73. (a)
74. (c)
75. (d)
76. (c)
77. (b)
78. (b)
79. (a)
80. (b)
81. (c)
82. (b)
83. (c)
84. (b)
85. (c)
86. (c)
87. (b)
88. (b)
89. (c)
90. (a)
91. (d)
92. (c)
93. (b)
94. (b)
95. (c)
96. (c)
97. (c)
98. (c)
99. (d)
100. (d)
101. (c)
102. (b)
103. (c)
104. (b)
105. (a)
106. (c)
107. (c)
108. (a)
109. (b)
110. (c)
111. (a)
112. (a)
113. (c)
114. (c)
115. (b)
116. (a)
117. (a)
118. (c)
119. (b)
120. (c)
121. (c)
122. (d)
123. (a)
124. (c)
125. (a)
126. (a)
127. (d)
128. (a)
129. (c)
130. (c)
131. (c)
132. (b)
133. (a)
134. (c)
135. (d)
136. (b)
137. (c)
138. (a)
139. (c)
140. (c)
141. (a)
142. (b)
143. (d)
144. (c)
145. (b)
146. (b)
147. (c)
148. (c)
149. (d)
150. (d)
151. (c)
152. (c)
153. (a)
154. (d)
155. (b)
156. (b)
157. (d)
158. (b)
159. (a)
160. (a)
161. (b)
162. (a)
163. (d)
164. (b)
165. (d)
166. (a)
167. (a)
168. (a)
169. (d)
170. (b)
171. (b)
172. (a)
173. (b)
174. (a)
175. (c)
176. (b)
177. (b)
178. (b)
179. (a)
180. (d)
181. (a)
182. (d)
183. (c)
184. (c)
185. (a)
186. (d)
187. (b)
188. (a)
189. (a)
190. (b) and (c)
191. (d)
192. (b)
193. (a)
194. (c)
195. (c)

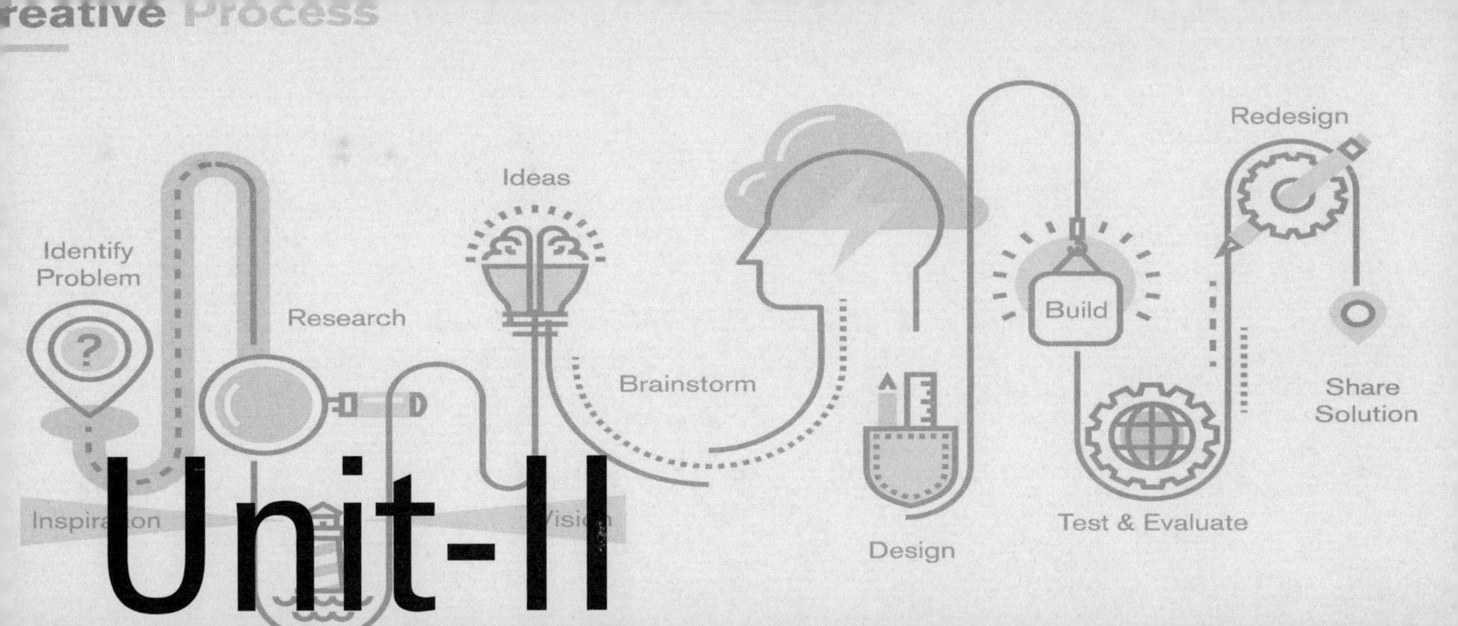

Unit-II

Research Methodology and Methods

CHAPTERS:

Top: Photo credit: mini.fini / Shutterstock
Below: Photo credit: PureSolution / Shutterstock

CHAPTER

1 Conceptualizing Social Reality

LEARNING OBJECTIVES:

In this chapter, we will discuss the following important topics.

- Philosophy of Science
- Scientific Method and Epistemology in Social Science
- Hermeneutic Traditions
- Objectivity and Reflexivity in Social Science
- Ethics and Politics

INTRODUCTION

Social reality clearly indicates that what we are referring to is actually society's ability to develop different ways of seeing the components of the visible aspects of reality. Berger and Luckman feel that studying the phenomena of social reality means that we use everyday common sense reality as a point of departure. This is what knowledge ultimately consists of: interaction and participation in social life and process. Thus "commonsense ideas" are one of the most important entrances to understanding sociology and phenomena of individuals, groups and societies. Thus it is clear that there are at least two sides to the existence and metaphysics of society—one is subjective and the other is objective.

PHILOSOPHY OF SOCIAL SCIENCE

Science

Science, you often tend to believe, is objective. Science is based on facts; science needs rational and dispassionate analysis, not an emotional or sentimental judgment. Science is based on hard facts and empirical evidence.

Social scientists, it is argued, are 'objective' and 'value-neutral'; they rely on hard empirical facts, and the social science account is, therefore, not an ideological, subjective, valorization (increasing value) or condemnation of social reality.

The two distinguished thinkers, Francis Bacon (1561–1626) and Rene Descartes (1564–1650), have provided the foundations of modern science.

Francis Bacon

Bacon taught us the first important lesson of objectivity, how to spell out the book of nature as it is how to observe it without any preselection and bias.

He argued that in order to be objective, we must overcome all the delusions that Bacon regarded as the "idols of mind" which are hurdles in the path of understanding truth.

Bacon has identified four species of 'idols of the mind' hidden in our brain, they are:

1. **Idols of the tribe:** These idols are common to the human species as such, and emanate from the typical human weakness: our urge to see what we like to see in the world, our search for regularity, and our obsession with our own beliefs. Human minds, Bacon argued, are like 'uneven mirrors' that distort reality. Superstitions and prejudices continue to prevail because of these idols. In fact, the human being's '"feelings imbue and corrupt his understanding in innumerable and sometimes imperceptible ways'.
2. **Idols of the den:** These idols, unlike the idols of the tribe, are unique to specific individuals. Each individual has his/her own dispositions and idols. Some, for instance, are inherently optimistic, some are pessimistic, and some strive for antiquity (ancient past); some love changes and innovation. All these individual peculiarities tend to affect one's ways of seeing, and hence distort reality.
3. **Idols of the market:** These idols are those that emanate out of human interaction, and cause severe linguistic confusion. Our language often proves to be inadequate to describe reality as it. No wonder, Bacon said that the great and solemn disputes of learned men often terminate in controversies about words and names.
4. **Idols of the theatre:** These are those idols that have crept into men's minds from the various dogmas of peculiar systems of philosophy.

For Bacon, these idols are essentially obstacles and must be overcome. Only then is it possible to see and observe the world without bias.

Rene Descartes

Rene Descartes taught us the fundamental lessons of rationalism (or deductive reasoning). Descartes privileged the mental and intellectual and argued that it was through clear ideas, or pure rationality, that human beings could arrive at truth and became free from all uncertainties and errors.

For him, the sense could not be a reliable source of knowledge, the senses could deceive one. As a result, in an act of meditation, Descartes began to doubt everything that he learned through the senses.

Descartes argued, '*man is a thing that thinks*'. This led him to privilege the indivisible mind that makes one think, and separate it from the non-thinking body.

According to Descartes, while one cannot separate oneself from one's mind, one can, however, exist without one's body.

'Although the whole mind seems to be united to the whole body, I recognize that if a foot or arm or any other part of the body is out off, nothing has thereby been taken away from the mind.'

It would not be wrong to say that the modern social sciences emerged out of this epistemological optimism.

Characteristics of Science

Merton argues that science is characterized by four interrelated organizational principles, which are ethical in nature and serve as structural imperatives for science.

1. **Universalism.** For him, science is universal because scientific produce is evaluated on the basis of merit and importance and not on the basis of value and norm.
2. **Organized Skepticism.** Merton suggests that all scientific claims should be open to critical investigation before being accepted as methodology and institutional codes of conduct
3. **Disinterestedness.** Merton states that scientists are committed to disinterestedness and do not consider self-interest as a viable motivation for scientific work. The aim of scientists is to advance scientific knowledge rather than personal interests.
4. **Communism.** For him, scientific knowledge that has been proven reliable and accurate shall be readily available to every member of the scientific community.

SCIENTIFIC METHODS AND EPISTEMOLOGY IN SOCIAL SCIENCE EPISTEMOLOGY

Epistemology

Aristotle began his work 'Metaphysics' with the observation that 'all human beings by nature want to know'. For this Kant poses the question 'What can I know?' Aristotle replied that the desire to know is fundamental to being human.

Epistemology tries to fulfill this desire. Epistemology is the branch of philosophy that deals with the nature, origin, and scope of knowledge. Epistemology focuses on our means of acquiring knowledge and how we can distinguish between truth and falsehood.

Scottish philosopher James Frederick Ferrier was the first to coin the term 'epistemology' in terms of study of knowledge. It comes from the Greek word 'episteme' meaning knowledge and 'logos' meaning principle or science. It focuses on how knowledge is originated. What is its nature and scope?

Epistemology has two major divisions one is called Rationalists and others are called Empiricists. Philosophers who believe that all knowledge is ultimately based on reason are called rationalists. Others, called empiricists, hold that all knowledge is ultimately based on experience.

Rationalist

The foundations of logical thinking go back to Greek philosophers, primarily Pythagoras, Plato, and Aristotle. The central tenet of rationalism or logical thinking is that truth is best discovered through reason and rational thought.

Rationalists believe that the world is deterministic, and that cause-and-effect accounts for all phenomena. They also believe that these can be understood through sufficient understanding and thought. A rational insight is the source of much wisdom. On the other hand, sensory experience is seen as highly illusory and tentative.

Like Logic and mathematics, philosophy too is a classic rational discipline. Rational reasoning is particularly attractive because it implies superior intelligence, and we all use it regularly, although the truth of our claims is often open to question. Prominent rationalists include Descartes, Spinoza, and Leibniz.

Empiricist

Empiricism emerged as a response to rationalist arguments, and events that changed British society and influenced the way the Anglo-Saxons understood social reality.

The first of these events which changed British society was the English Civil War in which the monarchy and feudalism were challenged. The second important event was the growing demand for individual rights and equality among all human beings.

HERMENEUTIC TRADITIONS

Hermeneutics

In earlier ages, the term 'hermeneutics' was used as a sacred term, used to describe a person who was close to God. Hermes was the person who brought the messages of the Greek gods to mortals. As a messenger, has first 'interpret' what the god has said and then 'understand' the meaning himself before he could convey their 'meaning' to the mortals.

Hermeneutics really came into its own during the Reformation period when the Protestants came up with alternative principles of the interpretation of the Bible, against the Catholic insistence on church authority and tradition in matters of understanding and interpreting the Holy Scriptures.

Hermeneutics is derived from the Greek word hermeneus, meaning translator or interpreter. Hermeneutics was initially applied to the interpretation or exegesis of scripture and has been later broadened to questions of general interpretation. Hermeneutics became a wider discipline that includes written, verbal, and non-verbal communication.

Therefore, Hermeneutics or the interpretation of tradition is:

1. a part of the methodological quest to understand the social reality.
2. It is a set of rules and procedures to interpret something.
3. It is the art of understanding and of making oneself understood.
4. It has been applied as a method in sociology.
5. It offers a toolbox for efficiently treating problems of the interpretation of human actions, texts, and other meaningful material.

Modern hermeneutics includes both verbal and non-verbal communication as well as semiotics, presuppositions, and pre-understandings. Hermeneutics has been broadly applied in the humanities, especially in law, history, and theology.

Aristotle introduced the word Hermeneia into philosophy mainly through his work '*Peri Hermeneius*', commonly referred to by its Latin title De Interpretatione and translated into English as On Interpretation.

Friedrich Schleiermacher (1768–1834), known as the father of modern hermeneutics, contributed to the introduction of a course on hermeneutics at the University of Berlin between 1810 and 1834.

Schleiermacher believed that human beings have a linguistic disposition and that their linguistic capacity enables them to understand the utterances of others. He considered hermeneutics to be an art and believed that every utterance, whether spoken or written, contemporary or historical, could be understood through an interpretation. Understanding and interpretation always have two aspects or components, a grammatical or linguistic component, and a psychological or theological component.

Understanding a speech always involves two moments

1. to understand what is said in the context of the language
2. to understand it as a fact in the thinking of the speaker

Johann Conrad Dannhauer was the first to produce a systematic textbook on general hermeneutics titled Hermeneutica. The work was intended to complement the Aristotelian Organon and its subject matter to distinguish between the true and false meaning of any text.

Hermeneutic Circle

Martin Heidegger developed the concept of the hermeneutic circle to conceive of the whole in terms of a reality situated in the elaborate experience of everyday existence by an individual. So understanding was developed on the basis of 'fore-structures', which allow external events to be interpreted in an elementary way. A process of interpretation in which we move continuously between smaller and larger units of meaning in order to determine the meaning of both.

OBJECTIVITY AND REFLEXIVITY IN SOCIAL SCIENCE

Objectivity

A researcher is said to be objective when he does not allow his values, biases, or his views to influence his research, analysis, or conclusions. Objectivity is paramount for research to be credible and considered scientific. However, some social scientists question whether sociology can ever be completely objective, as researchers' views and values are likely to influence their choice of topic.

Weber argued that while sociologists should be interested in the subjective views of their subjects, they should remain objective in their research; Others such as postmodernists argue that objectivity is impossible at all stages of research.

Many sociologists, not just those who consider their activities to be scientific argue that sociological research needs to be objective, and that their biases and values should never influence their research design, interpretation or analysis.

Reflexivity

Reflexivity refers to a situation where an individual becomes a self by being able to take the attitude of others and thereby reflect on his or her own behaviour. Reflexive means that the researcher can take stock of his/her own reservations, and prejudices and resolve them before recording responses obtained from the field.

In simpler terms, it implies that in participatory research, we deal with other human beings that look like us but may have different or even opposing customs, attitudes, social values, etc. The answer that they may give to an inquiry may be very different from the response that we expect or believe is the correct answer.

Reflexivity in participatory research methods helps to distinguish qualitative research methods from quantitative methods of research. It teaches us to delineate subjectivity from objectivity. Reflexivity refers to circular relationships between cause and effect, especially as embedded in human belief structures.

A reflexive relationship is bi-directional with both the cause and the effect affecting one another in a relationship in which neither can be assigned as causes or effects. It commonly refers to the capacity of an agent to recognize forces of socialization and alter their place in the social structure.

A low level of reflexivity would result in an individual being shaped largely by their surroundings or society. A high level of social reflexivity would be defined by an individual shaping their own norms, tastes, politics, desires, and so on, this is similar to the notion of autonomy.

As a sociological term, it first appears in the work of Talcott Parsons where it refers to the ability of social actors in modern societies to be aware and able to account for their actions. Another meaning of the term in sociology can be traced to the work of Harold Garfinkel, who used the term to refer to the process by which social order is created through ad hoc examples of communicative practice.

Giddens theorized that moving to a post-traditional culture causes individuals to perceive their self-identity as a reflexive project. Rather than simply assuming or passively inheriting who we are, we actively shape, reflect, and monitor ourselves, creating our biographical narratives as we go through life. We then treat our identity as a project, something we actively construct and are ultimately responsible for.

Giddens says, 'Self-identity, then, is not a set of traits or observable characteristics. It is a person's own reflexive understanding of their biography. Self-identity has a continuity that is, it cannot easily be completely changed at will but that continuity is only a product of the person's reflexive beliefs about their own biography'.

ETHICS AND POLITICS

In general, it is advisable for social scientists to research a topic that has the interest and support of local/national authorities. This will increase the likelihood that the results of the study will be implemented.

However, under certain circumstances, one may feel that a study is needed to show that the government's policy needs adjustment. If so, you should make an extra effort to involve relevant policymakers at an early stage to limit the potential for conflicts later.

The ethics of social work research are more concerned with the methods employed, while the political issues are more concerned with the practical cost and use of the research.

This means that the cost and use of research are of most concern from a political point of view. The political approach prioritizes low-cost research with high costs rather than an appropriate research methodology. Different research methods can affect the outcome of the research and error can arise due to using an inappropriate method in research.

Second, the ethical aspects can be separated from the political aspects of social work research because there are no formal codes of accepted political conduct comparable to codes of ethical conduct.

This shows that politics always influences social research in various aspects. Researchers should pay more attention to research that needs to deal with political issues.

Ethics in Social Science Research

Ethics, means rules of conduct or moral principles, gains importance when it comes to creating knowledge of any kind and specifically in the domain of research because the outcome of research is directly influenced by the integrity of the researcher.

Research ethics is concerned with the moral issues that arise during or as a result of research activities, as well as the ethical conduct of researchers. The management of research ethics is inconsistent across countries and there is no universally accepted approach to how it should be addressed.

Ethical issues may arise in the design and implementation of research involving human experimentation or animal experimentation. There may also be consequences for the environment, for society, or for future generations that need to be considered.

Research ethics is most developed as a concept in medical research, the most notable Code being the 1964 Declaration of Helsinki. Research in other fields such as social sciences, information technology, biotechnology, or engineering may generate different types of ethical concerns for those in medical research.

Paulo Freire (1997), said that it is impossible to think of or do something without being touched and incorporated by this ethical dimension: 'We are ethical beings, ethics pervades our entire existence'.

In everyday parlance it is commonly said - and this is not incorrect - that both ethics and morals are related to qualifications of good or bad. This question, however, becomes intriguing, and much more complex, when we come to ask about the fundaments of this 'good/bad'.

It is at this point that some begin to distinguish between ethics and morals: morals would be the customs and norms that are implicitly and tacitly established between peoples and groups, without questioning.

While ethics would be a critical philosophical reflection on this crucial question: based on which we can affirm that something is good or bad.

CHAPTER

2 Formulating Research Design

LEARNING OBJECTIVES:

In this chapter, we will discuss the following important topics.

- Research
- Reading social science research
- Data and documents
- Induction and deduction
- Fact, concept, and theory
- Hypothesis, research questions, objectives

INTRODUCTION

The research design is the blueprint of the planned main research. It includes the structure and background of the research methods, tools and techniques used. Research design is helpful because it allows the researcher to know which methods to use to investigate a particular problem and thus allows mastery of the method. This can lead to a successful research. Kerlinger defined research design as "the plan, structure, and strategy of an investigation conceived to obtain answers to research questions and to control variation".

RESEARCH

- The word 'Research' is a combination of 're' + 'search'. It is a journey from known to unknown. It is a careful investigation to search for new facts in any branch of knowledge. It is generally scientific in nature to provide an objective, which is an unbiased evaluation of data.
- Research always adds to the existing stock of knowledge. Research is a powerful tool which leads towards progress. It is conducted to verify the acceptability of some specific theory. It expands the limits of our knowledge.

Objectives of Research

i. It offers solutions to the problem.
ii. It helps to generate new knowledge.
iii. To test the hypothesis of a causal relationship between variables.
iv. To find out the truth, which has not been discovered yet
v. To construct a new procedure.

Characteristics of Research

1. **Objectivity:** It means to carry out research without any biases. Here results are not affected by the personal judgement.
2. **Validity:** Validity means, that research must be free from any systematic error. Validity is the main feature of research because without it research can go in the wrong direction. There should be the accuracy of the procedure, tests etc for the validity of the research. There are different types of validity that are given below:
3. **Reliability:** It refers to the consistency of a measure. It is the degree to which an assessment tool produces consistent results. There are

many types of reliability which includes. Test-retest reliability, internal consistency reliability etc. If the test is reliable there we can say that it should show high positive correlation.

4. **Accuracy:** Accuracy measure whether the research tools have been selected in the possible manner or not. It is very much closely related to validity. If we choose best tool for the collection of data, it improves the accuracy of research.
5. **Empirical research:** It refers to that research which is based on real-life experiences or observation by the researcher.
6. **Generalizability:** the sample is considered as representative of whole population, so that findings should be applicable to the whole population.
7. **Logical:** A good research is always followed by the rules of logical reasoning, which is of great importance in research
8. **Systematic:** there should be a definite procedure.

Types of Research

(A) Fundamental Research: Fundamental research is also known as basic or pure research. It gives answers to why, what and how. This research helps in developing theories by discovering broad principles. It is organized through different procedures of research. The basic purpose of this research is to add knowledge to the existing stock of knowledge. Fundamental research is a theoretical application of knowledge.

(B) Applied research: Applied research utilizes those applications which is set by fundamental research. It is done to solve the specific problem facing society. It is carried out by the academic institutions. Applied research is intensive in nature. In short we can say that it utilizes the principles to know the problems with the best possible immediate solution to the problem or issue. It is concerned with addressing the problems of the world. It is research that is aligned towards ascertaining economic, social or economic trends.

(C) Action research: It is a part of applied research. It gives an immediate solution to the problem. It is also known as the cycle of action. Action research was given by Kurt Levin in 1940. We can say that is a predefined process. Action research is carried out periodical assessment of projects. Here, direct action is taken with the objective of obtaining workable, solutions to the problems.

(D) Descriptive research: Field surveys and fact finding inquiries are the main contents of descriptive research. Nothing is manipulated in descriptive research. It is closely linked with historical, ex-post facto and analytical research. The main purpose of descriptive research is description of the state of affairs which exists at present.

- **(i) Historical research:** As we discussed earlier, historical research is linked with descriptive research. Historical research usually focuses on the historical aspect of the problem.
- **(ii) Analytical research:** Under this method, the researcher uses the information which is already available. It attempts to make critical evaluation of the given material.

(E) Correlational Research: Correlational research is a type of non-experimental research method in which a researcher measures two variables, understands and assesses the statistical relationship between them with no influence from any extraneous variable.

(F) Explanatory research: Explanatory research mainly gives answers to 'why'. It is used to connect different ideas and helps to understand the different reasons, causes and their effects. Types of explanatory research include two-cell design, Four-cell design, and Thatching design.

(G) Exploratory Research: This type of research is used to explore an area where little is known. It is normally done at the beginning of research. The main purpose of exploratory research is to clarify the problems and to develop hypotheses. It makes use of secondary data, case studies, projective techniques, interviews etc.

(H) Experimental research: It establishes cause and effect relationships. The fundamental feature of such research is that there is possibility of exercising control over independent variable. It identifies variables that changes the dependent variable.

Steps in Research

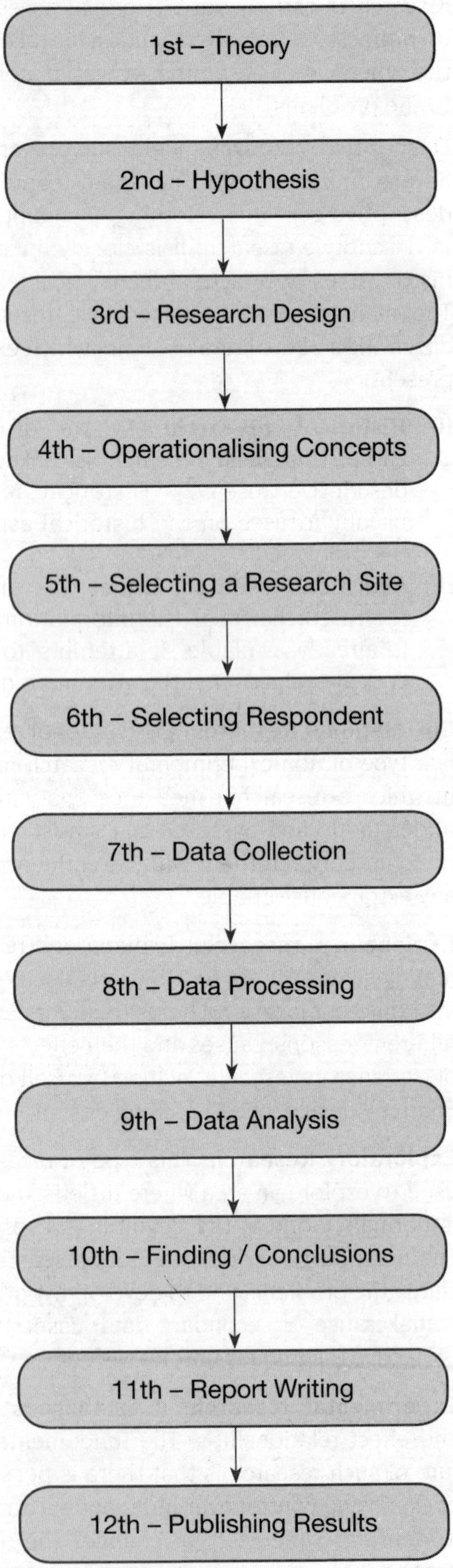

READING SOCIAL SCIENCE RESEARCH

There are many things to keep in mind while reading social research. Reading scholarly literature is different from reading other works.

- **i.** Begin by reading the abstract,
- **ii.** Skimming the piece, and
- **iii.** Reading the conclusion to get a good sense of what it's about.
- **iv.** Readers of social science literature should also form questions and take notes as they go along.
- **v.** When reading a research report, be sure to consider theoretical orientation, sampling, and other data-collection methods.

DATA AND DOCUMENT

Data

Data is the raw information from which statistics are created. Raw data is the direct result of research that was done as part of a study or survey. This is a primary source. Data can be analyzed and interpreted using statistical procedures to answer "why" or "how" questions. Data is used to create new information and knowledge. Research data is any information that has been collected, observed, generated, or created in order to validate original research findings.

Types of Data

The statistical data may be classified under two categories depending on the source utilized. These categories are as follows.

Primary Data

Primary data is that which is collected directly from the respondents using a data collection method such as a survey, interview, questionnaire, measurement, direct observation, or tabulation. Here, the researcher is directly involved in the collection of information needed to answer the research questions. Primary data can be classified on the basis of the following methods of primary data collection:

1. **Observation.** This method is generally used in traffic census or in surveys of car drivers carrying licenses. It is a relatively inexpensive method yielding accurate results.
2. **Experimentation.** This method was generally used in agricultural products. Recently, it has been used to collect data on consumer

behaviour to determine the effect on sales of new advertising methods, new packaging, alternative price policies, etc.

3. **Investigation.** Methods of investigation are
   i. **Direct Personal Inquiry.** Under this method, the investigator personally interviews each person who is in a position to provide the information required by him. It is suitable when the scope of inquiry is limited, or the nature of inquiry is confidential, and when maximum accuracy is required.
   ii. **Indirect oral Investigation.** This method is used when the informant is reluctant to give information or data that is of such a complex nature that it is difficult to obtain them directly. The merits of this method are wide coverage, economical, neutral, etc. The limitations of this method are indirect information, the bias of witnesses, etc.
   iii. **Information through correspondents.** Under this method, the investigator appoints local correspondents in different parts of the area of inquiry. They are instructed to regularly send information to the investigator on specific issues. This method is generally adopted by newspapers and magazines, which require information on a regular basis. This method is very cheap and gives results easily and quickly, and a wide area can be covered.
   iv. **Schedules to be filled by the informants.** A schedule or questionnaire is prepared under this method. The questionnaire consists of a set of questions on the problems being investigated. These questionnaires are addressed to individual informants and sent by post. They are requested to answer the questions and post them back to the investigator. This method of data collection is simple and cheap, reliable, and free from bias. But it suffers from demerits like non-response, limited range, and can be less accurate at times.

Advantages of Primary Data

i. Original in character.
ii. Meet the required need of the investigator without editing.
iii. Quality of data is better as have been collected by persons, who were specifically trained for that purpose. Thus, data is more accurate.
iv. Unbiased data.

Disadvantages of Primary Data

i. Expensive in terms of money and time
ii. Raw data
iii. Large volume of data
iv. Direct and personal intervention has to be there

Secondary Data

Secondary data is the data that already exists which has been collected by some other person or organization for their use and is generally made available to other researchers free or at a concessional rate. Sources of secondary data are journals, reports, government publications, or professional and research organizations. The collection of secondary data is less expensive in terms of money and time.

For example, if a researcher wants to analyze the weather conditions of different regions, he can get the required information or data records from the meteorology department. So, for the meteorology department, it is primary data, and for the researcher, the same data becomes secondary data.

Secondary data may not always answer the special questions of a researcher. Hence, a researcher should use a judicious mix of primary and secondary data to optimize the quality of research findings within the allotted time and money.

Classification of secondary data is based on source category medium and database.

On the basis of source, the classification of secondary data is as follows.

1. **Internal Source** – Internal source of secondary data that are available within the organization. e.g., Internal sources of secondary data such as departmental reports, production summaries, finance and accounting reports, and marketing and studies.
2. **External Source** – External sources of secondary data are those that exist outside the company in the form of books and periodicals, government sources, trade, and manufacturer's associations, publications, media sources, commercial sources, etc.

Advantages of Secondary Data Secondary Data can help to identify, clarify and redefine the research problem in situations, where the actual problems as a research study cannot be defined or are defined in an ambiguous way, the use of secondary data can help clear the confusion.

Secondary Data might also hold a solution to the problem sometimes; it happens that precise data regarding the current research is already available as secondary data. Hence, it might not be necessary to conduct a primary data collection increase at all. This saves time and money.

Secondary Data may provide alternative methods that can be used for primary research every research situation has custom-made primary research designed for it. When some published reports are gathered from secondary sources, they give an idea about the possible research alternatives.

Document

A document is anything in writing that contains a matter of sociological importance. In the case of social research, it has been used in the widest connotation and includes such written evidence as life histories, diaries, letters, official and unofficial records, proceedings of parliaments, committees, courts, societies, etc.

Classification of Documents

Documents can be classified under the following two heads: (a) personal documents, and (b) public documents.

Personal documents may be categorized as (i) Life History, (ii) Diaries, (iii) Letters, and (iv) Memoirs.

Public documents may be divided into the following two categories: (i) Unpublished Records, (ii) Published Records.

i. **Unpublished Records:** Such records, are not available to people in published form. It means, that everybody cannot have access to them. Proceedings of the meetings, noting on the files and memoranda, etc.
ii. **Published Records:** These records are available to people for investigation and perusal. Surveys, reports, reports of survey inquiries, and such other documents fall under this category.

INDUCTION AND DEDUCTION

Deduction is also known as general to a specific approach. In the deductive approach, we start from theory and try to prove it with the help of information available to us. Whereas, induction is a bottom-up approach. In this approach, we move from specific to general. It starts with specific observations and ends with generalizing theory.

Inductive Research Approach

It is common to conduct inductive research when there is little or no existing literature on a topic because there is no theory to the test. There are three steps in the inductive approach:

1. Observation
2. Observe a pattern
3. Develop a theory or general (preliminary) conclusion

Deductive Research Approach

When doing deductive research, one always starts with a theory. To reason deductively means to test these theories. You can't do deductive research if there isn't a theory yet. There are four steps in the deductive research approach:

1. Start with an existing theory and create a problem statement.
2. Formulate a falsifiable hypothesis based on existing theory.
3. Collect data to test the hypothesis.
4. Analyze and test the data.

FACT, CONCEPT, AND THEORY

Fact

Scientific research starts with facts and then moves toward theorizing. To be useful, facts must be organized, and the primary objective of the scientific method is to develop a mechanism for organizing facts, as they are collected, and become meaningful from the point of view of their objectives.

Fact is an empirically verifiable observation. It can be expressed in a proposition. But it is distinguishable from the proposition that a proposition is a statement—true or false, about phenomena phenomenon, a fact is one which is responsible to make the statement true or false.

For example, Taj Mahal is situated in Agra a city in Uttar Pradesh" is a proposition, because it is capable of testing. When the phenomenon is tested it becomes a fact.

Facts help to initiate theories. So, theory refers to the facts or to the ordering of the facts in some meaningful way.

Concept

A concept is an abstract symbol representing an object, a property of an object, or a certain phenomenon, e.g., book, person, intelligence, or meeting. A concept is, in reality, a definition in shorthand of a class or group of facts. Concepts are symbols that we attach to the bundle of meanings that we hold. Concepts represent only one part of reality.

For example, a concept like 'apple' means different things to different persons according to their needs. To the farmer, it is a product, to the seller, it is a commodity; to the transporter, it is a material object of a given weight and volume. Thus, different people hold different concepts of the same thing.

F.N. Kerlinger defines a concept as 'a word that expresses an abstraction formed by generalization from particulars,' thus indicating that not only is reality structured by concepts, but also reality affects the scientist's concepts. He adds that 'a construct is a concept with the additional meaning of having been created or appropriated for special scientific purposes'.

In the words of Goode and Hatt, 'A concept like a fact, is an abstraction, not phenomena. It takes its meaning from the thought framework within which it is placed.'

Types of Concepts

Concepts may be classified into (a) concrete concepts and (b) abstract concepts.

Concrete concepts symbolize material objects which can be seen, touched, and felt, e.g., books, tables, buildings.

Abstract concepts refer to properties or characteristics of objects, e.g., weight, height, attitude, intelligence, and leadership. They are constructs, i.e., they represent inferences deduced from observable events. They symbolize inferences "at a higher level of abstraction from concrete events and their meaning cannot be easily conveyed by pointing to specific objects, individuals or events".

Theory

Research is closely related to theory. The theory provides a conceptual model for research in turn contributes to theory. A theory is a scientific law. It is a summary of available knowledge of the relationship between the properties. The theory is a set of generalizations that are deduced from one another and are intimately interrelated.

Hypotheses lead to research; research leads to the discovery of new theories; new theories lead to new hypotheses. A theory is built upon collected facts. The investigator then searches, makes intelligent guesses as to how the facts are ordered, adds missing ideas or links, and puts forwards a hypothesis; deduces what consequence should follow from the hypothesis and looks for further facts which are consistent or otherwise with the deductions; builds a wider generalization or conceptual framework on more facts; and eventually outlines a theory.Kerlinger defined Theory as 'a set of interrelated constructs (concepts), definitions and propositions that present a systematic view of phenomena by specifying relations among variables, with the purpose of predicting and explaining the phenomena'.

HYPOTHESES, RESEARCH QUESTIONS, OBJECTIVES

Hypotheses

A hypothesis is a tentative statement, it is a relationship between two or more variables that direct the research activity to test it. A hypothesis is a testable prediction that is expected to occur. It can be a false or a true statement that is tested in the research to check its authenticity.

Sometimes, it is very difficult to start research without having a valid foundation. Hence, the research builds a logical relationship between various phenomena to start working on the research. This logical relationship is relevant to the theme of the research. This logical relationship between various phenomena is called a hypothesis. This logical relationship or testable assumption gives a direction to the research, specifies the focus of the research, and helps in framing research techniques.

For instance, a researcher, working on the topic 'Increasing number of Slums in Urban Society', will construct the following hypotheses:

i. Increase in rate of Urbanization (overurbanization), increase in the number of slums.
ii. Increase in rate of Rural migration, increase in the number of slums.
iii. Lack of basic amenities, and increase in the number of slums.

Characteristics of Hypothesis

- Empirically Testable
- Simple and Clear

- Specific and relevant
- Predictable
- Manageable

Importance of Hypothesis

- It gives a direction to the research.
- It specifies the focus of the researcher.
- It helps in devising research techniques.
- It prevents blind research.
- It ensures accuracy and precision.
- It saves resources – time, money and energy.

Types of Hypothesis

Simple Hypothesis A simple hypothesis is a hypothesis that reflects a relationship between two variables i.e., independent and dependent variables. Example, Higher the poverty, the higher would be the rate of crime in society. higher the use of fertilizers, the higher would be agricultural productivity. The higher the illiteracy in society, the higher would be the rate of unemployment.

Complex Hypothesis A complex hypothesis is a hypothesis that reflects a relationship among more than two variables. Examples: Higher the poverty, the higher the illiteracy in society, the higher will be the rate of crime (three variables – two independent variables and one dependent variable)

The lower the use of fertilizer, improved seeds, and modern equipment, the lower would be the agricultural productivity (Four variables – three independent variables and one dependent variable) Higher the illiteracy in society, the higher will be poverty and crime rate. (Three variables – one independent variable and two dependent variables).

Working Hypothesis A hypothesis, that is accepted to put to test and work on in research, is called a working hypothesis. It is a hypothesis that is assumed to be suitable to explain certain facts and the relationship of phenomena. It is hoped that this hypothesis would generate a productive theory and is accepted to put to test for investigation. It can be any hypothesis that is processed for work during the research.

Alternative Hypothesis If the working hypothesis is proved wrong or rejected, another hypothesis (to replace the working hypothesis) is formulated to be tested to generate the desired results – this is known as an alternate hypothesis.

As the name mentions, it is an alternate assumption (a relationship or an explanation) which is adopted after the working hypothesis fails to generate the required theory. Alternative Hypothesis is denoted by H1.

Null Hypothesis A null hypothesis is a hypothesis that expresses no relationship between variables. It negates the association between variables.

Examples: Poverty has nothing to do with the rate of crime in a society.

Illiteracy has nothing to do with the rate of unemployment in society.A null hypothesis has its purpose. A null hypothesis is made with the intention that the researcher wants to disapprove, reject or nullify the null hypothesis to confirm a relationship between the variables. A null hypothesis is usually made for a reverse strategy – to prove it wrong in order to confirm that there is a relationship between the variables. A null hypothesis is denoted by H0.

Statistical Hypothesis A hypothesis, that can be verified statistically, is known as a statistical hypothesis. It can be any hypothesis that has the quality of being verified statistically. It means using quantitative techniques, to generate statistical data, and can easily verify it. It can also be said that the variables in a statistical hypothesis can be transformed into quantifiable sub-variable to test it statistically.

Logical Hypothesis A hypothesis, that can be verified logically, is known as a logical hypothesis. It is a hypothesis expressing a relationship whose interlinks can be joined on the basis of logical explanation. It is can be verified by logical evidence.

Being verified logically does not necessarily mean that it cannot be verified statistically. It may or may not be verified statistically but it can be verified logically.

False Hypothesis A hypothesis that is bound to be unsatisfactory when verified is called a false hypothesis.

Barren Hypothesis A hypothesis from which no consequences can be deducted is called a Barren Hypothesis. It is a hypothesis that cannot test. For example, the child fell ill because a wicked women's eye fell upon it. This is a baseless hypothesis because it cannot be verified.

Research Questions

A research question is 'a question that a research project sets out to answer'. Choosing a research question is an essential element of both quantitative and qualitative research. The investigation will require data collection and analysis, and the methodology for this will vary widely. Good research questions seek to improve knowledge on an important topic and are usually narrow and specific.

To form a research question, one must determine what type of study will be conducted such as a qualitative, quantitative, or mixed study. Additional factors, such as project funding, may not only affect the research question itself but also when and how it is formed during the research process.

Research Objectives

The purpose of research is to discover answers to questions through the application of scientific procedures.

Research objectives can be categorized into a number of following broad groupings:

1. To gain familiarity with a phenomenon or to achieve new insights into it (studies with this object in view are termed as exploratory research studies);
2. To portray accurately the characteristics of a particular individual, situation or group (studies with this object in view are known as descriptive research studies);
3. To determine the frequency with which something occurs or with which it is associated with something else (studies with this object in view are known as diagnostic research studies);
3. To test a hypothesis of a causal relationship between variables.

CHAPTER

3 Quantitative and Qualitative Methods

Learning Objectives:

In this chapter, we will discuss the following important topics.

- Types of quantitative methods
- Types of qualitative methods
- Research design

INTRODUCTION

Quantitative research is based on the measurement of quantity or amount. It is applicable to those phenomena which can be expressed in the form of quantity. This type of research is based on the methodological principles of positivism and other strict sampling and research design standards. It is very similar to the deductive approach.

Qualitative approach is a non-quantitative analysis or deals with a qualitative phenomenon, which cannot be presented in the form of quantity. Qualitative research is particularly important in the behavioral sciences whose aim is to discover the underlying motives of human behavior.

Ramakrishna Mukherjee on the methodology of social research, clearly spelled out in the following words for him Quality and Quantity are not a dichotomy. There is no "either/or" between them. Quality refers to only "distances" in variations, which are not known to us and therefore, cannot be measured. Our job is to find out what are these, their distances, and how to measure them. This distance is the variation between entities we are concerned with. It may be individuals; it may be anything.

Qualitative research is similar to the inductive approach. It starts with observation and ends with a theoretical position. It is suitable when a subject requires in-depth study. Here researcher is more interested in the process as compared to the outcome.

TYPES OF QUANTITATIVE METHODS

Statistical Method

Positivists majorly depend upon this method because they think it is the most convenient and efficient way to see society and its problems. For example, the rate of sex ratio or the number of rapes happening in a particular area makes sociologists see the present scenario of society.

Survey Method

The social survey method consists of the collection of data concerning the living and working conditions of people in a given area with a view to formulating practical social measures for their betterment and welfare.

Some of the definitions of the social survey are:

i. For A. F. Wells, 'Social survey is fact-finding approach dealing chiefly with working-class poverty and with the nature and problems of a community'.

ii. E. W. Burgess, 'A social survey of a community is the scientific study of its conditions and needs for the purpose of presenting a constructive programme of social advance'.

iii. Mark Abrams defined, 'A social survey as a process by which quantitative facts are collected about the social aspect of a community's composition and activities'.

iv. For Bogardus, 'A social survey is the collection of data concerning the living and working conditions, broadly speaking, of the people in a given community'.

Comparative Method

It can be easily guessed from the name itself that the method includes comparing different values. For example, in sociology, different societies are compared by sociologists and after observing each and every factor they develop some theories under their research work. Marx, Durkheim, and Weber are said to be the inventor of this method which profoundly deals with logic.

TYPES OF QUALITATIVE METHODS

Ethnography

The term 'ethnography' is used to refer to 'empirical accounts of the culture and social organization of particular human populations'. On the other hand, ethnography is understood as a method of conducting research, which studies people according to certain procedures and rules in their natural settings or regions in order to capture the social meanings of their daily lives.

This indicates the intensive, field-based, and qualitative research of human groups through 'participant observation'. Ethnography may also refer to an academic discipline that involves the comparative study of ethnic groups.

Historical Method

Historical research is 'the systematic collection and objective evaluation of data relating to past events in order to test hypotheses concerning the causes, effects, or trends of those events that may help explain current events and predict future events'.

According to Isaac and Michael, historical research involves reconstructing 'the past systematically and objectively by collecting, evaluating, verifying, and synthesizing evidence to establish facts and reach defensible conclusions, often in relation to particular hypotheses'.

True historical research or historiography is concerned with analyzing and interpreting the meanings of historical events. It is the process by which a researcher is able to arrive at a conclusion about the probable truth of an event in the past by studying the objects currently available for observation.

Case-Study Method

A case study is defined as "an investigation of an individual or group in which the variables that are measured and whose empirical relationships are discovered are characteristics of the individuals or group." It is a form of qualitative analysis that involves very careful and complete observation of a person, situation, or institution.

According to Yang, 'The case study method may be defined as an all-inclusive and intensive study of an individual, in which the investigator brings to bear all his skill and methods or as a systematic gathering of enough information about a person to understand how he or she functions as a unit of society'.

RESEARCH DESIGN

Research design is a framework designed to find answers to research questions. It refers to the overall strategy used to conduct research that defines a systematic and logical plan for dealing with the established research question(s) through the collection, interpretation, analysis, and discussion of data.

The design of a study defines the study type (descriptive, correlational, quasi-experimental, experimental, review, meta-analytic) and subtypes (for example, descriptive-longitudinal case study), research problem, hypothesis, independent and dependent variables, experimental design, and, if applicable, data collection methods and a statistical analysis plan.

CHAPTER

4 Techniques

LEARNING OBJECTIVES:

In this chapter, we will discuss the following important topics.

- Sampling
- Questionnaire and schedule
- Statistical analysis
- Observation
- Interview
- Case study
- Data Analysis and report writing

INTRODUCTION

Tools and techniques in research are statistical methods of collection, analysis, interpretation, presentation and organization of data. Statistics provides a number of tools and techniques for analyzing data and interpreting the results of the analysis. Research techniques are important in sociology because they help sociologists conduct research and convert hypotheses into theories. Research techniques are essential, we need them to do research and make new discoveries.

SAMPLING

The sample is effectively representative of the population as a whole. After developing the data collection tools the next is to select the sample. This method is more desirable when the population is consistent. The data collection methods are known as sampling methods. The methods of sampling probability and non-probability sampling.

Probability sampling

In Probability sampling, each member of the target audience has an equal opportunity to be selected in the sample. Some of the important types of probability sampling or Random Sampling are:

i. **Simple Random Sampling:** As the name indicates, simple random sampling is nothing but a random selection of elements for sampling. This sampling technique is applied where the target population is large enough.
ii. **Stratified Random Sampling:** In the stratified random sampling method, a large population is divided into strata, and members of a sample are randomly selected from these strata. The strata are formed on the basis of shared attributes such as annual income, and educational qualification.
iii. **Cluster Sampling:** Cluster sampling is a probability sampling method using which the core

segment is divided into clusters, usually using geographic and demographic segmentation parameters. The items within a cluster should be heterogeneous, but there should be homogeneity between the clusters.

iv. **Systematic Sampling:** Systematic sampling is a technique in which starting point of the sample is chosen randomly, and all other elements are selected using a fixed interval. This interval is calculated by dividing the total size of the population by the target sample size.

v. **Multi-Stage Sampling:** Multi-stage sampling is the technique in which sampling is carried out in several stages so that the sample size gets reduced at every stage.

Non-probability Sampling

Non-probability sampling is a method in which the researcher involves his own knowledge and experience to create samples. It is a sampling technique in which a sample is collected without being given an equal chance to everyone. There are five non-probability sampling models:

i. **Convenience Sampling:** In convenience sampling, the elements of the sample are selected because of only one main reason, their closeness to the researcher. These samples are quick and easy to implement because there are no other parameters to choose from.

ii. **Consecutive Sampling:** Consecutive sampling is very similar to convenience sampling, except for the fact that the researcher here selects one sample or group of samples, conduct the research over them continuously over a significant period of time, collect the result, and then move on to another sample.

iii. **Quota Sampling:** Quota is similar to stratified sampling. Using quota sampling, researchers can use their knowledge of target traits and personalities to select elements to stratify. Members from different strata can then be selected to be part of the sample as per the understanding of the researcher.

iv. **Snowball sampling:** This sampling technique is used where the target audience for research is rare to put together. The information may be selected from the same individuals and they identify other people for the purpose of collecting information, which creates a network of sample elements. Snowball sampling is conducted with target audiences, which are difficult to contact and get information.

v. Judgmental sampling: Judgmental sampling is a non-probability sampling method where samples are made based only on the experience and skills of the researcher. It is a form of sampling in which the auditor selects a sample from a population on the basis of his or her own experience and assessment of the situation, rather than using statistical sampling techniques.

QUESTIONNAIRE AND SCHEDULE METHODS

Questionnaire and schedule methods are the popular and common methods for collecting primary data in business research. Both methods comprise a list of questions arranged in a sequence pertaining to the investigation.

Questionnaire Method

A questionnaire is a list of written questions which is to be answered by the respondent. These answers become primary data for investigation. According to Krishan Kumar (1992), 'a questionnaire is a written document listing a series of questions pertaining to the problem under study, to which the investigator requires the answers'.

In the word of Schvaneveldt questionnaire is 'a data-gathering device that elicits from a respondent the answers or reactions to printed i.e., pre-arranged questions presented in a given order'. Questionnaires are often used in surveys as the primary data collection instruments.

Under this method, questionnaires are sent personally or by post to various informants with a request to answer the questions and return the questionnaire. When the questionnaire is sent by post to informants, it is called a Mail Questionnaire.

Sometimes questionnaires may also be sent through E-mail depending upon the nature of the study and the availability of time and resources. After receiving the questionnaire, the informants read the questions and record their responses in the space meant for the purpose of the questionnaire. For a quick and high rate of response, the researcher is suggested to send the questionnaire in a self-addressed envelope.

Williams is of the opinion that the researcher should conduct some fieldwork with the target group in the form of interview or observation work. This in turn assists the researcher in knowing an in-depth understanding of the sample and also their reaction to a particular section of the questionnaire.

Types of Questionnaires

Mc Kornam grouped questionnaires into three types:

i. Mailed questionnaire
ii. Group administered questionnaire
iii. Personal contact questionnaire.

Out of these three types of questionnaires mailed one is a postal questionnaire. Williams calls this type a self-completion questionnaire. This type has a prearranged set of questions. The respondent is provided with a self-addressed stamped envelope to return within a specified period of time, after posting the questionnaire.

This type of questionnaire contains a cover letter, which explains the purpose, and objectives of the research. It also requests the respondent for cooperation and assures them of the confidentiality of their answers

The second type is a group-administered questionnaire. In this method, the researcher invites the respondents in a group to gather at one place and get the questionnaire completed. This type of method is basically used in schools by teachers to gather data on any research query.

The third one is the personal contact questionnaire; in this method, the researcher and the respondent come together and fill out the questionnaire in the presence of the researcher.

Types of Questions

Open-ended questions – Open-ended questions allow respondents the freedom to express their views. They give a lot of freedom to the respondents to answer according to their interpretation. Given below is an example of an open-ended question.

Close-ended question – Closed-ended questions are best suited for large-scale surveys. Limited questions are given with a list of acceptable answers. A respondent has to pick and choose the correct answer. The answers chosen by the respondents may be the most suitable for them but they may not be the correct answer. There is a possibility that the list of alternative answers may not be sufficient for the respondent, thus limiting his/her options.

Merits of Questionnaire Method

1. Respondents can take their own time to answer the questions. So, the researcher can obtain original data by this method.
2. This is a cheap method because its mailing cost is less than the cost of personal visits.
3. This method is free from the bias of the investigator as the information is given by the respondents themselves.
4. Large samples can be covered and thus the results can be more reliable and dependable.
5. You can use this method in cases where informants are spread over a vast geographical area

Limitations

1. Sometimes respondents chose not to return filled-in questionnaires, or they can delay their reply to the questionnaires.
2. This method is applicable only to the educated and co-operative respondents.
3. Once the questionnaire has been despatched, the investigator has no option to modify the questionnaire.
4. It cannot be ensured whether the respondents are truly representative.

Schedule Method

The schedule is also a list of questions, which is used to collect the data from the field. In this method, the responses are filled in by the researcher or the enumerator himself. When the scope of the study is wide, the researcher chooses to appoint people who are called enumerators for the purpose of collecting the data.

The enumerators go to the informants, ask them the questions from the schedule in the prescribed order and record the responses in the space provided for the answers in the schedule itself. For example, the census all over the world is conducted through this method.

The major difference between a questionnaire and a schedule is that the schedule is filled in by the informants, while the questionnaire is filled in by the researcher or enumerator.

Merits

1. This method is very useful where the informants are illiterates.
2. The researcher can overcome the problem of non-response as the enumerators go personally to obtain the information.
3. It gathers relatively more reliable data.

Limitations

1. It is a very expensive and time-consuming method as enumerators are paid persons and also have to be trained.
2. Since the enumerator is present, the respondents may not respond to some personal questions.
3. Reliability depends upon the sincerity and commitment of the enumerator.

STATISTICAL ANALYSIS

Meaning of statistics

The meaning of the word 'Statistics' is 'related to state'. Statistics is an independent discipline at present. In it, the methods of compilation, administration, classification, briefing, presentation, analysis, and explanation of data have been developed to study the problems of any field of life.

Statistics is the science that deals with, the methods of collecting, classifying, presenting, comparing, and interpreting numerical data collected to throw some light on any sphere of inquiry.

Characteristics of Statistics

In statistics, all the information is expressed quantitatively.

Statistics is an aggregate of facts.

In statistics, data are collected with a pre-determined purpose.

Cause and effect relationships should be established by standard techniques.

Statistical Methods

In every statistical investigation, the first thing is the collection of data. These data are so huge and complex in their nature that they do not give a clear and correct picture of the whole data. In order to have a clear and intelligible picture of the complex and bulky data, certain devices are applied. These devices are known as statistical methods.

These statistical methods are the techniques used for the collection, summarization, analysis, comparison, classification, and interpretation of huge and complex numerical data. Statistical tools such as tables, graphs, and diagrams are required for the analysis of data.

After the data have been collected, it is essential to put them in the form of tables with rows and columns. Tables should be prepared in such a way that they can be put to the best advantage with minimum effort.

For analyzing the data collected, tools such as tables, graphs, and diagrams are used. These tools are exhaustively used in data records, government reports, etc., in such a way that an ordinary person will be able to understand and draw a valid conclusion from the tools.

Measures of Central Tendency

The next step after classification, tabulation, and editing of data is its analysis and drawing conclusions. The activities before analysis and drawing conclusions only provide a shape and direction to the collected data. The information so collected becomes useful only when comparisons are drawn, correlation and other mathematical or statistical relationships are established between them and conclusions may be drawn.

According to Prof Bowley, 'Measures of central tendency (averages) are statistical constants which enable us to comprehend in a single effort the significance of the whole'.

The primary objectives of the Measure of Central Tendency are

1. To condense data into one value.
2. To facilitate comparisons between data.

In statistical methods the averages or measures of central tendency occupy an important place because the tools of statistical analysis are based upon them. Comparisons between various series are drawn through averages and it is the averages which represent the universe in condensed form.

The main types of averages are:

1. Arithmetic average or Mean
2. Median
3. Mode

Arithmetic Average/Mean

Arithmetic average or Mean is the most popular type of average. Arithmetic mean or average is used in some way or the other by all of us in our daily lives knowingly or unknowingly. The arithmetic mean of a series is obtained by adding the values of all the scores of the series and dividing the sum total by the number of scores.

The formula for arithmetic average/mean is (a) = (Sum of all the values/Total number of scores)

Median

Median is the value of the exact middle or central value of the items arranged in ascending order or descending order in a given series.

It divides the series in such a manner that the number of items before and after the median value is exactly equal in numbers.

If items are arranged in ascending order then all the items before the median are less in value and the items after it is more in value than the actual median.

In a series of individual observations, the median is determined by arranging the items in ascending or descending orders.

Advantages of Median

1. The calculation of the median is easy, particularly in a series of individual observations and discrete series.
2. Median is unaffected by the extreme and large values of variables.
3. As the median is a positional average and is influenced by the placement of items, the size or value of items does not influence the result.

Limitations of Median

1. For determining the median, the series has to be reorganized.
2. Unlike the mean, the median cannot be used as a measure for calculating the combined median of two or more groups.
3. In continuous series, the calculation of the median is a difficult affair.
4. Variation in sampling has a greater influence on the median than the mean
5. Median ceases to be typical of the series if a number of items in a series is small.

Mode

The word 'Mode' originated from the French word '*la-Mode*' which means fashion or the most popular phenomenon. Mode is the item in the series which has the maximum frequency and is located at the point of maximum concentration. In other words, the mode is the value of the variable which occurs or repeats itself the maximum number of times. Generally, the item having maximum frequency is determined as mode.

Advantages of Mode The mode has the following features:

1. Mode can be easily identified by having a look only.
2. Modal value can be diagrammatically determined.
3. Since it is a typical value, it is not affected by extreme values.

Limitations of Mode Mode has the following limitations:

1. In a small series of individual observation modes cannot be located.
2. Modal value overlooks the other items of the series.
3. Unlike other measures, the mode is an isolated value and through modal value and a total number of items, the aggregate cannot be determined.

Relationship between the Mean, Median, and Mode

In statistics, there is an empirical relationship between the mean, median, and mode. It is empirical because observations of countless data sets have shown that most of the time the difference between the mean and the mode is three times the difference between the mean and the median. This relationship in equation form can be expressed as:

$$\text{Mean} - \text{Mode} = 3\,(\text{Mean} - \text{Median}).$$

OBSERVATION

Observation in social science research is not merely watching but it is a careful process in which one or more persons observe some real-life situation and record pertinent occurrences.

Ram Ahuja defined observation as a planned methodical watching that involves constraints to improve accuracy.

Krishna Swami defined observation as a systematic viewing of a specific phenomenon in its proper setting for the specific purpose of gathering data for a particular study.

For Ronald R Powell observe means "to watch attentively in a scientific manner". In an observational study, the current status of the phenomenon is determined not by asking but by observing.

Participant Observation

In 'participant observation' the observer becomes more or less one of the group members and may actually participate in the activity of the group under study. The observer may play any one of the several roles in observation, with Interview, varying degrees of participation, as a visitor, an attentive listener, an eager learner, or as a participant observer.

A fine example of overt participant observation is the study "Street Corner Society" by William F. Whyte

(1943). He lived in a slum of Boston in the late 1930s that was inhabited by mostly first-generation and second-generation immigrants from Italy.

Non-participant Observation

In the 'non-participant observation' method, the observer takes a position where his/her presence is not felt by the group under study, the researcher here does participate in the group. He/she may follow closely the behaviour of an individual or characteristics of one or more groups. In this type of observation is like a one-way 'vision screen' which permits the observer to see the subject but prevents the subject from seeing the observer.

INTERVIEW

The basic instruments of data collection in survey research are questionnaires and interview methods.

Krishan Kumar (1992) defines 'interviewing is a process of personal interaction between a researcher and a respondent'.

Ranjit Kumar in his book Research Methodology (1999) opined that "any person-to-person interaction between two or more individuals with a specific purpose in mind is called an interview."

O'Leary (2004) of the view that 'Interviewing is a method of data collection which involves researchers asking respondents basically open-ended questions'.

According to Neuman (1991), 'the interview is a short duration, secondary social interaction between two strangers with the defined purpose of one person's obtaining specific information from the other. Information is obtained in a well-defined structured conversation in which the interviewer asks pre-arranged questions and records the answers of the respondent'.

In a simple sentence, we can say that survey interviewing is a face-to-face interaction with the respondents to get specific information.

Adams (1985) has compared questionnaires and interviews with surgical tools in medicine. He further stated that these tools are the most commonly used modes of data collection in many branches of social and behavioural sciences.

Types of Interviews

Structured Interview

A structured Interview is also called a directive interview. In a structured interview, the interviewer asks pre-drafted questions. Here, the interviewer is not allowed to change the question nor he can disturb the sequence of the question. And has no freedom to add new questions or delete any questions.

The interviewer is strictly instructed to ask only the predetermined questions and also to record them as it is. The interview schedule is prepared in advance. It may include both open-ended and closed-ended questions.

Ranjit Kumar suggested that an interview schedule is a tool to collect data while interviewing is a process/method of data collection.

In comparison to unstructured interview, structured interview generates uniform data. It does not require any professional training to conduct interview sessions because of predefined questions. It is required from the interviewer that he/she should remain unbiased. The interviewer can be biased in the case of an unstructured interview. The interviewer is supposed to give only clarifications on and when it is desired.

Krishan Kumar also said that it should restrict to only clarifications and no suggestions be given. This type of interview can be conducted person-to-person or through telephone or by using the electronic device.

Unstructured Interview

During the unstructured interview, the interviewer is free to ask whatever comes to his mind on the particular research problem under investigation. This type of interview can be conducted on a one-to-one basis or with a group of interviewees.

Depending on the nature of the research, the unstructured interview may allow the interviewee to give responses freely or it may impose restrictions over free responses. Hence, the interviewer is advised to ask the respondents only such questions, which strictly come under the area of research under study. There are no set typed questions. One question leads to another question and so on.

Here, the main aim of the interviewer is to get the personal opinion of the respondents on a given topic. The interviewer is always advised to keep an interview guide or schedule with him/her at the time of the interview. It helps him/her to know the areas to be covered and it also provides guidelines for the smooth conduct of the interview session.

The interviewer is free to ask additional questions and also repeat or delete questions as mentioned in the guide. If at any instance he/she feels that some questions are not very clear he/she has full freedom to change them.

At the time of the interview, if it is felt that putting certain questions or changing the sequence may yield some useful results, the interviewer can do it freely.

On the respondent's side, they are given the opportunity to give their views, opinions freely on the questions asked. An effort can be made during the interview to encourage them to speak freely. This level of freedom on both sides help generate spontaneous, useful responses in the area of research under study.

Focussed Interview

The aim of the Focussed interview is to get focussed, in-depth information on any given issue from the respondent. It is one of the types of unstructured interviews. The main task of the researcher here is to involve the respondent in a discussion on a specific topic so that the interviewer is able to get desired information. Here the interviewer has the freedom to decide the questions and their sequence.

Kothari is of the opinion that such interviews are helpful in the development of a hypothesis. Here the information is gathered from the respondent's area of experiences, effects, participation, etc. Here the interviewer is not only properly informed about the area of research but he/she also knowledgeable and skilled to get the required information from the experiences, and background of the respondent which has a direct bearing on the topic under study. The selection of respondents is done on the basis of knowledge experiences of the respondents on the area of study.

Non-directive Interview

Here in this type of interview, the Interviewer only acts as a catalyst, his position here is only of a prompter. He prompts the respondents to give information on the topic under investigation. The number of questions in this method is very less, and respondent express their views freely, but the area to be covered remains under the control of the interviewer. The interviewer allows free environment for the respondents so that they can express their opinion freely and to the point, the interviewer simply supports the views expressed by the respondent without approving or disapproving them.

Clinical Interview

Clinical Interview also comes under the category of unstructured interview.

Adams and Schvaneveldt reported that this type of interview has been used in social care work, counselling, and prison settings, and is also called personal history interviews. Here the interviewer records the feelings, and life experiences, of the respondents.

Here the interviewer is allowed to interact freely with the respondents to get information on the given topic. This type of interview is flexible and it includes introductory questions as well. Here the respondent can also give new information on related factors and elaborate on them.

It may prove very helpful in predicting, analyzing, and concluding some areas. The area under investigation, its objectives, and scope are the main determinants of the selection of questions and area to be covered in the clinical interview.

Telephonic Interview

As the name suggests, this type of interview is conducted over the phone. Here the researcher needs a telephone connection and an instrument, a phone directory, and a set of questions to be asked. It is best suited for market-type surveys, polling, etc.

It is one of the fastest ways of collecting data, it saves money and energy for the interviewer by avoiding a personal visit to the respondents. Conducting an interview session does not require special skills. No special skills are required to conduct such interview sessions.

A telephone interview is a faster and cheaper method for obtaining information. Extra staff i.e., field staff is not required in this method. Moreover, it is very flexible in comparison with the mailed questionnaire method. The case of non-response is very low in telephone interviews.

CASE STUDIES

Case studies are sources of informations about any situation, problems or the progress and experiences. It can also be a puzzle to the readers for which they are expected to analyse the information and to suggest possible solutions based on the problems and these are self-explanatory narrations.

The first case studies in the social sciences were likely conducted by Pierre Guillaume Frédéric Le Play, a 19th-century French sociologist and economist who studied family budgets. The method has been used in sociology, psychology, and anthropology since the early 20th century.

Charles H Cooley says that 'Case study deepens perception and gives a clear insight into life.'

Pauline Young opines that 'it is a method of exploring and analyzing the life of a social unit-be it a person, a family, an institution, cultural group or even an entire community'.

Goode and Hatt say, 'Case Study is a way of organizing social data so as to preserve the unitary character of the social object being studied'.

According to F.L. Whitney, 'A case study is a complete analysis and report of the status of an individual subject with respect as a rule to specific phases of his total personality'.

Sources of Data

Case studies are not limited to any single source of data. They employ a number of sources. The following are some of the identified sources of information for the case study method:

Life histories; Personal records; Personal documents; Personal letters; Confessions; Biographies; Interviewing individuals; Observations.

DATA ANALYSIS AND REPORT WRITING

Data Analysis

Once data is collected the researcher thinks about the processing and analysis of the data. This is a crucial stage of research work. Here, the researcher has to consult the guide and other academicians who have done research in the related field.

Therefore, it is advised that data processing must be planned in advance, and, necessarily, during the time of questionnaire formulation; and, during the time of data collection. Nowadays, with the advent of the computer, researchers might think it is the job of a computer assistant, but it is not so.

Before either giving it to the computer assistant or doing it manually, a lot of activities have to be completed:

i. editing of the data which you received from the field;
ii. coding of the data;
iii. preparation of the master chart if the data is to be computed manually; and
iv. presentation of data.

Editing of the Data

The editing of data is the first step of data processing and analysis. After collecting data, either through the questionnaire or schedule, you have to edit it. You have to carefully check for missing and wrongly entered data.

Coding of the Data

The questionnaire must be properly coded. The coding of data will make data entry easy. Coding of data means assigning a numerical symbol to each response to the question. The purpose of giving numerical symbols is to translate raw data into numerical data, which may be counted and tabulated.

Entering Data in the Master Chart

If you are doing tabulation manually, it is always wise to enter the data into a master chart. The master chart is a large sheet which will enable you to enter all the codes of different variables into it. It will help you to generate tables easily.

Data Tabulation

Tabulation is an orderly and systematic arrangement of numerical data presented in rows and columns for the purpose of information, comparison, and interpretation. So, a statistical table is a systematic arrangement of statistical data into rows and columns.

It summarizes the data in a logical and orderly manner for the purpose of presentation, comparison, and interpretation. Tabulation is, thus, a scientific process and means of recording, statistical data in a systematic and orderly manner.

Report Writing

A research report is considered a major component of any research study as the research remains incomplete till the report has been presented or written. No matter how good a research study, is and how meticulously the research study has been conducted, the findings of the research are of little value unless they are effectively documented and communicated to others.

The research results must invariably enter the general store of knowledge. Writing a report is the last step in a research study and requires a set of skills somewhat different from those called for in actually conducting research.

The research report will have, broadly, three parts.

Part I: The Preliminary Pages
Part II: The Main Text of the Research Report
Part III: The End Matter

ASSESS YOUR LEARNING

PRACTICE QUESTIONS

1. According to Bacon, there are many delusions that act as obstacles and divert us from the truth. These delusions that he regarded as the 'idols of mind'. There are four species of idols that Bacon identified which among the following is not one of them?
(a) Idols of the tribe
(b) Idols of the forest
(c) Idols of the market
(d) Idols of the theatre

2. In relation to Rene Descartes's fundamental lessons of rationalism (Philosophy of Science), which of the following statement is/are correct?
1. Descartes argued, 'man is a thing that thinks'.
2. One cannot separate oneself from one's mind, one can, however, exist without one's body

Chose the answer from the codes given below:
(a) Statement 1 only
(b) Statement 2 only
(c) Both are correct
(d) None of the statements are correct.

3. Sociology saw itself as a science: a scientific study of society. On what accounts it differentiated itself from religion, metaphysics, and common-sense?
(a) objectivity
(b) value neutrality
(c) empirical science
(d) subjectivity

4. Epistemology for a division includes which of the following?
1. Objectivity
2. Subjectivity
3. Empiricism
4. Rationalism

Choose the correct option:
(a) (1) and (2)
(b) (2) and (3)
(c) (3) and (4)
(d) (4) and (1)

5. Who coined the term 'epistemology'?
(a) Aristotle
(b) Immanuel Kant
(c) Johann Conrad Dannhauer
(d) James Fredrick Ferrier

6. Some knowledge is derived from sense experience while others is derived from reason. Epistemologists call these two types of knowledge as:
1. Empirical knowledge
2. Non-empirical knowledge
3. Objective knowledge
4. Subjective knowledge

Choose the correct option:
(a) (1) and (2)
(b) (2) and (3)
(c) (3) and (4)
(d) (4) and (1)

7. Hermeneutics (the interpretation of tradition) is
1. A part of the methodological quest to understand the social reality.
2. It is a rule or set of procedures to interpret something.
3. It is the art of understanding and of making oneself understood.
4. It has been applied as a method in sociology
5. It offers a toolbox for efficiently treating problems of the interpretation of human actions, texts, and other meaningful material.

Choose the correct option
(a) 1 and 2 only
(b) 1, 2, and 3 only
(c) 1, 2, 3 and 4
(d) 1, 2, 3, 4 and 5

8. Who is known as the father of modern hermeneutics?
(a) Friedrich Schleiermacher
(b) Johann Clauberg
(c) Dilthey
(d) Gadamer

9. The book '*hermeneutics*' is written by?
(a) Johann Conrad Dannhauer
(b) Friedrich Schleiermacher
(c) Johann Clauberg
(d) John Dilthey

10. Who developed the concept of the hermeneutic circle?
(a) Johann Conrad Dannhauer
(b) Martin Heidegger
(c) Friedrich Schleiermacher
(d) Johann Clauberg

11. Who is associated with the concept of 'Reflexive Modernization'?
(a) Edward Said
(b) J. Habermas
(c) Manuel Castells
(d) Anthony Giddens

12. Choose the incorrect statement?
(a) Reflexivity refers to circular relationships between cause and effect
(b) Methodology is the study of inter-relations among facts.
(c) Epistemology deals with the nature, origin, and scope of knowledge.
(d) Ethnography tries to study a socio-cultural phenomena.

13. Which of the following statement is/are correct?
1. Emic perspectives are the ethnographic approach under which the viewpoints and responses of the 'out groups' are noted down.
2. Etic perspective is the ethnographic approach under which the viewpoints and responses of the 'in group' or the members of the culture under study are noted down.

Chose the answer from the codes given below:
(a) Statement 1 only
(b) Statement 2 only
(c) Both are correct
(d) None of the statements are correct.

14. Which one of the following statements is correct with reference to a deductive argument?
(a) The relation between premises and conclusion is one of matter of fact
(b) The relation between premises and conclusion is one of logical necessity
(c) The relation between premises and conclusion is that of empirical necessity
(d) The relation between premises and conclusion is a matter of ascertainment of probability

15. Which of the following statements fails to indicate the intent of purposive sampling?
(a) Purposive sampling places the investigator's research questions at the forefront of sampling considerations
(b) Theoretical saturation is a useful principle for making decision about sample size
(c) Purposive sampling is not the fundamental principle for selecting cases and individuals in qualitative research
(d) There is considerable disagreement about what is an acceptable minimum sample size in qualitative research

16. Consider the following statements regarding the survey method of research:
1. Survey methods can be used in both, quantitative, as well as, qualitative studies.
2. Describing certain aspects or characteristics of the population and/or
3. Testing hypotheses about nature of relationships within a population.

Chose the correct statement/s from the codes given below:
(a) Statement 1 only correct
(b) Statements 1 & 2 only are correct
(c) All are correct
(d) None of the statements are correct.

17. The type of research that aims to solve a problem by adding to the field of application of a discipline is called as?
(a) Fundamental Research
(b) Applied Research
(c) Action Research
(d) Exploratory research

18. Which of the following research type discovers why, what, and how of actual life?
(a) Fundamental Research
(b) Applied Research
(c) Descriptive Research
(d) Exploratory research

19. A research type that is qualitative in nature, and is used in formulating and testing of hypothesis is called as?
(a) Fundamental Research
(b) Applied Research
(c) Descriptive Research
(d) Exploratory research

20. The research type which particularly deals with the 'cause and effect of the problem'?
(a) Experimental Research
(b) Survey Research
(c) Evaluative Research
(d) Exploratory research

21. Which research method is most suitable 'to measure the implementation and outcomes of programs for decision-making purposes'?
(a) Experimental Research
(b) Survey Research
(c) Evaluative Research
(d) Exploratory research

22. Which of the following is not a data-collection method?
(a) Research question
(b) Unstructured interview
(c) Postal survey questionnaire
(d) Participant observation

23. A deductive theory is one that
(a) Allows theory to emerge out of the data
(b) Involves testing an explicitly defined hypothesis
(c) Allows for findings to feed back into the stock of knowledge
(d) Uses qualitative methods whenever possible

24. It refers to inferring about the whole population based on the observations made on a small part.
(a) Deductive inference
(b) Inductive inference
(c) Pseudo-inference
(d) Objective inference

25. In which sampling method each member of the set has an equal chance of selection?
(a) Area sampling
(b) Non-random sampling
(c) Random sampling
(d) Systematic sampling

26. An example of probability sampling is
(a) Quota Sampling
(b) Snow-ball sampling
(c) Purposive sampling
(d) Lottery method

27. Questions that allow only a few alternative ways of answering are called as?
(a) Open-ended questions
(b) Unstructured questions
(c) Structural questions
(d) Dichotomous questions

28. A method of collecting primary data in which a number of individuals with a common interest interact is called?
(a) Telephone Interview
(b) Clinical Interview
(c) Focused Interview
(d) Group Interview

29. Readymade and readily available data is called as?
(a) Primary (b) Personal
(c) Organizational (d) Secondary

30. A Hypothesis from which no generalization can be made is known as?
(a) Null Hypothesis
(b) Barren Hypothesis
(c) Descriptive Hypothesis
(d) Analytical Hypothesis

31. When a hypothesis is stated negatively it is called as?
(a) Relational Hypothesis
(b) Situational Hypothesis
(c) Null Hypothesis
(d) Casual Hypothesis

32. A Hypothesis which develops while planning the research is?
(a) Null Hypothesis
(b) Working Hypothesis
(c) Relational Hypothesis
(d) Descriptive Hypothesis

33. Concepts can be divided into two types they are?
(a) Abstract and Coherent
(b) Concrete and Coherent
(c) Abstract and concrete
(d) None of the above

34. 'One of the methods of logical reasoning process' is called?
(a) Induction
(b) Deduction
(c) Research
(d) Experiment

35. It is a 'systematically conceptual structure of inter-related elements in some schematic form'?
(a) Concept
(b) Variable
(c) Model
(d) Facts

36. Who authored the book, '*Methods in Social Research*'?
(a) Wilkinson
(b) CR Kothari
(c) Kerlinger
(d) Goode and Halt

37. Who is the author of the book, '*Principia Ethica*'?
(a) G.E. Moore
(b) Martin Buber
(c) Gabriel Marcel
(d) Emmanuel Levinas

38. Choose the correct statements:
1. Deduction is a process of arriving at knowledge through experience.
2. Induction is a process of gaining knowledge independently of experience through pure logical reasoning.

Options:
(a) Statement 1 only
(b) Statement 2 only
(c) Both are correct
(d) None of the statements are correct.

39. The whole study of ethics can be divided into two types which are they?
(a) General ethics
(b Moral ethics
(c) Social ethics
(d) Special ethics

Choose the correct answer:
(a) (1) and (2)
(b) (2) and (3)
(c) (3) and (4)
(d) (4) and (1)

40. It is a way of indexing or categorizing the text in order to establish a framework of thematic ideas about it?
(a) Editing
(b) Coding
(c) Transcription
(d) Content Analysis

Answer Key

1. (b)
2. (c)
3. (d)
4. (c)
5. (d)
6. (a)
7. (d)
8. (a)
9. (a)
10. (b)
11. (d)
12. (a)
13. (d)
14. (b)
15. (c)
16. (c)
17. (a)
18. (b)
19. (d)
20. (a)
21. (c)
22. (a)
23. (b)
24. (b)
25. (c)
26. (d)
27. (c)
28. (d)
29. (d)
30. (b)
31. (c)
32. (b)
33. (c)
34. (a)
35. (c)
36. (d)
37. (a)
38. (d)
39. (d)
40. (b)

PREVIOUS YEARS' QUESTIONS

DECEMBER 2023

1. Which among the following are the elements of ethos of science propounded by Robert K. Merton?
   A. Universalism
   B. Humanism
   C. Communism
   D. Disinterestedness
   E. Organized scepticism
   Choose the correct answer from the options given below:
   (a) A, B, C and D only
   (b) B, C, D and E only
   (c) A, B, C and E only
   (d) A, C, D and E only

2. Which one is not a feature of qualitative methods?
   (a) Open-ended questions
   (b) Text and image analysis
   (c) Themes and pattern interpretation
   (d) Census data

3. A satisfactory statistical unit should possess the following qualities:
   A. Appropriateness
   B. Clarity
   C. Measurability and comparability
   D. Flexibility
   Choose the correct answer from the options given below:
   (a) A, B and C only
   (b) B, C and D only
   (c) A, B and D only
   (d) A, C and D only

4. Given below are two statements:
   Statement I: Sample size determination indicate the number of people in the sample and the procedures used to compute this number.
   Statement II: A large sample will provide less accuracy in the inferences made.
   In the light of the above statements, choose the correct answer from the options given below:
   (a) Both Statement I and Statement II are true.
   (b) Both Statement I and Statement II are false.
   (c) Statement I is true but Statement II Is false.
   (d) Statement I is false but Statement II is true.

5. Which is not a study design?
   (a) Cross-sectional
   (b) Interview
   (c) Cross-cultural
   (d) Longitudinal

6. The correct sequence of steps of conducting a research study are
   A. Research questions
   B. Data collection
   C. Literature review
   D. Writing-up
   E. Data analysis
   Choose the correct answer from the options given below
   (a) A, C, B, E, D
   (b) B, A, E, D, C
   (c) E, A, C, B, D
   (d) C, A, B, E, D

7. The characteristics of usable hypotheses are
   A. The hypothesis must be conceptually clear.
   B. The hypotheses should have empirical referents.
   C. The hypotheses should not be specific.
   D. The hypotheses should be related to a body of theory.
   Choose the correct answer from the options given below:
   (a) A, B and C only
   (b) A, C and D only
   (c) A, B and D only
   (d) B, C and D only

8. The graphic presentation of frequency distribution is done by using:
   A. Histograms technique
   B. Frequency polygons
   C. Percentile
   D. Smoothed frequency curves
   Choose the correct answer from the options given below:
   (a) A, B and Conly
   (b) B, C and D only
   (c) A, B and D only
   (d) A, C and D only

9. What are the steps in planning and implementation of a rural development project? Arrange in correct sequence.
   A. Selection of beneficiaries
   B. Base-line survey
   C. Monitoring and evaluation
   D. Selection of schemes
   E. Execution of the programme
   Choose the correct answer from the options given below:
   (a) C, A, B, D, E
   (b) A, B, C, D, E
   (c) B, A, D, E, C
   (d) B, D, E, C, A

10. One of the main characteristics of theories in modern science is
    (a) A theory is considered as a final explanation.
    (b) A theory is always held with some tentativeness.
    (c) A theory is just a hypothesis.
    (d) A theory is a description of facts.

11. Descriptive research design is used to
A. Portray accurately the characteristics of a particular individual, situation or group.
B. Determine the frequency with which it is associated with something occur or with which it is associated with something else.
C. Test a hypothesis of a causal relationship between variables.
D. Study to minimize bias and maximize reliability.
Choose the correct answer from the options given below:
(a) A, B and C only
(b) A, C and D only
(c) B, C and D only
(d) A, B and D only

12. Given below are two statements: one is labelled as Assertion A and the other is labelled as Reason R.
Assertion A: 'Dependent variables are the outcomes or results of the influence of the independent variables.
Reason R: 'Because independent variables are variables that are manipulated in the experiment'.
In the light of the above statements, choose the most appropriate answer from the options given below:
(a) Both A and R are correct and R is the correct explanation of A
(b) Both A and R are correct but R is NOT the correct explanation of A
(c) A is correct but R is not correct
(d) A is not correct but R is correct

13. Who has studied 'Lucknow Rickshawallas' in 1965?
(a) Harbert Risley
(b) Edward Shils
(c) Harold A. Gould
(d) Joseph Schumpeter

JUNE 2023

14. Karl Popper while following the deductive research strategy, advocated:
A. The natural and social words consist of essential uniformatives
B. The aim of science is to establish generalizations
C. Facts are analysed, compared, and classified without using hypothesis
D. It is not necessary that social facts are analysed by using falsifiability principle
Choose the appropriate answer from the options given below:
(a) A and B only
(b) B and C only
(c) C and D only
(d) A only

15. In the definition of knowledge, identify the elements which are valid:
A. Knowledge is a belief which is true.
B. Knowledge is a belief which is justified
C. Knowledge is a conjectured formation
D. Knowledge is a belief which is the true opinion of others
Choose the appropriate answer from the options given below:
(a) A and B only
(b) C and D only
(c) A and C only
(d) B and D only

16. Arrange the sources of knowledge in order of their usage of performance in social research.
A. Reasoning
B. Sense Perception
C. Intuition
D. Authority (Disciplinary)
Choose the correct answer from the options given below:
(a) A, B, C, D
(b) B, C, D, A
(c) B, A, D, C
(d) D, B, C, A

17. Arrange various sciences in a hierarchy from complex to simple as provided by Auguste Comte:
A. Physics
B. Biology
C. Astronomy
D. Chemistry
E. Sociology
Choose the correct answer from the options given below:
(a) A, C, E, B, D
(b) E, B, C, A, D
(c) C, B, E, D, A
(d) E, B, D, A, C

18. A merit of the interview method of data collection is:
A. It can cover a very wide geographical area
B. It can study quantitative aspects of any event
C. It is an effective way to study abstract personal factors
D. It is useful in the identification of unanticipated aspects of the respondent
Choose the appropriate answer from the options given below:
(a) A and B only
(b) Band C only
(c) C and D only
(d) A and D only

19. In social survey,
A. methods of questionnaire and structured interviews are used to gather data.
B. standardized information is collected from a sample selected as being representative of the selected population.

C. standardized information is obtained by asking diverse sets of questions to all members of sample.
D. standardized information is obtained by asking same sets of questions to all members of the sample.
E. both analytical and descriptive perspective can be made inbuilt in a social survey.

Choose the appropriate answer from the options given below:
(a) A, B, C, D only
(b) B, C, D, E only
(c) A, B, D, E only
(d) B, C, D only

20. Who among the following are not associated with hermeneutics?
A. Dilthey
B. Gadamer
C. Ricoeur
D. Popper
E. Husserl

Choose the appropriate answer from the options given below:
(a) A and B only
(b) B and C only
(c) A and C only
(d) D and E only

21. Arrange the following steps of research from initial to final stage:
A. Review of literature
B. Bibliography
C. Primary data collection
D. Statement of the problem

Choose the correct answer from the options given below:
(a) C, A, D, B
(b) D, A, C, B
(c) A, B, C, D
(d) B, D, A, C

22. Identify the type of sampling among the following in which the inferential statistics cannot be applied:
(a) Simple random sampling
(b) Stratified sampling
(c) Purposive sampling
(d) Multi-stage random sampling

MARCH 2023

23. Given below are two statements, one is labelled as Assertion (A) and the other is labelled as Reason (R).

Assertion (A): Sociologists must separate the empirical work from the conceptual universe that they construct.

Reason (R): In Weber's view, history is composed of unique empirical events; there can be no generalizations at the empirical level.

In light of the above statements, choose the *most appropriate* answer from the options given below:
(a) Both (A) and (R) are correct and (R) is the correct explanation of (A).
(b) Both (A) and (R) are correct and (R) is NOT the correct explanation of (A).
(c) (A) is correct but (R) is not correct.
(d) (A) is not correct but (R) is correct.

24. Standard deviation is a measure of dispersion around the:
(a) Mean
(b) Median
(c) Mode
(d) None of the above

25. According to Alex Inkeles, the three main paths available for delineating the subject matter of sociology are:
A. Analytical
B. Empirical
C. Historical
D. Philosophical
E. Theoretical

Choose the correct answer from the options given below:
(a) A, B, and C only
(b) A, C, and E only
(c) C, D, and E only
(d) A, C, and D only

26. Given below are two statements, one is labelled as Assertion (A) and the other is labelled as Reason (R).

Assertion (A): One of the most significant approaches to conducting ethnographic research on online communities is netnography which has been developed by Kozinets

Reason (R): Netnography is a form of ethnography because it entails the researcher's immersion in the on line worlds under investigation

In the light of the above statements, choose the most appropriate answer from the options given below.
(a) Both (A) and (R) are correct and (R) is the correct explanation of (A).
(b) Both (A) and (R) are correct and (R) is NOT the correct explanation of (A).
(c) (A) is correct but (R) is not correct.
(d) (A) is not correct but (R) is correct.

27. Match List I with List II

List I (Types of Variables)	List II (Definition)
A. Dependent variable	I. A variable whose categories can be rank ordered

B. Interval variable	II. A variable where the distances between categories are identical across its range
C. Ordinal variable	III. A variable that is influenced by another variable
D. Dichotomous variable	IV. A variable with just two values

Choose the correct answer from the options given below:
(a) A - IV, B - I, C - II, D - III
(b) A - I, B - IV, C - III, D - II
(c) A - II, B - III, C - IV, D - I
(d) A - III, B - II, C - I, D - IV

28. Participatory Action Research (PAR) is an example of
A. Public sociology
B. Classical sociology
C. Critical sociology
D. Theoretical sociology
E. Sociology in action
Choose the correct answer from the options given below:
(a) A, B, and C only
(b) B, D, and E only
(c) A, C, and E only
(d) C, D, and E only

29. The universe of units from which a sample is to be selected is called:
(a) Population
(b) Survey
(c) Reliability
(d) Validity

30. Deductive study represents the commonest view of the nature of the relationship between theory and social research. The chronological process of deduction is
A. Theory
B. Revision of theory
C. Hypothesis
D. Hypothesis confirmed or rejected
E. Data collection and findings analysis
Choose the correct answer from the options given below:
(a) A, B, C, D, E
(b) A, C, E, D, B
(c) E, C, D, A, B
(d) C, E, D, A, B

31. William Foote Whyte's 'Street Corner Society' is an example of:
(a) Participant observation
(b) Participatory Action Research
(c) Risk Society
(d) Globalization of labour

DEC 2021 & JUNE 2022

32. Select the correct statement/s
A. **Quantitative approach:** Post-positivist worldview, experimental strategy of enquiry and pre and posttest measures of attitudes
B. **Qualitative approach:** Constructivist worldview, ethnographic design and observation of behaviour
C. **Qualitative approach:** Pariticipatory worldview, narrative design and open-ended interviewing
D. **Mixed method approach:** Pragmatic worldview, collection of both qualitative and quantitative data sequentially
E. **Qualitative approach:** Post-positivist worldview, experimental strategy of inquiry and pre and post-test measures of attitudes
Choose the correct answer from the options given below:
(a) A, B and C only
(b) B and C only
(c) A,B, C and D only
(d) A and E only

33. Examples of nominal measures are:
A. Gender
B. Religious affiliation
C. Birth place
D. Social classes
E. Intellectual sophistication
Choose the correct answer from the options given below:
(a) D and E only (b) A, B and C only
(c) B, C and D only (d) A, B and D only

34. A. Quantitative research is any research method that involves the analysis of numerical data derived usually from surveys and experiments.
B. Qualitative research is any research method that involves the analysis of numerical data derived usually from surveys and experiments.
C. Inferential statistics does not allow researchers to use data from a relatively small group to speculate with some level of certainty about a larger group.
D. Quantitative research methods do not require statistical methods for collecting and reporting data.
E. Statistics is the mathematical method used to analyze numerical data.

Choose the correct answer from the options given below:
(a) A, B, C and D only
(b) A only
(c) B, C and D only
(d) A and E only

35. ________ was first developed by sociologists, B. Glaser and A. Strauss (1967), in an attempt to come to grips with their clinical research in medical sociology
(a) Conflict Theory
(b) Structural functionalist Theory
(c) Functionalist Theory
(d) Grounded Theory

36. __________ is an epistemological position that advocates the application of the methods of natural sciences to the study of social reality and beyond.
(a) Interpretivism
(b) Constructionism
(c) Positivism
(d) None of the above

37. The middle attribute in the ranked distribution of observed attributes is known as:
(a) Mean
(b) Mode
(c) Standard deviation
(d) None of the above

38. Given below are two statements:

Statement I: A major problem for empirical researchers is the connection between theory and observation referred to as rules of correspondence.

Statement II: In Sociology, the passage from observation to conceptualisation and back again requires a close examination of the manner in which our observations are organised and categorised, as well as, to the operationalisation of the concepts used to organise data.

In the light of the above statements, choose the most appropriate answer from the options given below

(a) Both Statement I and Statement II are correct
(b) Both Statement I and Statement II are incorrect
(c) Statement I is correct but Statement II is incorrect
(d) Statement I is incorrect but Statement II is correct

39. Match List-I with List-II

List I (Principles)	List II (Meaning)
A. Phenomenalism	I. Knowledge is arrived at through the gathering of facts that provide the basis for laws
B. Deductivism	II. Asserts that social phenomena and their meanings are continually being accomplished by social actors
C. Inductivism	III. The purpose of theory is to generate hypothesis that can be tested
D. Constructionism	IV. Only phenomena and hence knowledge confirmed by the senses can be warranted as knowledge

Choose the correct answer from the options given below:

(a) A - I, B - II, C - III, D - IV
(b) A - II, B - IV, C - I, D - III
(c) A - IV, B - III, C - I, D - II
(d) A - III, B - II, C - I, D - IV

40. A _______ entails the collection of data on more than one case (usually quite a lot more than one) and at a single point in time.
(a) Cross-sectional research design
(b) Longitudinal research design
(c) Both of the above
(d) None of the above

41. Given below are two statements:

Statement I: Correspondence analysis is a statistical method of analysis for cross-tabulated data by finding a geometrical representation.

Statement II: Well-known applications of correspondence analysis are presented by Pierre Bourdieu in Distinction.

In light of the above statements, choose the correct answer from the options given below

(a) Both Statement I and Statement II are true
(b) Both Statement I and Statement II are false
(c) Statement I is true but Statement II is false
(d) Statement I is false but Statement II is true

JUNE 2021

42. According to Durkheim, it is possible to make the claim of being Science, as systematization, classification and offering explanation on the basis of which of the following?
(a) Internality (b) Subjectivity
(c) Falsifiability (d) Externality

43. Which term is used to refer to the characteristics or properties of the studied object?
(a) Hypothesis/es (b) Research questions
(c) Ethics (d) Concepts

44. The reasoning which proceeds from a general truth to a particular truth is called:
(a) Inductive (b) Premise
(c) Deductive (d) Prediction

45. Which of the following are the four institutional imperatives, according to Robert K. Merton?

A. Universalism
B. Particularism
C. Communism
D. Disinterestedness
E. Organized scepticism

Choose the correct answer from the options given below:

(a) A, B, C and D
(b) B, C, D and E only
(c) A, C, D and E only
(d) A, B, D and E only

46. A relationship between two quantitative or qualitative variables is considered significant according to the $\chi 2$ (Chi-square) test at which of the following levels of error?

A. 1%
B. 2%
C. 3%
D. 5%
E. 10%

Choose the correct answer from the options given below:

(a) A, B, C and D only
(b) B, C, D and E only
(c) A, C, D and E only
(d) A, B, D and E only

47. Match List I with List II

List I (Book/Work)	List II (Sociologists)
A. Research Methods in Social Relations	I. Goode and Hatt
B. Methods in Social Research	II. Schuessler and Mueller
C. The Rules of Sociological Method	III. Seltiz, Jahoda et. al.
D. Statistical Reasoning in Sociology	IV. Emile Durkheim

Choose the correct answer from the options given below:

(a) A–I, B–II, C–III, D–IV
(b) A–III, B–I, C–IV, D–II
(b) A–II, B–III, C–IV, D–I
(d) A–III, B–IV, C–I, D–II

JUNE 2020

48. The primary philosophical assumption in 'null hypothesis' in social science research is
(a) Technicality
(b) Specification
(c) Falsifiability
(d) Distinctiveness

49. The study of people using participant observation and face-to-face interviewing is called
(a) Phenomenology
(b) Social mapping
(c) Ethnography
(d) Epidemiology

50. According to Durkheim, Indirect Experiment is ______
(a) Historical method
(b) Laboratory method
(c) Partial method
(d) Comparative method

51. Who used the 'historical approach' in his sociological analysis?
(a) A.R. Radcliffe - Brown
(b) C. Wright Mills
(c) E. Durkheim
(d) M. Ginsberg

52. Who used reflexive critique in his engagement with Kantian philosophy?
(a) Marx (b) Engels
(c) Hegel (d) Weber

53. Who was the first to use the word 'falsifiability' in the context of social science?
(a) Thomas Kuhn (b) George Ritzer
(c) William J. Goode (d) Karl Popper

54. Which term was used by Kuhn to state that science at any given time as being dominated by a specific ______
(a) Paradigm (b) Model
(c) Approach (d) Theory

55. Sample which fulfills the requirements of efficiency representativeness, reliability, and flexibility is called:
(a) Stratified sample
(b) Optimum sample
(c) Accidental sample
(d) Cluster sample

56. Which of the following are elements of induction?
1. General statements
2. Suggesting a regular association between two or more variables
3. Conclusion is the starting point
4. Derived from a series of empirical observations
5. Firm conclusion

Choose the correct answer from the options given below:

(a) 1, 2, and 3 only
(b) 3, 4, and 5 only
(c) 2 and 4 only
(d) 2, 4, and 5 only

57. Which of the following elements are involved in data analysis?
1. Data collecting
2. Coding

3. Editing
4. Classification
5. Observation

Choose the most appropriate answer from the options given below:

(a) 1, 2, and 3 only
(b) 2, 3, and 5 only
(c) 1, 4, and 5 only
(d) 2, 3, and 4 only

58. Match List I with List II:

List I (Research Work)	List II (Method)
A. Field observation	I. Survey
B. Looking at cause and effect relationships	II. Content analysis
C. Aim to describe a few characteristics of a large population	III. Empirical Research
D. Analysis of newspaper and media reports	IV. Explanatory Research

Choose the correct answer from the options given below:

	A	B	C	D
(a)	III	IV	I	II
(b)	IV	I	II	III
(c)	IV	II	III	I
(d)	I	II	III	IV

59. Arrange the following in a sequence according to the scheme given by Merton?

1. Observation of facts
2. Analysis of observed facts
3. Theory Building
4. Generalization
5. Conceptualization

Choose the correct answer from the options given below:

(a) 1, 2, 3, 4, 5
(b) 1, 2, 5, 4, 3
(c) 2, 4, 5, 1, 3
(d) 4, 5, 1, 2, 3

60. Given below are two statements: one is labelled as Assertion A and the other is labelled as Reason R.

Assertion (A): Objectivity in social science research can be maintained to some extent.

Reasons (R): Objectivity gives the account of the external world as it exists independently of our conceptions, but the social world cannot be observed from the outside alone.

In light of the above statements, choose the most appropriate answer from the options given below:

(a) Both (A) and (R) are correct and R is the correct explanation of A
(b) Both (A) and (R) are correct but R is not the correct explanation of A
(c) (A) is correct but (R) is not correct
(d) (A) is not correct but (R) is correct

61. Given below are two statements: One is labelled as Assertion A and the other is labelled as Reason R.

Assertion (A): In Sociology, we use the method of indirect experiment, that is. comparative method.

Reasons (R): In natural sciences, the establishment of causal connection is facilitated by experiments, but such experiments are impossible in social science.

In light of the above statements, choose the correct answer from the options given below :

(a) Both (A) and (R) are true and R is the correct explanation of A
(b) Both (A) and (R) are true but R is not the correct explanation of A
(c) (A) is true but (R) is not false
(d) (A) is false but (R) is true

Directions (62-66): Read the following passage carefully

In the field of human sciences, interdisciplinary research can result from two separate but interrelated needs. First is the need for information and more data, and the second is the need for more common structures or for analytical integration. At the first level, an interdisciplinary collaboration poses little or no problems. It involves the exchange of information among related disciplines in the belief that such exchange enriches a discipline's understanding of the phenomena under study. A discipline's boundaries and autonomy in explanatory terms are not eroded by interdisciplinary contacts at the level of information or data. It may sometimes lead to the adoption of common methods by related disciplines, which in turn, may pave the way for a possible integration at the level of analysis or perspectives, or interpretative scheme. The fulfillment of this second need for common structures, or what we have termed as analytical integration, is beset with several difficulties. Unlike in the natural sciences, in the social sciences, there is no linear order of sciences ranging between decreasing generality and increasing complexity. On the contrary, in some of the social sciences, there is a marked tendency to reduce explanations of diverse social phenomena to a single perspective peculiar to that science. Sociologists are often accused of reducing everything to sociology and their reductionism is often pejoratively dubbed as 'sociological imperialism Similar tendencies are noticeable, with differences in degree, among some economists, political scientists, linguists, psychologists, and so on.

Answer the following questions based on the facts/information described in the above passage:

62. The difficulties in analytical integration are due to:
(a) Social sciences having no linear order
(b) Social sciences have a pure experimental method
(c) Social sciences are simpler in nature
(d) Social sciences have more standardization

63. What is the common tendency among some social sciences?
(a) To expand the explanation of diverse phenomena to multiple perspectives
(b) To expand the explanation of one phenomenon to multiple perspectives
(c) To reduce explanations of diverse phenomena to one perspective
(d) None of the above

64. Sociological imperialism' is associated with ________
(a) Generalization of fact universally
(b) Social sciences are prejudiced
(c) Sociological reductionism
(d) Sociologists align with other social sciences

65. Inter-disciplinary research in human sciences results from
(a) Similar and diverse needs.
(b) Multiple and conflicting needs.
(c) Diverse and intra-related needs.
(d) Two separate but interrelated needs.

66. Interdisciplinary collaboration sometimes involves
(a) Adoption of different methods by discipline
(b) Adoption of a single method by diverse disciplines
(c) Adoption of common method by related disciplines
(d) Adoption of cross-method by one discipline

JUNE 2019

67. In which kind of research analysis of data is an ongoing process during data collection?
(a) Qualitative (b) Quantitative
(c) Survey (d) Experimental

68. Which test can be applied to measure the relationship between a qualitative and a quantitative variable?
(a) Correlation coefficient (r)
(b) Phi coefficient (0)
(c) Chi-square (yp)
(d) t-test

69. A null hypothesis tells us that two variables are
(a) partially related to each other
(b) conditionally related to each other
(c) not related to each other
(d) directly related to each other

70. Which of the following is NOT true about qualitative research?
(a) It uses an inductive approach
(b) Privileges positivism
(c) Involves interpretation
(d) Includes value judgment

71. A Likert scale measures
(a) correlation
(b) attitude
(c) deviation
(d) satisfaction

72. The value of the middle position in a distribution of values is called
(a) mean
(b) median
(c) mode
(d) mid-point

73. Which of the following is NOT true about survey research?
(a) It was a questionnaire
(b) It studies a sample drawn from a larger population
(c) It has reference to a single point in time
(d) It involves control variable

74. During which stage of research coding is essential?
(a) Before drawing a sample
(a) Before collecting data
(a) After cleaning of collected data
(a) After tabulation of data

75. What is meant by 'operationalization of a concept'?
(a) Indicating an empirical referent of a concept
(b) Linking a concept to a theory
(c) Doing conceptual research
(d) Operating in new situation

76. Theory and research are related to each other, because
A. theory guides research
B. theory is an outcome of research

Which of the following combinations is correct?
(a) A is true but B is false
(b) A is false but B is true
(c) A and B both are true
(d) A and B both are false

77. In research, what is meant by 'ethnographic allegory'?
(a) Reveals the underlying meanings of cultural practices
(b) Analyzing large-scale numerical data
(c) Explaining the type of population studied
(d) Comparing one field with another

78. A good set of research questions must NOT be
(a) clear
(b) broad
(c) connected to theory
(d) related to each other

Answer Key

1. (d)	**13.** (c)	**25.** (a)	**37.** (d)	**49.** (c)	**61.** (a)	**73.** (d)
2. (d)	**14.** (a)	**26.** (a)	**38.** (a)	**50.** (d)	**62.** (a)	**74.** (c)
3. (a)	**15.** (a)	**27.** (d)	**39.** (c)	**51.** (b)	**63.** (c)	**75.** (a)
4. (c)	**16.** (c)	**28.** (c)	**40.** (a)	**52.** (c)	**64.** (c)	**76.** (c)
5. (b)	**17.** (d)	**29.** (a)	**41.** (a)	**53.** (d)	**65.** (d)	**77.** (a)
6. (d)	**18.** (c)	**30.** (b)	**42.** (d)	**54.** (a)	**66.** (c)	**78.** (b)
7. (c)	**19.** (c)	**31.** (a)	**43.** (d)	**55.** (b)	**67.** (a)	
8. (c)	**20.** (d)	**32.** (c)	**44.** (c)	**56.** (b)	**68.** (c)	
9. (c)	**21.** (b)	**33.** (b)	**45.** (c)	**57.** (c)	**69.** (c)	
10. (b)	**22.** (c)	**34.** (d)	**46.** (a)	**58.** (a)	**70.** (b)	
11. (d)	**23.** (a)	**35.** (d)	**47.** (b)	**59.** (b)	**71.** (b)	
12. (a)	**24.** (a)	**36.** (c)	**48.** (c)	**60.** (a)	**72.** (b)	

Unit-III

Basic Concepts and Institutions

CHAPTERS:

Top: Photo credit: yupiramos / 123RF
Below: Cienpies Design / Shutterstock

CHAPTER 1

Sociological Concepts

LEARNING OBJECTIVES:

In this chapter, we will discuss the following important topics.

- Social structure
- Culture
- Network
- Status and role
- Identity
- Community
- Dispora
- Values, norms and rules
- Personhood, habitus and agency
- Bureaucracy, power and authority

INTRODUCTION

A concept is an abstract symbol that represents an object, a property of an object, or a certain phenomenon. Concepts are symbols that we associate with bundles of meaning that we hold. Concepts are essential in every science because accuracy is achieved through them. Each scientific discipline is continually developing a refined set of concepts, to those share same discipline, will mean the same thing at all times. Sociology also has a large number of concepts, which meanings are commonly shared by all sociologists. For example, Norm, Values, Status, etc. Here we will introduce you to some important sociological concepts.

SOCIAL STRUCTURE

Social structure is the patterned social arrangements found in a society that is both the product of social interaction and directly determines it. It is the organized set of social institutions and patterns of institutionalized relationships which together compose society.

Some examples of social structure are family, religion, law, economy, etc.

Definitions

Herbert Spencer was the first thinker to introduce the concept of social structure in Sociology, for him, a society is made up of different parts, all of which have to work in order to remain healthy, meet the demands of the environment, and to survive. Just like an organism, society adjusts and adapts itself to the demands and pressures of social change in order to survive. Spencer compared society's social structure with human ecology and thus his theory is called as 'organic analogy'.

S. F. Nadel defined social structure in his book, '*The Theory of Social Structure*' (1969). *He, too, has defined social structure in terms of the roles played by the individual actors in society and their consequent social status. He referred to the structure as the 'ordered arrangements of parts'.*

According to Radcliffe Brown, 'Human beings are connected by a complex network of actually existing relations.' He used the term social structure to refer to this 'network of actually existing relations'. He says that all the components of social structure have an indispensable function. The existence of a component is dependent on others.

Talcott Parsons defined social structure as the 'particular arrangements of interrelated institutions, agencies, and social patterns as well as the statuses and rules which each person assumes in the group'.

According to Harry M. Johnson, 'The structure of anything consists of the relatively stable interrelationships among its parts'. Moreover, the term 'part' itself indicates a certain level of stability.

According to MacIver and Page, various modes of grouping together comprise the complex pattern of social structure. They consider social structure as abstract which is composed of groups like family, class, caste, community, etc.

The study of social structure, according to Ginsberg, is concerned with the 'principal forms of social organizations' - types of groups, institutions, and the complex which constitute society.

Therefore, from the above definitions, it is clear that sociologist study 'social structure' at the micro level and macro levels. At the macro level they study social institutions like family, religion, law, education, etc., whereas, at the micro level, they study the everyday patterns of interactions (in the form of norms and customs) between the members of society.

But there are thinkers like Karl Marx who has written about the relations of production as constituting 'the economic structure, the real basis on which is erected a judicial and political superstructure and to which correspond the forms of the determined social conscience'. In this explanation, he used the term structure, not in the biological sense, but in the sense of a building or construction.

CULTURE

Culture is seen as a system of learned behaviour that is shared and transmitted among the members of society. It is acquired by man as a member of society and passed from one generation to other. It is socially transmitted rather than biologically in human society.

Culture in the field of sociology first emerged in Weimar Germany, where sociologists such as Alfred Weber used the term Kultursoziologie (cultural sociology).

Etymologically the word culture is derived from the Latin term 'colere' which means the natural process of tending or nurturing. Thus, the word culture was initially used to refer to the nurturing of the mind, cultivation of values, etc.

But today the word culture has multiple meanings. Culture is considered an umbrella term that encompasses social behaviour, morals, manners, customs, traditions, norms, laws, beliefs, knowledge, etc.

Definitions

E. B. Taylor gave one of the most important definitions of culture. According to him, 'Culture is that complex whole which includes knowledge, beliefs, arts, morals, laws, customs and any other capabilities acquired by man as a member of society'.

Malinowski describes culture as the 'handiwork of man and the medium through which he achieves his ends'. He believes that culture is that total way of life that secures an individual the satisfaction of his bio-psychic drives and the fulfillment of other wants and cravings and ultimately invests him with freedom.

Durkheim believes that shared culture is necessary for society to run smoothly. He also says that shared culture exists over and above the wishes of the individuals and it constrain their behaviour.

According to Redfield, 'culture is an organized body of conventional understanding manifest in art and artifacts, which persisting through tradition, characterizes a human group'.

According to George Simmel, culture means 'the cultivation of individuals through the agency of external forms which have been objectified in the course of history'.

F Walter defines culture as the 'totality of group ways of thought and action duly accepted and followed by a group of people'.

Robert Bierstedt describes culture as 'the complex whole that consists of everything we think and do and have as members of society'.

Claude Kluckhon says that 'Each specific culture constitutes a kind of blueprint for all of life's activities'.

According to MacIver, 'Culture is the expression of our nature in our modes of living and our thinking, intercourse, in our literature, in our religion in recreation and enjoyment'.

Herskovits says, 'Culture is the man-made part of society'.

David Bidney opines that culture is a product of:

1. Agro facts (cultivation)
2. Artifacts (industries)
3. Sociofacts (Social organizations)
4. Mentifacts (Beliefs, values, etc.)

From the analysis of the above definitions, it is clear that culture consists of two parts they are material culture and non-material culture

Material and Non-Material Culture

Material culture consists of man-made objects such as tools, clothing, automobiles, buildings, roads, etc. It is concerned with external, mechanical, and concrete objects.

Non-material culture includes the abstract ideas and the way of thinking that make up the culture. For example, words, values, beliefs, virtues, etc.

Analyzing the two, W.F. Ogburn has propounded the theory of Cultural Lag. According to him, technological progress produces rapid changes in the material aspects of our culture, but the non-material aspects fail to do so or manage to do only after a significant time lag. This is known as cultural lag.

Let us understand his theory with an example, suppose you have recently purchased the latest mobile, can you use it with the same ease as you are using your old mobile, your answer will be no, but after using it for a month definitely, you will know all the features of the mobile, this time is taken to learn the features he called 'Cultural lag'.

NETWORK

A social network indicates the way people in society are connected through various social familiarities. Social Networks are composed of nodes and ties. An actor participating in a network is called a node. Ties are the various types of connections between these nodes.

Network theorists believe that the life of an individual is dependent on how he/she is tied into the larger web of social connections. They argue that links or ties among actors are more important individual traits and characteristics.

Social Network Theory (SNT) uses a tool called Social Network Analysis (SNA) to evaluate the relationship between various actors using visualizations, mathematical algorithms, and computational tools.

Many principles of SNT are derived from the early works of Jacob Moreno, an Austrian-American psychiatrist. Working in the context of a girl's school in Hudson, Moreno created the technique of 'sociometry' that mapped the relationship among individuals.

Sociometry is used to enquire about the organization of a group. Moreno says that 'Sociometric explorations reveal the hidden structures that give a group its form'. According to him, large-scale social phenomena, such as economy and state, were sustained and reproduced over time by the small-scale configurations formed by patterns of friendships, likes, dislikes, etc.

Definitions

According to Peter. V. Marsden, a social network is a 'structure of relationships linking social actors'.

According to Georg Simmel, *'Society arises from the individual and induvial arises out of associations'*. He says that it is the nature of the ties themselves rather than the social groups per se that lay at the center of human behaviour.

STATUS AND ROLE

Status

Status is the position or rank that one holds in a given social group. It refers to the relative level of respect and honour granted to people in a given society.

Statuses are hierarchically arranged and are determined in relation to other members of society. Status is determined by a wide range of factors like sex, race, caste, class, physical features, etc.

Nature of Status

Every status has its own duties, rights, and responsibilities. For example, A father is expected to nurture, educate and protect his children. He also has the right to make various decisions that affect his children.

In a social situation, an individual's identity reveals his status. The dress pattern is one of the indicators. For example, a police officer in a social situation is identified through his dresses.

Each person holds a different status. For example, '*A woman can be a mother, wife, daughter, teacher, colleague, andmember of a book-reading club. In a modern complex society, an individual occupies various statuses during the course of a single day*'.

Ascribed and Achieved Status

Prof. Linton has divided status into two groups. These are:

Ascribed Status: It refers to the social status that is assigned at birth or assumed involuntarily later in life. It is a status that is neither earned nor chosen but assigned. For example, a person born into a rich family has a high ascribed status. Similarly, a person born into a Brahmin family automatically enjoys a higher status.

Achieved Status: This is based on merit. It is a status that is earned and reflects a person's skills, abilities, and efforts. It also refers to the status that is voluntarily chosen. For example, A doctor, a professional athlete, etc.

Status Set

It is coined by R K Merton. According to him, each person holds a different status. The status set is the sum total of all the statuses that a person occupies. A person can be a professor, father, husband, social worker, etc. The sum of all these statuses is called a status set.

Master Status / Key Status

The status that tends to overshadow all the other statuses or is given more importance is known as master status or key status. A master status is the primary identifying characteristic of an individual. The nature of master status varies from one society to another and also from one period of history to another.

Conflict theorists of the west often engage with the ascribed statuses of gender and race as they argue that these shape a person's life chances including income, education, occupation, etc.

Status Inconsistency

The concept of status inconsistency was propounded by Gerhard Lenski. It is a situation where an individual's social position has both positive and negative influences on his/her social status.

For example, a teacher may have a positive societal image (respect, prestige) which increases his status but he may have low income, which simultaneously decreases his status. Status inconsistency theory predicts that people whose statuses are inconsistent will be more frustrated and dissatisfied than people with consistent statuses.

Status Crystalization

Status crystallization (Status consistency) is another concept devised by Gerhard Lenski. Crystallized statuses are those which have various dimensions of statuses at approximately the same level.

When various measured dimensions of status are correlated then the status is said to be crystallized (or consistent). For example, when a person's educational qualification is consistent with the occupation held and salary received the status of an individual is considered to be crystallized.

Role

The role is the behaviour expected of an individual who occupies a given social position or status.

Roles are the socially defined attributes and expectations associated with a social position. When a person occupies a certain social position, his/her behaviour is determined by society's expectations rather than individual characteristics.

For example, a person who works as a waiter in a restaurant is expected to note down the orders, serve the food, etc.

According to Ralph Linton, the role is the dynamic aspect of status. The role is allocated according to the status people occupy in a social system. Each status has its own set of role requirements.

Nature of Role

Each and every member of society is bound to play social roles.

Some roles are enacted by only one or comparatively a few individuals in a particular social situation at a particular time.

Some roles are shared by multiple individuals.

Some roles are assumed voluntarily. The individual may choose to enact or not enact certain roles. On the other hand, the assumption of certain roles is largely involuntary.

Definitions

According to Duncan Mitchell, a social role is expected behaviour associated with a social position.

Ogburn and Nimkoff define the role as *'a set of socially expected and approved behaviour patterns, consisting of duties and privileges, associated with a particular position in a group'*.

According to Young and Mack, *'a role is the function of a status'*.

Robert Bierstedt says that role is the 'dynamic or behavioural aspect of status'.

Kingsley Davis described the role as the manner in which a person actually carried out the requirements of the position.

According to Fitcher, *'When a number of interrelated behaviour patterns are clustered around a social function, we call this combination a social role'*.

Turner defines a role as a 'cluster of behaviour and attributes'.

According to Banton, the concept of role *'provides one of the available means for studying elements of cooperation'*.

Role Set

According to Robert. K. Merton, each status has an array of roles associated with it. This is known as the role set. It is a "complement of role relationships in which persons are involved by virtue of occupying a particular status".

Merton offered the example of a medical student whose status as a student is not only related to teachers but to roles of others status occupants like nurses, physicians, social workers, etc.

Multiple Roles

Multiple roles refer to the roles associated with various social statuses of an individual at a given time. A person will be a lawyer, a father, a husband, a friend, etc.

Role Conflict

Role conflict as a concept was developed by R. K. Merton. It refers to the conflict that people experience when they find themselves pulled in various directions as they try to respond to the many statuses they hold.

The most obvious example of role conflict is work/family conflict, or the conflict one feels when pulled between familial and professional obligations. For example, a mother who is also a doctor has to work long hours and perform night duties. She at times, finds it difficult to perform the role of mother and doctor simultaneously.

Role Strain

Role strain occurs when people have difficulty meeting the expectations associated with social roles. William Goode defines role strain as the difficulty in fulfilling role obligations. Goode says that experiencing role strain is quite normal.

Role strain is different from role conflict. Role conflict occurs when two or more roles are at odds with each other. Role strain can be experienced in a single role. For example, Role conflict might occur if a sleep-deprived parent experiences the challenges of nurturing a baby.

Role Expectation

Role expectations may be viewed as actions or qualities expected of the occupant of a position. It is viewed as actions and codified. Expectations must be inferred from overt conduct, including self-reports, etc.

Role Behaviour

In their life people have to face different social roles, sometimes they have to face different roles at the same time in different social situations. There is an evolution of social roles: some disappear and some new developments. Role behaviour is influenced by:

- **i.** The norms that determine a social situation.
- **ii.** Internal and external expectations are connected to a social role.
- **iii.** Social sanctions (punishment and reward) are used to influence role behaviour.

IDENTITY

Identity is the combination of various factors like ethnicity, gender, beliefs, values, personality, physical features, etc. gives a distinguishing character to a person or a group. Our identity locates us in the social world, thoroughly affecting everything we do, feel, say, and think in our lives.

Erik Erikson became one of the earliest theorists to take an interest in identity. The Eriksonian framework rests upon a distinction among the psychological sense of continuity, known as the ego identity; the personal idiosyncrasies that separate one person from the next, known as the personal identity; and the collection of social roles that a person might play, known either as social identity or the cultural identity.

James Marcia identified four different identity statuses that people move through as they develop their identities:

- **i.** Foreclosure is when a person has made a commitment without attempting identity exploration.
- **ii.** Achievement occurs when an individual has gone through an exploration of different identities and made a commitment to one.
- **iii.** Diffusion occurs when there is neither an identity crisis nor commitment. Those with a status of identity diffusion tend to feel out of place in the world and don't pursue a sense of identity.
- **iv.** Moratorium is the status of a person who is actively involved in exploring different identities but has not made a commitment.

For Heidegger, people form an identity after facing death. It's death that allows people to choose from the socially constructed meaning in their world, and assemble a finite identity out of seemingly infinite meanings.

The essentialist favours a primordialist approach which takes the sense of self and belonging to a collective group as a fixed thing, defined by objective criteria such as common ancestry and common biological characteristics.

The social constructionist theory argues that identity is formed by a predominantly political choice of certain characteristics.

Personal Identity and Social Identity

Personal identity refers to the way people define themselves as an individual. It concerns individual characteristics that differentiate one human from another. For example, a person's skills, tastes, hobbies, etc.

Social Identity refers to people's self-categorization in relation to their group membership. Henry Tajfel defined social identity as "that part of an individual's self-concept which derives from his membership of a social group (or groups), together with value and emotional significance attached to this". For example, ethnicity, religion, gender, membership in a sports team, etc.

Identity Crisis

An identity crisis is a developmental event that involves an individual questioning their sense of self or place in the world. The concept has its origins in the work of developmental psychologist Erik Erikson, who believed that identity formation was one of the most important struggles that people face.

According to Erikson, an identity crisis is a time of deep analysis and exploration of different ways of viewing oneself. Erikson stated that it is important to develop a sense of identity during adolescence, although identity formation and development is not limited to adolescence alone.

COMMUNITY

A community can be described as people living together in common interdependence.

Sociologically, the idea of community often includes sharing of an identity, a sense of togetherness, and a common territorial basis.

Within the range of a community, the members may carry out their economic, political, religious, and other activities. Thus, a community can be referred to as the total organization of social life within a defined social space. For example: village, tribe, etc.

Definitions

F. Tonnies defines community as 'an organic, 'natural' kind of social collectivity whose members are bound together by a sense of belonging, created out of everyday contacts covering the whole range of human activities'.

R. E. Park says that *'community, in the broadest sense of the term, has a spatial and geographical connotation'*.

According to Talcott Parsons, 'A *community is that collectivity of members which share a common territorial area as their base of operations for daily activities'*.

Kingsley Davis says that a community is the 'smallest territorial group that can embrace all aspects of social life'.

MacIver and Page 'Wherever the members of any group—small or large—live together in such a way that they share, not this or that particular interest, but the basic conditions of life, we call that group a community'.

According to Bogardus (1952), 'a community is a social group with some degree of we feeling and living in a given area'.

Eshleman and Cashion (Sociology, 1983) defined it as 'a collection of people within a geographic area among whom there is some degree of mutual identification, interdependence or organization of activities'.

For Dotson (1991), "a community is a spatial or territorial unit of social organization in which people have a sense of identity and a feeling of belonging".

Mike O'Donnell (1997) has analyzed the various definitions of community and grouped them into three main categories:

1. The term 'community' is employed to describe a fixed locality (a given geographic area) as a basis of social organization.
2. Community is used to refer to a local social system or set of relationships that center upon a given locality. From a sociological point of view, it is the concentration of relationships, rather than the geographical factor that matters.
3. The term 'community' is also used to describe a quality of relationship that produces a strong sense of shared identity. This usage does not give any importance to the spatial or geographical aspect of the community. It does not depend on physical whereabouts or even on people having met each other.

Community and Society

Tonnies distinguished between two types of social groupings.

Gemeinschaft—often translated as a community—refers to groupings based on feelings of togetherness and on mutual bonds, which are felt as a goal to be kept up, their members being means for this goal.

Gesellschaft—often translated as a society—on the other hand, refers to groups that are sustained by it being instrumental for their members' individual aims and goals.

The equilibrium in Gemeinschaft is achieved through means of social control, such as morals, conformism, and exclusion, while Gesellschaft keeps its equilibrium through police, laws, tribunals, and prisons. Amish and Hassidic communities are examples of Gemeinschaft, while states are types of Gesellschaft. Rules in Gemeinschaft are implicit, while Gesellschaft has explicit rules (written laws).

The geographical area is an important aspect of a community. But a definite geographical area is not an important aspect of society.

Community is concrete whereas society is abstract.

Community and Association

The community has some general interests. Association has a specific interest.

The locality is essential for the community but an association may not be confined to a locality.

A community is a place where people of the same religion, values, norms, or beliefs live. They are identified by their culture and traditions, whereas, an association is formed by a group of people sharing common goals, and thoughts, or working for a common purpose.

DIASPORA

The term 'diaspora' was first used for Jewish people after they were exiled from their homeland. Although it started with a feeling of nostalgia and loss of homeland, 'diaspora' as a term is becoming increasingly contentious in the modern world.

Diaspora comes from the word 'diaspeirein,' from the Greek 'dia' which means 'across,' and 'speirein' which means 'scatter'. The term first appears in Septuagint, of the 2nd century BC, which is a primary Greek translation of the Old Testament.

Broadly it has now come to mean communities that migrated to another land due to various political, economic, or familial causes and now live away, but still maintain strong ties with their homeland.

Agnieszka Weinar (2010) defines diaspora as almost any population on the move and no longer referring to the specific context of their existence". It has even been noted that as charismatic Christianity becomes increasingly globalized, many Christians conceive of themselves as a diaspora, and form an image that mimics salient features of ethnic diasporas.

Vijay Mishra in his book, *'The Literature of the Indian diaspora: Theorizing the Diasporic Imaginary'* (2007) mentions that the one story that speaks to the heart of the diasporic experience is the Ramayana because the exile of Rama is characterized by loss and trauma.

Robert Cohen identified five types of diasporas:

1. Victim diasporas (e.g., classic diasporas forced into exile such as the Jewish, African, and Armenian diasporas)
2. Labour diasporas (e.g., mass migration in search of work and economic opportunities such as the Indian and Turkish diasporas)
3. Trade diasporas (e.g., migrations seeking to open trade routes and links such as the Chinese and Lebanese diasporas)
4. Imperial diasporas (e.g., migration among those keen to serve and maintain empires such as the British and French diasporas)
5. Cultural diaspora (e.g., those who move through a process of chain migration such as the Caribbean diaspora).

VALUES, NORMS, AND RULES

Values

Values are standards for discerning what is good and just in society. These are assumptions of what is right and important for society.

Values are expected to be followed for evaluating social interactions, goals, ideas, feelings, etc.

Values provide the general standard of behaviour that is expressed in a more specific, concrete form in social norms. Examples of values include kindness, justice, patriotism, etc.

Definitions

According to H. M. Johnson 'Values are general standards and may be regarded as higher-order norms'.

Young and Mack say that 'values are assumptions, largely unconscious, of what is right and important'.

G. R. Leslie, R. F. Larson, and H. L. Gorman define value as a 'group conception of the relative desirability of things'.

Some functions of values are:

1. Provide goals and ends for the member to aim for.
2. provide stabilities and uniformities in group interaction
3. brings legitimacy to the rules that govern specific activities.

Norms

Norms are the shared standards of behaviour that connote what is considered desirable and appropriate in society. These are the guidelines that direct our conduct in a given situation.

For instance, norms regarding clothes provide us guidelines for what to wear on particular occasions like funerals, dinner parties, office meetings, etc.

Every society has norms. But norms vary from one society to another. Sometimes within the same society, they differ from group to group.

Norms may be prescriptive (encouraging positive behaviour, for example, 'be honest') or proscriptive (discouraging negative behaviour, for example, 'do not cheat').

Formal norms are present in written form. Informal norms are generally understood but not precisely recorded.

Definitions

According to Young and Mack, 'Norms refer to group shared expectations'.

H. M. Johnson says, 'A norm is an abstract pattern held in mind that sets certain limits of behaviour'.

Robert Bierdstedt defines norm as 'the rule or standard that governs our conduct in the social situation in which we participate'.

Rules

Rules are constraints on behaviour that have known consequences for transgression and these consequences are made explicit to the people who are expected to follow the rules.

Rules are the actions that a group of individuals must obey. Not adhering to the rules set by society generally leads to penalties.

Rules are different from norms. Norms are the expected standards of behaviour that are followed by an individual or group. Whereas rules are standards made to be enforced by an individual or group.

PERSONHOOD, HABITUS, AND AGENCY

Personhood

Personhood, in simple terms, is the status of being a person. Some common elements in the definitions of personhood are human nature, agency, self-awareness, a notion of past and future, the possession of rights and duties, etc. However, the concept of personhood is difficult to define due to its historical and cultural variability.

Boethius, a philosopher of the early 6th century CE, gives the definition of 'person' as 'an individual substance of a rational nature'.

According to the naturalist perspective (Locke and Hume), the term designates any human who possesses continuous consciousness and who is capable of framing representations about the world.

Bruce Knauft's studies of the Gebusi people of Papua New Guinea depict a context in which individuals become persons incrementally, again through social relations. For him, in Papua New Guinea those who do not learn their culture is not people.

Charles Taylor argues that the naturalist view depends solely on performance criteria to determine what is a person. Thus, other things that exhibit 'similar complex adaptive behaviour' (like machines, and animals) could not be distinguished from persons.

According to Thomas White, the criteria for the person are as follows: alive, aware, feels positive and negative sensations, has a sense of self, controls own behaviour, recognizes other people and treats them appropriately, and has sophisticated cognitive abilities.

Habitus

The concept of habitus has been used as early as Aristotle but in contemporary usage was introduced by Marcel Mauss and later Maurice Merleau-Ponty. However, it was Pierre Bourdieu who turned it into a cornerstone of his sociology and used it to address the sociological problem of agency and structure.

The habitus is shaped by structural position and generates action, thus when people act and demonstrate agency they simultaneously reflect and reproduce social structure.

The term was earlier used in sociology by Norbert Elias in '*The Civilizing Process*' (1939) and in Marcel Mauss's account of 'body techniques' (techniques du corps). The concept is also present in the work of Max Weber, Gilles Deleuze, and Edmund Husserl.

The concept of habitus for Pierre Bourdieu refers to the socially ingrained habits, skills, and dispositions. It is the way individuals perceive the world around them and react to it.

For Bourdieu, habitus is the collective entity by which and into which dominant social and cultural conditions are established. It is the 'subjective but not individual system of internalized structures, schemes of perception, conception, and action common to all members of the class'.

According to Bourdieu, aesthetic sensibilities are shaped by culturally ingrained habitus. Upper-class people have a taste for fine art because they have been exposed to and trained to appreciate it since a very early age while the working-class individuals have generally not been exposed to "high art".

Agency

In sociology, agency is defined as the capacity of individuals to act independently and make their own choices. It refers to the thought and actions taken by individuals to express their individual power.

In '*American Journal of Sociology*', the agency is defined as a temporary embedded process that includes three different constitutive elements: iteration, projectivity, and practical evaluation.

The core challenge of sociology is understanding the relationship between agency and structure.

Social structure refers to the complex and interconnected set of social forces that work together to shape our interactions, behaviour, thoughts, and overall life courses.

On the other hand, the agency is the power people hold to shape their life experiences.

Sociologists understand the relationship between social structure and agency to be ever-evolving dialectic.

John Locke's concept of the social contract led to the conception of agency as the capacity of human beings to shape the circumstances in which they live.

BUREAUCRACY, POWER, AND AUTHORITY

Bureaucracy

Bureaucracy is the machinery, which implements rational-legal authority. Max Weber studied bureaucracy in detail and constructed an ideal type that contained the most prominent characteristics of bureaucracy.

Weber's ideal type of bureaucracy comprised various elements such as

(a) high degree of specialization and a clearly-defined division of labour, with tasks distributed as official duties,

(b) hierarchical structure of authority with clearly circumscribed areas of command and responsibility,

(c) establishment of a formal body of rules to govern the operation of the organization and administration based on written documents,

(d) impersonal relationships between organizational members and the clients,

(e) recruitment of personnel based on ability and technical knowledge,

(f) long-term employment, promotion on the basis of seniority and merit,

(g) fixed salary and the separation of private and official income.

Alvin Gouldner led an ethnographic study in a mine and identified three various patterns of bureaucracy and bureaucratization.

i. **Mock bureaucracy:** This type comes from an outside agency and is implemented officially, but not in daily behaviors. Both management and workers agree in this case to act the same way. The rules are enforced in this case, neither by management nor by the workers.

ii. **Representative bureaucracy:** Both management and workers enforced this rule and it generated very little tension. In this context, the focus was on the education of workers as management considered them as ignorant and careless regarding security rules. Meetings happened regularly to implement this program and it was as well the occasion to voice some concerns for workers. For the management, this program was a way to tighten the control over workers.

iii. **Punishment-centered bureaucracy:** this type of program was initiated by management and generated many tensions. Management viewed workers as deliberately willing to be absent. Therefore, the punishment was installed in order to force the workers not to be absent. For example, the "no-absenteeism" rule is an example of a punishment-centered bureaucracy.

The Italian Marxist Bruno Rizzi in '*The Bureaucratization of the World*' (1939) argues that the Soviet bureaucracy constituted a new ruling class that exploited the proletariat as much as the capitalists had in the past. It differed from capitalism only in that the new type of domination was based not on the individual but on group ownership of the means of production.

In his book, '*A General Theory of Bureaucracy*', first published in 1976, Dr. Elliott Jaques describes the discovery of a universal and uniform underlying structure of managerial or work levels in the bureaucratic hierarchy for any type of employment system.

Robert C. Stone's definition includes-red tape, rigid rules, and procedural emphasis, as features of bureaucratic organizations.

Power and Authority

Power is normally understood as the possession of control, authority, or influence over others, a relationship in which an individual or a group is able to exert influence over the minds and actions of others.

According to Arnold Woofers, it is defined as the ability 'to move others or to get them to do what one wants them to do and not to do, what one does not want them to do'.

Harold Lasswell and Abraham Kaplan construed exercises of power as 'acts affecting or determining other acts'.

Robert Dahl defined power as one actor's ability to make another do something that the latter 'would not otherwise do'.

Hannah Arendt argued that power is not the property of lone agents or actors, but of groups or collectivities acting together.

Marx on Power

Marx does not give a clear definition of power, for him, power means coercion. Marx views power to be held by a particular group in society at the expense of the rest of society. According to him the source of power in society lies in economic infrastructure and those who own the modes of production i.e., the dominant group uses power to further its own interest and thereby exploits those who are subject to power.

Max Weber on Power

For Max Weber, power is an aspect of social relationships. It refers to the possibility of imposing one's will upon the behaviour of another person.

Power is present in social interaction and creates situations of inequality since the one who has power imposes it on others this is called as constant sum concept of power.

Weber discusses two contrasting sources of power. These are as follows:

(a) Power which is derived from a constellation of interests that develop in a formally free market. For example, a group of producers of sugar controls the supply of their products in the market to maximize their profit.

(b) An established system of authority that allocates the right to command and the duty to obey. For example, in the army, a jawan is obliged to obey the command of his officer. The officer derives his power through an established system of authority.

Parsons on Power

Parsons regards power as something possessed by society as a whole. As such power is a generalized facility or resource in society. It is the capacity to mobilise the resources of the society for the attainment of goals for which a general public commitment has been made. In this sense, the amount of power in society is measured by the degree to which collective goals are realized.

Thus, the greater the efficiency of a social system for achieving the goals defined by its members, the more power exists in society. This view is known as a variable sum concept of power (different from Weberian and Marxian constant sum concept of power) since power in society is not seen as a fixed in contrast. Instead, it is variable in the sense it can increase or decrease.

Foucault: Power is Everywhere

In sociology, power knowledge is a term introduced by the French philosopher Michel Foucault. According to Foucault's understanding, power is based on knowledge and makes use of knowledge; on the other hand, power reproduces knowledge by shaping it in accordance with its anonymous intentions. Power creates/recreates its own fields of exercise through knowledge.

Power is also a major source of social discipline and conformity. In shifting attention away from the 'sovereign' and 'episodic' exercise of power, traditionally centered in feudal states to coerce their subjects, Foucault pointed to a new kind of 'disciplinary power' that could be observed in the administrative systems and social services that were created in 18th century Europe, such as prisons, schools and mental hospitals.

CHAPTER

2 Social Institutions

LEARNING OBJECTIVES:

In this chapter, we will discuss the following important topics.

- Marriage, family, and kinship
- Economy
- Polity
- Religion
- Education
- Customs and law
- Social stratification
- Caste and class
- Gender
- Sexuality and disability
- Race, tribe and ethnicity
- Social change and processes
- Modernisation and development
- Social transformation and globalisation
- Social mobility

INTRODUCTION

A social institution is an interrelated system of social roles and social norms, organized around the satisfaction of an important social need or social function. Social Institutions are organized patterns of beliefs and behaviour that are centered on basic social needs.

MARRIAGE, FAMILY, AND KINSHIP

Marriage

Marriage is a social contract between two or more people that is based on a sexual relationship and implies the permanence of the union. It is a legally and socially sanctioned union that is regulated by laws, rules, customs, beliefs, and attitudes that prescribe the rights and duties to their partner and accord status to their offspring.

Marriage is considered by sociologists to be a cultural universal. It exists in some form in all societies. Some basic functions of marriage are sexual gratification and regulation, division of labour between the sexes, economic production and economic production and consumption, procreation, and care of children.

Definitions

According to Malinowski, 'Marriage is a contract for the production and maintenance of children'.

Edward Westermark says 'Marriage is a relation of one or more men to one or more women which is recognized by customs or law and involves certain rights and duties both in case of parties entering into the union and in the case of children born of it'.

According to H.M. Johnson, 'Marriage is a stable relationship in which a man and a woman are socially permitted without loss of standing in the community to have children'.

Robert H Lowie describes marriage as a 'relatively permanent bond between permissible mates'.

Horton and Hunt say 'Marriage is the approved social pattern whereby two or more persons establish a family'.

According to Hoebel, 'The complexes of social norms that define and Control the relations of a mated pair to each other their kinsmen, their offspring and their society at large'.

Types of Marriage

On the basis of the number of spouse(s) marriages can be classified as:

Monogamy: Monogamy is the most common form of marriage. It is the union between one man and one woman. There are two types of monogamy- serial monogamy and non- serial monogamy. In serial Monogamous marriage, the possibility of remarriage exists in case of divorce or death. In the case of non-serial monogamy, the question of remarriage does not arise by either of the couples. Here a spouse has the same single spouse throughout his life.

Polygamy: Polygamy refers to the type of marriage where a man marries more than one woman at a time.

Polyandry: This is the type of marriage where a woman marries several men at a time.

On the basis of the selection of a spouse marriage can be classified as:

Endogamy: Endogamy or endogamous marriage refers to the marriage within one's own group such as within one's own caste, sub-caste, varna, and tribe (inside the same group).

Exogamy: It is just the opposite of the endogamy or endogamous marriage system. It refers to a system of marriage in which an individual has to marry outside one's own group such as gotra, caste, village, etc.

Anuloma: When a man of a higher caste or varna marries a woman of a lower caste or varna it is called as Anuloma.

Pratiloma: It is the opposite of Anuloma. When a man of lower caste or status marries a woman of higher caste or status it is known as Pratiloma.

Hypergamy: The practice of marrying a spouse of a higher caste or social status.

Hypogamy: It refers to marrying a person of a lower caste or social status.

In the Hindu religion, eight types of marriages are found, they are:

Brahma marriage: Brahma marriage is when a father gifts his daughter to a learned man of good character.

Daiva marriage: If the daughter is gifted to a priest, it is called Daiva marriage.

Arsha marriage: In Arsha marriage, the prospective man gifts the father of the girl a bull and cow before marriage.

Asura marriage: In Asura marriage, the bridegroom gets the bride in exchange for some money or articles given to the family members of the bride.

Gandharva marriage: Marriage based on mutual love is known as Gandharva marriage.

Prajapatya marriage: When a father gifts his daughter to a man, after duly honouring him, and exhorts the couple to perform their dharma together, it is called Prajapatya marriage.

Rakshasa marriage: Marriage by abduction is known as Rakshasa marriage and is regarded as lawful.

Paisacha marriage: The seduction of a girl who is asleep or intoxicated or of unsound mind is called Paisacha marriage. According to Manu, the two types i.e., Paisacha marriage and Asura marriage as unlawful.

Whereas Hindus after a long period of transition consider four types of marriage as the prashasta or acceptable types they are Brahma, Daiva, Arsha, and Prajapatya. While the other four are aprashasta or not acceptable.

Types of Marriages in Muslims

There are four types of marriages practiced by Muslims, these are as follows:

Sahih/Nikaah Marriage: This is the valid form of marriage as per the Sharia Law. The children born from this marriage are legitimate. It is obligatory for the husband to pay Mahr as a dower to his wife. The wife is entitled to get maintenance from her husband. The husband has the right to prohibit his wife's movements under this marriage.

Fasid Marriage: This marriage is an irregular marriage as the two parties fail to fulfill the prerequisite norms required for a valid marriage. Irregularities like marriage without a witness, marriage with a fifth wife, etc.

Muta Marriage {temporary marriage}: This marriage is carried out under a contract for a temporary period. It is legitimate in Shia Muslims only. Shia Muslims practice such marriage with a woman from Mahomedan, Jewish, or Christian religion.

Batil marriage: This type of marriage is completely unlawful according to Muslim law because the marriage takes place through forced consent of a woman and other prohibited grounds. The offspring from such marriage is illegitimate.

Family

A family is an intimate domestic group of people related to one another by bonds of blood, sexual mating, or legal ties. It is a socially recognized group usually joined by blood, marriage, or adoption that forms an emotional connection and serves as an economic unit of society.

Some features of family are:

- **i.** Family is a universal group. It is found in some form in all societies.
- **ii.** Family is responsible for the production and upbringing of children.
- **iii.** Family is a group through which descent can be traced.
- **vi.** Family is the unit of emotional and economic cooperation.

Definitions

MacIver defines family as 'a group defined by sex relationship sufficiently precise and enduring to provide for the procreation and upbringing of children'.

Eliot and Merrill state that 'Family is the biological social unit composed of husband, wife, and children'.

Burgess and Locke define family as 'A group of persons united by ties of marriage, blood or adoption constituting a single household, interacting and intercommunicating with each other in their respective social roles of husband and wife, father and mother, son and daughter, brother and sister, creating a common culture'.

According to Kingsley Davis, 'Family is a group of persons, whose relations to one another are based upon consanguinity and who are therefore kin to one another'.

Types of Family

On the basis of authority, family can be classified as:

The patriarchal family: In the patriarchal family the male head of the family is possessed of inclusive powers.

The matriarchal family: In a matriarchal family the authority is vested in the female head of the family.

On the basis of residence, family can be classified as follows:

Matrilocal family: In this type of family, the husband goes to live in the house of his wife.

Patrilocal family: In this type, the wife goes to live in the house of her husband.

Avunculocal family: The word 'avuncu' means maternal uncle. It is a family where the couple lives in their uncle's house after their marriage.

Amitolocal family: It is a family where the couple lives in father's sister's house after their marriage.

Neolocal family: The married couple stays in a completely new residence neither in the groom's family nor in the bride's family.

On the basis of structure, family can be classified as follows.

Nuclear family: Nuclear family is composed of a husband, wife, and unmarried children.

Joint Family: A joint family consists of three generations, living together under the same roof, sharing the same kitchen and purse or economic expenses. It is a family consisting of three nuclear families living together.

Extended family: The extended family is commonly defined as the nuclear family plus all kin belonging to either side, living together.

G.P. Murdock and W.I. Warner on the basis of birth and marriage identified two types of families, they family of orientation and the family of procreation. Family of orientation refers to the family into which a person is born and family of procreation refers to the one formed through marriage. In India, a very good example to understand is a marriage of a girl after marriage girl moves to her family of procreation, and her parents' house for her is a family of orientation.

Kinship

Kinship is one of the main organizing principles of society. The most basic bonds in society are based on marriage and reproduction. Thus, the institution of kinship primarily refers to the sets of relationships formed between individuals based on blood or marriage.

All societies use kinship as a basis for forming social groups and classifying people. But there is a great degree of variability in kinship patterns around the world.

Radcliffe Brown used the term kinship system to denote relationships that arose due to marriage and affinity. According to Radcliffe-Brown, the elementary family consists of a man, a wife, and their child/children; a compound family comprises a man with several wives (polygynous) or even a second marriage.

The kinship system thus refers to a network of social relations that is expressed through the family, clan, lineage groups, or moieties. He also speaks of the difference between clan and lineage. A clan is usually a group of people, who claim to belong to a kin group on the basis of an ancestor whom they may or may not have existed.

Claude Levi-Strauss' contribution to kinship studies is marked by his focus on studying the structural significance of ties underlying marriage and alliance. In his work, Elementary Structures of Kinship, Levi-Strauss speaks of the principle of exchange of women through marriage.

He sees marriage as the key in the system of the kinship of which reproduction is an essential part. This is questioned by Schneider and Boon, in reference to societies such as the Zulu, where marriage takes place between two women even though they might be impregnated by a man.

Robin Fox says that 'the study of kinship is the study of what man does with these basic facts of life- mating, gestation, parenthood, socialization, siblingship, etc'. He states that human society is 'working with the same raw material as exists in the animal world, but can conceptualize and categorize it to serve social ends'.

Types of Kinship

Consanguineal Kinship: It refers to the relationships based on blood, i.e., the relationship between parents and children, siblings, etc.

Affinal Kinship: It refers to the relationships formed on the basis of marriage. The most basic relationship that results from marriage is that between husband and wife.

Fictive kinship: These are forms of kinship or social ties neither based on blood nor marriage. Godparent is an example of fictive kinship.

On the basis of the degree of kinship G P Murdock classified three types of kinship:

i. **Primary Kinship:** It refers to direct relations. According to Murdock, there are 8 primary kins. These are father-son, husband-wife, mother-daughter, father-daughter, mother-son, younger-elder sisters, younger-elder brothers, and sister-brother.
ii. **Secondary Kinship:** It refers to the primary kin of primary kin. They are not our primary kin but they are the primary kin of our primary kin. For example, the father's brother (uncle) is secondary kin. According to Murdock, there are 33 types of secondary kin.
iii. **Tertiary Kinship:** They are the secondary kin of primary kin or primary kin of secondary kin. For example, the spouse of the sister-in-law is tertiary kin. According to Murdock, there are 151 types of tertiary kin.

ECONOMY

Economy refers to the way people use their environment to meet their material needs. It includes the production, exchange, distribution, and consumption of goods and services in a given area.

Three sectors that makeup the economy are:

I. **Primary sector:** The primary sector includes all those activities the end purpose of which consists in exploiting natural resources: agriculture, fishing, forestry, mining,
ii. **Secondary sector:** The secondary sector involves economic activities that generate finished products for consumption. Raw materials from the primary activities are taken and utilized to manufacture end products.
iii. **Tertiary sector:** The tertiary sector is the service sector. This sector is responsible for services delivered to both the primary and secondary sectors.

Economic Sociology

Economic sociology is a discipline that focuses on the application of sociological methods to the analysis of the production, distribution, exchange, and consumption of goods and services. It is the study of how material conditions of life are produced, influenced, and reproduced by various social processes.

Marxist economics focuses on the role of labour in the development of the economy. Marx argued that in a capitalist system, the specialization of labour force, coupled with the growing population, pushes wages down, adding that the value placed on goods and services does not accurately account for the true cost of labour.

The workers create value through their labour but are not properly compensated. They are exploited by the ruling class who generate profit by paying staff less than the value of their labour.

Weber's economic sociology focuses on social action. It emphasizes the role played by power, beliefs, and habits in the organization of economic life. Weber shows that political order linked to legal order provides the basis for economic order in a given society.

Karl Polanyi is viewed as the father of the concept of embeddedness. Embeddedness, according to Polanyi, economy is immersed in social relations. The economy cannot be a separate autonomous sphere. It has to be seen in relation to society as a whole.

POLITY

A polity refers to any group of people who have a collective identity, who are organized by some form of institutionalized social relations and have the capacity to mobilize resources.

The term polity is derived from the Greek word 'polis' which means an uncorrupted form of government in which a number of people together rule for the common good of the public. Thus, the term polity refers to the political system.

For maintaining an orderly arrangement of social relationships, we need to both resolve conflicts and coordinate diverse activities of people. This is generally done by exercising power and imposing some kind of constraint on people's behaviour.

When power relations are systematized and ascribed to specific functions, we speak of them as a political system.

According to Weber, those who hold power do so at the expense of others. It suggests that there is a fixed amount of power, and therefore if some hold power, others do not. This view is known as the constant-sum concept of power.

According to Talcott Parsons power is something that is possessed by society as a whole and power is a generalized facility or resource in society. This is known as the variable sum concept of power.

Sociologist Robert Michels developed 'the iron law of oligarchy' where, he asserts, social and political organizations are run by few individuals, and social organization and labour division are key.

C. Wright Mills coined the phrase 'power elite' to describe what he saw as the small group of powerful people who control much of society. Mills believed the power elite use government to develop social policies that allow them to keep their wealth.

Vilfredo Pareto propounded the concept of the circulation of elites. This means the process of replacement of one elite group by another because the governing elite decay in quality and lose their vigour.

According to Pareto Social system is made up of 2 kinds of people:

i. Elite class (Governing class or Ruling class)
ii. Non-elites (Mass or Ruled Class or subject)

According to Machiavelli, there are two main types of governing elites:

i. Those who achieve power because of their ability to take direct action-Lions
ii. Those who rule by diplomatic manipulation: Foxes

RELIGION

Religion is concerned with shared beliefs, practices, morals, worldviews, texts, sanctified places, prophecies, ethics, and organizations that relate humanity to supernatural, transcendental, and spiritual elements.

It is the human response to those elements of the life of mankind which are beyond their comprehension.

According to MacIver, 'Religion as we understand the term implies a relationship not merely between man and man but also between man and some higher power'.

Emile Durkheim states that 'Religion is a unified system of beliefs and practices relating to sacred things, that is to say, things set apart and forbidden'.

According to Ogburn, 'Religion is attitudes towards superhuman powers'.

J.M. Frazer believes that 'Religion is a belief in powers superior to man which are believed to direct and control the course of nature of human life'.

Malinowski defines religion as 'a mode of action as well as a system of belief and a sociological phenomenon as well as a personal experience'.

Thus, different scholars define religion according to their own views but it is very difficult to agree upon a universally accepted definition because religion is a very complex phenomenon. But one thing is clear belief and rituals are two main component parts of religion. Beliefs involve an understanding of truth, rights, and wrongs. Rituals are repeated behaviours based on understanding prescribed patterns of behaviour.

Religion in its primitive form: Totemism, Animism, and Naturism

Totemism

Durkheim believes that to understand the more complex religions, one must understand first the simple forms. Durkheim maintains that totemism is the simplest form of religion. He chose to study totemism as practiced by the aborigines of Central Australia. Totemism refers to the worship of totems.

The members of the clan believe themselves to have descended from some common ancestor — an animal, a plant, or even some non-living object. The "common ancestor" is the "totemic object". It is the totemic object that gives the clan its name and identity.

This totemic object of worship is called a totem, it can be a plant or an animal thought to possess supernatural powers. Each group within the society may have its own totem, including associated ceremonies.

Animism

Animism is the belief that spirits, apparitions, angels, or demons inhabit the earth. Either good or bad, these spirits interact with and/or influence humans in a variety of ways. For example, animists believe that malevolent spirits cause demonic possession, insanity, and disapproved behaviour.

According to animism, the idea of the soul (anima) is central to the religion. Hence the name animism. According to E.B. Tylor, a primitive man hit upon the idea of the soul because of an error. In his dreams, he walked about various places, engaged in various types of activities, and met his dead ancestors even while his body remained in one place.

Naturism

Naturism means the belief that the forces of nature have supernatural power. Andrew Lang and Max Muller develop the theory of naturism.

Max Muller, a great Sanskrit scholar, strongly advocates that the most ancient form of religious practice is naturism. Naturism, according to him, is primarily based on man's sensory experience out of which logical deductions are primarily made.

EDUCATION

Education is a social institution through which a society's children are taught basic academic knowledge, learning skills, and cultural norms in order to maintain the equilibrium in society. Every society in the world is equipped with some form of the education system, though those systems vary greatly.

Etymologically, the word 'Education' is derived from the Latin words 'educare' and 'educere'. Educare refers to 'to bring up' or ' to nourish', whereas the word 'educere' means ' to bring forth' or 'to drag out'.

Holistically education teaches us the standards of attitudes, behavior, and whatnot. It is beyond mere learning of information available. Education is the single most powerful weapon for socialization. Education is seen as a fundamentally optimistic human endeavor for progress and betterment of the society concerned.

Therefore, each and every individual acquires some sort of education, even if he has never spent a day in a school because his acquired characteristics are the products of experiences and activities which are the products of experiences and activities which are educational in nature. Education, in a wider sense, is used for the purpose of teaching people all characteristics which will enable them to live in society.

According to Manheim, 'Sociologists do not regard education solely as a means of realizing abstract ideals of culture such as humanism or technical specialization, but as part of influencing men and women'.

Froebel said, 'Education is the unfoldment of what is already enfolded in the gene. It is the process through which the child makes the internal external'.

According to Mahatma Gandhi, 'By education, I mean an all-round drawing out of the best in the child and man - body, mind and spirit'.

Types of Education

Formal Education

Formal education is imparted by an institution or agency specially established for this purpose. Such an institution has its own structure. For example, a school is an agency for formal education.

Non-Formal Education

Non-formal education has emerged as an alternative system of education. Due to limitations of the formal system of education and also because of individual requirements and circumstances, a child may not be able to attend school regularly.

Consequently, s/he may not be able to complete the education even at the primary level. Thus, a large number of children in India are not in a position to go to school. Therefore, the need for an alternative system of education was felt and non-formal education was organized to provide the facility of education to all the children who are not part of a formal system of education for whatever reason.

Informal Education

All the experiences gained by a child which can be used by him/her during lifetime are part of education. In a broad sense, education is a life-long process. While school provides education during fixed hours, the community and the media also function as sources of education. The education provided by the family, community, or media is called informal education.

Value Education

Value education has been mainly expressed in terms of the development of values and virtues like honesty, self-control, respect, responsibility, and loyalty for the personality/character development of the individual per se without situating them in the prevailing social, and cultural realities and conditions.

Functions and Importance of Education

1. A strong tool for socialization.
2. Learning and understanding of facts and information.
3. Intellectual and cognitive development of a person.
4. A vital weapon for social control both in a formal and informal ways.
5. It acts as a direction for individual growth and social establishment.
6. Ultimately generating social mobility and solidarity.

Provisions in the Constitution of India

Article 15(4) empowers the state to make special provisions for the advancement of any socially and educationally backward classes of citizens and for Scheduled Castes. This provision has enabled the state to reserve seats for Scheduled Castes in educational institutions in general and professional courses etc.

Right to Education Act (Article 21A): 'The state shall provide free and compulsory education to all children of the age of 6 to 14 years in such a manner as the state may, by the law, determine." Article 21(A) was added by the 86th constitution (Amendment Act) 2002.

Article 46: Promotion of educational and economic interests of Scheduled Castes, Scheduled Tribes, and other weaker sections. The state shall promote with special care the educational and economic interest of the weaker sections of the people and in particularly of the Scheduled Castes and the Scheduled Tribes and shall protest them from social injustice and all forms of exploitation.

CUSTOMS AND LAW

Customs

Customs are the unwritten laws that society follows. It basically emerges without proper authority and strict enactment having to restrictions to apply and protect. It can be described as some rules that we follow from generation to generation without citation. Another word for custom is 'folkways' (W.G. Sumner).

Customs are products of our day-to-day experience that can only be demolished when transformation takes place under circumstances. It has no direction and popularly exists for the sake of socio-cultural stability.

According to Kingsley Davis, 'The term custom is closer to folkways than to mores, but it tends to convey the traditional, automatic and mass character of both of them'.

According to MacIver, 'custom is a group procedure that has gradually emerged, without express enactment, without any constituent authority to declare it, to apply it, to safeguard it'.

L Bogardus says 'Customs and traditions are group accepted techniques of control that have become well established, that are taken for granted and that are passed along from generation to generation'.

M Ginsberg says 'Custom, in fact, is not merely, a prevailing habit, but also a rule or norm of action'.

Law

Law, on the other hand, is deliberately made by State or agency. It is external to humans. Laws are written, legitimate, and enacted by authorities bound to application and safeguard. Laws are also flexible rules that can be introduced, amended, and abolished if needed under some changing circumstances. Laws are quite adaptable than customs.

According to W.G.Sumner, 'Laws are codified mores'. Mores are strict than customs in application".

According to MacIver and Page, 'Law is the body of rules which are recognized, interpreted and applied to particular situations by the courts of the state'.

According to Max Weber, 'Law is an order that validity of which is guaranteed by the probability that deviation will be met by a physical or psychic sanction by a staff specially empowered to carry out this sanction'.

The law helps to maintain the fundamental order of society guaranteeing security and equal chance to opportunity. It is more precise than customs. It has boundaries and legitimacy is also concerned equally.

Comparative View of Custom and Law

According to Bushan and Sachdeva, '"The transition from custom to law is just a part of the general rationalization in modem society'.

In the words of Maclver and Page, custom establishes a social order of its own so that conflict arising between custom and law is not a conflict between law and lawlessness but between the orders of reflection (law) and the order of spontaneity (custom).

Laws can be changed very easily, but customs take a very long period of time to change, and they fade out or disappear without any formal abolition by any authority.

Customs are informal means of social control and repository of social heritage whereas laws, being a formal means of social control are essential for maintaining social security and stability.

SOCIAL STRATIFICATION

Social stratification is a process through which groups and social categories in society are ranked as higher or lower than one another based on their relative position in terms of prestige, privilege, wealth, and power. A distinction can be made between criteria that emphasize ascribed or innate qualities with which levels are relatively endowed and those that are acquired by the level through its own achievement.

So, in simple words, it is understood that when individuals and groups are ranked according to some generally accepted grounds of evaluation, social stratification occurs. Generally, the greater the social complexity of a society, the greater the social stratification.

Definitions

Ogburn and Nimkoff state that "the process by which individuals and groups are ranked in a more or less permanent hierarchy of status is known as stratification".

Melvin M. Tumin defines it as "any social group or society organized into a hierarchy of positions that are unequal with respect to power, wealth, social evaluation, and mental satisfaction".

Lundberg states that "a stratified society is marked by inequality, by differences between people in who they evaluate as low and high".

According to Gisbert, "Social stratification is the division of society into permanent groups of categories which are linked to each other by relations of superiority and subordination".

Parsons argues that stratification systems arise from common values. In the words of Parsons, 'Stratification, in its evaluative aspect, is the ranking of units in a social system according to a common value system.' Thus, those who perform successfully in terms of the society's values will be ranked higher and are likely to receive various types of rewards.

According to Kingsley Davis and Wilbert Moore, all social systems have certain prerequisites that must be met for the society to survive. One such condition is role allocation and performance. The greater the functional importance of the social role, the greater should be the reward. Some functions in society are more valuable than others. Qualified people filling those positions should be rewarded more than others.

Melvin Tumin refutes this thesis. He says that there is no objective way to measure the functional importance of posts. Whether lawyers and doctors are considered more important than agricultural labourers is a matter of opinion. He also argues that Davis and Moore ignored the effect of power on the unequal distribution of rewards.

Michael Dunlop Young was a British sociologist, social activist and politician who coined the term "meritocracy". Meritocracy is a political philosophy in which political influence is handed out largely according to an individual's intellectual talent and achievement.

Social Difference

Social stratification is the hierarchical ranking of people based on categories such as ethnicity, class, education level, and gender, whereas social difference is the differences between social groups and individuals based on physical, biological, and socio-cultural factors.

These categories can easily reflect differences between the people grouped in them. The underlying assumption here is that the differences between categories are important; however, the differences between them are not given any importance, that is, the categories are not given unequal status or unequal rewards.

Different categories of people are treated equally and one is not considered more important than the other. This is the concept of difference in social categories. When unequal conditions and rewards are associated with social categories and are ranked based on one or more defined factors, they are considered unequal.

According to Dipankar Gupta, differences become important when ranking the variations becomes difficult. Social stratification involves the concepts of both difference and inequality. For example, linguistic differences cannot be placed in hierarchical order.

Human differences, in themselves, are not particularly significant. What is important is the meaning of these differences. For example, a teacher is different from the students. However, if a teacher can direct and control the behaviour of students due to their differences, it becomes more important.

When we socially differentiate between a teacher and their students, we make judgments about their relative worth or status. What we are really saying is that these people are not only 'different', but that this difference is important because it lies in the nature of their relationship.

Hierarchy

In the social sciences, hierarchy describes a stratified system where people have clear positions or lines of authority. In other words, hierarchy means the ranking of positions within society or an organization according to certain criteria of evaluation accepted as relevant within the system.

For example, Brahmins as a caste group occupy the highest position and enjoy the privileges associated with it, while untouchable castes occupy the lowest position.

The word 'hierarchy' is derived from the Greek word 'hieros' meaning sacred and 'archin' meaning rule or order.

According to Marxist scholars, this hierarchy favours the dominant classes. Hierarchy promotes inequality between different classes which leads to conflict. Hierarchy is an informal structure of inequality in power.

Whereas functionalists argue that hierarchy symbolizes organized division of labour in society and is necessary for the smooth functioning of society. Like other functionalists, Parsons believed that order and stability in society were based on the values held by people in society. People who behave in accordance with these values are given a place above others.

Louis Dumont defined hierarchy as a characteristic of a social system where normative principles control or determine instrumental or utilitarian principles in the affairs of society. He calls this encircling. It is a process by which traditionally held values and beliefs incorporate rational utilitarian principles.

His work 'Homo hierarchicus' is important for understanding the caste hierarchy. It analyzes the caste system and the dominant tendency of lower castes to follow the habits of higher castes.

Inequality

The concept of inequality lies at the core of some major theoretical formulas of society. This is the basic component of the phenomenon of stratification in society. The term inequality generally refers to the phenomenon of unequal and/or unjust distribution of resources and opportunities among members of a given society.

In social sciences, inequality refers to the existence of unequal distribution of wealth, opportunities, respect, or rewards for different social positions or statuses within a group or society. For example, in the caste system, access to rights and resources is unfairly distributed based on the caste hierarchy.

Inequality in society can occur in two major ways:

Inequality of conditions: Inequality of conditions refers to unequal distribution of income, wealth and material goods.

Inequality of opportunities: Inequality of opportunities refers to the unequal distribution of life opportunities among individuals. This is reflected in measures such as level of education, health status, etc.

Types of Inequality

Rousseau identified two types of inequality between people: natural or physical inequality, referring to differences in age, health, physical strength, and mental abilities; and moral or political inequality implies a difference in privileges which are established or authorized by the consent of the people themselves. Power, respect.

According to Bataille, two aspects of social inequality deserve mention. The first is the distributional aspect which refers to various factors (income, wealth, occupation, education, power, skills) distributed in the population. It provides the basis for interpersonal interactions in society.

The second is the relational aspect which refers to the ways in which individuals differentiated by various factors relate to each other within a system of groups and categories. The emphasis here is on the interaction of a group or class of people.

In considering the concept of inequality, he distinguished between harmonic systems (in which society is divided into groups that are hierarchically placed and the order is considered appropriate) and disharmonic systems (in which there is no consistency between the order in which the groups are arranged). He defined a disharmonious system as one which maintains equality as an ideal but practices inequality.

Marginalization

Marginalization in society refers to the process of social exclusion in which individuals or groups are pushed to the margins of society, deprived of economic, political, social or cultural power and pushed towards being outsiders.

It is the process of marginalizing certain groups of people and denying them equal access to resources and opportunities, leading to poverty, discrimination and livelihood insecurity. As a result a large section of people have become socially ignorant, illiterate, illiterate and dependent.

Some of the factors leading to marginalization are:

1. Social exclusion
2. Globalization
3. Displacement (due to natural, industrial, political or economic causes)

Marginalization can also occur at the global level. Globalization, immigration, social welfare and policy are broad social constructs that have the potential to negatively contribute to access to resources and services. This results in marginalization of individuals and groups as well as nations.

Definitions

Peter Leonard defines marginality as "being outside the mainstream of productive activity and/or social reproductive activity".

Ghana S. Gurung and Michael Kollmeyer have noted that the concept of marginality is commonly used to analyze socioeconomic, political, and cultural areas where disadvantaged people struggle to gain access to resources and full participation in social life. We do.

In other words, marginalized people may be marginalized, excluded or ignored socially, economically, politically and legally, and may therefore be vulnerable to livelihood changes.

According to Somers, "Socio-economic marginality is a state of socio-spatial structure and process in which components of society and place in a regional unit are seen to lag behind the expected level of performance in economic, political and social well-being, as compared to average conditions for the region as a whole".

CASTE AND CLASS

Caste

Caste is generally understood as a uniquely Indian and Hindu system of social organization. It is characterized by endogamy, hereditary transmission of a style of life which often includes an occupation, ritual status in a hierarchy, and customary social interaction and exclusion based on cultural notions of purity and pollution. Caste system is a closed stratification system in which people can do little or nothing to change their social standing. A caste system is one in which people are born into.

Theories of the Origin of Caste System

Occupational Theory

Regarding the origin of caste system, Nesfield developed a theory known as occupation theory. This theory explains the connectivity between the caste on one side and the occupation on the other side. The occupation theory states that the origin of caste system can be found in the nature and quality of work performed by different groups of people in the society.

According to this theory, if a particular group follows a hereditary occupation, it evolves into a caste in course of time.

Traditional / Divine Theory

Caste system according to traditional theory is based on the Divine origin. The backup for this theory is to be found in the sacred books of Hindus like Purushasukta. Purushasukta reveals that the fourfold division of the society came into being from four different parts of Brahma or the viratpursha or the Divine or the Supreme Being.

The topmost Varna out of the Varna system is the Brahmans who, according to Purshasukta, were created from the topmost part of Brahma, i.e., mouth. The next Varna in descending order is the Kshatriyas who were created from arms, the Vaishayas were created from thighs of the Brahma and the last Varna, i.e., Shudras were created from the lower most part of Brahma, i.e., feet.

Racial Theory

Herbert Risley is the most ardent exponent of racial theory of the origin of caste system. Other supporters of this theory are the scholars like Ghurye, Majumdar, Westermarck and others. According to this theory, caste system came into existence due to clash of cultures and the contact of races.

Political Theory

According to this theory, caste system is a clever device invented by the Brahmins in order to place themselves on the highest ladder of social hierarchy. Dr. Ghurye states, 'Caste is a Brahminic child of Indo-Aryan culture cradled in the land of the Ganges and thence transferred to other parts of India.'

Guild Theory

According to Denzil Ibbetson, castes are the modified forms of guilds. In his opinion, caste system is the product of interaction of three forces: (i) tribes, (ii) guilds, and (iii) religion. The tribes adopted certain fixed professions and assumed the form of guilds.

Religious Theory

Hocart and Senart are the two main advocates of religious theory. According to Hocart, social stratification originated on account of religious principles and customs. In ancient India, religion had a prominent place. The king was considered the image of God. The priest kings accorded different positions to different functional groups. Senart has tried to explain the origin of caste system on the basis of prohibitions regarding sacramental food.

Class

A class is a collection of people who possess similar socioeconomic circumstances. Class is the division of society based on various socioeconomic factors.

Prior to the French Revolution, the term 'class' was used in a general sense as in the writings of Adam Smith, Madison and other scholars of the eighteenth century. Several of them used it interchangeably with 'group' or 'estate'. It was in the nineteenth century that class came to be recognized as a relevant concept in explaining social theories, ideologies, social structure, and social change.

According to Ossowski, the following three assumptions are common to all conceptions of 'class' society.

While classes are differentiated groups in society, they are not independent of each other. It is not possible to speak of one class without reference to other classes.

Division of people into classes concerns social status connected with a system of privileges and discriminations not determined by biological criteria. This means that each class is accorded certain privileges and discriminations that have a bearing on its social status and has nothing to do with sex or any other criteria that is biological in nature.

The membership of individuals in a social class is relatively permanent.This does not mean there is no possibility of transition from oneclass to another. But such transition ismade by some individuals only.

Aristotle states that people are differentiated into three elements: one class is very rich; the other class is very poor. The third class occupies a position between the two in being neither very rich nor very poor.

From Marxist viewpoint, a class is a social group whose members share relationship to the means of production. In a capitalist society, there are two main classes of people: the bourgeoisie, that controls the capital and means of production, and the proletariat, who provide the labour.

According to Weber, class is one dimension of the social structure. Social status, or 'social honour,' is another. Both are significant contributors of social difference. Those who share same class situation may not necessarily belong to the same status group. For example, the nouveaux riches (newly rich) are sometimes excluded from status groups of the privileges because their taste, dress, manner etc. are considered vulgar.

A. Gramsci refers to class domination as 'hegemony' known more generally in Marxian theory as the dominant ideology thesis, i.e., the existence of a powerful dominant class ideology that stresses the nature of private property and creates an acceptance of the whole capitalist social order among all classes.

GENDER

The term gender refers to the qualities, behaviours, norms, and rules that a society or culture associates with a person's sex.

Gender is not synonymous with sex. Sex is a biological classification. On the other hand, gender is the role that is assigned to individuals based on their sex. It is a concept that explains how societies determine and manage gender categories; the cultural meanings associated with a person's gender.

The World Health Organization (WHO) defines gender as 'socially constructed characteristics of women and men, such as norms, roles, and relationships between groups of women and men. This varies from society to society and can be changed."

Gender Identity

Gender identity is the personal understanding of one's own gender. Gender identity may relate to or differ from the sex a person was assigned at birth. The term gender identity was originally coined by Robert J. Coined by Stoller.

It is a person's deeply held internal perception of their gender. Individuals who identify with a role different from their biological sex are called transgender. Transgender individuals who attempt to alter their bodies through medical interventions such as surgery and hormonal therapy so that their physical existence better aligns with gender identity are called transsexuals.

Not all transgender individuals choose to change their bodies. Many people choose to retain their original anatomy but may present themselves as another gender to society. This is usually done by adopting dress, hairstyle, mannerisms, or other characteristics typically attributed to the other gender. (It is important to note that people who cross-dress, or wear clothing that is traditionally assigned to a gender different from their biological sex, are not necessarily trans-gender).

SEXUALITY AND DISABILITY

Sexuality

Sexuality is a broad field of study related to a person's gender, gender identity and expression, and sexual orientation. Human sexuality is the way people experience and express themselves sexually. This includes biological, sensual, physical, emotional, social or spiritual feelings and behaviour. Sexual orientation is the pattern of sexual interest one has toward the opposite or same sex.

According to WHO, 'sexuality is influenced by biological, physical, social, economic, political, cultural, legal, historical, religious and spiritual factors'.

Michel Foucault's Perspective on Sexuality

Foucault was influenced by the works of Georges Canguilhem in biology and medicine. Canguilhem argued that 'the abnormality arouses theoretical interest in the ordinary'. Foucault analyzed the relationship between sexuality, subjectivity, and truth.

On the other hand, Foucault argues that a new technology of sex became a major site of state-centric intervention in the late eighteenth century. These interventions sought to control social bodies and resulted in new forms of surveillance.

Repression of sexuality was a part of this process. It is argued that the term 'sexuality', as we now understand it, was absent in the period before the nineteenth century. In this context, it is important to understand Foucault's ideas about knowledge and power as he claims that power can produce knowledge.

He proposes four ways in which knowledge and power are linked to new practices and technologies of sex. These relate to Foucault's critique of psychoanalysis and the cultural construction of sexuality. Briefly, the four events can be listed as follows:

Hysterization of women's bodies: Women's bodies are considered saturated with sexuality. Therefore, women are depicted as having unstable bodies that can be prone to hysteria, resulting in images of 'nervous women'.

Pedagogization of children's sex: Children who engage in sexual activities are seen as acting contrary to the laws of nature. Parents, doctors, experts, and academics realized the consequences of children's sexual potential. The myths of masturbation are related to these notions.

Socialization of procreative behavior: Regulation of population operates as a means of controlling reproductive behaviour in accordance with the needs of society. Foucault claimed that this process of control is political in nature. For example, financial aid and contraception are embedded in this political discourse.

Psychiatrization of perverse pleasure: Sexuality is considered as a separate mental and biological tendency that can be subjected to psychiatry.

According to Foucault, these four phenomena related to knowledge and power result in the creation of four subjects – the hysterical woman, the masturbating child, the Malthusian couple, and the deformed adult.

Anthony Giddens' View on Sexuality

- The concept of plastic sexuality has been theoretically developed by Anthony Giddens (1992). 'Plastic' refers to the malleability of erotic expression, both in terms of individual choice and the framework of social norms. It is argued that 'flexible sexuality' emerges in the context of social changes during and after modernity.

- 'Fixed sexuality' is linked to the binary of modernity – either heterosexual or homosexual, either marital or extramarital, either committed or erotic, either normal or deviant.

Disability

- Disability has been a universal human experience since the beginning of history. It refers to a limitation in the functions and activities performed by individuals as members of society, thereby limiting their participation in the socio-cultural, political and economic life of their communities.
- The term 'disability' is not homogeneous; it includes a variety of physical variations, physical impairments, sensory deficiencies, and intellectual or learning disabilities that may either be congenital (present from birth) or acquired during life.
- Disability is variously seen as an indicator of illness, physical deficiencies, deformities and impairments. It is also seen as a condition that prevents a person from properly performing his or her 'expected' role within the family and community. It is also seen in the context of restricted economic and productive roles and/or social stigma and rejection.

Desexualistion of Disabled People

- When it comes to sexuality and disability, there is a sexual discourse around it. There is a perception in society that people with disabilities are asexual by nature and are not sexually active. Although some people with disabilities are asexual, it is a misconception to think that everyone is the same.
- Many people with disabilities lack the rights and privileges that would enable them to form intimacy and relationships. The perception that people with disabilities are unable to have sex, that they have low levels of sexual knowledge and inadequate sex education.
- As a result, they are more vulnerable to exploitation in sexual relationships. Therefore, proper sex education for youth with disabilities is not only important for them to learn about sexual rights, sexual identity, and sexual expression, but also how to ensure their sexual safety.

RACE, TRIBE AND ETHNICITY

Race

- For centuries, it was believed that race was based on biology and differed genetically between different subgroups. Now, race is far more widely accepted as a social construct and therefore cannot be distinguished based on biology alone.
- The term 'race' was originally used to refer to a nation or ethnic group. For example, the 13th-century traveler Marco Polo used the term 'Persian race' to describe the people living in the territory of the nation-state of Iran.
- According to historian Milton Meltzer, the rise of the Atlantic slave trade created another incentive to categorize human groups to justify the subjugation of African slaves.
- Sociologists say that race is a social construct because what it means to be a member of a certain race is defined by culture, time, and place.
- Stephen Palmi says that race is 'not a thing but a social relation'.
- According to Katya Giebel Mevorach, race is 'a human invention whose criteria of discrimination are neither universal nor fixed, but have always been used to manage difference.'

Although people differ in many of the physical characteristics that led to the development of such racial categories, anthropologists, sociologists, and many biologists question the value of these categories and thus the value of the biological concept of race.

- According to Carlton S. Coon, the world population can be divided into 4 major races, namely White/Caucasian, Mongoloid/Asian, Negroid/Black and Australoid.
- B.S. Guha detected six major racial types among the modern Indian population.
  1. Negrito
  2. Proto-Australoid
  3. Mongoloid
  4. Mediterranean Sea
  5. Western Brachycephals
  6. Nordics
- Sir Herbert Hope Risley tried to classify the Indian population on the basis of anthropometric measurements. He took the help of anthropometry to confirm his assumptions and published the results in 1915 under the title 'The People of India'. He identified three major racial types in India.

1. Dravidian
2. Indo-Aryan
3. Mongoloid

Tribe

- The word 'tribe' is derived from the Latin word 'tribus' which means 'one third'. The term originally referred to one of the three regional groups that united to form Rome. The Romans used the term 'tribus' for the 35 people who became part of Rome in 241 BC.
- A tribe is characterized by cultural uniformity, unified social organization and a defined territorial area. The identity and culture of tribes is deeply linked to the natural resources and environment in which they live.
- The term tribe has also been used by scholars to refer to any non-Western or indigenous society. Some use the term to refer to societies organized largely on the basis of kinship.
- Different sociologists and anthropologists have given importance to different aspects of tribal society and there is no universally accepted definition of tribe. For example:
  - o D.N. Majumdar describes the tribe as a social group with regional affiliation, endogamous and with no specialization in functions, hereditary or otherwise governed by tribal authorities, recognizing social distance with other tribes or castes based on language or Is united in speech.
  - o Lucy Mair defines tribe as an independent political division of a population having a similar culture.
  - o Gilin and Gilin consider any collection of pre-literate local group that occupies a common common territory, speaks a common language and practices a common culture as a tribe.
  - o According to Ralph Linton, tribe is a group of bands occupying a contiguous area or areas and having a sense of unity arising from many similarities in a culture, frequent contacts and a definite community of interests.
  - o Durkheim used the term 'poly-segment society' in place of the term 'tribe'. In his book 'The Division of Labor in Society (1839) Durkheim highlighted two types of solidarity in society: mechanical and organic. The social organization of primitive tribes is known as mechanical solidarity.
  - o Lewis H. Morgan in his book 'Ancient Society' (1877) has defined tribe as a fully organized society where kinship dominates all types of social relations.
  - o According to Marshall Shalins, tribe is a segmental organization composed of homogeneous and non-specific multi-family groups, clans or bands.
  - o He differentiates between state and non-state society. Non-state societies are divided into bands, tribes and chieftainships.
  - o D.N. Majumdar conducted an extensive study among the Khasa and brought out the characteristics of the tribal-Hindu continuum. He says that despite participating in Hindu rituals and worshiping gods and goddesses, the tribe considers them foreign and non-religious, whereas among the people of the caste these are an essential part of the religion.
  - o While studying the 'Kondh' and 'Oriya' political systems, F.G. Bailey saw tribe and caste as a continuum. He wants to distinguish not in terms of the totality of behaviour but in a more limited way in relation to the political economic system. He suggested, 'We see caste and tribe as opposite ends of the same line.
  - o According to Virginius Xaxa, the word 'tribe' was used in more than one sense by the British. In one sense, the term refers to a group of people with a common ancestor. In another sense it refers to a group of people living in primitive conditions. Virginius defines the Xaxa tribes as indigenous peoples.

Ethnicity

- Like race, the term 'ethnicity' is difficult to describe and its meaning has changed over time. Ethnicity should not be confused with nationality, which refers to citizenship. While some countries are composed largely of a single ethnic group (Egypt, Finland, Germany and China), others are composed of many different groups (United States, Australia and India).
- Max Weber claims that ethnic groups are socially constructed. First, they were based on subjective belief in a shared Gemeinschaft (community). Second, this belief in shared Gemeinschaft did not create the group; rather, the group built trust. Third, the group was formed as a result of a drive to monopolize power and position.

- Ronald Cohen claims that the identification of 'ethnic groups' in the usage of social scientists often represents inaccurate labels. They argue that an ethnic group is identified by outsiders, e.g., Anthropologists cannot match the self-identification of members of that group.
- Cohen also suggests that claims related to 'ethnic' identity are often effects of colonial practices and relationships between colonized peoples and nation-states.
- The terms 'ethnic categories,' 'ethnic networks,' 'ethnic communities' and 'situational ethnicity' were developed to distinguish instances when ethnic categorization is the labeling of others and when it is a matter of self-identification.
- 'Ethnic category' is a category established by people who are outside this category. Members of an ethnic category are classified by outsiders on the basis of a common name or symbol, a shared cultural element.

SOCIAL CHANGE AND PROCESSES

- Social change is understood as significant changes in various patterns of social relations, social processes, social patterns, actions and interactions, relationships and rules of conduct (norms), values, symbols and cultural products.
- The concept of social change also refers to changes in both material and non-material aspects of culture over time. These changes are brought about by external forces both from within the society (endogenous forces) and from outside (exogenous forces).
- Social change in society is brought about by two main processes which are evolution and diffusion.

Evolution

- The concept of development came into social science from the theories of biological evolution. With the advent of the Darwinian theory of biological evolution, society and culture began to be considered to undergo similar changes and exhibit similar trends. This theory is based on the assumption that society gradually changes from simple to more complex.
- Charles Darwin, the proponent of the theory of biological evolution, showed that species of organisms have evolved from simple organisms to more complex organisms through the processes of variation and natural selection.
- Many social scientists were influenced by this theory and applied it to human society and argued that society must have evolved from simple and primitive to complex and advanced.
- Herbert Spencer, known as the pioneer of evolutionary theory in sociology, described sociology as 'the study of evolution in its most complex form.' According to him, the society is gradually moving towards a better situation. He argued that it evolved from a military society to an industrial society. He claimed that Western societies survived and developed because they were better adapted to cope with the circumstances of life.
- L.H. Morgan believed that there were three basic stages in the process of development of society: savagery, barbarism and civilization.
- According to Auguste Comte, society develops through three mental conception stages:
    1. **Theological stage:** People believe that all the phenomena of nature are divine and supernatural creations.
    2. **Metaphysical stage:** People believe that God is an abstract being.
    3. **Positive stage:** A purely intellectual and rational view of life. People try to understand their environment through observations and experiments.
- Durkheim saw societies changing towards greater differentiation, interdependence and formal control under the pressure of increasing moral density. He advocated that society evolved from a more differentiated social structure with minimal division of labour and a type of solidarity called mechanical solidarity, giving rise to a type of solidarity with maximum division of labor which is called biological solidarity.
- The evolutionary approach was also used by Marx and Engels, who said that each stage of civilization, such as feudalism, prepared the ground for the next.
- Therefore, evolutionary theories in sociology made some basic assumptions such as:
    1. Change is inevitable and natural.
    2. Change is gradual and continuous.
    3. Change is progressive.
    4. The stages of change are irreversible.
    5. The direction of change is from simple to complex, from uniformity to heterogeneity, from indistinct to different in form and function.

6. All societies go through the same stage of development.

- Based on these assumptions, three types of evolution theories have been made,
  1. **Theory of linear evolution:** According to this theory, change always occurs in a linear manner. Followers of this theory believe that all societies gradually move towards higher stages of civilization.
  2. **Universal theory of evolution:** It states that every society does not necessarily go through the same definite stages of development. Rather, its argument is that the culture of mankind, as a whole, follows a definite line of development.
  3. **Multilinear Theory of evolution:** This is a relatively new framework of development. This theory recognizes that change can occur in many ways and that it does not necessarily go in one direction. Contemporary social evolutionists such as Gerhard Lenski, Jr. view social change as multilinear rather than linear.

Diffusion

- Diffusion, also known as cultural diffusion, is a social process through which elements of culture spread from one social group to another or it is the spread of cultural traits from one group to another.
- Diffusion theory originated in the mid-nineteenth century as a means of understanding the nature of the distribution of cultural traits around the world. Sociologists and anthropologists believe that cultural diffusion is the primary way through which modern societies developed the cultures they have today.
- Theorists of this school of thought observed how cultural diffusion occurs when societies with different lifestyles come into contact with each other.
- British anthropologist Tylor introduced the theory of cultural diffusion as an alternative to using the theory of cultural evolution to explain cultural similarities.
- Franz Boas used the concept of cultural diffusion to explain how this process works in areas that are close to each other. He considered culture to be composed of countless loose threads that were woven together to fit the new cultural context.
- Morgan believed that social change involved both independent innovation and diffusion.
- Cultural diffusion occurs at two levels:
  1. Diffusion of material culture
  2. Diffusion of non-material culture
- William F. According to Ogburn, elements of non-material culture are more resistant to change than material culture.
- According to him, technological progress brings about rapid changes in the material aspects of our culture, but the non-material aspects fail to do so or succeed in doing so only after a significant time lag. This is known as the cultural lag.

Types of Diffusion

Relocation Diffusion

- Relocation diffusion occurs when people move from their place of origin to another place and bring their innovations with them. As they relocate to a new place, they bring with them their own ideas, cultural traditions like food, music and more. Relocation diffusion may also be forced rather than chosen.
- For example, many cultural components of Southern American architecture, cuisine, and music are of African and Caribbean origin due to the forced relocation and enslavement of African people during the Trans-Atlantic slave trade.

Expansion Diffusion

- Expansion diffusion is the spread of an idea through a population where the number of people affected becomes increasingly large. There are three sub-types of extension spread:
  1. **Contagious Diffusion:** It is defined as the distance-controlled spread of an idea through a local population by person-to-person contact. It spreads rapidly from one source to another, from one person to another.

     For example, when videos or songs go viral, they spread contagiously with the help of modern technological innovations.
  2. **Hierarchical Diffusion:** This occurs when an idea spreads first among the most connected individuals, then to other individuals.

     For example, popular music reaches large urban centers before gaining popularity among the wider public.
  3. **Stimulation Diffusion:** Stimulation diffusion occurs when an idea spreads outward from its cultural center, but the original idea is replaced by new adopters.

For example, the changing interpretations of religious texts as they are translated into other languages.

Maladaptive diffusion

- Maladaptive diffusion is the adoption of diffuse traits that are not practical for or reflective of an area's environment or culture.
- For example, proliferation of grass lawns and monoculture crops which are very harmful to the environment.

MODERNIZATION AND DEVELOPMENT

Modernisation

- According to scholars, the process of modernization summarizes the changes that transform an agrarian or underdeveloped society with a weak state into an industrial society with a relatively efficient, active government. The modernization process embraces the changes that lead to industrialization and urbanization.
- Modernization gained great importance in the 1950s and 1960s, especially after the end of World War II. The Industrial Revolution in England and, to a lesser extent, the French Revolution in France brought modernization into the spotlight.
- According to Wilbert Moore, 'Modernization is the 'complete' transformation of a traditional or pre-modern society into the technology and associated types of social organization that characterize the advanced, economically prosperous, and relatively stable nations of the Western world'.
- Modernization refers to the transformation of society from 'traditional' to 'modern'.
- According to Krishna Kumar, 'Modernization: In sociology, the change from a traditional, rural, agrarian society to a secular, urban, industrial society'.
- D. Lerner, author of 'The Passing of the Traditional Society-Modernizing the Middle East', has also identified five characteristics of modernity, namely:
  1. Urbanization
  2. Literacy
  3. Mass media and mass communication
  4. Increasing political awareness,
  5. Skilled manpower to support economic growth and technological advancement for rapid industrialization
- Giddens said that to understand and conceptualize contemporary society, we need a new sociological theory capable of understanding its complexity. He describes the modern world as a 'juggernaut'.
- Modernity as a chariot is extremely dynamic, it is a 'world on the run' with huge leaps in the speed, scope and depth of change compared to prior systems.
- Giddens defines modernity in terms of four basic institutions.
- The first is capitalism, characterized by commodity production, private ownership of capital, propertyless wage labour, and a class system derived from these characteristics.
- The second is industrialism, which involves the use of non-living energy sources and machinery to produce goods. Industrialism is not limited to the workplace, and affects other settings such as 'transportation, communications, and domestic life'.
- Third, there is surveillance capacity which is defined as 'monitoring the activities of the subject population (primarily, but not exclusively) in the political arena.'
- Fourth is military power, or control over the means of violence, including the industrialization of war.

Development

- The term development is used in many ways, but most sociologists agree that development should mean improvement or progress at least for those who are in dire need of positive change in their lives.
- Most sociologists believe that development means economic growth and the positive outcomes arising from it, such as improved life expectancy, mass education and social welfare.
- Social scientists believe that modernization and development are interrelated concepts. He believes that modernization is a process of social change whereby less developed societies acquire characteristics similar to more developed societies.
- But there appear to be two main phases of modernization. Up to a certain point in its course, it takes with it the institutions and values of society, in what is generally considered a progressive, upward movement.

However, after some point, modernization begins to create dissatisfaction on an increasing scale. Groups make increasing demands on the community and these demands become increasingly difficult to meet. Modern society finds itself facing many new problems whose solutions often seem beyond the capacity of the traditional nation-state.

- Furthermore, there appears to be a dynamic principle built into the very structure of modern societies that does not allow them to settle down or achieve equilibrium. Their development is always irregular and uneven. Whatever the level of development, there are always 'backward' areas and 'peripheral' groups. It is a constant source of tension and conflict in modern societies.
- According to Daniel Lerner, to be successful and effective, the modernization process should not merely involve the mechanical 'transfer' of a few selected objects, but a complete 'transformation' of the society concerned.

SOCIAL TRANSFORMATION AND GLOBALIZATION

- The concept of social change has a very deep connection with social change. Social transformation is a relatively new term that has gained some popularity in social science discourse in recent decades. In fact, social transformation is a revolutionary form of social change. It is a more sudden transformation of society and/or the state, usually on a large scale, through agents such as revolution. The concept reflects the idea of a particularly deep and far-reaching change that changes people's way of life within a limited period of time.
- Globalization is one such process which has far-reaching impact on the lives of people and society. According to sociologists, globalization is a continuous process that involves interconnected changes in the economic, cultural, social and political spheres of society. As a process, it involves the ever-increasing integration of these aspects across nations, regions, communities, and even seemingly isolated places.
- In the context of economics, globalization refers to the expansion of capitalism to include all places around the world into one globally integrated economic system. Culturally, it refers to the global spread and integration of ideas, values, norms, behaviours, and ways of life.
- Luc Martel says that globalization is 'the integration of poor countries into a world economy of open competition'. Often the process of globalization starts with a single objective, such as market expansion. But there is usually a snowball effect, and globalization becomes a mixed bag of economic, philanthropic, entrepreneurial, and cultural endeavors.
- Proponents of globalization believe that it brings regions closer together that were never close before. As Marshall McLuhan, a Canadian thinker, coined the term 'global village' in the 1960s, it means that all parts of the world are being brought into one unit by the Internet and other electronic communication technologies.
- But social transformationists believe that globalization is slowing down the process of poverty reduction in some developing and underdeveloped countries of the world and is increasing the problem of inequality. Models of dependency and world systems theory can be used to understand this argument.

Dependency Theory

- First described in the late 1950s by Raoul Prebisch and Paul A. Proposed by Baran, dependency theory gained prominence in the 1960s and 70s. Dependency theory is the notion that resources flow from the 'periphery' of poor and underdeveloped states to the 'center' of rich states, enriching the latter at the expense of the former.
- According to the dependency theory, underdevelopment is mainly due to the peripheral position of the affected countries in the world economy. Generally, underdeveloped countries offer cheap labour and raw materials in the world market. These resources are sold to advanced economies, which have the means to transform them into finished goods.
- Underdeveloped countries buy finished products at high prices, which drains away the capital they could spend to upgrade their productive capacity. The result is a vicious cycle that divides the world economy between a rich center and a poor periphery.

World Systems Theory

- World systems theory is a further development of dependency theory, developed by sociologist Immanuel Wallerstein in the 1970s, an approach to world history and social change that suggests there is a world economic system in which some countries One benefits while others are exploited. Just as we cannot understand a person's behaviour without the context of their environment, experiences, and culture, a country's economic system cannot be understood without the context of the world system of which they are a part.

- The main features of this theory are:
  1. World systems theory is founded on a three-level hierarchy consisting of core, periphery, and semi-periphery regions.
  2. Core countries dominate and exploit peripheral countries for labour and raw materials.
  3. Peripheral countries are dependent on core countries for capital.
  4. Semi-peripheral countries share characteristics of both core and peripheral countries.
  5. This theory emphasizes the social structure of global inequality.

SOCIAL MOBILITY

- Social mobility is the movement of individuals, families, households or other categories of people within or between social strata in a society. It is a change in the social status of an individual relative to his or her current social status within a given society.
- Social mobility refers to movement from one social position to another within the social structure. It means change in social status. All societies provide some opportunities for social mobility. But societies differ from each other in the extent to which individuals can move from one level to another.
- According to Barber, social mobility refers to upward or downward movement between higher or lower social classes; or more precisely, movement between one relatively full-time, functionally important social role and another that is evaluated as higher or lower.
- Sorokin was the first sociologist on mobility who wrote the book 'Social and Cultural Mobility'. He believed that there is no society that is completely closed (caste) and there is no society that is completely open (class).
- He further argued that no two societies are exactly alike in the amount of movement permitted or discouraged. Furthermore, the speed or speed of change may vary from one time period to another. The rate of change depends on the level of modernization of a society.

Sorokin discussed three main types of mobility:

1. **Vertical Mobility:** It refers to the movement of people from one level to another or from one level to another. It brings changes in class, occupation and power. It involves movement from lower to higher or from higher to lower. There are two types of vertical mobility. One upward and the other downward mobility. When a person moves from a lower status to a higher status, it is called upward mobility. When it moves from top to bottom, it is called downward mobility.
2. **Horizontal Mobility:** It refers to the movement of people from one social group to another social group located at the same level. This means that the ranks of these two groups are not different. It indicates a change in position without a change in position.
3. **Intergenerational Mobility:** This type of mobility means that one generation changes its social status in contrast to the previous generation. With the help of education and skills, the young generation can get employment at higher positions. If the father is a cobbler but his son becomes a lawyer after getting education, then it is known as inter-generational mobility.

   The first major study on intergenerational mobility was conducted in England and Wales by David Glass in 1949. It was found that intergenerational mobility was quite high and almost two-thirds of the individuals interviewed were in a different occupational category as compared to their fathers.

Global Social Mobility Index

- It is an index prepared by the World Economic Forum in its Global Social Mobility Report. This index measures inter-generational social mobility in different countries in relation to socio-economic outcomes.
- The index is based on the following five factors:
  1. Health
  2. Education
  3. Technology
  4. Work
  5. Flexibility and Institutions

ASSESS YOUR LEARNING

PRACTICE QUESTIONS

1. Who said, 'man is a social animal and being social for man is both natural as well as necessary'?
(a) Socrates
(b) Aristotle
(c) Plato
(d) Rousseau

2. Who characterizes society in terms of 'social statics' and 'social dynamics', referring to social stability as well as social changes?
(a) Emile Durkheim
(b) Max Weber
(c) Herbert Spencer
(d) Aguste Comte

3. Comte emphasized that the evolution of society passed through three stages, which of the following is not one of them?
(a) Theological
(b) Metaphysical
(c) Sensate
(d) Scientific

4. Who defined culture as 'that complex whole which includes knowledge, belief, art, morals, law, custom, and any other capabilities and habits acquired by man as a member of society'?
(a) Alfred Kroeber
(b) B Malinowsky
(c) Edward B Tylor
(d) Ellenwood

5. Who defined culture in terms of the whole of man's material civilization like tools, weapons, clothing, shelter, machines, and even systems of industry, and on the other hand as man's non-material or spiritual civilization, such as language, literature, art, religion, ritual, morality, law, and government?
(a) W F Ogburn
(b) B Malinowsky
(c) Edward B Tylor
(d) Ellenwood

6. Which of the following thinker has made a distinction between society and culture in this way: 'Society means the totality of social facts projected onto the dimensions of relationships and groupings; cultures, the same totality in the dimensions of action'?
(a) S F Nadel
(b) Ogburn and Nimcoff
(c) MacIver and Page
(d) C.H. Cooley and L.L. Bernard

7. The process of learning the acceptable behaviour by individuals relevant to the group or the society to which they belong is called as?
(a) Assimilation
(b) Acculturation
(c) Melting Pot
(d) Cultural Contact

8. Which of the following statement is incorrect:
(a) The American sociologists C.H. Cooley and L.L. Bernard have described the forms of social control as conscious and unconscious.
(b) Karl Mannheim has discussed the direct and indirect forms of social control.
(c) George Simmel has described positive and negative forms of social control.
(d) Lapierre has identified autocratic and democratic forms of social control.

9. The word diaspora relates to the idea of a community longing for its homeland. In the beginning, this was applied to which community?
(a) Jewish (b) Indian
(c) Chinese (d) Canadian

10. The conflict between Tamils led by the Liberation Tigers for Tamil Eelam (LTTE) and the government led by the dominant Sinhalese community in Sri Lanka is an example of:
(a) Ethnic conflict (b) Communal Violence
(c) Naxalism (d) Ethnic Riots

11. Emile Durkheim has talked about two types of laws Repressive Laws and Restitutive laws in his book:
(a) Division of Labour in Society (1893)
(b) Elementary Form of Religious Life (1915)
(c) Education and Sociology (1922)
(d) Professional Ethics and Civic Morals (1950)

12. According to Sumner, '______ are actually codified mores'.
(a) Folkways (b) Tradition
(c) Custom (d) Law

13. Who said, 'Customs are social habits'?
(a) S F Nadel
(b) W F Ogburn
(c) MacIver and Page
(d) C.H. Cooley and L.L. Bernard

14. According to Freud, the human personality is made up of three major systems which of the following is not discussed by him?
(a) 'Id' (b) 'ego'
(c) 'supra ego' (d) 'superego'

15. The 'emigration of trained and talented individuals from the country of origin to another country resulting in a depletion of skills/resources in the former' is termed as:
(a) brain drain
(b) brain gain
(c) brain bank
(d) brain circulation

16. 'Community is the smallest territorial group that can embrace all aspects of social life', who gave this definition?
(a) E.S. Bogardus
(b) Kingsley Davis
(c) MacIver and Page
(d) Ogburn and Nimkoff

17. 'Culture is the man-made part of the environment', who said this?
(a) Robert Bierstedt
(b) E.A. Hoebel
(c) M.J. Herskovits
(d) B. Malinowski

18. Who said, 'Sociologists are the priest of modern society'?
(a) Emile Durkheim
(b) Max Weber
(c) Auguste Comte
(d) None of the above

19. 'Sociology is the study of the forms of social relation.' Who said this?
(a) E. Durkheim
(b) G. Simmel
(c) MacIver and Page
(d) Ginsberg

20. Every man in society occupies a number of statuses, different statuses associated with a single person are known as:
(a) status inconsistency
(b) status sequences
(c) status set
(d) status succession

21. Who has coined the terms status, status set, and status sequence?
(a) R. Linton (b) K. Davis
(c) MacIver & Page (d) R.K. Merton

22. 'Primary groups are nurseries of human nature.' Who said it?
(a) H.M. Johnson
(b) Herbert Spencer
(c) George Simmel
(d) Charles Horton Cooley

23. Sam, an American, assumes that the American culture and way of life are superior to all others. This is an example of
(a) culture shock (b) stereotyping
(c) ethnocentrism (d) endogamy

24. Emily, age 8, is able to grasp her own social position as well as that of the people around her. She begins to consider several tasks and relationships simultaneously. According to George Herbert Mead's theory, Emily is at the ________ stage.
(a) play (b) game
(c) imitative (d) preparatory

25. The concept of 'role' in Sociology refers to
(a) Positional aspect of individual
(b) Static aspect of the position
(c) Behavioural component of status
(d) Normative aspect of behaviour

26. Who defined culture as 'essentially a response to human needs.'
(a) Alfred Kroeber (b) B Malinowski
(c) Edward B Tylor (d) Ellenwood

27. Which one of the following does not constitute an element of social structure?
(a) Status and role (b) Groups and sub-groups
(c) Institutions (d) Sub-culture

28. Who among the following propounded the idea of transition from status to contract?
(a) Thomas Hobbes
(b) Henry Maine
(c) Montesquieu
(d) Rousseau

29. Which of the following concept is not propounded by Erving Goffman?
(a) Social Stigma
(b) Mystification
(c) Total Institution
(d) Political Management

30. Which of the following are the characteristics of a 'little community'?
1. Self-sufficiency
2. Hegemony
3. Homogeneity
4. Association

Choose the correct answer from the codes given below:
(a) 1, 2, and 3 (b) 1 and 2
(c) 2 and 3 (d) 1 and 3

31. Which of the following are the characteristics of values?
1. A generalized principle
2. Strong commitment for group members
3. Prescribed range of behaviour
4. A standard for judging goals

Choose the correct answer from the codes given below:
(a) 1, 2, and 3
(b) 1, 2, and 4
(c) 1, 3, and 4
(d) 2, 3, and 4

32. When cultural traits spread from one society to another, the process is called?
(a) Diffusion
(b) Parallelism
(c) Evolution
(d) Pluralism

33. Which of the following are the characteristics of a 'primary group'?
1. Small size
2. Self-interest
3. Similarity of background
4. Intensity of shared interest

Choose the correct answer from the codes given below:
(a) 1, 2, and 3 (b) 1 and 2
(c) 1, 3, and 4 (d) 1 and 4

34. Match list I with list II

List I	List II
A. Expected behaviour associated with a given status	I. Role
B. An array of roles that goes with a given status	II. Role conflict
C. The demand for two or more roles that do not mesh	III. Role strain
D. Conflicting demands of the same role	IV. Role set

Choose the correct answer from the codes given below:

	A	B	C	D
(a)	I	III	II	IV
(b)	II	I	III	IV
(c)	I	IV	II	III
(d)	II	III	IV	I

35. Ceremonies that mark a critical transition in the life of an individual from one phase of the life cycle to another are called?
(a) Role taking
(b) Rites of passage
(c) Status crystallization
(d) Role playing

36. The term 'status group' was coined by?
(a) Emile Durkheim
(b) Max Weber
(c) Herbert Spencer
(d) Aguste Comte

37. The concept of recruitment role was used by?
(a) Ralph Linton
(b) Talcott Parsons
(c) S F Nadel
(d) E. Goffman

38. Who said that 'role is the dynamic aspect of status'?
(a) Linton (b) Lundberg
(c) MacIver (d) Herskovitz

39. Match List-I with List-II:

List I (Concepts)	List II (Explanation)
A. Authority	I. Ideas and behaviour logically coherent
B. Power	II. Socially accepted norm
C. Rationality	III. The legitimate form of power
D. Legitimacy	IV. Depends on a personal source

Select the correct answer from the options given below:
(a) (A)-(II); (B)-(IV); (C)-(I); (D)-(III)
(b) (A)-(III); (B)-(I); (C)-(IV); (D)-(II)
(c) (A)-(III); (B)-(IV); (C)-(I); (D)-(II)
(d) (A)-(III); (B)-(IV); (C)-(II); (D)-(I)

40. 'A society of rationally coordinated un-equals in pursuit of large-scale tasks' is termed as?
(a) Bureaucracy (b) Organization
(c) Institution (d) Oligarchy

41. ________ descent is a kinship system that traces descent through the relatives of the mother.
(a) Bilineal (b) Matrilineal
(c) Trilineal (d) Patrilineal

42. Who wrote the book '*The Death of the Family*'?
(a) Edmund Leach
(b) T. Parsons
(c) David Cooper
(d) W. J. Goode

43. Who classified kinship terms into 'Classificatory' and 'Descriptive'?
(a) G.P. Murdock
(b) A.R. Brown
(c) B. Malinowski
(d) L.H. Morgan

44. Name the system adopted by a given society to guide family or blood relationships.
(a) Marriage (b) Culture
(c) Kinship (d) Taboos

45. Who defined 'family as a group defined by a sex relationship sufficiently precise and enduring to provide for the production and upbringing of children'?
(a) MacIver and Page
(b) Kingsley Davis
(c) Ogburn and Nimkoff
(d) Burgess and Locke

46. Who is the author of the book '*The Family*' (1953)?
(a) MacIver and Page
(b) Kingsley Davis

(c) Ogburn and Nimkoff
(d) Burgess and Locke

47. Talcott Parsons describes the two most important functions of family, which are they?
1. Primary socialization of children
2. Stabilization of adult personality
3. The regulation of sexual behaviour and reproduction
4. Primary group satisfaction

Choose the correct option:
(a) (1) and (2) (b) (2) and (3)
(c) (3) and (4) (d) (4) and (1)

48. The family in which one is born is known as:
(a) Family of Procreation
(b) Family of Birth
(c) Family of Orientation
(d) Consanguineous Family

49. Who divided the family into Family of Orientation and Family of Procreation?
(a) G P Murdock (b) Adrian Mayor
(c) R D Liang (d) None of the above

50. In such a family where authority is vested in the eldest male member of the family is known as:
(a) Authoritarian family
(b) Patrilocal family
(c) Patrilineal family
(d) Patriarchal Family

51. The type of family in which the couple live in the maternal uncle's house is known as?
(a) Amitolocal
(b) Virilocal
(c) Matrilocal
(d) Avanculocal

52. The type of family in which the couple after marriage live with the husband's father is known as?
(a) Virilocal (b) Matrilocal
(c) Patrivirilocal (d) Neolocal

53. In which book Edmond Leach has presented a pessimistic view of the family in industrial society?
(a) A Runaway World
(b) Rethinking Anthropology
(c) Culture and Communication
(d) Culture and Nature

54. In which of his book David Cooper has condemned family as an institution:
(a) The Language of Madness
(b) Existentialism
(c) The Death of the Family
(d) A Philosophies of Gardens

55. Who has called family as a group of nexus:
(a) R D Liang (b) David Cooper
(c) Edmund Leach (d) Talcott Parsons

56. The term which means the marriage of a woman with a man of higher varna is called as
(a) Hypogamy / Pratiloma
(b) Hypergamy / Anuloma
(c) Monogamy
(d) Polygamy

57. Which of the type of family not discussed by Frederic Le Play?
(a) Patriarchal (b) Stem
(c) Unstable (d) Atomistic

58. For LH Morgan the earliest type of family was?
(a) Monogamous
(b) Patriarchal
(c) Matriarchal
(d) Virilocal

59. To understand the pattern of kinship in India Irawati Karve explains the configuration of the linguistic areas, caste institution and organization of family as the most essential. She breakdown the whole nation into 4 parts which of the following is not among them?
(a) Western
(b) Central
(c) Northern
(d) Southern

60. Who said, 'Harmony between the emotional and intellectual aspects of religion can be conceived'?
(a) A R Radcliffe Brown
(b) Clifford Geertz
(c) Claude Levi Strauss
(d) B Malinowski

61. The use of phonemes in relation to the kinship system was done by whom?
(a) Levi-Strauss
(b) A. R. Radcliffe-Brown
(c) B. Malinowski
(d) S. F. Nadel

62. Alliance Theory in Kinship Studies is associated with which of the following scholars?
(a) Kathleen Gough
(b) Pauline Kolenda
(c) C. Levi-Strauss
(d) A. R Radcliffe-Brown

63. From among the following sociologists who have written on the '*Kinship Systems*' in different regions of India?
(a) P.N. Prabhu (b) G.S. Ghurye
(c) Irawati Karve (d) K.M. Kapadia

64. Who viewed education as the action exercised by the older generation upon those who are not yet ready for social life?
(a) Emile Durkheim (b) T B Bottomore
(c) R H lowie (d) Lord William Bentick

65. Which of the following is correct about informal education?

1. It helps to bring social equality
2. It helps to segregate people from the community
3. It focuses on the social aspect of learning
4. It does not bridge the gap between school and life

Choose the correct option:

(a) (1) and (2)
(b) (2) and (3)
(c) (1) and (3)
(d) (3) and (4)

66. Who proposed 'nai talim' or basic education which emphasized the introduction of productive handi-crafts in the school curriculum?

(a) Irawati Karve
(b) B R Ambedkar
(c) M K Gandhi
(d) R K Mukjerjee

67. It is formal sanction being used by the authorities for social control?

(a) Mores (b) Customs
(c) Law (d) Traditions

68. Weber defined law ' as an order, the validity of which is guaranteed by the probability that deviation will be met bya physical or psychic sanction by a staff specially empowered to carry out these sanctions' in which of the following book?

(a) The Sociology of Religion - 1920
(b) The City - 1921
(c) Basic Concepts in Sociology - 1922
(d) Economy and Society – 1922

69. Given below are two statements, one labelled as Assertion (A) and the other as Reason (R)

Assertion (A): Customs are more important in less developed societies.

Reason (R): As societies become complex and devel-oped, they are to loosen their hold and are, therefore, replaced by laws to a great extent.

Select the collect answer from the options given below:

(a) Both (A) and (R) are true and (R) is the correct explanation of (A)
(b) Both (A) and (R) are true, but (R) is not the cor-rect explanation of (A)
(c) (A) is hue, but (R) is false
(d) (A) is false, but (R) is true

70. Who coined the term 'Economic Sociology'?

(a) Max Weber
(b) William Stanley Jevons
(c) E A Gross
(d) Henry M Johnson

71. Elin Hildebrand classified economic system on the basis of?

1. Barter
2. Money
3. Consumption
4. Credit

Choose the correct answer from the codes given below:

(a) 1, 2, and 3 (b) 1, 2, and 4
(c) 1, 3, and 4 (d) 2, 3, and 4

72. Karl Polanyi, an economic historian has identified three different modes of allocation or principles of exchange which of the following is not one of them?

(a) Reciprocity
(b) Redistribution
(c) Market exchange
(d) Barter

73. Malinowski, studied the economic activities of which region?

(a) the kula of the western Pacific region
(b) the lovendu of South Africa
(c) the potlach of the North-West coast of America
(d) the Yoruba of Nigeria

74. Which one of the following is a process, by which parts of the middle class become effectively absorbed into the working class?

(a) Embourgeoisement (b) Proletarianization
(c) Alienation (d) Homogenization

75. The intra-tribal economic relations are mostly based on

(a) shell money
(b) jajmani system
(c) barter and exchange
(d) stone money

76. The institution of the Jajmani System implies:

1. The functional interdependence of castes
2. Absentee landlordism
3. The principle of social reciprocity
4. Structural mobility

Select the correct answer using the codes given below:

(a) 1 and 2 (b) 1 and 3
(c) 1 and 4 (d) 2 and 3

77. Match List I with List II and select the correct answer using the codes given below:

List I (Theory / Concept)	List II (Thinker)
A. Theory of the Leisure Class	I. Veblen
B. Circulation of the Elites	II. Malthus
C. Adaptive Culture	III. Ogburn
D. Survival of the Fittest	IV. Darwin
	V. Pareto

Codes:

	A	B	C	D
(a)	I	V	III	IV
(b)	V	I	III	IV
(c)	I	V	II	III
(d)	V	I	II	III

78. Consider the following features:
1. Fixed spheres of competence of different offices
2. Charismatic authority
3. Impersonality
4. Recruitment based on merit

Which of these are typical of the bureaucratic organisation?
(a) 1, 2, and 3 (b) 1, 3, and 4
(c) 2, 3, and 4 (d) 1 and 4

79. A legitimate right to give certain orders or commands is called
(a) power (b) authority
(c) influence (d) cohesion

80. Match List I and List II and select the correct answer:

List I (Concepts)	List II (Explanation)
A. Class	I. Politically sanctioned
B. Status group	II. Physical characteristics
C. Estate	III. Life chances
D. Race relations	IV. Life style

Codes:

	A	B	C	D
(a)	IV	III	I	II
(b)	IV	III	II	I
(c)	III	IV	II	I
(d)	III	IV	I	II

81. Match List I (Institution) with List II (People) and select the correct answer using the codes given below the Lists:

List I (Institution)	List II (People)
A. Potlatch	I. Naga
B. Genna	II. Trobrianders
C. Kula	III. Haitians
D. Pratik	IV. Kwakiutl
	V. Javanese

Codes:

	A	B	C	D
(a)	IV	II	V	III
(b)	III	I	II	IV
(c)	IV	I	II	III
(d)	III	II	V	IV

82. Crony capitalism is dominated by
(a) Medium-scale industries
(b) Powerful business families
(c) Partnership companies
(d) Group of powerful land owners practising mechanized farming

83. Who proposed the concept of a 'free economy'?
(a) Adam Smith (b) Niel Smelser
(c) Emile Durkheim (d) Max Weber

84. Match List I and List II and select the correct answer:

List I (Categories)	List II (Stages of evolution)
A. Agriculture	I. First
B. Industrial	II. Third
C. Pastoral	III. Second
D. Hunting	IV. Fourth

Codes:

	A	B	C	D
(a)	II	III	IV	I
(b)	I	IV	III	II
(c)	I	III	IV	II
(d)	II	IV	III	I

85. Who is the author of the book 'The Theory of Economic Development' in which he discusses the concept of 'entrepreneurship'?
(a) Adam Smith
(b) K Schumpeter
(c) T Veblen
(d) Henry Baverman

86. Who has discussed the concept of 'De skilling' in his book '*Labour and Monopoly Capital*'?
(a) Adam Smith (b) K Schumpeter
(c) T Veblen (d) Henry Baverman

87. The 'constant sum concept of power' is discussed by which of the following thinkers?
(a) Max Weber (b) Talcott Parsons
(c) Henry Baverman (d) Adam Smith

88. Who has discussed the concept of the 'iron law of oligarchies'?
(a) V Pareto (b) G Mosca
(c) R Michells (d) R A Dahl

89. Communist Manifesto was authored by:
(a) Stalin (b) Karl Marx
(c) Laski (d) George Bernard Shah

90. Manorial system of economy in England implied
(a) cultivation of land by the owners themselves.
(b) small-scale cultivation.
(c) feudal system i.e., lord employing labourers.
(d) Industrial system

91. Which one of the following statements about Rousseau is correct?
(a) He perfected the theory of the Social Contract
(b) He repudiated the theory of Contract altogether
(c) He transformed the theory of Contract into an idealist mode of political discourse
(d) He added nothing to the theories of Hobbes and Locke beyond combining their views

92. Who among the following described democracy as the 'tyranny of the majority'?
(a) J. Rousseau (b) De Tocqueville
(c) John Dunning (d) James Madison

93. Who among the following advocated party less democracy in India?
(a) M. N. Roy
(b) Jayprakash Narayan
(c) Acharya Narender Dev
(d) Ram Manohar Lohia

94. The concept of 'power elite' is connected with:
(a) Pareto (b) Mosca
(c) C. Wright Mills (d) James Burham

95. The Elitist theory holds that the power is always concentrated in the hands of:
(a) Priestly class (b) Military class
(c) Civil Servants (d) A small group of elites

96. Who of the following thinkers tried to combine the elitist theory with Marxism?
(a) Robert Michels (b) James Burham
(c) Vilfredo Pareto (d) None of the above

97. Who among the following held the view that family is an ideological conditioning device in an exploitative society?
(a) David Cooper (b) R D Liang
(c) Friedrich Engels (d) Edmund Leach

98. Karl Polanyi, an economic historian has identified three different modes of allocation or principles of exchange which of the following is not one of them?
(a) Reciprocity (b) Redistribution
(c) Market exchange (d) Barter

99. The study of social stratification is the study of
1. social problems
2. social differences
3. social inequalities
4. social disorganisation

Select the correct answer using the codes given below:

Codes:
(a) 1 and 2 (b) 1 and 3
(c) 1 and 4 (d) 2 and 3

100. Which three broad types of cultures succeeding each other have been analysed by P.A. Sorokin in his cyclical theory of social change?
(a) Ideational, Instrumental and Ethical
(b) Ideational, Idealist and Senate
(c) Idealist, Moral and Senate
(d) Idealist, Ethical and Modern

101. Given below are two statements, one labelled a Assertion (A) and the other as Reason (R)

Assertion: Differentiation refers to how things or pec ple can be distinguished from one another.

Reason: Stratification refers to the ranking of thing or people.

Select the correct answer from the options given below

a. Both (A) and (R) are true and (R) is the correc explanation of (A)
b. Both (A) and (R) are true, but (R) is not the co rect explanation of (A)
c. (A) is hue, but (R) is false
d. (A) is false, but (R) is true

102. Consider the following stages of Social Change as given by Karl Marx:
1. Feudal
2. Primitive Communism
3. Ancient
4. Capitalistic

The correct sequence of these stages of Soci Change is

(a) 2, 3, 1, and 4 (b) 1, 3, 4 and 2
(c) 4, 1, 2, and 3 (d) 3, 2, 1 and 4

103. Match List I and List II and select the correct answe

List I (Thinkers)	List II (Theories)
A. P. Sorokin	I. Evolutionary Theory of Change
B. A. Comte	II. Theory of Modernisation
C. K. Marx	III. Revolutionary Theory of Change
D. D. Lerner	IV. Cyclical Theory of Social Change

Codes:

	A	B	C	D
(a)	IV	III	II	I
(b)	I	II	III	IV
(c)	IV	I	III	II
(d)	I	III	II	IV

104. Which one of the following statements is correct?
(a) Social processes are always associative
(b) Social processes are always disassociative
(c) Social processes may be both associative ar disassociative
(d) Social processes are neither associative n disassociative

105. According to Max Weber, members of the same
(a) class have a common lifestyle
(b) class have common life chances
(c) class belong to the same status group
(d) status group belong to the same class

106. Which of the following types of authorities have been identified by Max Weber?
(a) Rational, emotional and traditional
(b) Rational, charismatic and traditional
(c) Traditional, ideal and rational
(d) Traditional, modern and post-modern

107. Which one of the following practices of bringing up children gives rise to the authoritarian personality in adult life?
(a) advice instead of domination
(b) matter of prestige instead of the situation
(c) encouragement instead of criticism
(d) withholding reward instead of punishment

108. Consider the following characteristics:
1. Patriarchy
2. Endogamy
3. Hierarchy
4. Equality

Which of these are typical of Hindu Caste System?
(a) 1 and 2 (b) 2 and 4
(c) 2 and 3 (d) 1 and 4

109. Assertion (A): Social mobility is necessarily more in class societies than in caste societies.

Reason (R): A single individual in a class society can move up to a class higher than that of his birth.
(a) Both (A) and (R) are true and (R) is the correct explanation of (A)
(b) Both (A) and (R) are true, but (R) is not the correct explanation of (A)
(c) (A) is hue, but (R) is false
(d) (A) is false, but (R) is true

110. Assertion (A): A low caste person usually sanskritises his style of life and ritual on becoming wealthy.

Reason (R): Sanskritisation resolves the inconsistency between newly acquired wealth and low ritual rank.
(a) Both (A) and (R) are true and (R) is the correct explanation of (A)
(b) Both (A) and (R) are true, but (R) is not the correct explanation of (A)
(c) (A) is hue, but (R) is false
(d) (A) is false, but (R) is true

111. Which one of the following is an integration of matter and concomitant dissipation of motion, during which matter passes from a definite coherent homogeneity to an indefinite incoherent heterogeneity?
(a) Development (b) Evolution
(c) Growth (d) Progress

112. The term 'Couvade' refers to
(a) husband practising magic during the pregnancy period of his wife
(b) husband looking after the first child during the second delivery of his wife
(c) husband leading the life of an invalid during the post-delivery period of his wife
(d) husband leading the life of a priest performing rituals for the safe delivery of his wife

113. Consider the following statements:
1. Equal access to property, power and prestige ends up in social stratification.
2. Differential access to property, power and prestige ends up in social stratification
3. Unequal access to property, power and prestige ends up in social stratification.

Which of these statements is/are correct?
(a) 1 only (b) 2 only
(c) 2 and 3 (d) 1 and 3

114. Who pointed out that social stratification is needed to ensure effective role allocation and role performance?
(a) Moore and Parsons
(b) Davis and Parsons
(c) Parsons and Weber
(d) Davis and Moore

115. Which one of the following represents a form of differentiation and not stratification?
(a) Class (b) Gender
(c) Caste (d) Sex

116. The concept of 'dominant caste' was first systematically developed by
(a) N.K. Bose
(b) A. Beteille
(c) M.N. Srinivas
(d) S.C. Dube

117. Who among the following emphasized the role of Charismatic Leadership in social change?
(a) Sorokin (b) Pareto
(c) Max Weber (d) Rajani Kothari

118. The Weberian model of social stratification has been applied to caste by
(a) M. N. Srinivas (b) S. C. Dube
(c) A. Beteille (d) G. S. Ghurye

119. Which among the following statement is incorrect in reference to ethnicity?
(a) Ethnicity refers to cultural practices and outlooks that distinguish a given community of people.
(b) Members of ethnic groups see themselves as culturally distinct from other groupings in society, and are seen by those others to be so."
(c) The main characteristics of distinction based on ethnicity are language, history or ancestry, etc.
(d) Ethnic differences are wholly biological.

120. Michael Mann observes that the social stratification theory centres around three nuclei, which of the following is not one of them?
(a) caste
(b) social class
(c) social status/ideology
(d) political power

121. Who is the author of the book *'The Rise of the Meritocracy'*?
(a) Eva Rosenfeld (b) Michael Young
(c) Anthony Giddens (d) Davis and Moore

122. Consider the following statements.
1. According to Dumont castes revolves around the rules of purity and pollution
2. Senart defines caste as a close corporation, exclusive, and in theory at any rate, rigorously hereditary.
3. Risley has defined caste as a collection of families, bearing a common name, claiming common descent from a mythical ancestor human or divine professing to follow the same hereditary calling.

Which of the above statement/s is correct?
(a) 1 and 2 only (b) 2 and 3 only
(c) 1 and 3 only (d) All are correct

123. Who said that 'Repressed sexuality was the cause of various neuroses and it was important to have an active and free sexuality'?
(a) Jean Khalf (b) Graham Burchel
(c) Michel Foucault (d) Anthony Giddens

124. Which of the following book is not written by Anthony Giddens?
(a) Modernity and Self-Identity
(b) A New Rules of Sociological Methods
(c) Classes Power and Conflicts
(d) Classes in Modern Society

125. Which of the following features of caste was discussed by G S Ghurye?
1. segmental division of society
2. hierarchy
3. restriction on dining
4. civil and religious disabilities
5. specific occupation
6. fixed rules

select the correct answer from the codes given below:
(a) 1, 2, 3, 4, 5, and 6
(b) 1, 2, 3, 4, and 6
(c) 1, 2, 3, 4, and 5
(d) 2, 3, 5, and 6

126. Which of the following is not the basic system of stratification?
(a) Intelligence (b) Slavery
(c) Caste (d) Estate

127. Who suggests that the social stratification system is just, right, and proper because it is basically an action of shared values?
(a) Talcott parsons
(b) Melvin M Tumin
(c) Eva Rosenfeld
(d) Kingsley Davis

128. Who said 'Social stratification is functional because it integrates various groups of people'?
(a) Talcott Parsons
(b) Melvin M Tumin
(c) Eva Rosenfeld
(d) Kingsley Davis

129. 'The caste is a closed organic group' said by?
(a) G S Ghurye
(b) F G Bailey
(c) Louis Dumont
(d) J H Hutton

130. Which of the following are forms of social stratification?
(a) Income Group
(b) Landlords and Tenants
(c) Caste and Class
(d) Racial Groups

131. Which of the following is not suggested by Max Weber as the bases of social stratification?
(a) Caste
(b) Class
(c) Status
(d) Power

132. According to ________ theory, African and South American countries will change by moving in the same direction as Western societies.
(a) evolutionary
(b) eurocentric
(c) world systems
(d) resource development

133. Who has proposed transitive and intransitive forms of inequality?
(a) Rousseau
(b) Ralph Dahrendorf
(c) Robert A Dahl
(d) Robert Redfield

134. Match List I and List II and select the correct answer:

List I (Theories related to origin of caste)	List II (Thinkers)
A. Political theory	I. Hocart and Senart
B. Occupational theory	II. Herbert Risley
C. Racial theory	III. Robert Nesfield
D. Religious theory	IV. Abbe Dubois

Codes:

	A	B	C	D
(a)	IV	III	II	I
(b)	I	II	III	IV
(c)	IV	II	III	I
(d)	I	III	II	IV

135. Who studied the Israeli Kibbutzim to describe the pattern of stratification there?
(a) Talcott parsons
(b) Melvin M Tumin
(c) Eva Rosenfeld
(d) Kingsley Davis

136. Which of the following thinker classified the social mobility into horizontal and vertical mobility?
(a) W Lyod Warner (b) S M Lipset
(c) D A Mitshel (d) Pitrim Sorrokin

137. Who is associated with the dialectical idealism of social change?
(a) Karl Marx
(b) Fredrich Engels
(c) G W Hegel
(d) Herbert Spencer

138. Which of the following thinker is called a social Darwinist?
(a) Karl Marx
(b) Fredrich Engels
(c) G W Hegel
(d) Herbert Spencer

139. The theory of 'response and challenge' in relation to social change is given by?
(a) W Llyod Warner
(b) S M Lipset
(c) Arnold Toynbee
(d) Herbert Spencer

140. Which of the following thinker is not associated with the technological theory of social change?
(a) W F Ogburn
(b) Mac Iver
(c) T Veblen
(d) H Risley

141. The name E.L. Bogardus is associated with one of the following concepts:
(a) Cultural Lag
(b) Social Differentiation
(c) Social Distance
(d) Cultural Diffusion

142. A biologically distinct group representing a common and distinctive heredity is referred to as
(a) caste
(b) estate
(c) ethnic group
(d) race

143. Who among the following considered social stratification as a functional necessity?
(a) Weber and Dahrendorf
(b) Bendix and Lipset
(c) Marx and Tumin
(d) Parsons and Moore

144. The defining feature of the traditional Jajmani System is the exchange of
(a) documents (b) land
(c) services (d) money

145. The caste becomes dominant when it pre-ponderates over the others numerically as well as with
(a) economic and political power
(b) social and religious power
(c) religious and economic power
(d) political and social power

146. Match List I with List II and select the correct answer using the codes given below the lists:

List I (Books)	List II (Authors)
A. Homo Hierarchicus	I. A. Beteille
B. Caste in Modern India	II. L. Dumont
C. Caste, Class, Power	III. R. Kothari
D. Caste in Indian Politics	IV. M.N. Srinivas

Codes:

	A	B	C	D
(a)	II	IV	III	I
(b)	IV	II	I	III
(c)	II	IV	I	III
(d)	IV	II	III	I

147. What is the central element in class-consciousness in Marxist theory?
(a) Class and culture
(b) Class and ranking
(c) Class-in-itself
(d) Class-for-itself

148. The 'concept of hegemony' was coined by
(a) Antonio Gramsci (b) D.R. Kelley
(c) L. Althusser (d) Talcott Parsons

149. Who looks at stratification as an integrative principle?
(a) Max Weber
(b) Ralph Dahrendorf
(c) Talcott Parsons
(d) C. Wright Mills

150. Who said that 'all permanently organized groups are stratified'?
(a) Melvin M Tumin
(b) Raymond W. Murray
(c) Pitirim Sorokin
(d) Max Weber

Answer Key

1. (a)	**23.** (c)	**45.** (a)	**67.** (c)	**89.** (b)	**111.** (b)	**133.** (b)
2. (d)	**24.** (b)	**46.** (d)	**68.** (d)	**90.** (c)	**112.** (c)	**134.** (a)
3. (c)	**25.** (d)	**47.** (a)	**69.** (a)	**91.** (a)	**113.** (c)	**135.** (c)
4. (c)	**26.** (b)	**48.** (c)	**70.** (b)	**92.** (b)	**114.** (d)	**136.** (d)
5. (d)	**27.** (d)	**49.** (a)	**71.** (b)	**93.** (b)	**115.** (d)	**137.** (c)
6. (a)	**28.** (b)	**50.** (d)	**72.** (c)	**94.** (c)	**116.** (c)	**138.** (d)
7. (b)	**29.** (d)	**51.** (d)	**73.** (a)	**95.** (d)	**117.** (c)	**139.** (c)
8. (c)	**30.** (d)	**52.** (c)	**74.** (b)	**96.** (b)	**118.** (c)	**140.** (d)
9. (a)	**31.** (b)	**53.** (a)	**75.** (c)	**97.** (a)	**119.** (d)	**141.** (c)
10. (a)	**32.** (a)	**54.** (c)	**76.** (b)	**98.** (d)	**120.** (a)	**142.** (d)
11. (a)	**33.** (c)	**55.** (a)	**77.** (a)	**99.** (d)	**121.** (b)	**143.** (d)
12. (d)	**34.** (c)	**56.** (b)	**78.** (b)	**100.** (b)	**122.** (d)	**144.** (c)
13. (b)	**35.** (b)	**57.** (d)	**79.** (b)	**101.** (b)	**123.** (d)	**145.** (a)
14. (c)	**36.** (b)	**58.** (c)	**80.** (d)	**102.** (a)	**124.** (d)	**146.** (c)
15. (a)	**37.** (d)	**59.** (a)	**81.** (c)	**103.** (c)	**125.** (a)	**147.** (d)
16. (b)	**38.** (a)	**60.** (b)	**82.** (c)	**104.** (c)	**126.** (a)	**148.** (a)
17. (c)	**39.** (c)	**61.** (a)	**83.** (a)	**105.** (b)	**127.** (a)	**149.** (c)
18. (a)	**40.** (a)	**62.** (c)	**84.** (d)	**106.** (b)	**128.** (a)	**150.** (c)
19. (b)	**41.** (b)	**63.** (c)	**85.** (b)	**107.** (b)	**129.** (b)	
20. (c)	**42.** (c)	**64.** (a)	**86.** (d)	**108.** (c)	**130.** (c)	
21. (d)	**43.** (d)	**65.** (c)	**87.** (a)	**109.** (a)	**131.** (a)	
22. (d)	**44.** (c)	**66.** (c)	**88.** (c)	**110.** (a)	**132.** (a)	

PREVIOUS YEARS' QUESTIONS

DECEMBER 2023

1. The sequence of Talcott Parson's Scheme of social evolution is:
A. Modern
B. Advanced primitive
C. Archaic
D. Primitive
E. Advanced intermediate
Choose the correct answer from the options given below:
(a) A, B, C, D, E (b) B, C, D, A, E
(c) D, B, C, E, A (d) A, C, B, D, E

2. Match List I with List II

List I	List II
A. The Post-modern condition; A Report on knowledge	I. Zygmunt Bauman
B. The Mirror of Production	II. Anthony Giddens
C. The Consequences of Modernity	III. Jean Baudrillard
D. Modernity and the Holocaust	IV. Jean-Francois Lyotard

Choose the correct answer from the options given below:
(a) A-I, B-II, C-IV, D-III
(b) A-II, B-I, C-III, D-IV
(c) A-IV, B-III, C-II, D-I
(d) A-III, B-IV, C-I, D-II

3. 'There are four important bases of socio-cultural identity in India: religion, caste, tribe and language'. Who said the statement?
(a) Yogendra Singh
(b) T.N. Madan
(c) T.K. Oommen
(d) Andre Beteille

4. Who among the following used the concept of globalization?
(a) R. Robertson (b) I. Wallerstein
(c) M. Waters (d) L. Martell

5. "Just as modernization dissolved the structure of feudal society, modernization today is dissolving industrial society and another modernity is coming into being" Who has given this statement?
(a) Zygmunt Bauman
(b) Anthony Giddens
(c) Ulrich Beck
(d) Jean Baudrillard

6. Emile Durkheim outlined a classification of societies. Arrange these societies in a proper sequence.
A. Simple society (the horde)
B. Simple polysegmentary societies
C. Simply compounded polysegmentary societies
D. Doubly compounded polysegmentary societies
Choose the correct answer from the options given below:
(a) A, C, B, D
(b) A, B, C, D
(c) A, D, B, C
(d) B, A, C, D

7. Totemism is a belief in:
(a) An image vested with a spirit and mind.
(b) A deity vested with power and spirit.
(c) A spirit vested with power and piety.
(d) An object vested with spirit and power.

8. L.T. Hobhouse proposed a classification of societies in terms of 'intellectual development.' Make a correct sequence of the categories.
A. Proto-science in the ancient east (Babylonia, Egypt and ancient China).
B. Formation of the elements of articulate thought in primitive societies.
C. The stage of critical and systematic thought in Greece.
D. The stages of reflection in the later East (China, Palestine and India).
E. The stage of 'experimental reconstruction' (modern science).
Choose the correct answer from the options given below:
(a) A, B, C, D, E
(b) B, A, D, C, E
(c) B, A, C, D, E
(d) C, A, B, D, E

9. A community is an area of social living marked by some degree of social coherence. The basis of community is:
A. Locality
B. Structure
C. Community sentiment
D. Stability
Choose the correct answer from the options given below:
(a) A, B and D only
(b) B and D only
(c) B, C and D only
(d) A and Conly

10. Which census introduced the category of person with 'physical infirmities' the blind, the deaf and the dumb?
(a) 1881 (b) 1931
(c) 1951 (d) 1961

11. The institution of education as a system of formal bureaucratic structure designed not to:
(a) Socialize.
(b) Store knowledge.
(c) Generate a new system of culture.
(d) Stratify.

12. Given below are two statements:
Statement I: Social positions, which one is born into or one acquires without one's own effort is, known as ascribed status.
Statement II: Achieved status is based on and defined by what people do or acquire through their own effort.
In the light of the above statements, choose the most appropriate answer from the options given below:
(a) Both Statement I and Statement II are true.
(b) Both Statement I and Statement II are false.
(c) Statement I is true but Statement II is false.
(d) Statement I is false but Statement II is true.

13. Functional approach in sociology appeared as a reaction against
(a) Methods of social anthropology
(b) Evolutionist method
(c) Economics method
(d) Interactionist method

14. Who coined the term 'credential society' for societies where people view diplomas and degrees as evidence of ability to perform specialized occupational roles?
(a) Anthony Giddens
(b) Randall Collins
(c) Ivan Illich
(d) P. Bourdieu

15. Who said traditional India did not have a developed socio-cultural foundation for the growth of rational legal authority and bureaucratic social structures?
(a) Daniel Lerner
(b) Max Weber
(c) F.W. Riggs
(d) Herold D. Lasswell

16. Who is associated with the Naturism?
(a) Max Muller
(b) E.B. Tylor
(c) R.R. Marett
(d) B. Malinowski

JUNE 2023

17. Match List I with List II

List I (Authors)	List II (Books)
A. G.S. Ghurye	I. The Indian Village Community
B. L.S.S. O'Mallay	II. Caste and Race in India
C. Sir H.H. Risley	III. Indian Caste Customs
D. B.H. Badew-Powel	IV. Tribes and Castes of Bengal, Ethnographic Glossary

Choose the correct answer from the options given below:
(a) A- II, B- III, C- IV, D-I
(b) A- III, B- IV, C-I, D-II
(c) A- IV, B- I, C-II, D-III
(d) A- I, B- II, C-III, D-IV

18. Given below are two statements: one is labelled as Assertion A and the other is labelled as Reason R.
Assertion A: Contemporary societies experiences the phenomena of ethnic identity assertion.
Reason R: The search of self-identity is intrinsic to human condition.
In light of the above statements, choose the most appropriate answer from the options given below.
(a) Both A and R are correct and R is the correct explanation of A
(b) Both A and R are correct but R is Not the correct explanation of A
(c) A is correct but R is not correct
(d) A is not correct but R is correct

19. Sociology of emotions examine the relations of feelings with the following:
A. Cultures
B. Structures
C. Interactions
D. Kingdom
E. Ocean
Choose the appropriate answer from the options given below:
(a) A, B, and C only
(b) A, B, and D only
(c) A, C, and D only
(d) A, D, and E only

20. L.H. Morgan in the book *Ancient Society* elaborated the progression of society through ______ stages.
(a) Savagery, barbarism, and civilization
(b) Savagery, barbarism, and primitivism
(c) Savagery, barbarism, and modernism
(d) Savagery, nihilism, and positivism

21. Given below are two statements: one is labelled as Assertion A and the other is labelled as Reason R.
Assertion A: According to H. Blumer, human beings act towards the things on the basis of meanings they have.
Reason R: The meanings are derived through the interpretative process while handling the things.

In the light of the above statements, choose the most appropriate answer from the options given below.

(a) Both A and R are correct and R is the correct explanation of A
(b) Both A and R are correct but R is Not the correct explanation of A
(c) A is correct but R is not correct
(d) A is not correct but R is correct

22. Explaining the effects of globalization, George Ritzer wrote a book titled:

(a) The Theory of the Leisure
(b) The Instinct of Workmanship and the State of the Industrial Act
(c) Social Network Analysis
(d) The McDonaldization of Society

23. Conceptually, what does incest taboo refer to?

(a) Alienation among close kin
(b) Paternal violence
(c) Avoidance of sexual relation of blood kin
(d) Marital violence

24. An aggregate which lacks structure or organization and whose members may be unaware or less aware of the existence of the grouping is known as:

(a) Quasi-group
(b) Peer group
(c) Primary group
(d) Secondary group

25. Who among the following has studied changing agrarian relations in Sripuram located in Tanjore district, Tamil Nadu?

(a) M. R. Srinivas (b) Andre Beteille
(c) Yogendra Singh (d) S.C. Dube

26. Auguste Comte has given three stages of thinking for the development of society. Which of the following is the third stage?

(a) Metaphysical (b) Positivistic
(c) Theological (d) Polytheism

27. Match List I with List II

List I (Concept)	List II (Explanation)
A. Status	I. A structural position within the social system
B. Imperatively Coordinated Association	II. Association of people controlled by a hierarchy of authority positions
C. Quasi group	III. A number of individuals who occupy positions that have the same role interest
D. Culture industry	IV. Industries such as movies and radio that were serving to make culture a more important factor in society than the economy

Choose the correct answer from the options given below:

(a) A - I, B - II, C - III, D - IV
(b) A - II, B - III, C - IV, D - I
(c) A - III, B - IV, C - I, D - II
(d) A - IV, B - I, C - II, D - III

28. Who amongst the following urges that the major function of religion is to maintain order in society?

(a) Ferdinand Tonnies (b) Herbert Spencer
(c) Max Weber (d) Emile Durkheim

29. Who among the following theorists regarded that population increase brings change in society?

A. Karl Marx
B. Max Weber
C. Emile Durkheim
D. Talcott Parsons

Choose the appropriate answer from the options given below:

(a) A and B only
(b) A and c only
(c) B and C only
(d) C and D only

30. David Held (1999) did not divide the globalization debate on which of the following aspects?

A. Sceptics
B. Transformationalists
C. Technocracy
D. Hyperglobalizer
E. Hypoglobalizer

Choose the appropriate answer from the options given below:

(a) A and B only
(b) A and D only
(c) C and E only
(d) B and D only

31. Identify those who identified the functions of conflict.

A. Karl Marx
B. Ralf Dahrendorf
C. George Simmel
D. C. Wright Mills
E. Lewis Coser

Choose the appropriate answer from the options given below:

(a) A, B, and E only
(b) C and D only
(c) C and E only
(d) B and D only

32. Which of the following sociologists is known for emphasizing the relation of morality and education?
A. J. Dewey
B. E. Durkheim
C. M. Weber
D. T. Parsons
E. R.K. Merton
Choose the appropriate answer from the options given below:
(a) A and B only
(b) B and c only
(c) C and D only
(d) D and B only

33. Who defined religion as 'a unified system of beliefs and practices relative to sacred things'?
(a) A.R. Radcliffe-Brown
(b) J.G. Frazer
(c) E. Durkheim
(d) M. Weber

34. Given below are two statements: one is labelled as Assertion A and the other is labelled as Reason R.
Assertion A: Theoretical synthesis of dialectic and functionalism underlines that 'society' is not a system of equilibrium but a nebulous structure of imperfectly coordinated elements which are held together by coercion of some elements and subjection of others.
Reason R: The social structure itself generates change through intra-conflicts and internal contradictions.
In light of the above statements, choose the most appropriate answer from the options given below.
(a) Both A and R are correct and R is the correct explanation of A
(b) Both A and R are correct but R is not the correct explanation of A
(c) A is correct but R is not correct
(d) A is not correct but R is correct

Read the following passage carefully and answer the question that follows:

In the present study, we are concerned exclusively with relations of authority, for these alone are part of the social structure and therefore permit the systematic derivation of group conflicts from the organization of total societies and associations within them. The significance of such group conflicts resets with the fact that they are not the product of structurally fortuitous relations of power but come forth wherever authority is exercised and that means in all societies under all historical conditions. (1) Authority relations are always relations of superordinate (2) Where there are authority relations, the super ordinate element is socially expected to control, by orders and commands, warning and prohibitions, the behaviour of the subordinate elements. (3) Such expectations attach to relatively permanent social positions rather than to the character of individuals; they are in this sense legitimate. (4) By virtue of this fact, they always involve specification of the persons subject to control and of the spheres within which control is permissible. Authority, as distinct from power, is never a relation of generalized control over others. (5) Authority being a legitimate relation, noncompliance with authoritative commands can be sanctioned; it is indeed one of the functions of the legal system (and of course quasi-legal customs and norms) to support the effective exercise of legitimate authority.

35. Select the incorrect statement.
(a) Authority founded on non-permanent relations
(b) Non-compliance to authority commands sanction
(c) Legal system supports effective execution of authority
(d) Quasi-legal customs cannot support effective exercise of authority

36. Authority relations are ____
(a) Relations of equality
(b) Relations of super ordination and sub ordination
(c) Authority relations are founded on the permanent social relations.
(d) Founded on character of individuals

37. Exercise of authority does not involve exercise of ____
(a) Control (b) Persuasion
(c) Warning (d) Prohibition

38. Exercise of authority produces ____
(a) Social cohesion
(b) Social conflict
(c) Egalitarian regime
(d) Totalitarian regime

39. Identify the incorrect statement with regard to the relationship of authority.
(a) Authority relations are a part of the social structure
(b) Authority relations are exterior to social structure
(c) Exercise of authority produces group conflict
(d) Authority relations are a part of all societies

MARCH 2023

40. Match List I with List II

List I (Concept)	List II (Theorist)
A. Delinquency area	I. Albert Cohen
B. Sub-cultural theory	II. Clifford Shaw
C. Differential opportunity theory	III. Howard Becker
D. Labelling theory	IV. Cloward and Ohlin

Choose the correct answer from the options given below:
(a) A - I, B - II, C - III, D - IV
(b) A - II, B - I, C - IV, D - III
(c) A - IV, B- III, C - I, D-II
(d) A - III, B - IV, C - II, D - I

41. Who gave the concept of 'sick role'?
(a) R.K. Merton
(b) Talcott Parsons
(c) N.J. Smelser
(d) C.W. Mills

42. Match List I with List II

List I (Term)	List II (Meaning)
A. Political elites	I. Elites of knowledge
B. Business elites	II. Elites of respect
C. Social elites	III. Elites of wealth
D. Intellectual elites	IV. Elites of power

Choose the correct answer from the options given below:
(a) A - I, B - II, C - III, D - IV
(b) A - IV, B - III, C - II, D - I
(c) A - I, B - III, C - II, D - IV
(d) A - II, B - IV, C - I, D - III

43. Given below are two statements:
Statement I: Disablism is the term used to describe an ideology that systematically marginalizes and isolates persons with disabilities through a range of social barriers: material, cultural, and psychological.
Statement II: Social and cultural barriers are not the root causes for the oppression faced by persons with disabilities in the society.
In light of the above statements, choose the most appropriate answer from the options given below:
(a) Both Statement I and Statement II are correct.
(b) Both Statement I and Statement II are incorrect.
(c) Statement I is correct but Statement II is incorrect.
(d) Statement I is incorrect but Statement II is correct.

44. Given below are two statements, one is labelled as Assertion (A) and the other is labelled as Reason (R).
Assertion (A): The term 'diaspora' denotes the dispersion of people throughout the world.
Reason (R): The Indian diaspora is known for its cuisine, cricket, and cinema.
In light of the above statements, choose the correct answer from the options given below:
(a) Both (A) and (R) are true and (R) is the correct explanation of (A).
(b) Both (A) and (R) are true but (R) is not the correct explanation of (A).
(c) (A) is true but (R) is false.
(d) (A) is false but (R) is true.

45. ____ refers to a family in which at least one of the adults has children from a previous marriage.
(a) Joint family
(b) Avanculocal family
(c) Step family
(d) None of the above

46. Match List I with List II

List I (Rule)	List II (Marriage)
A. Exogamy	I. Anuloma
B. Endogamy	II. Pratiloma
C. Hypergamy	III. Within own group
D. Hypogamy	IV. Outside own group

Choose the correct answer from the options given below:
(a) A - III, B - IV, C - II, D - I
(b) A - IV, B - III, C- I, D - II
(c) A - I, B - II, C - III, D - IV
(d) A - II, B - I, C - IV, D - III

47. Sociologist Ronald Robertson states that globalization at the cultural level began to occur because of:
A. Compression of the world and global consciousness.
B. Compression of time and contraction of space.
C. International recession and change in world order.
D. Increase in flows and global interaction.
E. Intensification of global economy.
Choose the correct answer from the options given below:
(a) A only
(b) B only
(c) A and B only
(d) C, D, and E only

48. Sanction refers to
A. A group of people who look after laws.
B. Codes which are very flexible.
C. Specific incidents of violation of law.
D. Specific penalty attached by the society to the violation of the code.
E. Those specific rewards attached to conformity.
Choose the correct answer from the options given below:
(a) D and E only
(b) A and D only
(c) B and C only
(d) A and B only

49. Caste is derived from a word from a language used in the Iberian peninsula. The word is:
(a) Casata (b) Cazata
(c) Casta (d) Castez

50. 'Totem' refers to
A. A group of people who live in hills and forests.
B. Unholy objects of everyday life.
C. Animals, plants or other objects which are held in special regard.
D. An individual who practices occultism.
E. An object, different from ordinary, that creates an attitude of reverence.

Choose the correct answer from the options given below:

(a) A, B, and C only
(b) B and D only
(c) C and E only
(d) A, B, C, and D only

51. Given below are two statements, one is labelled as Assertion (A) and the other is labelled as Reason (R).
Assertion (A): Cross-cousins are cousins whose parents are brothers and sisters.
Reason (R): In many tribal communities of Australia, cross-cousin marriages exist.

In light of the above statements, choose the correct answer from the options given below:

(a) Both (A) and (R) are true and (R) is the correct explanation of (A).
(b) Both (A) and (R) are true but (R) is NOT the correct explanation of (A).
(c) (A) is true but (R) is false.
(d) (A) is false but (R) is true.

52. Who among the following is associated with the concept of 'functional emphasis'?
(a) Davis and Moore
(b) T. Parsons
(c) Karl Marx
(d) Max Weber

DEC 2021 & JUNE 2022

53. Given below are two statements, one is labelled as Assertion (A) and the other is labelled as Reason (R).

Assertion (A): There is the increasing prevalence of borderless diseases.

Reason (R): There is the increase in global travel and an increasing rate of human migration.

In light of the above statements, choose the correct answer from the options given below:

(a) Both (A) and (R) are true and is the correct explanation of (A)
(b) Both (A) and (R) are true but (R) is NOT the correct explanation of (A)
(c) (A) is true but (R) is false
(d) (A) is false but (R) is true

54. Which one of the following is NOT correct?
(a) Status - Social position
(b) Role - Behavioural expectations
(c) Socialisation - Process of learning
(d) Values - Specific guidelines

55. The main features of class are
A. Homogeneity and Simplicity
B. Individualism
C. Economic and professional values
D. Rationalism
E. Traditionalism

Choose the correct answer from the options given below:

(a) A and E only
(b) B, C and D only
(c) B, C and E only
(d) B and D only

56. What is the appropriate term to describe a woman marrying the brother of her deceased husband?
(a) Sororate (b) Levirate
(c) Amitate (d) Avunculate

57. The academic journal published by Indian Sociological Society:
A. Man in India
B. Sociological Bulletin
C. Contributions to Indian Sociology
D. International Sociology
E. Annals of Indian Sociology

Choose the correct answer from the options given below:

(a) B, C and E only (b) B and C only
(c) B only (d) B, C, D and E only

58. In his famous work on the changing stratification of a Tanjore village, Andre Beteille observed the changes in-
(a) Caste system (b) Class system
(c) Power system (d) All of the above

59. Given below are two statements, one is labelled as Assertion (A) and the other is labelled as Reason (R)

Assertion (A): Prejudice is one thing. Discrimination is something else.

Reason (R): Prejudice is a matter of belief. Discrimination is a mode of behaviour.

In light of the above statements, choose the correct answer from the options given below:

(a) Both (A) and (R) are true and (R) is the correct explanation of (A)
(b) Both (A) and (R) are true but (R) is NOT the correct explanation of (A)
(c) (A) is true but (R) is false
(d) (A) is false but (R) is true

60. People under the class structure who are economically, politically and socially marginalised and excluded comprise the
(a) Economic class
(b) Oppressed class
(c) Underclass
(d) None of the above

61. Caste-based stratification is:
(a) Open
(b) Achieved
(c) Ascribed
(d) All of the above

62. The concept of "habitus" deals with
(a) Social status of the individuals
(b) Psychological orientations of the individuals
(c) Behavioural dispositions of the individuals
(d) Economic situation of the individuals

63. A structure of relationships linking social actors, or the set of actors and the ties among them:
(a) Social organisation
(b) Social network
(c) Social development
(d) Social institution

64. Match List-I with List-II

List I (Thinkers)	List II (Concepts/Ideas)
A. A. Comte	I. Size and density
B. E. Durkheim	II. Level of intellectual development
C. K. Marx	III. Evolution and Complexity
D. H. Spencer	IV. Economic Influence

Choose the correct answer from the options given below:
(a) A - III, B - IV, C - I, D - II
(b) A - II, B - I, C - IV, D - III
(c) A - I, B - III, C - IV, D - II
(d) A - II, B - III, C - I, D - IV

65. Who among the following used 'Comparative and Historical Research Method' in their study?
(a) Auguste Comte (b) Karl Marx
(c) Lewis Morgan (d) All of the above

66. Rewards and punishments associated with role expectations are called:
(a) Norms (b) Values
(c) Sanctions (d) Mores

67. Adopting a historical approach to the dispersal of people, R. Cohen identifies the following categories of diasporas:
A. Victim diasporas
B. Labour diasporas
C. Trading diasporas
D. Imperial diasporas
E. Cultural diasporas

Choose the correct answer from the options given below:
(a) A, B, D and E only
(b) A and E only
(c) A only
(d) A, B, C, D and E

68. A biological being is transformed into a social being with the help of the following:
(a) Socialisation (b) Institutionalisation
(c) Structuration (d) Alienation

69. Which one of the following influences deviance?
(a) Hierarchy
(b) Personality
(c) Status
(d) Norms

70. An Italian consuming paneer tikka in Rome and an Indian consuming pizza in Varanasi is an example of:
(a) Globalisation of food
(b) Globalisation of commodities
(c) Globalisation of culture
(d) All of the above

71. Given below are two statements, one is labelled as Assertion (A) and the other is labelled as Reason (R)
Assertion (A): Discrimination is a mode of behaviour.
Reason (R): To discriminate means to deny an individual or a group, a privilege or an opportunity or a pleasure that is thereupon reserved for one's own group.
In the light of the above statements, choose the correct answer from the options given below:
(a) Both (A) and (R) are true and (R) is the correct explanation of (A)
(b) Both (A) and (R) are true but (R) is NOT the correct explanation of (A)
(c) (A) is true but (R) is false
(d) (A) is false but (R) is true

72. Which of the following is NOT a defining feature of tribe?
(a) Food habits
(b) Common territory
(c) Kinship ties
(d) One language

73. Definite procedures or rules which people are expected to observe are known as:
(a) Norms (b) Values
(c) Sanctions (d) Mores

74. The structural features of caste system are:
A. Openness
B. Segmental division

C. Hierarchy
D. Non-hereditary occupations
E. Pollution and Purity

Choose the correct answer from the options given below:

(a) A, B and E only
(b) B, D and E only
(c) B, C and E only
(d) C, D and E only

Direction: Read the passage given below and answer the questions that follows.

Myrdal's well known position on theory of social change and development is that of circular causation and cumulative change. He suspects the validity of constructing universal evolutionary stage of 'growth'. These according to him tend to be teleological and often have conservative ideologies latent in them. The crucial factor in development is an 'upward' movement of the social system as a whole with all its component 'conditions: These conditions for the South Asian countries as described by Myrdal are: (1) output and income; (2) conditions of production ; (3) levels of living; (4) attitudes towards life and work; (5) institutions and (6) policies. He assumes a uni-directional causal relationship between these conditions; an 'upward and downward' movement in one would cause cumulative movement of similar nature in other conditions too. Value premises related to these conditions might differ from country to country specially in regard to conditions which are treated for their 'independent' (as a goal in themselves) values as different from those having 'instrumental' values. These valuations define ideological contexts of development in each national society, but their selectivity is organically linked with attributes of social system as a whole. The modernization process in India and other South Asian countries, according to Myrdal is heading fast towards a climax and the time for reasonable choice for them is limited. The opportunity for a 'gradualist' approach is also over. Myrdal thinks "it is not more difficult, but easier to cause a big change rapidly than a small change gradually. The prime areas for such big, rapid changes are social and institutional conditions in Indian society. These conditions (4 and 5 of the above) hold keys for mobilization of all other condtions of development.

75. According to Myrdal, it is easier
(a) To cause a small change gradually
(b) To cause a big change rapidly
(c) To cause a medium change slowly
(d) None of the above

76. Which of the following factors is NOT described by Myrdal for the development of South Asian countries?
(a) Environment
(b) Policies
(c) Institutions
(d) Output and Income

77. The modernization process in India is
(a) Heading fast towards climax
(b) Limited time for reasonable choice
(c) Both the above
(d) None of the above

78. Constructing universal evolutionary stage of growth may involve the following:
(a) Teleological ideologies
(b) Conservative ideologies
(c) Both the above
(d) None of the above

79. Myrdal's theory of social change and development is based on
(a) Cumulative change
(b) Circular causation
(c) Both the above
(d) None of the sbove

JUNE 2021

80. Who defined class as 'when a number of people have in common, a specific causal component of their life chances'?
(a) Karl Marx
(b) Max Weber
(c) Friedrich Engels
(d) Antonio Gramsci

81. Achievement, Self-discipline and Individualism that are instrumental on task-oriented represent which type of societies?
(a) Small societies
(b) Folk societies
(c) Advanced societies
(d) Peasant societies

82. Who among the following considered person-to-person relations and actually existing relations as constituting the social structure?
(a) M. Ginsberg
(b) A. R. Redcliffe Brown
(c) Raymond Firth
(d) R. K. Merton

83. Which one of the following is a suspicion of outsiders combined with a tendency to evaluate the culture of others in terms of one's own culture?
A. Assimilation B. Racism
C. Ethnocentrism D. Ethnography

84. An idea associated with Marshall McLuhan, who saw the spread of electronic communication as binding the world into a coherent single community called
(a) Global Village
(b) Global network
(c) Global sites
(d) Global city

85. Who has devised a theory of social conflict on understanding the central characteristics of the "nomadic" and "sedentary" societies of his time?
(a) Harriet Martineau
(b) Karl Marx
(c) Randall Collins
(d) Ibn Khaldun

86. The concept of Habitus as a basis for a cultural approach to structural inequality with a focus on the embodiment of cultural representation in human habits and routines was originally used by:
(a) Pierre Bourdieu
(b) Norbert Elias
(c) Anthony Giddens
(d) Richard Jenkin

87. Count Joseph Arthur de Gobineau is well known for his work on which of the following?
(a) Ethnicity
(b) Racism
(c) Migration
(d) Gender

88. Who among the following has divided globalization into two camps, the optimists and the pessimists?
(a) Anthony Giddens
(b) Mike O' Donnell
(c) Immanuel Wallerstein
(d) George Ritzer

89. Which one of the following is NOT a harbinger of cultural change?
(a) Contact with other cultures
(b) Revolution
(c) Spread of cultural traits
(d) Cultural conditioning

90. Robin Cohen argued for which of the following categories of diaspora?
A. Victim
B. Imperial
C. Labour
D. Culture
E. Community

Choose the correct answer from the options given below:
(a) B, E, A, C only
(b) C, D, E, B only
(c) A, B, C and D only
(d) E, C, B, A only

91. According to Ivan Illich, schools have developed which of the following four basic functions?
A. Provision of custodial care
B. Distribution of people within occupational rules
C. Learning of dominant values
D. Promote equality or the development of individual creativity
E. Acquisition of society approved skills and knowledge

Choose the correct answer from the options given below:
(a) B, C, D and E only
(b) A, B, C and D only
(c) D, C, B and A only
(d) A, B, C and E only

92. Which of the three primary models of ethnic integration are adopted by multi-ethnic societies?
A. Acculturation
B. Assimilation
C. Salad-bowl model
D. Melting pot
E. Cultural pluralism

Choose the correct answer from the options given below:
(a) B, C and D only
(b) A, C and D only
(c) A, D and E only
(d) B, D and E only

93. Which of the following scholar(s) has not emphasized the term 'Underclass'?
A. J. Goldthorpe
B. M. Savage
C. C. Murray

Choose the most appropriate answer from the options given below:
(a) A only (b) B only
(c) A and B only (d) C only

94. Which two of the following concepts are related with R. Robertson?
A. Differences-within-Sameness
B. Flow of gatherings and Squeezing
C. McDonaldization and Ethnicization
D. Homogeneity vs. Heterogeneity

Choose the correct answer from the options given below:
(a) A and C only (b) A and B only
(c) A and D only (d) B and C only

95. Match List I with List II

List I (Books)	List II (Authors)
A. Social Change	I. Neil J. Smelser
B. The Sociology of Economic Life	II. William J. Goode

C. The Family	III. Wilbert E. Moore
D. Social Stratification: The forms and Functions of Inequality	IV. Melvin Tumin

Choose the correct answer from the options given below:

(a) A–III, B–I, C–II, D–IV
(b) A–I, B–II, C–III, D–IV
(c) A–IV, B–III, C–II, D–I
(d) A–III, B–II, C–I, D–IV

96. Match List I with List II

List I (Book)	List II (Authors)
A. The Elementary Forms of Religious life	I. M. N. Srinivas
B. Religion and Society amog Coorgs of South India	II. A. Krober
C. The Science of Culture	III. Emile Durkheim
D. The Nature of Culture	IV. Leslie White

Choose the correct answer from the options given below:

(a) A–I, B–III, C–II, D–IV
(b) A–III, B–I, C–IV, D–II
(c) A–I, B–II, C–III, D–IV
(d) A–IV, B–III, C–I, D–II

97. Arrange the following three stages proposed by August Comte in the proper sequence
A. Theological stage
B. Positive stage
C. Metaphysical stage

Choose the correct answer from the options given below

(a) A, B, C
(b) A, C, B
(c) C, B, A
(d) B, C, A

98. Arrange the occurrence of the following technological revolutions in chronological order from the earliest to the latest
A. Printing revolution
B. Green revolution
C. Industrial revolution
D. Bio-technological revolution

Choose the correct answer from the options given below

(a) A, B, D, C
(b) A, C, B, D
(c) B, C, D, A
(d) C, A, B, D

99. Given below are two statements

Statement I: According to A. van Gennep, a direct rite is a curse or a spell.

Statement II: Direct rites are designed to produce results immediately, without intervention by any outside agent

In light of the above statements, choose the most appropriate answer from the options given below

(a) Both Statement I and Statement II are correct
(b) Both Statement I and Statement II are incorrect
(c) Statement I is correct but Statement II is incorrect
(d) Statement I is incorrect but Statement II is correct

100. Given below are two statements

Statement I: Some major concepts and approaches about social change in India can be grouped as Sanskritization and Westernization

Statement II: The term Sanskritization was used by M. N. Srinivas to describe the process of structural transformation in the Indian social structure

In light of the above statements, choose the most appropriate answer from the options given below

(a) Both Statement I and Statement II are correct
(b) Both Statement I and Statement II are incorrect
(c) Statement I is correct but Statement II is incorrect
(d) Statement I is incorrect but Statement II is correct

JUNE 2020

101. Radcliffe-Brown did not distinguish between social structure and
(a) Social system
(b) Social cognition
(c) Social relations
(d) Social conflict

102. Who said, 'social structure is the complex of the principal groups and institutions which constitute societies'?
(a) Emile Dukheim
(b) Radcliffe-Brown
(c) Raymond Firth
(d) M. Ginsberg

103. Who is of the view that incest taboo enables a relationship with wider society?
(a) C. Levi-Strauss
(b) H. Spencer
(c) K. Gough
(d) E. Westermarck

104. Which one of the following factors is negatively correlated with modernization?
(a) Achievement motivation
(b) Cosmopolitanism
(c) Individualism
(d) Religiosity

105. Who from among the following does see the relationship between the various strata in a stratified society as one of cooperation and interdependence?
(a) Marxists
(b) Functionalists
(c) Pluralists
(d) Interactionists

106. Choose the correct chronological sequence of Yogendra Singh's books:
1. Culture change in India: Identity and globalization
2. Essays on Modernization
3. Modernization of Indian Tradition
4. Ideology and theory in Indian Sociology
5. Social Stratification and social change

Choose the correct sequence from the options given below:
(a) 1, 3, 5, 4, 2
(b) 3, 4, 1, 5, 2
(c) 3, 2, 5, 1, 4
(d) 2, 3, 1, 5, 4

DECEMBER 2019

107. Which are the essential characteristics of bureaucracy?
A. Hierarchy of power
B. Unlimited power
C. channeling of communication
D. Informal relations between the officials

Choose the correct option:
(a) B and C
(b) A and D
(c) A and C
(d) B and D

108. Match List I with List II

List I (Sociologist)	List II (Book)
A. W.F. Ogburn	I. Social evolution and social progress
B. K. Marx	II. Civilization and culture
C. A. Weber	III. Basic and superstructure
D. L.T. Hobhouse	IV. Material and Non material culture

Choose the correct option:
(a) A–II, B–III, C–IV, D–I
(b) A–IV, B–III, C–II, D–I
(c) A–III, B–IV, C–II, D–I
(d) A–I, B–II, C–III, D–IV

109. Two statements are given below. One is labeled as Assertion (A) and the other as Reason (R).

Assertion (A): After the green revolution, inter-caste relations have changed from Jajmani to contractual relationships.

Reason (R): The green revolution has given opportunities to service castes in diverse occupations

Choose the correct option:
(a) Both (A) and (R) are true and (R) is the correct explanation of (A)
(b) Both (A) and (R) are true and (R) is not the correct explanation of (A)
(c) (A) is true but (R) is false
(d) (A) is false but (R) is true

110. Two statements are given below. One is labeled as Assertion (A) and the other as Reason (R).

Assertion (A): The globalization has intensified exclusion, marginalization and disconnection among different classes of people and regions.

Reason (R): It is due to economic reforms.

Choose the correct option:
(a) Both (A) and (R) are true and (R) is the correct explanation of (A)
(b) Both (A) and (R) are true and (R) is not the correct explanation of (A)
(c) (A) is true but (R) is false
(d) (A) is false but (R) is true

111. Who said that globalization is the growing reciprocal interdependence and integration of various economies around the globe?
(a) A. Giddens
(b) Meghnad Desai
(c) Henderson Hazel
(d) Martin Knor

112. Who has conceptualized social structure as a complex of principal groups and institutions which constitute societies?
(a) A.R. Radcliffe–Brown
(b) S.F. Nadel
(c) M. Ginsberg
(d) R. Firth

113. Who among the following viewed status as an 'effective claim to social esteem'?
(a) R. Linton (b) H. Maine
(c) M. Weber (d) R.K. Merton

114. Which of the following are examples of material culture?
A. Aspects of culture which govern the production and use of artifacts
B. Material production actually produced by society
C. Tools of governance in a community
D. Interaction of children with parents

Choose the correct option:
(a) B and C
(b) C and D
(c) D and A
(d) A and B

JUNE 2019

115. Match List-I with List-II:

List I (Concepts)	List II (Explanation)
A. Authority	I. Ideas and behaviour are logically coherent
B. Power	II. Socially accepted norm
C. Rationality	III. The legitimate form of power
D. Legitimacy	IV. Depends on a personal source

Select the correct answer from the options given below:

(a) A – II, B – IV, C – I, D – III
(b) A – III, B – I, C – IV, D – II
(c) A – III, B – IV, C – I, D – II
(d) A – III, B – IV, C – II, D – I

116. Which community has the majority of its population living in the diaspora than at home?

(a) Jewish (b) Indian
(c) Chinese (d) Canadian

117. A rule or standard of behaviour defined by shared expectations of two or more people regarding what behaviour is to be considered socially acceptable, is referred to as:

(a) custom (b) value
(c) tradition (d) norm

118. Who said that 'role is the dynamic aspect of status'?

(a) Linton (b) Lundberg
(c) MacIver (d) Herskovitz

119. When a newly married couple resides in the man's father's house this type of residence is termed as

(a) patrilocal (b) varilocal
(c) matrilocal (d) neolocal

120. Who said that 'role is the dynamic aspect of status'?

(a) Linton
(b) Lundberg
(c) MacIver
(d) Herskovitz

121. Which community has the majority of its population living in the diaspora than at home?

(a) Jewish (b) Indian
(c) Chinese (d) Canadian

122. Who has defined education as 'the action exercised by the older generations upon those who are not yet ready for social life.....'?

(a) R.H. Lowie (b) E. Durkheim
(c) D.P. Mukherji (d) P. Bourdieu

123. Among the following 'Couvade' is best described by

(a) Husband leads the life of invalid
(b) Practice both husband and wife follow
(c) A kinship usage
(d) Relationship of love and emotion between the husband and the wife

124. L. Dumont is the exponent of which of the following views of caste?

(a) Functional (b) Structural
(c) Bureaucratical (d) Mythological

125. The Weberian model of social stratification has been applied to caste by

(a) M.N. Srinivas (b) S.C. Dube
(c) A. Beteille (d) G.S. Ghurye

126. Consider the following statements:

A. Modernization is a consequence of development.
B. Development is progressive but all progress is not development.
C. Development is nothing but planned change.

Which of the above statements is correct?

(a) A, B and C (b) B and C only
(c) A and B only (d) A and C only

127. Who analyzed the ways in which economic and social transformation in capitalism connect to the information technology revolution?

(a) Edward Said (b) J. Habermas
(c) Manuel Castells (d) Clifford Geertz

128. Who is associated with the concept 'Reflexive Modernization'?

(a) Edward Said (b) J. Habermas
(c) Manuel Castells (d) Anthony Giddens

129. Which two of the following principles explain the Alliance theory?

A. Principle of reciprocity
B. Rules of Exogamy
C. Rules of Endogamy
D. Incest taboos

Choose the correct option:

(a) A and B (b) B and C
(c) C and D (d) A and D

Answer Key

1. (c)	**20.** (a)	**39.** (b)	**58.** (d)	**77.** (c)	**96.** (b)	**115.** (c)
2. (c)	**21.** (a)	**40.** (b)	**59.** (a)	**78.** (c)	**97.** (b)	**116.** (a)
3. (c)	**22.** (d)	**41.** (b)	**60.** (c)	**79.** (c)	**98.** (b)	**117.** (d)
4. (a)	**23.** (c)	**42.** (b)	**61.** (c)	**80.** (b)	**99.** (a)	**118.** (a)
5. (c)	**24.** (a)	**43.** (c)	**62.** (c)	**81.** (c)	**100.** (c)	**119.** (a)
6. (b)	**25.** (b)	**44.** (b)	**63.** (b)	**82.** (b)	**101.** (c)	**120.** (a)
7. (d)	**26.** (b)	**45.** (c)	**64.** (b)	**83.** (c)	**102.** (d)	**121.** (a)
8. (b)	**27.** (a)	**46.** (b)	**65.** (d)	**84.** (a)	**103.** (a)	**122.** (b)
9. (d)	**28.** (d)	**47.** (a)	**66.** (c)	**85.** (d)	**104.** (d)	**123.** (a)
10. (a)	**29.** (b)	**48.** (a)	**67.** (d)	**86.** (a)	**105.** (b)	**124.** (b)
11. (c)	**30.** (c)	**49.** (c)	**68.** (a)	**87.** (b)	**106.** (c)	**125.** (c)
12. (a)	**31.** (c)	**50.** (c)	**69.** (b)	**88.** (b)	**107.** (c)	**126.** (b)
13. (b)	**32.** (a)	**51.** (b)	**70.** (d)	**89.** (d)	**108.** (b)	**127.** (c)
14. (b)	**33.** (c)	**52.** (a)	**71.** (a)	**90.** (c)	**109.** (a)	**128.** (d)
15. (b)	**34.** (a)	**53.** (a)	**72.** (a)	**91.** (d)	**110.** (a)	**129.** (d)
16. (a)	**35.** (d)	**54.** (d)	**73.** (a)	**92.** (d)	**111.** (b)	
17. (a)	**36.** (b)	**55.** (b)	**74.** (c)	**93.** (c)	**112.** (c)	
18. (b)	**37.** (b)	**56.** (b)	**75.** (b)	**94.** (c)	**113.** (c)	
19. (a)	**38.** (b)	**57.** (c)	**76.** (a)	**95.** (a)	**114.** (d)	

Unit-IV

Rural and Urban Transformations

Chapters:

Chapter 1	Rural and Peasant Society
Chapter 2	Urban Society

Top: Photo credit: feodora52/ 123RF
Below: Photo Credit: Hurca. Shutterstock

CHAPTER

1 Rural and Peasant Society

LEARNING OBJECTIVES:

In this chapter, we will discuss the following important topics.

- Caste - tribe settlements
- Agrarian social structure and emergence of class relations
- Decline of agrarian economy, de-peasantization and migration
- Agrarian unrest and peasant movements
- Changing inter-community relations and violence

INTRODUCTION

When we talk about rural societies different countries define it in their own way, for example, the Bureau of the Census of the United States gave more importance to the size and density of the population in a specific area. They define a rural community on the basis of the size and the density of the population at a particular place. While in India, the term 'rural' is defined in terms of revenue: the village means the 'revenue village'. It might be one large village or a cluster of small villages. According to the Census Commission of India, a village is an entity identified by its name and a definite boundary.

The term 'rural society' is used almost synonymously with terms like 'village', 'countryside', or 'folk society'. Let us now understand the term 'folk', according to Robert Redfield's definition a 'folk' is a person or persons belonging to a small traditional and homogeneous community.

Hence from the above definition, it is clear that a folk society is traditional and homogeneous. This category is best understood in terms of culture and stands in contrast with the fast-changing and heterogeneous urban society. Redfield has written about the folk-urban continuum. For him a folk society is 'past-oriented', meaning that its members are content with their lot, with what they have, and they proudly hold their customs, norms, and traditions high. By tradition, sociologists mean the 'conventionalized modes of social behaviour and thought', that is the behaviour and thought that was established in the past are still considered valuable and applicable in the present and are going to persist in the future.

Let us now understand the term 'peasant', among the first thinker who elaborately discussed the term was American anthropologist, A. L. Kroeber. According to his definition 'Peasants are definitely rural but their day-to-day activity is in close relation to market towns; they form a class segment of a larger population which usually contains urban centers and sometimes metropolitan capitals. They constitute part societies with part-cultures. They do not have separate territory, they lack political autonomy, and the self-sufficiency of tribal populations, but their local units retain much of their old identity, integration, and attachment to the soil.'

CASTE-TRIBE SETTLEMENTS

Caste

Caste is generally understood as a uniquely Indian and Hindu system of social organization. It is characterized by endogamy, the hereditary transmission of a style of life that often includes an occupation, ritual status in a hierarchy, and customary social interaction and exclusion based on cultural notions of purity and pollution.

A caste system is a closed stratification system which means people get membership only when they are born into it, and they cannot do anything to change their social status.

Tribe

A tribe is a political community having a common territory and a common dialect. The members of a tribal group consider themselves to be descendants of a common ancestor and therefore all members are connected by blood relationship. The members of a tribe are generally endogamous and they have a common culture and religion. As they are political entities, they may have independent chiefs or heads on which social authority rests.

In Indian languages - including Sanskrit and Prakrit - Jana seems to have been the term to denote a tribe. These *Janas*, whom we call tribes were different from the other communities of people in the sense that they continued to remain outside the control of the Jati-system of social organization.

Caste-Tribe Continuum

The transition from tribe to caste can be viewed as one such change. The formation of institutions like private property, the caste system, the state, and the patriarchal family are the results of this process.

This process took a long period of time and passed through a lot of intermediate stages. As far as the gradual and constant cultural growth and modification are concerned, they were not uniform. We see periods of accretion of small changes during the Vedic period or within tribal systems.

There were also stages when major changes took place. There were periods when qualitative changes in ways of living took place. The concept of 'continuum' was initially propounded by R. Redfield in his work '*The Folk Culture of Yucatan*'. Other scholars used this work while trying to understand caste-tribe settlement.

For example, F.G. Bailey, while studying the '*Kondh*' and '*Oriya*' political systems, used this concept. According to him, 'sociologists view caste and tribe as the extreme ends of a single line. At different points along the line, the particular societies may be located according to their proximity to either the organic caste model or segmentary tribal model.'

The exponents of the tribe caste continuum argue that the transition was spread over a long span of time. About 70% of the tribal people have been characterized as Hinduized without being Hindus and as indistinguishable from the inferior ranks of caste order. The range of variations in this category of tribal is immense and the polar categories of tribe and caste do not longer prove useful.

It is felt that through cultural contact and diffusion of cultural traits, the guiding principles of socio-religious change are determined. According to Sachidananda, 'In India, most of the groups, which are regarded as tribal have been in close contact with Hindu society for many centuries and hence accepted the tradition, customs, occupational traits, and religious ceremonies. Directly or indirectly, he says tribes have imbibed influences from Hinduism.'

M. N. Srinivas and Redfield say that acculturation defines tribe-caste mobility in India. In the process of restructuring the normative content of social organization, individuals accept the dominant trends of the group to which they belong. They believe that tribes are in contact with a caste as a category and not with individuals in a society.

Michael York has studied three different tribes, "the *Gond*, *Kolam*, and *Naikpod*. For him these tribes though basically the same are separate. The similarity is affected by the fact that the Naikpod have now acquired the religious traits of the Telugu caste by prohibiting eating beef and pork in order to claim greater ritual purity."

According to D.N. Majumdar, 'The transformation of a tribal group into a group in the greater Hindu society with a higher position in the caste system may be absorbed without any occupational specialization within the group or by the group as a whole. It is seen that assimilation of a tribal group into the caste hierarchy has been achieved entirely through the process of imitating the behaviour of twice born caste group.'

There are several examples of tribal communities transforming into caste groups. This is done by accepting the ritual and social superiority of Brahmin and other twice-born castes. They accept a lowly occupation and the imposition of taboos in respect of food material comforts and social customs. They consequently accept the notion of rituals of purity and pollution.

Therefore, the tribe caste model is mainly of two types: The Hindu method of absorption assumes that the caste system protects tribal people, and the Sanskritization model emulates Brahminical or upper caste reference.

Scholars suggest that instead of adopting a particular caste, the tribal people attempt to get assimilated into the Hindu fold in general. G.S. Ghurye rejects this view. He argues that the position claimed or achieved by a tribal group in the caste hierarchy is determined by the ownership of land, possession of wealth, and past or present rank in the tribal structure.

But there are pieces of evidence of the phenomenon called 'tribalization', also exists. The traditional aspect of tribalization is defined by K.S. Singh as 'acceptance of tribal mores, rituals and beliefs by incoming communities.'

K.S. Singh suggests that acceptance of tribal mores is easier for the middle and lower segments of the caste hierarchical order. They move in search of land or to offer their services to their tribal masters. This process does not affect the Brahmin and other high-caste people.

There are examples of some tribes who manage to get into the Hindu fold by settling down at the peripheries of villages accepting menial jobs from caste Hindus. These tribal groups may adopt the surname or gotra of a caste and also marry into the caste.

For example, the study of two major Central Himalayan tribes Tharu and Khasa reveals that though they practice certain distinctive tribal customs, they also have been accepted as Kshatriya.

AGRARIAN SOCIAL STRUCTURE AND EMERGENT CLASS RELATIONS

The word 'agrarian' in general means anything related to land, its management, or distribution. It is any community whose economy is based on producing and maintaining crops and farmland.

According to Beteille, the term agrarian system is used to describe a more or less homogeneous and undifferentiated community of families characterized by small holdings operated mainly by family labor.

Study of agrarian social structure revolves around two major issues: Technological arrangements and social arrangements.

By technological arrangement, we mean the management of land which includes landownership, control of land, and use of land. The technological arrangement is discussed in relation to variations in ecological conditions. In other words, the land is looked at in terms of the geography which surrounds the land whereas the ecological setting of agriculture in India is highly variable.

The technological arrangements, thus, include ecological conditions along with the new agriculture technology, such as water pumps, threshers, chemical manure, improved seeds, etc. Another aspect is social management. It includes land control and land ownership. It is found that the Indian agricultural communities have recently been highly stratified. It shows that there is a close relationship between the system of stratification and the division of work.

For example, in Punjab and Haryana the proportion of agricultural laborers is relatively low and hence the laborers from Bihar migrate to Punjab and Haryana, whereas in West Bengal, Tamil Nadu, and Kerala, it is high therefore, in these three states the prevalence of sharecropping is also high.

K.L. Sharma in his study, discussed the problem of agrarian stratification and argues that agrarian structures in India have always been uneven. For him, these uneven structures of landholdings have resulted in diverse land tenure systems. The variations in the relationship between the land tenure system and social structure created an uneven feudal order in the pre-British and British periods.

When discussing agrarian social structure, we refer to land ownership, land control, and land use. Such an attitude towards land helps us to trace the agrarian hierarchy. What has happened so far is that the dominant castes, who control large tracts of land, oppress and exploit the subordinate classes.

According to Oliver Mendelson and Marica Vizziany, land control is the basis of the agrarian hierarchy and, therefore, the means by which the dominant caste has subjugated the untouchables in the village.

Another aspect of rural stratification is the farming pattern adopted by farmers. If the farmers take to those crops which require hard labour, naturally it would require a large number of agricultural labourers. In the states of Punjab and Bihar where paddy is grown, a large number of laborers are hired. Landless laborers also migrate from Bihar to Punjab for paddy transplanting.

Beteille has discussed the rural stratification pattern in the context of land control and land management. There are three main patterns in the productive organization of land: the first is based on family labour, the second on hired labour, and the third on the tenancy.

Daniel Thorner has analysed agrarian social structure on the basis of three criteria:

1. Income obtained from the soil (i.e., rent, own cultivation, or wages),
2. The nature of rights (i.e., ownership, tenancy, sharecropping, and no rights at all)
3. The extent of fieldwork actually performed (i.e., doing no work, doing partial work, doing total work, and doing work for others)

And hence on the basis of the above criteria, he described the following classes in agrarian social structure:

1. Malik (agricultural landlords)
2. Kisan (working peasants)
3. Mazdoor (agricultural laborers)

The Malik derives his agricultural income primarily from property rights in the soil, i.e., from a share of the produce of lands possessed by him. He may give his land either to tenants or may cultivate it by hiring labourers. The Maliks are further categorized into two types, first those who are absentee landlords and second those who reside in the village in which they own land.

The Kisans are the working peasants, who may be small landowners or tenants. The difference between the Malik and Kisan is the size of the land holding.

Whereas the Mazdoors are landless villagers, they do not owe any land and earn their living primarily from working on other people's land.

D.N. Dhanagre has suggested a different model of agrarian classes. He has proposed five classes:

1. Landlords (who derive income primarily from land- ownership by collecting rent from tenants, sub-tenants and sharecroppers)
2. Rich peasants (small landowners with sufficient land to support the family and who cultivate the land themselves)
3. Rich tenants (who have substantial holdings and have to pay a nominal rent to their landlords)
4. Middle peasants (landowners of medium size holdings and tenants with substantial holdings and paying higher rent)
5. Poor peasants (They sell their labor for money. They earn their livelihood by working as laborers on the land of others).

Land Ownership and Agrarian Relations

There were three types of land ownership and land revenue systems found in British India. The three major systems in India were – Zamindari, Ryotwari, and Mahalwari.

Zamindari system (permanent land revenue settlement) was introduced by Cornwallis in 1793 through the Permanent Settlement Act. It was introduced in the provinces of Bengal, Bihar, Orissa, and Varanasi. The Zamindars were recognized as the owners of the land. The Zamindars were given the right to collect rent from the farmers. While the zamindars became the owners of the land, the actual farmers became tenants.

Tax had to be paid even if the yield was less. It was to be paid in cash. Before this system was introduced, the tax could be paid in kind. The amount received was divided into 11 parts. 1/11th share of it belongs to Zamindars and 10/11th share belongs to the East India Company.

The Ryotwari system was started by Thomas Munro in 1820. This was the primary land revenue system in South India. Major areas that came under the Ryotwari system were Madras, Bombay, parts of Assam, and the Coorg province of British India. In the Ryotwari system, the ownership rights were handed over to the farmers. The British government used to collect taxes directly from the farmers. The revenue rates of the Ryotwari system were 50% where the land was dry and 60% in irrigated land. Although the land was owned by the peasants, excessive taxation impoverished them. In addition, tax rates were frequently increased.

The Mahalwari system was introduced by Holt Mackenzie in 1822. Later, the system was improved during the period of William Bentinck (1833). This was the primary land revenue system in North-West India. It was introduced in the Central Provinces, North-West Frontier, Agra, Punjab, Ganga Valley, etc. of British India. In this system, the land was divided into Mahals. Each Mahal includes one or more villages. The entire village (mahal) was treated as a unit for tax collection. The village headman or village committee was entrusted with the responsibility of collecting the tax. The right of ownership was vested with the farmers. The rate of tax in this system was also very high. The Mahalwari system had mixed provisions of both the Zamindari system and the Ryotwari system.

Land Acquisition in India

The first Land Acquisition Act in India was enacted in 1824 by the British Government. This act was popularly called Bengal Resolution I of 1824, this law ' applies to the whole of the province of Bengal under the presidency of Fort William'. The law enabled the government ' to acquire, at a fair valuation, land or other immovable property required for roads, canals or other public purposes'.

Land Acquisition Act, 1894

Until 2014, land acquisition in India was governed by the Land Acquisition Act of 1894 of the colonial era. The Land Acquisition Act of 1894 allowed the government to acquire private land. Under the 1894 Act, displaced people were only liable for monetary compensation linked to the market value of the land, which was still quite low considering the circle rates.

Right to Fair Compensation and Transparency in Land Acquisition, Rehabilitation, and Resettlement Act, 2013

The 2013 Act replaced the Land Acquisition Act, 1894, and provided for higher compensation to those dispossessed of land by the government for both public and private sector projects. It also mandates the consent of the majority of landowners and includes provisions for rehabilitation and resettlement.

DECLINE OF AGRARIAN ECONOMY, DE-PEASANTIZATION, AND MIGRATION

During the last two decades the agriculture sector has witnessed a decline in rates of growth, rising numbers of farmers' suicides, declining prices of several crops, and a widening gap between the agriculture and non-agriculture sectors. The agriculture sector is experiencing an unprecedented crisis and declining rural employment growth and as a result, food security and employment opportunities for the rural poor have reduced.

It is acknowledged that agricultural growth declined in the 1990s as compared to the 1980s. Production growth for both food grains and non-food grains has declined since the mid-1990s.

Falling food prices made the agriculture sector less profitable, leading to a decline in areas under cultivation, as non-food crops require more capital-intensive investment and could lead to a further decline in rural employment. According to the National Sample Survey (NSS), the annual growth rate of employment in rural areas was 2.07% in the 1980s, which declined to just 0.66% in 1992–2002.

It is believed that the root cause of the crisis was that agriculture is no more a profitable economic activity when compared to other enterprises' income. The income derived from these activities is not sufficient enough to meet the expenditure of the cultivators. And therefore, unless agriculture is made a profitable enterprise, the present crisis cannot be solved.

Related factors responsible for the crisis include dependence on rainfall and climate, liberal import of agricultural products, reduction in agricultural subsidies, lack of easy credit to agriculture and dependence on money lenders, the decline in government investment in the agricultural sector, and conversion of agricultural land for alternative uses.

The agricultural crisis affects the majority of the people in India and the economy as a whole in the long run. And therefore, it can be argued that the crisis in agriculture is a crisis for the country as a whole. The neo-liberal economic policy introduced in 1991 brought the Indian agriculture sector into the orbit of liberalization, privatization, and globalization.

Indian farmers were integrated into a new market economy and pushed towards commercial cropping. They were forced to use modern technologies, high-yield seeds, chemical fertilizers, pesticides, and irrigation facilities for cash crop cultivation. This policy of liberalization reduced the government's financial assistance and subsidies to the farmers.

In this situation, the big farmers could manage to do better by investing in irrigation and inputs and adopting new technologies but the small and marginal farmers faced greater hardships in managing their livelihood. The agrarian crisis, however, is not merely economic in nature. It has consequences beyond economic issues and concerns. The nature of the agrarian crisis is also social and cultural.

The agrarian crisis impacted social relations and affected the identities and cultural life of the community. Farmers are selling their land and cattle and migrating toward urban and industrial areas.

Bina Agarwal further points out two different processes - dissatisfaction and distress affecting the politically vocal farmers and poor farmers respectively. She suggests that the policies should, as a priority, address the concerns of the vulnerable sections that are in distress.

We can further point out another category, the 'dispossessed', the sections losing lands to the commercial non-agricultural sector. Women who are already marginalized, vulnerable, and deprived in a patriarchal society are the victims of the agrarian crisis. Their access and claims to livelihood, resources, and rights are threatened. A large number of women in rural areas are engaged in agriculture but they have never been recognized as farmers as traditionally land and resources are controlled by men.

The issues and concerns for the decline of agriculture can be listed as:

1. **Shrinking Land-base and Declining Access to Land:** One of the major issues facing Indian agriculture at present is the ever-shrinking land availability due to the conversion of agricultural land into non-agricultural uses. Coupled with this ever-shrinking land base is the problem of subdivision of holdings, particularly among small and marginal farmers, the issue of underutilization of available cultivable land, and the issue of land degradation. This issue influences the long-term structure of agriculture and its organisation.
2. **Irrigation System (Expansion and Utilisation):** Irrigation is one input for agricultural production, which can easily be separated from other inputs. The system of irrigation in India has received considerable importance in view of the shrinking land base.
3. **Availability and Access to Credit:** Some of the perennial issues concerning the availability and access to credit have continued to persist despite vast changes in the institutional support for the supply of credit to agriculture.
4. **Availability and Use of Other Inputs (Fertilisers, Seeds, and Pesticides):** The green revolution was propelled by the availability of high-yielding varieties (HYV) of seeds; of course, the need for the availability of other inputs like irrigation, credit, and pesticides was equally vital. Availability and use of quality seeds, fertilizers, and pesticides are essential for attaining higher crop yields and sustained growth in agricultural production.
5. **Prices, Costs, and Profitability:** The economic issues of income generation in agriculture critically hinge on the prices received by the farm sector, prices paid (costs), and profitability.
6. **Marketing System:** There are several problems in the agricultural sector, which are related to the system of marketing.

De-Peasantization and Migration

De-peasantization involves the erosion of peasant practices and the substitution of market rationality in agriculture. Both liberal and Marxist narratives of development view depeasantization as a precondition for liberal democracy or collective socialism, respectively.

Peasantries are considered obstacles to change given the modern view of "tradition" as pre-social and given an assumed resistance to technological change.

Modernization trajectories follow the rise of urban, industrial orders and the relocation of peasants into the urban proletariat as industrial production systems expand.

Araghi in his book '*Global Depeasantization*', identifies rural-urban migration as deruralization. This process causes depopulation and decline of rural areas and results in over-urbanization as people concentrates in urban areas.

It is the central feature of depeasantization, which he defines as a process where an increasing number of people who were involved in agriculture with direct access to the production of their means of subsistence become rapidly and massively concentrated in urban areas.

It is argued that within the peasant studies, there is a major gap between those that advocate the disappearance thesis and those that support the permanence thesis. Both attempts to situate the historical course of the peasantry within the development of society, although the disappearance thesis is far more common than the permanence thesis.

The disappearance thesis is based on the idea that capitalism will lead to the dissolution of the peasantry as individuals become wage workers in urban areas and capitalist farmers in the countryside.

The permanence thesis, by contrast, argues that peasant societies do not abide by the laws of individualistic capital and have a developmental logic of their own that will result in the survival of both the peasantry and the conditions of its reproduction.

A key component of the disappearance thesis, present in the work of Marx and Engels is the sense that peasants are a class representative of barbarism, unable to shape history and blocking the development of civilization. For civilization to progress, therefore, the peasantry must dissolve as society moves from a traditional to a modern state.

For rural agricultural populations in many countries, the policies implemented resulted in the removal of agricultural subsidies and price supports, land deregulation, wage freezes, and the devaluation of national currencies. In this context of high risks and low returns, small-scale peasant farmers were unable to compete.

De-peasantization as a process

The transformation of the workforce from farming to the non-farming sector can be divided into two categories: Growth-led shift and Distress-induced shift.

The growth-led shift is related to developmental factors like mechanization of agriculture, increasing employment, income, high education level, rampant urbanization, development of secondary and tertiary sectors, state intervention for generating employment opportunities, and so on. These factors are known as "pull factors" that attract the workforce from farming to more lucrative non-agricultural activities.

Distress-induced transformation is based on crisis-driven factors like falling productivity, increasing costs, decreasing returns, unemployment, underemployment, unproductive land, marketing problem, no or less subsidy provided by the government, etc. These factors are known as "push factors" which force the agriculture workforce from farming towards non-farm activities. These factors are responsible for depeasantization in rural Kashmir

K. Singh in his study points out that the crisis in agriculture has manifested itself in the form of:

1. stagnating productivity,
2. rising cost of production,
3. decelerating income,
4. shrinking employment,
5. mounting indebtedness, and
6. ecological imbalance.

For him, one of the main consequences of this agrarian distress has been that the marginal and small farmers, who find it increasingly hard to sustain on farming, are getting pushed out from the agricultural sector.

E. S. Dora in his study reveals that the process of liberalization in fact proved more disastrous for agriculture and peasantry in India because:

i. It was adopted without resolving the fundamental agrarian problems or contradictions such as an absolute egalitarian land structure, depeasantization, and abysmal condition of agricultural labour, tenants, and small peasants.
ii. Though India chiefly inherited most of these problems or contradictions from British rule, it did too little to resolve them after independence.
iii. During the period of economic reforms, the state did nothing to transform the depressed traditional institutional framework of agriculture.

Migration

Migration is the movement of people from one place to another and is often associated with a change of permanent residence. At the macro level, there are inter-regional and intra-regional disparities, and at the micro level, there is a fundamental lack of employment opportunities, resulting in low living standards among different socio-economic groups.

Migration is of the following types:

(i) Immigration and Emigration: When people from one country move to another country permanently, for example, if people from India move to America, for America it is called immigration, while for India it is called emigration.

(ii) In-migration and out-migration: In-migration refers to migration only within a region, while out-migration refers to migration outside the region. Both types of migration are called internal migration which takes place within the country. Migration from Bihar to Bengal is in-migration to Bengal, while it is out-migration to Bihar.

(iii) Gross and Net Migration: During any time period, the total number of people coming into the country and the total number of people going out of the country to live is called gross migration. Net migration is the difference between the total number of people coming to live in a country and the total number of people moving out of the country to live during a given time period.

(iv) Internal migration and international migration: Internal migration is the movement of people from one place to another within a country. International migration is the movement of people from one country to another in search of work, a place to call home, or a better standard of living.

Principles of Migration

E.G. Ravenstein's Law of Migration: Ravenstein developed his theory of migration by looking at migration in the United Kingdom. Under the law of migration, Ravenstein explains three basic reasons or categories for migration i.e., cause, distance, and migrant characteristics (ex.-gender).

Push-Pull Theory by Everett Lee: The push-pull theory was proposed by Lee. Lee explains that there are two reasons why people migrate. There is either a push factor or a pull factor. Push factors exist in the area you live in. It can be geographical factors, poverty, natural calamities, war, etc. It is several factors that lead people to opt-out. Pull factors are destination areas that attract people to move there. It could be a good economy, a high standard of living, and good job opportunities.

Gravitational Model by William J. Reilly: Gravitational model of migration is based on Newton's law of gravitation. The gravity model states that you have the area of area one's population multiplied by the area of area two's population, divided by the square of the distance between the two. Larger areas have greater attractive potential and with a small increase in separation the attraction can decrease.

Intervening Opportunities Model by Samuel Stauffer: An improvement to the gravity model was Intervening Opportunities by Stauffer. He points out that the number of trips an individual is willing to make is directly proportional to the number of destination opportunities and inversely proportional to the number of intervening opportunities.

Facts to Remember

Indian Immigrants by Country of Destination, 2020

Country of Destination	Number of Indian Migrants
United Arab Emirates	3,471,000
United States	2,724,000
Saudi Arabia	2,502,000
Pakistan	1,597,000
Oman	1,376,000
Kuwait	1,152,000
United Kingdom	835,000
Canada	720,000
Qatar	702,000
Australia	579,000
Total	**17,869,000**

Immigrants in India by Country of Origin, 2020

Country of Origin	Number of Migrants
Bangladesh	2,488,000
Pakistan	833,000
Nepal	734,000
Sri Lanka	185,000
China	108,000
Myanmar	57,000
Uganda	45,000
United Arab Emirates	38,000
United States	33,000
Brunei	24,000
Total	**4,879,000**

AGRARIAN UNREST AND PEASANT MOVEMENTS

The agrarian unrest, which emerged in India can broadly be grouped into three distinct time phases.

1. **The initial phase (1857–1921):** Characterized by the sporadic growth of peasant movements in the absence of proper leadership.
2. **The second phase (1923–1946):** Marked by the emergence of the class-conscious peasant organizations.
3. **Post-independence phase:** This era witnessed the uninterrupted continuity of the agrarian movements due to the failure of the ruling party to resolve any of the basic problems of the working masses of rural India.

   There are only two components of the peasantry that possess sufficient internal leverage to enter into sustained rebellion. These are a landowning middle peasantry and peasantry located in a peripheral area outside the domains of landlord control.

Some of the well-known Peasant Movements in India are:

The Santhal Rebellion of 1855: The Santhal rebellion, also known as a Santhal Hul, classified as a tribal movement by many scholars, took place in present-day Jharkhand and part of West Bengal (at the foothills of Rajmahal). The revolt broke out in July 1855, when thousands of Santhals assembled at Bhogandih village and declared themselves free. The movement was organized and led by two brothers namely Sidhu and Kanhu who claimed that they received messages from supernatural powers to put an end to the 'zhulum' of officers and the deceit of merchants.

Champaran Satyagraha (1917–18): The tenant farmers were forced by the British planters to cultivate indigo in three twentieth part of a bigha of their holding, this was known as 'Teen Kathia' system. The planters forced indigo cultivation at the best portions of land and offered very low prices for the indigo output. When the indigo market was adversely hit by the introduction of synthetic indigo in the world market in 1897 the planters started a new type of exploitation. This miserable scenario of indigo exploitation forced the ryots to resist, violently or otherwise, from time to time, against their oppressors but was cruelly crushed.

Raj Kumar Shukla and Sant Raut, a moneylender who owned some land, persuaded Gandhi to go to

Champaran and thus, the Champaran Satyagraha began. Gandhiji was joined and assisted in his protest against such exploitation by prominent personalities like J.B. Kripalani, Babu Brajkishore Prasad, and Babu Rajendra Prasad. The government had to relent and called Gandhiji for talks and also made him a member of the committee to enquire into the plight of the indigo peasants. Based on the committee's report the Teen Kathia system was abolished.

The Bardoli Movement in Gujarat: In 1925, the taluka of Bardoli in Gujarat suffered financial troubles. However, the government of the Bombay Presidency had raised the tax rate by 30% that year, and despite petitions from civic groups, it refused to cancel the raise in the face of the calamities. The situation for the farmers was grave enough that they barely had enough property and crops to pay off the tax, let alone feed themselves afterward. The activists of Gujarat such as Narahari Parikh, Ravi Shankar Vyas, and Mohanlal Pandya had a talk with the village leaders and sought the help of the prominent Gujarati freedom fighter Vallabhbhai Patel. The request made by Patel to reduce the taxes was ignored by the Governor of Bombay. Patel then instructed the farmers of Bardoli to refuse to pay the taxes. The Government decided to crush the revolt. In order to terrorize and seize the property of the villagers, bands of Pathans from northwest India were gathered. The Pathans and tax inspectors intruded into the houses of the farmers and took away their property which also included cattle. The government started to auction the houses and the lands of the farmers. But no one from Gujarat or from the entire India came forward to buy them.

Moplah Rebellion in Malabar (1921): The Moplah peasant movement was engineered in August 1921 among the peasants of the Malabar district in Kerala. The Moplah tenants were Muslims and they agitated against the Hindu landlords and the British government. While the elite among the Moplahs were traders and merchants, the Moplah masses of the Moplah worked as agriculturists who were tenants of Hindu landlords called Jenmis. The major grievances of the Moplah tenants were (i) Insecurity due to an unfavourable land tenure system due to which Moplahs could be ejected from their land without any appropriate notice (ii) High renewal of fees fixed by the Jenmis (iii) High rent fixed for Moplah and discriminating them against Hindu Tenants. During the same time, there was the Khilafat movement, in which Moplahs actively took part but finally ended up with agitation against the landlords. On Gandhi ji's call congress supported the Khilafat agitation which eventually led to the end of the Moplah Rebellion.

Tebhaga Movement in Bengal (1946–47): The word Tebhaga literally means three shares of harvests. The movement was started for the reduction in the share of the produce from one-half to one-third, which they traditionally used to pay to the jotedars, the intermediary landowners. The movement arose in North Bengal and included the districts of Dinaipur and Rangpur in East Bengal and Jalpaiguri and Malda in West Bengal. This was organised by the Kisan Sabha and marked a departure from the pattern of movements by the Indian National Congress.

Telangana Movement (1946–52): The Telangana Movement was a fight against the feudal oppression of the rulers and local landowners of Andhra Pradesh. It was launched by CPI through its peasant wing, the Kisan Sabha.

The Naxalite Movement in West Bengal (1967–71): The peasant uprising in May 1967 in the Naxalbari police station of Darjeeling district in the northern part of West Bengal is one of the major rebellions in post-colonial India. It was organized against the large-scale eviction of sharecroppers by the jotedars, resulting in the deteriorating condition of the poor peasants, and the failure of the government to effectively implement the land reform laws. The movement later spread to other regions of the state and elsewhere in Bihar and Andhra Pradesh in the form of the Naxalite movement.

Patiala Mujara Movement: The Mujara movement originated in the late 19th century when the princely state of Patiala faced oppression by the Maharaja of Patiala. The Biswadars (local landlords) had proprietary rights over the land but the tenants felt that these landlords had no legal rights over the land. The tenant grievance found an outlet in movements such as the Akali and Praja Mandal movements during the 1920s.

Srikakulam Movement in Andhra Pradesh: Srikakulam is located in the northernmost part of Andhra Pradesh bordering Orissa. The continuing backwardness of the area provoked the local communists of Palakonda, Parvathipuram, Kottur, and Patpatnam to organize local tribals like Jatapu and Savara under their banner. A movement that continued from 1957–58 to 1967 under the leadership of

Girijan Sangham and Mahila Sangham achieved some gains including the restoration of land illegally taken from tribals by moneylenders.

CHANGING INTER-COMMUNITY RELATIONS AND VIOLENCE

Inter-community relations refer to the particular state of affairs in an area where potentially conflicting ethnic, religious, cultural, political, or linguistic communities live together. It is the state of co-existence of two or more communities. Inter-community relations are not static; they change with time. Various reasons could lead to the changing inter-community relation. One major reason is communal violence.

Communal violence involves people belonging to two different religious communities mobilizing against each other and is characterized by feelings of enmity, emotional anger, exploitation, social discrimination, and social marginalization. A high degree of cohesion builds around tension and polarization in one community against another.

Indian law defines communal violence as 'any act or series of acts, whether spontaneous or planned, that results in injury or damage to any person or property, in relation to any religious or is referred to on the basis of membership of a deliberate or linguistic minority in any State of the Union of India within the meaning of clauses (24) and (25) of Article 366 of the Constitution of India, or the Scheduled Castes and the Scheduled Tribes.'

Colm Campbell proposed that sectarian violence generally occurs when

- the rule of law is eroded, the state fails or is grossly incapable of providing order, security, and equal justice which then leads to mass mobilisation, which is followed by radicalisation. Anger, and eventually violent mobilization, between one or more communities.

Features of Communal Riots

1. Communal riots are more politically motivated than religious. The Madan Commission, which inquired into the communal disturbances in Maharashtra in May 1970, emphasized that "the architects and builders of communal tension are communalists and a certain class of politicians - those all-India and local leaders who want to strengthen their political are out to seize every opportunity to do so." Giving a communal color to each incident enhanced his prestige and enriched his public image and thus projected himself in the public eye as a champion of the rights of his religion and his community.
2. Apart from political interests, economic interests also play an important role in fueling communal conflicts.
3. In a town where communal riots have taken place once or twice, the possibility of recurrence of communal riots is stronger than in a town where riots have never taken place.

Violence

Kenneth Waltz (1959) in his book, '*Man, the State, and War*' analytically examines violent conflicts from various perspectives, ranging from interpersonal conflict to interpersonal conflict, civil unrest, interstate wars, and global conflict. Dominant notions of evolutionary social change had come under increasing pressure and tended to offer functional and linear accounts of the increasing role of the nation-state in industrialisation, population growth, urbanization, education, and the bureaucratic management of everyday social relations.

Johann Galtung in 1969 articulated the notion of structural violence. He ran into some conceptual difficulties in trying to present the notion of structural violence as a response to rising radicalism and an attempt to reconcile his idolatry with the order of peace. He reiterated that as a result of extensive dialogue in many parts of the world, there are four categories of basic needs of the people.

According to his theory of basic needs, the first 'need set' category is survival and its negation is death or mortality. The second category is welfare and its taboos are poverty, disease, and misery. The third is identity, meaning, or purpose, the negation of which is dissociation. The fourth 'need group' category is that of freedom and its denial is oppression or suppression. Denial of these basic needs or 'need groups' results in eight types of violence with some subtypes that are easily recognized for direct violence, but structural violence is more complex to identify.

Direct violence is the only kind of violence that is accepted as real violence. At the interpersonal level, direct violence is the act or force used by one or more people to cause physical harm or injury to other people, including nature. This is also known as personal violence and is static.

These acts insult the basic needs of others. These acts are of war, torture, fighting, arms violence, physical abuse, and emotional abuse and are example of direct violence. Actor or actors are the fundamental ingredient of direct violence and make it a personal act. Structural violence is a permanent state of violence, which is embedded in the social, political, and economic structures that make up a society.

Due to the absence of a concrete person and its camouflaged nature, it is also known as indirect violence. Structural violence is often accepted as norm in society. Primarily, structural violence is the result of hierarchical relations within and between societies that privilege those who are on top and oppress, exploit and dominate those who are at the bottom.

CHAPTER 2

Urban Society

LEARNING OBJECTIVES:

In this chapter, we will discuss the following important topics.

- Urbanism, urbanity and urbanization
- Towns, cities and megacities
- Industry, service and business
- Neighbourhood, slums and ethnic enclaves
- Middle class
- Underclass
- Gated communities
- Urban movements and violence

INTRODUCTION

The term 'Urban society' refers to a set of specialized, non-agricultural activities that are characteristic of, but not exclusive to, city dwellers. Urban as a word has two meanings, one the demographic meaning which focus on the size and density of the population and the nature of work of most adult males are engaged in and second the Sociological meaning, which focuses on heterogeneity, impersonality, interdependence, and quality of life. As a sociologist we give prominence to the second aspect of meaning.

URBANISM, URBANITY, AND URBANIZATION

Urbanization

Urbanization is the movement of population from rural to urban areas and resulting in an increasing proportion of the population that lives in urban rather than rural locations. Thompson Warren defines it as "the movement from communities primarily or wholly concerned with agriculture to other communities, usually large ones whose activities are concentrated mainly in government, trade, manufacturing or allied interests".

In Anderson's opinion urbanization is not a one-way process but it is a two-way process. It not only includes movement from villages to cities and change from purely agricultural activities to non-agricultural activities such as business, trade, service, and profession, but also includes changes in attitudes, beliefs, values, and behavior patterns of migrants. He lists five major characteristics of urbanization they are- money economy, civil administration, cultural change, written records, and innovation.

As a country industrializes, the number of people living in urban areas tends to increase. Urbanization is the growth of cities, brought about by a population shift from rural areas and small communities to large ones, and the change from a largely agricultural economy to an industrial one.

For Marvin Olson, 'Urbanization is a process in which the size and strength of a community of a society increase'.

According to Srinivas, 'Urbanization does not simply mean an increase in population in a limited area, but it refers to a change in socio-economic relations.'

Kingsley Davis defined Urbanization as 'Urbanization is a definite process, the cycle of environments by which society changes from an agricultural to an industrial society.'

Mumford has given the evolutionary theory following the thesis of Petrick Geddes who viewed the development of urbanization as a cyclical growth. Mumford outlined several stages of urbanization as follows:

1. **Eopolis:** Collective village community.
2. **Polis:** This is the second stage which involves the association of villages or kin groups and the growth of a distinct division of labour.
3. **Metropolis:** This is the result of agricultural advances and the extension of trade networks. This is marked by the separation of classes. Mumford according to Maclver sees the beginning of a civilizational decline in which the city under the influence of capitalistic ethos concentrates upon bigness and power.
4. **Megalopolis:** This is marked by the dominance of profit motive, display speculation and triumph of mechanism', passivity, and the predominance of large cities over small.
5. **Tyrannopolis and Nekropolis:** This stage represents the combination of urban civilization because of the destruction of arts and sciences, the spread of war, famine, and disease.
    - While in his book 'the Death of the City' Spengler put forth the viewpoint of urbanizationas a social decay' he described the process of urbanization as the start of civilizational decay.

Some of the important causes of urbanization are:

1. Growing industrialization
2. Population pressure
3. Employment opportunities
4. In hope of a better standard of living people move to urban areas
5. Decrease in the death rate and growing birth rate leads to an increase in the urban population.
6. Seeking social mobility and good fortune rural people move to urban areas.

Over-urbanization

The concept of over-urbanization first emerged in the mid-20th century to describe cities whose rate of industrialization was growing more slowly than the rate of their urbanization.

According to sociologist Joseph Gugler, the concept was "widely accepted in the 1950s and 1960s". Kingsley Davis and Hilda Golden defined whether a country was hyper-urbanized based on how its relationship between industrialization and urbanization compared to other countries during the same time period.

Under-urbanization

Under-urbanization, defined as the achievement of high industrial growth without a parallel growth of urban population, can be plausibly viewed as a typical phenomenon of socialist economies and is widely recognized in the special case of China.

Urbanism

Urbanism is a way of life. It reflects an organization of society in terms of a complex division of labor, high levels of technology, high mobility, the interdependence of its members in fulfilling economic functions, and impersonality in social relations.

The emergence of urbanization in the early 20th century was associated with the rise of centralized manufacturing, mixed-use neighbourhoods, social organizations, and networks, and what has been described as a "convergence between political, social and economic citizenship".

Louis Wirth wrote that it is necessary to stop 'identifying urbanism with the physical entity of the city', and suggest that we should 'go beyond an arbitrary boundary line' and consider how 'technological advances in transport and communication has pervaded urban life, even beyond the city limits'.

Urbanity

Urbanity is defined as the state of people living in a city as compared to a village, i.e., a pattern of life e.g., Working conditions, food habits, etc. Urbanity represents the characteristics, personality traits, and attitudes associated with cities and urban area. People who can be described as urbanites are sometimes called citified.

According to Richard Sennett, public experience outside the private sphere of the home became a liability for men's self-development. Chatting in cafes or walking busy streets was, like traveling, a means of achieving sophistication and becoming comfortable with diversity.

For women, on the other hand, exploring the public sphere was considered immoral. Moving alone and freely in the city was associated with promiscuous sexual behaviour. It was in the sphere of the bourgeois household in the city that women acquired the manners and an accent of urbanity.

Urbanity is often regarded as the cultural capital of the upper social classes. For Pierre Bourdieu, there are three forms of cultural capital, each of them closely linked to the notion of urbanity. First, embodied cultural capital refers to investment in self-improvement. Thus, it focuses on urbanity as a personality trait that can be developed. second, objectified cultural capital is represented by material goods such as a car or a house in a trendy neighbourhood. Thus, it is closely related to the politics of space. Third, institutionalized cultural capital comprises an institution's formal recognition of a person's cultural capital, usually academic credentials or professional qualifications affecting everyday life in the city.

According to Lefebvre, after the agrarian, mercantile, and industrial ages, we are now passing through an urban revolution. This means not only that more than half of the world's population lives in cities, but also that the way we imagine the world has become urban. For Lefebvre personality, economic behaviour, spiritual beliefs, modes of social interaction, all aspects of human life have become urban.

TOWNS, CITIES, AND MEGACITIES

Town

According to the census 2011, places that can be categorized as Town:

1. Have a minimum population of 5,000
2. At least 75 percent of the male main working population is engaged in non-agricultural activities
3. Density of population at least 400 persons per sq km

Cities

The word city is derived from a French word meaning citizenship. A city is a large or important town. According to Louis Wirth 'cities have been melting pots of races, peoples, and cultures and the most favorable breeding ground of new biological and cultural hybrids'.

In the United States, cities are incorporated into municipalities with local governments. In Great Britain, the seat of a bishop is called a city.

According to the census 2011, towns with a population of 1,00,000 and above are called Cities.

Megacities

Megacities are urban areas with more than 10 million people. In 1950, only 3 cities were classified as megacities: London, New York, and Tokyo. Today this number is far greater. In India, there are three very large urban areas with more than 10 million people. These are:

1. Greater Mumbai (18.4 million),
2. Delhi (16.3 million) and
3. Kolkata (14.1 million).

Megacities play a huge role to play in both the global and regional economies in which they are located. This is because of 4 factors:

1. Production – manufacturing takes place in many cities but research and development and decision-making are often done in the biggest cities.
2. Migration – flows of migrants tend to be into major urban centers, so they directly affect the global and regional economies through labor.
3. Globalization - There are major links between megacities and this means that business, trade, and transport flow between these regions or nodes. Megacities are therefore central to the world economic system.
4. Governance - Many political decisions take place in megacities at both the national and regional levels. This means that these cities exert massive influence both globally and regionally.

Meta City

UN-HABITAT's State of the World's Cities report in 2006 specified a new class of urban form, the Meta city, defined as 'massive sprawling conurbations of more than 20 million people'.

The term Meta city was coined when the term megacity, designated as cities of more than ten million people became insufficient.

The idea of meta-polis was first introduced by French sociologist and philosopher Francois Ascher (1946–2009). According to Ascher, a metropolis is a heterogeneous area that constitutes an evolution of the former metropolis, and an attempt to assimilate a preconceived consciousness.

INDUSTRY, SERVICE, AND BUSINESS

Industry

Industry refers to a group of productive enterprises or organizations that produce or supply goods, services, or sources of income. Industries are generally classified as primary, secondary, tertiary, and quaternary.

Primary Industry: The sector includes agriculture, forestry, fishing, mining, quarrying, and the extraction of minerals. It can be divided into two categories: the genetic industry, including the production of raw materials, which can be increased by human intervention in the production process; and extractive industries, which involve the production of exhaustible raw materials that cannot be increased through farming.

The primary industry tends to dominate the economies of underdeveloped and developing countries, but as secondary and tertiary industries develop, their share in economic output tends to decline.

Secondary Industries: This sector, also called manufacturing industries, takes raw materials supplied by primary industries and processes them into consumer goods or other secondary industries to convert them into products. Secondary industry can be divided into heavy, large-scale, light, or small-scale industry.

Large-scale industry typically requires heavy capital investment in plant and machinery, has a complex industrial organization, a specialized labor force, and produces large volumes of output. Examples would include petroleum refining, steel, and iron manufacturing, automotive, etc.

Small-scale industries are those industries in which manufacturing, production, and rendering of services are done on a small or micro scale. Examples and ideas of small-scale industries are bakeries, beauty parlours, etc.

Tertiary Industry: It is also called the service industry. It includes industries that provide services or intangible benefits or generate wealth without producing tangible goods. This sector generally includes both private and government enterprises. Industries in this region include banking, finance, transportation, tourism, defense services, etc.

Quaternary Industry: It is an extension of the tertiary industry. It deals with information-based or knowledge-oriented products and services. Industries and activities in this sector include information systems and information technology, research, media, communication technology, etc.

Service

Service is a transaction in which no physical goods are transferred from the seller to the buyer. Services are generally intangible in nature. According to Kotler, Armstrong, Saunders, and Wong, a service is any activity or benefit that one party can provide to another, which is essentially intangible and does not result in ownership of anything. Its production may or may not be tied to the physical product.

According to Christopher Lovelock, 'Services are economic activities that create value and provide benefits for customers at specific times and places as a result of bringing about a desired change in or on behalf of the recipient of the service.'

Some characteristics of services are:

1. It is a core area or an activity or a task of business,
2. It is a major component and denotes a parallel size of the business,
3. Services may be collateral activity and have a supplementary service to support the core area of business,
4. It is an act or performance offered by one party to another,
5. It is an economic activity that creates value and provides benefits for customers,
6. Services are based on the concepts of rational behaviour and the norms of ethical values.
7. It is provided by a person, who processes particular skills, qualities, competencies, and learning aspects.

Business

Business is the activity of making one's living or making money by producing or buying and selling products. It is defined as an organization engaged in commercial, industrial, or professional activities. The term "business" also refers to the organized efforts and activities of individuals to produce and sell goods and services for profit. Businesses range in scale from a sole proprietorship to an international corporation.

Businesses are formed following the development of a business plan, which is a formal document detailing the goals and objectives of the business, and its strategies for how it will achieve the goals and objectives. Having a business name does not separate the business entity from the owner, which means that the business owner is responsible and liable for the debts incurred by the business. If the business obtains a loan, creditors can go after the owner's personal assets.

Types of Business

1. **Sole Proprietorship:** This is a business that is owned and operated by a single person. It is easy to set up, operate and register. All the profits of the business belong to the owner and he is also responsible for all the liabilities.
2. **Partnership:** When two or more persons join hands to run a business, they usually come under a partnership. The partnership comes in two forms – general and limited.
3. **Corporation:** A corporation is a business that has a separate legal identity from the people who own or run it. Ownership is usually represented in the form of shares of stock.
4. **Cooperative:** It is a private business organization owned and controlled by people for their mutual benefit. These people are called members and benefit from the goods and services offered by the cooperative.

NEIGHBOURHOOD, SLUMS, AND ETHNIC ENCLAVES

Neighbourhood

A neighbourhood is a geographic area surrounding a family's place of residence. Neighbourhood usually results from social interaction between people living near each other. Neighbourhoods also include a sense of shared identity and similar demographic characteristics such as living conditions and socioeconomic status.

The basic elements of a neighbourhood are people, place, connectivity system, shared identity, and public symbols. Putting the elements together, a neighbourhood can be described as a population living in an identifiable section of a city, whose members are organized in common contact networks of formal and informal relationships and associated with the area in public symbols. express identity.

American sociologist William Julius Wilson has discussed the role of neighbourhoods in human development through his theory of the "new urban poor". They argue that the experience of poverty has been more damaging for poor families since the late 20th century because the composition of such families' neighbourhoods has changed. Today, the poor live mostly in neighbourhoods made up of other poor families. The concentration of poverty and adult unemployment that accompanies it leads to the social isolation of poor children from higher education and stable employment.

Nearly all neighbourhood studies find that demographic or socioeconomic characteristics of neighbourhoods are associated with the outcomes of interest. According to Wilson, for example, living in a neighbourhood with many poor families cuts youth off from mainstream society and leads to violence and crime.

According to Kisar and Turkoglu, social ties such as neighbourhood and family ties are considered social networks at the micro level and these relationships serve the needs of security and support in the community at the basic level.

American sociologist Robert Sampson and his colleagues have demonstrated the importance of collective efficacy within neighbourhoods. Collective efficacy can be referred to as the shared belief among adults living in it that they can collectively achieve common goals.

It is associated with lower rates of crime and violence. Collective efficacy includes common goals regarding child-rearing, trusting one's neighbours, mutual exchange of favors, and willingness to informally supervise and sanction local youth.

Another important aspect is the quality of public institutions and services in the neighbourhood. Good schools, daycare, health care facilities, police protection, libraries, and parks are some of the important institutions that families consider when choosing to live in a neighbourhood.

A limitation of neighbourhood studies is that they assume that the neighbourhood has the same effect on all residents and that the causal effect flows in one direction, from the neighbourhood to the household. Similarly, a neighbourhood's impact on families must take into account the diversity of families within it and the fact that each may experience and respond to the neighbourhood differently.

Slum

A slum is usually a highly populated urban residential area, consisting mostly of dense, dilapidated housing units in a state of deteriorated or incomplete infrastructure, inhabited primarily by poor individuals.

According to the United Nations, the proportion of urban residents living in slums decreased from 47 percent to 37 percent in developing countries between 1990 and 2005. However, due to the increasing population, the number of slum dwellers is increasing. One billion people live in slums worldwide and this is expected to increase to 2 billion by 2030.

The Task Force on Housing and Slum Development appointed by the Planning Commission of India estimated that India has about 23% or more than 30 million persons as urban slum dwellers.

According to Mrs. Kumari Selja, India's largest slum population is in the country's financial and film capital Mumbai, where an estimated 6.5 million people live. While slums vary in size and other characteristics, most lack reliable sanitation services, clean water supplies, reliable electricity, law enforcement, and other basic services.

The main characteristics of the slum population are listed below:

1. High rate of poverty
2. They are the breeding grounds for social problems like crime, drug addiction, alcoholism, etc.
3. Low level of the economic status of its residents
4. High incidence of unemployment
5. Inadequate infrastructural facilities
6. Acute problem of malnutrition
7. Lack of drinking water
8. Lack of basic healthcare
9. Low standard of living
10. Huge extent of urban decay

Slums are still mainly found in urban areas of developing countries but are also found in developed countries. The lack of infrastructure in the slums is attributed to the informal nature of the settlement and no plans for the poor by the government authorities.

The National Institute of Urban Affairs, New Delhi mentions three forces in the emergence of slums. These are:

1. The demographic dynamism of a city attracts more people from rural areas which provide greater employment potential.
2. The existing urban land policies that prohibit the access of the poor to the urban land market.
3. Its inability to meet the growing demand for housing

In India, slums can be classified into three categories:

1. The old building that has become dilapidated and deteriorated in course of time.
2. The slums are characterized by poor and inadequate housing conditions constructed illegally around mills and factories.
3. The slums that illegally come up in different parts of the city through the unauthorized occupation of open land.

Top 5 states with largest slum population (census 2011)

1. Maharashtra
2. Andhra Pradesh
3. Tamil Nadu
4. West Bengal
5. Madhya Pradesh

Top 3 largest slums in the world

1. Khayelitsha, South Africa
2. Kibera, Kenya
3. Dharavi, Mumbai

Ethnic Enclaves

In sociology, an ethnic enclave is a geographic area with high ethnic concentration, distinct cultural identity, and economic activity. The term is generally used to refer to a residential area or work area with a high concentration of ethnic firms. Their success and development depend on self-reliance and are linked with economic prosperity.

The theory of social capital is very important in understanding the concept of ethnic enclaves. Douglas Massey explains how migrant networks provide new immigrants with social capital that can be transferred into other tangible forms.

As immigrants tend to cluster in close geographic spaces, they develop migrant networks, systems of interpersonal relations through which participants can exchange valuable resources and knowledge. Immigrants can take advantage of social connections by turning information into tangible resources. The exchange of information may include knowledge of employment opportunities, affordable housing, government assistance programs, and helpful nongovernmental organizations.

Enclave Economy Hypothesis

A study conducted by Alejandro Portes and Kenneth Wilson of the Cuban ethnic enclave economy in Miami led to conclude that participation in the enclave economy provided an alternative, quicker option for immigrants to achieve economic mobility in a host society. The discourse promoted by Portes and Wilson produced a body of literature that came to be known as the ethnic enclave hypothesis. The term "ethnic enclave" came to be widely used to represent two different definitions: an enclave of the economy and a residential area of high co-ethnic concentration.

Historically, the formation of ethnic enclaves has been the result of a variety of socioeconomic factors that attract immigrants to similar locations in the receiving country. Cultural diversity brings together people who do not understand each other's languages, but a group can communicate more easily with neighbours in an enclave. In some cases, enclaves have been enforced by law, as in ghettos.

During the decades of immigration restrictions, ethnic enclaves in the US were removed as economic and spatial barriers to successful assimilation into American life and to the upward mobility of immigrants. However, since the 1960s, ethnic enclaves have increasingly been seen as agents of economic and social mobility.

By providing space for co-ethnics to form potentially beneficial relationships, ethnic enclaves help members achieve economic mobility. Enclaves create an alternative labor market that is ethnic-specific and does not demand the social and cultural skills of the host country.

While ethnic enclave theory was developed to explain immigrant incorporation into the receiving society, it has also been linked to migration processes in large part because the successful incorporation of immigrants has the potential to reduce migration costs for future immigrants.

Despite their immediate benefits, the long-term implications of participation in an ethnic enclave are debatable. Enclave economies are bound by invisible barriers limiting immigrant growth and upward mobility. While participation in the enclave economy may assist in increasing the availability of employment opportunities in the enclave labor market, it may also prevent the acquisition of host country skills that may benefit the immigrant in the long run. Opportunities available in mainstream society may be out of reach of immigrants.

MIDDLE CLASS

Middle class refers to the class of people who fall in between the working class and upper class. B. B. Mishra in his book 'The Indian Middle Class' defined the middle class in terms of the independent small traders, professionals, and artisans who stood in between the bourgeoisie on the one side and the working class on the other. These classes grew in number with the development of towns and increasing urbanization that accompanied the development of industrial production. Direct trading between consumers and producers became more and more difficult with the growth of big towns and, cities. These groups were later called the 'old middle classes'.

The emergence of a "new middle class" is attributed to the further expansion of industrial capitalism and the rise of big corporations with large and complex organizational structures.

G D H Cole, a noted sociologist, attributes the birth of the new middle class to two important developments in Western industry. First, the increase in the number of public schools and the spread of education. and second, the spread of joint stock obesity. These developments gave rise to large-scale enterprises and brought into existence a new class of salaried people.

Lockwood, another sociologist, attributed the rise of the white-collar salaried class to the growth of any corporate capitalism and the rise of large organizations.

Karl Marx, on the other hand, referred to the middle class as part of the bourgeoisie i.e., the petty bourgeoisie or small business owners. The classical definition of the middle class can be found in Weberian socio-economic terms. Here, the middle class is defined as professionals or business owners who share domesticity, sub-urbanity, and a level of relative security (in the form of socially desired skills or wealth) against social distress.

Some modern theories of the political economy suggest that the middle class has a stabilizing influence on society, it bears neither possibly explosive (revolutionary) tendencies of the lower class nor absolutist (or oligarchic) tendencies of the upper class.

Therefore, the use of the term 'middle class' has often been ambiguous whether defined in terms of occupation, income, education, or social status. Social scientists have defined the term in various ways to serve their social and political ends.

Some theories such as the 'Paradox of interest' use wealth distribution data to determine the size and share of the wealth of the middle class. The middle class is a description given to individuals and families that typically fall between the working class and upper class within the socioeconomic hierarchy.

A group of people who regard themselves as middle class varies from one region to another. For instance, a middle-class standard of living in the United States has come to mean having "a secure job, a safe and stable home, access to health care, retirement security, time off for vacation, illness, and the birth or adoption of a child, opportunities to save for the future.

And the ability to provide a good education, including a college education, for one's children". But these criteria may not be needed to fit into the category of the middle class in other countries.

In February 2009, The Economist announced that more than half of the world's population now belonged to the middle class as a result of rapid growth in emerging countries. It characterized the middle class as having "a reasonable amount of discretionary income so that they have about a third of their income left over for discretionary spending after paying for basic food and shelter".

UNDERCLASS

The sociological concept of the underclass is relatively new. The underclass people are the ones who appear to stand out from the general society due to lack of employment, skill, income, wealth, or property.

It can be argued that the underclasses are those who have become surplus to a globalized economy because production can be moved anywhere in the world where unskilled labor is cheapest.

The underclass is the segment of the population that occupies the lowest possible position in a class hierarchy, below the core body of the working class. Gunnar Myrdal is generally credited as the first proponent of the term underclass. Writing in the early 1960s on economic inequality in the U.S., Myrdal's underclass refers to a 'class of unemployed, unemployable, and underemployed, who are more and more hopelessly set apart from the nation at large, and do not share in its life, its ambitions, and its achievements'.

According to sociologist Herbert Gans, while Myrdal's structural concept of the underclass remained relatively intact through the writings of William Julius Wilson and others, in many cases the structural definition was abandoned and replaced with a behavioral concept of the underclass which fuses Myrdal's term with Oscar Lewis's and others' conception of a 'culture of poverty'.

Marxist sociologist Eric Olin Wright views the underclass as "a category of social agents who are economically oppressed but not consistently exploited within a given class system". The lower class occupies the lowest possible rung on the class ladder.

According to Wright, the lower class is oppressed. He believes that this is because they are generally denied access to the labour market, and thus cannot easily rise above their status, but are thus "not constantly exploited" because the chance for economic exploitation is minimal.

GATED COMMUNITIES

A gated community (or walled community) is a form of residential community or housing estate that has strictly controlled entrances for pedestrians, bicycles, and automobiles, and is often characterized by a closed perimeter of walls and fences. Gated communities usually have small residential streets and include various shared amenities. For smaller communities, these amenities may include only a park or other common areas. For larger communities, it may be possible for residents to remain within the community for most daily activities.

One of the primary objectives of a gated community is to provide security to its residents that they would not experience in surrounding non-gated communities. Only residents have access to public areas, which may include parks and sports facilities such as tennis courts, community pools, etc., that are inside the gated community.

According to Vesselinov, 'physical barriers to entry' and 'restricted access' to non-residents are the two most important characteristics of 'gated communities'. From a neo-Marxist macro-perspective, 'gated communities' can be identified as a symptom of the growing gap between rich and poor in capitalist societies. Davis and others argue that the construction of 'gated communities' is an integral part of the project of building 'fortress cities'.

'Gated communities' are regarded as a strategy to control the urban poor and separate them from the shrinking middle class and upper class. From a micro-sociological as well as a psychological perspective, 'gated communities' can be discussed within the framework of an analysis of the sources of urban fear. Setha M. Low, an anthropologist, has argued that they have a negative impact on the net social capital of the wider community outside the gated community. He points out, social concerns expressed by residents of 'gated communities' include fear and prejudice based not only on class distinctions but also on notions of racial and ethnic exclusiveness. Apart from concrete fear, the lack of trust in the state and the willingness to pay taxes only for items used by the individual make proposals for 'gated communities' quite attractive to certain sections of society.

However, there is also another point of view, some researchers argued that GC's could have a positive effect on poor neighbourhoods and even promote social integration. In some cases, residential segregation in modern cities is beginning to acquire new and paradoxical features.

URBAN MOVEMENTS AND VIOLENCE

Urban Movements

Urban movements are social movements through which citizens attempt to gain some control over their urban environment. Urban social movement organizations are formed by residents to protest, or demand change, about the urban environment and urban services. The term was originally applied by Manuel Castells to urban movements that contributed to broad revolutionary social change.

Manuel Castells, in his book '*The Urban Question*', presented a model of the dynamics of the urban system that contained only one mechanism for structural change. He called this mechanism an 'urban social movement'.

The term was originally applied by Manuel Castells to those urban movements which contributed to wider revolutionary social change. Pickvance (2003) suggested that the term 'urban movements' is to be preferred because it is more straightforward, analogous to 'environmental movement' instead of 'environmental social movement'.

Urban movements tend to draw on a relatively stable set of familiar types of action. The actions found in urban movements overlap with the actions of other social movements. However, some items are specific for urban movements: the rent strike, squatting, and developing alternative spatial plans.

Organizational patterns can be bottom-up or top-down. Bottom-up mobilization involves building networks of activists and occasional participants, the creation of committees, possibly formal organizations, newsletters, and neighbourhood centers.

An example in which substantial bottom-up mobilization occurred was the 1970s Citizen Movement in Madrid. Top-down mobilization occurs when political parties build local organizations, such as in the case of the land squatter movement of Santiago de Chile from 1965-73, or when political groups try to take over or make use of a movement that started in a bottom-up fashion.

The literature related to urban movement illustrates a wide range of problems to which citizens have responded with collective action. A large set of problems in the urban area can be classified under the heading of "mass consumption" such as housing shortages, increase in rent, neglect of maintenance by landlords to the point of abandonment, and inadequate health care and education. In developing countries, slum dwellers face a lack of basic amenities like shortage in water supply, lack of sewer, and unavailability of electricity led to the urban social movement.

Another set of problems relates to urban planning is displacement and destruction of beloved urban landscapes. Specific groups mobilize around highly specific issues, such as squatters against anti-squatter policies, property owners against proposed social housing and against property taxes, and racist groups against migrants. According to Cassels, because women have a special role in mass consumption, they play a major role in urban movements.

Urban movements can achieve their maximum potential for social change when they are multi-issue and pursue the following three goals:

1. the realization of collective consumption demands as use value against commodification (such as those related to social housing).
2. to establish and strengthen an autonomous cultural identity and to promote communication rather than "programmed one-way information flow".
3. self-management on a territorial basis.

Urban Violence

Urban violence may be described as 'a complex spectrum of experiences', an understanding which is however limited to forms of physical violence, thereby downplaying the urban dimension itself.

Urban violence, in the simplest terms, can be described by some social researchers as a series of incidents that occur in urban spaces. Many social scientists believe that urban spaces have always been sites of conflict, struggle, and violence. Contemporary urban planning has been used in many instances as a tool to prevent, reduce and combat such disorderly activities.

Recent political events in urban squares and plazas draw on the symbolic power of these urban centers. Despite being mostly peaceful, such sites occasionally become sites of violent confrontations.

The urban, however, is much more than just the physical environment i.e., the city. Urban is also a social and existential condition (the urban 'way of life'), a historical and structural process (capitalist urbanism), and an ontological and affective simultaneous being. Overcoming the limitations of a simplistic and redundant definition of urban violence begins essentially, therefore, by rescuing the urban from its reductionism, and restoring it to its metaphysical value.

The urban can be rethought as the background from which violence appears and is experienced as a phenomenon, as well as the process that constitutes violence. Urban violence thus becomes a strategic concept emerging at the intersection between the structural, the representational, and the affective.

In *'Urbanism as a Way of Life'*, Louis Wirth systematized a series of equations that still hold today. Accordingly, the peculiar size, density, and heterogeneity of cities mean that urban ties inherently weaken social bonds, providing a fertile environment for violence.

This view of the city as unruly and chaotic naturalizes violence as a socially exogenous phenomenon that is kept in check through order and control. But this approach can be empirically disputed (quantitatively similar cities have very different patterns of violence) and also flawed conceptually.

It overlooks the extent to which violence is endogenous to the socio-spatial processes that produce the urban, politics pursuing certain kinds of order and control, and thus the role that questions of power, access, infrastructure, and regulations play in shaping its asymmetric and stratified impact.

Lourenco observes that urban violence is usually framed in two ways, sociologically, by focusing on social actors and relations, and anthropologically, by focusing on cultural definitions of violence.

ASSESS YOUR LEARNING

PRACTICE QUESTIONS

1. Which of the following is not one of the features of the urban community?
   (a) Face to face relationships
   (b) complex life
   (c) Materialistic
   (d) Glamour in life

2. Which among the following is not a cause of the growth of cities:
   (a) Trade & commerce
   (b) Industrialism
   (c) Development of transport
   (d) Hygienic outlook of people

3. Which among the following was an exclusive university town?
   (a) Taxila (b) Pataliputra
   (c) Nalanda (d) kashi

4. Who developed the concept of urbanism as a way of life?
   (a) Louis Wirth (b) Fisher
   (c) Lewis Coser (d) None of these

5. The world's first cities appeared about ________.
   (a) 3500 BC (b) 300 BC
   (c) 2000 BC (d) AD 100

6. Which of the following cities can be called a megalopolis?
   (a) Kochi (b) Chennai
   (c) Mumbai (d) Ahmadabad

7. Who coined the term post-industrial society?
   (a) D. Bell (b) Durkheim
   (c) Fisher (d) Louis Wirth

8. Durkheim's concept of organic solidarity is found in
   (a) Tribal society
   (b) Agricultural society
   (c) Traditional society
   (d) Modern society

9. Who has given the concept of rural-urban fringe?
   (a) M.N. Srinivas (b) K.M. Kapadia
   (c) S.C Dube (d) T L Smith

10. Industrialization weakens
    (a) role of religion in social life
    (b) father's authority in the family
    (c) caste system
    (d) All of the above

11. Which among the following meaning is closest to the term 'over urbanization'
    (a) Urbanization at the cost of village development.
    (b) Urbanization without the essential infrastructure.
    (c) rapid urbanization.
    (d) emergence of megalopolis.

12. Social distance in a city is due to:
    (a) The size of the city
    (b) the distance between residences
    (c) The social heterogeneity
    (d) The traffic problem in the city

13. Who says 'city life bombards the mind with images and impressions, sensations and activity'?
    (a) Simmel (b) Karl Marx
    (c) Webber (d) M.S.A. Rao

14. Conurbation means ________________.
    (a) cluster of cities & town
    (b) Cities of cities
    (c) group of slams
    (d) None of these

15. Who introduced the concept of Gesellschaft and Gemeinschaft?
    (a) George simmel (b) Durkheim
    (c) Tonnies (d) None of these

16. Who introduced the term white-collar crime?
    (a) Giddens (b) E burgess
    (c) Sutherland (d) Durkheim

17. Name the theory developed by D. Harris and Edward in analysing city.
    (a) Ecological theory
    (b) Zone theory
    (c) Sector theory
    (d) Multiple nuclei

18. Who developed the concentric- zone theory of the city?
    (a) Louis Wirth (b) E. Burgess
    (c) M.N Srinivas (d) M.S.A Rao

19. __________ refers to the number of people in an urban area per sq km.
    (a) Citification (b) Urban population
    (c) Urban density (d) Urbanism

20. Which of the following thinker called the village community a 'little community'?
    (a) Robert Redfield (b) M.S.A Rao
    (c) Mc Kim Marriot (d) Louis Wirth

21. The Mahalwari system was introduced in 1833 during the period of?
(a) William Bentick
(b) Thomas Munroe
(c) Lord Dalhousie
(d) Verrier Elwin

22. Which of the following concept refers to Third World cities which have a large population that cannot be absorbed into a formal economy?
(a) Over Urbanization
(b) Urbanism
(c) Urbanization
(d) Under Urbanization

23. Which of the following thinker shows the continuity between Rural/Urban social organizations on the basis of the study of Jatav's of Agra?
(a) M S A Rao (b) N K Bose
(c) B F Hoslitz (d) Owen Lynch

24. Which of the following term is said to be the 'city of cities'?
(a) Ecopolis (b) Polis
(c) Metropolis (d) Megalopolis

25. Who said that 'the urban groups have a reputation for namelessness'?
(a) Lewis Mumford
(b) Oskar lewis
(c) L Bogardus
(d) Owen Lynch

26. Who said that 'cities have been the melting pot of races, people, and cultures and are a most favourable breeding ground of new biological and cultural hybrids'?
(a) Robert Redfield
(b) M.S.A Rao
(c) Mc Kim Marriot
(d) Louis Wirth

27. Arrange the following forms of urban areas in ascending order:
(1) Megacity
(2) Meta city
(3) Metropolis
(4) City
Choose the correct option
(a) (1), (3), (2), (4)
(b) (4), (3), (1), (2)
(c) (2), (3), (4), (1)
(d) (1), (2), (3), (4)

28. Who is the author of the book, '*Rural Development: Putting the Last First*'?
(a) Robert Pritnam
(b) Jarte Krippers Black
(c) Dadabhai Naoroji
(d) Robert Chambers

29. Which one of the following states has the highest percentage of the metropolitan population in relation to the total urban population of the state?
(a) Kerala
(b) Maharashtra
(c) Gujarat
(d) West Bengal

30. Who has applied Robert Redfield's concept of 'Little and Great Tradition' to understand Indian society?
(a) S. C. Dube
(b) Yogendra Singh
(c) T. K. Oommen
(d) Milton Singer

31. Who refers to Indian villages as 'Little Republics'?
(a) Lord Ripon
(b) Charles Metcalfe
(c) Lord Macaulay
(d) Jawaharlal Nehru

32. Which of the following thinker is associated with the 'Central Place theory'?
(a) Harris and Ullman
(b) H.Hyot
(c) Walter Christaller
(d) R.D. Mackenzie

33. Which of the following is not the condition for defining a town in India?
(a) A minimum population of 5,000
(b) At least 75 percent of the male main working population engaged in non-agricultural pursuits
(c) A density of population of at least 400 persons per sq. km.
(d) A density of population of at least 500 persons per sq. km.

34. According to the census 2011, out of 4,041 Statutory Towns in Census 2011 Slums were reported from how many towns?
(a) 2253 (b) 2000
(c) 2543 (d) 4500

35. Which of the following state has the largest slum population in India (census 2011)?
(a) Maharashtra
(b) Andhra Pradesh
(c) Tamil Nadu
(d) West Bengal

36. The Gated communities or enclaves have originated in which of the following country?
(a) UK (b) USA
(c) Brazil (d) Nigeria

37. Community Development Program was the first major effort for rural development initiated in which year?
(a) 1950 (b) 1964
(c) 1952 (d) 1962

38. The Green Revolution strategy was driven by the use of High Yield Variety (HYV) seeds, fertilizers, irrigation, and mechanized farming. Who gave the term Green Revolution?
(a) Dr. William Gaud
(b) Amartya Sen
(c) Norman Borlaug
(d) M S Swaminathan

39. Bonded Labour System Abolition Act was passed in which year?
(a) 1976 (b) 1956
(c) 1948 (d) 1952

40. Who among the following described the city as a center of cultural innovation, diffusion, and progress?
(1) Robert Redfield
(2) William Foot Whyte
(3) Milton Singer
(4) Homer Hyot
Choose the correct option
(a) 1 and 2 (b) 2 and 3
(c) 3 and 1 (d) 3 and 4

41. Who among the following has classified the process of urbanization into two categories
I. Primary urbanization–It helps in spreading the values of Great Tradition.
II. Secondary urbanization–It leads to the overshadowing of values of the Little Tradition and hence, is also disintegrative.
1. Robert Redfield
2. William Foot Whyte
3. Milton Singer
4. Homer Hyot
Choose the correct option
(a) 1 and 2 (b) 2 and 3
(c) 3 and 1 (d) 3 and 4

42. Urbanization has led to the social and economic transformation of societies. Which of the following is not the outcome of urbanization?
(a) Decline of orthodoxies
(b) Liberation of women
(c) Promotion of democratic ideals
(d) Decline of slums

43. Who is the author of the book '***Urban Sociology in India***'?
(a) R K Mukherjee (b) M S A Rao
(c) M S Gore (d) M N Srinivas

44. Which of the following thinker studied the '***Rickshawallas of Lucknow***' in order to understand the Social Organization of an Occupational Category in urban areas?
(a) G S Ghurye
(b) Harold Gould
(c) M S A Rao
(d) M S Gore

45. It is the process in which people move from urban areas to rural areas.
(a) De-urbanization
(b) Rural migration
(c) Urbanization
(d) De-industrialization

46. Who defined the working class as a group which shares similar economic situation which distinguishes itself from others like property owners, managers, and employers. It, thus, refers to industrial workers and sometimes other wage earners and petty self-employed.
(a) Max Weber (b) M Holmstrom
(c) M S Gore (d) M S A Rao

47. Which of the following thinkers attributed the birth of slums to the rise of industrial cities and factory system?
1. Lewis Mumford
2. William Foot Whyte
3. Fredrich Engels
4. Homer Hyot
Choose the correct option
(a) 1 and 2 (b) 2 and 3
(c) 3 and 1 (d) 3 and 4

48. Who of the following are the author of the book 'Slums and Urbanization' (1990)?
1. Lewis Mumford
2. A R Desai
3. Devadas Pillai
4. Homer Hyot
Choose the correct option
(a) 1 and 2 (b) 2 and 3
(c) 3 and 1 (d) 3 and 4

49. Which of the following is not matched correctly?
(a) W H R River: Todas of Nilgiri
(b) W H Wiser: Town of Karimpur near Agra
(c) M N Srinivas: Rampura village near Mysore
(d) S C Dube: Village Sripuram near Hyderabad

50. Who is the author of the book '***The Hindu Jajmani System***'?
(a) W H R River (b) W H Wiser
(c) M N Srinivas (d) S C Dube

51. Who introduced the concepts of Universalisation and Parochialisation to describe the historical process of interaction between village and the greater culture?
(a) Mc Kim Marriott (b) W H R River
(c) W H Wiser (d) M S Gore

52. Who introduced the Mahalwari System in UP and Punjab in 1833?
(a) Lord Munro
(b) Lord Reed
(c) Lord McKenzie
(d) Lord Dalhousie

53. Who has written the book 'Coming of Post-Industrial Society' to describe the economic and social changes in the late 20th century?
(a) Robert Redfield
(b) M.S.A Rao
(c) Mc Kim Marriot
(d) Daniel Bell

54. The correct sequence of the process of Urbanisation, as seen in India is?
(a) Rural Village-Kasba-Small Town-Big Cities-Metropolitan city
(b) Kasba-Rural Village-Small Town-Big Cities-Metropolitan city
(c) Rural Village-Small Town- Kasba-Big Cities-Metropolitan city
(d) Rural Village-Small Town- Kasba - Metropolitan city-Big Cities

55. Which of the following is not correctly matched?
(a) Tonnies: 'Gemeinschaft' and 'Gesellschaft'.
(b) Durkheim: 'mechanical' solidarity and 'in-organic' solidarity.
(c) Henry Maine: 'status' and 'contract'.
(d) Spencer: 'militant' and 'industrial' societies.

56. The development of the ecological approach to urban analysis is attributed to
(a) Frankfurt School
(b) Vienna School
(c) Chicago School
(d) Manchester School

57. The haphazard outgrowth of cities, often mixing land-use in unplanned ways, is most precisely known as
(a) urban sprawl (b) strip cities
(c) megalopolis (d) urban periphery

58. Who coined the term 'folk-urban continuum'?
(a) R.E. Park (b) R. Redfield
(c) R. Dahrendorf (d) B. Malinowski

59. Which of the following sectors of economic activities will be predominantly found in post-industrial societies?
(a) Primary sector
(b) Primary and secondary sectors
(c) Tertiary sector
(d) Secondary and tertiary sectors

60. Inter-caste relations in rural India during the pre-independence phase were largely governed by
(a) Relationships of dominance and reciprocity
(b) Reciprocity of services
(c) Alliances with the governing elite
(d) Relations based on a sense of belongingness

61. It is a collection of families bearing a common name, speaking a common dialect, occupying or progressing to occupy a common territory, and is not usually endogamous, though originally it might have been so?
(a) Caste (b) Political group
(c) Political Party (d) Tribe

62. Which of the following is not correctly matched?

List I (Tribes)	List II (State/Region)
(a) Khasi	Meghalaya
(b) Toda	Nilgiri Hills
(c) Munda	Andhra Pradesh
(d) Khond	Odisa

63. Who said that 'tribalism is a pre-civilized storage of human society?
(a) Sir Henry Maine
(b) Triestske
(c) Oppenheimer
(d) Durkheim

64. Birsa Munda was associated with the tribal struggle of:
(a) North East Region
(b) Jharkhand
(c) Nagpur Division
(d) Deccan

65. Given below are two statements, one labelled as Assertion (A) and the other labelled as Reason (R)

Assertion (A): Naxalite movement is an armed struggle of the poor peasantry against the landlords.

Reason (R): Naxalite movement was born in the Naxalbari village of Darjeeling District.

In the context of the above two statements, which one of the following is correct?

Codes:

(a) Both A and R are true and R is the correct explanation of A
(b) Both A and R are true but' R is not the correct explanation of A
(c) A is true but R is false
(d) A is false but R is true

66. Which one of the following is not a peasant movement?
(a) Telengana Insurrection
(b) Tebhaga Movement
(c) Naxalvadi Movement
(d) Appiko Movement

67. Which one of the following is not a peasant movement?
(a) Kheda movement
(b) Tabligh movement
(c) Telangana movement
(d) Tebhaga movement

68. What led to the decline of the Guild System?
(a) Industrialisation
(b) Growth of Science
(c) Growth of Technology
(d) All of the above

69. Who described agrarian system as more or less homogeneous and undifferentiated community of families characterized by small holdings operated mainly by family labor?
(a) Andre Beteille (b) Harold Gould
(c) M S A Rao (d) M S Gore

70. Which of the following agrarian classes are identified by Daniel Thorner ?

1. Malik
2. Zamindar
3. Kisan
4. Krishak
5. Mazdoor

Chose the correct answer from the code given below:
(a) 1,3, and 5 (b) 1, 2, 3, and 5
(c) 2, 3, 4, and 5 (d) 1, 2, 3, and 4

Answer Key

1. (a)	**11.** (b)	**21.** (a)	**31.** (b)	**41.** (c)	**51.** (a)	**61.** (d)
2. (d)	**12.** (c)	**22.** (a)	**32.** (c)	**42.** (d)	**52.** (c)	**62.** (c)
3. (c)	**13.** (a)	**23.** (d)	**33.** (d)	**43.** (b)	**53.** (d)	**63.** (a)
4. (a)	**14.** (a)	**24.** (d)	**34.** (c)	**44.** (b)	**54.** (a)	**64.** (b)
5. (a)	**15.** (c)	**25.** (c)	**35.** (a)	**45.** (a)	**55.** (b)	**65.** (b)
6. (c)	**16.** (c)	**26.** (d)	**36.** (b)	**46.** (b)	**56.** (c)	**66.** (d)
7. (a)	**17.** (d)	**27.** (b)	**37.** (c)	**47.** (c)	**57.** (a)	**67.** (b)
8. (d)	**18.** (b)	**28.** (d)	**38.** (a)	**48.** (b)	**58.** (b)	**68.** (d)
9. (d)	**19.** (c)	**29.** (a)	**39.** (a)	**49.** (d)	**59.** (c)	**69.** (a)
10 (d)	**20.** (a)	**30.** (d)	**40.** (c)	**50.** (b)	**60.** (d)	**70.** (a)

PREVIOUS YEARS' QUESTIONS

JUNE 2023

1. Arrange peasant movements in chronological order:
   A. Tebhaga movement
   B. Champaran movement
   C. Telengana movement
   D. Naxalite movement

   Choose the correct answer from the options given below:
   (a) A, C, D, B
   (b) B, A, C, D
   (c) C, D, B, A
   (d) D, B, A, C

2. Who among the following has advocated for tribe-caste continuum?
   (a) Andre Beteille
   (b) Veena Das
   (c) Surajit Sinha
   (d) M.S.A. Rao

3. Match List I with List II

List I (Researchers)	List II (Specific Area of Research)
A.E.H. Sutherland	I. Marijuana Addicts
B.H. Becker	II. Street Comer Society
C.W.F. Whyte	III. White Collar Crime
D. Oscar Lewis	IV. Slums and Poor in Mexico

   Choose the correct answer from the options given below:
   (a) A - I, B - II, C - III, D - IV
   (b) A - III, B - I, C - II, D - IV
   (c) A - II, B - IV, C - III, D - I
   (d) A - IV, B - III, C - I, D - II

4. Arrange the rural-urban continuum from the units provided below:
   A. Hamlet
   B. Urban agglomeration
   C. Metropolis
   D. City
   E. Megapolis

   Choose the correct answer from the options given below:
   (a) A, B, D, C, E
   (b) A, B, C, D, E
   (c) E, D, C, B, A
   (d) A, D, B, C, E

5. Arrange the following events of Indian agrarian society in chronological order.
   A. Land reforms
   B. Farmer's movement
   C. Green revolution
   D. Permanent settlement

   Choose the correct answer from the options given below:
   (a) A, B, C, D
   (b) B, A, C, D
   (c) C, B, A, D
   (d) D, A, C, B

6. According to Eric R. Wolf, the prerequisites for sustained peasant rebellion are:
   A. Land owning middle peasantry
   B. Peasantry located in a peripheral area outside the domains of landlord control.
   C. Agricultural labour
   D. Rich peasantry

   Choose the correct answer from the options given below:
   (a) A and B only
   (b) B and C only
   (c) C and D only
   (d) D and A only

7. Who among the following has contributed in the mode of production debate by identification of agrarian classes in terms of Malik, Kisan, and Mazdoor?
   (a) P.C. Joshi
   (b) A.R. Desai
   (c) Daniel Thorner
   (d) Anand Chakravarti

Read the following passage carefully and answer the question that follows:

A main characteristic of rural caste is the coming together of various caste sections living in a village in order to produce food and other goods and services needed locally. In other words, caste system at the village level is locked into the production system and vice versa. Thus, the household of a landowner has enduring symbiotic relations with particular households of a blacksmith, carpenter, potter, oilman, barber, washerman, priest and a tenant or a labourer. The symbol of this is what is called the jajmani system in which specified quantities of grain-with-straw are paid by the landowner after harvest to the heads of the artisan, labouring and servicing households who have worked for him during the previous agricultural year. Traditionally, the rates remained stable over long stretches of time, and a landowner was expected to keep his workers so long as they did not persistently default on their tasks, and in turn, the workers could not change their masters without serious reason. Indeed, patron-client and master-servant relationships tended to be hereditary, a land-owner inheriting, as it were, a body of specialists to work on his land just as the latter inherited him. Inter-caste and inter-familial relations in the village were enduring and multi stranded.

8. Caste system at the village level is locked into the system of ______

(a) Production
(b) Communication
(c) Assimilation
(d) Commodification of services

9. Identify the correct statement.
Caste groups in rural areas come together in order to ________
(a) Produce food
(b) Produce services
(c) Produce goods
(d) Uniformity in social intercourse

10. Who among the following groups has enduring relationships with the service providers like blacksmith, carpenter, potter, barbers, etc.?
(a) Landowners
(b) Businessman
(c) Tenants
(d) Village tax collector

11. Service providers receive grain with straw after the harvest for the work they have done during the previous year under which one of the following systems?
(a) Zamindary (b) Jotedari
(c) Jajmani (d) Ryotwari

12. Traditional inter-caste relations in rural India are ________.
(a) Hereditary in nature
(b) Temporary in nature
(c) Commercial in nature
(d) Egalitarian in nature

MARCH 2023

13. Match List I with List II

List I (Author)	List II (Book)
A. A.R. Desai	I. Peasant Struggles in India
B. D.N. Dhanagare	II. Social Origins of Dictatorship and Democracy: Lord and Peasant in the Making of the Modern World
C. David Hardiman	III. Peasant Movements in India
D. Barrington Moore Jr.	IV. Peasant Resistance in India

Choose the correct answer from the options given below:
(a) A - I, B - II, C - III, D - IV
(b) A - III, B - I, C - II, D - IV
(c) A - I, B - III, C- IV, D- II
(d) A - II, B - III, C - IV, D - I

14. Match List I with List II

List I (Author)	List II (Book)
A. David Harvey	I. The Urban Question
B. Manuel Castells	II. Social Justice and the City
C. John Logan and Harvey Molotch	III. Wasted Lives: Modernity and its Outcastes
D. Zygmunt Bauman	IV. Urban Fortunes

Choose the correct answer from the options given below:
(a) A - I, B - III. C - IV, D - II
(b) A - II, B - IV, C - III, D - I
(c) A - II, B - I, C - IV, D - III
(d) A - I, B - II, C - III, D - IV

15. Who explained the possible reasons for the emergence of primate cities in 1939?
(a) Louis Wirth
(b) Ralph Linton
(c) Mark Jefferson
(d) Ashish Bose

16. Given below are two statements:
Statement I: Humans survived for tens of thousands of years without permanent settlements.
Statement II: The evolution of early cities began 12,000 years ago.
In light of the above statements, choose the most appropriate answer from the options given below:
(a) Both Statement I and Statement II are correct.
(b) Both Statement I and Statement II are incorrect.
(c) Statement I is correct but Statement II is incorrect.
(d) Statement I is incorrect but Statement II is correct.

17. Causes of the peasants' revolt against exploitation and oppression are:
A. Deterioration of their economic condition due to price rise, famine, etc.
B. Upliftment of their social status
C. Economic prosperity
D. Structural changes
E. Rising aspirations of peasants to improve their condition
Choose the correct answer from the options given below:
(a) A and B only
(b) A, B, C only
(c) D and E only
(d) A, D, and E only

Read the following passage carefully and answer the question that follows:

Recently, Ghanshyam Shah (7990) published a very important and well-documented review of literature on social movements in India in which, besides other dimensions, different typologies of tribal movements have also been described. L.K. Mahapatra (1972) applies the typologies widely used for social movements to tribal movements. He describes these as (1) reactionary (2) conservative, and (3) revisionary or revolutionary. The reactionary movement tries to launch a movement to bring back 'the good old days'; whereas the conservative movement tries to maintain the status quo. The revisionary or revolutionary movements are those which are organized for 'improvement' or 'purification' of the cultural or social order by eliminating 'evil' or 'low' customs, beliefs or institutions. Surajit Sinha (1968) classifies the movements into (1) ethnic rebellion (2) reform movements (3) political autonomy movements within the Indian Union (4) secessionist movements, and (5) agrarian unrest. K.S. Singh (1983a) makes more or less the same classification except that he uses the terms *Sanskritization* instead of reform movement and cultural movements instead of ethnic movements. For brevity, Ghanashyam Shah (ibid) has reformulated the typologies as follows: (1) ethnic movements (2) agrarian movements and (3) political movements. Not only is there a great deal of overlapping among all three types, but they are also interconnected and one leads to the other.

18. L.K. Mahapatra describes social and tribal movements as:
(a) Ethnographic conservative and innovative
(b) Reactionary, innovative, and evolutionary
(c) Reactionary, conservative, and revisionary
(d) None of the above

19. Who has recently published a well-documented review of literature on social movements In India?
(a) L.K. Mahapatra
(b) Ghanshyam Shah
(c) K.S. Singh
(d) All the above

20. The reactionary movement tries to launch a movement to:
(a) Bring back the good old days.
(b) Maintain the status quo
(c) Eliminate evil or low customs, beliefs or institutions.
(d) All the above

21. Who among the following has not classified and described social movements in India?
(a) Surajit Sinha
(b) K.S. Singh
(c) Ghanshyam Shah
(d) Dipankar Gupta

22. Who among the following has not classified and described social movements in India?
(a) Surajit Sinha
(b) K. S. Singh
(c) Ghanshyam Shah
(d) Dipankar Gupta

DEC 2021 & JUNE 2022

23. Match List-I with List-II:

List I (Tribe)	List II (Dormitories)
A. Gonds	I. Kichuki
B. Oraon	II. Dhumkuria
C. Bhutia	III. Gotul
D. Angami Naga	IV. Rangbang

Choose the **correct answer** from the options given below:

(a) A - II, B - III, C - I, D - IV
(b) A - III, B - II, C - IV, D - I
(c) A - I, B - IV, C - II, D - III
(d) A - I, B - II, C - III, D – IV

24. Which is the largest form of Urban life today?
(a) Edge city
(b) Megalopolis
(c) Metropolis
(d) None of the above

25. Match List-I with List-II

List I	List II
A. A person enumerated outside the place of normal residence	I. Migrant
B. Spouses and children joining the migrant in due course	II. Forced migration
C. Persons displaced by war or violence	III. Seasonal migration
D. Persons seeking work each year for a short time in a place other than their IV. normal residence	IV. Associative

Choose the **correct answer** from the options given below:

(a) A - I, B - IV, C - II, D - III
(b) A - I, B - III, C - IV, D - II
(c) A - I, B - II, C - III, D - IV
(d) A -I, B - II, C - IV, D – III

26. "Conurbation" means:
(a) A cluster of cities and towns forming a continuous network
(b) A confluence of different cultures
(c) A process by which identities are formed
(d) None of the above

27. Which one of the following was NOT a direct cause of the decline of the pre-British village artisan industries?

(a) Introduction of railways
(b) Growth of modern Industries in India
(c) Introduction of money economy in India
(d) Development of road transportation system

28. According to Louis Wirth, the following variables are important in making urban life impersonal:
A. Location
B. Affluence
C. Size
D. Density
E. Heterogeneity

Choose the correct answer from the options given below:
(a) A, B and C only
(b) B, C and D only
(c) C, D and E only
(d) A, C and E only

29. A. Fantasy city is a type of city in which great emphasis is placed on creating a spectacle, especially for consumption, leisure and tourism.
B. Edge cities are located at the innermost rings of large cities.
C. Megacities are cities with populations greater than 10 million people.
D. Megalopolis is a cluster of scantly populated cities that can stretch over great distances.
E. Metropolis is a large, powerful and cuturally influential urban area consisting of a central city and surrounding suburbs.

Choose the correct answer from the options given below:
(a) A only
(b) A and B only
(c) C and E only
(d) A, C and E only

30. Match List-I with List-II

List I (Thinkers)	List II (Concept/Theory)
A. Georg Simmel	I. Network Society
B. Louis Wirth	II. Metropolis and Mental life
C. Manuel Castells	III. Gesellschaft
D. Ferdinand Tönnies	IV. Urbanism as a way of life

Choose the correct answer from the options given below:
(a) A - II, B - IV, C - I, D - III
(b) A - II, B - IV, C - III, D - I
(c) A - IV, B - III, C - I, D - II
(d) A - III, B - IV, C - II, D - I

31. Which were the general land tenure systems prevalent in rural India before independence?
A. Jamindari
B. Sajhedari
C. Ryotwari
D. Hawaldari
E. Mahelwari

Choose the correct answer from the options given below:
(a) A, B and C only (b) B, C and D only
(c) C, D and E only (d) A, C and E only

JUNE 2021

32. Wangala village in Mysore was studied by which scholar?
(a) A. C. Mayer (b) M. Opler
(c) T. S. Epstein (d) H. S. Dhillon

33. Who said, "empty land sitting useless –if homeless people can live there", what is wrong?
(a) J. E. Perlman (b) R. Neurwirth
(c) V. Dupont (d) Ratna N. Rao

34. A megacity is one whose population is
(a) 15 million or more
(b) 10 million or more
(c) 5 million or more
(d) 1 million or more

35. Of the following, who has not worked on the functioning of the Jajmani system as a binding force among castes?
A. W. H. Wiser
B. K. Ishwaran
C. M. Opler
D. K. Gough
E. S. C. Dube

Choose the correct answer from the options given below:
(a) A and C only (b) C only
(c) D only (d) E only

36. Match List I with List II

List I (Authors)	List II (Books)
A. J. W. de Wit	I. Sociology of Slum
B. Vinit Mukhija	II. Shadow Cities: A Billion Squatters, A New Urban World
C. Robert Neuwirth	III. Policy, Poverty and Politics in Madras Slums
D. M. S. Dhadave	IV. Squatters as Developers? Slum Redevelopment in Mumbai

Choose the correct answer from the options given below:

(a) A–I, B–II, C–III, D–IV
(b) A–III, B–IV, C–II, D–I
(c) A–IV, B–II, C–I, D–III
(a) A–II, B–III, C–IV, D–I

37. Arrange the following states according to their level of urbanization in descending order as per the Census 2011

A. Himachal Pradesh
B. Tamil Nadu
C. Gujarat
D. Haryana
E. Punjab

Choose the correct answer from the options given below

(a) B, C, E, D, A
(b) A, C, D, B, E
(c) C, D, B, A, E
(d) E, D, C, A, B

JUNE 2020

38. Which one of the following is not a characteristic of a census town?

(a) A minimum population of 5000
(b) At least 75% of the male working population engaged in Non-agricultural occupations
(c) Presence of municipality/corporation cantonment board or notified town
(d) A density of population of at least 400 persons per sq. km.

39. Which one of the following is the least urbanized state in India?

(a) Bihar (b) Himachal Pradesh
(c) Assam (d) Odisha

40. During which decade increase in the total urban population was more than the total increase in the rural population of India?

(a) 1991–2001 (b) 2001–2011
(c) 1971–1981 (d) 1981–1991

41. Among the following which book is not written by M.N. Srinivas?

(a) India's Changing Villages
(b) India's Villages
(c) Social Change in modern India
(d) The Remembered Village

42. De-peasantization essentially means:

(a) the shrinking size of peasant's practices or small producers from the land
(b) the condition in which a person or community takes up corporate farming
(c) the condition in which a person changes his occupation and marriage pattern
(d) the condition in which a person becomes a millionaire

43. According to T. Shanin which of the following are characteristics of peasant societies?

(1) Family labour
(2) Production for Market
(3) Agriculture as a way of life
(4) Dependence on Urban means
(5) Underdog position

Choose the most appropriate answer from the options given below:

(a) 1, 2, and 3 only
(b) 1, 3, and 5 only
(c) 2, 3, and 4 only
(d) 3, 4, and 5 only

44. Which two of the following conditions are a must for an "Urban agglomeration"?

(1) Statutory Town
(2) Census Town
(3) All constituents must have 20,000 or more persons
(4) A degree college
(5) Primary Health Centre

Choose the most appropriate answer from the options given below:

(a) 1 and 2 only
(b) 1 and 3 only
(c) 2 and 4 only
(d) 1 and 5 only

45. Match List I with List II:

List I (Concept)	List II (Proponent)
A. Little and Great Tradition	I. Sorokin and Zimmerman
B. Parochalization and Universalization	II. M.N. Srinivas
C. Rural-Urban continuum	III. Robert Redfield
D. Sanskritization and Westernization	IV. Mckim Marriot

Choose the correct answer from the options given below:

	A	B	C	D
(a)	III	I	II	IV
(b)	I	IV	III	II
(c)	I	II	IV	III
(d)	IV	II	I	III

46. Match List I with II:

List I (Scholars)	List II (Work)
A. Oscar Lewis	I. Right to the City
B. Louis Wirth	II. Culture of Poverty
C. Janice Perlman	III. Myth of Marginality
D. David Harvey	IV. Urbanism

Choose the correct answer from the options given below:

	A	B	C	D
(a)	II	IV	III	I
(b)	III	II	IV	I
(c)	I	III	II	IV
(d)	IV	I	III	II

47. Match List I with List II:

List I (Works)	List II (Author/editor)
(1) India's Changing Villages	(i) M.N. Srinivas
(2) A Rajasthan Village	(ii) S.C. Dube
(3) The Remembered Village	(iii) McKim Marriott
(4) Village India	(iv) B.R. Chauhan

Choose the correct answer from the options given below:

(a) (1)-(i), (2)-(ii), (3)-(iii), (4)-(iv)
(b) (1)-(ii), (2)-(iii), (3)-(iv), (4)-(i)
(c) (1)-(ii), (2)-(iv), (3)-(i), (4)-(iii)
(d) (1)-(iv), (2)-(i), (3)-(ii), (4)-(iii)

48. Find the chronological sequence of the following.
(1) Implementation of Panchayat Raj
(2) Integrated Rural Development Programme
(3) Reservation of seats in Village Panchayats
(4) Community Development Programme

Choose the correct answer from the options given below:

(a) 1, 2, 3, 4 (b) 2, 3, 4, 1
(c) 3, 4, 1, 2 (d) 4, 1, 2, 3

49. Arrange the following cities according to their ranking in cleanliness given by the Ministry of Urban Development on the basis of the cleanliness index, 2017.
(1) Surat
(2) Bhopal
(3) Indore
(4) Vishakhapatnam

Choose the correct answer from the options given below:

(a) 1, 3, 4, and 2 (b) 3, 2, 4, and 1
(c) 2, 3, 4, and 1 (d) 4, 2, 3, and 1

50. In which census year data on slums was collected for the first time?
(a) 1991 (b) 2011
(c) 2001 (d) 1981

51. How many towns/cities were surveyed, and reported having a slum population in 2001?
(1) 740 (2) 743
(3) 540 (4) 640

Choose the correct answer from the options given below:

(a) 1 and 2 (b) 2 and 4
(c) 2 and 3 (d) 1 and 4

52. Calculate the % of Towns / Cities having slum population out of the total number of towns/Cities according to the census 2001.
(a) 15% (b) 12.3%
(c) 14.6% (d) 11.3%

53. In how many towns/cities slums were found in the 2011 census?
(a) 4041 (b) 2542
(c) 3213 (d) 7935

54. What was the slum population according to Pronab Sen Committee?
(a) 68 million (b) 93 million
(c) 170 million (d) 48 million

DECEMBER 2019

55. How many metropolises were there in India according to Census 2001?
(a) 53 (b) 35
(c) 55 (d) 17

56. The studies of Indian rural society by sociologists and social anthropologists largely focused upon:
(1) Categories of caste and community
(2) The analysis of rural and agrarian social structures
(3) Analysis of planned changes introduced by the state in the rural society
(4) Finding cultural impediments to the development of Indian rural society

Choose the correct option:

(a) 1 and 2 (b) 2 and 3
(c) 3 and 4 (d) 1 and 4

57. The earlier popular studies of Indian rural society were largely based on the interest of sociologists to:
(1) Understand Indian Village Society
(2) Document the structure of traditional Indian Village Society
(3) Understand the dynamics and change in Indian Village Society
(4) Document the contribution of Britishers to the Indian Village Society

Choose the correct option:

(a) 1 and 2 (b) 2 and 3
(c) 3 and 4 (d) 4 and 1

58. Who among the following is associated with the theory of "Urbanism as a way of life" and "Culture of Poverty"?
(1) Oscar Lewis
(2) William Foot Whyte
(3) Louis Wirth
(4) Homer Hyot

Choose the correct option:

(a) 1 and 2 (b) 1 and 3
(c) 3 and 1 (d) 3 and 4

59. Which of the following were the slum populations in India in 2001 and 2011 Census Years?

(1) 40.6 million (2) 42.6 million
(3) 68.0 million (4) 72.0 million

Choose the correct option:

(a) 1 and 2 (b) 2 and 3
(c) 3 and 4 (d) 1 and 4

60. Which two of the following are associated with the 'Right to City' and 'Slums' study?

(1) M. N. Srinivas
(2) H. Lefebvre
(3) R. Neuwirth
(4) I. P. Desai

Choose the correct option:

(a) 1 and 4 (b) 2 and 3
(c) 3 and 4 (d) 2 and 4

61. Which two of the following states are the most urbanized and least urbanized in India?

(1) Tamil Nadu
(2) Kerala
(3) Himachal Pradesh
(4) Assam

Choose the correct option:

(a) 1 and 2 (b) 1 and 3
(c) 2 and 3 (d) 3 and 4

62. Match List I with List II

List I (Peasant Movement)	List II (Place)
A. Bardoli movement	I. Malabar
B. Moplah rebellion	II. Andhra Pradesh
C. Peasant revolt in Telangana	III. Bengal
D. Tebhaga movement	IV. Gujarat

Choose the correct option:

(a) A – I, B - III, C - IV, D – II
(b) A – II, B - III, C - IV, D – I
(c) A – I, B - II, C - III, D – IV
(d) A – IV, B - I, C - II, D – III

63. Arrange the below-given states according to their level of urbanization in descending order:

(1) Tamil Nadu
(2) Maharashtra
(3) Kerala
(4) Punjab

Choose the correct option:

(a) 1, 2, 4, 3 (b) 1, 3, 2, 4
(c) 3, 1, 2, 4 (d) 1, 4, 2, 3

64. Arrange the following forms of urban areas in ascending order:

(1) Megacity
(2) Meta city
(3) Metropolis
(4) City

Choose the correct option:

(a) 1, 3, 2, 4 (b) 4, 3, 1, 2
(c) 2, 3, 4, 1 (d) 1, 2, 3, 4

65. Arrange the following mega cities in descending order according to their rate of growth during 2001–2011

(1) Kolkata Urban Agglomeration
(2) Greater Mumbai Agglomeration
(3) Delhi Urban Agglomeration

Choose the correct option:

(a) 3, 1, 2 (b) 1, 3, 2
(c) 2, 3, 1 (d) 1, 2, 3

66. What is the correct sequence of the publication year of the following books on Indian Rural Society?

(1) An Indian Village
(2) A Rajasthan Village
(3) India's Changing Villages
(4) The Remembered Village

Choose the correct option:

(a) 1, 2, 3, 4 (b) 2, 3, 4, 1
(c) 1, 3, 2, 4 (d) 3, 4, 1, 2

67. In which respect(s) Indian villages are undergoing change?

(1) Economic institutions
(2) Leadership style
(3) Relationships among castes
(4) Familial relationships

Choose the correct option:

(a) 1 and 2 (b) 2 and 3
(c) 1 and 3 (d) 2 and 4

68. Which of the following has a great impact on the units of social structure in the villages of India?

(a) Legislations
(b) Land reforms
(c) Education
(d) Political processes

69. Which are the measures of land reforms that have been implemented in the villages in India?

(1) Ceiling on land holding
(2) Panchayati Raj
(3) Bhoodan
(4) Law of Inheritance

Choose the correct option

(a) 1 and 2 (b) 2 and 3
(c) 1 and 3 (d) 2 and 4

70. How land reforms in different regions of India have been implemented?

(a) At the same time
(b) In the same manner
(c) Differently but at the same time
(d) Differently in different states at varying times

JUNE 2019

71. Two statements are given below. One is labeled as Assertion (A) and the other as Reason (R).

Assertion (A): Gated enclaves represent high income group residential areas.

Reason (R): Only rich can afford to live in such enclosures.

Choose the correct option:

(a) Both (A) and (R) are true and (R) is the correct explanation of (A)
(b) Both (A) and (R) are true and (R) is not the correct explanation of (A)
(c) (A) is true but (R) is false
(d) (A) is false but (R) is true

72. Which of the following states has the highest percentage of the metropolitan population in relation to the total urban population of the state?

(a) Kerala (b) Maharashtra
(c) Gujarat (d) West Bengal

73. By which year New Delhi is estimated to be the most populous city in the world?

(a) 2050 (b) 2040
(c) 2030 (d) 2025

74. Which of the following is NOT an attribute of rural society?

(a) Predominance of the natural environment
(b) Agrarian economy
(c) Manufacturing and industry
(d) Joint family

75. Who has applied Robert Redfield's concept of 'Little and Great Tradition' to understand Indian society?

(a) S. C. Dube (b) Yogendra Singh
(c) T. K. Oommen (d) Milton Singer

76. Given below are two statements, one labeled as Assertion (A) and the other as Reason (R):

Assertion (A): The absolute increase in population is more in urban areas than in rural areas during the 2001-2011 decade.

Reason (R): It is due to migration.

Select the correct answer from the options given below:

(a) Both (A) and (R) are true and (R) is the correct explanation of (A)
(b) Both (A) and (R) are true and (R) is not the correct explanation of (A)
(c) (A) is true, but (R) is false
(d) (A) is false, but (R) is true

77. The estate system is more often associated with

(a) ancient society (b) socialism
(c) feudalism (d) capitalist society

78. Who has written/edited the book, Peasants and Peasant Societies?

(a) Eric Wolf (b) Oscar Lewis
(c) Robert Redfield (d) Theodor Shanin

79. Who refers to Indian villages as 'Little Republics'?

(a) Lord Ripon
(b) Charles Metcalfe
(c) Lord Macaulay
(d) Jawaharlal Nehru

80. Who is the author of the book, Rural Development: Putting the Last First?

(a) Robert Pritnam
(b) Jane Krippers Black
(c) Dadabhai Naoroji
(d) Robert Chambers

Answer Key

1. (b)	13. (c)	25. (a)	37. (a)	49. (b)	61. (b)	73. (c)
2. (c)	14. (c)	26. (a)	38. (c)	50. (c)	62. (d)	74. (c)
3. (b)	15. (c)	27. (c)	39. (b)	51. (b)	63. (b)	75. (d)
4. (a)	16. (a)	28. (c)	40. (b)	52. (b)	64. (b)	76. (b)
5. (d)	17. (d)	29. (d)	41. (a)	53. (b)	65. (a)	77. (c)
6. (a)	18. (c)	30. (a)	42. (a)	54. (b)	66. (c)	78. (d)
7. (c)	19. (b)	31. (d)	43. (b)	55. (b)	67. (c)	79. (b)
8. (a)	20. (a)	32. (c)	44. (b)	56. (a)	68. (b)	80. (d)
9. (d)	21. (d)	33. (b)	45. (b)	57. (a)	69. (c)	
10. (a)	22. (d)	34. (b)	46. (a)	58. (c)	70. (d)	
11. (c)	23. (b)	35. (c)	47. (c)	59. (b)	71. (a)	
12. (a)	24. (b)	36. (b)	48. (d)	60. (b)	72. (a)	

Unit-V

State Politics and Development

CHAPTERS:

CHAPTER 1 Political Processes in India

CHAPTER 2 Social Movements and Protests

Top: Photo credit: bestdesign36 / 123RF

Below: Photo Credit: stoatphoto / Shutterstock

CHAPTER

1 Political Processes in India

LEARNING OBJECTIVES:

In this chapter, we will discuss the following important topics.

- Tribe, nation-state and border
- States Reorganization and Federalism in India
- Bureaucracy, Governance, and Development
- Public policy
- Political culture
- Grassroots democracy, Panchayati Raj under the 73rd Constitutional Amendment
- Law and Society
- Gender and development
- Corruption, Role of International Development Organizations

INTRODUCTION

Political process is the formulation and administration of public policy, usually done by interaction between social groups and political institutions, or between political leadership and public opinion. India, like any other third world country, after gaining independence from colonial rule, was engaged in a project of nation-building. But to carry out the project of nation building with the main objective of achieving democracy and development amidst ethnic diversities in the country. India has diversity in terms of caste, religious, tribal groups, linguistic groups and regional development. These diverse cultural groups in a country can pose a real challenge to the nation-building process.

TRIBE, NATION-STATE, AND BORDER

Tribe

Tribe is defined as a social group bound together by kin and duly associated with a particular territory having a common dialect. The members of the tribe consider themselves to be descended from a common ancestor and hence all the members are related by blood relation. The members of a tribe are generally endogamous and have a common culture and religion. They may also have independent heads or heads in whom social authority is vested. The replacement of customary law with formal law results in the establishment of a nation-state. The members of a tribe have a sense of unity, especially in time of external aggression.

Tribal Identity

Tribal populations are part of the diversity of India. But it was recognized that the tribal situation was very unique and a different approach was needed to deal with these issues.

There were mainly two approaches:

1. Isolationist
2. Assimilationist

The isolationist approach by Verrier Elwin and others advocated that the tribes should be isolated from the mainstream population and efforts were made to restrict the contact of tribes and outsiders. This would preserve tribal identity and their way of life.

On the other hand, the assimilationist approach favoured by Ghurye and Thakkar Baba advocated the assimilating of the tribes into the mainstream. They argued that most tribes were anyway part of India culturally and socially, and hence should be made part of the Indian mainstream.

Majumdar's model advocated that the mainstream and tribes can learn from each other's cultures, leading to a better quality of life. For example, the tribes can learn how to manage their assets and money while the mainstream society can learn certain aspects from tribes like the delayed age of marriage. However, the advocates of these approaches were non-tribes who had experienced tribal life from the outside.

T. K. Oommen in his work '*Insiders and Outsiders; Primordial Collectivism and Cultural Pluralism in Nation-Building*', said tribes in India is socially and culturally different from others.

i. Tribes are no longer isolated from non-tribes. Contact between the tribes and non-tribes is increasing due to migration and forced displacement. Everyday experiences in interacting with others are as important as government legislation ensuring equality and protection, in defining tribal perception of themselves and non-tribes.

ii. Tribal and non-tribal interactions take place in rural as well as urban areas. In rural areas, a number of studies have shown that the tribal experience has been largely negative. It has increased tribal alienation and caused frustration and anger among them.

Raja Kanti Das' studies of Oraons in Midnapore showed that the Oraons were adopting certain elements of Hinduism from their neighbours as an adaptive measure while striving for maintaining their identity and community organizations.

In urban areas, the nature of contact between the tribal and non-tribal has been different because of the relative anonymity prevailing in the cities. However, we see here too that people's perception of tribal people has negatively influenced the interaction patterns. Stereotypes about tribes are found in the language, representations, and nature of interactions in everyday situations.

Nation

A nation is a body of people belonging to a particular region. It is a nationality that has organized itself as a political body that is either independent or aspires to be independent. The nation reflects a consciousness of unity inspired by psychological and spiritual feelings that may or may not be sovereign. The physical element of sovereignty is not as important as the psychological element of a sense of unity.

A nation, in the sense of a common ethnicity, may include a diaspora or refugee who lives outside the nation-state, some nations in this sense do not have a state where ethnicity prevails. In a more general sense, a nation-state is simply a large, politically sovereign country or administrative territory.

Nation-State

A nation-state is a state in which a large majority share a common culture and are conscious of it. The nation-state is a concept in which cultural boundaries coincide with political boundaries.

According to a definition, "a nation-state is a sovereign state most of whose subjects are united by factors that define a nation such as a language or common ancestry." It is a more precise concept than "country", as a country need not have a dominant ethnic group.

Therefore, the most important attributes of a state are:

i. Territory
ii. Government
iii. Sovereignty

Therefore, members of a state can be of different nationalities. Nationality is subjective, statehood is objective. Nationality is psychological, statehood is political. Nationality is a state of mind while statehood is a condition of law. Nationality is a spiritual right while statehood is an enforceable obligation. Sovereignty is emphasized as an essential element of the state, not of the nation.

Border Issues with Tribes

Dr. Ajay Sahni, Executive Director of the Institute for Conflict Management, has done an extensive study on tribal conflicts in North East and found that there are three types of tribal conflicts:

i. Tribal conflicts with other tribal communities,
ii. Tribal conflicts with non-tribes, and
iii. Tribal conflicts with state agencies including police and military.

The major issues of tribal and non-tribal conflict have been discussed below.

Land Issues: Tribes in India have come in contact with outsiders throughout history. However, it was during the colonial period that the contact became common resulting in several conflicts Tribal land has been often communally owned rather than individually owned. However, under colonial law land had to be owned individually. Tribal land was alienated and unfortunately, the process continued even after India became independent.

Settling of Outsiders on Tribal Land: Outsiders (Non-tribes) have increasingly settled in tribal areas. The main reasons for this are the following: (i) tribal land is rich in natural resources (ii) Mining and development activities have increased job opportunities (iii) increase population and pressure on land, and (iv) the perception that tribes are gullible and can be exploited.

Myron Weiner in Sons of the Soil; Migration and Ethnic Conflict in India gives us an idea of tribal perception of the tribal themselves on the outsiders. They feel that the outsiders are not part of their community and are exploiting them.

Amita Baviskar asserts that the conflict between the state and the tribes is not only a right to livelihood but is also a clash of cultures. A culture that sees land and environment as assets to be exploited for development and a tribal culture that has learned to live with nature harmoniously.

For Instance, India, Pakistan, and Bangladesh are three nation-states born of British India, the division of colonial India into two countries was based on the criterion of religion the Muslim majority regions became Pakistan. And in 1971, Pakistan itself was divided and a new nation emerged – Bangladesh. The boundaries of these nations have divided many ethnic communities and placed them under different nation-states.

Members of these communities feel strongly that all their members should live together under one nation-state. For example, the Nagas are found in India and Burma. One of the demands of Naga separatists is that all Nagas unite under one state. Similar demands have been made by other separatist groups also.

STATES REORGANIZATION AND FEDERALISM IN INDIA

A Federal system of governance is a way of managing India, a vast country with its diversity. It is also a strategy to manage regional aspirations, some of which in the early days after independence had separatist tendencies. The main principle for awarding statehood is the linguistic basis- a common language.

The Government of India reorganized Assam and created Nagaland (1963), Meghalaya (1972), Mizoram (U.T. in 1972 and full-fledged statehood in 1987), and Manipur (1972). But often many areas in these regions are inhabited by more than one group which causes problems.

The tribal areas are even more pluralistic with a number of communities cohabiting in the same area. It is impossible to divide regions according to one community and grant statehood.

For example, in Manipur, the hills are dominated by the Nagas and the plains by Meiteis. The Nagas wants to integrate their areas into the state of Nagaland. But the division of Manipur will anger the people of the plains and some smaller non-Naga communities of the hills.

Similarly, the Santhals are divided between the states of Orissa, Madhya Pradesh, Bengal, and Chhattisgarh. In such a situation, the state's official language and medium of instruction in schools are in non-tribal language leading to the alienation of tribes.

The complex situation cannot be solved easily as granting statehood to the dominant often creates more problems than it addresses. The example of the division of the State of Assam into smaller states did not solve all problems of that region.

Administrative Arrangements, Inefficiency, and Insensitivity

Tribal communities during British rule were given considerable freedom to manage their own affairs. The autonomy given to these areas allowed the British to claim these areas as being under their control without using their administrative and military resources.

Separatists in the Northeast often justify their demand for a separate nation-state by claiming that the accession of the tribal areas was not legal and properly done. The consent of the people was not taken when it was determined whether these areas should join the Indian union.

Administrative inefficiency and insensitivity have contributed to the alienation of the tribal people. The use of armed forces to quell militancy has resulted in complaints of human rights violations.

BUREAUCRACY, GOVERNANCE, AND DEVELOPMENT

Bureaucracy is the machinery, which implements rational-legal authority. Max Weber studied bureaucracy in detail and constructed an ideal type that contained the most prominent characteristics of bureaucracy.

Alvin Gouldner led an ethnographic study in a mine and identified three various patterns of bureaucracy and bureaucratization.

- **i.** Mock bureaucracy: this type comes from an outside agency and is implemented officially, but not in daily behaviors. Both management and workers agree in this case to act the same way. The rules are enforced in this case, neither by management nor by the workers.
- **ii.** Representative bureaucracy: both management and workers enforced this rule and it generated very little tension. In this context, the focus was on the education of workers as management considered them as ignorant and careless regarding security rules. Meetings happened regularly to implement this program and it was as well the occasion to voice some concerns for workers. For the management, this program was a way to tighten the control over workers.
- **iii.** Punishment-centered bureaucracy: this type of program was initiated by management and generated many tensions. Management viewed workers as deliberately willing to be absent. Therefore, the punishment was installed in order to force the workers not to be absent. For example, the "no-absenteeism" rule is an example of a punishment-centered bureaucracy.

Robert Michels, in his *'iron law of oligarchy,'* postulates that intensifying complexity and bureaucratization of modern organisations are leading to the concentration of power at the top level, in the hands of a few who tend to rule in a dictatorial manner. He holds the increasing size of modern organisations and the increasing complexity of the problems responsible for this. The position of the topmost officials turns out to be invincible.

The Italian Marxist Bruno Rizzi in *'The Bureaucratization of the World'* (1939) argues that the Soviet bureaucracy constituted a new ruling class that exploited the proletariat as much as the capitalists had in the past. It differed from capitalism only in that the new type of domination was based not on the individual but on group ownership of the means of production.

Governance

The term, governance, is derived from the Greek term, kubernao, which means 'to steer'. So, governance is the process that steers the affairs of the State.

In ancient times, the Greek philosopher, Plato, also used the term, governance. A close examination of the literature on governance reveals that the term came into the limelight with the publication of the World Bank's report on sub-Sahara in 1989.

The World Bank report coined the term 'crisis of governance'. Thus, the focus was cast on improving governance by improving managerial and administrative competencies. Further, in 1992, the World Bank, in its publication, The World Development Report, focused on the renewed meaning of governance through a reconceptualization of the role of the State. It advocated an efficient and effective administrative state that is detached from its earlier omnipresent involvement in economic and administrative matters.

From the above discussion, it can be deduced that the different problems relating to administration can be tackled by institutions of the state, and by other actors as well.

Jon Pierre comments, in his book, *Debating Governance*, that the process of governance is no longer state-centric and that other actors have, also, emerged as critical players.

Stoker has identified the following features of governance while summarizing various perspectives on governance.

- **i.** It refers to a complex set of institutions and actors that are drawn not only from the government but from beyond.
- **ii.** Governance identifies the power dependence involved in the relationship between institutions that are involved in collective action.
- **iii.** It recognizes the blurring of boundaries and responsibilities for tackling social and economic issues.
- **iv.** It is about autonomous self-governing networks of actors.
- **v.** Governance ensures that the government is able to use new tools and techniques to steer and guide.

Prof. Kuldeep Mathur opines in his book, *From Government to Governance*, that governance is concerned with changes taking place in the organization of the state, and with changes in its relationship with the private sector and civil society actors (Mathur, 2009).

The World Bank defines governance as, 'The exercise of political authority, and the use of institutional resources to manage the society's problems and affairs.

'The World Bank interprets governance as the institutional capacity of public organizations to provide public and other goods demanded by a country's citizens in an effective, transparent, impartial, and accountable manner, subject to resource constraints.

Government and Governance

The concept of the state occupies a central place in discourses on politics and administration. Government is a critical and inseparable element of the state. The government is a constitutionally responsible state for administration through various institutions to ensure a better society and improved lives of citizens. So, the focus is on the state, and the state remains the principal actor in the entire process of administration.

In the course of administration, the government creates a relationship between its various institutions and citizens. The nature of this relationship depends on the nature of the state, e.g., whether it is a military state, autocratic state, democratic state, or any other form.

Moreover, the relationship between the state, the market, and civil society haveundergone rapid and huge change all over the world. With this background, 'governance' is recognised as an important concept in recent years both by the nation-states as well as by the international agencies giving funds for developing activities.

In India, it has gained prominence in academics, as well as other arenas, after the launch of liberal economic policies in 1991. As far as the meaning of the concept is concerned, it can be said that an exact inon of the concept of governance is still elusive.

However, there are various interpretations of the concept, and they seem to converge on a broad meaning, i.e., reform in the governing process for better and improved policy outcomes. So, the meanings include building and strengthening the capacities of various institutions of the state or public institution; encouraging and facilitating the participation of common citizens in the governing process.

But, with the beginning of the liberal economic policies, another actor, called the market, has entered into the scenario. Many people believe that the market has emerged as a viable alternative to the state as the latter has failed in ensuring effective development policies, and their proper implementation.

So, in this context, the meaning of governance includes the reduction of the role of the State in economic activities as well as the promotion of the role of the market.

Governance has a clear relationship to the redefinition of the role of the state in India. In many advanced countries, the redefinition of the role of the state has a direct bearing on the conceptualization of the term governance.

Governance and Development

The term development is closely related to the process of governance. Every state in the world initiates a series of development activities in order to bring about a positive change in the economy, society, and the lives of its citizens. In the entire process of development, the state has played a dominant role.

The United Nations General Assembly 2005 World Summit outcome envisaged that "...good governance is essential for sustainable development; that sound economic policies, solid democratic institutions responsive to the needs of the people, and improved infrastructure are the basis for sustained economic growth, poverty eradication, and employment creation; and peace and security, domestic stability, respects for human rights, including the right to development, the rule of law, gender equality and market-oriented policies and an overall commitment to just and democratic societies are also essential and mutually arcing".

The Asian Development Bank, while emphasizing the role of governance in development mentioned that poor governance holds back and distorts the process of development, and has a disproportionate impact on the poorer and weaker Governance: An Overview sections of society. Therefore, assisting developing countries in improving governance is a strategic priority of the ADB in eliminating poverty in Asia and the Pacific. The four key areas of the interrelationship between governance and development identified by the ADB:

- **i.** Accountability
- **ii.** Participation
- **iii.** Predictability
- **iv.** Transparency

Generally speaking, development implies the process of improving the standard of living and wellbeing of citizens by raising per capita income. Per capita income is definitely an important parameter of development, but the question is, how much benefit has it provided to common citizens in terms of availing the basic elements of life, such as health and education is an aspect to be taken into consideration.

Nobel prize winner Amartya Sen has contributed significantly towards changing the meaning of development and making it a broad and inclusive concept. He argued that one way of seeing development is in terms of the expansion of the real freedoms that the citizens enjoy to pursue the objectives, they have reason to value, and in this sense, the expansion of human capability can be, broadly, seen as the central feature of the process of development.

Governance and Globalization

The concept was again strengthened with the beginning of the process of globalization. It got additional emphasis with the beginning of the process of globalisation. Hence, the state-centric approach has changed, and the meaning of governance has also changed with the rise of the market as a player in development.

The market involves international and aid-providing agencies, and, with the rise to prominence of the market, these organizations have emerged as powerful players.

These agencies interpret governance as the set of guiding principles to improve and strengthen the capacity of the recipient countries towards better and effective implementation of development initiatives.

There is a quest for an alternative framework for policy making and implementation. Thus, with globalisation, a new set of actors, such as the state and its institutions, the market, civic organizations, and citizens have emerged.

This has resulted in a new pattern of relationship between these actors, giving a new twist to the meaning of the term, governance. It may be said that governance implies a renewed pattern of relationships between these actors.

PUBLIC POLICY

Public policy is a frequently used term in our daily life and in academic literature, where we often make references to national health policy, education policy, wage policy, agricultural policy, foreign policy, and so on. It is an area, which had to do with those spheres that are labelled as public. The concept of public policy presupposes that there is a domain of life that is not private or purely individual, but common.

Thomas Dye, a leading scholar of policy analysis, observes, 'Traditional (political science) studies described the institutions in which public policy was formulated. But unfortunately, the linkages between important institutional arrangements and the content of public policy were largely unexplored.'

- He further notes that today the focus of political science is shifting to public policy, that is, to the description and explanation of the causes and consequences of government activity.
- The study of public policy has evolved into what is virtually a new branch of social science, it is called policy science. This concept of policy science was first formulated by Harold Lasswell in 1951.

i. The Idea of Public

It is first important to understand the concept of 'public' for a discussion of public policy. We often use such terms as 'public interest', 'public sector', 'public opinion', 'public health', and so on. 'The starting point is that 'public policy' has to do with those spheres, which are so labelled as 'public'. The public dimension is generally referred to as 'public ownership' or control for 'public purpose.'

ii. The Concept of Policy

Like the idea of 'public', the concept of 'policy' Is not a precise term. Policy denotes, among other elements, guidance for action. It may take the form of a declaration of goals; a declaration of course of action; a declaration of general purpose; and an authoritative decision.

Hogwood and Gunn specify ten uses of the term 'policy', that is policy as a label for a field of activity; an expression of the desired state of affairs; specific proposals; decisions of government; formal authorisation; a programme; an output; an outcome; a theory or model; and a process. Unfortunately, the policy itself is something, which takes different forms. There is a thrust to designate policy as the 'outputs' of the political system, and to a lesser degree to define public policy as more or less inter-dependent policies dealing with different activities.

James Anderson suggests that policy be regarded as "a purposive course of action followed by an actor or set of actors in dealing with a problem or matter of concern".

David Easton defines public policy as "the authoritative allocation of values for the whole society". Public policies are formulated by what Easton calls the "authorities" in a political system, namely, "elders, paramount chiefs, executives, legislators, judges, administrators, councilors, monarchs, and the like".

POLITICAL CULTURE

Political culture describes how culture affects the political system; each political system is embedded in a particular political culture. Political culture is the set of attitudes, beliefs, and feelings that give order and meaning to a political process and that provide the underlying beliefs and rules that govern behavior in a political system. It encompasses both the political ideals and the operational norms of a polity.

Political culture, in political science, is a set of shared views and normative judgments held by a population regarding its political system. The notion of political culture does not refer to attitudes toward specific actors, such as the president or prime minister, but rather refers to how people view the political system as a whole and their belief in its legitimacy.

American political scientist Lucian Pye defined political culture as the combination of basic values, feelings, and knowledge that influenced the political process. Therefore, the building blocks of political culture are citizens' beliefs, opinions, and feelings toward their government.

Political culture has been most intensively studied in the context of the established democratic system of the west, the most notable study of political culture is 'The Civic Culture: Political Attitudes and Democracy in Five Nations' (1963) by American political scientists Gabriel Almond and Sidney Verba. Based on surveys conducted in the United States, Britain, West Germany, Italy, and Mexico, this historical investigation sought to identify the political culture within which liberal democracy is most likely to grow and strengthen.

Almond and Verba's argument is based on a distinction between three pure types of political culture: parochial political culture, subject political culture, and participant political culture.

1. In a parochial political culture, citizens are only implicitly aware of the existence of a central government. For example, tribal societies have few or no specialized political roles and low expectations for political change.
2. In a subject political culture, citizens view themselves not as participants in the political process but as subjects of the government. For example, totalitarian political structures, in which citizens have a high cognitive, affective, and evaluative orientation towards the political system with no active participation.
3. In a participatory political culture, citizens believe they can contribute to the system and are affected by it. For example, citizens of the United Kingdom and the United States, are well-informed and actively participate in the political process.

Daniel J. Eleazar identified three types of political culture:

1. Individualistic culture—In which politics is a marketplace between individuals seeking to maximize their self-interest, with minimal community involvement and opposition to the government, as well as a high degree of patronage.
2. Moralistic culture—Whereby government is seen as important and as a way to improve people's lives.
3. Traditionalistic culture—One which seeks to preserve the status quo under which elites have all the power and citizen participation is not expected.

   Ronald Inglehart proposes that political culture can determine the political system and that there is a correlation between Protestantism or societies with high secular, rational values and high self-expression values, and stable democratization.

GRASSROOTS DEMOCRACY, PANCHAYATI RAJ UNDER THE 73RD CONSTITUTIONAL AMENDMENT

Grassroots Democracy

Grassroots democracy is a tendency towards designing political processes that shift as much decision-making authority as practical to the organization's lowest geographic or social level of organization.

Grassroots organizations can have a variety of structures depending on the type of organization and what the members want. These can be non-structured and non-hierarchical organizations run by all members or run by members they want.

Ideally, a national grassroots organization would place as much decision-making power as possible in the hands of local people or common members instead of any centralized head office. The principle is that for democratic power to be best exercised it must be vested in a local community and common members rather than isolated individuals at the top of the organization.

Grassroots organizations can act as a building block for participatory systems. Grassroots systems are different from representative systems in many aspects. Grassroot system allows local communities or national memberships to elect representatives who then go on to make decisions.

Grassroots Democracy in India

Panchayat as an institutional instrument of development has been a part of ancient India as a self-governing institution which had distinct and well-defined functions, for example in ancient times, the Panchayati Raj system was prevalent during the Chola period, the institution of Panchayat represented not only the collective will but also the collective wisdom of the entire rural community.

During the British period, Ripon's resolutions of 1881 and 1882 can be considered the origin of modern local government in India. It introduced a highly decentralized system of administration of justice

Mahatma Gandhi saw the panchayat system in the form of Gram Swaraj. Interestingly, Dr. B.R. Ambedkar was not in favor of Panchayati Raj institutions. Nevertheless, he agreed to place it in the Constitution of India in Part IV through the Directive Principles of State Policy.

After independence, Prime Minister Jawaharlal Nehru inaugurated the Community Development Program (CDP) on October 2, 1952, the birth anniversary of Mahatma Gandhi.

The CDP was followed by the National Extension Service in 1953. NES block was identified as the lowest unit of development of the administration. But both programs had a limitation neither CDP nor NES was free from bureaucratic control.

- This limitation prompted the government to appoint a committee in 1957 under the chairmanship of Balwant Ray Mehta. The committee recommended a three-tier system of Panchayati Raj from village to district level, Gram Panchayat at the village level, Panchayat Samiti at the block level, and Zilla Parishad at the district level.

Panchayati Raj under the 73rd Constitutional Amendment

P.V. Narasimha Rao's government enacted the 73rd Constitutional Amendment, which was passed by Parliament on 23 December 1992 and came into effect on 24 April 1993. This Act added Part - IX to the Constitution of India. It is entitled as 'Panchayats' and includes the provisions of Articles 243 to 243-O.

The Act has given practical shape to Article 40 of the Constitution and has given constitutional status to Panchayati Raj Institutions. Which states that State shall take steps to organise village panchayats and endow them with such powers and authority as may be necessary to enable them to function as units of self-government.

The Constitutional Amendment ensures a three-tier structure at the zilla, block, and village levels, an election commission to hold elections periodically.

74th Constitutional Amendment Act (CAA), 1992

74th Amendment of 1992: It was passed by Parliament in December 1992 and came into force on 1 June 1993 adding Part IX A (Articles 243-P to 243-ZG) and the 12th schedule in the Constitution.

It made municipal governments a formal part of the three-tier governing system

- **i.** Nagar Panchayat for an area in transition from rural to urban area.
- **ii.** Municipal Council for a smaller urban area.
- **iii.** Municipal Corporation for a larger urban area.

Demographic and other conditions, which are determining factors for constituting a particular type of municipality differ a great deal from one State to another. It has, therefore, been left to the State Legislatures to decide which specific type of municipality will be constituted for a particular urban area. With this amendment act 12th schedule was added to the constitution of India, this schedule has 18 items.

LAW AND SOCIETY

Social control is a concept within the disciplines of the social sciences. Social control is described as a fixed set of rules and standards in a society that bind individuals to traditional norms as well as the use of formal mechanisms. The term "social control" was first introduced into sociology by Albion Woodbury Small and George Edgar Vincent.

Law and Society is an American movement, established after World War II primarily through the initiative of sociologists who had a vested interest in the study of law.

The argument for the law and society movement is summarized by Lawrence Freedman in two short sentences, 'The law has a highly significant presence in the United States. Second, this is so important that it cannot be left to the lawyers alone'.

Its founders believed that 'the study of law and legal institutions in their social context can be constituted as a scholarly field distinguished by its commitment to interdisciplinary dialogue and multidisciplinary research methods.'

As such, 'The basic assumption behind this movement is that law is not autonomous i.e., it is not independent of the society.' While traditional legal scholars look inside the legal system to answer questions of society, the 'law and society movement' looks outside and considers the level of autonomy as an empirical question.

Furthermore, law and society scholars express deep concern with the impact that law has on society once it is enacted, a concern that is either ignored or unaddressed in the conventional legal system. The founding of the Law and Society Association in 1964 and the Law and Society Review in 1966 guaranteed the continuity of the scholarly activities of the Law and Society movement and allowed its members to influence legal education and policy-making in America.

From one perspective, the main difference between the Sociology of law and law and society is that the latter does not limit itself theoretically or methodologically to sociology and instead tries to accommodate insights from all social science disciplines. 'Not only does it provide a home for sociologists and social anthropologists and political scientists interested in law, but it also seeks to include psychologists and economists who study law.'

Another perspective says that both the sociology of law and law and society should be viewed as multidisciplinary or inter-disciplinary enterprises, although the sociology of law has a special relationship to the methods, theories, and traditions of sociology.

During the 1970s and 1980s, several studies were conducted by scholars of law and society on conflict and dispute resolution methods. For example, William Felstiner, in his early work, focused on alternative methods of resolving conflicts, employing avoidance, mediation, litigation, etc. In another study, Felstiner, along with Richard Abel and Austin Sarat, developed the idea of a conflict pyramid, naming the formula 'Naming, Blaming, Claiming', which refers to the different stages of conflict resolution and the levels of the pyramid.

GENDER AND DEVELOPMENT

Development has been differently defined as, progress, positive change in the socioeconomic position of the people, a community, or a nation.

The Marxist understanding of the primacy of the economic basis of exploitation added extra merit to such ideas.

The Libertarians like Margaret Thatcher and Ronald Reagan argued for what is known as complete freedom to the individual and the withdrawal of the state from affairs of individual freedom. They insist that it is the individual and her merit that alone counts.

The communitarian view, has gained some popularity these days due to two factors.

First, the most powerful women's movement over the last three decades has been fought by women with the help of the local communities. They have thus inspired other struggles.

Second, western aid agencies are also propagating the communitarian idea in their programmes. Often, they are projected in opposition to the state. The basic proposition is that women's development and freedom lie in the community where their rights are vested.

Ester Boserup in her work, *Woman's Role in Economic Development*, argued that the economic work of the female is never accounted for in the analysis of economic activities, the Green Revolution she says is focused on technology and training of men while conveniently forgetting the women whose work, quite a substantial economic activity in the fields.

The poor women of the Third World were doubly exploited. First, they are women and secondly, they come from Third World and poor backgrounds. Thus, class, and gender both fuse in them. Their issues were not merely related to domestic violence -or demand for sexual choices but to the very basic human development items, i.e., education, health, and employment.

It began to be argued that for the end of the subordination of the female, the beginning should be made from the lower end, i.e., the poor women of the Third World.

Critics of the Green Revolution have pointed out that it has brought uneven distribution of benefits and its emphasis on new technologies in fact was creating more inequality between men and women.

The green revolution resulted in monoculture crops, droughts, etc., and thus not only reduced food security at the local level but environmental hazards like increased salinity, etc. started affecting the lives of the people. And in all these events women faced a major casualty.

One of the most crucial issues that face the woman's question today is the relationship between larger political processes, the idea of justice, and the role of women. There is no confusion today that men's well-being depends on women's well-being.

This close relationship has been reflected in the very high human development indicators from several states in India, like Kerala, Himachal Pradesh, Tamilnadu, etc., where general improvement in the health status of women led to improvement in the health status of both the male child and the female child.

Amartya Sen has pointed out, 'freedom in one area fosters freedom in other areas as well'. Development is seen as the only way possible to bring out a positive change in the status of women and change gendered exploitation.

The Indian development experience can show that through the development process, there has been a revolutionary change in the basic indicators of women's lives. The indicators like education, health, or life expectancy do not simply reflect the well-being of the woman involved, but as commented by many economists or sociologists, its fruits are shared by the coming generations too.

CORRUPTION, ROLE OF INTERNATIONAL DEVELOPMENT ORGANIZATIONS

Corruption

Corruption is a type of dishonesty or criminal offense committed by a person or organization to gain an illegal advantage or abuse power for one's personal gain. Corruption can include a range of activities, including bribery and embezzlement, although it can also include practices that are legal in many countries. Political corruption occurs when an officeholder or other public servant acts in an official capacity for personal gain. Corruption is most common in kleptocracies, oligarchic systems, narco-states, and mafia states.

Stephen D. Morris, a professor of politics, has written that political corruption is the illegitimate use of public power to benefit a private interest.

Economist Ian Senior has defined corruption as an act of secretly providing a good or service to a third party in order to influence some action that benefits the corrupt, the third party, or both.

World Bank economist Daniel Kaufman expanded the concept to include 'legal corruption' in which power is abused within the limits of the law because those in power often have the ability to legislate to protect them. The impact of corruption in infrastructure is increased cost and construction time, lower quality and decrease the benefit.

Corruption can Occur on Different Scales

Petty Corruption

Petty corruption is small-scale corruption and occurs at the end of the implementation of public services when public officials meet the public. For example, in many small places such as registration offices, police stations, state licensing boards, and many other private and government sectors.

Grand corruption

Grand corruption is defined as corruption occurring at the highest levels of government, requiring a significant impairment of political, legal, and economic systems. This type of corruption is usually found in countries with authoritarian or dictatorial governments, but also in countries where there is not enough policing of corruption. Government systems in many countries are divided into legislative, executive, and judicial branches in an effort to provide independent services that are less subject to major corruption because of their independence from each other.

Systemic corruption

Systemic corruption or endemic corruption is corruption that occurs primarily due to weaknesses in an organization or process. This can be compared to individual officials or agents who act corruptly within the system.

Role of International Development Organizations

World Bank

Founded	1945
Headquarters	Washington D.C. (U.S.A.)
India and World Bank	India was one of the 17 countries, that prepared the agenda for the Bretton Woods Conference (June 1944), it is a founding member of the World Bank

Remarks	The World Bank Group works in every major area of development. It provides a wide array of financial products and technical assistance, and help countries share and apply innovative knowledge and solutions to the challenges they face.

International Monetary Fund (IMF)

Founded	1944
Headquarters	Washington D.C. (U.S.A.)
Members	The International Monetary Fund (IMF) is an organization of 189 countries.
India and IMF	India joined the IMF on December 27, 1945, as one of the IMF's original members.
Remarks	The IMF's primary purpose is to ensure the stability of the international monetary system—the system of exchange rates and international payments that enables countries (and their citizens) to transact with each other. The Fund's mandate was updated in 2012 to include all macroeconomic and financial sector issues that bear on global stability solutions to the challenges they face.

World Trade Organization (WTO)

Founded	1 January 1995
Headquarters	Geneva, Switzerland
Members	The WTO has 164 members and 22 observer governments. Liberia became the 163rd member on 14 July 2016, and Afghanistan became the 164th member on 29 July 2016.
India and WTO	India has been a WTO member since 1 January 1995 and a member of GATT since 8 July 1948.
Remarks	The WTO provides a forum for negotiating agreements aimed at reducing obstacles to international trade and ensuring a level playing field for all, thus contributing to economic growth and development. Their interpretation and application. The current body of trade agreements comprising the WTO consists of 16 different multilateral agreements (to which all WTO members are parties) and two different plurilateral agreements (to which only some WTO members are parties).

World Economic Forum (WEF)

Founded	1971
Headquarters	Geneva, Switzerland.
Members	The World Economic Forum provides a platform for the world's 1,000 leading companies to shape a better future. As a membership organization, the Forum engages businesses in projects and initiatives – online and offline – to address industry, regional and systemic issues.
Remarks	The World Economic Forum, committed to improving the state of the world, is the International Organization for Public-Private Cooperation. The Forum engages the foremost political, business, and other leaders of society to shape global, regional, and industry agendas.

The Asian Development Bank

Founded	19 December 1966
Headquarters	Mandaluyong, Metro Manila, Philippines
Members	From 31 members at its establishment in 1966, ADB has grown to encompass 67 members—of which 48 are from within Asia and the Pacific and 19 outside.
India and ADB	India is a founding member of the ADB and is now the fourth largest shareholder.
Remarks	The Asian Development Bank aims for an Asia and Pacific free from poverty. Its mission is to help developing member countries reduce poverty and improve the quality of life of their people. As a multilateral development finance institution, ADB provides: • loans • technical assistance • grants

New Development Bank

Founded	During the sixth BRICS Summit in Fortaleza (2014), the leaders of BRICS nations signed the Agreement establishing the New Development Bank (NDB).
Headquarters	Shanghai, China
Members	The Bank's Articles of Agreement specify that all members of the United Nations could be members of the bank, however, the share of the BRICS nations can never be less than 55% of the voting power. At present BRICS nations are the members of NDB
India and NDB	As a member of BRICS, India is one of the founding members of NDB, India has 20% shareholding and 20% of voting rights in NDB.
Remarks	The Bank will provide technical and financial assistance for projects to be supported by the NDB and engage in information, cultural, and personnel exchanges with the purpose of contributing to the achievement of environmental and social sustainability.

European Union

Founded	1 November 1993
Headquarters	Brussels, Belgium
Members	28 European countries
Remarks	The Treaty of Maastricht established the European Union in 1992. Recently, United Kingdom has initiated a process for withdrawing from European Union.

SAARC

Founded	1985
Headquarters	Kathmandu (Nepal)
Members	Afghanistan, Bangladesh, Bhutan, India, Nepal, the Maldives, Pakistan, and Sri Lanka
Remark	The organization promotes the development of economic and regional integration. It launched the South Asian Free Trade Area in 2006.

International Court of Justice (ICJ)

Founded	1945
Headquarters	Hague, Netherland
India and ICJ	India is a member of ICJ

The important fact about ICJ	The Court has a twofold role: to settle, in accordance with international law, legal disputes submitted to it by States (Contentious cases) and to give advisory opinions (Advisory proceedings) on legal questions referred to it by duly authorized United Nations organs and specialized agencies.

Amnesty International

Founded	1961
Headquarters	London
Important facts about Amnesty International	Focused on human rights. The objective of the organization is "to conduct research and generate action to prevent and end abuses of human rights and to demand justice for those whose rights have been violated
India and Amnesty	HQ of Amnesty International in India is in Bangalore

International Solar Alliance (ISA)

Founded	2015
Headquarters	Gurugram
India and ISA	India is a founding member of ISA
Important facts about ISA	• Alliance of more than 121 countries, most of them being sunshine countries, which come either completely or partly between the Tropic of Cancer and the Tropic of Capricorn. • Launched by India at the India Africa Summit, and a meeting of member countries ahead of the 2015 United Nations Climate Change Conference in Paris in November2015
Member Countries	121 members

CHAPTER

2 Social Movements and Protests

LEARNING OBJECTIVES:

In this chapter, we will discuss the following important topics.

- Political factions and pressure groups
- Movements based on Caste, Ethnicity, Ideology, Gender, Disability, Religion, and Region
- Civil Society and Citizenship
- NGOs, Activism and Leadership
- Reservations and Politics

INTRODUCTION

Collective attempts to bring social change are defined as a social movement. It is an attempt to bring change in certain social institutions and to create a Social Movements entirely new social order. Or the attempts may represent a socially shared demand for change in some aspects of the social order. Turner and Kilhan define a social movement as a 'collectivity which acts with some continuity to promote or resist change in the society or group of which it is a part'.

Hans Toch in his book *'The Social Psychology of Social Movements'* defined the social movement as an attempt by a large number of people to collectively solve a problem that they feel they share in common. These definitions, above al0l, bring out two important qualifications of a social movement. First, social movements involve collective action against the actions of a small group of individuals. Second, the collective effort is designed to promote change or to resist change in the society in which the effort is made. The collective effort may therefore be to reform, inaugurate, transform, restore, or reinstate all or some aspects of the social order.

POLITICAL FACTIONS AND PRESSURE GROUPS

Political Factions

A political faction is any part of a political system, the term is most often applied to the parts of political parties, pressure groups, and interest groups. In general, the term is a grouping of individuals, especially within a political organization, such as a political party, a trade union, or another group with a political purpose. It may also be called a power bloc, or a voting bloc.

The individuals within a faction are united in a common goal for the organization they are a part of. They stick together to achieve this goal and improve their position within the organization.

The objectives of a political group are as varied as the variety of bodies within which they appear. Typically, however, they include, advancing a particular policy or policy agenda, preventing the adoption of alternative policies, and supporting a specific individual to positions of power within the organization or in the wider political system.

A faction may be organized with the primary aim of supporting a given individual or group, or with a major objective, with little in common otherwise, or it can have a comprehensive and definitive set of policies.

Either way, factional politics usually revolve around personality, with certain individuals playing a key role, acting as a magnet for like-minded people, leading faction activities, and to serve as a leading voice for the group's shared objectives. Such individuals may be referred to by various names, such as 'power brokers' or 'factional chiefs'.

Functioning of Political Faction

In democratic structures, factions rely heavily on securing enough votes to win crucial ballots. This process is sometimes called "doing the numbers". Gaining numbers will help the faction push the policies it supports and propel its members to powerful positions within the wider organization.

If one faction develops within an organization, there will usually be at least one other that develops in opposition to it. Opposing factions will try to match each other's level of organization and internal discipline but will also engage in negotiations and tradeoffs to ensure that the organization's activities are not compromised and that every group has a chance to obtain at least some of its goals.

The key to the operation of an organized faction is the existence of a power base. This will usually be an office, division, or branch of the wider organization over which the faction has effective control. Sometimes a power base may be an external or affiliated organization that is linked in some way to the wider organization.

A power base serves several key functions:

1. It acts as a recruitment center for new members, and promotes homogeneity within the membership (crucial for maintaining factional cohesion).
2. It can be used as an organizing center for factional events and activities.
3. It functions as a springboard, advancing the career of selected factional members and allowing them to gain skills that will increase their effectiveness and clout.

Aim of Political Faction

The existence of a factional system can have serious negative consequences for a political organization. If factional strife becomes intense and public, there may be a perception of disunity in the organization. Taken a step further, if the conflict is particularly severe, it can cause rifts within the organization that seriously impair its effectiveness, causing the organization to break down or collapse.

An environment of intense factional conflict may also lead individuals to focus on attacking their factional enemies rather than on advancing the wider organization.

Any political organization is likely to have many highly opinionated and passionate people. The existence of a factional system allows its operations to be more predictable and stable. Compromise and give-and-take between factions allow the organization to operate without having to satisfy the whims of many different, uncompromising individuals that might otherwise lead to division. So, somewhat counterintuitively, factionalism can actually promote organizational harmony.

Factions also help broaden and diversify the organization's appeal. Just as a democratic government is often invigorated by strong opposition, having an organization with many different points of view can energize it and allow it to perform its role more effectively.

The Founding Fathers of the US Constitution, Madison, Hamilton, and Washington explicitly warned against the dangers of party factionalism. In their words, the factions would create divisions that would eventually destroy the government.

Pressure Groups

In democratic politics, pressure groups are organizations that attempt to influence the government. The International Encyclopaedia of the Social Sciences describes the groups as representing the interest of the sections into which society is divided. With advanced specialization, groups will be more numerous and specialized.

Such groups represent the interests of various sections of society such as farmers, labourers, government employees, businessmen, professional people, and even students.

Pressure groups also known as interest groups are forms of organizations that exert pressure on the political or administrative system of a country to extract benefits from it and advance their own interests.

Pressure groups are formed by both dominant groups and the deprived ones as the dominant group pushes states for economic concessions, and the deprived one demands basic amenities in a competing environment.

The primary aim of any pressure group is to influence the government on a specific public policy issue or problem. According to V. O. Key, a striking feature of American politics is the extent to which political parties are supplemented by private associations formed to influence public policy. These organizations are commonly called pressure groups.

David B. Truman defines an interest group as "a shared attitude group that makes certain claims upon the other groups in the society."

The vitality of the pressure groups is mainly determined by their ability to influence the government. Influencing the government involves influencing the public policy decision-makers, lawmakers, implementers of policies and decisions, etc. The role of pressure groups is closely connected with politics.

The importance of pressure groups is primarily determined by their ability to influence the government. Influencing government involves influencing public policy decision-makers, lawmakers, implementers of policies and decisions, etc in their own or larger interest. The role of pressure groups is closely linked to politics.

Harold D. Lasswell in his early work on politics, uses the subtitle, 'who gets what, when, how?' and says that, 'the study of politics is the study of influences and influential.'

Robert Dahl, Hunter, etc., believe that pressure groups act as multiple power centers in modern liberal democracies.

Characteristics of Pressure Group

i. They are collections of individuals who hold a similar set of values and beliefs on the basis of religion, ethnicity, political philosophy, or a common goal.

ii. They are a –non-political group.

iii. The main concern of a pressure group is to influence the government for promoting its specific interest

iv. They play the mediatory role between the people and the government.

v. They balance the national interest and the interest of individuals.

vi. They help in social integration and political articulation and act as a catalyst for change.

vii. They, in many ways, provide alternatives to the inadequacies of political parties and government.

viii. Pressure groups are formed not only to promote and preserve economic interests but they are also used to protect and promote linguistic, cultural, and religious interests.

ix. Pressure groups act as vehicles for mobilization of the masses and hence, promote political and administrative participation.

x. They have, in a way, deepened the roots of participatory democracy.

Maurice Duverger mentions two types of pressure groups—Promotional and Protective pressure groups.

i. Trade Unions and professional associations like ASSOCHAM and CII are examples of protective groups.

ii. PETA, Greenpeace, etc. are examples of promotional groups as they promote some cause. These usually have a wider membership base than protective groups that protect the interests of a narrow group.

MOVEMENTS BASED ON CASTE, ETHNICITY, IDEOLOGY, GENDER, DISABILITY, RELIGION, AND REGION

Social Movement

A social movement is a loosely organized effort by a large group of people to achieve a particular goal, usually a social or political goal. It can be to implement, oppose or undo any social change. It is a type of group action and may involve individuals, organizations, or both.

Sociologist Charles Tilly defines social movements as a series of controversial demonstrations, displays, and campaigns by which ordinary people make collective claims about others. For Tilly, social movements are a major vehicle for the participation of ordinary people in public politics. He argues that there are three major elements of a social movement:

1. Campaigns. It is a sustained, organized public effort making collective claims of target authorities.
2. Repertoire. employment of combinations from among the following forms of political action: the creation of special-purpose associations and coalitions, public meetings, solemn processions, vigils, rallies, demonstrations, petition drives, statements to and in public media, and pamphleteering; and
3. WUNC displays participants' concerted public representation of worthiness, unity, numbers, and commitments on the part of themselves and their constituencies.

Sociologist David Aberle described four types of social movements, are Alternative, Redemptive, Reformative, and Revolutionary social movements.

Alternative movements are typically focused on self-improvement and limited, specific changes to individual beliefs and behavior. These include things like Quit smoking, Mothers Against Drunk Driving (MADD), Planned Parenthood, etc.

Redemptive movements (sometimes called religious movements) are "meaning-seeking movement" that are focused on a specific category of the population, and their goal is to provoke inner change or spiritual growth in individuals. For example, Sree Narayana Dharma Paripalana Yogam (S.N.D.P) movement seeks to bring inner change in the life of the Ezhava community of Kerala.

Reformative social movements advocate bringing some minor change instead of radical change in the social structure. But are targeted at the entire population. For example, switching from incandescent light bulbs to energy-saving compact fluorescent bulbs in order to protect the environment.

Revolutionary movements seek to completely change every aspect of society, their goal is to change the structure of society in totality. It is an attempt to change the government, regime, or society through violence. Examples include Bolsheviks in Russia, the Chinese Communist Party, and other communist movements in Southeast Asia.

Caste Movements

The nature of caste movements in India were mainly reformative and revolutionary. The reformative movements were run to improve the present condition of the lower castes under the caste system. The main objective of these movements was to bring about positive changes by spreading education among the low caste and weaker groups, improving the social status of women, etc. Whereas the revolutionary movements completely rejected the traditional social system and emphasized on radical change. They were against the orthodox ideology of Brahminism.

Jyotiba Phule Movement

The movement was founded by Jyotirao Phule in Maharashtra in the 1870s. On 24 September 1874, Phule formed the Satyashodhak Samaj to protect the rights of depressed groups such as women, Shudras, and Dalits. Phule's theory of lower caste exploitation was based on cultural and ethnic groups rather than political and economic factors.

Jyotirao Phule was against the orthodox Brahmins and other upper castes and termed them 'hypocrites'. He worked against the tyranny of the upper caste people and urged the farmers and lower-class people to disobey the restrictions placed on them. He wrote books named Gulamgiri and Sarvajanik Satyadharma.

Shri Narayana Dharma Paripalana Yogam Movement (SNDPY)

The movement was founded in 1903 by the religious leader Shri Narayana Guru in Kerala. It is a charitable society that seeks to bring inner change through spiritual and educational upliftment of the Ezhava community for 114 years.

Congress and the Harijan Movement

Gandhiji started this movement to remove untouchability from India. The movement began to lay emphasis on uplifting the social status of the lower caste and backward castes. Congress passed various resolutions with the help of Gandhiji.

In 1921, Congress made an appeal for removing untouchability. Later a committee was set up in 1922 and a resolution was passed in 1923 for this purpose. In 1932, Gandhiji started the All-India Anti Untouchability league known as Harijan Sevak Sangh in order to improve the condition of untouchables by providing them with all kinds of facilities.

Dr. Bhimrao Ambedkar and His Depressed Class Movement

B.R. Ambedkar's movement provides an all-India organization for the rejection of all forms of feudal bondage imposed on Dalits. He launched a major anti-untouchability movement in the 1920s, which continues in various forms even today. He did many reforms and movements for the upliftment of the downtrodden and depressed class.

In 1924, he founded the Depressed Classes Institute i.e., Bahishkrit Hitakarini Sabha in Bombay. He also founded the Samaj Samata Sangh to propagate the teaching of social equality between the upper castes and the lower class. He led the famous Mahad Satyagraha or Chavdar Tale Satyagraha on 20 March 1927 for the right of untouchables to draw water from wells and ponds, temple entry, etc.

Gender Movement

Gender movements in the contemporary context are a part of new social movements which have become the basis for active participation of the women in community life. Organized around issues such as civil liberties, equality, ecology, identity, ethnicity, education, health, etc., these movements operate outside party politics and shift the nature of participation from traditional modes of representation to direct collective action.

Some of the women reformers who worked towards their upliftment are discussed below.

Raja Ram Mohan Roy: Raja Ram Mohan Roy did a great job in abolishing the biggest evil custom of Sati Pratha. He organized the Atmiya Sabha in 1815 and also founded the Brahmo Samaj on 20 August 1828. Brahmo Samaj fought against sati pratha, child marriage, caste system, purdah system, untouchability, drug addiction, etc.

Ishwar Chandra Vidyasagar: Ishwar Chandra Vidya Sagar was a reformer in Bengal, he was a strong supporter of widow remarriage and also worked for women's education. Vidyasagar made a great effort to get the Hindu Remarriage Act passed in 1856, he presented a petition in favor of this Act in the Indian Legislative Council and the British Government.

Kandukuri Veeresalingam Pantulu: He was the social reformer and writer of Andhra Pradesh; he also published the book *Viveka Vardhani*. He is considered as the father of the renaissance in Telugu. He was an ardent supporter of women's education, and widow remarriage and strictly opposed the dowry system. He started 'Brahmo Mandir' in 1887 and 'Hitkarni School' in 1908.

Mahadev Govind Ranade: He along with his wife Ramabai worked towards widow remarriage, and female education and opposed child marriage. He organized the National Social Conference which became a prestigious institution for social reforms. For the first time in India, his wife Ramabai made the biggest effort to educate widows.

Swami Dayanand Saraswati: Swami Dayanand Saraswati was the founder of the Arya Samaj, and was a great supporter of women's education and widow remarriage and condemned the custom of many social evils such as child marriage, dowry, and polygamy.

Dhondo Keshav Karve: Dhondo Keshav Karve strongly supported widow remarriage and worked for the longest time for the emancipation of women. She established women's schools and widow homes in Pune.

Disability Movement

The Disability Rights Movement started in the USA, is a global social movement to secure equal opportunities and equal rights for all people with disabilities.

Disability activists are working to break down the institutional, physical, and social barriers that prevent people with disabilities from living their lives like other citizens.

Disability rights are complex because there are many ways in which a person with a disability›s rights can be violated. It is a form of discrimination in which others fail to meet the needs of a person with a disability.

Disability Rights in India

The Rights of Persons with Disabilities Act, 2016 is a disability law enacted by the Parliament of India to fulfill its obligation to the United Nations Convention on the Rights of Persons with Disabilities, which India ratified in 2007. It came into force on 28 December 2016. The Act replaced the existing Persons with Disabilities (Equal Opportunities, Protection of Rights and Full Participation) Act, 1995.

CIVIL SOCIETY AND CITIZENSHIP

Civil society is an organization apart from the state. It is an area in which individuals come together and form groups, pursue common enterprises, share interests, and communicate on important and sometimes not-so-important matters.

The term 'civil society' can be traced through the works of Cicero and other Romans to the ancient Greek philosophers. In its classical usage civil society was largely equated with the state.

The modern idea of civil society found expression in the Scottish and Continental Enlightenment of the late 18th century.

The Marxist theorist Antonio Gramsci revived the term to portray civil society as a special nucleus of independent political activity, a crucial sphere of struggle against tyranny. Although Gramsci was amongst persons fighting against dictatorships of all political stripes in Eastern Europe and Latin America.

Understanding the importance of the given concept, recently David Held tried to give shape to the concept of 'civil society' through a sociological definition. In his words, Civil society retains a distinctive character to the extent that it is made up of distinct areas of social life such as the domestic world, the economic sphere, cultural activities, and political interaction which are organized by private or voluntary arrangements between individuals and groups outside the direct control of the state.'

Civil society suddenly became a mantra for everyone from the president to political scientists in the

1990s. The global trend towards democracy opened up space for civil society in former dictatorships around the world. In the United States and Western Europe, public fatigue with entrenched party systems sparked interest in civil society as a means of social renewal.

Especially in the developing world, privatization and other market reforms have given civil society an opportunity to intervene as governments scale back their reach. And the information revolution provided new tools for making connections and empowering citizens. Civil society became a major element of the post-Cold War consciousness.

Civil Society and Social Movement

Social movements and civil society have structures like organizations and well-identified leadership and ideology. Civil society initiatives and social movements are social processes that undergo several stages of progression from mobilization to intensive collective action.

Social movements and civil societies pledge to change the established order of society. However, some of them also work to resist change in society. They both occupy civil space in society. The creation of a new collective identity is an essential part of both social movements and civil society. They are based on identified ideological choices.

Social movements and civil society have structures such as organizations and well-recognized leadership and ideology. Civil society initiatives and social movements are social processes that go through several stages of progression from mobilization to intensive collective action.

Social movements and civil society both promise to bring change to the established order of society. However, some of them also work to resist change in society. They both occupy a civil place in society. The construction of a new collective identity is an essential part of both social movements and civil society. Both are based on the identified ideological alternatives.

NGOS, ACTIVISM AND LEADERSHIP

Organizations that are independent of government involvement are known as non-governmental organizations. NGOs are a subgroup of organizations founded by citizens, which include clubs and associations that provide services to their members and others.

NGOs are usually non-profit organizations, and many of them are active in humanitarianism or the social sciences. Surveys indicate that NGOs have a high degree of public trust, which can make them a useful proxy for the concerns of society and stakeholders.

According to NGO.org (the non-governmental organizations associated with the United Nations), an NGO is any non-profit, voluntary citizens group that is organized on a local, national, or international level.

NGOs perform a variety of service and humanitarian functions, bring citizen concerns to Governments, advocate and monitor policies and encourage political participation through the provision of information.

In social movements, Non-Governmental Organisations (NGOs) play a very important role. They represent the interests of civil society and participate vitally in the political system.

They contribute valuable information and ideas, advocate effectively for positive change, provide essential operational capacity in emergencies and development efforts, and generally increase the accountability and legitimacy of the governance process. NGOs are essential partners of the government in the process of deliberation and policy formation as well as in the execution of policies.

Importance of NGOs

1. NGOs play an important supportive role as mediators and facilitators to ensure equity and participation in the development process.
2. NGOs endeavour to plug gaps in the government's programmes and reach out to sections of people often left untouched by state projects. For example, during the Covid crisis, several NGOs came forward to provide aid to migrant labourers.
3. They are engaged in diverse activities, relating to human and labour rights, gender issues, healthcare, environment, education, legal aid, and even research.
4. There are political NGOs that mobilise public opinion against the government's policies and actions.
    - An activist is a person who works to change a community, aiming to make it a better place. To be a strong and effective activist, a person must have the capacity to lead others, be dedicated to a cause, and be able to persuade or influence others in the community to believe in the cause.

Leadership in Social Movement

Leaders are critical to social movements: they inspire commitment, mobilize resources, create and recognize opportunities, devise strategies, frame demands, and influence outcomes.

According to Robert Michels' theory of political leadership, followers voluntarily cede agency to their leaders. The public is grateful to leaders for speaking and acting on their behalf, even when leaders become political elites whose interests' conflict with those of their followers.

Large bureaucratic organizations are, in Mitchell›s view, necessary for mass movements and parties, but they inevitably become oligarchies as leaders are motivated to maintain their own power and positions. Leaders become part of the power elite, more concerned with organizational maintenance than with the core goals of the movement. The type of leadership affects the centralization of decision-making, division of labor, and the extent to which the organization is subject to schism.

Eichler similarly associates bases of leadership with organizational characteristics and outcomes. Leaders of social movements are not a representative assortment of individuals randomly chosen from the populations they lead. V. I. Lenin, Mahatma Gandhi, Martin Luther King, Jr., and Betty Friedan were leaders of very different types of social movements, yet they all enjoyed at least middle-class status and were highly educated.

Leaders can advance poor people's movements through their commitment to education for themselves and their followers.

Functions of Leadership

Leadership functions are related to goal attainment and maintenance and strengthening of the group. Goal attainment functions are critical to achieving group goals, including making suggestions for action, evaluating movement toward goals, stopping activities irrelevant to goals, and presenting effective solutions for goal achievement.

The functions related to the maintenance and strengthening of the group include the functions of encouraging members, removing tension-causing situations, and giving everyone a chance to express themselves. The main functions of leadership are to contribute to the achievement of group goals and to help hold the group together. The leader alone cannot achieve the goal of the group and helps in maintaining its cohesion and strength.

Leadership is not the activity of an individual alone. In a large-scale organization it becomes a collective activity for no single individual can meet the tremendous demands of working out the whole organization. This has led to the view that leadership-like power is dispersed throughout the organization. No one person has all the leadership functions.

The functions of an organization are divided and each individual in his respective position provides leadership in so far as he contributes to the attainment of the group goal and the maintenance of group cohesiveness. Leadership is provided at several levels in the hierarchy but at the same time, individual leadership is important. The leader is the symbolic spokesman, the coordinator supreme, the important participant in decisions as to goals, the primary change content, and the example to the organization.

RESERVATIONS AND POLITICS

Reservation

Reservation is a device through which some proportions of positions are fixed in employment, seats in representative bodies such as parliament, state legislatures, and local self-government institutions, for the weaker sections of society such as SCs, STs, OBCs, women, or EWS.

It is needed to help those sections of society who cannot meet their needs without the help of the state or any other agency. It is discriminatory in a positive sense, not in a negative sense. That means the purpose of such discrimination is to bring at par with the unreserved category of people who need the state's help. In this sense, reservation is also known as positive discrimination.

As reservation is initiated by the state, is also known as affirmative action. The Indian state provides reservations to different categories on different grounds. For the Scheduled Castes (SCs), the principal ground for reservation has been the experience of untouchability undergone by the castes identified as SCs.

The Scheduled Tribes get it because of their disabilities faced on account of their geographical locations and other characteristics. The OBCs get it because of their social and educational backwardness.

Women get it because of their discrimination due to patriarchal values in society. And the Economically Weaker Section gets it because of their poor economic status. The latter generally belong to those communities which cannot get reservations in other categories but need state devices for betterment. They belong to poor persons from the high castes.

Since independence two types of caste politics can be discerned. The first type involved the caste groups clamoring either for being recognised as OBC by the state governments or those already recognised for getting a higher quota in the reservations.

The decision of the State governments to appoint the Backward classes Commission from time to time provided the occasion for such caste politics to flourish.

The second type of caste politics involved the of social and political forces for and against reservations for the OBC based solely on caste criteria. The extent of castes' involvement in politics can be appreciated by noting the simple fact that over 50% of the populace belongs to the category of the OBCs.

While the first type of caste politics sought to influence the reservation policy of the state government, the second type of caste politics was aimed to resist the reservation policy of the central government.

Reservations for SCs and STs

The constitution provides for three types of reservations for the SCs and STs. These are

i. reservation of jobs in government services and in the public sector,
ii. reservation in educational institutions, and
iii. reservations in legislative representations.

Under Articles 16(A), 320(4), and 333, 15% and 7% of the jobs are reserved at all levels in the public services for the SCs and STs respectively.

Article 15(4) deals with the reservation of seats in educational institutions.

Articles 330 and 332 provide for the reservation of seats in the Lok Sabha and State Legislative Assemblies.

Reservations for the OBCs

The Union government had as early as 1953 appointed the Kalelkar Commission under Article 340. The Commission submitted its report in 1956, but its recommendations were not implemented by the Union government.

The second Commission under Article 340 was appointed by the Janata Party Government in 1978. This Commission known as Mandal Commission submitted its report in 1982. It identified 3943 castes as OBC and recommended 27% reservation in government and semi-government jobs and admission to educational institutions.

On 13th August 1990, the Union Government headed by V.P. Singh issued an office memorandum extending reservation to the OBCs on the lines recommended by the Mandal Commission.

The Ramanand Prasad committee was set up by the Union government to identify the "creamy layer". Once it had done its job, the government executed the order of 13th August 1990 in September 1993.

Women's Reservation Bill

The Women's Reservation Bill or The Constitution (108th Amendment) Bill, 2008, is a pending bill in the Parliament of India that proposes to amend the Constitution of India to reserve 1/3rd of all seats in the Lower house of Parliament of India, the Lok Sabha, and in all state legislative assemblies for women. The seats were proposed to be reserved in rotation and would have been determined by draw of lots in such a way that a seat would be reserved only once in three consecutive general elections.

ASSESS YOUR LEARNING

PRACTICE QUESTIONS

1. It is a collection of families bearing a common name, speaking a common dialect, occupying or progressing to occupy a common territory and is not usually endogamous, though originally it might have been so.
(a) Caste
(b) Political group
(c) Political Party
(d) Tribe

2. The statement 'History is the graveyard of Aristocracies' is attributed to
(a) G. Mosca (b) K. Marx
(c) V. Pareto (d) L. Feuerbach

3. Which of the following is NOT an essential attribute of a state?
(a) Territory
(b) Government
(c) Sovereignty
(d) Civil society

4. Which set of International Development organizations work towards fighting against poverty?
(a) ILO, UNICEF, WHO, UNHCR, The Red Cross
(b) Oxfam, UNDP, UNICEF, The Red Cross, The Hunger Project
(c) World Bank, WHO, IMF, UNDP, ILO
(d) UNHCR, CEDAW, UNICEF, IMF, Oxfam

5. Which of the following is not correctly matched?

List I (Tribes)	List II (State/Region)
(a) Khasi	Meghalaya
(b) Toda	Nilgiri Hills
(c) Munda	Andhra Pradesh
(d) Khond	Odisa

6. Which are the essential characteristics of bureaucracy?
1. Hierarchy of power
2. Unlimited power
3. Channelling of communication
4. Informal relations between the officials

Choose the correct option:
(a) (2) and (3)
(b) (1) and (4)
(c) (1) and (3)
(d) (2) and (4)

7. The Historical Theory of the Origin of the State was propounded by:
(a) Sir Henry Maine (b) Triestske
(c) Oppenheimer (d) Durkheim

8. Which one of the following theories held that the State is a product and manifestation of the irreconcilability of class antagonisms?
(a) Evolutionary Theory
(b) Anarchist Theory
(c) Marxist-Leninist Theory
(d) Guild-Socialist Theory

9. Which one of the following political thinkers was the first exponent of the liberal theory of States?
(a) John Locke
(b) T.H. Green
(c) Jean Jacques Rousseau
(d) Hobbes

10. Which one of the following statements about the welfare state is correct?
(a) A welfare state is the same as a socialist state
(b) The welfare state is based on the principles of classical liberalism
(c) The welfare state is a collectivist state
(d) The welfare state embodies the principles of neoliberalism

11. Who among the following thinkers held that 'Human consciousness postulates liberty, liberty involves rights and rights demand the State'?
(a) Hegel (b) Green
(c) Bosanquet (d) Laski

12. Who said that 'tribalism is a pre-civilized storage of human society?
(a) Sir Henry Maine (b) Triestske
(c) Oppenheimer (d) Durkheim

13. The doctrine of proportionate equality was propounded by:
(a) Aristotle (b) Rousseau
(c) Marx (d) Rawls

14. In their book *The Civic Culture* (1963), American political scientists Gabriel Almond and Sydney Verba identified three pure types of political culture, which among the following is not one of them?
(a) Parochial (b) Subject
(c) Participant (d) Universal

15. The principle of distributive justice was first propounded by?
(a) Aristotle (b) Godwin
(c) Herbert Spencer (d) Rawls

16. Which of the following pairs is not correctly matched?
(a) Karl Marx : The Poverty of Philosophy
(b) V.I. Lenin : State and Revolution
(c) Josef Stalin : Wage, Labour and Capital
(d) Friedrich Engels : Origin of Family, Private Property and the State

17. Who believes 'Means are after all everything. As the means, so the end; there is no wall of separation between means and end.'?
(a) M.K. Gandhi (b) B.R. Ambedkar
(c) Mao Zedon (d) Karl Marx

18. In India, partyless democracy was first advocated by?
(a) Jayprakash Narayan
(b) M. N. Roy
(c) Vinoba Bhave
(d) Mahatma Gandhi

19. Birsa Munda was associated with the tribal struggle of:
(a) North East Region
(b) Jharkhand
(c) Nagpur Division
(d) Deccan

20. Given below are two statements, one labelled as Assertion (A) and the other labelled as Reason (R)

Assertion (A): Naxalite movement is an armed struggle of the poor peasantry against the landlords.

Reason (R): Naxalite movement was born in the Naxalbari village of Darjeeling District.

In the context of the above two statements, which one of the following is correct?

Codes:
(a) Both A and R are true and R is the correct explanation of A
(b) Both A and R are true but R is not the correct explanation of A
(c) A is true but R is false
(d) A is false but R is true

21. Which one of the following is not a Peasant movement?
(a) Telengana Insurrection
(b) Tebhaga Movement
(c) Naxalvadi Movement
(d) Appiko Movement

22. Which one of the following is not a peasant movement?
(a) Kheda movement
(b) Tabligh movement
(c) Telangana movement
(d) Tebhaga movement

23. Given below are the two statements, one labelled as Assertion (A) and the other labelled as Reason (R):

Assertion (A): The challenge that the Indian state is facing today is how to achieve an equivalence between the state and the civil society within a democratic framework.

Reason (R): Criminalization of politics, political corruption and communal violence stand in the way of creating a value-based political culture.

In the context of the above two statements, which one of the following is correct?

Codes:
(a) Both A and R are true and R is the correct explanation of A
(b) Both A and R are true but R is not the correct explanation of A
(c) A is true but R is false
(d) A is false but R is true

24. Which of the following pairs is not correctly matched?
(a) Aristotle : The Politics
(b) Plato : The Republic
(c) Henry Maine : The Social Contract
(d) Montesque : The Spirit of the Laws

25. Who defined Bureaucracy as - The purest type of exercise of legal authority with a hierarchy of paid, full-time officials, who formed a chain of command'?
(a) Amitai Etzioni
(b) Peter Blau
(c) Max Weber
(d) R K Merton

26. Who has discussed the dysfunctions of bureaucracy?
(a) Amitai Etzioni
(b) Peter Blau
(c) Max Weber
(d) R K Merton

27. Which of the following amendments were related to grass root democracy (local self-government) in India?
(a) the 73rd and 74th amendment
(b) the 74th and 75th amendment
(c) the 75th and 76th amendment
(d) the 76th and 77th amendment

28. Who is known as the father of local self-government in India?
(a) Lord Mayo
(b) Lord Ripon
(c) Lord Dalhousie
(d) Lord Minto

29. Which of the following book is not written by Ragini Kothari?
(a) Politics in India
(b) Caste in Indian Politics
(c) Rethinking Democracy
(d) Citizenship and Social Class

30. Who propounded the concept of '*Hegemony*'?
(a) Antonio Gramsci
(b) Karl Marx
(c) Max Weber
(d) R. Dahrendorf

31. Who defined citizenship as a status, which is enjoyed by a person who is a full member of a community?
(a) Thomas Paine (b) R. Bendix
(c) T.H. Marshall (d) Bryan S. Turner

32. Who is the author of the book '*Second Sex*'?
(a) Kate Millet
(b) Margaret Thatcher
(c) Ronald Reagan
(d) Simone De Beauvoir

33. The Persons With Disabilities (Equal Opportunities, Protection of Rights and Full Participation) Act came into force in which year?
(a) 1990 (b) 1995
(c) 2000 (d) 2005

34. David Aberle has described four types of social movements, which of the following is not one of them?
(a) Transformative movements
(b) Reformative movements
(c) Redemptive movements
(d) Resistive movements

35. Raja Ram Mohan Roy campaigned against which evil practice prevailed in India?
(a) Alcoholism
(b) Dowry
(c) Inter-Caste Marriage
(d) Sati Pratha

36. Who was associated with Bhoodan Movement?
(a) Ishwar Chandra Vidyasagar
(b) Acharya Vinoba Bhave
(c) Rabindranath Tagore
(d) J P Narayan

37. Which of the following match is incorrect?
(a) Dalit Movements : B.R. Ambedkar
(b) Naxalite Movement : Charu Majumdar
(c) Chipko Movement : Swami Shajanand
(d) S.N.D.P. Movement : Shri Narain Guru

38. Consider the following statements:
Dalit Movement seeks
1. to raise social awareness among Dalits about their rights
2. privileges for the Dalits
3. to bring social change through revolution

Which of these is correct?
(a) 1 and 2 (b) 2 and 3
(c) 1 and 3 (d) 1, 2, and 3

39. Reservation for Scheduled Castes is provided in terms of their?
(a) Poverty (b) Economic necessities
(c) Population (d) Low ritual positions

40. The process of acquisition of a political culture is known as
(a) Political modernization
(b) Political socialisation
(c) Political stratification
(d) Political legitimation

41. Law and Society movement started in which of the following country?
(a) Germany (b) USA
(c) Finland (d) Sweden

42. What measure did libertarians Margaret Thatcher and Ronald advocate for complete freedom of the individual?
(a) basic services such as health and education, should be free of charge through state funding.
(b) the model which is characterised by a free economy regulated by competition.
(c) The withdrawal of the state from affairs of individual freedom.
(d) The development and freedom lie in the community itself where rights are enshrined.

43. Which of the following thinker argued that the green revolution is the gender-biased process?
(a) Riley Dunlap (b) William R. Catton
(c) Allan Schnaiberg (d) Ester Boserup

44. Which wave of feminism originated in two branches, the liberal feminists and the radical feminists?
(a) First (b) Second
(c) Third (d) Fourth

45. Which of the key areas of interrelationship between governance and development does not identified by the ADB?
(a) Accountability (b) Participation
(c) Predictability (d) Transdisciplinary

46. Which of the following thinker is not associated with 'The Civic Culture'?
(a) Almond, Gabriel, and Verba, Sidney
(b) Cook, T. E., and Morgan P. M
(c) John Pierre
(d) R Paul Brass

47. '*Crisis of Governance*' is coined by which of the following institution?
(a) World Trade Organization
(b) United Nations Development Programme
(c) World Bank
(d) Asian Development Bank

48. Which of the following thinker points out a correlation between Protestantism and stable democratization?
(a) R Ingelhart (b) J Bongart
(c) C Holdgate (d) R Riverstein

49. Which of the following statement is or are incorrect?
1. Nationality is subjective, statehood is objective.
2. Nationality is psychological, statehood is political.
3. Nationality is a condition of mind whereas statehood is a condition of law.

Chose the correct option from the codes given below:

(a) 1 and 2 only
(b) 2 only
(c) 1 and 3 only
(d) None of the above

50. The book *'The Bureaucratization of the World'* is written by?

(a) Herbert Blumer
(b) Bruno Rizzi
(c) Manuel Castells
(d) Max Weber

Answer Key

1. (d)	**9.** (a)	**17.** (a)	**25.** (c)	**33.** (b)	**41.** (b)	**49.** (d)
2. (c)	**10.** (b)	**18.** (a)	**26.** (d)	**34.** (d)	**42.** (c)	**50.** (b)
3. (d)	**11.** (b)	**19.** (b)	**27.** (a)	**35.** (d)	**43.** (d)	
4. (b)	**12.** (a)	**20.** (b)	**28.** (b)	**36.** (b)	**44.** (b)	
5. (c)	**13.** (a)	**21.** (d)	**29.** (d)	**37.** (c)	**45.** (d)	
6. (c)	**14.** (d)	**22.** (b)	**30.** (a)	**38.** (a)	**46.** (a)	
7. (a)	**15.** (a)	**23.** (a)	**31.** (c)	**39.** (d)	**47.** (c)	
8. (c)	**16.** (c)	**24.** (c)	**32.** (d)	**40.** (b)	**48.** (a)	

PREVIOUS YEARS' QUESTIONS

DECEMBER 2023

1. Who among the following have drawn attention to the 'dark side' of the family life?
   (a) Liberals
   (b) Functionalists
   (c) Structuralists
   (d) Feminists

2. Match List I with List II.

List I	List II
A. Ho	I. Dhangarbassa
B. Bhotia	II. Sing-bonga
C. Oraon	III. Rangbang
D. Bhuiya	IV. Jonkerpa

   Choose the correct answer from the options given below:
   (a) A-I, B-II, C-III, D-IV
   (b) A-III, B-II, C-I, D-IV
   (c) A-IV, B-III, C-II, D-I
   (d) A-II, B-III, C-IV, D-I

3. Who among the following uses the phrase 'anti-politics machine'?
   (a) Robert Chambers
   (b) James Ferguson
   (c) Keith Hart
   (d) Thomas B. Hansen

Read the following passage and answer the questions.

A sociological study was focussed on two villages—one a large settlement of some 5142 people and the other, a small village of only 759 people. Despite their differences in size, both villages exhibited a roughly similar caste and religious structure. Each settlement contains both Hindu and Muslim families which are internally divided into caste or caste-like groupings; and each possesses a dominant caste that tends to control a substantial part of the economic and political resources of the village. The village population is divided into three socio-economic groups: (1) A group of agriculturists who are of high status and high income that make up the dominant caste, together with certain individuals from other caste who have achieved a better economic status than their fellows; (2) A middle group of less wealthy agriculturists, artisans, and members of the occupational castes; and (3) A group of individuals of low status and income made up of the lowest order caste and poor agricultural labourers. In both villages, there is a small but powerful segment that constitutes the elite. This comprises people mostly of high social status and income who are better educated, have urban contacts and play an active part in village and inter-village politics.

4. The power structure of the study villages comprised those having
   A. Better education and high social status.
   B. Urban contact.
   C. Neutral attitude.
   D. Active participation in village politics.
   Choose the correct answer from the options given below:
   (a) A, C and D only
   (b) A, B and D only
   (c) B, C and D only
   (d) A, B and C only

5. The lower class in the village was comprised of
   A. Lowest order caste.
   B. Agricultural labourers.
   C. Rich farmers.
   D. Marginal farmers.
   Choose the correct answer from the options given below:
   (a) A, B, C only
   (b) A, C, D only
   (c) A, B and D only
   (d) B, C and D only

6. The peasant class in the village has following characteristics:
   A. High status.
   B. Make up a 'dominant caste'.
   C. High income.
   D. Landlessness.
   Choose the correct answer from the options given below:
   (a) A, B and C only
   (b) A, B and D only
   (c) B, C and D only
   (d) A, C and D only

7. In what ways are two villages similar to each other?
   A. In caste and religious structure.
   B. Both religious groups divided in caste/caste-like structures.
   C. Both the villages had almost same settlement pattern.
   D. Both the villages had a dominant caste.
   Choose the correct answer from the options given below:
   (a) A, B and D only
   (b) A, B and C only
   (c) B, C and D only
   (d) A, C and D only

8. The structure of middle class in the study villages comprised
   A. Less wealthy agriculturalists.
   B. Artisans.
   C. Occupational castes.
   D. Lowest order caste.

Choose the correct answer from the options given below:
(a) A, B and D only
(b) A, B and C only
(c) B, C and D only
(d) A, C and D only

JUNE 2023

9. Who among the following has written the book *Civilizing the Savage*?
(a) Verrier Elwin
(b) Ramachandra Guha
(c) Radha Kamal Mukherjee
(d) Joan P. Mencher

10. Who gave the concept of anti-Minotaur to demolish the myth of 'value neutral sociology'?
(a) Anthony Giddens
(b) Alvin Gouldner
(c) Robert Merton
(d) Thurston Veblen

MARCH 2023

11. The First wave of feminism was synonymous with:
(a) 'Me-too' movement.
(b) 1960's Civil Rights Movement.
(c) Queer Movement.
(d) Women's Suffragette Movement.

12. Who wrote the book *Who Governs*?
(a) Domhoff (b) Robert Dahl
(c) Lasswell (d) Reisman

13. Who wrote the book *Women's Role in Economic Development*?
(a) Ester Boserup
(b) Judith Butler
(c) Martha Nussbaum
(d) Ann Oakley

14. Match List I with List II

List I (Terminologies)	List II (Used by the theorist)
A. Governing elite	I. Marx
B. Ruling class	II. Pareto
C. Veto group	III. Floyd Hunter
D. Top leaders	IV. Riesman

Choose the correct answer from the options given below:

(a) A - I, B - II, C - III, D - IV
(b) A - II, B - I, C - IV D - III
(c) A - III, B - IV, C - I, D - II
(d) A - IV, B - I, C - II, D - III

15. The following scholars have written extensively on the relationship between caste and politics in India.
A. Rajni Kothari
B. Norman Palmer
C. D. Miller
D. Colin Campbell
E. Key
Choose the correct answer from the options given below:
(a) A, B, and C only
(b) D and E only
(c) A, B, C, D, and E
(d) B, C, and D only

16. Who among the following talks about three dimensions of power, (a) decision making (b) non-decision making and (C) shaping desires?
(a) Alvin Genldner
(b) Anthony Giddens
(c) Steven Lukes
(d) Max Weber

17. Match List I with List II

List I (Books)	List II (Authors)
A. *Bureaucracy in Modem Society*	I. Milton Singer
B. *The McDonaldization of Society*	II. Peter M. Blau
C. *Nation Building in Independent India*	III. George Ritzer
D. *When a Great Tradition Modernizes*	IV. M.N. Srinivas

Choose the correct answer from the options given below:
(a) A - II, B - III, C - IV, D - I
(b) A - I, B - II, C - III, D - IV
(c) A - III, B - IV, C -I, D-II
(d) A - IV, B - I, C - II, D - III

DEC 2021 & JUNE 2022

18. Use of public office for private gain is known as:
(a) Abuse
(b) Corruption
(c) Insincerity
(d) None of the above

19. Given below are two statements, one is labelled as Assertion (A) and the other is labelled as Reason (R).

Assertion (A): N.K Bose emphasised the need to bring ethnology and Indology together in the study of Indian Society,

Reason (R): It is possible to reconstruct the structure of the Indian Constitution through these two approaches.

In the light of the above statements, choose the correct answer from the options given below:

(a) Both (A) and (R) are true and (R) is the correct explanation of (A)
(b) Both (A) and (R) are true but (R) is NOT the correct explanation of (A)
(c) (A) is true but (R) is false
(d) (A) is false but (R) is true

20. The #MeToo movement is a part of which wave of feminism?

A. First Wave
B. Second Wave
C. Third Wave
D. Fourth Wave
E. Fifth Wave

Choose the correct answer from the options given below:

(a) A and B only
(b) B and C only
(c) C and E only
(d) D only

21. What are the main features of the Rights of Persons with Disabilities Act, 2016?

(a) Number of disabilities increased from 7 to 21
(b) Percentage of reservation increased from 3% to 4%
(c) Special courts, to handle cases related to violation of rights of person with disabilities, set up in each district
(d) All of the above

22. Who has classified political institutions into republic, aristocracy, monarchy and autocracy?

(a) Robert Michels
(b) Montesquieu
(c) Harold Gould
(d) Rajani Kothari

23. Match List-I with List-II

List I	List II
A. Harijan	I. Constitutional and administrative
B. SC/ST	II. Political and cultural
C. Dalit	III. Political and administrative
D. Maha-Dalit	IV. Moral and ethical

Choose the correct answer from the options given below:

(a) A - I, B - II, C - III, D - IV
(b) A - IV, B - I, C - II, D - III
(c) A - IV, B - II, C - I, D - III
(d) A - III, B - II, C - IV, D - I

JUNE 2021

24. Given below are two statements, one is labelled as Assertion A and the other is labelled as Reason R

Assertion A: Democracy has become a global force; while it has become widespread, but all is not well with this political system and it has got into some difficulties almost everywhere.

Reason R: For its failure, it is not the institution itself that is to be blamed; it is the way it has worked or the way its working has been distorted and manipulated by those in power.

In light of the above statements, choose the correct answer from the options given below

(a) Both A and R are true and R is the correct explanation of A
(b) Both A and R are true but R is NOT the correct explanation of A
(c) A is true but R is false
(d) A is false but R is true

25. Match List I with List II

List I (Authors)	List II (Books)
A. Ann Oakley	I. The Future of Feminism
B. Erwing Goffman	II. The Captured Womb: A History of the Medical Care on Pregnant Women
C. Richard Jenkins	III. Forms of Talk
D. Sylvia Walby	IV. Social Identity

Choose the correct answer from the options given below:

(a) A–III, B–II, C–I, D–IV
(b) A–II, B–III, C–IV, D–I
(c) A–IV, B–I, C–III, D–II
(d) A–III, B–IV, C–II, D–I

26. Of the following, what are the causes of the weakening of the Nation-State?

A. Rise of post-national membership
B. Increasing significance of transnational corporations
C. Decrease of political interest in the rights of 'first nations'
D. The growing strength of supranational institutions
E. Smooth process of governance

Choose the correct answer from the options given below:

(a) A, C and D only
(b) B, D and E only
(c) A, B and D only
(d) C, D and E only

27. Who among the following traced the evolution of citizenship in three key stages of Civil rights, Political rights and Social rights?

(a) T. H. Marshall
(b) Gordon Marshall
(c) R. J. Marshal
(d) Martin Marshall

28. The Munda and the Oraon of the Chotta Nagpur who live close to each other and share much of their cultural life, belong to which speech group, respectively?
(a) Austric and Dravidian speech group
(b) Negrito and Nordic speech group
(c) Mongoloid and Mediterranean speech group
(d) Western Brachycephals and Mongoloids speech group

JUNE 2020

29. Which one of the following incidents prompted Vinobha Bhave to initiate the Bhudan Movement in India?
(a) Nalgonda Incident
(b) Srikakulam Incident
(c) Naxalbari Incident
(d) Madhubani Incident

30. Who among the following started the self-respect movement in Tamilnadu?
(a) E.V. Ramaswamy Naicker
(b) Jyotiba Rao Phule
(c) Narayana Guru
(d) Sri Guruji Golwalkar

31. In which state Champaran Satyagraha movement was initiated?
(a) Odisha (b) Madhya Pradesh
(c) Uttar Pradesh (d) Bihar

32. Which of the following are characteristics of a social movement?
1. It is a collective behaviour
2. It is oriented towards goals
3. It can bring or resist change
4. Causes of movement are always real, known or unknown
5. Movement is caused by deprivation only

Choose the most appropriate answer from the options given below:
(a) 1, 2, 4 only (b) 2, 3, 5 only
(c) 1, 2, 3 only (d) 3, 4, 5 only

33. Given below are two statements: One is labelled as Assertion A and the other is labelled as Reason R.

Assertion (A): The Preamble of the Constitution seeks to spread fraternity among all Indians.

Reasons (R): The Preamble of the Constitution of India guarantees to all citizens of India. Social, Economic and Political Justice

In light of the above statements, choose the correct answer from the options given below:
(a) Both (A) and (R) are true and R is the correct explanation of A
(b) Both (A) and (R) are true but R is not the correct explanation of A
(c) (A) is true but (R) is false
(d) (A) is false but (R) is true

DECEMBER 2019

34. Which set of International Development organizations work towards fighting against poverty?
(a) ILO, UNICEF, WHO, UNHCR, The Red Cross
(b) Oxfam, UNDP, UNICEF, The Red Cross, The Hunger Project
(c) World Bank, WHO, IMF, UNDP, ILO
(d) UNHCR, CEDAW, UNICEF, IMF, Oxfam

35. Match List I and List II

List I (Tribes)	List II (State/Region)
A. Khasi	I. Nilgiri Hills
B. Toda	II. Meghalaya
C. Munda	III. Odisa
D. Khond	IV. Chota Nagpur

Choose the correct option:
(a) A - II, B - I, C - IV, D - III
(b) A - I, B - II, C - IV, D - III
(c) A - III, B - I, C - II, D - IV
(d) A - IV, B - III, C - I, D - II

36. Match List I with List. II

List I (Feminist Perspective)	List II (Gender Issues)
A. Cultural	I. Gender Inequality
B. Liberal	II. Gender Oppression
C. Radical	III. Structural Oppression
D. Socialist	IV. Gender differences

Choose the correct option:
(a) A - IV, B - I, C - II, D - III
(b) A - I, B - III, C - IV, D - II
(c) A - II, B - IV, C - III, D - I
(d) A - III, B - II, C - I, D - IV

37. Tamilian movement in Srilanka is an example of :
1. An Ethnic movement
2. A Regional movement
3. A Religious movement
4. A social reform movement

Choose the correct option:
(a) 1 and 2
(b) 2 and 3
(c) 3 and 4
(d) 4 and 1

38. Who has criticized the emerging political culture of corruption and criminality in his/her work on Indian Politics?
(1) D.N. Dhanagare
(2) Zoya Hasan
(3) Rajni Kothari
(4) Anand Kumar

Options:

(a) 1 (b) 2
(c) 3 (d) 4

39. Match List I with List II

List I (Peasant Movement)	List II (Place)
A. Bardoli movement	I. Malabar
B. Moplah rebellion	II. Andhra Pradesh
C. Peasant revolt in Telangana	III. Bengal
D. Tibhaga movement	IV. Gujarat

Choose the correct option:

(a) A - I, B - III, C - IV, D - II
(b) A - II, B - III, C - IV, D - I
(c) A - I, B - II, C - III, D - IV
(d) A - IV, B - I, C - II, D - III

40. What are the essential characteristics of bureaucracy?

1. Hierarchy of power
2. Unlimited power
3. Channelling of communication
4. Informal relations between the officials

Choose the correct option:

(a) 2 and 3 (b) 1 and 4
(c) 1 and 3 (d) 2 and 4

41. Bhil and Meena's tribes are largely living in the state of—

(1) Gujarat (2) Maharastra
(3) Rajasthan (4) Jharkhand

Options

(a) 1 (b) 2
(c) 3 (d) 4

42. Where was the largest and longest protest in 1980 organised by Bhartiya Kisan Union under the leadership of Mahendra Singh Tikait?

(a) Hyderabad (b) Banglore
(c) Delhi (d) Meerut

43. Sociology originated largely in a philosophical ambition to

1. Account for the course of human history
2. Explain the social crisis of the 19th Century Europe
3. Explain the origin of Industrialization
4. Account for the French revolution

Select the correct option:

(a) 1 and 2 (b) 2 and 3
(c) 3 and 4 (d) 4 and 1

44. Which one of the following metropolises has the highest percentage and lowest percentage of scheduled castes?

(a) Bengaluru (b) Mumbai
(c) Chennai (d) Delhi

Choose the correct option:

(a) 1 and 2 (b) 2 and 3
(c) 3 and 2 (d) 4 and 1

45. From among the classical sociologists, who have used the comparative method but in different ways?

1. Emile Durkheim 2. Karl Marx
3. Max Weber 4. Auguste Comte

Choose the correct option

(a) 2 and 3 (b) 3 and 4
(c) 4 and 1 (d) 1 and 3

JUNE 2019

46. Match List-I with List-II

List I (Author)	List II (Contribution)
(A) Max Weber	I. Interaction Ritual
(B) E. Goffman	II. The Nation State and Violence
(C) A. Giddens	III. The Religion of India
(D) David Held	IV. Models of Democracy

Chose the correct option from those given below:

(a) A - I, B - IV, C – III, D – II
(b) A – III, B - IV, C – II, D – I
(c) A - III, B - I, C – II, D – IV
(d) A - IV, B - I, C – II, D – III

47. According to Max Weber, which entities are always struggling for domination?

(a) Class (b) Parties
(c) Class Situation (d) Status

48. Which one of the following countries is an example of 'state capitalism'?

(a) China (b) India
(c) Switzerland (d) France

49. Which section of Indian Penal Code deals with LGBT?

(a) 376 (b) 377
(c) 487 (d) 497

50. Which ruling party in Cambodia was associated with mass killing in the 20th century?

(a) National Socialist
(b) Bosnian Nationalist Group
(c) Khmer Rouge
(d) Republican Party

51. Who propounded the concept of 'Hegemony'?

(a) Antonio Gramsci (b) Karl Marx
(c) Max Weber (d) R. Dahrendorf

Answer Key

1. (d)
2. (d)
3. (b)
4. (b)
5. (c)
6. (a)
7. (a)
8. (b)
9. (a)
10. (b)
11. (d)
12. (b)
13. (a)
14. (b)
15. (a)
16. (c)
17. (a)
18. (b)
19. (c)
20. (d)
21. (d)
22. (b)
23. (b)
24. (a)
25. (b)
26. (c)
27. (a)
28. (a)
29. (a)
30. (a)
31. (d)
32. (c)
33. (b)
34. (b)
35. (a)
36. (a)
37. (a)
38. (c)
39. (d)
40. (c)
41. (c)
42. (c)
43. (a)
44. (c)
45. (d)
46. (c)
47. (b)
48. (a)
49. (b)
50. (c)
51. (a)

Unit-VI

Economy and Society

Chapters:

Top: Photo credit: elenabsl.Shutterstock
Below: Photo Credit: Morrowind.Shutterstock

CHAPTER

1 Relationship between Economy and Society

LEARNING OBJECTIVES:

In this chapter, we will discuss the following important topics.

- Exchange, gift, capital, labour, and Market
- Property and property relations
- State and Market: Welfarism and neoliberalism
- Poverty and exclusion
- Factory and industry systems
- Business and family
- Tourism

INTRODUCTION

Sociologists, while analyzing the relationship between economy and society, argued that society affects the economic structure and economic processes in turn affect the society's environment. Economic sociology is the application of sociological methods to understand the production, distribution, exchange, and consumption of goods and services. Economic sociology is particularly attentive to the changes caused by society's actions on the economic system and vice versa.

EXCHANGE, GIFT, CAPITAL, LABOUR, AND MARKET

Exchange

- Karl Polanyi, an economic historian, has identified three different methods of allocation or theories of exchange:
    i. reciprocity,
    ii. redistribution and
    iii. market exchange.

Reciprocal Exchange

This method refers to the transfer of goods or services between two people or groups based on their role obligations. For example, we visit our grandparents with gifts during the holidays, offer a ride to school to a friend, etc. We behave according to rules defined by reciprocal exchange, revolving around the notion of role obligation.

The reason for their reciprocal exchange is not necessarily dictated by the desire for the material goods as it is in the market. Certainly, when mother and son make an effort to give each other gifts they know will be appreciated, but the reason for the exchange is their obligation to each other, an obligation they assume when they are mother and son. He plays the role of a son. If the son fails to give anything to his mother, she will be hurt and disappointed. Similarly, a mother who did not give gifts would also have to face very disappointed children. For this reason, reciprocal exchange between strangers usually does not occur.

Furthermore, the reciprocal exchange is not determined by maximization which is the basic principle operating in market exchange. When a mother gives a gift to her son, she does not care what the son is going to give her in return.

There are two kinds of reciprocity:

i. **Generalised reciprocity:** It is a type of reciprocal exchange in which neither the value of the gift nor what is given is calculated nor the time of repayment is specified. Such transactions do not involve economic or other self-interest. This means that generalized reciprocity is the giving of gifts without any immediate return or conscious thought of return.

ii. **Balanced reciprocity:** It is a type of reciprocal exchange in which goods and services of proportionate value are traded within a finite period (direct exchange). This kind of reciprocity is motivated by the desire or need for certain objects in exchange.

Redistribution

This system of exchange refers to the transfer of goods and services between a group of people and a central collecting source based on role obligation. In this kind of exchange, a central collecting agency first collects the goods at some central point and then redistributes them among the members of the group. Like reciprocity, the redistributive exchange also occurs because people are obligated to each other.

In other words, goods collected or contributed from members of a group flow to some central point from which they are redistributed to society. Redistribution is a process that is found in all societies but it becomes an important mechanism of distribution only in societies with a relatively complex system of political organisation and substantial economic surplus.

In all societies, there is some voluntary redistribution, at least within the family. The members of the family pool their labor or products or income for their common good. But redistribution exists in most hunting and fishing societies, in some horticultural societies, and in nearly all pastoral and agricultural societies, which have political machinery of one sort or another to coordinate centralized collection and distribution, for example, Potlatch celebrations.

The Potlatch Ceremony

Potlatch is a gift-giving ceremony among indigenous peoples of the Pacific Northwest Coast of Canada and the United States, it is also a form of redistribution. Traditionally its function was to act as a primary government institution, legislative body, and economic system. It involves the ritual display of privileges and titles and the distribution of goods among the guests for the purpose of validating and enhancing the host's privileges and prestige.

A potlatch involves giving away or destroying wealth or valuable items in order to demonstrate a leader's wealth and power. For example, the house-building potlatch is most important ceremony practiced by almost all the members. For about 10 years a man and his wife work hard to accumulate the required property. A year before the potlatch ceremony, the wife lends furs or blankets from the common store to various members of her clan. The clan members return them at the time of potlatch with a hundred percent interest. At the time of the potlatch, the guests assemble in the new house and are seated according to their rank. Through this ritual, while the recipients gain material goods, the hosts acquire social and political prestige.

Market Exchange

It is the exchange of goods and services according to the law of supply and demand. The market exchange system is controlled by the circulation of money in which goods and services are bought and sold at a money price that is determined by the impersonal forces of supply and demand.

Unlike reciprocity and redistribution, in which the social and political roles of those who exchange are important, market exchange is impersonal and occurs no matter what the social position of the participants is.

Market exchange is thus the most purely economic model of exchange. In a market exchange system economic goals play a more important role than social or political goals. Therefore, market exchange is also known as money exchange or commercial exchange.

This system of exchange involving money came into being when an economy developed to the point where the food supply regularly exceeded the needs of those engaged in food production. Market exchange depends on the fact that how much people want a particular commodity or service and how much they have to pay to get them.

Every time we speak of selling something or buying something we need, we are using terms associated with market exchange such as buy, sell, discount, price, money, cost, profit, loss, etc. These words express various aspects of the many different transactions that characterise our complex market economy.

Following are some of the important types of economic exchange.

i. Barter System
ii. Silent Trade
iii. Jajmani System
iv. Ceremonial Exchange
v. Reciprocity
vi. Redistribution
vii. Market or Commercial Exchange

Barter System

Barter system is the direct exchange of goods and services i.e an exchange may be goods for goods, goods for services, service for service, etc. It is considered to be the earliest form of exchange in Human society. Barter usually replaced money as the method of exchange during crises like war, natural calamity, etc.

Silent Trade

Silent trade (also known as silent barter or trade and dumb barter) is a peculiar form of exchange where the exchanging parties do not come into face-to-face interaction during the process of exchange. The exchanging partners could be enemies or antagonised. One group of people leaves a certain quantity of products at a customary place to be taken by another group, who in turn leaves back some other products. The pygmy Semang and Sakai of Malaya and the Vedda and Sinhalese of Sri Lanka practice silent trade.

Jajmani System

William H Wiser (1988) introduced the term Jajmani system in his book, The Hindu Jajmani System: A Socio-Economic System Interrelating Members Of A Hindu Village Community In Services, where he described in detail how different caste groups interact with each other in the agriculture-based system of production, distribution, and exchange of goods and services.

In different parts of India different terms are used to describe this economic interaction among the castes, for example in Maharashtra the term Balutedar or bara balute and mera or mirasi in rural Rayalaseema of Andhra Pradesh, jajmani in North India, mirasi in Tamil Nadu and adade in Karnataka.

Jajmani system, (Hindi: deriving from the Sanskrit yajamana, "sacrificial patron who employs priests for a ritual") is reciprocal (usually asymmetrical and some scholars term its non-reciprocal) social and economic arrangements between families of different castes within a village community in India for the exchange of goods and services.

Here, one family exclusively performs certain services for the other, such as ministering to the rituals or providing agricultural labour, or some goods such as agricultural implements, pots, baskets, etc in return for payment, protection, and employment security. These relations are supposed to continue from one generation to the next, and payment is normally made traditionally, in the form of a fixed share in the harvest rather than in cash.

Ceremonial / Gift Exchange

It is a kind of social system in which goods and services are given to relatives, friends, and neighbours on various social occasions like birth rituals, marriage, death rituals, etc. The basic initiative of this exchange is to establish good relations between the various social groups in society.

Kula Ring of Exchange

According to Malinowski (1922), Kula is a ceremonial exchange among Trobriand Islanders of New Guinea. Kula is also known as kula exchange or kula ring. It is a complex system of visits and exchange of two kinds of ornaments as well as trading of food and other commodities with the people of other (nearby or far off) islands.

The Kula ornaments are of two types. One consists of shell-disc necklaces (veigun or Soulava) that are traded to the north (circling the ring in a clockwise direction) and the other are shell armbands (Mwali) that are traded in the southern direction (circling counter-clockwise).

These are exchanged in a ceremonial ambiance purely for the purposes of enhancing mutual trust relationships, securing trade, and enhancing one's social status and prestige.

Market

As we generally understand that market is a place where things are bought and sold. Adam Smith, in his book 'The Wealth of Nations', described a market economy as a series of individual exchanges or transactions that automatically constitute a functioning and orderly system. Sociologists view markets as social institutions that are constructed culturally. For example, markets are often controlled or organized by particular social groups or castes or classes, and have specific relationships to other institutions, social processes, and structures.

Capital Market

A capital market is a market where buyers and sellers engage in the trade of financial securities like bonds, stocks, etc. The buying/selling is undertaken by participants such as individuals and institutions.

Capital markets help channelise surplus funds from savers to institutions that then invest them into productive use. Generally, this market trades mostly in long-term securities.

The capital market consists of primary markets and secondary markets.

Primary markets deal with the trade of new issues of stocks and other securities, whereas secondary market deals with the exchange of existing or previously-issued securities. Another important division in the capital market is made on the basis of the nature of security traded, i.e., stock market and bond market.

Labour Market

In order to understand the meaning of labour markets, one needs to understand who are the demanders and suppliers in the labour market. Firms and other employers demand labour to produce goods and services. Households supply their labour services and in return, get wages.

The labour market is studied by microeconomists as well as macroeconomists as both use the tools of demand and supply. The labour market refers to the supply and demand for labour, in which employees provide the supply and employers the demand. It is a major component of any economy and is intricately tied in with markets for capital, goods, and services.

At the macroeconomic level, supply and demand are influenced by domestic and international market dynamics, as well as factors such as immigration, the age of the population, and education levels. Commonly used measures in labour markets are the unemployment rate, labour productivity, labour intensity, participation rates, and total wage income as a percentage of GDP.

Wages represent the price of labour, which provides income to households and represents a cost to firms. In a hypothetical free market economy, wages are determined by the unregulated interaction of demand and supply. However, in real mixed economies, governments and trade unions can exert an influence on wage levels.

At the microeconomic level, individual firms interact with employees, hiring them, firing them, and raising or cutting wages and hours of work. The interaction between supply and demand influences the hours the employees work and the compensation they receive in form of wages, salary, and other benefits.

Mode of Production Debates

Utsa Patnaik She has authored several books–Peasant Class Differentiation–A Study in Method, The Long Transition (1999), and The Republic of Hunger and Other Essays.

She has also edited and co-edited several volumes Chains of Servitude–Bondage and Slavery in India, Agrarian Relations and Accumulation–the Mode of Production Debate in India, The Making of History –Essays Presented to Irfan Habib, The Agrarian Question in Marx and his Successors in two volumes, andA Theory of Imperial Capitalism

The discussion, which developed into a wide-ranging debate, on the growth of capitalist production in Indian agriculture, began in the early sixties with a few papers by authors of broadly Marxist persuasion, in diverse journals some of which are now defunct. The debate gathered momentum towards the end of the decade and reached its most intensive phase in the seventies, with a large number of participants writing in Economic and Political Weekly. The starting point of the broader debate lay in a dual dissatisfaction as far as this author was concerned:

First, with the idea that the mechanisms and trajectory of development of an ex-colonial country like India were in their essentials the same as those for the western capitalist countries; and secondly, with the idea that India was part of a world capitalist 'periphery', a mere agreement integrated through the exchange, with the western world.

From the beginning broadly two approaches or points of view emerged. First, did not see any major qualitative 'break' between the colonial and post-independence periods with respect to the growth of capitalist relations of production, other than perhaps one of the varying speeds of transition.

According to this interpretation, colonial exploitation involved the growing commercialisation of agriculture and the growth of wage-paid labour, and such commodity production inevitably implied also that capitalist production relations were developing.

If these relations did not take the pervasive form of direct employment of hired labour for profit, this was sought to be explained by invoking Marx's distinction between the 'formal' versus 'real' subsumption of labour under capital, with the argument that peasants indebted to merchants and moneylenders were 'formally subsumed under capital'.

The landlord-petty tenant relation was also interpreted by some as a 'capitalist' one, i.e., the analytical distinction between profit and rent was considered unimportant. Post-independence developments, on this view, continued the same trends, only at a much faster pace.

The second approach, to which this author subscribed, on the other hand, identified a definite qualitative 'break' between the colonial and subsequent period with respect to the growth of capitalist production in agriculture and related this break primarily to the question of accumulation.

It argued that colonial revenue-cum-rent exploitation promoted not the proletarianization of peasants so much as their pauperisation since a substantial share of the economic surplus was transferred abroad to finance metropolitan industrialisation.

Consequently, these forms mediated a process of 'forced' commercialisation of agriculture ('forced' because peasants had to sell to pay rent-cum-revenue), marked by a relative absence of transformation of the productive base and structural deformation of the economy.

The post-independence agrarian structure carried the legacy of this process in the form of endemic underemployment and unemployment. While the new economic environment of state investments and encouragement of capitalist production initiated a new phase of agrarian accumulation, it was constrained by inherited production relations and in particular by the petty tenancy.

Hamza Alavi Important issues have been raised by Indian Marxist agricultural economists in the debate on the 'Mode of Production in Indian Agriculture'. That debate is taking place in the context of the far-reaching changes which have taken place in Indian agriculture in recent years — changes that were once celebrated as 'the Green Revolution'.

Today, its conservative authors, as well as its radical critics, are compelled, by the force of the surfacing contradictions in rural class relations (as well as in the economy as a whole), to move beyond the limits of justification or condemnation, and to analyse and assess the nature and significance of the structural changes that have taken place.

The Indian debate on the mode of the production revolves around the question of whether, in the last 15 or 20 years, there has been a decisive movement in Indian agriculture from a feudal mode of production to a capitalist mode of production.

Similar questions have been raised elsewhere. In fact, a theoretical point of departure for the Indian debate is the well-known polemical exchange between A Gunder Frank and Ernesto Laclau about feudalism and capitalism in Latin America.

A more serious criticism could be that, by focusing on the agrarian economy, the debate conceptualizes 'mode of production' too narrowly — although it must be said that, on specific issues, the wider contexts of the developments in agriculture and some of the implications arising therefrom are considered.

We would like to emphasize that, both the concept of 'feudalism' in India (during the period of direct colonial domination) as well as the contemporary phenomenon of rural 'capitalism' cannot be grasped theoretically in all their implications except specifically, in the context of the world-wide structure of Imperialism into which it is articulated.

A consideration of that fact should lead us towards a conception of a colonial mode of production and the structural specificity that distinguishes it from both feudalism and capitalism in the metropolis.

The contemporary changes and the issues in the debate must be looked at in the context of the demands made on the Indian agrarian economy by Imperialism and industrial development since Independence, as well as in the context of the successful policies that were instituted to realise the objectives for those purposes and the dilemmas and contradictions underlying such policies

Ashok Rudra Ashok Rudra (Marxist) states that contrary to the general tendency of dividing the farmers into three categories – small, middle, and big, there are only two classes in Indian agriculture:

i. big landowners and
ii. agricultural labourers

PROPERTY AND PROPERTY RELATIONS

Property

Property refers to the rights that the owner of the object has in relation to others who are not owners of the object. Property rights are backed by the state and enforced through its legal institutions. According to Kingsley Davis, property "consists of the rights and duties of one person or group (the owner) as against all other persons and groups with respect to some scarce good.

According to Morris Ginsberg, property may be described as the set of rights and obligations which define the relations between individuals or groups in respect of their control over material things or persons treated as things.

According to Anderson and Parker, "Property consists of those goods and services which society grants to an individual or a group of individuals the exclusive right to possess, use and dispose of." This right to goods and services is expressed in the value system of society.

For MacIver, "property is not wealth or possessions, but the right to control, exploit, use or enjoy wealth or possessions that may be owned by a person or several persons belonging to the same social group or relative or clan.

Hobhouse states that property "must be conceived of in terms of man's control over things", a control that is recognized by society as more or less permanent and exclusive.

Harry M. Johnson states, "In popular speech, the word property often refers to things as well as to property rights". Therefore, according to him, property means both things and rights.

Types of Property

Property can be broadly classified into two types, private property, and public (common) property.

Private Property: The term private property is usually applied to rights held by individuals or groups acting in their own interests. Private property can further be classified into two types: individual property and collective property. In individual property, the control is vested in one person. Collective property can take various forms depending on the collective entity that holds ownership and control.

Public Property: The term 'public property' refers to rights held by the community at large and administered by individuals or groups acting as agents of the community. Public property is a property that is subscribed to public use. The term can be used either to describe the use of the property or to describe the character of its own i.e. collectively owned by the population of the state.

State ownership, also called public ownership, government ownership, or state property, are property interests that are vested in the state rather than in individuals or communities.

Difference between private property and public property:

- **i.** The ownership of Private property is controlled by an individual or group of individuals, while the public property is owned by the community.
- **ii.** Private property is generally used by its owner for his own good, while the public property is used for the public good.
- **iii.** Private property is regulated by state laws, and rights over private property is proved by a legal document, while public property belongs to the state and is not subject to regulation by any external group.

STATE AND MARKET: WELFARISM AND NEOLIBERALISM

Welfarism

The term welfarism was coined by the British economist John Hicks. It has been introduced into contemporary debate about social justice by Amartya Sen. Welfarism is a term denoting all theories that demand that we judge the state of society in general, and just distributions in particular, by the welfare of the people concerned, and by their welfare only.

Welfare is an emotional state, subjectively experienced by the person herself. The concepts synonymous with welfare are the terms well-being, happiness, desire fulfillment, utility.

On the other hand, it is also obvious that welfare is influenced by economic goods. Man does not live by bread alone, but the welfare of a hungry person increases when she/he is given bread to eat or money to buy bread. Man does not live by bread alone, but the welfare of a hungry person increases when he is given bread to eat or money to buy bread. Thus, the distribution of economic goods is the distribution of welfare up to a point. Welfarism implies that the distribution of economic goods is evaluated by the effect it has on the welfare of the persons concerned.

Welfare State

The term 'welfare state' describes collectively a range of social policies that aim to provide basic services such as health and education, according to the need and normally, free of charge through state funding. It is sometimes extended more loosely to areas such as social security in which individuals are legally required to make substantial contributions in order to receive the benefits.

The theory of the welfare state is the basis of positive liberalism. It is a sort of state, which provides extensive social services to all the citizens, protects the weaker sections, provides economic and social security, and tries to reduce the gap between the rich and the poor.

It makes laws to control the economy, nationalized industries, makes laws to protect the weaker sections, arranges the supply of essential commodities, maintains essential services, and through progressive taxation and income redistribution tries to reduce the gap between the rich and the poor and thereby, harmonizes the different interests in society.

A welfare state is a form of government in which the state protects and promotes the economic and social welfare of citizens, based on the principles of equal opportunity, equitable distribution of wealth, and public responsibility for citizens unable to avail themselves of the minimum provision for a good life.

Sociologist T. H. Marshall described the modern welfare state as a distinctive combination of democracy, welfare, and capitalism. As a type of mixed economy, the welfare state funds the governmental institutions for health care and education along with direct benefits given to individual citizens.

Early features of the welfare state, such as public pensions and social insurance, developed from the 1880s onwards in industrializing Western countries. The Great Depression, World War I, and World War II have been characterized as important events that ushered in expansion of the welfare state.

Neoliberalism

Neoliberalism is the policy model that favours free markets and minimal government intervention in the economy. It is usually associated with laissez-faire economics.

It is generally associated with policies of economic liberalization, including privatization, deregulation, globalization, free trade, austerity, and reductions in government spending in order to increase the role of the private sector in the economy and society.

In particular, neoliberalism is often characterized by

i. its belief in sustained economic growth as the means to achieve human progress,
ii. its confidence in free markets as the most-efficient allocation of resources,
iii. its emphasis on minimal state intervention in economic and social affairs, and
iv. its commitment to the freedom of trade and capital.

The initial use of the term neoliberalism in English was by the French economist Charles Gide in 1898 to describe the economic beliefs of the Italian economist Maffeo Pantaleoni, first in French with the term neoliberalism, and the term was later used by others including classical liberal economist Milton Friedman in his 1951 essay "Neo-liberalism and its Prospects".

Since the 1990's activists have used the word 'neoliberalism' for global market liberalism ('capitalism') and for free-trade policies. In this sense, it is widely used in South America.

'Neoliberalism' is often used interchangeably with 'globalization'. But free markets and global free trade are nothing new, and the use of the term tends to ignore developments in advanced economies. Around the world, neo-liberalism has been imposed by powerful financial institutions such as

- International Monetary Fund (IMF),
- World Bank and
- Inter- American Development Bank

A general characteristic of neoliberalism is the desire to intensify and expand the market, by increasing the number, frequency, repeatability, and formalization of transactions.

MODELS OF ECONOMIC DEVELOPMENT

Capitalist Model of Development

The main characteristics of the capitalist model of development are:

(a) Private ownership of property and means of production,
(b) promotion of economic activities through private enterprises, and
(c) minimum possible state regulation and control on private enterprises.

Thus, the capitalist model is characterised by a free economy regulated by competition.

Socialist Model of Development

The socialist path of development adopted by the Second World is seen to be opposite or dichotomous to the capitalist path of development. The former, contrary to the latter, is characterized by state ownership of property and means of production, public enterprises, and complete state regulation of economic activities. Thus, the socialist model refers to a controlled economy.

Mixed Model of Development

In a mixed economy, private and public sectors go side by side. The government directs economic activity in some socially important areas of the economy, the rest being left to the price mechanism to operate.

Theory of Modernization

According to Smelser's analysis, modern societies are characterized by social structural differentiation, i.e., clear definition of functions and political roles from national institutions.

"Structural differentiation is the process by which a social role or organization differentiates into two or more roles or organizations. The new social units are structurally distinct from each other, but together they are functionally equivalent to the original unit." Smelser's definition, shared with some variations by recent theoretical analyses, establishes a significantly more inclusive concept than the older "division of labor".

It does not limit itself to the economic sphere, and it deals with more complex structural elements than roles-with organizations and on occasion with even broader and less tangible phenomena such as institutions, values, and cultural complexes. While there is considerable merit in this broader concept, which derives from Spencer, it requires further theoretical distinctions. For instance, it is necessary to recognize that differentiation at the level of roles can go hand in hand with an agglomeration of functions at the level of organizations or broader institutional complexes, and vice versa.

In his book 'The stages of economic growth' Walt Rostow said that modernization is a phased process; he has suggested 5 phases of economic growth: these five stages are:

1. **Traditional society:** In this society barter trading was still practiced to exchange goods, here people use primitive and rudiment technology and are heavily reliant on subsistence farming.
2. **Pre-conditions for takeoff:** Urbanization begins here, people move from subsistence farming to commercial farming, and transportation networks such as roads and railways improve.
3. **The take-off process:** In this stage urbanization increases, industrialization progresses, and technological breakthroughs occur. The "secondary" (goods-producing) sector expands and the ratio of secondary versus primary sectors in the economy moves increasingly towards the secondary. Textiles and apparel are usually the first "take-off" industries, as was the case in Great Britain's classic "Industrial Revolution". An example of a take-off phase is the Agricultural (Green) Revolution in the 1960s.
4. **The drive to maturity:** Here diversification of the industrial base, and expansion of multiple industries take place and new industrial units take root quickly. Manufacturing has shifted from investment-driven (capital goods) to consumer durables and domestic consumption.
5. **Rapid development of transportation infrastructure:** Large-scale investment in social infrastructure (schools, universities, hospitals, etc.). This stage is also known as the age of high mass consumption in this the industrial base dominates the economy; the primary sector is greatly diminished from the economy and society, there is wide and normative consumption of high-value consumer goods (e.g. automobiles), and consumers typically have disposable income, beyond all basic needs. A large scale movement from rural countryside to cities or urban society takes place.

Theory of Dependency

Dependency theory is the notion that resources flow from a "periphery" of poor and underdeveloped states to a "core" of wealthy states, enriching the latter at the expense of the former. Andre Gunder Frank, Raul Prebisch, and P Baran are among the main authors of dependency theory.

The foundations of the theory of dependency emerged in the 1950s from the research of the Economic Commission for Latin America and the Caribbean ECLAC. One of the most representative authors was Raul Prebisch.

The underdeveloped countries were able to purchase fewer and fewer manufactured goods from the developed countries in exchange for a given quantity of their raw materials exports.

Theory of World Systems

Immanuel Wallerstein has developed the best-known version of world-systems analysis, beginning in the 1970s. "World-system" refers to the inter-regional and transnational division of labor, which divides the world into core countries, semi-periphery countries, and periphery countries.

Core countries are the most economically diversified, wealthy, and powerful (economically and militarily).

Peripheral countries are the least economically diversified.

Semi-peripheral nations are those that are midway between the core and periphery.

POVERTY AND EXCLUSION

Poverty is often defined in terms of the income levels of a set of population. The income criteria are preferred as an indicator of poverty as it is easy to establish the income earned by a person or a household. A number of other indicators can be added to these measurements based on their monetary value to arrive at a comprehensive measurement of poverty. Money values denote objective standards of poverty measurement.

Poverty can be conceived as absolute or relative. Absolute poverty is defined as a lack of income or failure to attain capabilities. It can be chronic or temporary, is sometimes closely associated with inequity, and is often correlated with vulnerabilities and social exclusion. The concepts used to define poverty determine the methods employed to measure it and the subsequent policy and programme packages designed to address it.

The Human Development Report 1997 (published by UNDP) distinguishes between poverty and underdevelopment by associating the former with individuals and the latter with an aggregate perspective. The process of development informs us about the degree of progress made by society but this picture would not be complete unless the advances made by each segment and strata in society are assessed.

To maintain development gains and accelerate progress, the Sustainable Development Goals present a roadmap to end poverty in all its dimensions, protect the planet and ensure that all people enjoy peace and prosperity. Three years into the 2030 Agenda, governments, citizens, and the private sector are working together to meet the Goals' targets and ensure dignity and well-being for everyone.

Poverty has been defined differently in developed and developing countries because of their different levels of economic development. There are two main approaches to the problem of poverty-the 'nutritional' approach and the 'relative deprivation' approach.

Nutritional Approach

This approach has been adopted in developing countries. In this case, poverty is measured on the basis of minimum food requirements. This is calculated in terms of consumption of adequate calories (generally 2250 calories) to maintain the working capacity of a person.

People who are unable to fulfill this bare minimum in food consumption due to their low income are placed below the 'poverty line'. The concept of the poverty line is used to demarcate the poor from the non-poor.

It is formulated in terms of an income level, which is considered to be adequate for enabling a person to maintain a minimum level of consumption of goods and services. Persons whose income level is below the poverty line are identified as poor. This is a measure of 'absolute' poverty i.e., poverty defined with reference to some predetermined standard or norm.

Relative Deprivation Approach

In the case of developed countries, the 'relative deprivation' approach has been adopted for measuring poverty because the fulfillment of the minimum need for food is not the major problem. Here, poverty is seen in terms of the relative deprivation of a class or a section of the population against the privileged ones.

Poverty is perceived in terms of an exclusion of a class or section of the population from average living patterns, activities, and participation in social life because of a lack of resources e.g., wealth, income, education and political power.

The emphasis is more on social inequalities than nutritional requirements. The 'nutritional' approach to poverty is highly deficient in nature because it excludes essential non-food requirements for human living. In defining poverty, we must include essential non-food requirements like clothing, housing, education, and health-care facilities, which are as important as the essential food requirements for an average human life in a civilized society.

Culture of Poverty

Poverty forces the poor and deprived to develop certain patterns of behaviour enabling them to survive the sordid conditions of poverty. This pattern has been termed 'Culture of poverty'. The concept was developed by an anthropologist, Oscar Lewis, based on his studies in Mexico. He suggests that the poor develop a culture of their own, or rather a subculture that is not part of the behaviour pattern or the value system of the society in which they live. Lewis says that the poor tend to be socially isolated.

FACTORY AND INDUSTRY SYSTEMS

Factory system, a system of manufacturing that began in the 18th century and is based on the concentration of industry in specialized and often large establishments. The system originated during the Industrial Revolution. The factory system replaced the domestic system, in which individual workers used hand tools or simple machinery to make goods in their homes or in workshops attached to their homes.

The use of waterpower and then the steam engine to mechanize processes such as cloth weaving in England in the late 18th century marked the beginning of the factory system. The system that arose, in which work was organized using power-driven machinery and the production of goods on a large scale, had important social consequences:

- **i.** In the past, workers used to be independent craftsmen who had their own tools and set their own working hours, but in the factory system, the employer owned the tools and raw materials and set the hours and other conditions under which the workers worked.
- **ii.** The location of work also changed.
- **iii.** Under the domestic system workers had inhabited rural areas, whereas in the factory system workers moved to cities and towns because the new factories had to be located near waterpower and transportation.

The movement toward industrialization often led to overcrowded substandard housing and poor sanitary conditions for workers. Furthermore, many of the new unskilled jobs could be performed equally well by women, men, or children, thus tending to reduce factory wages to subsistence levels.

Factories tend to be poorly lit, cluttered, and unsafe places where workers work long hours for little pay. These harsh conditions gave rise to the trade-union movement of the late 19th century, in which workers attempted to improve their conditions through collective action.

Two major advances in the factory system occurred in the early 20th century: management science and the assembly line.

Scientific management, such as time and motion study, helped to rationalize production processes by reducing or eliminating unnecessary and repetitive tasks performed by individual workers.

The old system in which workers carried their parts to a stationary assembly point was replaced by the automatic assembly line, in which the product being assembled moved on a mechanized conveyor from one stationary worker to the next until it was completely assembled properly.

Changing Nature of Labour Relations

Industrial relations means the relationship between a worker on the one hand and his employer on the other. Workers in industrial relations provide their services for wages. But their performance depends upon the environment provided during work, i.e., working conditions apart from wages are responsible for good performance, how the management treats its workers and how the workers act in the interest of their employers is the essence of industrial relations.

In most industrial units of modern organized industry, workers organize themselves into unions and use their common interests as a force that keeps them unionized. They use unions as a means to ensure a good work environment. On the other hand, employers may also prefer to help improve the work environment, as long as the cost of improving the environment results in increased productivity to offset the costs incurred.

Production is the result of joint efforts of management and workers in any producing unit. Therefore, harmonious industrial relations are essential for achieving the targets of production and enhancing productivity. In the absence of good relations, industrial conflicts surface and adversely affect all sections of society.

Other consequences of bad industrial relations are work stoppage and impoverishment of the workers and retrenchment. Management faces loss due to stoppage of production, rise in the cost of production, and damages to machines and equipment.

Disruption in production activities reduces the national income. This leads to a decline in government revenue through the reduced collection of excise and corporate income taxes, increased administrative expenses for maintaining law and order and controlling criminal activities during periods of industrial conflict.

In 1974, Harry Braverman wrote 'Labor and Monopoly Capital', which provided a critical analysis of scientific management. In this book capitalist productive relations are analyzed from Marxist point of view. Following Marx, Braverman argued that work within capitalist organizations was exploitative and alienating and that workers were therefore to be forced into servitude. For Braverman, the capitalist system over time eventually leads to deskilling and routinization of the worker.

Andrew Freidman, in his work 'Industry and Labor (1977)', suggested that while direct control of labor is beneficial to the capitalist under certain circumstances, a degree of "responsible autonomy" may be granted to unionized or "core" workers, in order to harness their skill under controlled conditions.

Furthermore, Richard Edwards showed in 1979 that although hierarchies remain stable in organizations, additional forms of control such as technical control through email monitoring, call monitoring, procedures for leave, illness, etc. have been added to gain the interests of the capitalist class versus the workers.

Duncan Galley has shown in his study that is important to look at the question of skill from the point of view of social class, he observed that most non-manual, intermediate, and skilled manual workers believed that their work demanded a high level of skill. But at the same time, most manual workers felt that the responsibility and skills required in their work either remained constant or declined.

BUSINESS AND FAMILY

Joint Hindu Family Firm

Joint Hindu Family Firm is a unique form of business organization practiced only in India. It is a firm belonging to a Joint Hindu family and is governed by the provisions of Hindu law.

In Hindu Law there are two schools:

i. **Mitakshara Law:** It is applicable to the whole of India except Bengal and Assam. According to this school of thought, a Hindu inherits property from his father, grandfather, and great-grandfather. Thus, in the male line, three successive generations (son, grandson, and great-grandson) inherit the ancestral property. They are called coparceners and the senior most member of the family is called 'Karta'. The Hindu Succession Act, 1956 has extended the extent of coparcenary interest to female relatives of a deceased coparcener or to male relatives claiming through such female relatives.

ii. **Dayabhaga Law:** It is applicable in Bengal and Assam. According to this, male heirs become members only after the death of the Hindu karta. According to Hindu law, a business is an inheritable asset and after the death of the Hindu, the business will be owned by all the coparceners. The eldest of the co-parceners becomes the new Karta and manages the business.

If a property is inherited from another relative, or acquired from personal resources, such property is treated as personal property and is to be distinguished from ancestral property.

Some of the significant characteristics of the Joint Hindu Family Firm are:

i. The business is managed by the senior most member of the family called the Karta. Other members do not have the right to participate in the management of the firm.
ii. Other members cannot question the authority of the Karta. If other members of the family want to have rights over the business, the only way is to dissolve the family by mutual consent.
iii. Only the Karta has the power to borrow money for the business. Karta's liability is also unlimited while other members are liable only to the extent of their share in the
iv. If the Karta has misappropriated the funds of the business, he has to pay compensation to the other co-members to the extent of their shares in the business.
v. The death of any member of the family does not lead to the dissolution of the business or the family.
vi. Through the mutual agreement the joint Hindu family firm can be dissolved.

Difference between the Joint Hindu family Firm and the Partnership Firm

A joint Hindu family firm is the result of the operation of Hindu law. No formal agreement is required for the new member of the family to become a member of the joint Hindu family business, he automatically becomes a coparcener. While a legal agreement is necessary for individuals to become partners in a partnership firm.

In a joint Hindu family firm only, the Karta can participate in the management. The liability of the Karta is unlimited but the liability of the other coparceners is limited to their share in the business. The rights, duties, and liabilities of the coparceners are governed by the provisions of Hindu law. On the other hand, in a partnership firm, each partner has the right to participate in the management of the business. The liability of each partner is also unlimited. The duties, rights, and liabilities of the partners are governed by the Indian Partnership Act, 1932.

Digital Economy and E-Commerce

'Digital Economy 'means an economy which is based on digital computing technologies or doing business through 'internet' and 'world wide web'. The digital economy has also been referred to as the online economy, internet economy, new economy, or e-economy.

Thomas Mesenboargy identified three main components of the digital economy i.e.

i. e-business infrastructure,
ii. e-commerce, and
iii. e-business.

E-commerce has been growing rapidly across the world. It helps companies or individuals to conduct business over the electronic network and internet. There are three types of e-commerce business models in India.

These are (i) inventory base; (ii) market base; and (iii) hybrid model of inventory or marketplace model. E-commerce or e-business uses Electronic Data Interchange (EDI), Electronic mail, or Electronic Fund Transfer (EFT) for less paper or paperless exchange of information.

It means the ability to conduct business electronically or by the internet. It is a platform for selling services and products through the internet.

The advantages of e-commerce/e-business are that it (i) increased purchasing opportunities for the buyers; (ii) lowers staff costs; (iii) helps the market expand; (iv) decreases the cost of advertisement; (v) enhances the opportunities for the globalization of business; (vi) maximize the profit; and (vii) improved customer service and loyalty.

E-marketing like the online economy, internet marketing, web marketing, digital marketing, and online marketing terms are being used for e-marketing.

It is a set of tools and methodologies used for advertisements of products and services through the internet. It not only includes marketing on the internet but also includes marketing through email/or using social media like WhatsApp, LinkedIn, and Facebook.

The advantages of e-marketing are, it (a) reduces marketing costs of the product; (ii) helps to reach the right consumer; (iii) helps in monitoring the marketing process; (iv) increases sales of the product; and (v) increase profit. To conclude it can be said that, 'online marketing connects organisations with qualified and knowledgeable potential customers and takes business development to a much higher level than traditional marketing'. It is further stated that online marketing combines the internet's creative and technical tools, including design and development for sales and advertising.

Uses of the internet: The Internet provides information to customers on his/her individual accounts/mobile. It helps the customer to know the low price of the individual product. It also helps the company to know which products are selling well and see the profit through day to day operations.

The internet can be used for customer relationship management, enterprise resource planning, supply chain management, and procurement. Many people use the internet as a source of information to compare prices or look at the latest products on offer before making a purchase online or at a traditional store.

E-business is sometimes used as another term for the same process. More often, though, it is used to define a broader process of how the Internet is changing the way companies do business, of the way they relate to their customers and suppliers, it also functions as marketing and logistics.

At present, the number of internet users is estimated to be 566 million as of December 2018. About 87% of them are regular users, 97% of users access the internet on mobile devices. About 250 million users belong to rural India.

Digital Divide

The term 'Digital Divide' combines two words in itself: 'Digital' & 'Divide'. The term 'Digital' here refers to Information & Communication Technology (ICT) while 'Divide' means differences, disparity or gaps.

In general, the digital divide is a phenomenon wherein those who have access to ICT are benefit by its use of it. Their economic well-being is ensured in the form of highly paid jobs and more business opportunities, while those who do not have the access to ICT remain aloof with these benefits and hence comparatively they are in a disadvantageous position.

The divide does not affect only economically but socially as well. Hence the digital divide is the socio-economic difference between people in their access to ICT.

The term also refers to gaps between groups in their ability to use ICTs due to varying literacy and technical skills, and the gap in the availability of quality, useful digital content. The divide is seen as a socioeconomic problem.

The term was used for the first time in the mid-1990s in reference to the disparity in Internet access between rural and urban United States of America. The idea of the digital divide, as put by some scholars, echoes reservations against claims of the revolutionary power of ICT.

It is commonly suggested that ICT is transforming society by bridging the distance or gap. Against this, the skeptics have pointed out that ICT is forming a new kind of gap and this gap is known as the digital divide. Their argument is based on a hypothesis found in Communications Studies i.e., 'the knowledge gap hypothesis'.

Knowledge-gap Hypothesis

The knowledge-gap hypothesis suggests that each new medium of information increases the gap between the informed class and the uninformed class in society. Those who have access to the new medium will get more information than their counterparts. It was first proposed by Phillip J. Tichenor and his colleagues.

TOURISM

England's Sporting Magazine introduced the word "tourism" in 1911.' Feifer proposes that the word tourist 'was coined by Stendhal in the early nineteenth century [1838].' Mieczkowski defined tourists as 'persons who travel out of curiosity and idleness.'

Kaul argues that even though the word tourist is of comparatively recent origin, nevertheless invaders were commonly referred to as tourists in the hope that one day they would leave.

According to Hunziker and Krapf tourism is "the sum of the phenomena and relationships arising from the travel and stay of non-residents, in so far as it does not lead to permanent residence and is not connected to any earning activity".

Erik Cohen (1972) outlined four types of tourists which are as follows:

- **Organised Mass Tourists:** These are the least adventurous tourists. On buying their package holiday they remain encapsulated in an "environment bubble" divorced from the host community as they remain primarily in the hotel complex. They make few decisions about their holiday.
- **Individual Mass Tourists:** They are similar to organised mass tourists in that they utilise the facilities made available by the tour operator, but they have some control over their own itinerary. They may use the hotel as a Concept in the Tourism base and hire a car for their own trips. However, many will tend to visit the same places as the mass organised tourist.
- **Explorer:** The explorer arranges his or her trip alone, and attempts to get off the beaten track.
- **Drifter:** Drifters will live with the locals and adopt many of the practices of that community. Income is generated by working with the community, but often through low-skilled work, which creates a tendency to mix with the lower socio-economic groups.

ASSESS YOUR LEARNING

PRACTICE QUESTIONS

1. Which of the following statement is incorrect?
   (a) After the green revolution, inter-caste relations have changed from Jajmani to contractual relationships.
   (b) The green revolution has given opportunities to service castes in diverse occupations.
   (c) Green Revolution can be considered a failure in terms of human needs although it has succeeded in its goal of producing more food.
   (d) Most of the groups affected by the green revolution belonged to the lower backward classes.

2. Who suggests that modernization has 5 stages they are: traditional society, a precondition for take-off, the takeoff process, the drive to maturity, and high mass consumption society?
   (a) Neil J. Smelser
   (b) W. W. Rostow
   (c) Daniel Lemer
   (d) E. M. Rogers

3. Equal Remuneration Act was enacted in which year?
   (a) 1986 (b) 1976
   (c) 1966 (d) 1956

4. Which of the following statement about Child Labour (Prohibition and Regulation) Amendment Act, 2016 is incorrect?
   (a) It prohibits "the engagement of children in all occupations and of adolescents in hazardous occupations and processes".
   (b) Adolescents refers to those under 14 years.
   (c) The Act also imposes a fine on anyone who employs or permits adolescents to work.
   (d) It allows child labour in "family or family enterprises" or allows the child to be "an artist in an audio-visual entertainment industry".

5. A set of policies that emphasizes the rule of the market, cutting public expenditure for social services, deregulation puritization, and elimination of the public good or community is conceptualized as which of the following?
   (a) Neo-Marxism
   (b) Neo-functionalism
   (c) Neo-liberalism
   (d) Fordism

6. India imposed a cess on domestically produced and imported coal which was earlier known as 'clean energy cess', now it is renamed as?
   (a) GST Compensation Cess
   (b) Clean Environment Cess
   (c) GST Environment Cess
   (d) GST Energy Cess

7. What percentage of the total profit a corporate must invest for the purpose of 'Corporate Social Responsibility (CSR)' in India?
   (a) 5% (b) 4%
   (c) 3% (d) 2%

8. According to the World Bank, if you're living on $1.90 a day or less, you're living in?
   (a) Extreme Poverty
   (b) Absolute Poverty
   (c) Relative Poverty
   (d) Above Poverty Line

9. According to "Piecing together the poverty puzzle" a report on poverty in 2018 published by the World Bank, which of the following country has the largest number of people living in extreme poverty?
   (a) India
   (b) Nigeria
   (c) Democratic Republic of Congo
   (d) Ethiopia

10. Who is the author of the book, "Poverty and Unbritish Rule in India"?
   (a) Dadabhai Naoroji
   (b) G S Ghurye
   (c) Verrier Elwin
   (d) Yogendra Singh

11. What is the measure of the poverty line as per the Asian Development Bank?
   (a) $2.9 per person per day.
   (b) $3.5 per person per day.
   (c) $4.5 per person per day.
   (d) $ 1.51 per person per day.

12. The intra-tribal economic relations are mostly based on?
   (a) shell money
   (b) jajmani system
   (c) barter and exchange
   (d) stone money

13. The poverty line in India is estimated on the basis of the?
   (a) Income level
   (b) Consumption Expenditure
   (c) Living standard
   (d) Conspicuous Consumption

14. Who said that globalization is the growing reciprocal interdependence and integration of various economies around the globe?
(a) A. Giddens
(b) Meghnad Desai
(c) Henderson Hazel
(d) Martin Knor

15. Who is the author of the book 'Spending the Kids' in which he described the growing number of older people in Western society spending their money on travel, cars, and property, in contrast to previous generations who tended to leave that money to their children.
(a) Annie Hulley
(b) Die Broke
(c) Jacob Mincer
(d) Jonathan Friedman

16. Who is the author of the book '*Consumption and Identity*'?
(a) Annie Hulley
(b) Die Broke
(c) Jacob Mincer
(d) Jonathan Friedman

17. Digital economy is the result of increasing
(a) Online shopping
(b) Automatic machines in production
(c) Computer technology
(d) Imparting technology for industrialization

18. The process by which technology lowers the cost of storing, sharing, and analyzing data is known as:
(a) Mechanization
(b) Commercialization
(c) Digitalization
(d) Globalization

19. World Bank comprises two institutions, which are they?
(1) the International Bank for Reconstruction and Development (IBRD)
(2) the International Development Association (IDA)
(3) the World Intellectual Property Organization (WIPO)
(4) the United Nations Development Programme (UNDP)

Codes:
(a) 1 and 2
(b) 2 and 3
(c) 3 and 4
(d) 1 and 4

20. The Gini coefficient, sometimes called Gini index is used to measure?
(a) Happiness
(b) Inequality of income or wealth
(c) Distribution of taxes
(d) Poverty

21. Which of the following statement is incorrect in relation to "World-system theory"?
(a) Core countries are the most economically diversified, wealthy, and powerful.
(b) Peripheral countries are the least economically diversified.
(c) Semi-peripheral nations are those that are midway between the core and periphery.
(d) The theory divides the world on the basis of differentiation of political structure.

22. Which one of the following statements substantiates the findings of Lambert's study of the Indian factory?
(a) Social structure of the factory maintains many elements of traditional social structure
(b) Indian factory system is basically effective in its orientation
(c) Factories in India are open to all for recruitment purposes
(d) Employment in factories ensures up-ward social mobility

23. Who among the following said that 'Industries are the Temples of Modern India'?
(a) Ambedkar
(b) Jawaharlal Nehru
(c) Mahatma Gandhi
(d) S. Radhakrishnan

24. Which of the match given below is incorrect

List I (Institution)	List II (People)
(a) Potlatch	Kwakiutl
(b) Genna	Naga
(c) Kula	Trobrianders
(d) Pratik	Javanese

25. Price mechanism means
(a) Price Manipulation by producers
(b) Price Manipulation by consumers
(c) Spontaneous play of market forces which determines prices
(d) Regulated market

26. What is the purpose of giving gifts by the host to all the attendance at the end of the Potlatch ceremony?
(a) To achieve a high status
(b) To show his wealth
(c) To enhance the trade
(d) To establish friendly relations

27. Who said that the Kula ring is a classic example of distinction between gift and commodity exchange?
(a) B Malinowski
(b) Marcel Mauss
(c) Maurice Godelier
(d) Radcliffe Brown

28. Which of the following statement is incorrect in relation to ceremonial exchange that existed worldwide?
(a) Potlatch, a practice among some Native American and peoples of west coast North America
(b) Koha, a practice among the Māori
(c) Moka, a similar practice in the Mt. Hagen area of Papua New Guinea
(d) Kula ring is a ceremonial exchange system conducted on the coast of Mexico

29. Who is the author of the book "The Gift"?
(a) B Malinowski
(b) Marcel Mauss
(c) Maurice Godelier
(d) Radcliffe Brown

30. Soulava, Mwali, Gimwali, etc are terminologies associated with which of the following ceremonial exchange?
(a) Potlatch
(b) Moka
(c) Koha
(d) Kula

31. ________ poverty can be defined as the state of severe deprivation of basic human needs such as food, safe drinking water, sanitation facilities, health, shelter, education and information.
(a) Absolute
(b) Relative
(c) Collective
(d) Cyclical

32. Which among the following is NOT one of the three obligations of gift exchange identified by Marcel Mauss?
(a) Giving
(b) Acknowledging
(c) Receiving
(d) Repaying

33. Which theory is associated with Immanuel Wallerstein?
(a) Weak tie theory
(b) World-system theory
(c) Structuration theory
(d) Surplus value theory

34. Which among the following is not a feature of a laissez-faire economy?
(a) Self-regulating market forces
(b) Free trade
(c) Individuals are driven by self-interest
(d) Tight rules and regulations by the government

35. Who authored '*Citizenship and Social Class*'?
(a) T. H. Marshall
(b) Stuart Hall
(c) Friedrich Engels
(d) Antonio Gramsci

36. Who introduced the phrase "invisible hand"?
(a) John Locke
(b) David Hume
(c) Adam Smith
(d) Immanuel Kant

37. Esping-Andersen identified three types of welfare state regimes. Which among the following is not one of them?
(a) Liberal
(b) Authoritarian
(c) Social democratic
(d) Conservative

38. "'The theory of Communism may be summed up in the single sentence: Abolition of private property.' This statement belongs to:
(a) David Ricardo
(b) Anthony Giddens
(c) Adam Smith
(d) Karl Marx

39. Who wrote '*Capitalism and the Production of Poverty*'?
(a) Hamza Alavi
(b) Utsa Patnaik
(c) Uma Chakravarti
(d) Amartya Sen

40. It is a gift-giving ceremony practiced among indigenous groups of the Pacific Northwest Coast of Canada and the United States.
(a) Potlatch
(b) Sundance
(c) Burbung
(d) Jajmani

41. Which among the following is incorrectly matched?
(a) Culture of poverty: Oscar Lewis
(b) Dependency theory: Andre Gunder Frank
(c) Knowledge-gap hypothesis: Jurgen Habermas
(d) Embeddedness: Karl Polanyi

42. Which of the following is not a part of World System Theory?
(a) Core
(b) Periphery
(c) Semi-periphery
(d) Concentric zone

43. ________ is a phenomenon whereby an individual or group is in a state of poverty over an extended period of time.
(a) Near poverty
(b) Relative poverty
(c) Chronic poverty
(d) Situational poverty

44. In the following question, two statements are given. One is the assertion (A) and the other is a reason (R). Examine the statement carefully and mark the correct answer according to the instruction given below

Assertion (A): It is extremely important to bridge the gender digital divide.

Reason (R): The gender digital divide is a major roadblock to women's economic empowerment.

(a) Both (A) and (R) are true and (R) is the correct explanation of (A)
(b) Both (A) and (R) are true but (R) is not the correct explanation of (A)
(c) (A) is false but (R) is true
(d) (A) is true but (R) is false

45. The Head of the Joint Hindu Family Firm is known as:
(a) Karta (b) Director
(c) Rakshak (d) Heritor

46. Opening up the economy to the economy of the world so that the Indian economy can compete at the international level is called
(a) Neoliberalism
(b) Welfarism
(c) Globalization
(d) Liberalization

47. Who is the author of the book '*Collective Choice and Social Welfare*'?
(a) John Hicks
(b) Adam Smith
(c) Joan Robinson
(d) Amartya Sen

48. **Assertion(A):** Capital market is a market where buyers and sellers engage in trade and financial securities like bonds, stocks, etc.

Reason(R): Capital market consists of primary and secondary markets.

Choose the correct answer from the codes given below:

(a) Both A and R are true and R is the correct explanation of A
(b) Both A and R are true, but R is not the correct explanation of A
(c) A is true, but R is false
(d) A is false, but R is true

49. An economy based on digital computing technologies or doing business through the help of the internet is called
(a) E-business
(b) E-government
(c) Digital economy
(d) Digital marketing

50. Who is the author of the book '*India's Path of Development*'?
(a) Yogendra Singh
(b) A.R Desai
(c) M.K Gandhi
(d) Jawaharlal Nehru

Answer Key

1. (d)	**9.** (a)	**17.** (c)	**25.** (c)	**33.** (b)	**41.** (c)	**49.** (c)
2. (b)	**10.** (a)	**18.** (c)	**26.** (a)	**34.** (d)	**42.** (d)	**50.** (b)
3. (b)	**11.** (d)	**19.** (a)	**27.** (b)	**35.** (a)	**43.** (c)	
4. (b)	**12.** (c)	**20.** (b)	**28.** (d)	**36.** (c)	**44.** (a)	
5. (c)	**13.** (b)	**21.** (d)	**29.** (b)	**37.** (b)	**45.** (a)	
6. (a)	**14.** (b)	**22.** (a)	**30.** (d)	**38.** (d)	**46.** (c)	
7. (d)	**15.** (a)	**23.** (b)	**31.** (a)	**39.** (b)	**47.** (d)	
8. (a)	**16.** (d)	**24.** (d)	**32.** (b)	**40.** (a)	**48.** (b)	

PREVIOUS YEARS' QUESTIONS

DECEMBER 2023

1. Which among the following statements are true about relative poverty?
A. It is universal and unavoidable.
B. It refers to the deprivation of some people in relations to those who have more.
C. It depends upon a universally agreed minimum for adequate nutrition and living
D. It depends on the values and standard of living that a particular society sets.
Choose the correct answer from the option given below:
(a) A, B and C only (b) B, C and D only
(c) A, B and D only (d) A, B, C and D only

2. Social justice is justice in terms of the distribution of:
A. Wealth
B. Ownership of resources
C. Opportunities
D. Privileges
Choose the correct answer from the options given below:
(a) B and C only (b) A, B and D only
(c) A, C and D only (d) C and D only

3. The Information, Communication Technological Revolution has contributed in the growth of post-industrial society through
A. Shifting the production of tangible product to commodified ideas.
B. Shifting from mechanical skills to digital Skills.
C. Minimization of supervision of educated and creative force.
D. Centralization by work from factories.
Choose the correct answer from the options given below:
(a) A, C and D only
(b) A, B and C only
(c) B, C and D only
(d) A, B, C and D only

4. Match List I with List II.

List I	List II
A. Imaging the Modern City (1999)	I. Mannel Castells
B. Post Modern Urbanism (1995)	II. Jane Jacobs
C. Urban Question; A Marxist approach (1977)	III. Nan Ellin
D. The Death and life of Great American Cities (1961)	IV. James Donald

Choose the correct answer from the options given below:
(a) A-IV, B-III, C-I, D-II
(b) A-II, B-III, C-IV, D-I
(c) A-III, B-II, C-I, D-IV
(d) A-I, B-IV, C-III, D-II

5. What changes were brought by industrialization in society?
A. New forms of energy.
B. Manufacturing and mass production.
C. Division of labour and specialisation.
D. Introduction of wage labour.
E. Decentralization of work.
Choose the correct answer from the options given below:
(a) A, B and C only
(b) B, C, D and E only
(c) A, B, C, D and E only
(d) A, B, C and D only

6. Given below are two statements:
Statement I: The informational economy is global.
Statement II: A global economy is historically a new reality, distinct from a world economy.
In the light of the above statements, choose the correct answer from the options given below:
(a) Both Statement I and Statement II are true.
(b) Both Statement I and Statement II are false.
(c) Statement I is true but Statement II is false.
(d) Statement I is false but Statement II is true.

7. P.P. Rey describes three stages through which transition from feudal to the capitalist mode of production takes place. What is the sequence of the following three stages?
A. Capitalism becomes dominant; it still makes use of feudalism; capitalism destroys all peasant handicrafts and forms of production.
B. Capitalism is subordinated to feudalism and depends on landed property to get both raw materials and workers.
C. Feudalism becomes an obstacle to the development of capitalism and so it is dismantled.
Choose the correct answer from the options given below:
(a) A, B, C
(b) B, A, C
(c) A, C, B
(d) C, B, A

8. A worker who possesses a diversity of skills or qualifications and is therefore able to move easily from job to job is called
(a) Industrial worker
(b) Portfolio worker
(c) Participatory worker
(d) Organizational worker

9. What are the different types of society?
A. Agrarian societies
B. Industrial societies
C. Modern societies
D. Hunting and gathering societies

Choose the correct answer from the options given below:

(a) B and D only
(b) A, C and B only
(c) A, B and D only
(d) B, C and D only

JUNE 2023

10. Arrange the order of economy in Economic Sociology.
A. Neo-liberal
B. Mixed
C. Primitive
D. Colonial
Choose the correct answer from the options given below:
(a) A, B, C, D
(b) C, D, B, A
(c) D, C, B, A
(d) B, C, A, D

11. The classical notion of poverty includes
A. Surplus poverty
B. Absolute poverty
C. Obsolete poverty
D. Relative poverty
Choose the appropriate answer from the options given below:
(a) A and C only
(b) B and D only
(c) A and B only
(d) C and D only

12. Match List I with List II

List I (Social Scientists)	List II (Contributions)
A. G. Ritzer	I. Ethnic Groups and Boundaries
B. F. Tonnies	II. The McDonaldization
C. I. Wallerstein	III. Gemeinschaft and Gesellschaft
D. F. Barth	IV. The Modem World System

Choose the correct answer from the options given below:

(a) A - II, B - Ill, C - IV, D - II
(b) A - Ill, B - IV, C - I, D - II
(c) A - IV, B - I, C - II, D - III
(d) A - I, B - II, C - III, D - IV

13. Who introduced the idea of the global village in the study of mass media?
(a) Marcuse (b) Mc Lellan
(c) Mc Luhan (d) Miliband

14. Match List I with List II

List I (Concepts)	List II (Sociologists)
A. Hegemony	I. Immanuel Wallerstein
B. Fordism	II. Max Weber
C. World system	III. Antonio Gramsci
D. Verstehen	IV. Henry Ford

Choose the correct answer from the options given below:

(a) A - III, B - IV, C - I, D - II
(b) A - IV, B - I, C - II, D - III
(c) A - I, B - II, C - III, D - IV
(d) A - II, B - III, C - IV, D - I

MARCH 2023

15. Match List I with List II

List I (Models of Urban Ecology)	List II (Proponents of Models)
A. Concentric zone model	I. Homer Hoyt
B. Sector model	II. Harris and Ullman
C. Multiple-nuclei model	III. Amos Howley
D. Ecological analysis	IV. Burgers

Choose the correct answer from the options given below.
(a) A - III, B - I, C – II, D - IV
(b) A - II, B - III, C - IV, D - I
(c) A - I, B - II, C - III, D - IV
(d) A - IV, B – I, C – II, D - III

16. An economy in which much of the work force is involved not in the physical production or distribution of material goods but in their design, development, technology, marketing, sales, and servicing, is known as
(a) Industrial economy
(b) Knowledge economy
(c) Pastoral economy
(d) None of the above

17. Which of the following statements are correct?
A. The modern working class in India was the offspring of the modern industries, transport, and plantation established in India during the British period.

B. The Indian proletariat was formed out of the pauperized peasant and ruined artisans, who became wage earners.
C. The Indian working class developed national and class consciousness much later than the educated middle class.
D. During the pre-British period, the workers of India were protected against risks of sickness, unemployment, old age, and death.
E. A larger proportion of the workers were prosperous in colonial India.

Choose the correct answer from the options given below:
(a) A, B, and C only
(b) D and E only
(c) A, B, C, and D only
(d) A, D, and E only

18. Given below are two statements:
Statement I: Gentrification is a process of moving wealth back into the metropolis.
Statement II: Gentrification in Europe and the United States is a process which has often worked to the benefit of ethnic minorities at the expense of white people.
In light of the above statements, choose the correct answer from the options given below:
(a) Both Statement I and Statement II are true.
(b) Both Statement I and Statement II are false.
(c) Statement I is true but Statement II is false.
(d) Statement I is false but Statement II is true

19. Who described land use in Chicago in terms of concentric zones rather like a Bull's-eye?
(a) Kevin Bales
(b) Howard Becker
(c) Ulrich Beck
(d) Earnest W. Burgess

20. According to a popular estimate, the decline of common property resources can take forms listed below.
A. Physical loss of resources due to natural calamity.
B. Deterioration of productivity of resources.
C. Re-assignment of usage and property rights.
D. Use of mechanization and sharecropping.
E. Buying and selling of property.

Choose the correct answer from the options given below:
(a) A and B only
(b) A, B, and C only
(c) A, B, C, and D only
(d) E only

21. Feminization of labour force denotes
A. A process of empowerment of women.
B. Globalization, creating more jobs for women.
C. Increase in participation of women in the labour market.
D. A process of subjugation of women.
E. Decrease in participation of women in labour market.

Choose the correct answer from the options given below:
(a) A only
(b) B only
(c) C only
(d) D and E only

22. The author of the book, *The Gift: The Forms and Functions for Exchange in Archaic Societies* is:
(a) Howard Becker
(b) Ulrich Beck
(c) Marcel Mauss
(d) Alain Touraine

23. Which one of the following has analysed patterns of Conspicuous Consumption and Conspicuous Waste?
(a) Thorstein Veblen
(b) V. Pareto
(c) W.G. Ogburn
(d) Max Weber

24. Match List I with List II

List I (Concepts/ Ideas)	List II (Thinkers)
A. Tragedy of culture	I. Pitrim A. Sorokin
B. Idealist culture	II. Thorstein Veblen
C. Industrial society	III. George Simmel
D. Conspicuous consumption	IV. Herbert Spencer

Choose the correct answer from the options given below:

(a) A - III, B - I, C - IV, D-II
(b) A - I, B - II, C – IV, D - III
(c) A - III, B - II, C - I, D - IV
(d) A - IV, B - II, C - I D - III

25. Who coined the term 'Megalopolis'?
(a) George Ritzer
(b) Jean Piaget
(c) Jean Paul Sartre
(d) Jean Gottmann

DEC 2021 & JUNE 2022

26. The concept of "conspicuous consumption" denotes:
A. Fetishism of commodities.
B. People want to show that they are simple-living.
C. People want to show others what they are consuming.
D. People have access to commodities.
E. Tragedy of Culture,

Choose the correct answer from the options given below:

(a) A and B only
(b) B only
(c) C only
(d) D and E only

27. Production characterised by large number of standardised products made by highly specialised workers is known as
(a) Factory production
(b) Capitalistic production
(c) Mass production
(d) All of the above

28. The durable relations between a food-producing family and the families that supply them with goods and services are known as-
(a) Service caste- higher caste relations
(b) Producer-supplier relations
(c) Caste relations
(d) Jajmani relations

29. Match List-I with List-II

List I (Thinkers)	List II (Theory/Approach/Model)
A. W. W. Rostow	I. World Systems Theory
B. Paul Baran	II. Take-off Model
C. Amartya Sen	III. Capabilities Approach
D. Immanuel Wallerstein	IV. Dependency Theory

Choose the correct answer from the options given below:
(a) A - II, B - I, C - III, D - IV
(b) A - II, B - IV, C - I, D - II
(c) A - I, B - II, C - IV, D - III
(d) A - II, B - IV, C - III, D - I

30. Relative poverty refers to:
(a) Poverty of the people who are relatively marginalised
(b) Deprivation of resources that is life threatening
(c) Deprivation of some people in relation to those who have more
(d) None of the above

31. Given below are two statements, one is labelled as Assertion (A) and the other is labelled as Reason (R)

Assertion (A): Sociologists usually distinguish between absolute and relative poverty.

Reason (R): In developed countries, with established welfare systems, absolute poverty is rare.

In the light of the above statements, choose the most appropriate answer from the options given below:
(a) Both (A) and (R) are correct and (R) is the correct explanation of (A).
(b) Both (A) and (R) are correct but (R) is NOT the correct explanation of (A).
(c) (A) is correct but (R) is not correct.
(d) (A) is not correct but (R) is correct.

32. ________ is the channelling of an increasing number of women into low-status, poorly paid manual work.
(a) Feminisation of poverty
(b) Female proletarianization
(c) Feminisation of labor
(d) None of the above

33. The unit of production in tribal economy is
(a) Clan (b) Village
(c) Family (d) None of these

34. The features of "Kula Ring", described by Malinowski are:
A. It is an exchange cycle
B. It had no monetary value
C. It was seen as an exchange of gifts
D. It provided internal status to men
E. It did not weld together, a large number of islands

Choose the correct answer from the options given below:
(a) A, B, D and E only
(b) A, C, D and E only
(c) A, B, C and D only
(d) B, C, D and E only

35. Given below are two statements

Statement I: Some of the developing countries have embarked successfully on a process of rapid industrialization.

Statement II: They are referred to as the Newly Industrializing Countries.

In light of the above statements, choose the most appropriate answer from the options given below
(a) Both Statement I and Statement II are correct
(b) Both Statement I and Statement II are incorrect
(c) Statement I is correct but Statement II is incorrect
(d) Statement I is incorrect but Statement II is correct

Direction: Read the passage given below and answer the questions that follows.

Property, in Hobhouse's phrase, 'is to be conceived in terms of the control of man over things', a control which is recognized by society, more or less permanent and exclusive. Property may be private (individual or collective) or common. In his account of the development of property, Hobhouse observed that there is some personal private property in all societies, but that in many primitive societies the principal economic resources are communally owned (e.g. hunting land, grazing land, pasture). In more developed agricultural societies, private ownership comes to predominate. But Hobhouse pointed out that although tribal common ownership disappears, common ownership may be maintained for the joint-family, R. H. Lowie, in an excellent short account of property, which uses much comparative material from primitive and civilized societies, presents much of the same view. There is personal private property among all primitive people, including names, dances, songs, myths, ceremonial regalia, gifts, weapons, household implements. So far as the 'instruments of production' are concerned there are differences between hunters and food-gatherers, where the land is tribal property (not always well-defined), and agriculturalists and pastoralists. Among agriculturalists individual private property in land is frequently found, though the clan or tribe may still exercise some control over its use or alienation. In the case of pastoralists, land may be communally owned but not the livestock; 'the ownership of livestock strongly develops the sense of individual property'.

36. For the pastoralists:
(a) Livestock may be communally owned
(b) Land may be communally owned
(c) Both the above
(d) None of the above

37. Which among the following are possessed by primitive people as personal private property?
(a) Songs, myths, dances and names
(b) Weapons, gifts, ceremonial regalia & household implements
(c) Both the above
(d) None of the above

38. In primitive societies, the principal economic resources are:
(a) Privately owned
(b) Personally owned
(c) Communally owned
(d) All the above

39. "Property is to be conceived in terms of the control of man over things". Who said this?
(a) R. H. Lowie (b) Hobhouse
(c) Both the above (d) None of the above

40. In more developed agricultural societies
(a) Communal ownership dominates
(b) Pastoral ownership dominates
(c) Private ownership dominates
(d) Social ownership dominates

JUNE 2021

41. Given below are two statements, one is labelled as Assertion A and the other is labelled as Reason R

Assertion A: Eradicating poverty in all its forms including extreme poverty is the greatest global challenge

Reason R: It is an indispensable requirement for sustainable development

In light of the above statements, choose the most appropriate answer from the options given below
(a) Both A and R are correct and R is the correct explanation of A
(b) Both A and R are correct but R is NOT the correct explanation of A
(c) A is correct but R is not correct
(d) A is not correct but R is correct

42. The Exchange Theory was propounded and/or advanced by which one of the following sociologists?
A. B. Malinowski
B. P. M. Blau
C. A. R. Radcliffe Brown
D. G. Homans
E. Talcott Parsons

Choose the correct answer from the options given below
(a) A, B and C
(b) A, B and D
(c) B, C, D and E
(d) A, C, D and E

43. Which of the following are true about the sociology of consumption?
A. Focus on material culture
B. Focus on mass culture
C. New approach to the analysis of equality and political power
D. Largely emerging from capitalist societies
E. New approach to the analysis of inequality and political alignments

Choose the correct answer from the options given below:
(a) A, B, C and D only
(b) B, C, D and E only
(c) A, C, D and E only
(d) A, B, D and E only

44. In which one of the following approaches, sexual division of labour was taken for granted and as natural?
(a) Women in Development (WID)
(b) Women and Development (WAD)
(c) Gender and Development (GAD)
(d) Postmodernism and Development (PAD)

45. According to new ideas in the industry:
(a) human work is no longer considered as a pure economic activity
(b) Worker is not supposed to work only for the sake of wages
(c) Both (1) and (2)
(d) None of the above

JUNE 2020

46. In modern Industrialized society the status of women in the industry

(a) Has considerately gone down
(b) Has gradually risen
(c) Has remained unchanged
(d) Has not been defined

47. Yellow revolution is related to
(a) Oilseed (b) Milk
(c) Telangana (d) Tiger conservation

48. Which of the following three characteristics did the feudal estates of medieval Europe have?
1. Had a Status
2. Serfdom was decreasing
3. Were political groups
4. Had division of labour
5. Serfs had the ability to appeal for justice

Choose the most appropriate answer from the options given below:
(a) 1, 2 and 5 only
(b) 1, 3 and 4 only
(c) 4, 5 and 2 only
(d) 3, 4 and 2 only

49. Which two of the following are the biggest dams in India?
1. Sardar Sarovar Dam
2. Bhakra Dam
3. Tehri Dam
4. Hirakud Dam

Choose the most appropriate answer from the options given below:
(a) 1 and 2 only (b) 2 and 4 only
(c) 2 and 3 only (d) 4 and 1 only

50. Which of the following are characteristics of the pre-capitalist mode of production?
1. Unfree labour
2. Commodity production
3. Fusion of economic and political power
4. Mechanisation
5. Subsistence

Choose the most appropriate answer from the options given below:
(a) 1, 2, 3 only (b) 2, 3, 5 only
(c) 3, 4, 5 only (d) 1, 3, 5 only

51. Sylvia Walby in her book *'Theorising Patriarchy'* talks of elements of patriarchy. Which of the following is <u>not</u> one of them?
1. Women are likely to be paid less
2. Sexuality is to be treated positively
3. Women are likely to raise children
4. Men and women are likely to be treated equally

Choose the most appropriate answer from the options given below:
(a) 1, 2, 3 only (b) 2, 3, 4 only
(c) 1, 3, 4 only (d) 4 only

52. Match List I with List II:

List I (Author)	List II (Book)
A. P.L. Berger	I. Economy and Society
B. T. Parsons and N. Smelser	II. Social Theory and Social Structure
C. T.B. Bottomore	III. Invitation to sociology
D. R.K. Merton	IV. Classes in modern society

Choose the correct answer from the options given below:

	A	B	C	D
(a)	IV	III	I	II
(b)	III	IV	II	I
(c)	III	I	IV	II
(d)	I	IV	II	III

DECEMBER 2019

53. Two statements are given below. One is labelled as Assertion (A) and the other as Reason (R).

Assertion (A): After the green revolution of inter-caste relations have changed from Jajmani to contractual relationships.

Reasons (R): The green revolution has given opportunities to service castes in diverse occupations

Choose the correct option:
(a) Both (A) and (R) are true and (R) is the correct explanation of (A)
(b) Both (A) and (R) are true but (R) is not the correct explanation of (A)
(c) (A) is true but (R) is false
(d) (A) is false but (R) is true

54. 'Kula' exchange is associated with which tribe?
(a) Krowe tribes
(b) Azande tribes
(c) Tikopians
(d) Trobriand Islanders

55. The ability of workers to use muscles and brain to transform their environment is called
(a) labour union
(b) labour power
(c) labour unrest
(d) labour movement

56. Who said that globalization is the growing reciprocal interdependence and integration of various economies around the globe?
(a) A. Giddens
(b) Meghnad Desai
(c) Henderson Hazel
(d) D.Martin Knor

57. Which one of the following metropolises has the highest percentage and lowest percentage of scheduled castes?

A. Bengaluru
B. Mumbai
C. Chennai
D. Delhi

Choose the correct option:

(a) A and B
(b) C and B
(c) B and C
(d) D and A

58. Given below are two statements, one is labelled as Assertion (A) and the other as Reason (R):

Assertion (A): Globalisation has intensified exclusion, marginalisation and disconnection among different classes of people and regions.

Reasons (R): It is due to economic reforms.

Choose the correct option:

(a) Both (A) and (R) are true and (R) is the correct explanation of (A)
(b) Both (A) and (R) are true, but (R) is not the correct explanation of (A)
(c) (A) is true, but (R) is false
(d) (A) is false but (R) is true

59. Given below are two statements one is labelled as Assertion (A) and the other as Reason (R)

Assertion (A): Women's participation in the industrial workforce has reduced over the years.

Reasons (R): There has been an expansion of the industry and increasing automation

Choose the correct option

(a) Both (A) and (R) are true and (R) is the correct explanation of (A)
(b) Both (A) and (R) are true, but (R) is not the correct explanation of (A)
(c) (A) is true, but (R) is false
(d) (A) is false but (R) is true

60. Given below are two statements, one is labelled as Assertion (A) and the other as Reason (R):

Assertion (A): Green revolution in Punjab has resulted in many ecological problems.

Reasons (R): It is due to over-exploitation of land and underground water, and overuse of pesticides and fertilizers for more production.

Choose the correct option:

(a) Both (A) and (R) are true and (R) is the correct explanation of (A)
(b) Both (A) and (R) are true, but (R) is not the correct explanation of (A)
(c) (A) is true, but (R) is false
(d) (A) is false but (R) is true

61. Which set of International Development organizations work towards fighting against poverty?

(a) ILO, UNICEF, WHO, UNHCR, The Red Cross
(b) Oxfam, UNDP, UNICEF, The Red Cross, The Hunger Project
(c) World Bank, WHO, IMF, UNDP, ILO
(d) UNHCR, CEDAW, UNICEF, IMF, Oxfam

62. How many educated unemployed were in India, according to the census counting of 2011?

(a) 84 million (b) 79 million
(c) 74 million (d) 81 million

63. What term is used to describe a system of ceremonial exchange by certain groups of tribes in the Trobriand Islands?

(a) Kula Ring (b) Potlatch
(c) Connubium (d) Jajmani

64. What term is best suited to describe an ideology based upon a rethinking and a reassertion of classical liberalism?

(a) Welfarism
(b) Neo-functionalism
(c) Neo-Liberalism
(d) Neo-Marxism

65. The process of buying and selling products by electronic means is known as

(a) e-pathshala
(b) e-governance
(c) e-commerce
(d) e-tourism

66. The stages in the development of property according to Marx can broadly be classified as

(a) Classless society, primitive communism, class differentiation and inequality
(b) class differentiation and inequality, Classless society, primitive communism
(c) primitive communism, Classless society, class differentiation and inequality
(d) primitive communism, class differentiation and inequality, classless society

JUNE 2019

67. Structural-differentiation model of economic development was formulated by

(a) Neil J. Smelser (b) W. W. Rostow
(c) Daniel Lemer (d) E. M. Rogers

68. The proportion, of women workers in labour force in India as per the World Bank Report 2017 is

(a) 15.6% (b) 24.5%
(c) 27.9% (d) 31.8%

69. Around the world, neo-liberalism has been imposed by powerful financial institutions.

Which of the following is one of such institution?

(a) International Labour Organization (ILO)
(b) United Nations Educational Scientific and Cultural Organization (UNESCO)
(c) Inter-American Development Bank (IDB)
(d) BRICS

70. Which one of the following countries is an example of 'state capitalism'?

(a) China (b) India
(c) Switzerland (d) France

71. A set of policies which emphasizes the rule of the market, cutting public expenditure for social services, deregulations puritization and elimination of the public good or community is conceptualized as which of the following?

(a) Neo-Marxism (b) Neo-functionalism
(c) Neo-liberalism (d) Fordism

72. What is the measure of extreme poverty internationally in terms of per day per head of purchasing parity?

(a) \$1.0 (b) \$1.9
(c) \$3.5 (d) \$4.5

73. Who has written/edited the book, *Peasants and Peasant Societies*?

(a) Eric Wolf (b) Oscar Lewis
(c) Robert Redfield (d) Theodor Shanin

74. What percentage of the total profit a corporate must invest for the purpose of 'Corporate Social Responsibility (CSR)' in India?

(a) 5% (b) 4%
(c) 3% (d) 2%

75. Who analyzed the ways in which economic and social transformation in capitalism connect to the information technology revolution?

(a) Edward Said (b) J. Habermas
(c) Manuel Castells (d) Clifford Geertz

Answer Key

1. (c) **2.** (c) **3.** (b) **4.** (a) **5.** (d) **6.** (a) **7.** (b) **8.** (b) **9.** (c) **10.** (b) **11.** (b) **12.** (a)
13. (c) **14.** (a) **15.** (d) **16.** (b) **17.** (a) **18.** (c) **19.** (d) **20.** (b) **21.** (c) **22.** (c) **23.** (a) **24.** (a)
25. (d) **26.** (c) **27.** (d) **28.** (d) **29.** (d) **30.** (c) **31.** (b) **32.** (b) **33.** (c) **34.** (c) **35.** (a) **36.** (b)
37. (c) **38.** (c) **39.** (b) **40.** (c) **41.** (a) **42.** (b) **43.** (d) **44.** (a) **45.** (c) **46.** (b) **47.** (a) **48.** (b)
49. (c) **50.** (d) **51.** (d) **52.** (c) **53.** (a) **54.** (d) **55.** (b) **56.** (b) **57.** (c) **58.** (a) **59.** (a) **60.** (a)
61. (b) **62.** (a) **63.** (a) **64.** (c) **65.** (c) **66.** (d) **67.** (a) **68.** (b) **69.** (c) **70.** (a) **71.** (c) **72.** (b)
73. (d) **74.** (d) **75.** (c)

Unit-VII

Environment and Society

CHAPTERS:

Top: Photo credit: Lightspring / Shutterstock
Below: Photo Credit: chayanuphol / Shutterstock

CHAPTER

1 Culture, Society, and Environment

LEARNING OBJECTIVES:

In this chapter, we will discuss the following important topics.

- Social and cultural economy: Various forms
- Technological change
- Agriculture and biodiversity
- Indigenous knowledge systems and ethno-medicine
- Gender and environment
- Forest policies
- Adivasis and exclusion
- Ecological degradation and migration
- Development and environment
- Water and social exclusion
- Disasters and community responses
- Environmental pollution
- Public health and disability
- Climate change and international policies

INTRODUCTION

Have you ever thought that whatever we have or we do is directly or indirectly related to the environment around us. Even our culture, customs etc. or material things are the product of our ecology. The term ecology refers to the trap of physical and biological systems and processes in which humans are an element. The social environment in which we live arises from the mutual action between biological ecology and human interventions. This is a two-way process. Just as nature shapes society, in the same way society shapes nature. For example, the fertile soil of Gangetic plains enables intensive agriculture. Its high productivity allows dense population settlements and generates enough surplus to support other, non-agricultural activities, giving birth to complex hierarchical societies and states. In contrast, Rajasthan's desert can only support shepherds that move from one place to another to supply fodder to their animals. These are examples of environment shaping forms of human life and culture. Various relations between the environment and society show various social values and norms as well as knowledge systems.

SOCIAL AND CULTURAL ECOLOGY: VARIOUS FORMS

Ecology is the study of the interrelationships between organisms and their environment. It is viewed as an interdisciplinary or multidisciplinary field of science that systematically draws knowledge from several disciplines such as genetics, anthropology, sociology, etc.

Sociologists are primarily interested in the interrelationships between humans and their environment. Here, by environment, we mean the natural environment, which includes forests, rivers, lakes, seas, mountains, plants, etc.

Social Ecology

Social ecology is the study of relationships between people and their environment, often the interdependence of people, collectives, and institutions. Social ecology is concerned not only with the direct response to an environment where technology is unsophisticated but also with the distribution and composition of groups necessary for the exploitation of natural resources, the indirect relationships that arise from these groups, and the evolution of the cosmos related to the specific habitat.

It emerged in the mid-1960s under the influence of both the global environmental and American civil rights movements, and by the late 1970s played a more visible role in the upward movement against nuclear power. According to this school of thought, ecological problems arise primarily from social problems, particularly from various forms of hierarchy and domination.

Social ecology is a theory of radical political ecology based on communalism, which opposes the current capitalist system of production and consumption. The theory of social ecology is established by Murray Bookchin. Bookchin proposes ethical principles to replace society's propensity for hierarchy and domination with democracy and freedom.

For Bookchin, social ecology is an approach to society that adopts an ecological, reconstructive, and community perspective on society. This ideology reconstructs and transforms current attitudes on both social issues and environmental factors while promoting direct democracy. It eschews scarcity and hierarchy in the economy in favor of a world in which human communities work closely with nature to accept and promote diversity as well as creativity and freedom.

Cultural Ecology

Cultural ecology deals with the effect of culture on nature. There are occasions when this effect is beneficial, other times it is not. Today there is an imbalance towards forests in India and the world.

It is the study of human adaptation to the social and physical environment. Human adaptation refers to both biological and cultural processes that enable a population to survive and reproduce in a given or changing environment.

Cultural ecology is a theory that attempts to explain the similarities and differences in culture in relation to the environment. With an excessive focus on how material culture, or technology, relates to basic survival, cultural ecology was the first theoretical approach to provide an explanation for those similarities and differences.

An important aspect of cultural ecology is the study of adaptation, how people deal with, affect, and are affected by their changing environment. It is important for our existence on the planet as it provides understanding and solutions to problems like deforestation, loss of species, lack of food, loss of soil, etc.

Cultural ecology became an influential approach within anthropology. Elements of the approach are still seen today in political ecology, human behavioral ecology, and the ecosystem approach.

The concept of cultural ecology was first propounded by Julian Steward. According to Steward:

i. Cultures in similar environments can have similar adaptations.
ii. All adaptations are short-term and continuously adjusted to local conditions.
iii. Changes can either elaborate on earlier cultures or may generate entirely new ones.

Using Steward's approach, anthropologists compare cultures to determine what factors influenced similar cultural evolution, in other words, similar adaptations. In cultural ecology, cultures, not individuals, adapt. This approach assumes that culture is superorganic, a concept Steward learned from Alfred Krober.

Steward proposed that we can begin to understand these adaptations by first examining the cultural core. The cultural core included the technology, knowledge, labor, and family organization used to collect resources from the environment.

Then he thought it necessary to investigate the practices associated with the cultural core, which includes the organization of labour. Steward also advocated examining how social institutions and belief systems were influenced by subsistence behaviours.

In 1962, Anthropologist Charles O. Frake defined cultural ecology as 'the study of the role of culture as a dynamic component of any ecosystem'. Cultural ecologists study how and why cultures do what they do to solve their subsistence problems, how people understand their environment, and how they share that knowledge.

TECHNOLOGICAL CHANGE

Technology can be defined as the application of scientific purposes to the practical purposes of human life. It is the sum total of the techniques, skills, and methods used in the production of goods and services or in the achievement of services such as scientific investigation. Technology can refer to methods ranging from as simple as stone tools to the complex genetic engineering and information technology that have emerged since the 1980s.

The word technology comes from the Greek word techne, meaning art and craft, and the word logos, meaning word and speech. It was earlier used to describe applied arts but is now used to describe advances and changes that affect the environment around us. Some, such as Lewis H. Morgan, Leslie White, and Gerhard Lensky, have declared technological progress to be the primary factor driving the development of human civilization.

Morgan's concept of three major stages of social development (savageness, barbarism, and civilization) can be divided by technological milestones such as fire. White argued the measure by which to judge the development of culture was energy.

White distinguishes between five stages of human development: In the first, people use their muscle energy. In second, they harness the energy of domesticated animals. In third, they harness the energy of plants (agricultural revolution). In fourth, they learn to use the energy of natural resources: coal, oil, and gas. In fifth, they harness nuclear power.

Lenski's approach focuses on information. The more information and knowledge a given society has, the more advanced it is.

Using different techniques for the construction of new things is a determining characteristic of humanlike species. The first major technologies were tied to survival, hunting, and food preparation. Stone tools and weapons were major technological developments of the Stone Age. Another important technological development of this period is the invention of the wheel.

One of the most significant developments of the medieval era was the development of economies where water and wind power were more significant than animal and human muscle power. Most water and wind power were used for milling grain. Water power was also used for blowing air in blast furnaces, pulping rags for paper making, and felting wool.

Some significant technological inventions of this period include mechanical clocks, spectacles, vertical windmills, etc.

Papermaking, a 2nd-century Chinese technology, was carried to the Middle East when a group of Chinese papermakers was captured in the 8th century. In Germany, around 1440, goldsmith Johannes Gutenberg invented the printing press, which started the printing revolution. In Renaissance Europe, the arrival of mechanical movable printing introduced the era of mass communication.

The Industrial Revolution was the transition to new manufacturing processes in Europe and the United States, in the period from about 1760 to sometime between 1820 and 1840. This transition included going from hand production methods to machines, new chemical manufacturing and iron production processes, the increasing use of steam power and water power, the development of machine tools, and the rise of the mechanized factory system.

The Second Industrial Revolution is also known as the Technological Revolution. This revolution led to the widespread adoption of technological systems such as telegram, railroad networks, sewage systems, etc.

Electrification spread rapidly in the 20th century. At the beginning of the century, electric power was for the most part only available to wealthy people in a few major cities such as New York, London, Paris, and Newcastle upon Tyne, but by the time the World Wide Web was invented in 1990 an estimated 62 percent of homes worldwide had electric power, including about a third of households in the rural developing world.

AGRICULTURE AND BIODIVERSITY

The term 'Biodiversity' was first conceptualized by Edward O Wilson in 1988. It refers to the variety of life on earth i.e., the variety of animals, plants, fungi, bacteria, etc. that make up our natural world. The agricultural biodiversity constitutes plants, animals, soil organisms, insects, and other flora and fauna in agro-systems as well as elements of natural habitats that pertain to food production.

Components of Biodiversity

It consists of three components, which are as follows.

1. **Species Diversity:** It refers to the variety of different types of species found in a particular area. For example, humans show a lot of diversity among themselves.
2. **Genetic Diversity:** This refers to the variation in terms of genetic makeup within species, which is transferred across generations. For example, there are different varieties of the same species of rice, wheat, maize, barley, etc.
3. **Ecosystem Diversity:** This refers to the variety of associations among organisms and with the environment for utilizing resources. For example, diversity in different ecosystems like deserts, rainforests, mangroves, etc.

Importance of Biodiversity for Agriculture

The knowledge of biodiversity and its conservation has multiple proven benefits for agricultural productivity, sustainability, and food security at all scales and in all types of agricultural systems and can benefit agriculture in the following ways:

1. Increases productivity, yields, and food security.
2. Reduce the pressure of agriculture on fragile areas, forests, and endangered species.
3. Builds stability, robustness, and sustainability of farming systems.
4. Contribute to sound pest and disease management.
5. Conserve soil and increase natural soil fertility and health.
6. Diversify products and income opportunities from farms.

Loss of Biodiversity: Threat to Agriculture

The direct and indirect causes of loss of biodiversity in agriculture are:

1. Monoculture
2. Use of pesticide
3. Deforestation
4. Impact of climatic changes
5. Excessive Application of HYV technology

INDIGENOUS KNOWLEDGE SYSTEMS AND ETHNO-MEDICINE

Indigenous Knowledge Systems

Indigenous knowledge is understood as local or traditional knowledge that indigenous people have brought down with them from earlier times via oral tradition. Indigenous knowledge (IK), Traditional knowledge (TK), and Local knowledge (LK), generally refer to 'A body of knowledge built up by a group of people through generations of living in close contact with nature'.

Characteristics of Indigenous Knowledge

1. It is dynamic, systematic, and universal in principle. It is unwritten and known through oral traditions.
2. It is practically common sense, based on teachings and experience passed on from generation to generation.
3. It is holistic–it cannot be compartmentalized and it is rooted in the spiritual health, culture, and language of the people.
4. It sets out the rules governing the use of resources - respect; an obligation to share. It is dynamic, cumulative, and stable.
5. It is a way of life - wisdom is using knowledge in good ways. It is using the heart and the head together. It comes from the spirit in order to survive.
6. It gives credibility to people.
7. It is based on experience, acquired from observations over time – it is argued that it may be most useful for local-scale decision-making.
8. It can show an understanding of the complex relationships between these individual components and the dynamic ecosystems within which they act.
9. It describes the health of the local environment, wildlife, etc., and promotes consideration of the relationships between human and biological systems.
10. It often describes these symbiotic relationships and provides the basis for life-sustaining decisions about how to relate to the environment.

Importance of Indigenous Knowledge

1. Indigenous knowledge contributes to local empowerment and development, enhances self-reliance, and strengthens self-determination.
2. The use of IK in research and management plans gives legitimacy and credibility in the eyes of both local people and outside scientists, increases cultural pride, and thus motivation to solve local problems with local resources and resources.
3. Indigenous peoples can provide valuable information on how to effectively manage the local environment and its natural resources.
4. There are situations in which modern science is not appropriate, and the use of simpler techniques and procedures is required. Learning from Indigenous knowledge can therefore improve understanding of local conditions and provide a productive context for activities designed to help communities.
5. Indigenous knowledge systems and technologies are found to be socially desirable, economically affordable, and sustainable and involve minimal risk to rural farmers and producers, and above all, they are widely believed to conserve resources.
6. Investing in the dissemination of indigenous knowledge can help reduce poverty.

7. The sharing of indigenous knowledge within and between communities can increase cross-cultural understanding.

Benefits of Indigenous Knowledge

1. **Moderation in the exploitation of resources:** Production is only for subsistence needs. What is necessary for immediate survival is taken from the environment.
2. **Diversified production systems:** No single resource is over-exploited; the risk can be minimized by using several subsistence strategies.
3. **Respect for nature:** A 'conservation ethics' is often present. The land is considered sacred, humans depend on nature for survival, and all species are interconnected.
4. **Flexible:** Indigenous knowledge is able to adapt to new situations and incorporate external knowledge.
5. **Social responsibility:** There are strong family and community ties and with them a sense of obligation and responsibility to preserve the land for future generations.

Application of Indigenous Knowledge

1. **Cultural preservation:** Knowledge and images of the past keep a culture alive and reinforce a sense of place and the notion of home.
2. **Land claim processes:** Indigenous geography is used as a basis for land selection and to develop approaches to native control.
3. **Resource management practices:** Incorporating a wide range of knowledge relating to species and species habitats.
4. **Land use regulation:** Indigenous Knowledge is used in locally based planning processes to determine the local and regional approaches most affected by development.
5. **Environmental monitoring:** Reflecting and recording changes related to people's well-being over time.
6. **Conservation of plant diversity:** Indigenous Knowledge can reduce over-exploitation; habitat loss and fragmentation; global climate change; species introduction and invasion.
7. **Agriculture:** Knowledge related to crop selection, intercropping, and planting time.
8. **Animal husbandry and ethnic veterinary:** Knowledge of breeding strategies, livestock characteristics, requirements, and use of plants to treat common ailments.
9. **Use and management of natural resources:** Soil Fertility Management, Knowledge of Sustainable Management of Wild Species.
10. **Health care:** Knowledge of the properties of plants for medicinal purposes.
11. **Community development:** Common or shared knowledge provides links between community members and generations; and
12. **Poverty alleviation:** Knowledge of survival strategies based on local resources.

Challenges to Indigenous Knowledge

1. **IK is easily overlooked:** Indigenous practices sometimes do not seem to be sophisticated. Despite their effectiveness, they can easily be overlooked. For example, a traditional irrigation system consisting of earthen canals and bamboo pipes seems to be less efficient than an introduced system of straight and cemented canals.
2. **IK is an endangered species:** Since most of it is not documented and is passed orally from one generation to another. They are threatened by modernization, urbanization, and globalization.
3. **IK is not well managed:** The people who created the content (IK) had no interest in preserving it, and those who held the content had no control over its creation. Library and information professionals have not been at the forefront of managing IK, despite the fact that it is becoming an important resource in the planning and management of sustainable development projects.
4. **Limited access to Indigenous Knowledge:** Access to indigenous information collected so far is very limited as it is not well organized in terms of being indexed and abstracted.
5. **Reluctance to share IK:** It is common that some local people are not willing to share their IK. Some IKs are generic and can be used freely in many communities by both members and outsiders.
6. **IK may not always be accurate:** Like other knowledge systems, IK has its limitations and weaknesses. IK may not be fair and accurate in all circumstances. It may be unwise to accept all traditional knowledge as good practice or sustainable practice.

How to Protect Indigenous Knowledge

1. **Raise Awareness:** There is a need to raise awareness in the community about the value of their IK. This can be done through recording and shar-

ing IK success stories in songs, sketches, puppet plays, storytelling, plays, videos, and other traditional or modern means of communication.

2. **Documentation:** Libraries should record and document IK. Since IQ is essential for development, it should be gathered, organized, and disseminated in a systematic way similar to western knowledge.
3. **Digital Libraries:** To enhance IK documentation, digital libraries based on IK can also be developed. These are known for preserving indigenous culture and making relevant information readily available locally.
4. **Establishing the value of IK:** It is important to find out what people value most in a specific IK, why they chose it, what they see as its strengths and weaknesses, what if IK was not available, what would be most affected if IK was not available and what features do people look for when testing a technology.
5. **Capacity building:** IK specialists need to develop relevant capacity through training, who will integrate IK into development projects but are also knowledgeable in recording, storing, disseminating, and matching IK to development projects.

Rights of Indigenous Knowledge and International Initiatives

Several international conventions and agreements address the subject of traditional knowledge and the rights of indigenous and local communities, such as:

1. Convention on Biological Diversity (CBD) and related protocol (Nagoya Protocol),
2. United Nations Educational Scientific and Cultural Organization (UNESCO)
3. International Treaty on Plant Genetic Resources for Food and Agriculture (ITPGRFA),
4. Convention for the Safeguarding of the Intangible Cultural Heritage,
5. Permanent Forum on Indigenous Issues and Food and Agriculture Organization (FAO).
6. World Intellectual Property Organization (WIPO),

Ethno-medicine

Ethno-medicine or traditional medicine is a term that refers to a wide range of healthcare systems/structures, practices, beliefs, and remedial techniques arising from indigenous cultural development. Such healthcare systems do not necessarily follow the structure of modern or 'Western' medicine. Instead, these healthcare practices are based on the unique culture that originated from the native/indigenous groups of people.

Ethno-medicine isn't limited to conventional things, like using indigenous plants and materials to treat the sick. It also includes studying or using:

1. How disease/sickness arises according to the native cultural view.
2. Indigenous beliefs about what a person's signs and symptoms really mean.
3. The way a disease/illness progresses.
4. The best ways by which a disorder should be managed and who should manage it and how.

Types of Ethno-medicine

1. Ayurveda
2. Yoga
3. Tai Chi
4. Attention
5. Dance and Music
6. Reiki
7. Qigong
8. Aromatherapy
9. Herbal Therapy
10. Acupressure / Acupuncture

GENDER AND ENVIRONMENT

Natural resources are an integral part of a rural household. Women, especially those living in rural areas, play a major role in the management of natural resources, including soil, water, forests, and sources of energy. Their function in agriculture and animal husbandry, as well as their central role in the home, make them daily managers of the living environment.

As women work further in the environment, they suffer more from the adverse effects of environmental degradation. Nevertheless, women are no longer seen as mere victims, it is increasingly recognized that women can play an important role in natural resource management because of the knowledge and experience they have gained from working together with their environment. To have a sustainable development perspective on environmental studies, we need to include women's knowledge systems in mainstream understanding.

Key Theories and Approaches in Gender and Environment

Gender is an important symbolic and material dimension of environmental relations and has important implications for ecological relations. There are various theories and approaches to studying the interrelationship of gender and environment such as:

Eco-feminism and the environment: Eco-feminism was coined as a term in 1974 when Frenchwoman Francoise d'Eubonne called for an ecological revolution led by women to save planet Earth. Eco-feminism has developed as an analysis of the society-nature relationship and as a prescription for how these relationships can be transformed. There are many different approaches to ecological feminism approach such as cultural eco-feminism and social eco-feminism.

Cultural ecological feminism identifies a powerful and positive link between women and nature, particularly through female reproductive functions such as childbirth and menstruation. This connection between women and nature is used to argue that women are better placed as advocates of nature than men.

Social eco-feminism argues that because both women and nature have been subjugated by a society dominated by men, women, in the roles they play, are in a better position than men to speak up for nature, the subject of domination. Because of this shared experience.

FOREST POLICIES

Forests are an important part of any nation, not only for their commercial value but also for the quality of life that it guarantees. Therefore, it was considered important even during British rule that India should have a forest policy. The British were the first to officially recognize India's natural wealth and initiated the process of formulating a forest policy during the late nineteenth century.

But their policies were mostly aimed at keeping himself in an advantageous position and exploiting the resources as much as possible. Their plan was to plunder the natural wealth of the nation as much as possible. The sequence of their efforts in this direction through acts and policies are as follows:

1. The first Conservator of Forests was appointed in Bombay by the British in 1850 and the first Forest Department was established in 1864.
2. To generate income, the Forest Act of 1865 was brought, which classified forests into reserved forests and unclassified forests.
3. The former was off limits to local people and the latter un-surveyed forests were progressively reclassified as reserve forests before the end of the century and the process was accelerated by the inclusion of a provision in the Revised Forest Act of 1878.
4. The Forest Act, 1865 was enacted for the first time to combat the diverse local population.
5. By the Forest Act of 1878 the village forests were also closed and the rights which belonged to the people were converted into privileges and that too for a fee.
6. The first forest policy was made in the year 1894, in which agriculture was given priority over forests.
7. The next Forest Act was enacted in the year 1927, which made the rules more stringent and further curtailed the privileges of the people.

Post-Independence Era

After independence, importance was given to the sector of forestry, but only after the priority sectors of agriculture and industry.

The Central Forestry Board was established in the year 1950 followed by a National Policy on Forests in the year 1952. In this National Forest Policy of 1952, the target was to cover 33% of the total land with forests established.

The National Forest Policy of 1952 was replaced by the National Forest Policy of 1988. This policy was considered better than the previous one, as it emphasized the conservation of our existing forests through deforestation and soil conservation.

Organization of Forest Sector in India

Forests in India are almost all owned by the government and any problem with the forests must be reported to the forest departments, which are agencies of the Indian government. In each state, the forestry sector is headed by a Principal Chief Conservator of Forests.

The Ministry of Environment and Forests is the principal administrative agency for the planning and coordination of environment and forestry programs.

National Forest Policy of 1988

The revised National Policy was called the "National Forest Policy 1988" and was placed in the Parliament on 7 December 1988 and approved by the House. The following are the basic objectives that govern the National Forest Policy:

i. Maintaining environmental stability through conservation and, where necessary, restoration of ecological balance that has been adversely affected by the country's severe depletion of forests.
ii. To conserve the natural heritage of the country by conserving the remaining natural forests containing a large variety of flora and fauna, which

represent the remarkable biological diversity and genetic resources of the country.

iii. To check soil erosion and denudation in the catchment areas of rivers, lakes, and reservoirs in the interest of soil and water conservation, to reduce flood and drought, and to reduce the siltation of reservoirs.

iv. To investigate the extent of sand dunes in desert areas and coastal areas of Rajasthan.

v. To substantially increase the forest/tree cover in the country, especially on all bare, degraded, and unproductive lands, through large-scale afforestation and social forestry programs.

vi. To meet the requirements of the rural and tribal population for fuelwood, fodder, minor forest produce, and small timber.

vii. To increase the productivity of forests to meet the essential national requirements.

viii. To encourage efficient use of forest produce and maximize wood substitution.

ix. To create a mass movement with the participation of women to achieve these objectives and reduce the pressure on the existing forests.

National Forest Commission

The National Forest Commission was established in 2003. It submitted its report in March 2006. Some of the recommendations of the commission are:

i. Emphasis on the need to conduct scientific research to assess the optimum forest/tree cover according to forest type and topography to meet the desired objectives.

ii. Amendment to the Indian Forest Act, 1927.

iii. The Forest Department should implement the Biological Diversity Act, 2002 and the Environment Protection Act.

iv. Re-scheduling of species under the Wildlife Protection Act to avoid man-animal conflict.

v. No further amendment to the Forest Conservation Act, 1980.

vi. No change in the National Forest Policy of 1988.

ADIVASIS AND EXCLUSION

Adivasis is the collective name used for many indigenous peoples of India. The word 'tribal' is derived from the Hindi words 'Adi', meaning from ancient times or from the beginning, and 'Vasi', meaning inhabitant or inhabitant.

It was coined in the 1930s, largely the result of a political movement to create a sense of identity among the various indigenous peoples of India. Adivasis are officially called 'Scheduled Tribes', but this is a legal and constitutional term, which varies from state to state and region to region, and therefore excludes some groups that may be considered indigenous. Could

Tribals have always been victims of extreme injustice and social exclusion. They have been denied almost everything, most importantly, their forest rights. For example, the right to reside, the right to collect, the right to use forest produce, etc. were taken away under Article 21 of the Constitution of India.

After independence, efforts have been made to ensure justice. It is because of these efforts that at least a very small (almost negligible) fraction of the ST community is now a part of mainstream society. More than 95 percent of Scheduled Tribes still live in rural areas, and economic exploitation remains their most pressing problem. Less than 10 percent are hunter-gatherers, but more than half depend on forest produce for their livelihood, many in the form of tendu leaves, which are used to produce bidis (cigarettes).

Since the time of the British administration, there have been laws regulating the ownership and use of forests, and today most forest land is effectively nationalized, with large areas contracted out to private commercial interests. This has deprived tribal communities of rights in the land, and they can be fined or imprisoned for taking forest produce that has traditionally belonged to them. Deforestation has many causes, although it is often attributed to the shifting agricultural practices of tribals.

A serious threat to the tribals is the massive dam construction for irrigation and hydroelectricity. According to local indigenous activists, thousands of residents were displaced due to the construction of the Sardar Sarovar Dam. Furthermore, policies are strictly limited to the public sector. They have not improved the prospects of tribals in the growing private sector.

There has been a lack of support from the state towards the tribal community when it comes to land redistribution rights and rights of marginal farmers and daily labourers. Tribals are the poorest constituents in various states of India, irrespective of the political composition of the state governments.

Tribals often face hardships and exclusion due to physical distance, poverty, and prevailing social prejudices. Whenever the word tribal comes, it always means a group of rural illiterate uncivilized people who live in forests.

This concept of describing tribals as backward Hindus were promoted by GS Ghurye. Though the government has taken some measures to promote their economic upliftment, a lot more needs to be done to uplift their economic and social status.

Social Forestry 1976

The National Commission on Agriculture (NAC, 1976) while emphasizing the commercial importance of forests alleged that the rural communities are the main culprits for its destruction.

But despite stressing the primacy of ensuring the supply of timber to industry, it recognized the need for at least a subsistence forest product and proposed alternative systems, woodlots, and agroforestry. The new concept of social forestry (SF) was introduced to reduce the pressure of the local population on forests.

But social forestry did not become a real substitute for the supply of produce from natural forests, and was unpopular in many areas, leading to further degradation due to conflicts between local communities and the forest department.

ECOLOGICAL DEGRADATION AND MIGRATION

Ecological degradation is the deterioration of the environment through the depletion of resources such as air, water, and soil; destruction of ecosystems; habitat destruction; extinction of wildlife; and pollution. It is defined as any change or disturbance in the environment that is considered harmful or undesirable.

Historical ecologists are interested in the history of resource use. He argues that 'people construct (or change) their environment over time, not just, meekly, adopt it' (Srivastava).

Migration on a permanent or temporary basis has always been one of the most important survival strategies adopted by people at the time of natural or man-made disasters. However, knowledge of the complex two-way relationship involving environmental change as both a cause and consequence of migration is limited.

Historically, migration caused by environmental change has occurred within national boundaries, as have environmental impacts resulting from population movements. Till recently the international dimensions of this relationship have been neglected. Today, mass migration at an accelerated pace is associated with the processes of globalization.

Some key points while studying environmental migration are:

1. Migration induced by environmental disasters, which are caused by environmental degradation.
2. Movement inspired by environmental change due to large-scale projects.
3. Environmental consequences of international population movements.
4. The implications of these relationships for economic growth and poverty reduction.
5. Ethical and policy dimensions of emerging international migration-environment-development trends.

Before examining environment-migration interrelationships and their implications for development in some detail there are several generalizations that can be drawn from the limited literature on migration and environment (Hugo 1996):

1. Most migration that is environmentally motivated occurs as internal migration within nations rather than as international migration.
2. While in the past the migration destination options for eco-migrants have been overwhelmingly to relocate within their country of origin, the importance of international destinations is increasing.
3. Migration occurs primarily in poor, less developed countries (LDCs), both as a cause and consequence of environmental change.
4. As the scale and pace of environmental change have accelerated, climate-driven migration is also on the rise.

Castells (2002) suggests that there are three key elements in the debate on environmentally motivated migration:

1. Debate over the terminology and definition of 'environmental refugee'.
2. Can environmental factors be identified as the root cause of migration?
3. Who will provide protection to the displaced people from the environment?

Speare says that 'migration in the strict sense can be considered involuntary only when a person is physically taken from a country and has no opportunity to escape from those who take him. Movement under danger, even immediate danger to life, has a voluntary element, as long as there is an option to flee, hide, or stay in another part of the country and hope to escape persecution.

On the other hand, some scholars of migration argue that most population mobility, traditionally viewed as voluntary, occurs in situations in which migrants actually have little or no choice. Samir Amin, discussing migration in West Africa, states that: 'A comparative cost and benefit analysis carried out at the individual level of the migrant is of no value. In fact, it only gives an appearance of objective rationality to a 'choice' (of the migrant), which in fact does not exist, because, in a given system, he has no choice.'

Peterson distinguished between 'induced migration' when the migrants retain some power to decide whether or not to leave, and 'forced migration' when they do not have this power.

In cases of environmental migration, poorer countries and groups may suffer because they do not have the resources to set up sophisticated warning systems or for a quick, planned, well-provisioned flight from the disaster and to aid afterward to recover the victims.

While the occurrence of a catastrophic environmental event is an important and increasingly important cause of environmentally induced migration, less dramatic, gradual, environmental deterioration causes greater migration.

Billsborrow, in his case studies of Indonesia, Guatemala, and Sudan, shows that environmental degradation is one of the leading causes of migration. He suggests that environmental changes induce migration through their 'social' effects:

1. reduce income
2. increasing risk of future loss of income
3. Making the environment less healthy.

Environmental degradation occurs when population growth exceeds the carrying capacity of the land, leading to the degradation of natural resources. Population pressure, especially in Least Developed Countries (LDCs), can lead to settlement expansion in ecologically fragile areas that are particularly vulnerable to degradation.

Since climate change does not occur as suddenly as a catastrophic environmental disaster, its effects often go unnoticed. Spitz characterizes the progressive onset of food shortages associated with drought, famine, and the gradual degradation of the environment as 'silent violence'.

DEVELOPMENT AND ENVIRONMENT

Development refers to the improvement in the economic and social conditions of a country. It refers to improving the management of natural and human resources of an area in order to create wealth and improve the lives of the people.

It is a well-known fact that the growth and development of human society, even the survival of human beings, requires a number of natural resources, both physical and biological. The land is limited for all practical purposes and although water can be replenished, it may also become scarce over time. Air is seemingly renewable but may become unusable due to severe degradation of its quality through changes in its composition.

Energy in its natural form like sunlight appears to be abundant but it is severely lacking at the consumer level. Fossil fuels such as coal, petroleum, natural gas, and radioactive elements are certainly finite. As a result of their increasing use, they are rapidly depleting.

The unprecedented growth in world production and consumption are causing environmental stress through irreversible impacts at the local, regional, and global levels. Global warming and ozone layer depletion are examples of global environmental degradation; Acid rain and the state of the oceans in many countries are of international concern and the more local effects are due to air and water pollution, soil degradation, deforestation, etc.

Still, in most developing countries poverty, malnutrition, infectious and parasitic diseases, lack of food and water, poor sanitation and lack of proper housing are major concerns rather than issues of global warming or ozone depletion.

Sustainable Development

The concept of sustainable development was first introduced during the Stockholm Intergovernmental Conference on the Human Environment in June 1972 to emphasize the relationship between development and environmental problems and to promote political and economic change at the local, national, and global levels to deal with these problems.

The World Commission on Environment and Development (1987), also known as the "Bruntland Report", defined the concept of sustainable development as "development that meets the needs of the present without compromising the ability of future generations to fulfill their own needs".

The United Nations Conference on Environment and Development, held in Rio de Janeiro in 1992, affirmed the pursuit of economic and social progress and equity within the limits of the world's natural resources as a practical goal for everyone from individuals to governments.

The measures needed to ensure sustainable development were further outlined in Agenda 21 to promote sustainable development at the local level in developed and developing countries. Although Agenda 21 was a voluntary declaration, it has become part of the local government of many countries. India is at the forefront of developing countries and has implemented Agenda 21.

Displacement and Rehabilitation

Displacement is much more than a physical dislocation. The socioeconomic fabric of life is being uprooted by traumatic experiences. This results in a spiral of poverty. Displacement threatens the existence and identity of the people. Displacement involves a process of eviction. It is a process in which the poorer sections are 'pushed out' from their own residence. It is a situation where underprivileged people have no option but to move from their village or native place to another place. Local residents lose their control over resources.

Given the number of displacements, the types of displacements, and the plight of the displaced, many are now asking: whose nation is this? Who is getting good? Is it for planners, administrators, implementing agencies, or upper middle class or marginalized sections of society? (Fernandes 1997) Planners and administrators invariably exploit and manipulate the relatively vulnerable socio-economic and political position of displaced persons. Their numbers are underestimated. They are treated with indifference and given only minimal cash compensation. They are rarely provided security of tenure or alternative developed land. Often after a traumatic and painful period of establishing a new lifestyle, they are informed again they must move again to make way for another project.

In addition to immediate economic loss, displacement also brings social, cultural, and psychological dislocation. Physical displacement of people leads to uprooting from their socio-cultural base which is no less pathetic than the dispossession of land. They lose their traditional mechanisms of social control, and as a result, social tensions increase among them (Fernandes, 1997).

The history of tribals has been one of displacement without rehabilitation. If the history of Jharkhand is traced back to the Muslim, British, and post-colonial times, one wonders how involuntary displacements have taken place over the centuries without any rehabilitation or adequate resettlement. One excuse given by various governments is that there is no policy on rehabilitation. Yet, what is a matter of serious concern is the partisanship at the expense of the wealthy few. It is precisely this approach that is discriminatory towards the weaker sections, especially the tribals.

The land is sacred to the tribals as it is the only resource they have for their sustenance. About 70 percent of India's population, most of whom are tribals, mainly depend on land-related work and agricultural production. Thus, for them, the land is the means of livelihood and the basis of socio-economic relations. Alienation from land and displacement have threatened the livelihoods of millions of people.

People are displaced without any consultation or participation in the development process. Furthermore, they are denied their due share in the benefits of the development project that displaces them. A sizable number of the displaced belong to the Scheduled Castes and Scheduled Tribes and women are the worst sufferers. Furthermore, resettlement is still not an integral part of any displacement plan.

WATER AND SOCIAL EXCLUSION

Mehmet Murat Ildan's most quoted statement "'For every drop of water you waste, you should know that somewhere on earth someone is looking for a drop of water!' Explains the real importance of water.

The social exclusion of certain sections of society on religious, caste, social or other grounds from the water sector in India needs to be seen in the context of the overall concept of 'social exclusion'. Viewed from a broader perspective, the concept of 'social exclusion' refers to the systematic exclusion of individuals and groups from one or more dimensions of society, such as structures of power and privilege, opportunities, and resources.

Social exclusion also describes what happens when people or regions are excluded from essential services or daily aspects of life that most take for granted. Water is an important livelihood asset for all. But water is not easily and equally accessible to all. The availability of water in a society depends on various social factors like class, caste, etc.

Poverty and social exclusion are closely related – the poorest people are often socially excluded, have fewer opportunities for development, and have an unheard voice in the decisions made on their behalf. This means that often water, sanitation, and hygiene services do not meet the needs of the least powerful. People with disabilities and older people are excluded from water points and toilets if they cannot reach them easily.

The concept of 'social exclusion' analyzes how inequalities are mediated through complex intersections of social, economic, political, and cultural processes and resources as well as opportunities are provided or denied, and how these are shaped by policies, and institutions and are reflected in the institutional norms and rules. For traditionally prosperous families, well-being and security revolved around adequate and reliable water. This view explains the continued focus on the development or exploitation of water, even in the face of water scarcity.

Inequalities in access to water are largely ignored in current drinking water policy and practice, which assumes an altruistic and unitary user community and divided water use and/or need. Unless the Demand-Response Approach (DRA) formulates a new plan to incorporate poverty and livelihood perspectives, the drinking water sector will struggle to raise and address demand.

Not explicitly addressing these issues will mean that the intended and potential benefits of DRA are unlikely to be realized both in terms of sustainability (planning and finance) and poverty reduction. In theory, DRA aims to improve the financial and technical stability and efficiency of distribution systems and places a heavy emphasis on user 'communities' to act as management and financing institutions.

In policy, the DRA aims to enable a voice and choice for all, including the poorest. However, in practice, the implications of poverty in demanding and accessing water are poorly understood and addressed in the currently implemented demand-responsive approach to water supply management.

Water resources, both communal and individual, remain under the control of socially, politically, and economically powerful, usually upper-caste men. The current emphasis on cost recovery over equity means that DRA, as currently practiced, primarily benefits economically better-off households. Furthermore, domestic water sector policy is narrowly focused on providing safe drinking water and does not recognize the importance of the productive use of water at the household level.

Nor does the practice of demand-based approaches take into account the competing and conflicting demands on the resource base. This makes it difficult, if not impossible, for water supply projects to guarantee access to safe water for domestic use.

Given the deep roots of exclusionary attitudes and practices, understanding exclusion requires studying the dynamic interrelationships between the excluded and the excluded actors, with an emphasis on the processes and mechanisms of exclusion, as well as the institutions of power, agency, the competitive and emergent nature of culture and social identity.

Water has been both a medium and a source of exclusion for Dalits in the fourfold varna hierarchy of Hindu society (Sharma 2003; Joshi and Fawcett 2006). Only 62.3 percent of Indian households have access to safe water – 81.4 percent of urban and 55.5 percent of rural households. This means that women spend a lot of time fetching water from distant wells and other sources, adding to the burden on women.

DISASTERS AND COMMUNITY RESPONSES

A disaster is a disruption that occurs over a short or long period of time that causes widespread human, physical, economic, and environmental loss. The community has always been an important element. Community resilience and capacity in disasters are important elements in preparedness for a crisis event. The role of education and learning in disasters is becoming increasingly important. Organizations such as UNESCO, the European Commission, and other international and national bodies consider education to be an important factor in enabling people to prepare for emergency situations.

Within education, community education is an important feature of disaster response, especially in countries that experience natural disasters, such as New Zealand and Japan. According to Klein, disasters of various kinds have been used as a form of 'disaster capitalism', where catastrophic events are used as neoliberal projects for profit to rebuild communities and the environment. Klein refers to the use of catastrophes in this way as the shock principle. The theory of shock works like this: A basic disaster—coup, terrorist attack, market downturn, war, tsunami, hurricane—puts a population into a state of collective shock.

In some countries that experience a high degree of natural disasters, community education is very important. Community education is an important part of the culture of disaster preparedness in Japan. In New Zealand, there is also an emphasis on community learning and resilience, but with an orientation towards lifelong learning, rather than top-down. Wilson believes that community learning in a disaster can only be understood in the context of community history and culture. He believes that community education is rooted in the 'social memory' of communities.

According to Sapirstein, community learning is an important outcome after a disaster and can be 'locked' into efforts to build resilience by integrating lessons learned with existing educational curricula.

Designing and implementing an effective disaster response during disasters requires recognizing the vulnerabilities and capabilities of affected populations. To identify these strengths and weaknesses, the Capabilities and Vulnerability Analysis (CVA) model can be used to examine three aspects of the information:

1. **Physical factors:** What productive resources, skills, and threats (such as land, environment, health, skills and labor, infrastructure, food, housing, capital, and technologies) are available?
2. **Social organization:** What are the relationships and organization between communities (for example, formal political structures and informal systems such as decision-making, establishing leadership, or organizing various socio-economic activities)? When prejudice or conflict is present in a community, social and organizational vulnerability is inevitable.
3. **Attitude:** How does the community view its ability to adapt to changes? Strengths and weaknesses can make a significant difference in the ability of communities to rebuild and improve their physical base and social institutions. A community is psychologically more vulnerable when its people feel victimized, fatalistic and dependent.

World's Biggest Man-made Disasters

1. Nuclear power plant explosion in Chernobyl, Russia—A major meltdown occurred in April 1986 at the nuclear power plant in Chernobyl, Russia. The release of radioactive material into the atmosphere is calculated to be four hundred times more radioactive than the bomb dropped on Hiroshima. Caused many birth defects and other health problems. The total number of fatal cancer deaths caused by the recession is estimated to be around 100,000. The land around Chernobyl would remain unusable for two centuries.
2. Kuwait oil fires—When Saddam Hussein invaded Kuwait in 1991, triggering the Gulf War, an environmental catastrophe ensued when Iraqi troops blew up Kuwaiti oil wells. 600 wells were set on fire and burned for seven months, making it the largest oil spill in history.
3. The Bhopal gas leak disaster was the release of methyl isocyanate, a highly toxic flammable, colorless liquid, along with several other toxic substances, into the atmosphere around the city of Bhopal in India on 3 December 1984. A large amount of water inadvertently entered a tank containing methyl isocyanate, creating the deadly chemical. More than 500,000 people were exposed and of these, 15,000 died within the first few days. In addition, more than 20,000 people have died in the region from gas-related diseases.
4. The Three Mile Island Nuclear Plant Partial Meltdown on March 28, 1979, the United States was about to suffer the most significant nuclear accident in history. A partial meltdown due to a fault in the secondary cooling circuit was responsible for a 'small' amount of radiation leakage, fortunately, a radiation control system did its job and no direct casualties were recorded at the time of the accident.
5. The Jilin chemical plant explosion was a series of explosions that occurred on November 13, 2005, at a petrochemical plant in Jilin city, Jilin province, China, over a period of one hour. The explosions killed six, injured dozens, and caused the evacuation of thousands of residents.
6. The Deepwater Horizon oil spill was an industrial disaster that began on 20 April 2010 in the Gulf of Mexico, which is considered the largest marine oil spill in the history of the petroleum industry. The US federal government estimated total discharges at 4.9 million barrels. After several failed attempts to stop the flow, the well was declared sealed on 19 September 2010. The leak threatened 8,332 marine species, some of which were already endangered and under federal protection.
7. The Fukushima Daiichi nuclear disaster was a 2011 nuclear accident at the Fukushima Daiichi Nuclear Power Plant in Okuma, Fukushima Prefecture, Japan. Following a major earthquake, a 15-meter tsunami disabled the power supply and cooling of the three Fukushima Daiichi reactors, triggering a nuclear accident on 11 March 2011. All three cores melted largely in the first three days. There have been no deaths or cases of radiation sickness from the nuclear accident, but more than 100,000 people were evacuated from their homes as a preventive measure.

ENVIRONMENTAL POLLUTION

Environmental pollution is defined as contamination of the physical and biological components of the Earth/atmosphere system to such an extent that normal environmental processes are adversely affected.

Environmental pollution is an adverse change in our environment that is caused entirely or largely as a byproduct of human actions. Human activities through urbanization, industrialization, mining, and exploration are at the forefront of global environmental pollution.

Environmental pollution is a global problem and is common in both developed and developing countries, with serious long-term consequences. Degradation of environmental quality as a result of pollution is evidenced by the loss of vegetation, biological diversity, excess amounts of harmful chemicals in the ambient environment and overconsumption of food grains, and increased risks of environmental accidents and threats to life support systems.

Holdgate defined environmental pollution as the introduction, into the environment, of substances or energy liable to interfere with the legitimate uses of the environment.

Singh defined pollution as 'a state of disequilibrium in any system from a state of equilibrium'.

The substances which cause pollution are called pollutants. A pollutant can be any chemical (toxic metals, radionuclides, organophosphorus compounds, gases) or geochemical substance (dust, sediment), biological organisms or products, or physical substances (heat, radiation, sound waves) that are intentionally produced by humans. or is inadvertently released. With actual or potential adverse, harmful, unpleasant, or inconvenient effects on the environment.

On the basis of the nature of pollutants and post-pollution of environmental components, pollution can be classified as follows:

Air pollution

Release of chemicals and particles into the atmosphere. Common gaseous pollutants include carbon monoxide, sulfur dioxide, chlorofluorocarbons (CFCs) and nitrogen oxides produced by industry and motor vehicles. Photochemical ozone and smog are formed as nitrogen oxides and hydrocarbons react with sunlight.

Air pollution can result from both human and natural actions. Natural events that pollute the air include forest fires, volcanic eruptions, wind erosion, pollen dispersal, evaporation of organic compounds, and natural radioactivity. Pollution is often not caused by natural phenomena.

The major effects of air pollution are:

i. Acidification: Chemical reactions associated with air pollutants can create acidic compounds that can damage vegetation and buildings. Sometimes, when an air pollutant, such as sulfuric acid, combines with water droplets to form clouds, the water droplets become acidic, causing acid rain. When acid rain occurs in an area, it can kill trees and harm animals, fish, and other wildlife. Acid rain destroys the leaves of plants.

ii. Eutrophication: Rain can carry and deposit nitrogen in rivers and some pollutants in the soil. This will have an adverse effect on the nutrients in the soil and water bodies. This may result in a large increase in lakes and water bodies and may create harmful conditions for other living organisms.

iii. Ground-level ozone: Chemical reactions involving air pollutants create ozone (O3), a toxic gas. Gas ozone can affect people's health and can also harm vegetation types and some animal life.

iv. Particulate Matter: Air pollutants can be in the form of particulate matter which can be very harmful to our health. The level of effect generally depends on the length of time of exposure, as well as the type and concentration of chemicals and particles exposed. Short-term effects include irritation of the eyes, nose, and throat, and upper respiratory infections such as bronchitis and pneumonia. Others include headaches, nausea, and allergic reactions.

Water Pollution

Discharge of wastewater from commercial and industrial effluents into surface water; Discharge of untreated domestic sewage, and chemical contaminants, such as chlorine, from treated sewage; The release of waste and contaminants into surface runoff flowing into surface water, including urban runoff and agricultural runoff, which may contain chemical fertilizers and pesticides.

Water pollution affects drinking water, rivers, lakes, and oceans all over the world. In many developing countries, it is a leading cause of death, usually by people drinking from polluted water sources.

Organic pollutants – sewage and municipal organic waste, agricultural residues, dairy activity as well, depletion of dissolved oxygen in the body of water body leading to the death of marine organisms, emission of methane,

Easy to leach out chemicals in household and municipal waste - not easy to leach out, such as soaps and detergents, contain lead, mercury nickel zinc, and chromium, causing heavy metal pollution of water.

Industrial Effluents. Effluents are released into lakes, rivers, and seas. They contain acids and toxic substances. Agricultural wastes such as Chemical fertilizers, pesticides, insecticides, herbicides, etc.

The effects of water pollution are varied. These include poisoned drinking water, poisoned food animals (due to bioaccumulated toxins from the environment over the lifetime of these organisms), unbalanced river and lake ecosystems that can no longer support full biological diversity, loss of forests from acid rain, Harvesting, and many other effects. Waterborne diseases caused by contaminated drinking water: typhoid, amebiasis, giardiasis, ascariasis, hookworm

Soil/Land Pollution

It is caused by the presence of xenobiotics chemicals or other changes in the natural soil environment. Most land pollution affects animals that live on lands, such as cows, goats, and other herbivores. If these animals feed on plants that have been exposed to toxic chemicals, they can pass on deadly diseases to animals higher up the food chain, including humans causing harmful effects:

- causes cancer, including leukemia
- Lead in soil is especially dangerous for young children harming brain development
- Mercury can increase the risk of kidney damage; cadmium can cause liver toxicity
- Neuromuscular blockade as well as depression of the central nervous system causing headache, nausea, fatigue, burning of the eyes, and skin rash.

Noise Pollution

This includes road noise, aircraft noise, industrial noise as well as high-intensity sonar.

Radioactive Pollution

Radioactive contamination that results from nuclear power generation and nuclear weapons research, manufacture, and deployment.

Thermal Pollution

Temperature change in natural water bodies due to human influence, such as the use of water as a coolant in a power plant.

Plastic Pollution

Covers the accumulation of plastic products and microplastics in the environment that adversely affects wildlife, wildlife habitats, or humans.

Although environmental pollution can be caused by natural events such as wildfires and active volcanoes, the use of the term pollution generally indicates that the pollutant has an anthropogenic source—that is, a source created by human activities.

Efforts are made to limit the release of harmful substances into the environment through air pollution control, wastewater treatment, solid waste management, hazardous waste management, and recycling. Unfortunately, pollution control efforts often outweigh the scale of the problem.

High levels of air pollution are common in many large cities, where particles and gases from transportation, heating, and construction accumulate and persist.

The problem of plastic pollution on land and oceans has only increased because the use of single-use plastics has increased around the world.

Furthermore, greenhouse gas emissions, such as methane and carbon dioxide, continue to drive global warming and pose a major threat to biodiversity and public health.

States with the most deaths due to air pollution are

1. Uttar Pradesh
2. Maharashtra
3. Bihar
4. West Bengal
5. Rajasthan

PUBLIC HEALTH AND DISABILITY

It is estimated that more than 1 billion people are living with some form of disability. This corresponds to approximately 15% of the world's population, with up to 190 million (3.8%) people aged 15 years and over experiencing significant difficulties with functioning, often requiring health services.

Disability is extremely diverse. While some health conditions associated with disability result in poor health and the need for comprehensive health care, others do not. However, all people with a disability have the same general health needs and therefore need access to mainstream health services.

Article 25 of the United Nations Convention on the Rights of Persons with Disabilities (CRPD) reinforces the right of persons with disabilities to access the highest standard of health care without discrimination. However, the reality is that few countries provide adequate quality services for people with disabilities.

People with disabilities face a number of barriers when trying to access healthcare. These:

1. **Prohibitive cost:** Two of the main reasons why people with disabilities in low-income countries may not be able to access essential health care are the affordability of health services and transportation. More than half of people with disabilities are unable to afford health care, compared to about a third of people without disabilities.
2. **Limited availability of services:** There is a lack of suitable services for people with disabilities. Several studies suggest that there is a high unmet need for health care among people with disabilities due to the non-availability of services, especially in rural and remote areas.
3. **Physical barriers:** Unequal access to buildings (hospitals, health centres), inaccessible medical equipment, poor signage, narrow doorways, internal staircases, inadequate bathroom facilities, and inaccessible parking areas create barriers to health facilities. For example, women with mobility difficulties are often unable to undergo breast and cervical cancer screening because exam tables are not height-adjustable and mammography equipment only accommodates women who are able to stand.
4. **Inadequate skills and knowledge of health workers:** People with a disability were more than twice as likely to report that healthcare provider skills were insufficient to meet their needs, were four times more likely to report being treated poorly, and were almost three times more likely to report having been denied care.

Too often, disability is not seen as a public health issue. Therefore, the health sector does not take action toward disability inclusion. Thus, the inclusion of disability in the health sector remains a breach of the health agenda of countries.

Health ministries need to commit to disability inclusion. This includes action to achieve equality for people with disability in three areas:

1. access to effective health services,
2. safety during health emergencies, and,
3. Access to cross-sectional public health interventions such as water, sanitation, and hygiene services to achieve the highest attainable standard of health.

Governments can improve health outcomes for people with disabilities by improving access to quality, affordable health services. Assessing existing policies and services, identifying priorities to reduce health disparities, and ensuring disability inclusion in the health sector are critical to closing the gap between disability and health care.

People with disabilities not only experience low levels of health due to their primary and secondary health conditions, but also the effects of social marginalization, poverty, denial of access to health and social services, and discrimination. These important environmental factors either cause disability or worsening disability.

Swavlamban Health Insurance Scheme for Persons with Disabilities

- Launch date: 2nd October 2015
- Swavlamban Health Insurance Scheme to provide affordable Health Insurance to persons with disabilities (PwDs)
- Swavlamban Health Insurance Scheme for Persons with Disabilities is a Prestigious Health insurance Scheme for Persons with Disabilities (As Per PWD Act 1995) launched by The New India Assurance Company Limited, in Association with the Ministry of Social Justice, Dept of Empowerment of Persons with Disabilities.

Its mission is:

1. to Provide affordable Health Insurance to persons with Blindness, Low Vision, leprosy-Cured, Hearing Impairment, Loco-Motor disability, Mental-Retardation, and mental illness.
2. to Improve general Health conditions & Quality of life of persons with Disabilities.

CLIMATE CHANGE AND INTERNATIONAL POLICIES

Climate change

Climate change can be expressed as any significant change in Earth's climate that lasts for an extended period of time while global warming refers to changes in climate that cause an increase in the average temperature of the lower atmosphere.

But, according to the Intergovernmental Panel on Climate Change (IPCC), climate change "refers to any change in climate over time, whether due to natural variability or as a result of human activity" (IPCC, 2001).

Article 1 of the United Nations Framework Convention on Climate Change (UNFCCC) defines it as 'Climate change refers to changes in climate that are directly or indirectly attributable to human activity that alter the composition of the global atmosphere changes and that is in addition to natural climate variability observed over comparable time periods' (IPCC, 2001).

Causes of Climate Change

- The causes of climate change can be divided into two categories: natural and human causes.
- Natural Causes. Earth's climate is influenced and changed by natural causes such as volcanic eruptions, ocean currents, Earth's orbital changes, and solar variability.
- Anthropogenic Causes. Green House Gases (GHGs) – While natural GHGs have been showing an increase for decades, there is also a concern for emissions of purely man-made GHGs, which include many ozone-depleting substances.
- Cryogenic Processes - The processes of permafrost, glaciation, defrosting, and deglaciation are known as cryogenic processes. Recent evidence has shown that the ice sheets of Antarctica, Greenland, Baffin Island, etc. are throbbing, thinning, and melting.
- Black carbon – This is a solid resulting from the incomplete combustion of carbon-containing materials and is responsible for more than 30% of the recent warming in the Arctic region.
- Tackling climate change is one of the greatest global challenges of the 21st century. The average global temperature at Earth's surface continues to rise due to increased carbon dioxide (CO_2) and other greenhouse gas concentrations in the atmosphere, the effects of which are already evident today.

International Policies Related to Climate Change

At the United Nations Conference on Environment and Development, also known as the Rio Summit or Earth Summit, held in Rio de Janeiro in 1992, the United Nations Framework Convention on Climate Change (UNFCCC) was adopted to stabilize greenhouse gas concentrations in the atmosphere. was adopted for the purpose of at a sustainable level and thus counteract the severe consequences.

The UNFCCC aims to stabilize atmospheric concentrations of greenhouse gases at a level that would prevent dangerous anthropogenic interference with the climate system. It came into force in 1994, following ratification by the 50th state.

Signatory states meet at regular intervals in the COP (Conference of the Parties) to agree on further action in climate protection.

Kyoto Protocol

In 1997, this meeting was held in Kyoto, Japan, during which the Kyoto Protocol (2008–2012), the first document containing legally binding obligations to limit and reduce, was adopted by ratified countries.

Cancun Agreement

The Cancun Agreement, adopted at the United Nations Climate Conference in Mexico (December 2010), includes a timetable for a review of the objective of keeping the average global temperature rise well below 2 °C. The agreements confirm that developed countries will mobilize US$100 billion in climate finance annually for developing countries by 2020, and establish a Green Climate Fund through which much of the funding will be channeled.

Environmental Movements

Bishnoi Movement

In the 1700s, at Khejarli in the Marwar region of Rajasthan, trees were ordered to be cleared for the construction of a new palace. The Bishnoi tree was influenced by the teachings of the martyr Guru Maharaj Jambaji, who founded the Bishnoi religion in 1485.

Harming plants or animals was forbidden in the Bishnoi religion. Amrita Devi, a female villager, could not bear the destruction of both her faith and the sacred trees of the village. She hugged trees and encouraged others to do the same. 363 Bishnoi villagers were killed in this movement.

The king who came to know about these incidents reached the village and ordered the soldiers to stop the logging process. Soon after, the Maharaja designated the Bishnoi state as a protected area, forbidding harm to the trees and animals. This law still exists in the region today.

Chipko Movement:

The Chipko movement in 1973 under the leadership of Sunderlal Bahuguna, Gaura Devi, Sudesha Devi, Bachni Devi, Chandi Prasad Bhatt, Govind Singh

Rawat, Dhoom Singh Negi, Shamsher Singh Bisht, and Ghanshyam Raturi aimed to protect trees from axes of forest contractor.

Bahuguna told the villagers about the importance of trees and how they prevent soil erosion and benefit the environment through rain and pure water. The main demand of the protests was that trees should not be cut as it benefits the local people. The Chipko movement gained momentum in 1978 when women faced police firing and other torture.

Appiko Movement

Similarly, the Uttara Kannada and Shimoga districts of Karnataka saw a southern version of the Chipko movement, known as the Appiko movement or Appiko Chaluvali. The movement used various methods to raise awareness such as foot marches in the interior forest, slide shows, folk dances, street plays, etc. This movement was against the commercialization of natural forests.

Save Silent Valley Movement

Silent Valley is a tropical region of Kerala that is rich in biodiversity. However, in 1978, the lush evergreen cover had to be deforested for the construction of a hydroelectric dam on the Kuntipuzha River in Kerala by the Kerala State Electricity Board.

Locals feared that the project would submerge at least 8.3 square kilometers of green cover around the dam area. Several NGOs opposed the project and urged the government to abandon it.

Kerala Shastra Sahitya Parishad (KSSP), an NGO, and poet-activist Sugathakumari played a key role in the Silent Valley protest. In January 1981, bowing to unrelenting public pressure, the government called off the project and declared Silent Valley a protected area.

Jungle Bachao Andolan

This movement started in 1982 in the Singhbhum district of Bihar. The tribals of Singhbhum district started protesting when the government decided to replace natural Sal forests with highly-priced teak. The move was called by many as "greed game political populism". Later this movement spread to Jharkhand and Orissa.

Narmada Bachao Andolan

Narmada Bachao Andolan took place in the year 1985. The movement was led by Medha Patkar along with Arundhati Roy, Baba Amte, and Aamir Khan along with tribals, farmers, environmentalists, and human rights activists.

The main objective of the movement was to oppose the construction of several big dams on the Narmada River. It started when the people displaced by the construction of the Sardar Sarovar Dam were not provided proper rehabilitation and resettlement.

Tehri Dam Struggle

The Tehri Dam attracted national attention in the 1980s and 1990s. Major objections include seismic sensitivity of the area, submergence of Tehri town as well as forest areas etc. Despite the support of other prominent leaders such as Sunderlal Bahuguna, the movement failed to garner sufficient popular support at the national and international levels.

ASSESS YOUR LEARNING

PRACTICE QUESTIONS

1. The 'Jungle Bachao Andolan' began in the state of?
   (a) Karnataka (b) Bihar
   (c) Uttarakhand (d) Himachal Pradesh

2. Thomas Malthus regarded war, famine, and disease as:
   (a) Malthusian Catastrophe
   (b) Preventive Check
   (c) Positive Check
   (d) Population Hazard

3. In which year was the first National Forest Policy formulated?
   (a) 1880 (b) 1894
   (c) 1926 (d) 1937

4. Match the following:

List I (Environmental Day)	List II (Date)
A. National Science Day	I. March 23
B. World Meteorological Day	II. February 28
C. Anti Tobacco Day	III. October 3
D. Word Habitat Day	IV. May 31

   Choose the correct codes given below:
   (a) A–II, B–I, C–IV, D–III
   (b) A–I, B–II, C–IV, D–III
   (c) A–IV, B–II, C–III, D–I
   (d) A–I, B–II, C–III, D–IV

5. Under which ministry, the Centre has set a target of providing clean drinking water to all by the year 2024?
   (a) Jal Shakti Ministry
   (b) SwachhBharat Mission
   (c) Swajal Ministry
   (d) All of the above

6. The unfavourable alteration of the environment due to human activities is termed as
   (a) Catastrophe
   (b) Ecological imbalance
   (c) Ecological conservation
   (d) Pollution

7. Select the three indicators of Human Development?
   1. Life Expectancy
   2. Social Inclusion
   3. Education
   4. Per capita income

   Choose the correct option below:
   (a) 1, 2 and 4 (b) 1, 2 and 3
   (c) 2, 3 and 4 (d) 1, 3 and 4

8. Which of the following is a type of forced migration?
   (a) Immigration (b) Diaspora
   (c) Displacement (d) Refugees

9. Concept of 'The Human Development Index Was developed by whom?
   (a) A. R. Desai (b) Mahbub Ul Haq
   (c) M. Desai (d) Manmohan Singh

10. Which of the following factors Everett S. Lee included in his theory of migration?
    (a) Factors associated with the area of origin.
    (b) Factors associated with the area of destination.
    (c) Intervening and personal factors.
    (d) All of the above.

11. The slogan "Save planet earth" was generated at:
    (a) Rio Earth Summit
    (b) Jakarta Summit
    (c) Copenhagen Summit
    (d) Brazil Summit

12. Which among the following countries is known to be the only carbon-negative country in the world?
    (a) Norway (b) Bhutan
    (c) South Korea (d) Switzerland

13. On which date did the UN General Assembly adopt the 2030 Development Agenda titled, "Transforming Our World: The 2030 Agenda for Sustainable Development"?
    (a) 26th June, 2015
    (b) 25th September, 2015
    (c) 19th July, 2014
    (d) 1st January, 2015

14. When is 'National Pollution Control Day' celebrated?
    (a) December 2 (b) November 2
    (c) October 2 (d) None of the above

15. People who have left their home country, usually involuntarily to foreign countries
    (a) Diaspora (b) Tourist
    (c) Ethnic groups (d) Pilgrimage

16. Which of the following is an ecofeminism movement?
    (a) Self-Respect Movement
    (b) Santhal Movement
    (c) Chipko Movement
    (d) All of the above

17. Farming which aims at achieving maximum productivity on the limited land with all efforts possible is called:
    (a) Mixed farming
    (b) Shifting agriculture
    (c) Intensive farming
    (d) Subsistence agriculture

18. Who amongst the following is an environmental activist?
(a) Vandana Shiva (b) Amartya Sen
(c) M.N. Srinivas (d) None of these

19. What was the aim of the United Nations Framework Convention on Climate Change, 1992?
(a) To maintain better ecosystem management
(b) To assist developing countries in implementing environmentally sound policies
(c) To stabilize greenhouse gas concentration in the atmosphere
(d) None of the above

20. A wide range of healthcare systems/techniques that arise from indigenous cultural development is known as?
(a) Indigenous knowledge
(b) Ecosystem
(c) Ethnomedicine
(d) Technology

21. The basic elements of social ecology as given by Mackenzie include:
1. Environment
2. Polity
3. Population
4. Settlement Pattern
5. Connectivity
6. Economy

Choose the most appropriate answer from the options given below:
(a) 2, 3, 5, and 6 only
(b) 1, 3, 4, and 5 only
(c) 1, 3, 4, and 6 only
(d) 2, 3, 4, and 6 only

22. Who is considered the propounder of Cultural Ecology?
(a) Daniel Bookchin
(b) Julian Steward
(c) Theodore Adorno
(a) Don Tapscott

23. Assertion (A): Ecofeminism draws parallels between women and nature.
Reason (R): Both women and nature are oppressed by men.
(a) Both (A) and (R) are true and (R) is the correct explanation of (A)
(b) Both (A) and (R) are true but (R) is not the correct explanation of (A)
(c) (A) is true but (R) is false
(d) Both (A) and (R) are false

24. The apex body for Disaster Management in India is
(a) National Institute for Disaster Management
(b) National Disaster Response Force
(c) National Disaster Management Authority
(d) None of the above

25. Who coined the slogan for the Chipko movement "Ecology is the permanent economy"?
(a) Sunderlal Bahuguna
(b) Gaura Devi
(c) Chandi Prasad Bhatt
(d) Sudesha Devi

26. Why is World Environment Day celebrated?
(a) To encourage awareness and action for the protection of the environment
(b) To increase deforestation
(c) To encourage littering
(d) To increase the concentration of greenhouse gases

27. Where is the 'Centre for Science and Environment' (CSE) headquartered?
(a) New Delhi (b) Bengaluru
(c) Pune (d) Bhopal

28. Total Number of biodiversity hotspots in India:
(a) Four (b) Three
(c) Six (d) Five

29. Who is the author of Staying Alive: Women, Ecology and Development?
(a) Vandana Shiva (b) Amitav Ghosh
(c) Sanjeev Sanyal (d) Medha Patkar

30. When is World Forest Day celebrated?
(a) 5th April (b) 7th November
(c) 21 March (d) 22 July

31. Which of the match given below is incorrect

List I (Environmental Law)	List II (Year)
(a) The Environment (Protection) Act	1973
(b) The Biological Diversity Act	2002
(c) The Wildlife Protection Act	1972
(d) The Water (Prevention and Control of Pollution) Act	1974

32. In which of the following book did anthropologist Julian Steward (1902-1972) coin the term Cultural Ecology?
(a) The Concept and Method of Cultural Ecology
(b) Evolution and Ecology
(c) Theory of Culture Change
(c) Area Research, theory and practice

33. Earth Day is an annual event celebrated around the world on which date?
(a) 22nd April (b) 5th June
(c) 31st May (d) 11th May

34. When was the term 'Social Forestry' used for the first time in India?
(a) 1972 (b) 1976
(c) 1978 (d) 1979

35. The report named 'Our Common Future' (1987), also known as the Brundtland Report, a document that coined and defined the meaning of the term?
(a) Agenda 21
(b) Sustainable Development
(c) Earth Summit
(d) Biodiversity

36. Which of the match given below is incorrect

List I (Disasters)	List II (Causes)
(a) Bhopal Gas Tragedy	Oil Spill
(b) Chernobyl	Nuclear Disaster
(c) The Minamata Disease	Mercury Poisoning
(d) Tambura Disaster	Volcanic Eruption

37. Who among the following was the first to use the term 'Environmental Sociology' in his book '*Man in His Environment*'?
(a) Max Weber (b) Riley Dunlap
(c) Craig Humphrey (d) Samuel Klausner

38. The book 'Environment, Energy, and Society' is written by?
(a) Lester W. Milbrath and Barbara V. Fisher
(b) Daniel Stokols and Irwin Altman
(c) Craig R. Humphrey and Frederick H. Buttel
(d) William R. Catton and Riley Dunlap

39. According to the United Nations Framework Convention on Climate Change (UNFCCC) secretariat, the overwhelming direct cause of deforestation is?
(a) Agriculture (b) Mining
(c) Climate Change (d) Desertification

40. Who coined the term Ecology?
(a) Ernest Haeckel (b) Murray Bookchin
(c) Gilbert White (d) Frederic Clements

41. Who said, 'Social ecology emphasizes that the destiny of human life goes hand-in-hand with the destiny of the non-human world'?
(a) Ernest Haeckel (b) Murray Bookchin
(c) Gilbert White (d) Frederic Clements

42. Who among the following suggested the establishment of the 'National Park' theory'?
(a) Jawaharlal Nehru (b) Verier Elwin
(c) M Gadgil (d) B. K. Roy Burman

43. National Forest Policy came into existence in which year?
(a) 1927 (b) 1939
(c) 1865 (d) 1988

44. Land Acquisition Act in 1894 This Act authorized the Government to have control over?
(a) Public Land (b) Private Land
(c) Both A and B (d) None of the above

45. Which of the following match is incorrect:
(a) Verier Elwin: A Philosophy of NEFA
(b) N. K. Dixit: Tribals in India
(c) M Gadgil: India's Deforestation
(d) K Padhi: Impact of Forest Policies on the Indigenous People

46. Which of the following personalities is not associated with the 'Chipko Movement"?
(a) Amrita Bai
(b) Sundarlal Bahuguna
(c) Gaura Devi
(d) Kinkari devi

47. Which of the following leader is associated with Narmada Bachao Andolan (NBA)?
(a) Kinkari devi (b) Sarla Tripathi
(c) Medha Patkar (d) Maneka Gandhi

48. Wangari Mathai is associated with which of the following environmental movement?
(a) Friends of the Earth
(b) Green belt movement
(c) Green Polities
(d) Green Peace Movement

49. Green Peace was founded by?
(a) Irving Stowe and Dorothy Stowe
(b) Wangari Mathai
(c) ennifer Morgan
(d) Patrick Geddes

50. Match List I with List II (Sustainable Development Goals)

List I (Goals)	List II (Title)
A. Goal 1	I. Clean Water and Sanitation
B. Goal 6	II. No Poverty
C. Goal 7	III. Climate Action
D. Goal 13	IV. Affordable and Clean Energy

Codes:

	A	B	C	D
(a)	I	II	III	IV
(b)	II	I	III	IV
(c)	II	I	IV	III
(d)	III	I	IV	II

51. The term Biodiversity was first conceptualized by?
(a) Norwood Russell Hanson
(b) Edward Wilson
(c) Karl Wilhelm Friedrich Schlegel
(d) M Friedman

52. Eco-feminism is a term coined by
(a) Ariel Salleh
(b) Andree Collard
(c) Sherry Ortner
(d) Françoise d'Eubonne

53. Which of the following statements is incorrect?
(a) Traditional Knowledge is distinctly associated with an indigenous or local community, which preserves and transmits it from generation to generation.
(b) Traditional Knowledge is old and static.
(c) Traditional Knowledge is generated, preserved, and transmitted in a traditional and intergenerational context.
(d) Traditional Knowledge is not limited to any specific technical field.

54. The Cancún Agreements, adopted at the UN Climate Conference in Mexico (December 2010), including a time schedule for reviewing the objective of keeping the average global temperature rise below?
(a) 2 °C (b) 1.5 °C
(c) 2.5 °C (d) 1 °C

55. Who led The Narmada Bachao Andolan movement?
(a) Medha Patekar
(b) Amrita Bai
(c) Sundarlal Bahuguna
(d) Gauri Devi

56. Wangari Mathai is associated with which of the following environmental movement?
(a) Friends of the Earth
(b) Green belt movement
(c) Green Polities
(d) Green Peace Movement

57. Which field studies the relationship between environments and the cultural communities that exist within those particular settings?
(a) Social ecology
(b) cultural ecology
(c) ecology
(d) environmental psychology

58. The National Disaster Management Authority functions under the Union Ministry of
(a) Environment (b) Water Resources
(c) Home Affairs (d) Defense

59. The Disaster Management Act came into force in which year?
(a) 2000 (b) 2005
(c) 2010 (d) 2015

60. Who merged the feminism in "ecofeminism" with "womanism"?
(a) Ariel Salleh (b) Andree Collard
(c) Sherry Ortner (d) Riane Eisler

Answer Key

1. (b)	**10.** (d)	**19.** (c)	**28.** (a)	**37.** (d)	**46.** (d)	**55.** (a)
2. (c)	**11.** (a)	**20.** (c)	**29.** (a)	**38.** (c)	**47.** (c)	**56.** (b)
3. (b)	**12.** (b)	**21.** (c)	**30.** (c)	**39.** (a)	**48.** (b)	**57.** (b)
4. (a)	**13.** (b)	**22.** (b)	**31.** (a)	**40.** (a)	**49.** (a)	**58.** (c)
5. (a)	**14.** (a)	**23.** (a)	**32.** (c)	**41.** (b)	**50.** (c)	**59.** (b)
6. (d)	**15.** (a)	**24.** (c)	**33.** (a)	**42.** (b)	**51.** (b)	**60.** (a)
7. (d)	**16.** (c)	**25.** (a)	**34.** (b)	**43.** (d)	**52.** (d)	
8. (c)	**17.** (c)	**26.** (a)	**35.** (b)	**44.** (c)	**53.** (b)	
9. (b)	**18.** (a)	**27.** (a)	**36.** (a)	**45.** (d)	**54.** (b)	

PREVIOUS YEARS' QUESTIONS

DECEMBER 2023

1. Which among the following is not the principles of 'deep ecology?
   (a) The wellbeing and flourishing of human and non-human life on earth have value in themselves.
   (b) The flourishing of human life and culture is compatible with a substantial decrease of human population.
   (c) Humans have no right to reduce the richness and diversity of nature to satisfy their vital needs.
   (d) Present human interference with non-human world is excessive and the situation is rapidly worsening.

2. Match List I with List II.

List I	List II
A. Cultural ecology	I. It shows the pattern by which environmental hazards are greatest in proximity to poor people, especially minorities.
B. Carbon footprint	II. It refers to human demand hectare of land per person.
C. Environmental racism	III. A theoretical paradigm that explores the relationship of human culture and the physical environment.
D. Ecological footprint	IV. A personal measure of how much carbon dioxide you create and how much you contribute to climate change.

   Choose the correct answer from the options given below:
   (a) A-III, B-IV, C-I, D-II
   (b) A-IV, B-III, C-I, D-II
   (c) A-I, B-II, C-IV, D-III
   (d) A-IV, B-III, C-II, D-I

3. Which among the following are the critique of the 'precautionary principle'?
   A. It concentrates only on one side of risk the possibility of harm.
   B. It warns us against interfering with natural processes as a matter of principle.
   C. There is no hope of responding to climate change unless we are prepared to take bold decision.
   D. Risk taking is essential to new thinking.
   Choose the most appropriate answer from the options given below:
   (a) A, B and C only
   (b) B, C and D only
   (c) A, C and D only
   (d) A, B, C and D

4. Given below are two statements: one is labelled as Assertion A and the other is labelled as Reason R.
   Assertion A: The average temperature has risen 0.8°C around the world since 1880. It has caused massive climate changes reflected in forms of heatwaves, ocean warming, rise in sea level and glacier melting.
   Reason R: From the time of the Industrial Revolution, the amount of carbon dioxide that humanity has produced has risen tenfold.
   In the light of the above statements, choose the correct answer from the options given below:
   (a) Both A and R are correct and R is the correct explanation of A.
   (b) Both A and R are correct but R is NOT the correct explanation of A.
   (c) A is correct but R is not incorrect
   (d) A is not correct but R is correct.

Read the following passage and answer the questions.

The term 'environment' implies all the external factors—living and non-living, material and non-material—which surround man. However, the newer concept also includes the social and economic conditions under which we live. For better understanding, environment can be divided into three components—physical (water, air, soil, housing, etc.), biological (plants and animal life including viruses, insects, rodents and social customs, cultures, income, occupation, etc.).

The key to man's health lies largely in his environment. In fact, much of man's ill-health can be traced to environmental factors like poor housing, presence of animals, air, water and soil pollution, etc. Often, man is responsible for the pollution of his environment through urbanization, industrialization and other human activities his which is bringing profound social and environment changes all over the world. Hence, to address this problem, a combined multi-disciplinary programme of action is needed to achieve a healthy environment.

Hence, two of the changes needed to achieve 'health for all' are concerned with a healthy environment and healthy life style and require initiatives by the individual, the family and the community.

5. The newer concept of environment, apart from external factors, also includes:

A. Economic conditions.
B. Non-living factors.
C. Social factors.
D. Bacteria and viruses.

Choose the most appropriate answer from the options given below:

(a) B, C and D only
(b) B and D only
(c) A and C only
(d) A, C and D only

6. The adverse environmental factors which can affect human health are:
A. Poor housing conditions.
B. Water contamination.
C. Waste segregation.
D. Presence of animal reservoirs.

Choose the correct answer from the options given below:

(a) A and D only
(b) B, C and D only
(c) A, B and D only
(d) C and D only

7. What are the basic requirements to ensure 'health for all'?
A. Healthy behaviour patterns.
B. Healthy environment.
C. Friendly government.
D. Healthy lifestyle.

Choose the correct answer from the options given below:

(a) B and D only
(b) A and B only
(c) B, C and D only
(d) A, B and D only

8. Man is responsible for the pollution of his environment through various activities like:
A. Urbanization.
B. Water conservation.
C. Industrialization.
D. Migration.
E. Waste disposal.

Choose the correct answer from the options given below:

(a) B, C and D only
(b) A, B and E only
(c) C, D and E only
(d) A, C and D only

9. Which cannot be considered as social component of environment?
(a) Income
(b) Wastes
(c) Religion
(d) Customs

JUNE 2023

10. Match List I with List II

List I (Name of social movements)	List II (States)
A. Chipko	I. Andhra Pradesh
B. Anti Arrak	II. West Bengal
C. Naxalbari	III. Uttarakhand
D. Shetkari movement	IV. Maharashtra

Choose the correct answer from the options given below:

(a) A-III, B- I, C-II, D-IV
(b) A-I, B-II, C-III, D-IV
(c) A- IV, B- III, C-II, D-I
(d) A-II, B-I, C-III, D-IV

MARCH 2023

11. The term 'Biocitversity' was coined by
(a) A.G. Tansley
(b) E. Clement
(c) E.O. Wilson
(d) E. Odum

DEC 2021 & JUNE 2022

12. Match List-I with List-II

List I (Personalities)	List II (Recognition)
A. Pandurang Hegde	I. Goldman Environmental Prize
B. M. C. Mehta	II. Bishnoi Movement
C. Marimuthu Yoganathan	III. Appiko Movement
D. Amrita Devi	IV. Eco-warrior

Choose the **correct answer** from the options given below:

(a) A - III, B - I, C - IV, D - II
(b) A - IV, B - I, C - II, D - III
(c) A - IV, B - II, C - I, D - III
(d) A - III, B - IV, C - I, D - II

13. Match List-I with List-II

List I (Books)	List II (Authors)
A. The Sociology of Disaster	I. Jeffery D. Sachs
B. Environmental Sociology	II. Ram Ahuja

C. The Age of Sustainable Development	III. Thomas E. Drabek
D. Social Problems in India	IV. John Hannigan

Choose the correct answer from the options given below:

(a) A - IV, B - I, C - II, D - III
(b) A - I, B - III, C - IV, D - II
(c) A - III, B - IV, C - I, D - II
(d) A - IV, B - I, C - III, D - II

14. Match List-I with List-II

List I (Books)	List II (Authors)
A. World Risk Society	I. M. Castells
B. End of Millennium	II. V. Shiva
C. Development as Freedom	III. A. Sen
D. Ecofeminism	IV. U. Beck

Choose the **correct answer** from the options given below:

(a) A - IV, B - I, C - III, D - II
(b) A - III, B - II, C - IV, D - I
(c) A - II, B - IV, C - I, D - III
(d) A - I, B - II, C - III, D – IV

15. Which one of the following is NOT correctly matched?
(a) Park and Burgess: Ecological School
(b) H. W. Odum: Regional School
(c) Dexter, Huntington: Impact of climatic conditions on human society
(d) Maclver: Human Geography

16. Given below are two statements, one is labelled as Assertion (A) and the other is labelled as Reason (R)

Assertion (A): Enhancing global conciousness is a vital dimension of increasing environmental awareness.

Reason (R): Our choices and actions are responsible for our actions towards ecology.

In light of the above statements, choose the most appropriate answer from the options given below

(a) Both (A) and (R) are true and (R) is the correct explanation of (A)
(b) Both (A) and (R) are true but (R) is NOT the correct explanation of (A)
(c) (A) is true but (R) is false
(d) (A) is false but (R) is true

JUNE 2021

17. Who is the author of the book 'Human Ecology'?
(a) R. Park (b) A. Hawley
(c) E. Burgess (d) G. Simmel

18. The title of the Brundtland Report is
(a) 'Environment-friendly Resource Consumption'
(b) 'Our Common Future'
(c) 'Caring for Earth'
(d) 'Caring and Sharing'

19. Which one of the following environmentalists got the Nobel Prize for Peace in 2004 for contribution to Sustainable Development, Democracy and Peace?
(a) Sundarlal Bahuguna
(b) M. C. Mehta
(c) Wangari Mathai
(d) Anil Agarwal

20. Depletion of the ozone layer in the stratosphere is responsible for:
(a) Increase in Carbon dioxide
(b) Skin cancer
(c) Cholera
(d) Increase in Sulphur dioxide

21. Which two of the following are the cleanest cities of India, as per the Government of India Survey of 2020?
(a) Chandigarh
(b) Indore
(c) Navi Mumbai
(d) Surat

Choose the correct answer from the options given below:

(a) B and D only
(b) A and C only
(c) A and D only
(d) B and C only

22. Which two of the following major greenhouse gases contribute to global warming?
A. Nitrous oxide
B. Carbon dioxide
C. Methane
D. Chlorofluorocarbons

Choose the correct answer from the options given below:

(a) A and D (b) A and C
(c) B and D (d) B and C

23. Match List I with List II

List I (Author)	List II (Book)
A. C. Geertz	I. Staying Alive: Women, Ecology and Development
B. A. Agarwal	II. Agricultural Involution: The process of Ecological Change in Indonesia
C. V. Shiva	III. Environmentality
D. G. A. Gajeta	IV. Indigenous Community: Rekindling the Teaching of the Seventh Fire

Choose the correct answer from the options given below:

(a) A–I, B–II, C–III, D–IV
(b) A–IV, B–III, C–II, D–I
(c) A–II, B–III, C–I, D–IV
(d) A–III, B–I, C–II, D–IV

24. Arrange the following activities in sequence as per their occurrence during a year

A. World Forestry day
B. World Heritage day
C. World Environment day
D. World Ozone day
E. World Population day

Choose the correct answer from the options given below

(a) A, B, C, E, D
(b) A, C, D, B, E
(c) A, D, B, E, C
(d) D, A, B, C, E

JUNE 2020

25. On which of the following dates Earth Day and World Environment Day are celebrated?

1. April 22
2. April 18
3. June 5
4. June 11
5. February 2

Choose the most appropriate answer from the options given below:

(a) 1 and 4 only
(b) 1 and 3 only
(c) 2 and 3 only
(d) 4 and 5 only

26. Match List I with List II:

List I (Author)	List II (Book)
A. A. Agarwal	I. Sacred Ecology
B. J.M. Acheson	II. Cows, Kin and Globalization
C. S.A. Crate	III. Capturing the commons
D. F. Berkes	IV. Environmentality

Choose the correct answer from the options given below:

	A	B	C	D
(a)	III	II	I	IV
(b)	IV	III	II	I
(c)	II	IV	III	I
(d)	I	III	II	IV

DECEMBER 2019

27. Two statements are given below. One is labelled as Assertion (A) and the other as Reason (R).

Assertion (A): Green revolution in Punjab has resulted in many ecological problems.

Reason (R): It is due to over-exploitation of land and underground water and overuse of pesticides and fertilizers for more production.

Choose the correct option:

(a) Both (A) and (R) are true and (R) is the correct explanation of (A)
(b) Both (A) and (R) are true and (R) is not the correct explanation of (A)
(c) (A) is true but (R) is false
(d) (A) is false but (R) is true

28. Match List I with List II

List I (Author)	List II (Book)
A. A. Bateson	I. Nature's Economy
B. F. Berkos	II. The Ascent of Man
C. J. Beonowski	III. Sacred Ecology
D. D. Worster	IV. Steps to Ecology

Choose the correct option:

(a) A – IV, B – III, C – II, D – I
(b) A – II, B – III, C – I, D – IV
(c) A – III, B – IV, C – II, D – I
(d) A – I, B – II, C – III, D – IV

29. Which one of the following is not the objective of Green peace Movement?

(a) protection of Oceans
(b) Elimination of toxic waste
(c) Eradication of poverty
(d) Safe and Sustainable trade

30. In which year Government of India promulgated the National Rehabilitation policy for project displaced persons?

(a) 2002 (b) 2004
(c) 2006 (d) 2001

31. What term is best suited to describe an ideology based upon a rethinking and a reassertion of classical liberalism?

(a) Welfarism (b) Neo-Functionalism
(c) Neo-Liberalism (d) Neo-Marxism

JUNE 2019

32. Famous environmental NGO 'Tarun Bharat Sangh' was founded by

(a) Rajendra Singh (b) Kailash Satyarthi
(c) Rukmini Banerji (d) Bharat Vatram

33. When was the term 'Social Forestry' used for the first time in India?
(a) 1972 (b) 1976
(c) 1978 (d) 1979

34. Who among the following coined the term 'Cultural Ecology' in his famous book,
Theory of Culture Change: The Methodology of Multilinear Evolution?
(a) J. H. Steward (b) G. L. Young
(c) W. R. Catton Jr. (d) R. Dunlop

35. 'Momentum for Change: Climate Neutral Now' is an initiative which was launched by
(a) The United Nations Environment Programme (UNEP)
(b) The United Nations Framework Convention on Climate Change (UNFCCC)
(c) The World Meteorological Organization
(d) The Inter-Governmental Panel on Climate Change

36. What was the theme of 'World Environment Day, 2018'?
(a) Connecting People of Nature
(b) Beat Plastic Pollution
(c) Go Wild for Life
(d) Seven Billion Dreams One Planet

37. Who is the author of the monograph An Environmental History of the World?
(a) Ramchandra Guha
(b) L. Feuerbach
(c) Francis Zimmerman
(d) Donald Hughes

38. Match List-I with List-II:

List I (Acts and Policies)	List II (Year)
A. Biological Diversity Act	I. 1972
B. Environmental Protection Act	II. 2002
C. Wild Life Protection Act	III. 1986
D. Plastic Waste Management Rules	IV. 2016

Select the correct answer from the options given below:
(a) (A)–(I); (B)–(II); (C)–(III); (D)–(IV)
(b) (A)–(II); (B)–(I); (C)–(III); (D)–(IV)
(c) (A)–(II); (B)–(III); (C)–(I); (D)–(IV)
(d) (A)–(III); (B)–(I); (C)–(IV); (D)–(II)

39. In which state was the 'Appiko' movement launched?
(a) Kerala (b) Karnataka
(c) Andhra Pradesh (d) Telangana

Answer Key

1. (c)	**7.** (a)	**13.** (c)	**19.** (c)	**25.** (b)	**31.** (a)	**37.** (d)
2. (a)	**8.** (d)	**14.** (a)	**20.** (b)	**26.** (b)	**32.** (a)	**38.** (c)
3. (c)	**9.** (b)	**15.** (d)	**21.** (a)	**27.** (a)	**33.** (b)	**39.** (b)
4. (a)	**10.** (a)	**16.** (a)	**22.** (d)	**28.** (a)	**34.** (a)	
5. (c)	**11.** (*)	**17.** (b)	**23.** (c)	**29.** (c)	**35.** (b)	
6. (c)	**12.** (a)	**18.** (b)	**24.** (a)	**30.** (b)	**36.** (b)	

NOTE: The correct answer to Q. 35 is Walter G. Rosen.

Unit-VIII

Family, Marriage, and Kinship

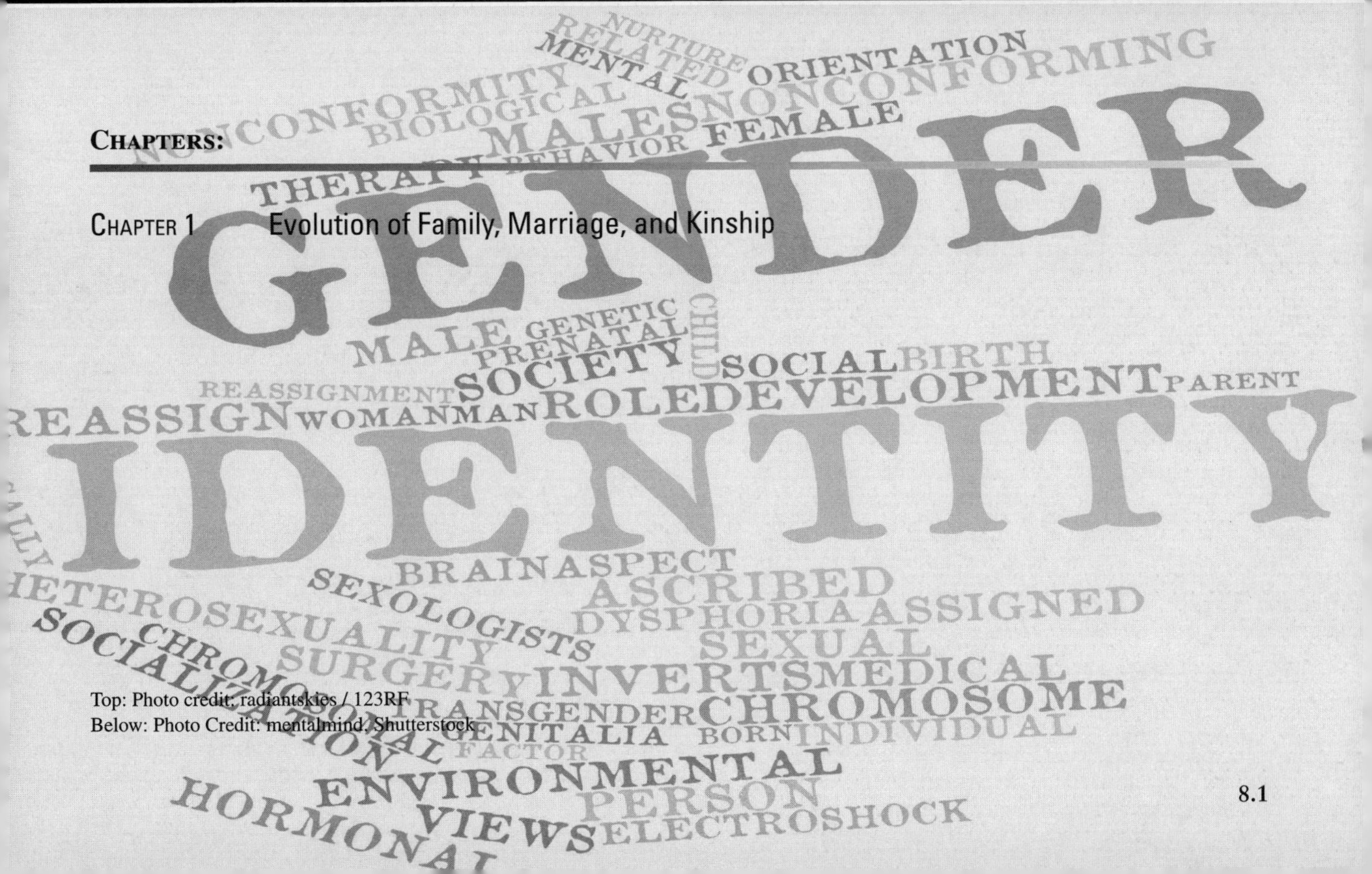

CHAPTERS:

Top: Photo credit: radiantskies / 123RF
Below: Photo Credit: mentalmind, Shutterstock

CHAPTER 1

Evolution of Family, Marriage, and Kinship

LEARNING OBJECTIVES:

In this chapter, we will discuss the following important topics.

- Theoretical approaches
- Cultural perspective
- Gender relations and power dynamics
- Gender, sexuality, and reproduction
- Children, youth, and elderly
- Changing marriage practices
- Family law

INTRODUCTION

Family, marriage and kinship are the most essential functional units of society. Learning about the main features of these institutions, their definitions and social significance becomes essential for understanding any society. The primary reason for this is that they play a major role in social systems. Family is the smallest and most basic social unit based on descent and filiation. While marriage provides accepted social status to the offspring, it plays a very important role with regard to matters such as inheritance and succession. And kinship refers to human relations by blood or by marriage. This unit discusses in depth the rules of these basic institutions family, marriage and kinship prevailing in the society.

THEORETICAL APPROACHES

Structural Functionalist Perspective

Structural functionalism is a school of thought according to which each of the institutions, relationships, roles, and norms that together constitute a society serves a purpose, and each is indispensable to the continued existence of the others and of the society as a whole.

Structural-functional theory studies groups of people or organizations in society and looks for events or other things that hold that group together. The question that fits this principle is, "What are the consequences of marriage for the operation of society?" In looking at the outcomes of marriage, structural functionalists are looking at the most important functions that hold a marriage together and make it work.

Structural-functionalists study marriage from a macro perspective. This lets them focus on the less common tasks that affect some marriages, but on the biggest, most important tasks that affect almost every marriage.

Structural functionalists believe that families are an important social institution and that they play an important role in stabilizing society. The family and its members perform certain functions which facilitate the prosperity and development of society.

Structural functionalism is a sociological theory that states that the way society function is determined by emphasizing the relationships between the various social institutions (for example, government, law, religion, education, etc.) that make up the society.

Radcliffe-Brown defines the social function of a socially standardized way of activity (or way of thought) as its relation to the social structure, existence, and continuity to which it contributes something.

He applied his structural-functional theories primarily to his analysis of work structure and kinship systems at work in primitive societies. His discussion of the role of the mother's brother in the kinship system of some South African tribes (such as the Bathonga, Nama-Hottentots, and Tongans) is very typical.

Avanculate refers to the privileged relationship that exists between a mother's brother and a sister's son. Radcliffe-Brown interprets this relationship from a structural-functional perspective, focusing on kin and the roles (or functions) they play in the kinship structure.

Radcliffe-Brown considers ties on the father's side and then looks at how these are balanced by ties on the mother's side. He demonstrated that in a patrilineal system, authority over a person is vested in his father's lineage, enjoyed by his mother's lineage, and by extension from the males of his mother's lineage.

Thus, while respect characterizes the relationship on the father's side, it is structurally balanced by indulgence in the relationship on the maternal side. The opposite happens in matriarchal systems. To explain the comma, he used the functional expansion of emotions and the structural similarity of siblings.

George Murdock conducted a survey of 250 societies and determined that there are four universal residual functions of the family: sexual, reproductive, educational, and economic. In every society, although the structure of the family varies, the family performs these four functions.

According to Murdock, the family (which for him includes the status of marriage) regulates sexual relations between individuals. He does not deny the existence or impact of premarital or extramarital sex but states that the family provides a socially legitimate sexual outlet for adults. This outlet gives way to reproduction, which is a necessary part of ensuring a society's survival.

- Radcliffe-Brown states that most stateless, 'primitive' societies that lack strong centralized institutions are based on a federation of corporate-dynastic groups.

Alliance Theory

Alliance theory, also known as general exchange theory, is a structuralist method of studying kinship relationships. It has its origins in Claude Lévi-Strauss's Elementary Structures of Kinship (1949) and is opposed to Radcliffe–Brown's Decent theory.

Alliance theory seeks to inquire about how inter-individual relationships are woven and how they ultimately constitute society. This theory is inspired by Marcel Mauss's idea of reciprocity.

The main exponent of coalition theory was Claude Lévi-Strauss. Other important contributors are Rodney Needham and Louis Dumont. The Alliance principle is based on the prohibition of incest. According to it, this universal prohibition of incest is what drives human groups towards exogamy. Thus, within a given society, certain categories of relatives are prohibited from intermarrying. The incest taboo is thus a negative prescription. Without this negative prescription males would not be motivated to seek females outside their internal kinship circle.

The incest taboo of alliance theory, in which one's daughter or sister is offered to someone outside the family circle, initiates a cycle of exchange of women. In return, the donor is entitled to a woman from the other's intimate kinship group. Thus, negative prescriptions of prohibition have positive counterparts. The idea of alliance theory is thus a reciprocal or a generalized exchange that finds affinity.

The prohibition of adultery is universally recognized. It is seen as a fundamental condition of human social life. A man is not allowed to take as his wife a woman who is his near relative and in fact, he must give her to another man. It is the prohibition of incest that prompted human groups to practice exogamy. This theory has some similarities with Sigmund Freud's work 'Totem and Taboo'.

CULTURAL PERSPECTIVE

The cultural theoretical approach to understanding the social institutions of marriage, family, and kinship calls for a comparative approach rather than other universal approaches. The aim is to look at these practices as different in different cultures and to recognize differences within communities or nations.

It is the cultural anthropological approach that helps to understand the different types of family, marriage, and kinship. Cultures elaborate on that basic relationship and build upon it to create units that are culturally regarded as central to social life.

In a basic biological sense, women give birth and form the minimum family unit in most societies, although not all societies have mothers and children. Cultures elaborate on that basic relationship and build upon it to create units that are culturally regarded as central to social life.

In our society, it is culturally acceptable to be married to only one spouse at a time. It is reinforced by religious systems and laws. When anthropologists speak of family structures, we distinguish several standard family types, any of which may be the typical or preferred family unit in a culture.

The first is the nuclear family: parents who are in a culturally recognized relationship, such as a married couple, with dependent children. This type of family is also called the conjugal family. A non-conjugal nuclear family may be a single parent with dependent children because one of the spouses has died or divorced or never married.

Next is the extended family: a family of at least three generations who share a household. A stem family is a variant of an extended family consisting of an older couple and one of their adult children, a spouse (or spouse), and children.

In stem families, Le Play says that the father selects one of his children to live near the parent's home to work the farm and eventually inherit it, thus continuing the family line. All the other children left the parent's family to make nuclear homes of their own. Le Play argued that the stem family was the dominant form of a peasant family in most parts of Europe.

Shah (1998) comments on the norms and values held by different members of a family and their attitudes and behaviour in relation to others for commonality in the family.

Dubey (1997) acknowledges the importance of the mother in shaping the child's identity, as the caste of both parents places the child in the caste hierarchy.

GENDER RELATIONS AND POWER DYNAMICS

One of the most enduring patterns in the distribution of power is the inequality between women and men. Gender places people in different positions in the hierarchy of society.

The set of roles, behaviours, and attitudes that society defines as appropriate for women and men can be both a cause and a consequence of power relations ranging from the intimate sphere of domestic relations to the highest levels of political decision-making.

According to Burns and Kinder, gender is a site of 'enduring inequality'. Gender categories are learned very early in life and form a core part of a person's identity.

Feminists view the family as an institution that has perpetuated and perpetuated sexual inequalities.

Feminists argue that the so-called private realm of family, sex, and reproduction should be part of the political realm and thus subject to principles of justice. Families are not 'natural' orders, but social institutions supported by laws. For example, marriage is a social institution. Therefore, the state cannot choose not to intervene in families. (The only question is how and on what grounds it should intervene)

Feminists believe that gender is socially constructed. This means that gender roles are learned rather than determined by biology, and the most important institution where we are socialized into our appropriate roles and norms of behaviour is the family.

Gender roles are socially constructed and reinforced through the family and education system. For example, there is a tendency to give dolls and tea sets to girls and toy cars and construction sets to boys (Firestone).

Feminists have also pointed out that gender socialization is evident in a hidden curriculum in the education system where books representing men and women in 'traditional' roles reinforce the view that men and women follow different paths in life. Are.

Feminist activists often point to the historical, legal, and social inequalities of marriage, family life, and divorce in their criticism of marriage.

In feminist theory, wives are seen as subordinate, economically dependent, and separate (Johnson).

Atkinson was particularly critical of love and marriage as the ideal relationship because, in accepting women for a subordinate role, they are complicit in their own oppression. According to her, love becomes a political institution that is a necessary part of male supremacy, and that women are 'innately trying to reclaim'., .] certain and political loss by merging with the enemy'

Carol Pettman considered marriage in terms of a social contract in which men have dominance over women.

According to Gail Rubin 'women are given in marriage, taken in war, exchanged for favours, sent as gifts, traded, bought and sold'.

Marriage is rooted in a discourse of monogamy that 'privileges the interests of both men and capitalism as it operates through mechanisms of exclusivity, ownership and jealousy' (Robinson).

Inheritance, Succession, and Authority

Inheritance, also called succession, is the distribution of property to heirs or successors upon the death of the owner. The term inheritance also refers to the property itself. In modern society, this process is regulated by law to the smallest detail. Inheritance laws coordinate with the reckoning of lineage in most societies, but not necessarily in a one-to-one manner.

In fact, it is often the case that some types of property pass from father to son, and other types of property pass from mother to daughter. In most parts of India, in the past, fixed assets such as land and housing were inherited only by sons. In the absence of a son, except in rare circumstances, by the nearest male relatives on the father's side.

- On the other hand, movable property in the form of cash and jewellery was given to the daughter at the time of her marriage, as well as a certain amount of jewellery from the mother-in-law to the daughter-in-law. In addition to different types of property, rights and obligations, esoteric knowledge, crafts, and skills, etc. could be passed down according to kinship roles, the succession of office and other social roles and statuses are also very often determined by kinship criteria.

In such cases, the person's position is said to be 'ascribed', not 'achieved'. It is commonly asserted that the ascriptive status of modern, industrial societies. There is a lot of truth in this statement, but the importance of kinship ties should not be underestimated even in modern society. It is often seen that if the father is a doctor or a lawyer in a family, then there is a possibility of the son or daughter also choosing the same profession. Most Indian women who have been successful in the political field are either daughters, sisters, or wives of people active in politics. One such example is the Nehru family of India.

On the basis of authority, families can be classified into:

i. **Patriarchal family:** In a patriarchal family, the male head of the family has reclusive powers.
ii. **Matriarchal family:** In the matriarchal family the authority is vested in the female head of the family.

On the basis of rules of residence, families can be classified into:

Rules of residence, meaning residence after marriage, are an important variable in kinship systems, and substantially affect the quality of individual relationships within kinship networks. Therefore, on the basis of residence, the family can be divided into the following parts:

i. **Matrilocal family:** In this type of family the husband goes to live at his wife's house.
ii. **Patrilocal family:** In this type, the wife goes to live at her husband's house.
iii. **Avanculocal family:** The word 'Avancu' means maternal uncle. This is the family where the couple lives in the maternal uncle's house after their marriage.
iv. **Neo-local family:** The married couple in the new residence is neither in the family of the bridegroom nor in the family of the bride.
v. **Virilocal:** In this type of family the wife goes to live at her husband's house.
v. **Matri-patrilocal residence:** In this type of family the couple lives for a time with the bride's parents, then go to live permanently with the groom's parents

On the basis of structure families can be classified into:

i. **Nuclear family:** Nuclear family consists of a husband, wife, and their unmarried children.
ii. **Joint family:** Joint families are made up of a group of siblings, their spouses, and their dependent children. According to M.S. Gore, the joint family consists of a man and his wife and their adult sons, their wives and children, and the younger children of the parental couple. The size of the joint family is very large. Generally, the eldest male is the head of the family. In this type of family, the rights and duties of the members are determined by the hierarchical order of power and authority.
iii. **Extended family:** The term extended family is used to indicate a combination of two or more nuclear families based on the extension of the parent-child relationship. According to Murdock, an extended family consists of two or more nuclear families that are connected through the extension of the parent-child relationship, i.e., the involvement of a married adult in his parent's nuclear family. According to Bottomore, there are different types of extended family: 1. Patriarchally extended family- based on an extension of father-son relationship 2. Matriarchally extended family- based on the

mother-daughter relationship. 3. Fraternal or Collateral Family – A horizontally extended family consisting of two or more brothers, their wives, and children. In India, the family season extended vertically and/or horizontally is called a joint family. Strictly speaking, it is a property-sharing unit.

- On the basis of marriage and birth, G. P. Murdock divided the family into two types: Family of Orientation: Refers to the family into which a person is born. and the family of procreation: it refers to the one formed through marriage.

GENDER, SEXUALITY, AND REPRODUCTION

Gender

The term gender refers to the characteristics, behaviours, norms, and rules that a society or culture attaches to a person's gender. Gender is not synonymous with sex. Sex is a biological classification. Gender on the other hand is the roles assigned to individuals on the basis of their sex. It is a concept that describes how societies determine and manage sex categories, and cultural connotations attached to a person's gender.

In an effort to clarify the use of the terms sex and gender, US Supreme Court Justice Antonin Scalia wrote in a 1994 briefing. 'The term gender has acquired new and useful meanings of cultural or behavioural characteristics (as opposed to physical characteristics)". That is to say that a woman is related to feminine and a man is related to masculine in a similar way Gender is related to sex.

The World Health Organization (WHO) defines gender as "socially constructed characteristics of women and men, such as norms, roles, and relationships between groups of women and men. It varies from society to society and can be changed."

Gender Construction

According to sociologists, gender is a social construct. People learn gender through the process of socialization. For most people, this process begins when they are born, with parents choosing a gender name based on the child's sex and decorating the child's room, and color-coding and matching its toys and clothes. Gender chooses in ways that reflect cultural expectations and stereotypes.

Then, from infancy, they are socialized by family, teachers, religious leaders, peer groups, and the wider community, who teach them what is expected of them in terms of appearance and behavior based on their gender. Media and popular culture also play an important role in gender teaching.

One consequence of sexual socialization is the formation of gender identity, which is the definition of oneself as a man or a woman. Gender identity shapes how we think about others and ourselves, and it affects our behaviours.

The term gender role refers to society's concept of how men and women are expected to look and how they should behave. These roles are based on the norms or standards created by society.

Gender Identity

Gender identity is an individual's sense of one's own gender. Gender identity can relate to or differ from the sex a person was assigned at birth. The term gender identity was originally coined by Robert J. Stoller in 1964.

Gender identities are fluid. It is a person's deeply held internal belief about his or her gender. Individuals who identify with a role different from their biological sex are called transgender. Transgender individuals who attempt to change their bodies through medical interventions such as surgery and hormonal therapy so that their physical existence is better aligned with their gender identity are referred to as transsexuals.

Not all transgender persons choose to change their bodies. Many choose to retain their original anatomy but may present themselves to society as the other gender. This is usually done by adopting dress, hairstyle, mannerisms, or other characteristics typically assigned to another gender. (It is important to note that people who cross-dress or wear clothing that is traditionally assigned to a gender different from their biological sex are not necessarily transgender).

GLAAD (formerly the Gay and Lesbian Alliance Against Defamation) describes gender identity as 'an inner, personal sense of being a man or a woman'. For transgender people, their own internal gender identity does not match the gender they were assigned at birth. Most people have a gender identity of either male or female. For some people, their gender identity doesn't fit neatly into either of those two options.

They define gender expression as 'the external manifestations of gender, expressed through one's name, pronouns, clothing, haircut, mannerisms, voice, or body features'. Society identifies these signs as masculine and feminine, although what is considered masculine and feminine has changed over time and varies by culture.

Sexuality

Human sexuality is the way people experience and express themselves sexually. It includes biological, sensual, physical, emotional, social, or spiritual feelings and behaviour.

Alfred Kinsey was among the first to see sexuality as a continuum rather than a strict dichotomy of gay or straight. They constructed a six-point rating scale that ranges from exclusively heterosexual to exclusively homosexual.

In his book *'Sexual Behaviour in the Human Male'*, Kinsey writes, 'Males do not represent two discrete populations, heterosexuals and homosexuals. The world is not to be divided into sheep and goats. The living world is a continuum in every aspect of it.'

Some common forms of sexuality are:

i. **Heterosexual:** A person is physically and emotionally attracted to someone of the opposite sex, so a man is attracted to a woman, and a woman is attracted to a man.
ii. **Homosexual:** Homosexual people are attracted to the same sex.
iii. **Bisexual:** People who are bisexual are attracted to both men and women.
iv. **Pansexual:** People who are attracted to other people regardless of their gender or sexual identity.
v. **Asexual:** People who are asexual or ace do not feel sexually attracted to anyone and do not feel the desire to have sex.

But these are not the only forms of sexuality. Sexuality can be self-defined. Everyone is allowed to talk and feel about their sexuality in their own way that makes sense to them. The physical and emotional aspects of sexuality include bonds between individuals that are expressed through intense feelings or physical expressions of love, trust, and care.

Sexual orientation is the pattern of one's sexual interest in the opposite or same sex. Sexuality is a broad concept. It is a composite term for one's sexual behaviour, attraction, likes, dislikes, etc. Sexuality also influences and influences social, cultural, political, legal, philosophical, spiritual, moral, ethical, and religious aspects of life.

Sexuality is understood as a person's capacity for sexual feelings. The study of sexual attitudes and practices in sociology is interesting because sexual behavior is a cultural universal. Throughout time and space, most humans have participated in sexual relations (Brood 2003).

However, each society interprets sexuality and sexual activity in different ways. Many societies around the world have different attitudes about premarital sex, the age of sexual consent, homosexuality, masturbation, and other sexual behaviors that do not conform to universal cultural norms (Widmer, Trese, & Newcomb 1998).

What is considered "normal" in terms of sexual behavior is based on a society's customs and values. For example, societies that value monogamy will oppose sex outside marriage. Individuals are socialized into sexual behavior by their family, education system, peers, media, and religion.

Reproduction

Reproduction (or reproduction or breeding) is the biological process by which new individual organisms – "offspring" – are produced from their "parent" or parents. Reproduction is a fundamental feature of all known life; Each individual organism exists as the result of reproduction.

Although reproduction is a biological process, there are many social factors that influence the pattern of reproduction. For example: In many societies, preference is given to boys. There are also certain obligations and norms that people follow when it comes to choosing a mate for breeding. Factors such as social status, social education, and social obligations play an important role in influencing reproductive preferences.

Fecundity refers to the physical ability to reproduce, and fertility refers to the actual production of live offspring. So, fecundity refers to the potential production of living offspring, and fertility to the actual production.

Human fertility depends on a long list of factors, including physical health and nutrition, sexual behavior, culture, instinct, endocrinology, time, economics, lifestyle, and emotions. Fertility rates vary between countries and cultures because these factors vary.

In some places, government policies have focused on reducing the birth rate by improving women's sexual and reproductive health and rights. Generally, a high birth rate is associated with health loss and low life expectancy, low standard of living, low status of women, and low level of education.

Breeding patterns vary widely within India. Racial and ethnic minorities have higher fertility rates than the majority, and families with low incomes or low levels of education generally have more children than those who are affluent or well-educated.

India's child sex ratio declined from 927 in the 2001 census to 919 in the 2011 census, despite several laws to prevent female feticide and schemes to encourage families to produce girl children.

Although India was one of the first countries in the world to develop a legal and policy framework guaranteeing access to abortion and contraception, women and girls still face many barriers to the full enjoyment of their reproductive rights, including the poor quality of health services and the denial of women. Decision-making rights of girls.

Children, Youth, And Elderly

Biologically, a child is a human being between the stages of birth and puberty, or between the developmental period of infancy and youth. Puberty is best understood as a period of transition from childhood dependency to adulthood independence. Puberty is more fluid than in other fixed age groups. Youth is generally defined in relation to education and employment, as 'youth' is often referred to as a person between the age of leaving compulsory education and finding their first job.

The United Nations, for statistical purposes, defines 'youth' as persons between the ages of 15 and 24. However, apart from that statistical definition, the meaning of the word 'youth' varies in different societies around the world.

Veteran refers to an age approaching or exceeding the life expectancy of a human, and thus the end of the human life cycle. The biological process of aging is called gerontology, the medical study of the aging process is called gerontology, and the study of diseases affecting the elderly is called geriatrics.

There are about 104 million elderly persons (aged 60 years or more) in India as per Population Census 2011; 53 million females and 51 million males. The size of the elderly population is increasing over time due to better education, health facilities, and an increase in life expectancy.

This proportion has increased from 5.6% in 1961 to 8.6% in 2011. The total number of children in India is 164.5 million, which is about 660 thousand more than the number recorded in 2001. The proportion of young children in the 0-4 age group as well as the proportion of the population in the 0-14 age group is higher in rural areas than in urban areas for both males and females.

Urban areas have a higher proportion of males and females aged 15–59 than rural areas. India has the largest proportion of the population in youth age groups in the world i.e., 35.3% of the country's population is in the age group of 0-14 years in the 2011 census and 41% of the population is under 18. years of age. More than 50% of India's population is below the age of 25 and more than 65% is below the age of 35.

A report released by the United Nations Population Fund and HelpAge India states that the number of elderly is expected to increase to 173 million by 2026. By 2025, the world will have more old people than young people and will cross the two billion marks.

Laws Related to Children and Elderly in India

Article 24 of the Indian Constitution clearly states that 'No child below the age of fourteen years shall be employed to work in any factory or mine or employed in any hazardous employment.'

Child Labor (Prohibition and Regulation) Act 1986

The Child Labour (Prohibition and Regulation) Act 1986 designates a child as a person who has not completed his 14 years of age. It aims to regulate the working hours and conditions of child labor and to prevent child labor from being employed in hazardous industries.

Child Labour (Prohibition and Regulation) Amendment Act, 2016

The Government has enacted the Child Labour (Prohibition and Regulation) Amendment Act, 2016 which came into force on 1/9/2016. The Amendment Act completely bans the employment of children below the age of 14 years.

Maintenance and Welfare of Parents and Senior Citizens Act, 2007

It is legislation introduced by the Ministry of Social Justice and Empowerment, Government of India to provide for more effective provisions for the maintenance and welfare of parents and senior citizens. It creates a legal obligation for children and heirs to provide maintenance to senior citizens and parents by monthly allowance. It also provides a simple, quick, and inexpensive mechanism to protect the life and property of older persons.

Emotions and Family

A family is an intimate domestic group of people who are related to each other by bonds of blood, sexual intercourse, or legal relations. It is a socially recognized group usually linked by blood, marriage, or adoption that forms an emotional connection and serves as the economic unit of society. Burgess and Locke defined the family as "a body of persons united by the ties of marriage, blood or adoption, who constitute a single household, interacting and inter-communicating with each other in their respective social roles as, husband and wife, father and mother, son and daughter, brothers and sisters, creating a common culture. According to Kingsley Davis, 'A family is a group of individuals who are related to each other on the basis of consanguinity and are therefore kin to each other'.

The primary function of the family is to ensure the continuity of society through socialization. Affective (emotional) accountability is very important because family members interact with each other during difficult times. Affective (emotional) reactivity is a person's ability to respond with appropriate emotions.

The family is the first and foremost influence on a child's social and emotional development. For the most part, families naturally fulfil this responsibility by being responsive to their child's needs and providing a safe environment to grow and learn.

Emotional regulation is a term generally used to describe a person's ability to effectively manage and respond to emotional experience. People unconsciously use emotion regulation strategies to cope with difficult situations many times each day. In addition to more obvious benefits such as good health, strong emotional regulation skills can also enrich personal relationships.

CHANGING MARRIAGE PRACTICES

Marriage is a social contract between two or more people that is based on sexual relations and enforces the permanence of the union. It is a legal and socially sanctioned union regulated by laws, rules, customs, beliefs, and attitudes that determine the rights and duties of their partner and confer status on their offspring.

Some of the basic functions of marriage are sexual gratification and regulation, division of labour between the sexes, economic production and economic production and consumption, procreation, and child care.

Marriage is considered by sociologists to be a cultural universal. It is present in all societies in some form or the other. The importance attached to marriage is reflected in the fact that only a small percentage of men and women remain unmarried. The Report of the Committee on the Status of Women in India indicated that only 0.5 percent of women in India never marry. Only a very small percentage of men and women remain single by choice.

While marriage is still considered important and necessary, there are visible changes in marriage patterns. Old notions about large family size, (i.e., that large numbers of children especially sons are a source of status for parents) are being replaced by a preference for smaller family sizes. Marriage is also becoming prevalent mainly for self-fulfilment rather than procreation or social welfare.

Child marriage is still prevalent in India. Although there are differences between different religious groups, classes, and castes in terms of the age of marriage, the average age of marriage in India is low. The 1971 census data on the marital status of women shows that in more than one-third of the total districts of our country, the average age of marriage of girls was less than 15 years. Although early marriages are still prevalent in India, their rate has decreased due to various efforts made by government and non-governmental organizations.

Women's age at marriage increased from 16.1 years in 1961 to 19.3 in 1991. The rural-urban difference in the age of women at the marriage in 1991 is 2 years and this indicates that despite the increase in the age of marriage, there remains a wide gap between rural and urban. regions of the country. Research shows that the need for education and employment of boys has raised the age of marriage in urban areas and to do well in rural areas. The age of marriage is also much higher in the states which have high literacy rates as compared to the states which have low literacy levels.

- Caste endogamy is still highly relevant in terms of mate selection patterns. Many caste organizations devise all kinds of strategies to limit marriages within their own castes and sub-castes. However, inter-caste marriages are now recognized by law and occur on a larger scale than before. Although most marriages are arranged by parents/elders, today there have been some modifications in the pattern of choosing a life partner. These patterns can still be seen today

i. marriage by parents'/elders' choice without consulting either the boy or girl

ii. marriage by self-choice without parent's consent

iii. marriage by self-choice but with parents' consent

iv. marriage by parents' choice but with the consent of both the boy and the girl involved in the marriage.

v. marriage by parents' choice but with the consent of only one of the two partners involved.

Marriage of their own free will (with or without parental consent) is an increasingly common occurrence. Love, personal commitment, and inner satisfaction are now seen as the cornerstones of marriage (Allen & Grow, 2001)

While rites are an important component of marriage among many communities, there are classes or groups that do not have religious rites in marriage. A marriage without rites is called a customary marriage. These marriages are based on simple rituals. Customary forms of marriage are generally found in groups where divorce and secondary marriages are permitted and practiced. The second marriage of a widow or a separated or divorced woman is usually celebrated in a simple manner.

The Special Marriage Act of 1954 provides for secular and civil marriages before a registrar. The Act applies to all Indian citizens who choose to make use of its provisions, irrespective of their religious affiliation. Civil marriage enables people to avoid the expense of traditional weddings.

However, weddings are still an expensive affair for most people. Large sums have to be bought, gift jewellery, furniture, utensils, clothes and generally the expenditure is more for the bride's side as compared to the groom's side.

Bride-price is the money, property, or other forms of wealth paid by the groom or his family to the family of the woman he is to be married to. The tradition of bride price is found in some patriarchal tribes and some castes in the middle and lower rungs of the caste ladder. Under the local influence of upper caste values and practices, some groups have given up their practice of bride price and adopted the practice of dowry. For example, peasants in villages in Karnataka and the Godiya caste in Andhra Pradesh abandoned their practice of bride price and adopted the practice of dowry.

Dowry refers to a specific category of gifts given by the bride's side to the groom's side. This set of gifts symbolizes the transfer of wealth from the bride's side to the groom's side. Dowry has been a prevalent practice even in modern India. Some parents are often unable to get their daughters married because of dowry. If they do so, they marry out of their status and are subject to pressures of various kinds in the form of dowry demands from the groom's side. We often hear about dowry deaths or a girl being sent back to her parents' home for not meeting dowry demands.

Today, we also hear of cases of unmarried girls who commit suicide to reduce the burden of their anxious, guilt-ridden parents who have not been able to fix their marriages. Many women become victims of domestic violence when dowry demands are not met. In 1961, the Government of India passed the Dowry Prohibition Act. In 1984 and again in 1986, the Act was amended to make the law more stringent and effective. For example, today a husband and his family can be punished for demanding dowry if his bride dies under circumstances other than normal within seven years of marriage. There is also a Dowry Prohibition Cell to deal with dowry complaints.

In the past, due to strong social codes and the stigma attached to divorce, married couples were not allowed to separate. But today divorce is a relatively common occurrence. Now there are more divorce cases due to legislation, education, and less rigid social rules.

The concept of an Indian wedding has seen a drastic change over the years. In the past, the ceremony was a family affair, restricted to an affordable budget, even though the guest list was long. In contrast, in present times, the occasion is generally celebrated in an elaborate manner. A huge amount is spent to make the ceremony a 'grand gala'.

Cohabitation occurs when a couple moves from dating to living together which may or may not lead to marriage. Today, it is more socially acceptable for couples to initiate sexual relations, build homes, and have children outside of formal marriage. Today there has been a drastic change in the division of labour among married couples. It is now common for women to enter the public sector and engage in economic activities.

Same-sex marriage is a new social phenomenon. This phenomenon began in the 21st century when many countries began allowing same-sex couples to legally marry. This has given rise to a new form of family formation.

CHANGING CARE AND SUPPORT SYSTEMS

The family as a social institution is undergoing changes. There have been changes in both its structure and functions. In India, as in many traditional societies, the family has been not only central to social and economic life, but also the primary source of support for family members. The increasing commercialization of the economy and the development of the infrastructure of the modern state brought about a significant change in the structure of the family in India in the 20th century.

India's fertility rate has fallen, and couples have started having children at a later age. An inevitable consequence of declining fertility rates and increasing age at first birth is a reduction in family size in most countries of the world, including India. The combined effect of substantial socioeconomic development achieved during the last two decades and effective implementation of family planning programs has led to a decline in fertility. In traditional societies, where human labour was the source of power for the family, the priority was to have more children. But as the economic contribution of children to a family diminished, the need for a large number of children diminished. Emphasis was placed on the quality of life rather than the number of children, and a new concept was added to the family.

The process of commercialization that opened up markets in many developing countries has succeeded in changing traditional cooperation in economic relations. The economics of the family and the gendered division of labour within the family is determined to a large extent by opportunities in the labour market. Developing economies have facilitated the release of women from household chores and their entry into the labour market.

The joint family was prevalent in ancient times. But today, nuclear families are more common. Parsons argues that modern industrial society has led to the development of the 'isolated nuclear family'. The family is structurally isolated as it is not an integral part of the wider kinship group.

Leena Kashyap suggested that 'For India, the twentieth century and the Second World War brought about devastating changes in all aspects of its society, including changes in the family's structure, functions, and the roles of its members'. With political independence from the British in 1947, India embarked on the task of nation-building and economic independence, enthusiastically and somewhat uncritically welcoming Western ideals of modernization and development.

According to Kashyap, 'Economic liberalization, as well as technological progress that has come in the wake of globalization has had a profound impact on the socio-economic, political and cultural life of Indian society, deeply affecting the traditional family pattern.'

In the Indian context, the responsibility of elders is usually taken up by the family members. (Rita Sonawat, 2001). However, some factors have changed this process.

First, migration has left the elderly with a sense of lack of support from their children. Also, if they are given an opportunity to migrate, they may not be willing to do so because of not changing their lifestyle after so many years. (Rita Sonawat, 2001)

Secondly, earlier a child had a support system in the form of elders in the house. But in a nuclear family, the child does not get this support.

Third, abuse has also been reported in many cases. Older women have been found to be abused more than men.

Fourth, the tradition of 'compulsory dependence' on boys is also changing. In recent times daughters are taking equal responsibility of caring and supporting their parents.

In urban areas, the use of day care facilities for children has increased due to the increase in the number of women working outside. But formal day-cares are generally used by the wealthier sections of the society. Low-income families have to rely on informal childcare arrangements. Many families depend on relatives to look after their children.

According to Leena Kashyap, earlier marriages were completely arranged by the elders. Now, often the youth have the autonomy to make decisions. If their parents arrange a marriage, their choice is usually considered. An increase in the trend of love marriage can be seen. Marriage was not a matter of choice but in many cases a matter of convenience. Now the ideas of love, companionship and personal happiness are also given importance.

With the advent of labour intensive industries and the resultant impetus to earn, there has been a large-scale movement from rural to urban areas. Due to these individuals are not getting in touch with their roots and thus cut off from the support of kin and community.

Due to economic demands in urban areas, many expatriates are unable to adequately support their families. 'Gender role convergence' can be observed, with men and women working towards a more egalitarian relationship, contributing to the paid labour force, housework and child care.

FAMILY LAW

Family law (also called matrimonial law or domestic relations law) is an area of law that deals with family matters and domestic relations. The subjects commonly covered by the family law of a nation are:

i. Marriage, Civil Union, and Domestic Partnership.
ii. Entering into legally recognized husband-wife and domestic relations.
iii. Termination of legally recognized family relationships and ancillary matters, including divorce, annulment, property settlement, alimony, child

custody and visitation, child support, and alimony awards.

iv. **Adoption:** the act of adopting a child and, in some cases, an adult.

v. **Surrogacy:** The Law and Process of Giving Birth as a Surrogate Mother.

vi. **Child protection proceedings:** court proceedings that may result from state intervention in cases of child abuse and child neglect.

vii. **Juvenile Law:** Matters relating to minors including status offenses, delinquencies, emancipation, and juvenile adjudication.

viii. **Paternity:** Proceedings to establish and disestablish paternity, and administration of paternity tests.

In the past, family law was closely linked to the law of property and succession. This may have arisen primarily in questions of economics and property created by the transfer of a woman from her father's family to the power and guardianship of her husband.

Even in relation to the relationship between parent and child, legal concepts such as guardianship, custody, and legitimacy were linked to family power structures and family economic interests.

Family law has also traditionally been concerned with matters of personal status – for example, the question of whether a person should be considered married or single, legitimate or illegitimate although the incidence and significance of these distinctions often derive from the law of property.

Family law shares an interest in some social issues with other areas of law, including criminal law. For example, one issue that has received considerable attention since the late 20th century is the very difficult problem of violence within the family, which can be physical violence perpetrated by one adult member on another or by one adult on a child or another. Can take Violent or abusive behaviour within the family circle. In severe cases, the only real solution may be to end cohabitation or to remove the abused child from the family unit into some form of public or foster care.

Today, the nuclear family is the more common family structure. Therefore, the law mainly deals with the rights of the couple and their children and the duties of the couple towards the children and each other.

For example, in a strictly monogamous society, the law would forbid a person from being married to more than one person at the same time. Traditionally, family law has not concerned itself much with unions that did not begin by legal marriage, although some systems of law allow the recognition of a 'natural' child by the father for purposes such as inheritance and support. given.

More recently, the family law of several European countries and some jurisdictions in the United States was amended to recognize civil unions or domestic partnerships, which led to a number of legal incidents of marriage for same-sex couples.

Since the 1970s, one-parent families have acquired an importance that is not adequately reflected in traditional law. It may be necessary to adapt the law to a greater extent to the needs of one-parent families in areas such as the organization of family and child-welfare services and the legal and administrative machinery for family support, employment support, day nurseries, and the likes

Head of a single-parent household may find it difficult to afford the high cost of child care while working or training, especially on a modest or low income. In some legal systems, a contract in its traditional form is the core of the constitution of a marriage. Contracts can be complex, with various clauses as in Islamic law. In most countries today, however, the legal documentation of a marriage is primarily a registration of the event.

Basically, then, marriage in the legal sense is the implied creation of certain rights or obligations such as maintenance, rights to marital property and inheritance, and custody of minor children. Older laws in many countries considered decision-making regarding children to be a private family matter in which courts should not interfere, except in cases of serious child abuse or similar. In modern law, courts must take jurisdiction and intervene in family decision-making when there is injustice, oppression, or cruelty.

The history of marriage is linked to women's legal and economic dependence on men and women's legal disabilities to own and deal with property. In earlier legal systems, especially in Asia, a woman's consent was often unnecessary or of minor importance; The marriage was negotiated between the woman's father and the man or his family. In modern law, voluntary consent is important.

To satisfy the requirement of voluntary consent to marriage, a party must have reached the age at which he or she is capable of giving meaningful consent, and it is also implied that a person may be legally unfit on mental grounds ability to marry.

In most modern societies, the marriage of young children, arranged by their parents, is prohibited. The term 'Hindu' in post-independence Hindu law governing marriage, divorce, adoption, maintenance, guardianship, and succession describes not only persons who are Hindu by religion, but also Sikhs, Buddhists, and Jains. Broadly speaking, the term "Hindu" includes those Indians who are not Christians, Parsis, Muslims, or Jews for the purposes of the law.

The Special Marriage Act, 1954

Special marriage laws apply to citizens of India irrespective of their religion, caste, or culture. Under the provisions of the Act, people belonging to a different religion, caste, or community are allowed to marry, provided certain conditions are met:

- **i.** Marriage registration in India is compulsory to solemnize a marriage under this Act. A family lawyer can be hired to complete marriage registration in India
- **ii.** The age of both bride and groom must be 18 and 21 years respectively
- **iii.** Both of them must be of sound mind
- **iv.** Both the bride and groom cannot share common ancestors or be blood relatives. In accordance with the Act, there are 37 relations forbidden, in which no wedding can be performed between them

The special marriage laws are applicable to citizens of India irrespective of their religion, caste, or culture. Under provisions of the Act, people from a different religion, caste, or community are allowed to get married, provided certain conditions are met:

The Hindu Marriage Act, 1955

The Hindu Marriage Act, 1955 lays down the law for divorce.

It applies to Hindus, Buddhists, Jains, and Sikhs.

Under Section 13 of the Act, the grounds for divorce include:

- **i.** voluntary sexual intercourse with any person other than his or her spouse
- **ii.** cruelty
- **iii.** desertion for a continuous period of not less than 2 years immediately preceding the presentation of the petition
- **iv.** ceasing to be a Hindu by conversion to another religion
- **v.** being "incurably of unsound mind"

The Family Court Act, 1984

The Family Courts Act, 1984 provides for the establishment of Family Courts for the promotion of reconciliation and speedy redressal of disputes relating to marriage and family matters and for matters connected therewith.

Family courts hear matters related to marriage, divorce, and the welfare of children. These courts are trial courts and are presided over by additional district judges who conduct trials and review evidence.

Family courts follow the Civil Procedure Code. Family proceedings are usually public but may be held in private at the request of the parties or if circumstances require.

Domestic Violence and Crime Against Women

Domestic violence is violence or other abuse in a domestic setting. Domestic violence is often used synonymously with intimate partner violence, which is perpetrated by one person against another in an intimate relationship.

In its broadest sense, domestic violence also includes violence against children, adolescents, parents, or elders. It takes many forms, including physical, verbal, emotional, economic, religious, reproductive, and sexual abuse, which can range from subtle, coercive forms to marital rape and violent physical abuse such as kneeling, beatings, female genital mutilation, and acid throwing leads to disfigurement or death.

Domestic murders include stoning, bride burning, honor killings, and dowry deaths. The victims of domestic violence are mainly women and young girls.

The United Nations defines violence against women as "any act of gender-based violence that results in or is likely to result in, physical, sexual or psychological harm or suffering to women, including threats of such acts, coercion, or deprivation of liberty, whether occurring in public or in private life."

It includes "physical, sexual and psychological violence occurring within the family and community, including beatings, child sexual abuse, dowry-related violence, rape, female genital mutilation and other traditional practices harmful to women, non-marital violence and Others include violence related to exploitation, sexual harassment and bullying at work, in educational institutions and elsewhere, trafficking of women, forced prostitution, and violence perpetrated or condoned by the state.

UN Declaration on Elimination of Violence Against Women

The United Nations General Assembly adopted the Declaration on the Elimination of Violence against Women in 1993. It testifies to the international recognition and understanding that violence against women is a violation of their human rights and a form of discrimination against women.

Following UN initiatives, the Platform for Action was adopted by the Fourth World Conference on Women held in Beijing in 1995.

The Beijing Declaration and Platform for Action identified three strategic objectives for addressing violence against women:

1. Take integrative measures to prevent and eliminate violence against women.
2. Study the causes and consequences of violence against women and the effectiveness of preventive measures.
3. Eliminate trafficking in women and assist victims of violence due to prostitution and trafficking.

Kofi Annan, Secretary-General of the United Nations, declared in a 2006 report posted on the United Nations Development Fund for Women (UNIFEM) website: Violence against women and girls is a problem of pandemic proportions. At least one out of every three women around the world has been beaten, coerced into sex, or otherwise abused in her lifetime by the abuser usually someone known to her.

The Committee on Family Violence of the National Institute of Mental Health (1992) included in its definition of violence 'acts that are physically and emotionally harmful or that carry the potential to cause physical harm ... [and] may also include sexual coercion or assaults, physical intimidation, threats to kill or to harm, restraint of normal activities or freedom, and denial of access to resources.'

The Task Force on Male Violence Against Women of the American Psychological Association defined violence as 'physical, visual, verbal, or sexual acts that are experienced by a woman or a girl as a threat, invasion, or assault and that have the effect of hurting her or degrading her and/or taking away her ability to control contact (intimate or otherwise) with another individual.'"

Violence against women (VAW), also known as gender-based violence and sexual and gender-based violence (SGBV), are violent acts primarily or exclusively committed against women or girls. Such violence is often considered a form of hate crime, committed against women or girls.

Cases of violence against women can be found in all parts of the world though the incidents and intensity of such violence have varied over time and even today vary between societies.

Such violence is often seen as a mechanism for the subjugation of women, whether in society in general or in interpersonal relationships. Power inequalities between women and men and the masculine culture are the major sources of violence.

Domestic Violence in India

Domestic violence is widely prevalent in India. The National Crime Records Bureau (NCRB) 2019 reports that a majority (30.9%) of all the 4.05 lakh cases under crimes against women are registered under Section 498A of the Indian Penal Code (IPC). The section deals with 'cruelty by husband or his relatives'.

According to a National Family and Health Survey in 2005, the total lifetime prevalence of domestic violence was 33.5%, and 8.5% for sexual violence among women aged 15–49.

One in three women in India is likely to have been subjected to intimate partner violence of a physical, emotional, or sexual nature reveals research published online in the Journal of Epidemiology & Community Health. Yet only one in 10 of these women formally report the offense to the police or healthcare professionals, the findings show.

These figures suggest that India is unlikely to meet Sustainable Development Goal (SDG-5) 5, which focuses on gender equality and the elimination of all forms of violence against women and girls by 2030, say the researchers.

Domestic Violence Act, 2005 Protection of Women from Domestic Violence Act, 2005 President A.P.J. Abdul Kalam has given assent to the Protection of Women from the Domestic Violence Act, 2005, which seeks to provide protection to victims of violence within the family.

Under the new Act, any woman subjected to mental or physical injuries, physical abuse, criminal intimidation or force, or sexual abuse (any conduct of a sexual nature that abuses, humiliates, degrades, or otherwise violates the dignity of a woman), will be covered under domestic violence.

Domestic violence, as per the Act, constitutes physical or mental harm, including sexual, verbal, emotional, or economic abuse by a male member of the family or anyone living under the same roof.

Crimes Identified Under the Special Laws in India

Sati (Prevention) Act: Sati, the custom of burning widows on the funeral pyre of their husbands was banned through legislation in 1829.

Roop Kanwar's Sati case in 1987 raised this issue again. There was a large protest by women's organizations all over the country against Sati and its glorification. As a consequence, in December 1987, Parliament passed the Commission of Sati (Prevention) Act 1987. But this had some shortcomings like it accepted Sati as suicide. The Act does not notice that women usually do not have a choice.

The Dowry (Prohibition) Act, 1961 made demanding and accepting dowry from the bride's family a criminal offense. Later amendments to the Act made the punishment for offenses more stringent and shifted the burden of proof (that there was no demand for dowry) to the person who is alleged to have taken or abetted the taking of dowry.

The Indecent Representation of Women (Prohibition) Act, 1986, prohibits the indecent representation of women through advertisements, books, pamphlets, etc.

This crime against the unborn girl child is sought to be tackled by banning sex selection under the Pre-natal Diagnostic Techniques (Regulation and Prevention of Misuse) Act, 1994. It is an Act of the Parliament of India enacted to stop female feticides and arrest the declining sex ratio in India. The act banned prenatal sex determination.

Feticide is an offense under the Indian Penal Code and infanticide is tantamount to murder.

The practice of flesh trade or trafficking in women is another crime committed against women. In order to control this, the Immoral Traffic (Prevention) Act, 1986 was enacted. This Act covers all those persons who are sexually exploited for commercial purposes.

Honour Killing

Honour killing or shame killing is the killing of a family member, due to the perpetrator's belief that the victim has brought shame or dishonor on the family, or has violated the tenets of a community's or an honor culture's religion.

In a patriarchal society, the activities of girls and women are closely monitored. The maintenance of a woman's virginity and "sexual purity" is considered the responsibility of male relatives. The mere suspicion that a woman has acted in a way that brings a bad name to her family can trigger an attack.

Victims of honour killings are usually accused of engaging in "sexually immoral" acts, including openly conversing with men who are not related to them, to having sex outside marriage (even if They are victims of rape or sexual assault).

A woman may be targeted for murder for many other reasons, including refusing to enter into an arranged marriage, marrying out of caste/religion, seeking divorce or separation (even from an abusive husband), etc.

The United Nations Population Fund estimates that at least 5,000 women are killed in honor killings each year. These crimes occur all over the world and are not limited to a specific religion or faith. Although they have occurred more frequently in various parts of the Middle East and South Asia, India, and Pakistan account for about half of all honor killings.

According to Amnesty International, honor killing is most widespread in Pakistan. A report by the Human Rights Commission of Pakistan (HRCP) said that 647 women were killed in the name of 'honour' in 2009 – 13 percent more than in 2008 when 574 such killings were recorded.

It is said that more than 1,000 young people are killed every year in India due to 'honour killings' linked to forced marriages. In 2015 alone, 251 honour killings were recorded in India and honor killings are mainly reported in the Indian states of Punjab, Haryana, Rajasthan and Uttar Pradesh. It is also widespread in South India and the western Indian states of Gujarat and Maharashtra.

National Crime Records Bureau, Data 2015 India reported 251 cases of honor killings in 2015, showing a significant increase in killings of people who feel they are acting to protect the integrity of their families.

The decisions of patriarchal khap panchayats have often been linked to the practice of honor killings. Khap panchayats oppose and punish couples who marry within the same gotra (lineage) or violate other social norms. Men can also be victims of honor-based violence. But women are the primary target. Honour killings are related to gender roles and the patriarchal structure of society.

ASSESS YOUR LEARNING

PRACTICE QUESTIONS

1. The following items consist of two statements, Statement I and Statement II. Examine these two statements carefully and select the correct answer using the options given below.

   Statement I: Fertility is the physiological capability of an individual to reproduce.

   Statement II: Fecundity is the actual reproductive performance of an individual.

   (a) Statement I and Statement II are correct
   (b) Statement I is correct but Statement II is incorrect
   (c) Statement I is incorrect but Statement II is correct
   (d) Statement I and Statement II are incorrect

2. **Assertion (A):** Infertile couples have reproductive alternatives in modern society.
   Reason (R): The introduction of newer reproductive technologies has assisted in overcoming biological limitations.
   (a) Both (A) and (R) are correct, and (R) is the correct explanation of (A).
   (b) Both (A) and (R) are correct, but (R) is not the correct explanation of (A).
   (c) (A) is correct, but (R) is not correct.
   (d) (A) is wrong, and (R) is correct.

3. Who gave the statement 'polyandry is an ethnographic curiosity'?
   (a) B Malinowski
   (b) G. P. Murdock
   (c) Radcliffe-Brown
   (d) Levi Strauss

4. **Assertion (A):** Incest is best described as a taboo.
   Reason (R): It is an extremely negative prohibition that is impossible to breach.
   (a) Both (A) and (R) are correct, and (R) is the correct explanation of (A).
   (b) Both (A) and (R) are correct, but (R) is not the correct explanation of (A).
   (c) (A) is correct, but (R) is not correct.
   (d) (A) is wrong, and (R) is correct.

5. How many primary Kins does an individual possess?
   (a) 8 (b) 15
   (c) 3 (d) 5

6. What are the two principles used by Levi-Strauss to explain alliance theory?
   A. incest taboo
   B. principle of monogamy
   C. principle of reciprocity
   D. principle of equity
   (a) A, B (b) A, C
   (c) B, C (d) B, D

7. When did The Hindu Adoptions and Maintenance Act come into force?
   (a) 1956 (b) 1964
   (c) 1967 (d) 1972

8. Couvade refers to:
   (a) Certain rituals that are carried out by the husband of a pregnant woman
   (b) Marriage by abduction or marriage by capture
   (c) Relationship between men and the children of their siblings
   (d) Marriage-like arrangement where three or more adults live together

9. The custom in which a woman is asked to marry the brother of her deceased husband is known as?
   (a) Levirate
   (b) Polyandry
   (c) Sororate
   (d) Hypergamy

10. Who argued that the nuclear family suffers from an emotional overload which increases the level of conflict between its members?
    (a) E. Leach (b) T. Parsons
    (c) G. Murdock (d) B. Malinowski

11. Who argued that the nuclear family suffers from an emotional overload which increases the level of conflict between its members?
    (a) E. Leach
    (b) T. Parsons
    (c) G. Murdock
    (d) B. Malinowski

12. **Assertion 'A':** Caste endogamy is still widely prevalent in Indian society.

    Reason 'B': Marrying outside the rigid boundaries of caste remains taboo in many parts of India.

    Codes:

    (a) Both 'A' and 'R' are true and 'R' is the correct explanation of 'A'
    (b) Both 'A' and 'R' are true, but 'R' is not the correct explanation of 'A'
    (c) 'A' is true, but 'R' is false
    (d) 'A' is false, but 'R' is true

13. Who said, 'The nuclear family becomes like an overloaded electric circuit'?
(a) G. P. Murdock (b) Friedrich Engels
(c) Edmund Leach (d) Talcott Parsons

14. Who is the author of 'World Revolution and Family Patterns'?
(a) G. P. Murdock
(b) Talcott Parsons
(c) William J. Goode
(d) A. G. Frank

15. Which marriage practice was prevalent among the Todas of Nilgiri Hills?
(a) Polyandry
(b) Polygyny
(c) Monogamy
(d) Same-sex marriage

16. Who formulated the distinction between classificatory and descriptive kinship terminologies?
(a) Claude Levi Strauss
(b) Lewis Morgan
(c) Bronisław Malinowski
(d) A R Radcliffe-Brown

17. A principle of succession where the subject is succeeded by the youngest child is known as:
(a) Ultimogeniture
(b) Primogeniture
(c) Agnatic seniority
(d) Matrilineal succession

18. When a newly married couple establishes their own residence that is separate from both husband's and wife's natal household, it is known as:
(a) Duolocal residence
(b) Patrilocal residence
(c) Neolocal residence
(d) Avunculocal residence

19. Who has said that marriage is rooted in the family rather than family in marriage?
(a) Malinowski (b) Murdock
(c) Westermarck (d) Weber

20. Who argued that an isolated nuclear family is the typical form of family in modern industrial society?
(a) Talcott Parsons (b) A M. Shah
(c) R. K. Merton (d) G. P. Murdock

21. When a special role is given to a father's sister, it is known as:
(a) Teknonymy (b) Amitate
(c) Avunculate (d) Couvade

22. Who defined marriage as a "contract for the production and maintenance of children"?
(a) Lundberg (b) Murdock
(c) Malinowski (d) Westermarck

23. Adelphic polyandry stands for:
(a) Husbands of women are brothers
(b) Husbands of women are engaged in one type of economic activity
(c) Husbands are not related to each other
(d) Marriage with a second husband without the approval of the first husband

24. Which of these is NOT a type of family identified by Zimmerman?
(a) trustee (b) atomistic
(c) domestic (d) blended

25. '*Urbanization and family change*' is authored by:
(a) K. M. Kapadia (b) M. S. Gore
(c) Erich Goore (d) A M. Shah

26. Which theory, created by A. Giddens, argues that individuals now choose to look for someone to create meaningful relationships that are based on mutual love and respect?
(a) Liquid Love
(b) Confluent Love
(c) Agape Love
(d) Empathy Love

27. Choose the correct factors that are responsible for the change in the structure of the family.
(1) Industrialization
(2) Women's economic participation
(3) Urbanization and migration

Choose the correct options below:
(a) 1 and 3 only (b) 1 and 2 only
(c) 1 only (d) 1, 2, and 3 only

28. Match the following:

List I (Constitutional Provisions for Children)	List II (Aims/Objectives)
A. Article 23 (1)	I. Children below 14 years to be discouraged from being employed in any factory
B. Article 45	II. Protection from being trafficked and forced to bonded labour
C. Article 39 (f)	III. Free and compulsory education till the age of 14
D. Article 24	IV. Protection of children and youth against exploitation

Choose the correct codes below:
(a) A–III, B–I, C–II, D–IV
(b) A–IV, B–III, C–I, D–II
(c) A–II, B–III, C–I, D–IV
(d) A–II, B–III, C–IV, D–I

29. Among Muslim marriages, what is given as an obligation to the bride from the husband?
(a) Dinar (b) Mahr
(c) Kohl (d) Mubarat

30. Which among the following is NOT one of the three stages of the family mentioned by Michael Young and Peter Willmott?
(a) early industrial family
(b) symmetrical family
(c) dispersed family
(d) pre-industrial family

31. Child Labour (Prohibition & Regulation) Amendment Act was passed in:
(a) 2019 (b) 2014
(c) 2016 (d) 2011

32. Who conducted a detailed study of the kinship system of the Nayar community?
(a) Talcott Parsons
(b) Kathleen Gough
(c) G. P. Murdock
(d) Claude Levi-Strauss

33. Match the following:

Book	Author
A. The Family in India	I. A. R. Desai
B. Kinship Organization in India	II. M. N. Srinivas
C. Marriage and Family in Mysore	III. Irawati Karve
D. Urban Family and Family Planning in India	IV. A. M. Shah

(a) A–IV, B–II, C–I, D–III
(b) A–III, B–I, C–II, D–IV
(c) A–II, B–IV, C–III, D–I
(d) A–IV, B–III, C–II, D–I

34. Polygamy exists in two main forms. These are:
(a) Endogamy and Exogamy
(b) Polygyny and Polyandry
(c) Hypergamy and Hypogamy
(d) Isogamy and Anisogamy

35. On the basis of _______ a family may be patriarchal or matriarchal.
(a) Blood Relations (b) Marriage
(c) Authority (d) Size

36. Who argued that most stateless, 'primitive' societies that lack strong centralized institutions are based on an association of corporate-descent groups?
(a) Radcliffe-Brown
(b) Murdock
(c) Lévi-Strauss
(d) Dumont

37. 'Women are given in marriage, taken in battle, exchanged for favours, sent as tribute, traded, bought, and sold.' Who said that?
(a) Gayle Rubin
(b) Mary Wollstonecraft
(c) Susan B Anthony
(d) Jane Alpert

38. The Household Dimension of the Family in India: A Field Study in a Gujarat Village and a Review of Other Studies is written by:
(a) Irawati Karve
(b) S. C Dube
(c) A M Shah
(d) Andre Beteille

39. The Alliance Theory of Claude Lévi-Strauss has similarities with:
(a) Ideal Type by Max Weber
(b) Self-Fulfilling Prophecy by Robert K. Merton
(c) Structural Functionalism by A R Radcliffe-Brown
(d) Totem and Taboo by Sigmund Freud

40. Who defined gender as a site of 'durable inequality'?
(a) Atkinson
(b) Burns and Kinder
(c) Mauss
(d) Murdock

41. A family wherein two nuclear families have split up to form a new family is called
(a) Patrifocal lone-parent family
(b) Matrifocal lone-parent family
(c) Empty nest family
(d) Reconstituted family

42. **Statement 1:** In couvade, the husband leads the life of an invalid along with his pregnant wife.
Statement 2: The usage of couvade is prevalent among the Toda and Khasi tribes.
Choose the correct options given below:
(a) Statement 1 is correct, and Statement 2 is incorrect
(b) Statement 1 is incorrect, and Statement 2 is correct
(c) Both Statement 1 and Statement 2 are correct
(d) Both Statement 1 and Statement 2 are incorrect

43. Who wrote the book '*The History of Human Marriage*'?
(a) Murray Bookchin
(b) EO Wilson
(c) Janet Carsten
(d) Edvard Westermarck

44. In which year was the Preconception and Prenatal Diagnostic Techniques Act implemented?
(a) 1990
(b) 1994
(c) 2000
(d) None of these

45. Match the following:

List I (Books)	List II (Scholars)
A. Kinship and Marriage: An Anthropological Approach	I. David M. Schneider
B. Systems of Consanguinity and Affinity of the Human Family	II. Radcliffe Brown and Daryll Forde
C. A Critique of the Study of Kinship	III. L. H. Morgan
D. African Systems of Kinship and Marriage	IV. Robin Fox

Choose the correct codes below:

(a) A–IV, B–III, C–I, D–II
(b) A–III, B–IV, C–I, D–II
(c) A–I, B–II, C–III, D–IV
(d) A–II, B–IV, C–III, D–I

46. The Evil practice of Sati Pratha was abolished in which year:

(a) 1929 (b) 1956
(c) 1829 (d) 1856

47. The Hindu Widow Remarriage Act came into existence in:

(a) 1856 (b) 1829
(c) 1956 (d) 1929

48. Hindu Marriage Act which allows divorce in Hindus, Buddhists, Sikhs, and Jains (except in J & K) came into existence in:

(a) 1955 (b) 1956
(c) 1958 (d) 1962

49. The type of family in which the couple lives in the maternal uncle's house are known as:

(a) Avanculocal (b) Amitolocal
(c) Virilocal (d) Neolocal

50. The type of family in which the couple lives in the husband's house are known as:

(a) Avanculocal (b) Amitolocal
(c) Virilocal (d) Neolocal

Answer Key

1. (d)	**9.** (a)	**17.** (a)	**25.** (b)	**33.** (d)	**41.** (d)	**49.** (a)
2. (a)	**10.** (a)	**18.** (c)	**26.** (b)	**34.** (b)	**42.** (c)	**50.** (c)
3. (b)	**11.** (a)	**19.** (c)	**27.** (d)	**35.** (c)	**43.** (d)	
4. (a)	**12.** (a)	**20.** (a)	**28.** (d)	**36.** (a)	**44.** (b)	
5. (a)	**13.** (c)	**21.** (b)	**29.** (b)	**37.** (a)	**45.** (a)	
6. (b)	**14.** (c)	**22.** (c)	**30.** (c)	**38.** (c)	**46.** (c)	
7. (a)	**15.** (a)	**23.** (a)	**31.** (c)	**39.** (d)	**47.** (a)	
8. (a)	**16.** (b)	**24.** (d)	**32.** (b)	**40.** (b)	**48.** (a)	

PREVIOUS YEARS' QUESTIONS

DECEMBER 2023

1. Match List I with List II.

List I	List II
A. Robin Fox	I. Regional difference in family structure in India
B. Leela Dube	II. Kinship organization in India
C. Iravati Karve	III. Sociology of kinship
D. Pauline Kolenda	IV. Kinship and marriage

Choose the correct answer from the options given below:
(a) A-I, B-II, C-III, D-IV
(b) A-II, B-I, C-IV, D-III
(c) A-IV, B-III, C-II, D-I
(d) A-III, B-II, C-IV D-I

2. Who among the following said that family was the outcome of male possessiveness and jealousy, and a growth in property and
of the sense of property?
(a) Lewis Morgan
(b) Westermarck
(c) R. Lowie
(d) P.N. Prabhu

3. L.H. Morgan listed five different and successive forms of family. Arrange them in the order of evaluation.
A. The Punaluan family.
B. The Consanguine family.
C. The Patriarehal family.
D. The Syndyasmian family.
E. The Monogamous family.
Choose the correct answer from the options given below:
(a) A, B, C, D, E
(b) B, A, D, C, E
(c) B, A, C, E, D
(d) E, D, C, B, A

4. Who among the following coined the term 'intersectionality'?
(a) Barbara Smith
(b) Combahee River
(c) Kimberle Crenshaw
(d) Patricia Hill Collins

5. Who among the following has used the term 'unstable family' for the first time?
(a) C.H. Cooley
(b) Le Play
(c) Georg Simmel
(d) F. Engels

6. Which of the following is associated with transvestite woman?
(a) A woman who regularly dresses as a man.
(b) A man who regularly dresses as a woman.
(c) A man who becomes a woman.
(d) A woman who becomes a man.

7. Who among the following is associated with the study of family in Mahuva, a town in Saurashtra?
(a) I.P. Desai
(b) A.M. Shah
(c) Iravati Karve
(d) Mandelbaum

8. Who among the following is the author of the essay 'Why marriage matters'?
(a) Jesse Ellison
(b) Caitlin Flanagan
(c) John Gottman
(d) Robinson

9. Who among the following used the 'alliance approach' to understand the patterns of kinship?
(a) Louis Dumont
(b) T.N. Madan
(c) K. Gough
(d) Oscar Lewis

JUNE 2023

10. Who among the following did psychoanalytic study of childhood in Hindu families?
(a) Ashis Nandy
(b) A.M. Shah
(c) Sudhir Kakkar
(d) Leela Dube

11. *World Revolution in Family Patterns* was written by
(a) William J. Goode
(b) Sylvia Walby
(c) Belly Friedan
(d) Simone de Beavoir

12. Domestic violence, according to the feminist scholars, is related to ________
A. Gender inequalities
B. Secondary status of women
C. Patriarchy
D. Education of children
E. Advertisements

Choose the appropriate answer from the options given below:

(a) A, B, and C only
(b) A, B, and D only
(c) A, B, and E only
(d) A, C, and E only

13. Which of the following sociologists have discussed the family from functionalist perspective?
A. G.P. Murdock
B. T. Parsons
C. Sherry B. Ortner
D. Norman W. Bell

Choose the appropriate answer from the options given below:

(a) A, B, and C only
(b) A, C, and D only
(c) A, B, and D only
(d) B, C, and D only

14. Who wrote the book *The Subjection of Women*?
(a) Sylvia Walby
(b) Bob Connell
(c) S. Firestone
(d) John Stuart Mill

MARCH 2023

15. Arrange the following social legislations in chronological order on the basis of year of enactments:
A. The Equal Remuneration Act
B. Abolition of Sati Act
C. The Sati Prevention Act
D. The Hindu Marriage Act
E. The Maternity Benefit Act

Choose the correct answer from the options given below:

(a) B, D, E, A, C
(b) A, B, C, D, E
(c) B, C, D, E, A
(d) A, B, D, E, C

16. Which of the following facts are correct about the concept of gender?
A. Ann Oakley's 'Sex, Gender and Society (1972)' made the sex-gender distinction popular in Sociology.
B. Gender is a matter of culture, it refers to the societal classifications into masculine and feminine.
C. Margaret Mead's study of the 3 societies in the New Guinea Islands contributed to the shaping of the concept of gender in the latter half of the 20th century.
D. Gender is not socially constructed.
E. Gender is not a matter of culture.

Choose the correct answer from the options given below:

(a) C, D, and E only
(b) A, B, and D only
(c) A, B, C, and E only
(d) A, B, and C only

17. Which of the following facts pertaining to conceptual shifts in the Women In Development (WID) discourse are correct?
A. WID considers women as a homogenous group.
B. WID does not consider women as a uniform group.
C. WID projects the myth that women's development can be achieved by addressing economic issues alone.
D. In WID, women are treated as 'beneficiaries of development' and not as active agents of development.
E. Decade for women (1975–85) signified a new visibility of Women in Development (WID) in International Forums.

Choose the correct answer from the options given below:

(a) A, B, and E only
(b) A, B, D, and E only
(c) A, C, D, and E only
(d) A, B, and D only

18. Chronologically arrange the following historical events–
A. French Revolution
B. Rise of Feminism
C. Rise of Socialism
D. American Revolution
E. European Renaissance

Choose the correct answer from the options given below:

(a) A, E, B, C, D
(b) E, D, A, C, B
(c) D, A, C, B, E
(d) E, A, C, B, D

19. Which of the following practices prevents sex relations between a parent and child or between brother and sister?
(a) Rules of Commensality
(b) Rules of Succession
(c) Incest taboo
(d) None of the above

20. The study of the processes of ageing, old age and the elderly is known as
(a) Gerontology
(b) Genealogy
(c) Human Ecology
(d) None of the above

21. A type of marriage in which two or more women are legally mated to one man is known as:
(a) Hypogamy
(b) Sororate
(c) Polyandry
(d) None of the above

DEC 2021 & JUNE 2022

22. Who has conducted the study on Nayars of Kerala?
(a) George Peter Murdock
(b) Kathleen Gough
(c) Edward Westermarck
(d) William N. Stephens

23. Who has written the book, '*The Family in India: Critical Essays*'?
(a) P. Uberoi (b) Irawati Karve
(c) A. M. Shah (d) I. P. Desai

24. ________________ is an approach originally developed by Dorothy Smith (1978) to better understand women's everyday experiences by discovering the power relations that shape those experiences.
(a) Case study
(b) Content analysis
(c) Institutional ethnography
(d) Participatory Action Research

25. Which one of the following practice matrilineal family structure?
(a) Garo (b) Koya
(c) Garasia (d) Gond

26. __________is a set of socially constructed ideas that accommodate the interests of men and patriarchy and involve the compliance of females.
(a) Hegemonic masculinity
(b) Emphasized femineity
(c) Both of the above
(d) None of the above

JUNE 2021

27. If nephews and nieces are brought up in their maternal uncle's family, the arrangement is referred to as
(a) Avunculocal residence
(b) Neolocal residence
(c) Matrilocal residence
(d) Patrilocal residence

28. Who said that monogamous marriage developed not to unite men and women in marital bliss, but to protect private property?
A. Friedrich Engels
B. Karl Marx
C. Schulasmith Firestone

Choose the correct answer from the options given below:
(a) A only (b) B only
(c) C only (d) A, B and C

29. According to P.M. Kolenda, which family types were not discussed for a comparative evaluation?
A. Single person household
B. Sub-nuclear family
C. Juvenile family
D. Supplemented sub-nuclear family
E. Singular family

Choose the correct answer from the options given below:
(a) C and E only (b) A and B only
(c) B and D only (d) A and D only

30. A Hindu marriage ceremony consists of a series of ritual performances, which are:
A. Kanyadan
B. Prajapatya
C. Vivaha-havan
D. Pani-grahan
E. Sapta-padi

Choose the correct answer from the options given below:
(a) A, B, C and D only
(b) A, C, D and E only
(c) B, C, D and E only
(d) A, B, C, D and E

JUNE 2020

31. Match List I with List II:

List I (Author)	List II (Book)
A. P.L. Berger	I. Economy and Society
B. T. Parsons and N. Smelser	II. Social Theory and Social Structure
C. T.B. Bottomore	III. Invitation to sociology
D. R.K. Merton	IV. Classes in modern society

Choose the correct answer from the options given below:

	A	B	C	D
(a)	IV	III	I	II
(b)	III	IV	II	I
(c)	III	I	IV	II
(d)	I	IV	II	III

32. In modern Industrialized society the status of women in the industry
(a) Has considerately gone down
(b) Has gradually risen
(c) Has remained unchanged
(d) Has not been defined

33. Yellow revolution is related to
(a) Oilseed
(b) Milk
(c) Telangana
(d) Tiger conservation

34. Which of the following three characteristics did the feudal estates of medieval Europe have?
1. Had a Status
2. Serfdom was decreasing
3. Were political groups
4. Had division of labour
5. Serfs had the ability to appeal for justice

Choose the most appropriate answer from the options given below:

(a) 1, 2, and 5 only (b) 1, 3, and 4 only
(c) 4, 5, and 2 only (d) 3, 4, and 2 only

35. Which two of the following are the biggest dams in India?
1. Sardar Sarovar Dam
2. Bhakra Dam
3. Tehri Dam
4. Hirakud Dam

Choose the most appropriate answer from the options given below:

(a) 1 and 2 only (b) 2 and 4 only
(c) 2 and 3 only (d) 4 and 1 only

36. Which of the following are characteristics of the pre-capitalist mode of production?
1. Unfree labour
2. Commodity production
3. Fusion of economic and political power
4. Mechanisation
5. Subsistence

Choose the most appropriate answer from the options given below:

(a) 1, 2, 3 only (b) 2, 3, 5 only
(c) 3, 4, 5 only (d) 1, 3, 5 only

37. Sylvia Walby in her book *'Theorising Patriarchy'* talks of elements of patriarchy. Which of the following is not one of them?
1. Women are likely to be paid less
2. Sexuality is to be treated positively
3. Women are likely to raise children
4. Men and women are likely to be treated equally

Choose the most appropriate answer from the options given below:

(a) 1, 2, 3 only (b) 2, 3, 4 only
(c) 1, 3, 4 only (d) 4 only

DECEMBER 2019

38. In Indian weddings there is a predominance of what is called 'Conspicuous consumption'. This can be applied to indicate two things:
A. Reflection of the caste of a person
B. Display of wealth
C. Providing expensive food
D. Demonstration of one's status

Choose the correct option:

(a) (A) and (B) (b) (C) and (D)
(c) (A) and (C) (d) (B) and (D)

39. Identify the correct sequence of different laws passed in India to improve women's status in society:
(a) Protection of Women from Domestic Violence Act, Panchayati Raj Act, Hindu Succession Act
(b) Panchayati Raj Act, Hindu Succession Act, Protection of Women from Domestic Violence Act
(c) Hindu Succession Act, Protection of Women from Domestic Violence Act, Panchayati Raj Act
(d) Hindu Succession Act, Panchayati Raj Act, Protection of Women from Domestic Violence Act.

40. Which two of the following principles explain the Alliance theory?
A. Principle of reciprocity
B. Rules of Exogamy
C. Rules of Endogamy
D. Incest taboos

Choose the correct option:

(a) A and B (b) B and C
(c) C and D (d) A and D

41. Which of the following family law in India was enacted in 1956?
(a) Adoption and Maintenance Act
(b) Dowry Prohibition Act
(c) Hindu Marriage Act
(d) Special Marriage Act

42. Which one of the following tribes is patrilineal?
(a) Garo (b) Maliku
(c) Khasi (d) Toda

43. Given below are two statements, one is labelled as Assertion (A) and the other as Reason (R):

Assertion (A): Representation of women by media reinforces the stereotype rather than challenging them.

Reasons (R): Media serves the power elite.

Choose the correct option:

(a) Both (A) and (R) are true and (R) is the correct explanation of (A)
(b) Both (A) and (R) are true and (R) is not the correct explanation of (A)
(c) (A) is true, but (R) is false
(d) (A) is false, but (R) is true

44. Which among the following is the most common form of domestic violence in the world?
(a) Wife battering
(b) Child Abuse
(c) Elderly Abuse
(d) Sibling violence

45. By which year the number of older persons is expected to be more than children aged less than 10 years?
(a) 2030 (b) 2040
(c) 2050 (d) 2060

46. Two statements are given below. One is labelled as Assertion (A) and the other as Reason (R).

Assertion (A): Social institution of marriage has undergone many changes in modern India

Reason (R): Indian youth are getting influenced by western ideas

Choose the correct option:
(a) Both (A) and (R) are true and (R) is the correct explanation of (A)
(b) Both (A) and (R) are true and (R) is not the correct explanation of (A)
(c) (A) is true but (R) is false
(d) (A) is false but (R) is true

47. From among the following sociologists who have written on the 'Kinship Systems' in different regions of India?
(a) P.H. Prabhu
(b) G.S. Ghurye
(c) Irawati Karve
(d) K.M. Kapadia

48. Match List I with List II

List I (Sociologist)	List II (Book)
A. K.M. Kapadia	I. Human society
B. G.F. Murdock	II. Marriage and Family in India
C. Kingsley Davis	III. Social structure
D. P.N. Prabhu	IV. Hindu Social Organization

Choose the correct option:
(a) (A)–(II), (B)–(III), (C)–(I), (D)–(IV)
(b) (A)–(I), (B)–(II), (C)–(III), (D)–(IV)
(c) (A)–(IV), (B)–(III), (C)–(II), (D)–(I)
(d) (A)–(III), (B)–(II), (C)–(IV), (D)–(I)

49. Match List A with List B:

List I (Books)	List II (Authors/Editors)
A. Family, Kinship, and Marriage in India	I. T.N. Madan
B. Changing Kinship, Family, and gender relations	II. Rajni Parliwala
C. Family and Kinship	III. Rajni Parliwala
D. Marrying in South Asia	IV. Patricia Uberoi, Ravinder Kaur, and Rajani Palriwala

Choose the correct option:
(a) (A)-(I), (B)-(III), (C)-(IV), (D)-(II)
(b) (A)-(II), (B)-(IV), (C)-(III), (D)-(I)
(c) (A)-(IV), (B)-(II), (C)-(I), (D)-(III)
(d) (A)-(III), (B)-(II), (C)-(I), (D)-(IV)

JUNE 2019

50. Match List-I with List-II:

List I (Books)	List II (Authors)
A. After Kinship	I. David M. Schneider
B. American Kinship	II. Janet Carsten
C. Structural Anthropology	III. Bob Simpson
D. The Theory of Social Structure	IV. Claude Levi-Strauss
	V. V. S. F. Nadel

Select the correct option from the options given below:
(a) (A)–(IV); (B)–(V); (C)–(II); (D)–(I)
(b) (A)–(III); (B)–(IV); (C)–(V); (D)–(I)
(c) (A)–(II); (B)–(I); (C)–(IV); (D)–(V)
(d) (A)–(I); (B)–(II); (C)–(III); (D)–(IV)

51. Kinship terminologies reflect a great deal about preferences and prohibitions of marriage. Which categories of relatives are preferred in Dravidian marriage as reflected in the terminology?
(a) Preference for 'sapinda' marriage
(b) Preference for cross-cousin marriage
(c) Preference for parallel cousin marriage
(d) Prohibited cross and parallel cousin marriage

52. 'Punaluan' as a form of family has been classified by
(a) G. P. Murdock
(b) P. N. Prabhu
(c) L. H. Morgan
(d) K. M. Kapadia

53. Which of the following practices do PNDT (1994) Act and its Amendments aim to prohibit?
(a) Abortion in India
(b) Sex-selective abortion in India
(c) Autonomy of women to abort a child
(d) Legal right to abort a fetus

54. When a newly married couple resides in the man's father's house this type of residence is termed as
(a) patrilocal
(b) virilocal
(c) matrilocal (d) neolocal

55. Which section of Indian Penal Code deals with LGBT?
(a) 376 (b) 377
(c) 487 (d) 497

56. Honour killing is aimed at protecting which of the following social institutions?
(a) Family and Caste
(b) Caste and Law
(c) Law and Marriage
(d) Women and Khap

57. Among the following 'Couvade' is best described by
(a) Husband leads the life of invalid
(b) Practice both husband and wife follow
(b) A kinship usage
(d) Relationship of love and emotion between the husband and the wife

58. Alliance Theory in Kinship Studies is associated with which of the following scholars?
(a) Kathleen Gough
(b) Pauline Kolenda
(c) Levi-Strauss
(d) A. R. Radcliffe-Brown

59. Why has ultrasound technology in reproductive medicine led to 'missing girls' in India but not in the West?
(a) High value of daughter
(b) Aversion to daughter
(c) Aversion to son
(d) Aversion to marriage

Answer Key

1. (c)
2. (b)
3. (b)
4. (c)
5. (b)
6. (a)
7. (a)
8. (b)
9. (a)
10. (c)
11. (a)
12. (a)
13. (c)
14. (d)
15. (a)
16. (d)
17. (c)
18. (b)
19. (c)
20. (a)
21. (d)
22. (b)
23. (c)
24. (c)
25. (a)
26. (b)
27. (a)
28. (a)
29. (a
30. (b)
31. (c)
32. (b)
33. (a)
34. (b)
35. (c)
36. (d)
37. (d)
38. (d)
39. (d)
40. (d)
41. (a)
42. (d)
43. (b)
44. (b)
45. (a)
46. (b)
47. (c)
48. (a)
49. (d)
50. (a)
51. (b)
52. (a)
53. (b)
54. (b)
55. (d)
56. (c)
57. (b)
58. (c)
59. (b)

Unit-IX

Science, Technology, and Society

Chapters:

Top: Photo credit: melitas / 123RF
Below: Photo Credit: wrightstudio / 123RF

CHAPTER

1 Evolution of Society with Science and Technology

LEARNING OBJECTIVES:

In this chapter, we will discuss the following important topics.

- History of technological development
- Virtual community
- Media: Print and electronics
- e-governance and surveillance society
- Technology and emerging political processes
- Technology and changing family relationships
- Technology and the changing healthcare system
- Food and technology
- Cybercrime

INTRODUCTION

Technology can be defined as the application of scientific theories to the practical purposes of human life. It is the sum total of the techniques, skills, and methods used in the production of goods and services or in the achievement of services such as scientific investigation.

Technology can refer to methods ranging from as simple as stone or wooden stick tools such as pully to the complex genetic engineering and information technology that has emerged since the 1980s.

The word 'technology' comes from the Greek word 'techne', meaning art and craft, and the word 'logos', meaning word and speech. It was earlier used to describe applied arts but is now used to describe advances and changes that affect the environment around us.

HISTORY OF TECHNOLOGICAL DEVELOPMENT

Thomas S. Kuhn in his book '*The Structure of Scientific Revolutions*' described, Science as a cycle of normal science and revolutionary science, Science is basically a normal science when it is used as it is for long period, but when it is interrupted by crises, it Leads to a shorter period of revolutionary science. The main engagement in the general science period is puzzle-solving activities. All scientists work as collaborators, not innovators, applying known solutions to problems.

Some, such as Lewis H. Morgan, Leslie White, and Gerhard Lenski, have declared technological progress to be the primary factor driving the development of human civilization. Morgan's concept of three major stages of social development (savageness, barbarism, and civilization) can be divided by technological milestones such as fire. White argued the measure by which to judge the development of culture was energy.

White distinguishes between five stages of human development:

i. First stage, people use their muscle energy.
ii. Second stage, they harness the energy of domesticated animals.

iii. Third stage, they harness the energy of plants (agricultural revolution).
iv. Fourth stage, they learn to use the energy of natural resources: coal, oil, and gas.
v. Fifth, they harness nuclear power.

Lenski's approach to development focuses on information. The more information and knowledge a given society has, the more advanced it is. He identifies four stages of human development based on the progress made in the history of communication.

i. First stage, information is passed on by genes.
ii. Second stage, human receives information through sensation, they can learn and impart information through experience.
iii. Third stage, humans begin to use signs and develop logic.
iv. Fourth stage, they can form symbols, and develop language and writing.

T. Veblen considered technology as the only explanation of a social change. For Veblin change in society can only be introduced by the change in technology. WF Ogburn states that technology changes society by changing our environment to which we in turn adapt. This change usually occurs in the physical environment and the adjustments we make to these changes often modify customs and social institutions.

Modern Technology which Changed the World

Printing press – The printing press was invented in the Holy Roman Empire by the German Johannes Gutenberg around 1440. The printing press spread over several decades to more than 200 cities in a dozen European countries.

By 1500, printing presses operating throughout Western Europe had already produced over 20 million volumes. In the 16th century, with the press spread far and wide, their production increased tenfold to an estimated 150 to 200 million copies. Operating a press became so synonymous with the printing enterprise that it gave its name to a whole new branch of media, the press.

Water and steam power – The Industrial Revolution was the transition to new manufacturing processes in Europe and the United States from approximately 1760 to the period between 1820 and 1840. The increasing use of steam power and water power, the development of machine tools, and the rise of the mechanized factory system.

Communication technology – The Second Industrial Revolution (starting around 1850) is also known as the Technical Revolution. This revolution led to the widespread adoption of technological systems such as telegram, railroad networks, sewage systems, etc.

The Green Revolution, or Third Agricultural Revolution, is a set of research technology transfer initiatives occurring between the late 1950s and 1960s that increased agricultural production worldwide.

The key processes of the Green Revolution include:

1. Utilization of final capital and technical inputs,
2. Adoption of modern scientific methods of farming,
3. Use of high-yielding seeds,
4. Rational use of chemical fertilizers,
5. Agriculture Consolidation of land holdings.

Biotechnology – Modern biotechnology originated in the mid-1970s with new advances in genetics, immunology, and biochemistry. Biotechnology includes all techniques that use living organisms or substances from organisms to produce or alter a product, cause changes in plants or animals, or develop microorganisms for specific purposes.

Electrification – Electrification spread rapidly in the 20th century. At the beginning of the century electric power was for the most part only available to the wealthy in a few major cities such as New York, London, Paris, and Newcastle upon Tyne, but it was not until the invention of the World Wide Web in the 1990s that it was estimated that more electricity could be supplied worldwide. 62 percent of households in the U.S. have electricity, including about a third of households in the rural developing world.

Changing Notions of Time and Space

The sociology of space is a subdiscipline of sociology. It is based on the social as well as the physical constitution of space. It is concerned with understanding the physical complexity of social practices, institutional forces, and the interaction of humans and space.

Simmel wrote on the sociology of space in his book 'Sociology: Investigations on the Forms of Society'. His concerns included the process of cosmopolitanization and the separation of places of leisure in modern economic societies. Other eminent people who have dealt with the concept of space are Henri Lefebvre, David Harvey, Manuel Castells, Edward Soja, etc.

Martina Low developed the idea of a 'relational' model of space, which focuses on the 'ordering' of living beings and social objects, and examines how space is created in processes of perception, memory, or thought and expresses itself in the form of social structures.

From a sociological perspective, Martina Low follows the 'theory of structuration' proposed by Anthony Giddens, whose concept of 'duality of structure' extends Low's sociological terms to '"duality of space'. For Low like agency and structure, living being and space determine each other.

The most important exponent of Marxist spatial theory was Henri Lefebvre. He proposed a 'social space'" where the relations of production are reproduced and dialectical contradictions were spatial rather than temporal. Lefebvre sees the social production of space as a dialectical interaction between three factors. The space is formed:

i. By 'spatial practice', means reproduced space in everyday life
ii. By '"representation of space', meaning the space as it is developed cognitively
iii. From 'spaces of representation', by which Lefebvre meant complex symbols and conceptual spaces

A decisive new impetus was given to Marxist spatial theory by David Harvey, who was interested in the effects of the transition from 'Fordism' to 'flexible accumulation' on the experience of space and time. He shows how various innovations at the economic and technological levels have dissolved the crisis-prone inflexibility of the Fordist system, thus increasing the turnover rate of capital. This causes a general acceleration of economic cycles. According to Harvey, the result is 'time-space compression'.

Henri Lefebvre in his work *'the production of Space'* says that space embraces many intersections. This means that we need to consider how the different modes of spatial production relate to each other. He argues that there are three aspects to our spatial existence. These are:

i. The First space is a material place, 'the spatial practice of a society conceals the place of that society, it proposes and presupposes it in a dialectical conversation, it produces it slowly and surely as it owns and appropriates'.
ii. The second space is mental space or imagined space, it is 'the conceptual space, the space of scientists, planners, urbanites, technocratic subversives, and social engineers, as a certain kind of artist with a scientific bent, all of whom identify with that which remains and that which is conceived is reckoned with'.
iii. The third space (social space/living space) '"space is perceptibly alive through its associated images and symbols'.

Flows and Boundaries

Flow – The concept of flow from psychological perspectives represent an optimal state of consciousness, a positive psychological state. It is a condition in which people become so engrossed in a task that nothing else seems important.

The idea of flow is similar to the feeling of being in the zone or groove. The flow state is the best state of essential motivation, where one is fully engaged in what one is doing.

Boundaries – Social boundaries are established social rules that control individuals in society, they are considered typical because most people in a society agree that they suggest the proper way to live. Social boundaries also allow people to quickly assess others.

We categorize people into various descriptions within the first few seconds of meeting them. Social boundaries make it easy to determine what is similar and different about us in comparison to the people we meet.

Symbolic boundaries are a theory of how people form social groups. Symbolic boundaries are conceptual distinctions made by social actors that separate people into groups and generate a sense of equality and group membership.

Symbolic boundaries are a necessary but insufficient condition for social change. Only when symbolic boundaries are widely agreed upon can they take on a constraining character.

Émile Durkheim regarded the symbolic boundary between the sacred and the profane as the deepest of all social facts, and the one from which lesser symbolic boundaries derive. Mary Douglas has emphasized the role of symbolic boundaries in private and public events experienced even in a secular society. Erving Goffman has emphasized symbolic boundaries in his analysis of dramaturgical analysis.

In recent years, the idea of 'boundaries' has come to play an important role in the social sciences. It is linked to social and collective identity, census categories, cultural capital, racial and ethnic group status, hegemonic masculinity, group authority, immigration, etc.

In the Context of Globalization

In the context of globalization, flow means the exchange and interaction of international trade, ideas, culture, etc. The term "flow" is used to describe any type of domestic, cross-border, and broad international movement of goods, services, capital, people, thought, or culture. Globalization involves the linking of people and places to each other by various types of global flows. This includes:

Capital flow–There is a huge flow of money through the stock markets of the world every day. Investment banks, pension funds, and private citizens buy and sell shares and money in different currencies in order to make a profit.

Labour flow–Record migration has been recorded in recent years despite restrictions imposed by several governments. Soon a quarter billion in the world will be economic migrants. Some states have special needs for migrant workers. For example, Qatar is dependent on Indian construction workers.

Product flow–The size of the flow of manufactured goods has increased manifold in recent years, driven by low production costs in China and even lower-wage economies such as Bangladesh and Vietnam.

Service flows – By 2040, India is expected to be the second-largest economy in the world and some of its economic success is attributed to the call center services that Indian workers provide to large US and EU companies.

Information Flows

The Internet has brought real-time communication between distant locations, allowing goods and services to be purchased at the click of a button. As of June 2019, Facebook reports an estimated 2.4 billion Monthly Active Users generating countless numbers of "likes" daily.

According to social scientists, globalization has blurred economic distinctions between countries, creating a "borderless world" in which economic decisions are made without reference to national boundaries.

Globalization has had an impact on world cross-border flows. There has been an increase in international economic activity which has expanded world trade and general capital flows. Goods are flowing easily across national borders through reduced trade barriers and new transportation methods.

Economic integration lowers barriers between national economies, and governments lower tariffs and other trade barriers to strengthen trade and help create a borderless world. Technological advances in communication have also led to the integration of economies.

VIRTUAL COMMUNITY

A virtual community is a social grouping of individuals who connect through specific social media to advance mutual interests or goals, potentially crossing geographical and political boundaries. Some of the most widespread virtual communities operating under social networking services are online communities or inter-communities. A virtual community is a group of people who may or may not meet each other face-to-face, and who exchange words and ideas through the mediation of a digital network.

The first use of the term virtual community appeared in an article by Gene Youngblood written in 1984 but published in 1986 about the Electronic Cafe (1984), an art project created by Kit Galloway and Sherry Rabinowitz, based in Los Angeles. The project connected the five restaurants and an art museum through a live video link.

The term gained popularity when Howard Reingold wrote the article '*The Virtual Community*' (1993). Rheingold defines virtual communities as social groupings that emerge from the net when enough people engage in those public discussions with enough human emotion for long enough to form webs of personal relationships in cyberspace.

For Steven Jones a virtual community is a 'space' in cyberspace that is ' based on knowledge and information on the common beliefs and practices of a society separated from the physical space'.

According to Sandy Stone 'Virtual communities are passage points for collections of common beliefs and practices that unite people who are physically separated.' (Stone, 1991).

Preece identifies four components of an online community:

i. People
ii. Shared purpose
iii. General policies
iv. Information Systems

Fernbach and Thompson consider virtual communities as a set of social relationships constructed in cyberspace through repeated interactions within a specific boundary. Here are some of the most prominent features of virtual communities:

i. Participants are often anonymous or use pseudonyms, for example, 007.
ii. Groups can be quite large, with hundreds or thousands of participants.
iii. There are active participants, but there are also many passive readers.
iv. Group membership is often temporary
v. group structure is highly flexible

Virtual communities are used for a wide variety of social and professional groups. Interaction between community members varies from personal to purely formal. Early research into the existence of media-based communities was concerned with the nature of reality, and whether communities could actually exist through media, which may place virtual community research within the definition of social science.

In the seventeenth century, scholars belonging to the Royal Society of London formed a community through an exchange of letters. Melvin Weber, in 1963, coined the concept '*Communities without propinquity*' to express such groupings. And '*Communities liberated*' was the name given by Barry Wellman in 1979, which began the modern era of thinking about non-local communities.

Also, Benedict Anderson's '*Imagined Communities*' in 1983 described how various technologies such as national newspapers contributed to the development of national and regional consciousness among early nation-states.

Sherry Turkle, professor of Social Studies of Science and Technology at MIT, analyzed such groups in her 1995 book '*Life on the Screen: Identity in the Age of the Internet*' and concluded that the Internet is a place where acts of discrimination are less likely to occur. she argues that discrimination is easier in a reality where it is easier to identify the identity of a person.

Virtual World

Virtual worlds are the most interactive of all virtual community forms. In this type of virtual community, people stay connected by becoming avatars in the computer-based world. Users create their own avatar character, from choosing the avatar's outfit to designing the avatar's home and controlling their character's life and interactions with other characters in a 3-D virtual world.

It is similar to a computer game, although there is no objective for the players. A virtual world gives users the opportunity to create and operate imaginary lives in a virtual world. The characters within the world can talk to each other and have conversations almost exactly like people actually do. For example, characters can socialize with each other and have intimate relationships online.

Cyberspace

Cyberspace is a virtual space characterized by the use of electronics and the electromagnetic spectrum to store, modify, and exchange data through network systems and associated physical infrastructure. In fact, cyberspace can be seen as an interconnection of human physical geography. William Gibson is sometimes credited with inventing or popularizing the term in his novel Neuromancer.

MEDIA: PRINT AND ELECTRONICS

Media refers to various means of communication. It refers to a communication outlet or tool used to store and distribute information or data. The term media refers to components of the mass communications industry, such as print media, publishing, photography, cinema, radio, television, news media, digital media, and advertising.

In the general sense, the word media is the plural form of medium. In mass communication, media refers to the basic means of mass communication, which help in the dissemination of messages related to the latest news, education, sports, entertainment, and promotion of goods and services to a large group of people in a short period of time.

Print Media

Print media is a form of mass media in which news or information is shared through printed publications. Print media is the oldest medium of sharing information/news. Print media use printing to spread news, information, or message among a large number of people.

Print provides wider access to knowledge about a particular subject and enables future generations to build directly on earlier intellectual achievements without the changes that result from oral traditions. Print media is today being challenged by its electronic counterpart.

The earliest known form of printing on paper was woodblock printing, which appeared in China before 220 AD for printing cloth. However, paper printing did not come into existence till the seventh century. Later developments in printing technology include movable type invented by Bei Sheng around 1040 AD and the printing press invented by Johannes Gutenberg in the 15th century, who introduced printing to Europe with his mechanical movable type printing press.

Printing consists of at least four distinct items: (i) the manuscript, that is, the text to be printed; (ii) the composition of matter either by hand or by machine; (iii) the physical medium, say, paper on which the material is to be printed; and (iv) the ink with which the material is to be printed.

Electronic Media

Electronic media is a form of mass media in which news or information is shared through an electronic medium. Electronic media uses electronics or electromechanical energy for the audience to access the content. This electronic information can be accessed in a number of ways, via the Internet, television, or radio.

The main types of electronic media include television news, news through mobile apps, etc. Live show, live discussion, and live reporting is possible in electronic media as it is based on the instant update method. Electronic media has emerged as a powerful source for making people aware. Latest happenings around the world.

Electronic media are used for the storage, distribution, and transmission of information in electronic form. It includes magnetic, optical, digital, and magneto-optical media. It is making a profit from electronic publishing all over the world.

Difference between Print Media and Electronic Media

- **i.** Print media is a form of mass media that creates, and distributes news and information through printed publications. Electronic media is a form of mass media that creates and distributes news and information through electronic means.
- **ii.** Print media is the older form of media. Electronic media is a relatively new and advanced form of media.
- **iii.** One must be literate to go through the print media as one needs to read the information in it. Literacy is not a primary requirement to go through electronic media as one can see or hear the information.
- **iv.** Editing and updating print media requires more time as new printed material needs to be issued. Electronic media can be edited and updated on real-time basis.
- **v.** Print media is not available 24*7 rather it comes in intervals like daily printed newspapers, monthly magazines, etc. Electronic media is available 24x7, for example, news apps on smartphones, news channels on TV, etc.
- **vi.** The main types of print media include printed newspapers, magazines, journals, and books. The main types of electronic media include information or news through Television, smartphones, laptops, etc.
- **vii.** Live show, live discussion, and live reporting is not possible in print media. Live show, live discussion, and live reporting is possible in electronic media.
- **viii.** Print media is more reader-friendly. Electronic media is more audience friendly.

Visual Media

Visual media is a visual mode of disseminating information which includes, blueprints, slides, transparencies, photographs, illustrations, and drawings:

Blueprint – 'A blueprint is a photographic copy of a preliminary plan for a building or machine with white lines on a blue background'. Many libraries of industrial enterprises, consultancy firms, etc. have a huge collection of blueprints.

Slides – 'A slide is a small piece of photographic film in a frame which, when light is passed through it, shows a large image on a screen or plain surface'. A projector is required to use the slides. Slides are used when presenting papers at conferences; delivering a lecture to a class or any other gathering; Demonstration of the working of a machine, the side effects of a medicine, the usefulness of a specific fertilizer, etc.

Slide shows are also organized in villages to educate illiterate farmers, artisans, and others about better methods of farming, healthy living, low-cost housing, the utility of family planning, etc.

Audio-visual media (A-V media) combine both audio media and visual media. With the help of this medium people not only see but also hear. Movies, video recording, and television are some examples of A-V media. Many documentary films have been produced on almost any topic in the world.

Social Media

Social media are interactive technologies that allow the creation, sharing, and exchange of information, ideas, career interests, and other forms of expression through virtual communities and networks. Social media is a computer-based technology that facilitates the sharing of ideas, thoughts, and information through the creation of virtual networks and communities.

Social media is Internet-based and provides instant electronic communication of content to users. Content includes personal information, documents, videos, and photos. Users engage with social media via a computer, tablet, or smartphone through web-based software or applications.

Some of the most popular social media websites with over 100 million registered users include Facebook, Instagram, QZone, Weibo, Twitter, Tumblr, Baidu Tieba, and LinkedIn. Depending on the definition, other popular platforms sometimes referred to as social media services include YouTube, QQ, Quora, Telegram, WhatsApp, LINE, Snapchat, Pinterest, Viber, Reddit, Discord, VK, Microsoft Teams, and many more.

Social media originated as a way to interact with friends and family but was later adopted by businesses that wanted to take advantage of a popular new communication method to reach customers. The power of social media is the ability to connect and share information with anyone or many people on earth at once.

According to the latest data, as of January 2023, there were 5.16 billion Internet users worldwide, which is 64.4 percent of the global population. However, current trends suggest that two-thirds of the world's population should be online by the end of 2023. These figures suggest that more than 9 out of 10 Internet users now use social media every month.

Social media can take the form of a variety of technology-enabled activities. These activities include photo sharing, blogging, social gaming, social networks, video sharing, business networks, virtual worlds, reviews, and more. Even governments and politicians use social media to connect with electors and voters.

For individuals, social media is used to keep in touch with friends and extended family. Some people will use various social media applications to network for career opportunities, find like-minded people around the world, and share their thoughts, feelings, insights, and emotions. People who engage in these activities are part of a virtual social network.

For businesses, social media is an important tool. Companies use the platform to find and connect with customers, drive sales through advertising and promotion, measure consumer trends, and provide customer service or support.

E-GOVERNANCE AND SURVEILLANCE SOCIETY

e-Governance

Generally, governance refers to the system of directing and controlling the actions, affairs, policies, and actions of a political entity, organization, or nation. The concept of e-governance has arisen recently, e-governance is an attempt by the government to use information technology to improve the efficiency or effectiveness of the executive function of the government.

e-Governance is the application of ICT to government business processes for good governance. In other words, e-governance is the use of ICT by the public sector with the aim of improving information and service delivery, encouraging citizen participation in decision-making, and making the government more accountable, transparent, and efficient.

The Ministry of Information and Technology says that e-governance goes far beyond the computerization of stand-alone back-office operations. It implies a fundamental change in government functioning and a new set of responsibilities for the legislature, executive, judiciary, and citizens. According to the Comptroller and Auditor General of the UK, e-governance refers to providing public access to information through the Internet by government departments and their agencies.

e-Governance can be defined as the application of communication and information technology for providing government services, exchange of information, transactions, and integration of already existing services and information portals.

e-Governance (Electronic Governance) is the integration of ICT (Information and Communication Technology) in all processes, with the aim of increasing government capacity to meet the needs of the general public. The basic objective of e-governance is to simplify the processes for everyone at the national, state, and local levels, i.e., government, citizens, businesses, etc.

Good governance can be viewed as the application of economic, political, and administrative authority to smoothly manage the business activities of a country at the national and local levels.

The perspective of e-Governance is 'the use of technologies that help govern and control'. The central goal of e-Governance is to reach the beneficiary and ensure that their service needs are met. Ideally, the government would automatically recognize the importance of achieving this goal in order to maximize its efficiency.

e-Governance in India

In India, the main thrust for e-Governance was provided by the launch of NICNET - National Satellite-based Computer Network - in 1987. This was followed by the District Information System of National Informatics Center (DISNIC) program to computerize all district offices in the country, for which free hardware and software were offered to state governments. NICNET was extended to all district headquarters through state capitals by 1990. In the ensuing years, a large number of e-Governance initiatives were set up at both the Union and State levels with ongoing computerization, tele-connectivity, and internet connectivity.

Types of Participation in e-Governance

G2G (Government to Government): When the exchange of information and services takes place within the perimeter of the government, it is called G2G interaction. It can be horizontal, that is, between different government entities, and vertical, that is, between national, state, and local government entities, and within different levels of the entity.

G2C (Government to Citizen): The interaction between the government and the general public is G2C interaction. Here an interface has been established between the government and the citizens, which enables the citizens to get access to a variety of public services. Citizens have the freedom to share their views and grievances on government policies anytime, anywhere.

G2B (Government to Business): In this case, e-Governance helps the business class to interact seamlessly with the government. It aims to eliminate red tape, save time, and cost, and establish transparency in the business environment while interacting with the government.

G2E (Government to Employees): The government of any country is the largest employer and hence it also deals with the employees on a regular basis, as do other employers. ICT helps in making the interaction between the government and the employees faster and more efficient, as well as increasing their satisfaction level by providing perquisites and additional benefits.

National e-Governance Plan

The National e-Governance Plan (NeGP) was prepared by the Department of Electronics and Information Technology (DeitY) and the Department of Administrative Reforms and Public Grievances (DARPG) in 2006.

NeGP aims at improving the delivery of government services to citizens and businesses with the following vision: "Making all government services accessible to the common man through Common Service Delivery Outlets and providing efficiency, transparency, and reliability of such services at affordable cost" To ensure that the basic needs of the common man are met.

In India, the government is also providing investment incentives in terms of tax concessions and setting up e-zones for ICT-based industries. There are agencies such as the Indian National ICT Council and projects such as the e-Governance Initiative that are responsible for e-Governance.

The National Informatics Center is credited with helping the Government of India adopt IT in the 1990s and has also helped spread the technology to e-Governance. In India, the main thrust for e-governance was provided by the launch of NICNET, a national satellite-based computer network, in 1987.

Based on the advice of the Second Administrative Reforms Commission, the Government of India formulated a National e-Governance Plan (NeGP) in 2003.

Advantages of e-Governance

Speed – Digital technology makes communication faster, the internet, and smartphones have enabled the instant transmission of high amounts of data all over the world.

Cost-effective – In the traditional system, a major portion of the government expenditure goes into the cost of purchasing stationery for official purposes. Letters and written records consume a lot of stationery. However, replacing them with smartphones and the internet could save crores of rupees in expenditure every year.

Transparency – The use of e-Governance helps in making all the operations of the business transparent. All government information can be uploaded on the Internet. Citizens have access to particular information whenever they want it, at the click of a mouse, or at the touch of a finger.

Accountability – Transparency is directly linked to accountability. Once the actions of the government are available, we can hold them accountable for their actions.

Some other benefits of e-Governance include reduced corruption, increased convenience, increased GDP, the direct participation of constituents, and expanded reach of the government.

Disadvantages of e-Governance

High setup cost and technical difficulties. Technology also has its disadvantages. In particular, the setup cost is very high and the machines have to be maintained regularly. Often, computers and the Internet can also break down, disrupting government work and services.

Cybercrime or leakage of personal information. There is always a risk of theft of private data of citizens stored in government servers. Cybercrime is a serious issue; a data breach can cause the public to lose faith in the government's ability to govern.

Surveillance Society

Surveillance is the monitoring of behavior, activities, or information for the purpose of gathering, influencing, managing, or directing information. This may involve remote observation via electronic devices, such as closed-circuit television (CCTV), or the interception of electronically transmitted information, such as Internet traffic. It can also include simple technical methods, such as human intelligence gathering and mail interception.

Surveillance societies are societies that function, in part, because of the extensive collection, recording, storage, analysis, and application of information about individuals and groups in those societies as they go about their lives.

Since the early 1990s surveillance technologies such as closed-circuit television (CCTV) and biometric identification documents for use in crossing national borders have been increasingly deployed in an effort to monitor and protect public spaces, particularly those which are considered 'risky places'.

Many organizations are using technology, such as facial recognition, in an effort to help reduce crime. The danger with surveillance is that it becomes embedded within the systems, the structures, and the interests it represents. Its use is taken for granted and its consequences go unnoticed.

As data travels silently across international borders, between national states, and within transnational corporations, the impact of surveillance becomes even more difficult to identify, regulate, and debate. For us, it is important that this power is used fairly, responsibly, and with due respect for human rights, civil liberties, and the law, based on oversight of activities and personal data.

Surveillance\Panoptic Society of Michel Foucault

In his 1975 book '*Discipline and Punish*', Foucault argued that French society redefined punishment through new 'humane'" practices of 'discipline' and 'surveillance', which were used in prisons, mental asylums, and schools, carried out in new institutions such as workplaces and factories.

Michel Foucault's seminal contribution to criminology focused on how the nature of crime control shifted from using the threat of violence and fear of being physically punished to controlling through fear of surveillance.

Foucault argues that disciplinary power developed significantly at the end of the 19th century with Jeremy Bentham's new design of the prison, known as the panopticon, which included a central observation tower and prison cells surrounding its walls. The enclosures were arranged in such a way that prisoners could potentially be subject to observation at any time, but could not see if they were being watched. Because of this, prisoners had to self-monitor their behavior so that, in effect, they could discipline themselves as a result of being under constant surveillance.

Mass Surveillance

Mass surveillance is the complex surveillance of an entire population or a large portion of a population. Surveillance is often carried out by local and federal governments or government organizations, such as the National Security Agency (NSA) and the Federal Bureau of Investigation (FBI), but it can also be carried out by corporations either on behalf of governments or on their own initiative.

The legality and permissions required to engage in mass surveillance vary, depending on the laws and judicial systems of each country. This is the single most indicative distinguishing feature of totalitarian regimes. It is also often contrasted with targeted surveillance.

Mass surveillance has often been cited as necessary to fight terrorism, prevent crime and social unrest, protect national security, and control populations. In contrast, mass surveillance has been equally criticized for violating privacy rights, limiting civil and political rights and freedoms, and being illegal under some legal or constitutional systems.

Another criticism is that increased mass surveillance may lead to the development of a surveillance state or an electronic police state where civil liberties are violated or political dissent is curtailed by programs such as COINTELPRO, the FBI began a counterintelligence Program launched in 1956 to disrupt the activities of the Communist Party of the United States. Such a state can be called a totalitarian state.

Smart City

A smart city is an urban area that uses a variety of electronic methods and sensors to collect data. Insights derived from that data are used to efficiently manage assets, resources, and services. In turn, that data is used to improve operations across the city.

The development of smart cities has seen an increase in the adoption of surveillance technologies by governments, although the primary purpose of surveillance in such cities is to use information and communication technologies to control the urban environment making the city livable.

The implementation of such technology by many cities has resulted in increased efficiency in urban infrastructure as well as improved community participation. Sensors and systems monitor the infrastructure, operations, and activities of a smart city and aim to help it run more efficiently.

For example, the city may use less electricity. Its traffic moves more smoothly with less latency. Its citizens use the city with greater security. Threats can be dealt with faster. prevent civil violations of regulations, and city infrastructure. Power distribution and roads with traffic lights, for example, dynamically adjust to respond to varying conditions.

TECHNOLOGY AND EMERGING POLITICAL PROCESSES

Science and technology began in Europe as a revolt against medieval intellectual attitudes and technology as a new mode of production. It was only through two to three centuries of social and political struggle that they were able to establish science as a major intellectual and social activity.

Based on the approach they have applied to the study of science, philosophers, and historians of science can be mainly divided into two schools of thought known as 'internalists' and 'externalists'.

The 'internalist'" school holds that science, both in its content and pace of development, is independent of social and political forces. For those who regard science as nothing less than an "institutional truth", the community of scientists is very special and exemplary.

Unlike most human communities, the community of scientists is often seen by them as democratic, disinterested, tolerant, and above all, rational. While there are many variations of such a view, this position has been largely supported by such scientist-philosophers as Jakub Bronowski, Anatole Rappaport, and Jacques Monod.

However, many modern accounts of the development of science are 'externalist' to a greater or lesser extent and reflect the belief that social and political factors play an important role in the development of both science and technology.

This approach values science as a social activity adapted to the socio-political and economic context in which it develops. Those who have supported such a view of science include John Bernal, Thomas Kuhn, and Paul Feyerabend.

Politics and Technology

Politics and technology involve the concepts, systems, personalities, efforts, and social movements that include the Internet and other information and communication technologies (ICTs). Social scientists have begun to explore how internet technologies influence political communication and participation, especially in terms of what is known as the public sphere.

The increased availability of mobile phones, and subsequent access to the public sphere, has increased the ability of individuals and groups to focus on and organize particular issues.

Recently, social media has emerged as one of the major platforms of politics. Millions of users can learn about policies and statements, interact with political leaders, and organize and voice their opinion on political matters. Political campaigns are also using social media sites to reach voters using political advertising.

In the 2008 US presidential campaign, the Obama campaign's use of Facebook, YouTube, and Twitter was widely credited with helping President Barack Obama achieve a historic victory.

The Internet enables civic participation, gives people a platform to voice their opinions, holds politicians accountable, and improves human rights in the larger context. Information technology tools are influencing political events and revolutionizing the political process all over the world. Technological tools have been used in innovative ways to improve accountability and contribute to the welfare of people during the Ebola epidemic, the Syrian refugee crisis, etc.

YouTube and Twitter have become the main means of communication used by the government and dissidents, as seen in Libya and the Syrian uprising.

The concept of the public sphere can be understood as public spaces in which private citizens interact and share information and ideas relevant to society. These may include, for example, town halls, public places, markets, and tea shops.

In Jürgen Habermas' book *'The Structural Transformation of the Public Sphere – An Inquiry into a Category of Bourgeois Society'*, he defines the public sphere as 'a sphere of social life in which public opinion can be formed'.

Howard Rheingold states that the virtual spaces created through the Internet and related information and communication technologies have led to the emergence of a new type of digital public sphere.

Some scholars have alternatively conceptualized it as a virtual public realm. These new virtual spaces can be used in much the same way as traditional, offline spaces: i.e., as 'free spaces' to discuss and debate ideas of public importance.

Just as the public sphere is a composite of 'every interaction in which private individuals come together to form a public', the digital public sphere also includes all forms of new media, such as chat rooms, website comment sections, and social media, in Private citizens who engage in discourse as a public.

Research has shown that increased use of social media leads to an increase in some types of political engagement and participation. Rabia Karakaya Polat, a politics and technology scholar, finds that the Internet leads to a more informed and better society. The Internet enables information to be disseminated at a greater rate than traditional means at a lower cost.

The digital public sphere has the potential to promote democratic culture and enhance citizens' ability to challenge the political and economic power of governments and corporations, such as through online protests, activism campaigns, and social movements.

The most obvious way that technology affects politics is as a tool for political actors such as politicians, governments, and other organizations to better identify, engage and rally members of the public to their cause, as well as disseminate political messages. as a tool to do.

According to author Bruce Gronbeck, the various functions of campaigns, winning the idea battle, converting and mobilizing supporters, and providing informational claims and themes to supporters, are normally performed through technologically mediated communication channels.

State Policy, and Science and Technology

Pierre Lorty, President of the Canadian Academy of Engineering says that 'As governments grapple with ever more complex policy problems, science, and technology must support government efforts to provide an evidence base for making decisions and manage risk and uncertainty'.

Government, at any level, 'can be viewed as an information system in which data is collected, organized, stored, managed, analyzed and retrieved, all ultimately for the purposes of decision-making'.

There is increasing use of information technology (IT) in decision-making within city governments to meet the demands of result-oriented management to make governments more efficient by reducing administrative costs and improving service delivery.

IT can contribute to the policy decision-making process by providing accurate and timely information to the decision-makers. Managing information is essential for city government managers to reduce uncertainty and ambiguity about goals and cause-effect relationships in the decision-making process.

Digital Services provided by the Government of India

Bharat Broadband Network Limited (BBNL), a Government of India entity that executes the BharatNet project, is the custodian of the Digital India (DI) project. Some of the facilities provided through this initiative are Bharat Net, Digital Locker, E-Education, E-Health, E-Sign, E-Shopping, and National Scholarship Portal. As part of Digital India, the Government of India planned to start botnet cleaning centers.

The National e-Governance Plan aims to bring all front-end government services online. MyGov.in is a platform for sharing inputs and views on matters of policy and governance. It is a platform for citizen engagement in governance through 'Discuss', 'Do' and 'Disseminate' approaches.

UMANG (Unified Mobile Application for New-Age Governance) is the Government of India's all-in-one single unified secure multi-channel multi-platform multi-lingual multi-service freeware mobile apps for over 1,200 central and state government services.

The e-Sign Framework allows citizens to digitally sign a document online using Aadhaar authentication.

- Swachh Bharat Mission (SBM) mobile app is being used by people and government organizations to achieve the goals of the Swachh Bharat Mission.
- The Digital Locker facility will help citizens to digitally store their important documents like PAN Card, Passport, Marksheet, and Degree Certificates. Digital Locker will provide secure access to government-issued documents. It uses the authentication services provided by

Aadhaar. It aims to eliminate the use of physical documents and enables the sharing of verified electronic documents across government agencies.

Information Technology Act 2000–2008 (Amendment)

The Indian Parliament passed the Information Technology Amendment Act of 2008 without much debate, giving the government the legal power to tap all communications without a court order or warrant. Section 69 of this Act states that the Central Government or a State Government or any officer thereof specially authorized by the Central Government or a State Government may if satisfied that it is necessary so to do in the interest of sovereignty or integrity, access any computer resource intercept, monitor, or decrypt any information received or stored through.

With every Indian being given a UID from the Unique Identification Authority of India since February 2011, the government will be able to track people in real-time. A national population registry of all citizens will be established by the 2011 census, during which fingerprints, and eye irises will be scanned along with GPS records of each household.

Digital Divide and Inclusion

The digital divide refers to the gap between haves and has not of ICT, it is about how people in less developed countries have less access to information and communication technologies than people in more developed countries. For example, the world's most developed regions, such as North America and Western Europe, each have the highest Internet penetration rates of over 80%, while the least developed countries, such as Africa and South Asia, have less than 30%.

However, other research has shown that even within more developed countries such as the United States, the digital divide between high and low socioeconomic classes and different education levels persists. Therefore, a digital divide is an unequal distribution in access, use, and influence of information and communication technologies (ICT) among any number of district groups.

The divide between different countries or regions of the world is referred to as the global digital divide, which examines this technological gap between developing and developed countries internationally.

Until well before the turn of the 20th century, the digital divide primarily referred to the divide between people who did not have telephone access, after the late 1990s the term came to be used primarily to describe the divide between those with and without Internet access, especially broadband access.

Social scientists argue that the traditional online public sphere has historically not been open or accessible to disadvantaged or marginalized groups in society, such as women or people from the lower classes. They believe that online spaces are more open and thus can help increase inclusive political participation from marginalized groups. In particular, anonymous online spaces should allow all individuals to speak on an equal footing with others.

Digital India is a campaign launched by the Government of India on 1 July 2015 by Indian Prime Minister Narendra Modi to ensure that government services are made available to citizens digitally by improving online infrastructure and increasing internet connectivity or the country. The initiative includes plans to connect rural areas with high-speed internet networks. It includes three main components-

i. development of secure and stable digital infrastructure,
ii. digitally delivering government services and
iii. universal digital literacy.

TECHNOLOGY AND CHANGING FAMILY RELATIONSHIPS

Science and technology are essential elements of modern life. They transcend local boundaries and touch the lives of all. The development of mankind can also be seen in the context of technological development. The invention of fire and the wheel changed the face of mankind. Different historical eras such as hunter-gatherers, farming societies, and industrialist societies, differ from each other in terms of technological progress.

Technological factors represent conditions created by men that have a profound effect on their lives. Technology is a product of civilization. According to Karl Marx, the formation of social relations and mental perceptions and attitudes are also dependent on technology.

Thorsten Veblen considered technology as the only explanation of the social change. W.F. Ogburn states that technology changes society by changing the environment to which we adapt. This change usually occurs in the physical environment and the adjustments we make to these changes often modify customs and social institutions.

Gerhard Lenski emphasizes the importance of technology within a society and how it causes a society to grow and change. But communication technologies, while functional, can produce unintended consequences, such as a reduction in family interaction.

Symbolic interactionism, introduced by George Herbert Mead, highlights the importance of social interaction for the development of the individual, the formation of social roles, and the strengthening of social bonds. If the use of communication technology increases isolation and interferes with social interaction, it will be very problematic, especially as the types of family interactions explained by Mead are so important to socialization and the integrity of social groups.

Today's family is gradually moving towards materialism, individualism, and liberalism. The task of setting moral standards for children and adolescents has been largely taken over by peer groups, mass media, etc. In other words, the influence of the family on the socialization and personality development of individuals is gradually diminishing.

The results of these changes are visible in the form of child neglect, behavioral problems in children, indiscipline among youth, alcoholism, neglect of elders, abuse of elders, abandonment, divorce etc.

Many functions of the family have been taken over by other agencies. Marriage is losing its sanctity. It is treated as a civil contract rather than a sacred bond. Marriages are becoming more and more unstable. Cases of divorce, abandonment, and separation are on the rise.

Technology has raised the status of women, but it has also contributed to tension and stress in the relationship between men and women in the home. The religion is losing its hold on the members.

In The Big Disconnect, Dr. Steiner-Adair describes how electronic devices are shaping children's lives, especially their relationships with important people in their lives. And while the "disconnect" is most apparent in homes with teenagers, where parents and children often tend to live on different planets, electronic devices have exposed older children to a host of new dangers, from nude selfies to cyberbullying.

In '*Is Technology Creating a Family Divide*', Dr. Jim Taylor discusses how the more time individuals spend on technology, the more time they pull away from their family lives.

In '*Technoference: How Technology Can Hurt Relationships*', Brandon McDaniel outlines the damage that technology can do to relationships.

The Internet has certainly provided new possibilities for electronic communication, but critics argue that it also has a dark side too. One area of particular concern for young children is the ability to access and download pornographic material. Internet users can download pornographic photos, have frank sexual conversations with distant 'playmates', play erotic games, or purchase tickets for a solo cruise. In recent years, sexual predators have also used the Internet to identify potential victims.

Technological determinism is a reductionist theory that holds that a society's technology determines the development of its social structure and cultural values. The term is believed to have originated from Thorstein Veblen.

Technological determinism seeks to show technological development, the media, or technology as a whole, as a major factor in social change. According to this theory, changes in family patterns and relationships are determined by technology.

Social constructivist approaches oppose the key assumption underpinning technological determinism that technology is an independent, exogenous, and autonomous entity or force that drives social change.

Social scientists such as Pinch and Bijker (1984) and Grint and Woolgar challenge the essential assumption that technologies have inherent characteristics, they suggest that the characteristics, functioning, and successes of technologies derive not from their intrinsic characteristics, but from the broader socio-political contexts in which they are designed, developed, and adopted. Technologies can shape and influence human actions, but ultimately human actors have full control over the socio-technological change.

- Wajcman uses a feminist approach to social constructivism to argue that gender identity and power relations influence the development, design, and use of household technologies.
- Sociology professor Elizabeth Silva argues that technological change occurs because people's lives change. For example, the increase in the number of working mothers leads to labor-saving hardware such as washing machines, dishwashers, etc.
- 'Women no longer have the time to shop for food every day, so there is a need to have a freezer for food storage,' says Dr. Silva. That need to cook food more easily and quickly means you have developments in cooking technology like the microwave oven. The microwave oven already

existed as it was developed for the Navy during WW2, but in the 1980s It was not launched for domestic use until the early 1990s.

According to Giddens, social networking sites have become the most popular online destination in recent years. One of the main concerns over the use of social networking sites is that as people spend more and more time online in cyberspace communicating and handling their daily tasks, it may be that they spend less time interacting with each other in the physical world.

Positive Impacts of Technology

Better communication–It has been made easier for people to check in on their family members. Parents can watch their kids while they are away. If something does go wrong, a phone call can ease the anxiety.

It has made tracking easy. Most of the tech apps have tracking apps like GPS. With such an app, it is easy for family members to track and provide assistance when a person is in trouble.

Better security–There are a lot of devices in the home that has implemented home security systems. For example, an emergency alarm can be used in the event of a robbery or a fire. This ensures that the family, neighbours, and all concerned authorities are alerted in time.

Virtual interaction–People can use technology to connect with their family members virtually. For example, they can video call them virtually. It doesn't matter how far you are, even if you are abroad, you can still keep in touch with your family members through virtual interaction.

Adverse Impacts of Technology

Too much screen time. The amount of time people spends looking at their phones, tablets, iPads, computers, and laptops is at an all-time high. While technology has introduced new forms of communication, it has considerably decreased the amount of time families spend communicating with each other.

Negative lifestyle–Since family members spend most of their time looking at their gadgets, it means they have limited outdoor activities. Not only does this spoil the quality of their relationships, but it also leads to leading an unhealthy lifestyle.

Poor face-to-face communication –Today the mode of communication has changed from direct face-to-face communication to just chatting. Family relationships are seriously affected by this. Less communication leads to less bonding and it is also very difficult for families to build strong relationships.

Separation of children–Media and other forms of technology are creating division in the family, as parents are too immersed in their own tech lives instead of trying to connect with their kids, on the other hand, children spent too much time in technology any interference from parents is considered as an intrusion in their lives. So, technology is destroying the parent-child relationship.

Impact socialization–The socialization of the family is severely affected due to the inappropriate use of technology by the family members. Socialization is a very important function of a family as it builds a strong emotional bond, teaches each member about their values, norms, and beliefs, and helps them to realize their support and guidance throughout life.

TECHNOLOGY AND THE CHANGING HEALTHCARE SYSTEM

Health care –Since health is affected by many factors such as adequate food, housing, basic sanitation, a healthy lifestyle, and protection from environmental hazards and communicable diseases, the boundaries of health extend beyond the narrow confines of medical care.

Thus, it is clear that "health care" implies more than "medical care". Medical care is a subset of the health care system. Health care is a public right and it is the responsibility of the government to provide this care equally to all people. These principles have been recognized by almost all the governments of the world and hence, have been enshrined in their respective constitutions. In India, health care is wholly or substantially a government function.

Technology has brought many changes in the healthcare industry over the years. This has allowed many cures to be created and beneficial changes in treatment and care.

Healthcare systems changed dramatically due to technological advances, from anesthetics and antibiotics to magnetic resonance imaging scanners and radiotherapy. Future technological innovations will continue to transform healthcare.

Digital technology has become an integral part of healthcare and is all set to revolutionize medical practice. Digital technology has greatly improved operational efficiency with respect to standards of medical care. The change has significantly enhanced the overall experience for both healthcare professionals and patients.

Some of the areas where digital technology has made an enormous impact in healthcare include:

Better access to medical information and data: One of the biggest benefits of the digital revolution has been the ability to store and access data. Healthcare professionals can now access patient data from anywhere. In addition, intranets and the Internet have allowed health professionals to rapidly share medical information with each other, resulting in more efficient patient care.

Big data: Another great advantage of digital technology is that it allows physicians to collect big data in the least amount of time. Access to big data allows clinicians to identify risk factors and recommend appropriate preventive and intervention steps more effectively.

Information and communication technology: The healthcare industry is constantly improving with the development of information and communication technology. Medical experts have access to extensive research studies as well as diverse population groups that provide new insights into genetics, diseases, and outcomes of care. Care providers can compare patient data with many other patients, identify risk factors, and recommend preventive treatments using this new technology.

Telemedicine/Telehealth: There is still a shortage of healthcare providers in many areas. An important advantage of digital technology is video conferencing. Telehealth is not only cost-effective, but it can also help determine who needs emergency assistance. Telecom is also being used to provide education and training to health workers living in remote areas.

Online education: Another important advantage of digital technology is the availability of online education, especially with regard to health-related degrees. Today, students interested in pursuing careers in healthcare can complete their healthcare degree entirely online. With this, they can study wherever they want, from any school they want and in their own time. The availability of online education for health professionals has eliminated the need to travel long distances and take time off from work.

Health Apps: Health apps enable patients to monitor their health and illness, provide them with medical information, allow them to access test results, and prompt them when it is time to get a check-up. In addition, the healthcare app enables healthcare workers to quickly check test results, drug dosage recommendations, and other information they need immediately.

FOOD AND TECHNOLOGY

The Agricultural or Neolithic Revolution occurred during the Neolithic Age, a period that began 11,000 years ago in southern Asia and 9,000 years ago in the Tigris and Euphrates River basins. The Agricultural Revolution provided more and better food, promoted better human fertility and longevity, and so increased human population numbers.

But it wasn't until the Enlightenment and the Industrial Revolution that food became a focus of scientific study. This was the period when mechanization in public health, medical nutrition, and food processing, especially for mass production, developed on a large scale.

The adaptation of agricultural production and food processing to large-scale production technologies has significantly changed the human-food relationship. Those processes made it possible for a small number of food workers to support a large number of food consumers.

Over the years technology has changed how we produce and receive our food through applications, robotics, data, and processing techniques. Technology helps food manufacturers produce more efficiently for the world's growing population. There are 7.5 billion people in the world now and that means there is more demand for food every year.

Charles Darwin, in developing his theory of natural selection, relied heavily on the knowledge and experiences of plant and animal breeders.

According to biological anthropologist Richard Wrangham, food processing began about 2 million years ago by a distant ancestor who discovered cooking, the basic form of food processing. Thus, humans first learned how to cook food, then how to transform, preserve and store it safely. This experience-based technique gave birth to modern food processing.

According to Harold McGee (1990), chemistry began with the 'food chemistry' of ancestral cooks. The molecules the cook changes and manipulates were the molecules of the food. Every time contemporaries prepare food to eat, whether in a large food processing plant or in a kitchen, they repeat the origins of an art form practiced since the harnessing of fire 125,000 years ago.

Canning is the most remarkable achievement in food technology. It was invented by Nicolas Appert, who preserved hot foods in bottles in Paris in 1790. Twenty years later the food-canning industry was born when the first "tin" cans were produced in England.

Louis Pasteur's 1864 work on bacteria and asepsis made it possible to understand the principles behind this food preservation technique.

It was not until 1928 that Charles Olin Ball worked out the mathematical formula that made the thermal processing of foods possible. In the early twenty-first century, all heat sterilizing processes in the food and pharmaceutical industries depend on ball work.

World Risk Society

Over the last 30 years, the increasingly globalized food production systems upon which people have relied have become ever more subject to crises that can have long-term effect. From pandemics such as swine flu and chicken flu, through mad cow disease and outbreaks of foot-and-mouth disease, to ethical and health concerns about factory-farmed animals, genetically modified crops, and world agricultural contribution to environmental crises like global warming, food production across the world today is in a state of risk and vulnerability.

The German sociologist Ulrich Beck (1992) has conceptualized these as a 'world risk society', whereby human activities create problems that may be out of control, beyond the reach of any specialized institution to effectively deal with.

Eric Schlosser expresses similar concerns in his book Fast Food Nation, divided into two sections: 'The American Way' and 'Meat and Potatoes'. 'The American Way', the first part, takes a historical view of the fast-food business by analyzing its beginnings within post-World War II America, while 'The Meat and the Potato' examines the specific mechanisms of the fast-food industry.

'The American Way' – The first section of Fast-Food Nation examines the relationships between the fast-food industry and the entertainment industry of Ray Kroc and Walt Disney making the industry profitable by advertising to children.

Next, Schlosser visits Colorado Springs, CO, and investigates the life and working conditions of the typical fast-food industry employee, learning how fast-food restaurants pay minimum wage to a higher proportion of their employees than any other American industry.

'Meat and Potatoes'—The second section of the text begins with a discussion of the chemical components that make food taste so good making the industry the most dangerous job in America. Furthermore, meat produced by slaughterhouses has become increasingly more dangerous since the centralization of the industry, due to the way cattle are raised, slaughtered, and processed, creating an ideal setting for the spread of E. Coli.

Schlosser reflects on how fast food has matured as an American cultural export after the Cold War and how the collapse of Soviet communism led to the mass spread of American goods and services, especially as a result, the rest of the world is catching up to America's rising obesity rates.

CYBERCRIME

Cybercrime is a criminal activity that either targets or uses a computer, a computer network, or a network device. Cybercrime can threaten the security and financial health of an individual, company, or country.

Internationally, both state and non-state actors engage in cybercrimes, including espionage, financial theft, and other cross-border crimes. Cybercrimes that cross international boundaries and involve the actions of at least one nation-state are sometimes referred to as cyberwarfare.

Some cybercriminals are organized, use advanced techniques, and are highly technically proficient. Others are novice hackers. Cybercriminals can infect computers with viruses and malware to damage devices or prevent them from functioning. They can also use malware to delete or steal data. The biggest threat of cybercrime is to the financial security (of an individual as well as the government).

Types of Cybercrime

Hacking: It is an illegal act by which a hacker breaks the security system of someone's computer for personal gain.

White hat: White hat hackers are those individuals who hack systems to find out the security vulnerabilities of the systems and inform the organizations so that preventive actions can be taken to protect the systems from external hackers.

Black hat: Unlike white hat, black hat hacks the system with malicious intent. They may hack the system for socially, politically, or economically motivated motives. They find security flaws in systems and own information and exploit systems for personal or organizational gains, as long as the organizations whose systems are compromised are aware of it, and security patches are applied. We do. They are popularly known as crackers.

Gray hat: Gray hat hackers find and report security vulnerabilities to site administrators and offer to fix security bugs for a consulting fee.

Blue hat: A blue hat hacker is someone outside of computer security consulting firms, used to perform bug-testing prior to the launch of systems, looking for exploits so that they can be closed.

Unwanted mass surveillance: Mass surveillance refers to the monitoring of a large section of a group of people by authorities, especially for security purposes, but if someone does it for personal interest, it is considered a cybercrime.

Child pornography: It is one of the most heinous crimes which is done shamelessly all over the world. Children are sexually abused and videos are uploaded on the internet.

Child grooming: This is the practice of establishing an emotional relationship with a child, especially for the purpose of child trafficking and child prostitution.

Copyright infringement: If a person violates the protected copyright of someone without permission and publishes it in his own name, then it is known as copyright infringement.

Money laundering: Illegal possession of money by an individual or organization is known as Money Laundering. This usually involves the transfer of funds through foreign banks and legitimate businesses. It is the practice of converting illegally earned money into a legitimate financial system.

Cyber Extortion: When a hacker hacks someone's email server or computer system and demands money to reinstall the system, it is known as cyber extortion.

Cyber terrorism: It refers to unlawful attacks and threats of attacks against computers, networks, and the information stored therein in order to intimidate or coerce a government or its people into furthering political or social objectives.

Cyber Security

Cyber security is the activity by which information and other communication systems are secured or protected from unauthorized access or modification or exploitation or even theft. It is the practice of protecting computers, servers, mobile devices, electronic systems, networks, and data from malicious attacks. It is also known as information technology security or electronic information security. The term is applied in a wide variety of contexts, from business to mobile computing.

ASSESS YOUR LEARNING

PRACTICE QUESTIONS

1. **Statement I:** Today's world is shrinking.

   Statement II: Advancement in technology has blurred the boundaries of nation-states.

   Choose the correct option from those below:

   (a) Statement I is correct, and Statement II is incorrect.
   (b) Statement I is incorrect, and Statement II is correct.
   (c) Both Statement I and Statement II are correct.
   (d) Both Statement I and Statement II are incorrect.

2. Who coined the term *'information overload'*?
   (a) Marshall McLuhan
   (b) Manuel Castells
   (c) Bertram Gross
   (d) Ulrich Beck

3. Who is the author of *'The Production of Space'*?
   (a) Henri Lefebvre (b) Michel Foucault
   (c) Nigel Thrift (d) Georg Simmel

4. Which of the following is an example of new media?
   (a) Newspaper (b) Radio
   (c) Television (d) Twitter

5. Who wrote the essay 'Of other spaces'?
   (a) Georg Simmel (b) Michel Foucault
   (c) David Harvey (d) Manuel Castells

6. Who is the author of the book *'New Technology and the Workers' Response'*?
   (a) K.C Agrawal (b) A K. Bagchi
   (c) N.K. Banerji (d) N.R. Sheth

7. Which of the following is a radio programme hosted by Prime Minister Narendra Modi where he addresses the people of the nation on a monthly basis?
   (a) Akashvani
   (b) All India Radio
   (c) Maan Ki Awaaz
   (d) Mann Ki Baat

8. Two statements are given below. One is labelled as Assertion (A) and the other as Reason (R).

   Assertion (A): Representation of women by media reinforces the stereotype rather than challenging them.

   Reason (R): Media serves the power elite.

   Choose the correct option:

   (a) Both (A) and (R) are true and (R) is the correct explanation of (A)
   (b) Both (A) and (R) are true and (R) is not the correct explanation of (A)
   (c) (A) is true but (R) is false
   (d) (A) is false but (R) is true

9. Arrange the following technological revolutions in chronological order.
   A. Green Revolution
   B. Printing Revolution
   C. Industrial Revolution
   D. Biotechnological Revolution

   Choose the correct option:
   (a) B, A, C, D (b) B, C, A, D
   (c) D, C, B, A (d) A, B, C, D

10. Match the type of technology with the time period in which they broadly originated and evolved:

Type of Technology	Time Period
A. Electronic computing, nuclear power, genetic engineering	I. Medieval Period
B. Textile, Mining, Metallurgy	II. 19th Century
C. Sugar mills, paper mills, wind mills	III. 18th Century
D. Transportation, construction, manufacturing	IV. 20th–21th Century

   Choose the correct option:
   (a) A – I, B – II, C – III, D – IV
   (b) A – IV, B – III, C – I, D – II
   (c) A – III, B – IV, C – II, D – I
   (d) A – II, B – I, C – III, D – IV

11. Who among the following has conceptualized media as a 'Cultural Industry'?
   (a) Functionalists
   (b) Political–Economists
   (c) Neo–Marxists
   (d) Post Modernists

12. Who is the author of the book "Metaphysical Foundations of Natural Science"?
   (a) Plato
   (b) Aristotle
   (c) St. Augustine
   (d) Immanuel Kant

13. Arrange the following in sequence order the development of human communication,
   (1) Age of Information
   (2) Age of Speech

(3) Age of Writing
(4) Age of Electronics
(5) Age of Signs

Choose the correct sequence from the options given below:

(a) 1, 2, 3, 4, 5 (b) 3, 2, 1, 4, 5
(c) 5, 2, 3, 4, 1 (d) 5, 2, 4, 3, 1

14. Who is the author of the book, '*The Virtual Community*'?
(a) Melvin Webber
(b) Howard Rheingold
(c) Barry Wellman
(d) Benedict Anderson

15. Who authored the book '*The Digital Divide*'?
(a) Jan Van Dijk
(b) Carl Osunde
(c) William F. Ogburn
(d) Franz Boas

16. A domain describing a widespread interconnected digital technology characterized by the use of electronics and the electromagnetic spectrum is called?
(a) Virtual reality (b) Internet
(c) Cyberspace (d) Augmented reality

17. National Cyber Security Policy 2013 is drafted by:
(a) Ministry of Information and Broadcasting
(b) Ministry of Science and Technology
(c) Ministry of Electronics and Information Technology
(d) Ministry of Social Justice and Empowerment

18. Which year's Science Policy Resolution centered on the issues 'foster, promote and sustain'?
(a) 2003 (b) 1958
(c) 2013 (d) 1983

19. Under which Science and Technology Policy, 'Science Technology and Innovation' system has been introduced?
(a) Science & Technology Policy 1958
(b) Science & Technology Policy 2013
(c) Science & Technology Policy 2003
(d) Science & Technology Policy 1983

20. Society that extensively collects information to monitor and control the activities of individuals and groups is described by sociologists as:
(a) Information Society
(b) Controlled Society
(c) Closed Society
(b) Surveillance Society

21. Who coined the term '*Third Culture Kid*'?
(a) Ruth Useem
(b) Peter Blau
(c) Patricia Hill Collins
(d) John Goldthorpe

22. Who analyzed the ways in which economic and social transformation in capitalism connect to the information technology revolution?
(a) Edward Said (b) J. Habermas
(c) Manuel Castells (d) Clifford Geertz

23. Who is the first person who developed the concept of information society?
(a) Fritz Machlup
(b) Frank Webster
(c) Michael Buckland
(d) Boyles James

24. Frank Webster discussed five major types of information that can be used to define information society which of the following is not one of them?
(a) Technological
(b) Economic
(c) Temporal
(d) Spatial and Cultural

25. It is an online research method originating in ethnography, is understanding social interaction in contemporary digital communications contexts?
(a) Netnography
(b) Informography
(c) Digitography
(d) Webography

26. Which of the following thinker is associated with the term "information overload?
(a) Michael Buckland
(b) Alvin Toffler
(c) Antonio Negri
(d) Michael Hardt

27. Who believed that 'social space' is where the relations of production are reproduced and that dialectical contradictions were spatial rather than temporal?
(a) Martina Löw (b) Henri Lefebvre
(c) David Harvey (d) George Simmel

28. Who developed the idea of a 'relational' model of space?
(a) Martina Löw
(b) Henri Lefebvre
(c) David Harvey
(d) George Simmel

29. It is a term coined by US sociologist Ruth Hill Useem in the 1950s, for children who spend their formative years in places that are not their parents' homeland.
(a) Adopted Children
(b) Third Culture Kid
(c) Future Kid
(d) New Age Kid

30. Who said that the more information and technology a society had, the more advanced it would become?
(a) W. F. Ogburn (b) Gerhard Lenski
(c) Herbert Spencer (d) Leslie White

31. Who made a distinction between 'hot' and 'cool' media?
(a) Marshall McLuhan
(b) David Harvey
(c) Manuel Castells
(d) Anthony Giddens

32. Who described the concept of 'big disconnect' where parents and kids often seem to inhabit different planets?
(a) Steiner Adair
(b) Jim Taylor
(c) Elizabeth Silva
(d) Gerhard Lenski

33. Who said that 'the primary function of culture' and the one that determines its level of advancement is its ability to 'harness and control energy'?
(a) Leslie White
(b) Lewis H. Morgan
(c) Gerhard Lenski
(d) B Malinowski

34. Who said that chemistry began with the "'food chemistry' of ancestral cooks?
(a) Harold McGee
(b) Nicolas Appert
(c) Louis Pasteur
(d) Ulrich Beck

35. Canning is the most noteworthy achievement in food technology. It was invented by
(a) Harold McGee
(b) Nicolas Appert
(c) Louis Pasteur
(d) Ulrich Beck

36. Who authored '*World Risk Society*'?
(a) Harold McGee
(b) Nicolas Appert
(c) Louis Pasteur
(d) Ulrich Beck

37. Digital divide is the result of increasing
(a) viewership of television
(b) usage of automatic machines in production
(c) computer technology in everyday life
(d) imparting technology for industrialization

38. '*The Network City*' is the work of which thinker?
(a) Gene Youngblood
(b) Murray Turnoff
(c) Barry Wellman
(d) Manuel Castells

39. '*Surveillance Society: Monitoring Everyday Life*' is the work of which thinker?
(a) David Lyon
(b) Steve Mann
(c) Shoshana Zuboff
(d) James Rule

40. Who defined the concept of 'Surveillance Capitalism'?
(a) David Lyon
(b) Steve Mann
(c) Shoshana Zuboff
(d) James Rule

41. A mode of monitoring in which citizens watch governing bodies is called as?
(a) Surveillance Capitalism
(b) Disaster Capitalism
(c) Sousveillance
(d) Surveillance

42. Who defined surveillance as the "operations and experiences of gathering and analyzing personal data for influence, entitlement or management"?
(a) David Lyon
(b) Steve Mann
(c) Shoshana Zuboff
(d) James Rule

43. Who said that 'Virtual communities unite people who were physically separated'?
(a) Melvin Webber
(b) Howard Rheingold
(c) Barry Wellman
(d) Sandy Stone

44. Who coined the word 'Imagined Communities'?
(a) W. F. Ogburn (b) Gerhard Lenski
(c) Herbert Spencer (d) Benedict Anderson

45. What is the primary goal of an ethical hacker?
(a) Avoiding detection
(b) Testing security controls
(c) Resolving security vulnerabilities
(d) Determining return on investment for security measures

46. The Information Technology Act 2000 is an Act of the Indian Parliament notified on
(a) 27th October 2000
(b) 15th December 2000
(c) 17th November 2000
(d) 17th October 2000

47. Which amongst the following does not fall under types of Cyber Crime?
(a) SQL Injections
(b) Denial-of-Service attack
(c) Logic bombs
(d) Card attack

48. They aim to hack into any system for their own profit or out of malice?
(a) White Hat
(b) Grey Hat
(c) Red Hat
(d) Black Hat

49. Who was the founder of the 'ideal type' of a 'total surveillance society'?
(a) David Lyon
(b) Steve Mann
(c) Shoshana Zuboff
(d) James Rule

50. Who is the author of the work "Theory and Progress in Social Science"?
(a) David Lyon
(b) Steve Mann
(c) Shoshana Zuboff
(d) James Rule

Answer Key

1. (c)
2. (c)
3. (a)
4. (d)
5. (b)
6. (b)
7. (d)
8. (b)
9. (b)
10. (b)
11. (c)
12. (d)
13. (c)
14. (b)
15. (a)
16. (c)
17. (c)
18. (b)
19. (b)
20. (d)
21. (a)
22. (c)
23. (a)
24. (c)
25. (a)
26. (b)
27. (b)
28. (a)
29. (b)
30. (b)
31. (a)
32. (a)
33. (a)
34. (a)
35. (b)
36. (d)
37. (c)
38. (c)
39. (a)
40. (c)
41. (c)
42. (a)
43. (d)
44. (d)
45. (c)
46. (d)
47. (d)
48. (d)
49. (d)
50. (d)

PREVIOUS YEARS' QUESTIONS

DECEMBER 2023

1. Which cannot be considered as qualitative audio-visual digital method?
(a) Film (b) Newspaper
(c) Photographs (d) Computer messages

2. Social factors fostering technological development are:
A. Social mobility.
B. Policy of rewarding the inventors.
C. Social conservatism.
D. Specialization.
Choose the correct answer from the options given below:
(a) A, B and D only
(b) A and B only
(c) B, C and D only
(d) B and C only

3. Which among the following is true about 'Collingridge dilemma' which is related to regulation of technology?
A. Regulating a technology in the initial stage of its adoption, when its potential dangers are not evident is easy.
B. Regulation becomes harder by the time the dangers of technology are identified.
C. If early regulation is applied, it may restrict further growth of technology.
D. Regulation at a more mature stage could be restrictive in its efficacy and its ability to prevent accidents.
Choose the most appropriate answer from the options given below:
(a) A, B and C only
(b) A, B, C and D only
(c) B and C only
(d) A and D only

4. Which among the following acts are cybercrimes?
A. Illegal hacking
B. Ethical hacking
C. Unleasing of malware
D. Uploading illegal materials
E. Cyber stalking
Choose the most appropriate answer from the options given below:
(a) A, B, C, and D only
(b) B, C and D only
(c) A, C, D and E only
(d) B, C, D and E only

5. Who said this; 'we now live in the time of the tribe'?
(a) R. Reader
(b) G. Davie
(c) M. Maffesoli
(d) C. Barone

6. Which of the following are the stages of information technology revolution?
A. Microelectronics, computers and telecommunications convergence
B. The innovations in the field of environment.
C. The creation of the Internet.
D. Network technologies and pervasive computing.
E. Technologies of Life—bio-technology (genetic engineering).

Choose the correct answer from the options given below:

(a) A, B, C and D only
(b) B, C, D and E only
(c) A, C, D and E only
(d) A, B, D and E only

7. Which of the following societies is a 'mass society'?
(a) Industrial society
(b) Tribal society
(c) Peasant society
(d) Feudal society

8. Which among the following are true about technological revolution?
A. They create objective needs for social and political innovation.
B. They create a need for identifying the areas in which new institutions are needed and old one required to modify.
C. The new institutions have to be appropriate to specific new needs.
D. Social responses to technological revolution vary from society to society.

Choose the most appropriate answer from the options given below:

(a) A, B and D only
(b) B, C and D only
(c) A, B, C and D only
(d) A, C and D only

JUNE 2023

9. The biomedical model refers to:
A. The application of science to medical diagnosis and cure as the main feature of modem health care system.
B. Disease defined objectively
C. Medical care by trained experts
D. Symptoms experienced by the relatives

Choose the appropriate answer from the options given below:

(a) A, B, and C only
(b) B, C, and D only
(c) A, C, and D only
(d) C, D, and A only

10. What does not refer to the rites of passage?
(a) Ceremonies
(b) Rituals
(c) State
(d) Symbols

MARCH 2023

11. Social aggregations that emerge from the Net when enough people carry on public discussions to form webs of personal relationships in cyberspace is known as
(a) Virtual community
(b) Residential community
(c) Non-residential community
(d) None of the above

12. SPSS is a computer application that allows quantitative data to be managed and analysed. SPSS stands for:
(a) Statistical Package for Social Studies.
(b) Statistical Package for Social Sciences.
(c) Statistical Package for Sociology and Social Anthropology.
(d) Statistical Package for Scientific Study.

13. The coming of an artificial intelligence society is immediately preceded by:
(a) First stage of knowledge society
(b) Second stage of primitive communism
(c) Third stage of feudalism
(d) Agrarian social structure

14. Given below are two statements:
Statement I: Inventions are the wheels on which technology advances
Statement II: Inventions do not affect social or cultural orders
In light of the above statements, choose the correct answer from the options given below:
(a) Both Statement I and Statement II are true.
(b) Both Statement I and Statement II are false.
(c) Statement I is true but Statement II is false.
(d) Statement I is false but Statement II is true.

15. Match List I with List II

List I (Concepts)	List II (Thinkers)
A. Disembedding	I. Donna Haraway
B. Scientific management	II. Anthony Giddens
C. Cyborg	III. F.W. Taylor
D. Hyperreality	IV. Jean Baudrillard

Choose the correct answer from the options given below:
(a) A- I, B- IV, C- III, D- II
(b) A - IV, B – III, C- II, D - I
(c) A - III, B - I, C - II, D - IV
(d) A - II, B - III, C - I, D - IV

DEC 2021 & JUNE 2022

16. The disharmony between the rapid growth of technology and slower transformation of social institutions and beliefs is known as
(a) Technological lag
(b) Communicational lag
(c) Cultural lag
(d) Informational lag

17. Who among the following criticised the effects of "mass media" and "culture industry" on population?
(a) Ulrich Beck
(b) Alfred Schutz
(c) Theodor Adorno
(d) Ernest Burgess

18. Who has written the book, 'World Revolution and Family'?
(a) William Goode
(b) David Cooper
(c) Michael Anderson
(d) Ronald Fletcher

19. Who wrote the book, "*The Lonely Crowd*"?
(a) Howard Rheingold
(b) Bruno Latour
(c) David Riesman
(d) Georg Simmel

JUNE 2021

20. According to Pippa Norris, the concept of the digital divide encompasses which three of the following distinct aspects?
A. Global divide
B. Local divide
C. Social divide
D. Democratic divide
E. Economic divide

Choose the correct answer from the options given below:
(a) A, B and C
(b) C, D and E
(c) A, C and D
(d) B, D and E

21. Serviceable tools were needed to supplement the deficiencies of
(a) Bodily organs
(b) Knowledge
(c) Machines
(d) Nuclear power

22. Technological progress is the result of the accumulation of ________

(a) Wealth (b) Knowledge
(c) Surplus (d) Raw-material

23. Archaeologists can detect in the form of hand axes and change in________

(a) Cost of manufacture
(b) Use of manufacture
(c) Inputs in manufacture
(d) Techniques of manufacture

24. The distinction in knowledge has emphasized through ___________

(a) Myths (b) Manufacturing
(c) Memories (d) Machines

25. What was the knowledge embodied in the hand axes of the Old Stone Age?

(a) Creative (b) Scientific
(c) Useful (d) Progressive

JUNE 2020

26. Which of the following books is authored/co-authored by Stanley Cohen?

1. Folk Devils and Moral Panics: The creation of Mods and Rockers
2. Frontiers of Identity: The British and others
3. Visions of Social control
4. The Urban Question
5. The Manufacture of News

Choose the most appropriate answer from the options given below:

(a) 1, 2, 3 only (b) 2, 3, 4 only
(c) 1, 3, 5 only (d) 3, 4, 5 only

27. Michio Kaku in his *'Three Pillars of Revolution'* talks of which of the following?

1. Quantum Revolution
2. Silicon Revolution
3. Computer Revolution
4. Bio-molecular Revolution
5. Green Revolution

Choose the most appropriate answer from the options given below:

(a) 1, 2, 3 only (b) 1, 3, 4 only
(c) 4, 3, 5 only (d) 2, 3, 4 only

28. Match List I with List II:

List I (Scientist)	List II (Scientific contribution)
A. Kepler	I. Mechanical Philosophy
B. Boyle	II. Planetary orbits
C. Descartes	III. Gas law
D. Harvey	IV. Classification of plants

Choose the correct answer from the options given below:

	A	B	C	D
(a)	I	IV	III	II
(b)	II	III	IV	I
(c)	II	III	I	IV
(d)	IV	II	I	III

29. Arrange the following in sequence order the development of human communication,

1. Age of Information
2. Age of Speech
3. Age of Writing
4. Age of Electronics
5. Age of Signs

Choose the correct sequence from the options given below:

(a) 1, 2, 3, 4, 5 (b) 3, 2, 1, 4, 5
(c) 5, 2, 3, 4, 1 (d) 5, 2, 4, 3, 1

DECEMBER 2019

30. The process by which technology lowers the cost of storing, sharing, and analyzing data is known as :

(a) Mechanization
(b) Digitalization
(c) Commercialization
(d) Globalization

31. Who is the author of the book, 'The Virtual Community'?

(a) Melvin Webber
(b) Howard Rheingold
(c) Barry Wellman
(d) Benedict Anderson

32. Who among the following has conceptualized media as a 'Cultural Industry'?

(a) Functionalists (b) Political - Economists
(c) Neo - Marxists (d) Post Modernists

33. Who among the following considered 'time' and 'space' as 'a priority'?

(a) Plato (b) Aristotle
(c) St. Augustine (d) Immanuel Kant

34. Arrange the following technological revolution in chronological order

A. Green Revolution
B. Printing Revolution
C. Industrial Revolution
D. Bio-technological Revolution

Choose the correct option:

(a) B, A, C, D
(b) B, C, A, D
(c) D, C, B, A
(d) A, B, C, D

35. Match the type of technology with the time period in which they broadly originated and evolved:

Type of Technology	Time Period
A. Electronic computing, nuclear power, genetic engineering	I. Medieval Period
B. Textile, Mining, Metallurgy	II. 19th Century
C. Sugar mills, paper mills, wind mills	III. 18th Century
D. Transportation, construction, manufacturing	IV. 20th–21th Century

Choose the correct option:

(a) (A)–(I), (B)–(II), (C)–(III), (D)–(IV)
(b) (A)–(IV), (B)–(III), (C)–(I), (D)–(II)
(c) (A)–(III), (B)–(IV), (C)–(II), (D)–(I)
(d) (A)–(II), (B)–(I), (C)–(III), (D)–(IV)

36. What are the two main factors that can help in bridging the digital divide?
A. Higher education and employment
B. Ownership of property and wealth
C. Access to Computer and Internet
D. Computer literacy and information

Choose the correct option:

(a) (C) and (D) (b) (A) and (B)
(c) (B) and (C) (d) (A) and (D)

JUNE 2019

37. Why has ultrasound technology in reproductive medicine led to 'missing girls' in India but not in the West?
(a) High value of daughter
(b) Aversion to daughter
(c) Aversion to son
(d) Aversion to marriage

38. Who has written the book, *The Structure of Scientific Revolution*?
(a) John Dewey (b) Thomas S. Kuhn
(c) David Held (d) Manuel Castells

39. Who has authored the book, '*What is This Thing Called Science*'?
(a) C. Wright Mills
(b) A. F. Chalmers
(c) Y. Singh
(d) B. K. Pattanaik

40. Digital divide is the result of increasing
(a) viewership of television
(b) usage of automatic machines in production
(c) computer technology in everyday life
(d) imparting technology for industrialization

41. Internet originated in which one of the most innovative research institutions of the world?
(a) Defence Research Establishment, Ottawa
(b) US Defence Department's Advanced Research Project
(c) Bell Laboratory
(d) Microsoft

42. Why 'Nestle' received negative criticism on social media over the lead issue in the product 'Maggi'?
(a) They abused the users on social media
(b) They did not reply to the user's complaints
(c) They refused to apologize and digitally deleted protesters' links
(d) They did not explain if anything was wrong with their product

43. Which one of the following describes all the forms of information technology that involve communication?
(a) Electronic Communication Technology
(b) Interpersonal Communication Technology
(c) Mass Communication Technology
(d) Official Communication Technology

44. To protect yourself from a computer hacker, you should turn on a
(a) Script (b) VLC Media Player
(c) Antivirus (d) Firewall

45. Which one of the following cities has changed from a 'pensioners' paradise to the 'silicon valley of India'?
(a) Hyderabad (b) Pune
(c) Bengaluru (d) Gurugram

Answer Key

1. (b)	**8.** (d)	**15.** (d)	**22.** (b)	**29.** (c)	**36.** (a)	**43.** (a)
2. (a)	**9.** (a)	**16.** (c)	**23.** (d)	**30.** (b)	**37.** (b)	**44.** (d)
3. (b)	**10.** (c)	**17.** (c)	**24.** (c)	**31.** (b)	**38.** (b)	**45.** (c)
4. (c)	**11.** (a)	**18.** (a)	**25.** (c)	**32.** (c)	**39.** (b)	
5. (c)	**12.** (b)	**19.** (c)	**26.** (c)	**33.** (d)	**40.** (c)	
6. (c)	**13.** (a)	**20.** (c)	**27.** (b)	**34.** (b)	**41.** (b)	
7. (a)	**14.** (c)	**21.** (a)	**28.** (c)	**35.** (b)	**42.** (c)	

Unit-X

Culture and Symbolic Transformation

CHAPTERS:

Top: Photo credit: stoatphoto. Shutterstock
Below: Photo Credit: 3D_creation. Shutterstock

CHAPTER 1

Signs and Symbols, Rituals, Beliefs and Practices

LEARNING OBJECTIVES:

In this chapter, we will discuss the following important topics.

- Sign and symbols
- Rituals
- Belief and practices

INTRODUCTION

Signs, symbols, rituals, beliefs and practices are concepts that are related to each other in some way or the other. In fact, all these words serve as an image or representation of something in the mind. According to Radcliffe-Brown's definition "everything that has meaning is a symbol". The meaning here is that which is expressed by the symbol, or what is meant by the symbol. Rites are those formal actions which are expressed by symbols. A ritual is a patterned, repetitive, and symbolic enactment of a cultural belief or value. Rituals usually serve to enhance social cohesion, as their primary purpose in most cases is to align the individual's beliefs and practices with those of the group.

SIGNS AND SYMBOLS

Sign

A sign can be any object, phenomenon, quality, or entity whose presence or occurrence indicates the possible presence or occurrence of something else. Signs are informative, advisory, mandatory, prohibitive, and warning in nature. For example, red is a stop sign in traffic. Depending on whether the language is spoken, signed, or written, signs may include sounds, gestures, letters, or symbols.

Symbol

The term symbol originates from the Greek word *Symbolon* meaning token or sign.

According to Radcliffe-Brown, 'everything that has a meaning is a symbol'. Any type of physical, social, or intangible object to which people assign a name, meaning, or value. A Symbol is anything that represents something else. It can be signs, gestures, physical objects, words, or events. For example, A cross symbol represents Christianity.

Semiotics

The study of symbols and signs, which is any form of activity, conduct, or process that involves symbols and signs, including the production of meaning is called Semiotics.

Semiotics can be broadly defined as a branch of communication theory that analyzes the various modes of representation and systems of signs employed by human beings to transmit thoughts, feelings, ideas, and ideologies. It is used in analyzing a wide range of disciplines like anthropology, sociology, art, literature, and mass media.

Modern semiotic studies stemmed from two major branches: one was the European tradition developing from ideas presented by the Swiss-French linguist Ferdinand de Saussure and the other emerging from ideas forwarded by Charles Sanders Peirce.

Saussure, in his book, '*Course in General Linguistics* (1916)' posits that signs are made up of two parts:

- **i.** a signifier can be a sound, an object, an image, and
- **ii.** a signified concept generated by the signifier.

For example, in the word 'cat', the letters separately i.e., 'c', 'a', 't', form the signifier. When we read the word, a mental picture of a cat is conjured up in our minds. This mental picture or the concept, which the signifier calls forth, is signified.

Charles S. Pierce (1931), on the other hand, proposed a different theory of signs, which he called semiotics, and was interested in analyzing the manner in which humans extract meaning from different categories of signs.

Kristeva critically interacts with ideas forwarded by psychoanalysis, anthropology, philosophy, linguistics, and phenomenology to create her concept of '*Semanalysis*'.

Umberto Eco's well-known work, A *Theory of Semiotics* (1976) rejects both the theory that it is the objects (things or events) that determine the meaning of signals or signs, and the notion that "iconic" signs must mirror their objects.

Eco argues that the proper approach to formulating a unified semiotic theory would be to assess the means by which signs can function as signs and the manner in which they are produced and interpreted.

He distinguishes between 'signification' and 'communication'; arguing that while the former is a semiotic event by which a sign 'stands for' something, the latter is primarily concerned with the transmission of information.

Interactionists focus on how symbols are used during interactions. This is known as Symbolic interaction. Symbols provide a means of expressing ideas of importance to people. This is the reason why sociologists consider symbols to be very important to study. For example, Durkheim was interested in the study of the 'totem' because he believed it symbolized the idea of collective solidarity among Australian aborigines.

Symbols are operators in the social processes because they help the actors move from one status to another and also to resolve social contradictions. Symbols bind actors to the categories and norms of their society. Turner argued that the meaning of symbols can be understood only in their 'action-field' context.

For Turner, 'symbol is always the best possible expression of a relatively unknown fact, a fact which is nonetheless recognized or postulated as existing'.

Symbolic Nature of Culture

According to Max Weber, symbols are important element of culture, people use symbols to express their spirituality and the spiritual side of a real event. Cultures are shared systems of symbols and meanings. While different cultures have varying systems of symbols, one symbol that is common to all is language.

Language is a symbolic system through which people communicate and through which culture is transmitted. Some languages have a system of symbols used for written communication, while others rely only on spoken communication and non-verbal actions.

The Sapir-Whorf hypothesis is based on the idea that people experience their world through their language, and so they understand their world through the culture embedded in their language.

The Linguistic Relativity hypothesis states that language shapes thought.

Types of Symbols

1. **Religious Symbols** –Religious symbols are used by religion as a set of symbols that include archetypes, works, artifacts, events, or natural events. Religions see religious texts, rituals, and works of art as symbols of compelling ideas or ideals. For example, the Cross of Jesus is a religious symbol that represents Christianity.
2. **Cultural Symbols** –A cultural symbol is a physical manifestation that signifies the ideology of a particular culture or that merely has meaning within a culture. Cultural symbols do not necessarily have to be actual symbols or signs, they can also be gestures such as handshakes and hand signals.
3. **Significant Symbols** –A significant symbol is a gesture that evokes the same response in the person to whom the gesture is directed. These symbols are described by social behaviorist G H Mead. For example, one dog barks, and the other dog either barks or runs away.

RITUALS

What are Rituals?

A ritual is an act performed repeatedly and according to custom. It is ceremonial and formal. Rituals are a series of symbolic actions which have a specific meaning in relation to religious beliefs. Rituals tend to be standardized, repeated, and condensed.

They are behaviours or practices that are either required for or expected of the members of a particular group. For example, kneeling in prayer faces Mecca five times.

Religions view religious texts, rituals, and works of art as symbols of compelling ideas or ideals.

In the ethnographic description of rituals in diverse cultures given by scholars like Edward Tylor, James Frazer, Bronisław Malinowski, Emile Durkheim, and many others, the term ritual is used to denote two separate sets of activities:

1. The first is strictly in the sphere of religious practice and refers to a wide range of religious activities such as prayer, ceremonial worship, chanting, a range of gestures and movements, activities with sacred objects, etc. all done with the specific intention of spiritual communication with a Supreme Being. Thus, the various religious activities and practices engaged in by the Hindus, Muslims, Christians, Sikhs, etc. in their respective temples, mosques, churches, and gurdwaras, etc. may be referred to as rituals.
2. A second group of rituals is those human activities that are associated with the individual's life cycle as they move from one social setting to the next, Arnold Van Gennep called these types of rituals as 'rites of passage'. In all societies, the individual passes through several stages of life, marking the transition from one stage of life to another. Such changes are often marked by activity that is ritualistic in character, for example, marriage allows a person to move from student life to married life.

Evolutionist Understanding of Ritual

The early evolutionary scholars on religion like Tylor, Frazer, Morgan, and others located religion like most other institutions of society within an evolutionary mold. Both Tylor and Frazer were inclined to explain religion as an evolving belief system. Rituals are understood as the first stage of this evolution. This original stage was termed as 'magic' or the pre-religious stage or the animistic stage by Tylor.

He observed rituals as resulting from the cult of the dead-the early need of human beings to understand dreams, hallucinations, sleep, and death led them to believe in a soul or an indwelling personality which became the object of ritual worship. This indwelling personality in the animistic stage is extended outwards to cover animals, plants, and even inanimate practices.

Tylor in his book, *Primitive Culture* (1958) goes on to define rituals as practices in this animistic stage that are highly emotive, and expressive to the point of being dramatic, non-rational, and rooted in magical beliefs.

Functionalist Understanding of Ritual

According to Durkheim, ritual is human behavior that occurs in the realm of the sacred. By specifying the particular space within which religious activities take place, Durkheim laid the groundwork for an empirical examination of the religious domain as well as the relationship of practices and beliefs within this domain to the larger human society.

Parsons reformulated the definition of rituals given by Durkheim, and orienting the meaning of rituals within a theory of social order, Talcott Parsons, reviewing the work done in the sociology of religion, observes that rituals fall within the realm of the sacred. There are human practices that are characterized by a non-rational or transcendental nature. By this Parsons means that ritual behavior exists outside the means-ends relationship, in contrast to human rational behavior that occurs within the means-ends relationship. They are an end in themselves.

Psychoanalytic Understanding of Ritual

Using almost identical ideas of the means-end relationship in understanding human activity, Sigmund Freud in his book Totem and Taboo (1918) defined rituals as those specifically non-rational or formalized symbolic beliefs of any kind, that are different from the practical belief that the belief that is rationally linked to empirical goals.

Symbolic Component of Ritual

Treating rituals as symbolic components of a culture, Social and Cultural Anthropology have tried to provide a new interpretation of religious practices. The Cultural Anthropologist, Edmund Leach defined rituals as culturally oriented behavioral patterns which seek to make a symbolic statement about human beings' relationship with a Supreme Being.

Characteristics of Rituals

1. Ritual as Conscious and Voluntary
Ritual behaviour is not part of the common behaviour of individuals in everyday life. On the contrary, participation in ritual behaviour demands a conscious engagement on the part of these believers to submit to very highly patterned rules and roles which conform the self to all others who have embodied these 'typical' roles in the past.
The voluntaristic component of ritual must be understood from the larger context of ritual being part of a religious system of beliefs and practices. The believer of a faith voluntarily submits to his/her personal will to be the collective will of the group engaged in the ritual. It is only through this voluntaristic submission of the self that the believer can enter the realm of the sacred to achieve communion with that which is 'divine'.
2. Ritual as Repetitions and Stylized Bodily Actions
At the manifest level, rituals are clearly and evidently expressions that the human body articulates in the act of worship. The human body becomes an extremely important organ of religious experience i.e., not only does it pattern itself in terms of movements and gestures within a given religious practice but it also becomes the subject of internalizing the experience contained in the given religious practices.
Within ritual, the stylized patterned and the repetitious nature of actions (for e.g., the chanting of mantras in a temple or the 1 offering of the 'Namaaz' by the Muslims) brings out not only the patterned movements of the body but also serve as vehicles or communication through which the body relates to the sacred.

Types of Rituals

On the basis of intention and occasion, Evans Pritchard, a social anthropologist, classified rituals into two main types:

1. **Confirmatory Rituals:** These are rituals that are concerned with the changes in social status and those concerned with the interaction of social groups. Thus, rituals performed at the time of birth, marriage, death, etc. tend to be present in all cultures of the world and they symbolize a change in the status of the individual in any social group.
2. **Piacular Rituals:** Evans Pritchard categorized this second type as rituals concerned with the moral and physical well-being of the individual or the social group. The need to emphasize this state of moral or physical well-being arises from the fact that occasions arise in the life of an individual and group when such a state of moral and physical well-being is threatened. An individual faced with catastrophe, an epidemic, or the failure of rains, etc. are situations that call for the performance of Piacular rituals. Such rituals incorporate intentions such as appeasement and atonement.

Other Types of Rituals

Rite of Passage: Rite of Passage is a ritual event that marks the transition of an individual from one status to another, including birth, coming of age, marriage, death as well as initiation into groups that are not bound by formal stages of life. Arnold van Gennep said that the rites of passage in any individual's life are marked by three stages: separation, transition, and incorporation.

Calendrical and commemorative rites: They are ritual events marking a particular time of year or a certain period of time since an important event. Calendar events give social meaning to the passage of time, creating repeating weekly, monthly, or annual cycles.

Rites of Exchange and Communion: This style of ritual includes forms of sacrifice and offering meant to praise, please, or propitiate divine powers. According to early anthropologist Edward Tylor, such sacrifices are gifts in expectation of return.

Rites of Affliction (Grief rites): Anthropologist Victor Turner defines rites of affliction as actions that seek to mitigate spirits that inflict humans with misfortune. These rites may include forms of spirit divination to establish cause and rituals that purify and protect.

Rites of feasting, fasting, and festivals: they are those rites through which a community publicly expresses adherence to basic, shared religious values, rather than to the overt presence of deities as is found in rites of affliction where fasting or feasting may also take place.

Political rituals: According to anthropologist Clifford Geertz, political rituals are practiced to construct power, he argued that rituals are not the ornaments of political power, but rather that political actors' power depends on their ability to create rituals and the cosmic framework within which the social hierarchy headed by the king is considered natural and sacred.

Role and Functions of Ritual

1. **Socialization:** Rituals, ceremonies, etc. act as a socializing force. They bring the individuals within the defined society and integrate them.
2. **Social Control:** They act as instruments of social control. They are linked with worldly rewards and punishments. The priest often controls society by asking followers to perform these for some reason or the other.
3. **Merit and Status:** At times they are performed with a view for getting social prestige and status. Like performing some sacrifice or conducting yagna etc.
4. **Identification:** Certain rituals are performed to have a specific identity. Putting vermilion by married women or circumcision among Muslims or piercing of earlobes in some communities are a few examples.
5. **Spiritual Advancement:** The performance of customs and rituals is closely linked with people's desire to achieve spiritual satisfaction and advancement. Prayers, pilgrimage, fasting, sacrifices, and various forms of worship are followed for this purpose. It applies to all religions and communities.
6. **Systems of Healing or Therapy:** One of the most widespread functions of ceremonies and rituals has been to use these for healing purposes. This takes various forms in different religions, social groups, and tribes.

BELIEFS AND PRACTICES

A belief refers to a state or habit of mind. In this state one places trust or confidence in some person or thing. A belief is a notion or idea which has the same value as a statement of knowledge or truth.

In this sense, religious beliefs refer to a religious doctrine or body of doctrines held by a group. Most of the religious doctrines are generally related to the worship of God or the supernatural. For example, Tylor regarded animism as the first stage in the development of religion. He defined religion as a belief in supernatural beings such as ghosts, spirits, and gods.

Practices are related to sacred and spiritual concerns in every culture FUNERAL RITES are being practiced.

Sociologists study religion as both a belief system and a social institution.

As a belief system, religion shapes what people think and how they see the world.

As a social institution, religion is a pattern of social action organized around the beliefs and practices that people develop to answer questions about the meaning of existence.

Types of Beliefs and Practices	What/Who Is Divine	Example
Pluralism	Multiple gods	Ancient Greeks and Romans
Monism	Single god	Judaism, Islam
Atheism	No deities	Atheism
Animism	Nonhuman beings (animals, plants, natural world)	Indigenous nature worship (Shinto)
Totemism	Human-natural being connection	Ojibwa (First Nations)

CHAPTER

2 Changing Material Culture, Moral Economy

LEARNING OBJECTIVES:

In this chapter, we will discuss the following important topics.

- Changing material culture
- Moral economy

INTRODUCTION

Change is the only constant thing in this world. Just like seasons, life and people changes too. Our culture is constantly changing. This doesn't always happen in an "obvious" way–developments in material culture have a domino effect on non-material culture that isn't always immediately visible. Change in material things like railroads or cellphones creates new opportunities, and cultures evolve when new concepts are introduced into a culture, for example, as a result of diffusion or globalization. Most sociologists like W.F. Ogburn believe that material culture changes much faster than non-material culture. This chapter deals with impact of change in non-material culture over society.

CHANGING MATERIAL CULTURE

Culture

Culture in sociology means learned behaviour. The sociologist understood culture as the language, customs, beliefs, rules, arts, knowledge and collective identities and memories developed by members of social groups that make sense of their social environment.

Sociologists study cultural meaning by exploring individual and group communication; meaningfulness is expressed in social narratives, ideologies, practices, tastes, values, and norms as well as in collective representations and social classifications.

According to E.B. Tylor, 'Culture is that complex whole which includes knowledge, belief, art, morals, law, custom and any other capabilities and habits acquired by man as a member of society'.

Malinowski defines Culture as it is the handiwork of man and the medium through which he achieves his ends.

In his book, *Knowledge, Culture and Man*, Pritibhushan Chatterji says that culture "means something cultivated or ripened. 'Culture' refers to some kind of refinement which is born of education and enlightenment." This seems to be very close to culture as envisioned in our ancient Vedic view.

In her book, *Culture and Modernity*, Roop Rekha Verma defined culture as 'a system of the patterns and the modes of expectations, expressions, values, institutionalization and enjoyment habits of people in general'.

Characteristics of Culture

Culture is a complex whole: All the elements and traits of culture are to be understood in relation to one another. All of them, in this respect, constitute a whole, called culture, and are complex in nature.

Culture is learned. The culture of mankind is not instinctive, or innate, or transmitted biologically. It is composed of habits, i.e., learned tendencies to react, acquired by each individual through his own life experiences after birth.

Culture is a complex whole. All elements and traits of culture must be understood in relation to each other. All of them, in this regard, constitute a whole, called culture, and are complex in nature.

Culture is learned. The culture of mankind is not biologically transmitted. It is composed of habits, that is, learned tendencies, acquired by each individual through his own life experiences after birth.

Culture is inculcated. All animals are capable of learning, but humans alone are capable of transmitting acquired habits and behavior to the next generation. Animals can be trained to learn many tricks, but they cannot pass them on to their puppies. However, humans are capable of passing on all their learning and habits to their offspring.

Culture is social. The habits of a cultural system not only develop and circulate over time but are shared by all human beings living together in a society. The habits shared by the members of a society together constitute their culture.

Language act as a carrier of culture. It is the language through which we transmit our culture from one generation to another. Without it man cannot transmit culture from one generation to another and from one place to another.

Culture is adaptive. Culture is not static it is dynamic. It is adaptive through the process of change. Over time, culture adapts to the geographical environment and the biological and socio-psychological demands of the human organism.

Culture is cumulative. We acquire knowledge or skill from our previous generations.

Culture is gratifying. Culture always satisfies our biological and social needs.

Culture is integrative. In the process of adaptation, all the elements of culture form a coherent and integrated whole. Some anthropologists believe that culture is actually an integrated system with most of its elements in perfect balance with each other.

Classification of Culture

Sociologists describe two interrelated aspects of human culture: the physical objects of the culture and the ideas associated with these objects. So, culture is classified into two categories:

1. Material Culture
2. Non-Material Culture

Sociologist William F. Ogburn distinguished between material and non-material culture. Material culture refers to those things which satisfy the material needs of a man like houses, means of transport, factories, food items, etc. They are tangible aspects of society.

On the other hand, non-material culture refers to non-tangible aspects of culture such as customs, norms, ideas, beliefs, language, etc. There is much debate over what should be included in the purview of culture. Some anthropologists believe that only those aspects can be part of the culture which can be communicated. Many others also include objects in the definition of culture.

Giddens and Sutton argued that culture has always dealt with the non-material aspect, this traditionally did not include material objects such as buildings, and furniture, but this thinking has gradually changed. Sociologists have started taking interest in 'material culture' too. So, both material and non-material things are part of the culture. Culture not only includes knowledge, beliefs, art, and practices but also includes manmade objects such as tools, buildings, means of transport and communication or various artifacts.

Green (1964) defined culture as 'a socially transmitted system of knowledge, practice and normative modes of belief as well as the artifacts that generate and maintain knowledge and practice as they pass through time'.

Characteristics of Material Culture

1. It renders culture manifest in physical, palpable, measurable form.
2. It includes what archaeologists typically refer to as artifacts, collectors as relics, and art historians as objects d'art.
3. All writing and symbolic expression, from pictographs, graffiti, iconography, and tattoos to cuneiform tablets and comic books can be considered material culture.
4. Material culture communicates, expresses meaning, conveys experience, disciplines, and exhibits agency.

Different Perspectives on Material Culture and Non-material Culture

1. **Evolutionists:** They believe that material and non-material culture are the results of social evolution. Morgan, Tyler, Haddon, Marx, Spencer, and Durkheim are the main propounders of this view.
2. **Modified Evolutionism:** Based on basic principles of evolutionism. It holds the view that

social institutions do not evolve in a linear upward line. The growth is marked by a recurring development in the opposite direction, best manifested in a parabolic curve.

3. **Functionalists:** They argue that in order to understand the culture, it is necessary to understand how the various agglomerates and elements of culture function. Malinowski is considered to be the father of this theory. He holds that the various elements of culture contribute to the whole society while fulfilling man's needs.
4. **Expansionist(diffusion):** Ralph Linton's name is especially associated with this theory. The propounders of this theory believe that special elements of culture develop in a particular place and from there expand toward other places and groups.
5. **Culture Area Approach:** Clark Wissler defined the restricted area of culture as a cultural area. He demonstrated that in a cultural area, comprising a set of culture complexes a central point of dispersal. People living on the borders of two cultural areas would share the features of both. Such areas were called marginal areas.

Change in Material Culture

Culture is always evolving. New things are added to material culture every day, and they affect non-material culture as well. Cultures change when something new (say, railroads or smartphones) opens up new ways of living and when new ideas enter a culture (say, as a result of travel or globalization).

The first great revolution or radical change in material culture came between 14,500 and 12,000 before the present, when the shift from food collecting to food producing, the Agricultural Revolution, was well underway.

About 1800 the second great change in technology, the Industrial Revolution, took place based on the harnessing of the energy of coal, oil, gas, and heat for use in methods of production.

The harnessing of atomic energy marked the beginning of the third great revolution in material culture and culture as a whole.

Characteristics of Change

The main characteristics of change are given below:

1. Change is universal: No society is static, whether it is the primitive society or the most civilized one. The speed and rate of change is relative, it differs from society to society, and from time to time.
2. Social change is community change: It does not refer to the change in the life of an individual or the life patterns of several individuals. It is a change, which occurs in the life of the entire community.
3. The speed of social change is relative: It is not the same throughout society. Social change in urban areas is faster than in rural areas. The speed and rate of social change are relative because the nature and speed of social change are affected by, and related to the time factor. The speed of social change differs from time to time because the factor which causes change does not remain the same with the change of time.
4. Change is a law of nature: It is natural. It can occur either in the natural course or, as a result of planned efforts. It is also a natural tendency that our needs keep changing. To satisfy our desire for change and our changing needs, social change becomes a necessity.
5. It is difficult to predict the exact form of social change: There is no inherent law of social change according to which it assumes a definite form. For example, it is assumed that industrialization will increase the speed of urbanization, but we cannot predict the exact forms, and which social relationships will be impacted in the future, on account of industrialization.
6. One change lead to many changes in a chain-reaction sequence. For example, technology has changed the domestic system of production. The changed domestic system of production brought women from the home to the factory and the office. The employment of women resulted in their independence from the bondage of man, and it brought about a change in women's attitudes, and ideas. It meant a new social life for women. It, consequently, affected every aspect of family life.
7. Social change is multifactorial: Many factors work together to induce a change. This is because social phenomena are complex and mutually interrelated, and interdependent.
8. Social change may be broadly classified as modifications or replacements. For example, the joint family system is changing to nuclear family. The Gurukul system has changed to a

centralized school system. Society's ideas about women's rights, religion, government, and citizens' right to information and education stand modified today.

Types of Changes

The following are the types of change:

1. Planned change entails mutual goal setting by one, or both parties, an equal power ratio, and deliberateness, eventually, at least, on the part of both sides.
2. Indoctrinal change involves mutual goal setting and is deliberate, but involves an imbalanced power ratio. Many schools, prisons, and mental hospitals, or other 'total institutions' fall into this category.
3. Coercive change is characterized by non-mutual goal setting (or, goals set only by one side), an imbalanced power ratio, and one-sided deliberateness. Coercive change, as we are using the term, may be exemplified by the thought control and brainwashing practices of the communists. Here, there is little, or, no opportunity to engage in mutual goal-setting. The deliberateness originates from one party, the change agent.
4. Technocratic change may be distinguished from planned change by the nature of the goal setting. Technocratic means to bring about change are solely dependent on collecting and interpreting data. The technocratic change follows primarily an engineering model, where a client defines his difficulties as deriving from inadequate knowledge, and assumes that his lack of knowledge is accidental, or, a matter of neglect - not something that is functionally a part of him. The technocrat colludes in his assumption and merely makes and reports his findings.
5. Interactional change is characterized by mutual goal setting and fairly equal power distribution, but with no deliberateness on either side of the relationship. Unconsciously either may be committed to changing the other in some direction. Such changes can be observed among good friends who help each other.
6. Socialization change has a direct kinship with interactional hierarchical control. Parent-child relationships would be the most obvious example, although counselor-camper and teacher-student relationships would also be applicable here. Greater deliberateness on the 'adult' side of the relationship.
7. Emulative change is the sort of process we associate with the formal organization, where there is a clear-cut superior-subordinate relationship. To this extent, it closely resembles Kelman's concept of influence through the process of identification. Change is brought about, possibly unconsciously, through a form of identification with and emulation of power figures.
8. Natural change refers to changes brought about with no apparent deliberateness and no goal-setting on the part of those involved. It is a residual category or encompassing all 'accidents', unanticipated consequences, and changes brought about in connection with cataclysms such as earthquakes and floods. It may be that this category includes the operation of all those factors and comes with our limited knowledge which cannot be properly defined.

Factors responsible for the change in Material Culture

1. Discovery,
2. Invention,
3. New technology, and
4. Contact with other cultures involving diffusion and cultural borrowing.

MORAL ECONOMY

Moral economy is an economy that is based on goodness, fairness, and justice as opposed to one where the market is assumed to be independent of such concerns.

The concept was elaboration by English historian E.P. Thompson, '*The Making of the English Working Class* (1961)'.

In the 1970s the concept of a moral economy was developed further in anthropological studies of peasant economies. The notion of a non-capitalist cultural mentality using the market for its own ends has been linked by others.

The concept was widely popularized in anthropology through the book, '*The Moral Economy of the Peasant: Rebellion and Subsistence in Southeast Asia by James C. Scott* (1976)'.

A moral economy, in one interpretation, is an economy that is based on goodness, fairness, and justice.

Such an economy is generally only stable in small, closely knit communities, where the principles of mutuality i.e., 'I'll scratch your back if you'll scratch mine' operate to avoid the free rider problem.

In a related sense, moral economy is also a name given in economics, sociology and anthropology to the interplay between cultural mores and economic activity.

It describes the various ways in which customs and social pressure compel economic actors to conform to traditional norms even at the cost of profit.

In modern times, 'utopian moral economies' have arisen to systemically reorganize their economic system to reflect a particular moral or ethical code that rejects the free-market ethos of capitalist economies.

Societies following some derivative of socialism or communism are the obvious examples.

Rather than economic exchanges being motivated by self-interest, greed, or profit, moral economy exchanges are driven by moral obligations created by kinship structure and relations, gift-giving, and rituals.

CHAPTER

3 Education: Formal and Informal, Religious Organizations

Learning Objectives:

In this chapter, we will discuss the following important topics.

- Education: Formal and informal
- Religious Organisations

INTRODUCTION

Education is a social process, which prepares individuals to lead a meaningful and dignified life. Together with other social forces, it plays an important role in shaping the structure of society. Through education, the society imparts its knowledge, skills, values and behavioral patterns to its young generation. Thus, ensuring self-preservation and continuity. In this sense, education is a process of socialization. Religious socialization is an interactive process through which social agents influence individuals' religious beliefs and understandings. People interact with various agents of socialization throughout life, and these individuals, organizations, and experiences channel the beliefs and understandings that constitute religious preferences, and these preferences help inform commitment to religious organizations.

EDUCATION: FORMAL AND INFORMAL

The term 'education' is derived from the Latin word, educare which means, 'to bring up', 'to lead out', and 'to develop'. In a simple sense, education refers to the process of bringing up, leading out, and developing individuals into mature, adult members of society.

In its widest possible sense, education is characterized by the moral, intellectual, and spiritual development of a person. It may be noted that the conception of education as the all-around development of an individual, as distinct from training, emerged in the nineteenth century.

The process of education comprises the cultivation of distinct qualities and traits through explicit instructions or through implicit inhibition as part of growing up amidst family members, kin, and peer groups.

Swami Vivekananda has defined education as a "Manifestation of perfection already in man."

Aristotle defined education as "Creation of a sound mind in a sound body'.

Pestalozzi said, 'Education is a natural, harmonious, and progressive development of man's innate powers'.

According to Mahatma Gandhi, education is 'an all-round drawing out of the best in child and man = body, mind, and spirit'.

John Dewey, an eminent American educationist saw, 'education as the power by which man is able to control his environment and fulfill his possibilities'.

Sociological Perspective on Education

The sociological perspective on education focuses on both the process of education and the interrelationship between education and different aspects of society. The chief concern is with understanding how education influences social processes and gets influenced by them. The seeds of the sociology of education were laid in the writings of Plato and others who focused on the role of education in laying the foundation of social order and supporting the state.

The sociology of education was, however, carved as a specialized domain of enquiry much later. Emile Durkheim, the French Sociologist, stresses the need for a sociological approach to the study of education.

In the words of Mannheim, 'Sociologists do not regard education solely as a means of realizing abstract ideals of culture, such as humanism or technical specialization, but as part of the process of influencing men and women. Education can only be understood when we know for what and for what social position the pupils are being educated'.

The sociological perspective on education establishes the importance of the social and cultural context of education. While Durkheim focuses on the role of education in the preservation of society and culture which happens through the transmission of values, knowledge, beliefs, and skills of culture through the family, kinship group, and school. Dewey distinguishes between the growth of the individual in accordance with the expectations of a specific society and the natural growth of an individual. We need to understand that the goals, values, and skills identified as critical by the social order are transmitted through the process of education. Now, these undergo change as social order itself transforms. It is for this reason that education is spoken of as a dynamic process.

Theoretical Approaches

Functionalism: Functionalism treats society as a self-regulating system of interrelated elements with structured social relationships and observed regularities. Functionalists perceive society as similar to a biological organism which is composed of many distinct but interdependent parts with each part contributing to the functioning or survival of the whole system. All the parts are not only interdependent but also coordinated and complementary to each other. A change in one part is believed to affect other parts; the malfunctioning of one part is dealt with by other parts in a coordinated way so as to maintain the equilibrium of the whole system.

According to Durkheim, the major function of education is to transmit society's norms and values. The survival of society or collective life is possible only with a sufficient degree of homogeneity among various members of the society. Homogeneity among members is reached by adhering to rules and regulations laid down by society.

Education preserves and reinforces these homogenizing principles of the society in a child from the beginning. Durkheim writes, 'Education is the influence exercised by the adult generation on those that are not yet ready for social life. Its object is to arouse and to develop in the child a certain number of physical, intellectual and moral states which are demanded of him by both political societies as a whole and the social milieu for which he is specifically destined'.

He highlights the role played by education in instituting 'social being' in the 'individual being'. The individual being is made up of mental states that apply only to himself/herself and to the events in his/her personal life. The social being embodies a system of ideas, sentiments, and practices of the group of which a person is a part.

According to Durkheim, specific skills imparted in educational institutions are necessary to maintain the division of labour in society. As society shifts from simple to complex form there is a corresponding increase in the complexity of the division of labour and the emergence of more specialized occupations.

Educational institutions give the required specified skills to their members according to the demands of society and prepare them to play role sets offered by society.

Parsons' views on the educational system are similar to Durkheim's. According to Parsons, two critical issues are paramount in the context of education in society. The first is that of the internalization of commitments and capacities among children in classrooms for adult roles. Here, the school class may be treated as an agency of socialization through which children are motivated and trained to perform adult roles.

The second is the allocation of human resources within the role structure of the adult society. He recognizes the role played by various socialization agencies like family, informal peer groups, and others in moulding the youth by society. He lays importance on school class as a focal agency of socialization that begins with the entry of children to first grade (standard) and lasts till their entry into the labour market or marriage.

Emile Durkheim states that "each society, considered at a given stage of development, has a system of education which exercises an irresistible influence on individuals. It is idle to think that we can rear our children as we wish. There are customs we are bound to follow, If we violate them too much, they take revenge on our children. Children, when they are adults, are unable to live up to their peers with whom they do not agree. Whether he was raised according to ideas that were either out of date or premature did not matter. In one case as in the other, they are not of their time and, therefore, they are outside the conditions of normal life. Then, in every period, there is a prevailing kind of education from which we cannot deviate without encountering the lively resistance that restrains the whims of dissent".

Functionalists are criticized for their perception that the educational systems operate as an integrative mechanism of society and treat children equally. These criticisms arise from critical theorists who argue that the educational system is a medium of the ruling elite and not representative of the entire society. According to Collins, the functional role played by education in fulfilling the needs of a division of labour is criticized as an exaggeration. There is no evidence to prove that education supplies the knowledge and skills necessary for occupations.

Conflict Theory: According to conflict theorists, society is in a state of perpetual disequilibrium, yet it is maintained as a body by powerful social groups that coerce cooperation from the less powerful. They treat society as divided into dominant and subordinate groups that are characterized by a constant power struggle between themselves. It is not necessary that different units would operate in a way that solidarity of the whole society is maintained. There is a strong possibility of social instability. Society and its units are continuously changing. This dynamism needs to be accepted as a normal characteristic of any society. An interaction between two units involves some form of conflict which is essential for the continuity of society.

According to Althusser whose ideas are derived from Marxism, society is divided into the capitalist class (which owns the modes of production and exercises control) and the labour class (which renders service in the production systems and remains subordinate to the former). The capitalist class requires a continuous supply of labour power the exploitation of which generates profits. Educational systems are used by the capitalist class to produce the required labour power. Workers are socialized to accept the ideology of the ruling class which legitimizes the capitalist system and submit to the exploitation of the capitalists.

Bowles and Gintis explain that the capitalist system requires a surplus amount of labour power to enhance its bargaining potential while employing the workers. The educational system raises a surplus of workers whose skill set is suited to cater to lesser-paid menial jobs. Unemployment and the availability of replaceable labour bring control over the workers and keep wages to a minimum. The governing structure and curricula of the educational systems are determined by the capitalist class.

According to Bourdieu and Passeron, the major role of the educational system is the reproduction of the culture of dominant classes. Dominant classes are able to impose their own meanings as legitimate the basis of the educational system. They maintain that educational systems tend to hide their objective function, which means masking the objective truth or its relationship to the structure of class relations.

Interactionism: interactionism emerged as an alternative perspective to understand the relationship between individuals and society. In its unit of analysis, interactionism shifts importance from the larger society to the individual. Drawn largely from a social psychological perspective, interactionism starts by examining the nature of interaction itself and thenceforth explores the nature of the interaction between members of the society.

Employing the interactionist perspective, sociologists of education seek to explore the ways in which teachers and students interpret and assign meaning to their interactions. Interactionism suggests that the status of the students in an educational system is decided by the nature of interactions with teachers where meanings are constructed beyond academic parameters.

Another study by Cicourel and Kitsuse confirms that students were classified based on their class background rather than academic performances and other non-academic factors Like their appearance, manners, etc.

Keddie finds that social class is an important factor in defining and classifying students. Though students were supposedly divided in terms of ability, students within each group exhibited similar socio-economic backgrounds.

Postmodernism: Postmodernism is emerging as an alternative theoretical framework to modernism in understanding the real world, but has not yet developed as a single coherent thought or theoretical perspective. Practitioners have appropriated, transformed, and transcended ideas from various theories and there is a lack of consensus on the nature of ideas that can be covered,

Echoing postmodern concerns, Tillich questions the notion of compulsory education followed almost all over the world mentioning that in the process traditional skills of self-sufficient people were being discarded. Schools work as repressive systems that induce students to passively consume whatever is taught to them. They are not allowed to think critically. They are made to conform to the rules laid down by the ruling class. Students are expected to follow whatever is taught in education.

A similar argument is evident in the work of Freire who suggests the replacement of curriculum-based education with dialogue-based informal education. He criticizes the existing educational system as being akin to the banking process in which the student is viewed as an empty account waiting to be filled by the teacher. He seeks to abandon the teacher-student dichotomy and favours the introduction of reciprocity in the minds of teachers and students.

Formal Education

Formal education is a set of clearly established goals, a definite structure, and procedures for reaching specific goals. Education is thus not only deliberate instruction, but organized instruction as well.

Educational institutions such as schools and colleges are formal learning environments or systems of education. They are called formal system of education because they apply a formal process to educate the child. Coombs and Ahmed defined "Formal education as a hierarchically structured, chronologically graded education system, which runs from elementary school through university and includes, in addition to general academic studies, a variety of specialized institutions for full time technical and professional training".

Characteristics of Formal Education

- **i.** Formal education is a purposeful, planned effort to impart specific skills or information.
- **ii.** It is a systematic process in which someone designs the educating experiences.
- **iii.** It is considered a success when those being instructed acquire skills, thoughts, and information that those designing the experience seek to impart.
- **iv.** It is intentional learning leading to degrees and certifications.
- **v.** Formal learning is a structured model that present the right curriculum, corresponding to laws and norms. It is rather presentational education.
- **vi.** Example-education imparted by an institution such as a school or college.

Informal Education

In the informal process of education, the social skills and values learned through interaction with family members, peers, and other social groups are those that are largely useful in mundane life. They enable an individual to deal with a range of people and situations, which he/she is likely to encounter in his/her life.

It occurs in a spontaneous, unplanned way.

Experiences that educate informally occur naturally, someone to stimulate specific thoughts or to impart specific skills does not design them.

It is an education that is seen as learning which goes on in our daily life or learning projects undertaken by us to teach ourselves.

This learning is based on daily life experiences like peer groups, family,media, or any other influence in the learner's surroundings. Example-Informal education may be a parent teaching a child.

Characteristics of Informal Education

- **i.** Informal education is not pre-planned or deliberate. It is indirect, incidental, and spontaneous.
- **ii.** No specific agencies or institutions are there like schools to impart this type of education.
- **iii.** No formal ends or goals or objectives are present.
- **iv.** Takes place from the day-to-day activities, experiences, and living in the family or community or even in the school and colleges incidentally either through informal interaction or by observation of various things.
- **v.** There is no prescribed timetable or curriculum.
- **vi.** There are no qualified or trained teachers.
- **vii.** No examinations or awarding of certificates take place.
- **viii.** It is provided by informal agencies such as home or family or community.

RELIGIOUS ORGANIZATIONS

Religion is not only a body of belief but it is practiced. Almost all major religions of the world are found in organized forms. A religious organization grows out of and after the religious experience of a charismatic personality (for example, Christ, Mohammad, Buddha). This religious experience of a charismatic personality gets organized and institutionalized.

Its developmental process operates at three levels:

1. formation of the pattern of worship, i.e., the cult;
2. formation of the pattern of ideas and definitions, i.e., development of myths and theology; and
3. formation of association and organization.

Sociologists generally speak of four types of religious groups they are: the ecclesia (The Church), the sect, the denomination, and the cult. This differentiation of religious groups is based mainly on the pioneering work of Max Weber and Ernst Troeltsch and on the basis of the development of Christianity in the West.

Genesis of Religious Organizations

Religious groups originate and sustain, over a period of time due to the following factors:

1. **Social Factors.** The genesis of religious organization lies in social groupings which are a part of society. It also lies in the routinization and institutionalization of charisma and in the structural differentiation of society. The solid foundations of a religious organization are often laid down by the disciples and not by the founder. His religious experience provides a breakthrough.

The death of the originator of the religion or preceptor creates a crisis of continuity and succession. The way they are met has a significant bearing on the subsequent religious organization.

The crisis of continuity is usually accomplished by collecting, recording, and transmitting the sayings, teachings, precepts, and deeds of the founder. But, socially, more significance is the emergence of a system of worship, a cultic philosophy that binds and inspires subsequent religious brotherhood, the cult is the center of every religious organization.

The crisis of succession can be met in a number of ways, by the customary law of succession i.e. by primogeniture or by nominating a successor, by consensus among disciples, by appointment, or through the struggle for power among disciples/colleagues or among group members.

Since the founder of Islam did not have a successor, Khilafat had come to occupy a cardinal place in the organization of Islam. Christ, too, did not have a successor, nor did he name one but Christianity grew into an ecclesiastical-apostolic order. The Buddha ordered that the Sangha he founded would be guided by Dhamma (Dharma) and Vinaya after his death. It is said that the oligarchic-democratic tradition of the Sangh grew out of the republican traditions of Sangh grew out of the republican traditions of the tribes among which Buddha was popular.

2. **Development Process.** The formation of a cult is one level of this process, the other being the formation of myths and theology. The formation of the group is the third level. These three operate simultaneously and inter-relatedly.

Myth is a dramatic story in which the Supernatural interacts with humans in the human form(s), the myth reinforces belief in the cultic pattern. Theology rationalizes the belief system. Both constitute 'the intellectual level of rationalization of religion'. The development of theology goes along with the development of a professional priestly class - the religious specialist.

3. **Universal Features.** Symbolized by its rituals, beliefs, and organization, a religious group displays a new spirit of coherence and unity. Nevertheless, it adjusts to the differences based on position and function and often tolerates the order system of statuses that it desires. Nevertheless, it adjusts to differences depending on the situation and function and often tolerates the ordering system of statuses that it seeks.

Types of Religious Organizations

Ecclesia (The Church)

Ecclesia was founded on the religious experience of Christ as described in the Bible. Christ being the divine mediator between man and God, in the ecclesia, his experience is viewed as revealed and, hence, infallible. Since this revelation is for man's salvation, man must adopt it. It must be followed by many and people who oppose it (heretics) must be punished or converted.

This doctrinal and rigid approach has tended to make Ecclesia a highly proselytizing religion.

Sect

The sect as a religious organization stands for those who disagree with the interpretation of doctrine from an established church and as a unity of religious brotherhood with a well-defined creed. Unlike a church, membership in a sect is not compulsory. It is voluntary, relatively exclusive, and often qualified ritually. The fact is that the sect arises from people's dissent with the Church over many differences in dogma and perception of the social Denominations situation. These make the sect have clear dogmas and values of its own.

The sect is often intolerant of other religious groups. It may or may not convert. Its main feature is the elimination of the distinction between clergy and worshippers. In its organization, the sect is usually democratic. It can be worldly as well as otherworldly. Sects are born in protest and rebellion. Its relationship with the political authority may or may not be smooth. If rebellious, the sect could be prosecuted.

Denomination

The Denomination grows out of the Sect as the latter grows out of Ecclesia. As Johnson observes, "The line between ecclesia and denomination is not always clear-cut nor is the line between sect and cult.

The denomination is what usually results when a sect becomes 'respectable' in the eyes of middle-class society and relaxes its religious vigour. It is also observed that a conservative type of sect is more prone to change into a denomination.

A denomination, thus, grows out of a sect and shares many similarities with Ecclesia. Socially, it is a middle-class phenomenon, bound essentially by middle-class status identity, and respectability. Its membership is voluntary and relatively open but is largely defined by the class-status-consciousness.

The denomination is thus the result of the Sect becoming larger in terms of members and is in fact much closer to the Church than the Sect ever was. It also means a change of the various dogmas, ethics, and codes of the denomination.

Cult

The cult is a voluntary organization, open to all who wish to join or participate. But, where there it is secretive, there is a tendency to be highly exclusive. It regulates its members according to its system of doctrine and rituals which are well-defined.

A cult emphasizes one principle (above all others) or it focuses on a god or goddess with certain characteristics. Cults seem to flourish in metropolitan centers where culturally heterogeneous populations live together and they widely feel the effects of rapid and impactful social change. It creates situations of contingency and powerlessness and thus creates problems of adjustment.

CHAPTER

4 Piety and Spirituality, Commodification of Rituals

LEARNING OBJECTIVES:

In this chapter, we will discuss the following important topics.

- Piety and spirituality
- Commodification of Rituals

INTRODUCTION

Both spirituality and piety involve a regular spiritual discipline on the part of the believer. This discipline may include meditation, sacred reading, prayer, Eucharistic adoration, attending Mass and other devotions, as well as writing/journaling. From the point of view of piety, these disciplines are taken as an expression of devotion to God. The goal is not simply to practice something, but the goal is the integration of religious experience, practice, and one's life. The danger is that in piety, spiritual practice becomes an end in itself and its effect remains on the surface.

PIETY AND SPIRITUALITY

Piety

The word 'Piety' has its roots in the Ancient Latin 'pietas', a word denoting filial duty and respect for elders, obligations that were religious duties in ancient times.

Piety refers to the virtue of reverence for God and devotion to religious obligations. The term has long been used by people in the medieval and early modern periods to describe the rites and devotion practiced in their daily religious rituals.

Pietism is the term applied to the theological awakening that developed from within Protestantism in the seventeenth century. It constituted neither a unified religious trend nor a structured orientation.

It can be said that Pietism is a reaction to the secular and intellectual tendency of Protestantism, a reaction that emphasizes the personal religious experience of each believer as well as the mediation of the Bible in everyday Christian practice.

Pietism stems not only from the growth and intensification of inner life but also from the establishment of schools, orphanages, and missions. It represents a theology of the heart, which is relatively indifferent to doctrinal matters and for which the fundamental criterion is authenticity.

Sociologically, Pietism is a popular and entrepreneurial movement that crosses a range of diverse Protestant denominations. This is particularly evident in Lutheranism, Methodism, and several revivalist religious movements that punctuated the history of Protestantism.

Historically, pietism appeared in German Protestantism in the seventeenth century. Philipp Jacob Spener's book, *Pia Desideria (Sacred Desires)*, published in 1675, is one of the outstanding works of this period.

Spirituality is more important than theological competence in the training of priests. Pietism is a form of protest, developed out of the Protestant Church, against dogmatic orthodoxy and routine liturgy of the Christian life, and for a revival of faith understood as feeling and action.

Pietism had considerable influence because of its charitable work, its distribution of the Bible, and its educational and charitable institutions.

Through and through its influence, Pietism has largely transcended German Protestantism and Lutheranism. It also appeared in the Reformed Church.

Spirituality

Spirituality is an experiential, inner aspect of consciousness. It is the ability to directly experience the sacred. Such experience may be cognitive, emotional, and/or motivational. For many people, the sacred can be experienced in a wide variety of situations such as in nature, in relationships, in music, dance, and art, in religious devotion, and in inspirational texts and speeches.

Experiences of spirituality begin in childhood for many people and have an element of upliftment in the sense that the experience enables the individual to see things in a wider context than their traditional perceptual sphere.

Both spirituality and piety involve a regular spiritual discipline on the part of the believer. This discipline may include meditation, sacred text, and prayer.

From the point of view of piety, these disciplines are taken as an expression of devotion to God. From a spiritual perspective, these disciplines are performed not only as an expression of devotion but as a means of our conversion to Christ. The goal isn't just to do some exercise; Rather the goal is the integration of religious experience, practice, and one's life. The danger is that in piety, spiritual practice becomes an 'end in itself' and its effect remains on the surface.

For example, one might keep a journal as a form of spiritual discipline. A person may enter their journal every day without gaining much insight. It is a worthy pious practice but when the practice leads to insight and a deeper understanding of how God is working in his life then the practice has contributed to the transformation and spiritual growth of the individual.

COMMODIFICATION OF RITUALS

Commodification

Commodification is the transformation of goods, services, ideas, nature, personal information, or people into objects or items of trade. According to Arjun Appadurai, a commodity, in its most basic form, is 'any object intended for exchange' or anything of economic value.

The commodification of culture thus involves the construction of culture in which cultural objects and traits are promoted as symbols of a particular culture.

According to Karl Marx, commodification is 'the expropriation of the means of production from the overpopulated population in order to supply the laborers who labor to buy them, and the consumers are unable to produce for their direct use'.

Pop culture, advertising, the mainstream, and capital. These are all aspects of commoditization – the act of taking something original and commercializing it, turning it into an object of trade and capital.

Commodification is socially constructed and involves businesses taking things like identity and language and turning aspects of them into a service or good. Commodification plays a large role in how society views subcultures and deviance.

Commodification of Rituals

The commoditization of rituals refers to the conversion of religious symbols into commodities, items of readily available consumption in the "supermarket of religion", economic life, and the media landscape.

It is a process of recontextualizing religious symbols, language, and ideas from their original religious context into media and consumer culture.

In this process, religious symbols become commodities, 'supermarkets of religion' and objects of readily available consumption in the media landscape.

The business of rituals works on many levels. The two most obvious are the (often commercial) offerings of blessings, prayers, etc. through the purchase of religious artifacts, books, figures, etc. The second important - and obvious - level is the association of religious values through a religious aesthetic. for consumer products. Often, the objectification of rituals is related to the loss of power to shape religious practices.

For example—traditionally marriages were arranged by families, but there are now professional marriage bureaus and websites that help people find brides and grooms for a fee.

The commodification of rituals occurs when aspects of rituals are turned into property that can be sold for profit. This has negative aspects as some say it can leave less developed societies open to abuse.

On the positive side, it allows less developed societies to develop and share their cultural knowledge with the rest of the world. According to Shepherd, cultural commodification is considered by many scholars as a component of cultural tourism that can help revive local interest in traditional cultural forms, thus both reviving disappearing cultural traits and can provide material benefits to the host.

It also brings to the fore the fact that in the commodification of culture, the host can easily differentiate between the 'sacred' (and not open to tourism) and the 'profane' (and therefore open to commodification). In this regard, Goldstein's work on the objectification of beliefs may be cited.

It has examined the role of commodification in very different contexts as manifested in the exploration and expression of beliefs. The work looks at the practice of advertisements for ghost tours, haunted hotels, and haunted restaurants in Scotland.

In a modern world of rational and scientific beliefs, the concept of ghosts and haunted houses holds an aura of thrill and mystery that adds to the overall excitement of travel. Therefore, elements associated with ghosts are a major attraction for tourists visiting Scotland.

Such reworkings and revivals of old myths and old wives' tales are part of contemporary consumer culture. Haunting elements are introduced as part of Scotland's history, witch hunts, wars, and plagues that have ravaged the country in the past, giving it an appearance of authenticity.

Every tourist who has visited the Scottish Highlands has been on a tour of Loch Ness and was presented with the Loch Ness monster story, known as Nessie, who lived in the waters of the lake. In the next section, we will discuss some of the areas that have been affected by the commodification of culture in the tourism industry.

CHAPTER

5 Communalism and Secularism

Learning Objectives:

In this chapter, we will discuss the following important topics.

- Communalism
- Secularism

INTRODUCTION

Secularism in practice has existed since ancient times. In societies such as Ancient Greece, a limited secularism was practiced in which religion was not included in the political system, although it was still prevalent in public life. It referred to the laws related to ethics and social values made by the human society to ensure the well-being and harmonious functioning of the society. These laws were not the creation of God. The law was derived from reason and sensitivity to do what was best for the society, keeping in mind the generally accepted values of tolerance and social responsibility that constituted the society. Power was exercised through laws. This means that the laws and social values that govern society are to be seen as laws in their own right, not because they have some divine sanction. Religion or caste or whatever, have their own rights.

COMMUNALISM

Communalism is an ideology that states that society is divided into religious communities whose interests differ and are, at times, even opposed to each other. The antagonism practiced by the people of one community against the people of another community and religion can be termed as 'communalism'.

This antagonism goes to the extent of falsely accusing, harming, and deliberately insulting a particular community and can extend to looting, burning of houses and shops of the helpless and weak, insulting women and even murder.

Yerankar defines communalism as an expression of the heightened sense of community feeling.

- According to Seth, it refers to inter-communal rivalries and social tensions, economic, political, or cultural differences between the rulers and the ruled. It is an ideology that determines the gradual development of relations between two communities within and outside their respective folds.

Dixit argues that communalism is a political doctrine that makes use of religio-cultural differences to achieve political ends.

Sabrewal argues that communalism as a concept emerged due to the fact that members of a multi-religious society had to witness and confront the behavioral pattern practiced by specific communities per se.

According to Kamath, whenever such groups, either ethnic or religious, fight for their exclusiveness, group identity, or group interest even at the cost of national interest or try to impose their way of life on other groups, there is communal disharmony and this is termed as communalism.

Origin and Growth of Communalism in India

It is widely felt that communalism in India was born, nurtured, and propagated deliberately by British imperialism to sow discord. This served the divide-and-rule objective of the colonial administration.

Thus, the prevailing religious differences were first used to project the social and cultural variations and then to promote political divisions by treating Indians not as Indians but as members of different religious communities.

Causes

The term came into use in the early 20th century during British colonial rule. Lord Minto was called the father of communal electorates for legalizing communalism by the Morley-Minto Act in 1909. which faced strong resistance from Gandhi ji and others.

All these acts were done by the British government to appease Muslims and other communities, for their own social needs. This feeling of communalism has deepened since then, fragmenting Indian society and being a cause of unrest.

The main forces which encouraged the growth of communalism in contemporary India are:

1. Economic backwardness of Muslims.
2. Growth of communal parties and organizations.
3. Electoral compulsions of political parties.
4. Communal media, literature, and textbooks
5. Separatism and isolation among Muslims.

Major Communal Riots in India

- Partition of India,1947
- Anti-Sikh riots, 1984
- Ethnic cleansing of Kashmiri Hindu Pundits in 1989
- Babri masjid demolition in Ayodhya, 1992
- Assam Communal violence,2012
- Muzaffarnagar violence, 2013

Important Perspectives on Communalism in India

1. **Colonialist Viewpoint.** The British seemed to see 'Hindu-Muslim antagonism' much earlier than the term 'communalism' emerged. Colonial thinkers like Hugh McPherson in his work 'Origin and Growth of Communal Antagonism' reject the idea that 'communalism' is 'a modern invention, the product of recent political developments', which refers specifically to the politics of separate electorates.

   McPherson emphasizes that 'the religious basis of communal dissension' began to be "reinforced by political factors" with Tilak's establishment of the 'Anti-Cow Killing Society' in 1893, which he suggests was designed to 'stimulate the militant spirit of Hinduism and establish its domination of the Indian political system'.
2. **Nationalist Viewpoint.** For the colonialist, 'communalism' is a pre-colonial problem that is irremediable. For the nationalist, 'communalism' is a colonial problem with its remedy being nationalism. Under this rubric, communalism in India develops as a concomitant to Indian nationalism and is nothing but nationalism driven into religious channels. For the nationalist, while both nationalism and 'communalism' were responses to colonialism, the former was the 'right' response and the latter was the wrong one.

   The nationalist project was a unitary and symbiotic culture of historic cooperation between Hindus and Muslims which was thwarted by colonial rule, especially with the policy of Divide and Rule, of the British rulers in India which gave rise to communalism.
3. **Some Scholarly Responses.** The most notable theorist on 'communalism', Bipan Chandra, who wrote Communalism in Modern India in 1984, worked very clearly within a nationalist framework. Chandra and other nationalist historians emphasized that the phenomenon of 'communalism' is a 'modern' one and did not exist before colonialism. Clearly, since any form of 'popular' politics could not have existed before the British advent, Chandra attributed 'communal politics' to colonial origins.

Communal Violence

Communal violence is common all over the world nowadays. These are known by various alternative names, such as in Xinjiang province in China called ethnic violence. Communal violence and riots are also called non-state conflict, violent civil or minority unrest, mass racial violence, social or inter-communal violence, and ethno-religious violence. Violence between Buddhists and Muslim Rohingya living in Rakhine state which extends along most of Myanmar's coast to the Bay of Bengal and borders Bangladesh's Chittagong province, erupted in 2013.

Such violence in neighboring countries like Myanmar, Bangladesh, and Pakistan leads to retaliatory violence in India as well. It also triggers the problem of refugees, as in the case of Pakistani Hindus, etc. Sri Lanka has also been facing international criticism and the United Nations is concerned with the ethnic conflict and the government's crackdown against the minority Tamils, which has a direct bearing on the relations between India and Sri Lanka. and internal security of India.

SECULARISM

Secularism is the doctrine that seeks to govern human affairs on the basis of secular, naturalistic ideas. It is generally defined as the separation of religion from civil affairs and the state and can be elaborated to a similar position relating to the need to suppress religion in any public sphere.

Secularism has a variety of connotations in India. As Madan notes these dimensions are:

- the separation of state from religion.
- equal and impartial treatment of all communities by the state.
- approaching religious beliefs in a spirit of objective rationality.
- ensuring a just standard of living for all people irrespective of community.

As Madan points out, India is defined in the Preamble to the Constitution as a secular republic. Secularism in India does not mean the abolition of religion but the separation of state from religion. However, the separation of politics from religion is not envisaged. People are free to form religion-based political parties.

The word secularism was coined by George Jacob Holyoake in the middle of the nineteenth century based on the Latin word saeculum (complete renewal of a human population). Apart from implying a separation of the Church from the state, it also suggests freedom to the individual.

In India, secularism is popularly understood as the best philosophy that would enable people belonging to diverse religious backgrounds to live together in a harmonious manner and create a state that would accord the same degree of respect and freedom to all religions.

Secularism, as an ideology, consists of the following five ideas-

Firstly, it stresses the role of human autonomy. This means that secularism recognizes the right of an individual to order her life independent of authority.

Secondly, secularism asserts that not only state and laws but family relations, education, morality, knowledge, and values are also completely free from the dominance of religion.

Thirdly, secularism seeks not just the autonomy of the individual but also the autonomy of reason. The reason is made the sole criterion of truth and this undermines the faith in religion and the authority of the church.

Fourthly, secularism makes room for the values of pluralism and religious toleration because it does not make any religion final, infallible, and beyond rational scrutiny. A plurality of religious worldviews is therefore considered natural by secularists and tolerance is an attitude they value towards other religions and value systems.

Fifthly, secularism is not anti-religion. Instead, it is concerned with the affairs of this world and considers that secular life and knowledge are autonomous.

Philosophy of Indian Secularism

The term 'secularism' is similar to the Vedic concept of '*Dharma Nirapakshata*', i.e., the indifference of the state towards religion.

This model of secularism has been adopted by western societies where the government is completely separated from religion (i.e., separation of church and state).

The Indian philosophy of secularism deals with '*Sarva Dharma Sambhava*' (literally meaning that the paths of all religions have the same destination, though the paths themselves may differ) which means equal respect for all religions.

This concept, adopted and propagated by personalities like Vivekananda and Mahatma Gandhi, is called 'positive secularism' which reflects the dominant ethos of Indian culture.

India has no official state religion. However, various personal laws - on matters such as marriage, divorce, inheritance, and alimony - differ with a person's religion.

Indian secularism is not an end in itself but a means to address religious pluralism and seeks to achieve peaceful coexistence of different religions.

Indian Vs Western Model of Secularism

Over the years, India has developed its own unique concept of secularism which is fundamentally different from the parallel western concept of secularism in the following ways:

According to the Western model of secularism, the 'state' and 'religion' have their own separate spheres and neither the state nor the religion shall interfere in each other's affairs. Thus, the western concept of secularism requires a complete separation of religion and state.

However, in India, there exists no 'wall of separation' between religion and the state, neither in law nor in practice. In India, both the state and religion can and often do, as legally prescribed and judicially, interact and interfere in each other's affairs. established criteria. In other words, Indian secularism does not require the complete removal of religion from the affairs of the state.

As per the western model, the state cannot provide any financial support to educational institutions run by religious communities.

On the other hand, the Indian model has chosen a positive mode of engagement. In India, the state provides all religious minorities with the right to establish and maintain their own educational institutions that can receive aid from the state.

In the Western model, the state does not interfere in matters of religion as long as the religion is operating within the bounds of the law.

On the other hand, in Indian secularism, the state should intervene in religion to remove evil from it. India has intervened by enacting laws against the practices of sati or widow-burning, dowry, animal and bird sacrifice, child marriage, and abstinence. preventing Dalits from entering temples

In the Western concept of secularism, religion is relegated entirely to the private sphere and has no place in public life. The Western model forbids the formulation of any public policy on the basis of religion; The state is completely aloof from the religious activities and practices of its citizens.

In India, the state has a policy of setting up Departments of Religious Endowments, Wakf Boards, etc. It is also involved in appointing Trustees of these boards.

Threats to Secularism

While the Indian constitution declares the state to be absolutely neutral to all religions, our society is steeped in religion. The mixing of religion and politics, which is the mobilization of votes based on primitive identities like religion, caste, and ethnicity, has put Indian secularism at risk.

Communal politics operates through the communalization of social space, by spreading myths and stereotypes against minorities, through attacks on rational values, and by practicing divisive ideological propaganda and politics.

The politicization of any one religious group leads to the competitive politicization of other groups, resulting in inter-religious conflict. Communal riots are one of the manifestations of communalism. Even in recent times, communalism has proved to be a major threat to the secular fabric of Indian politics.

The rise of Hindu nationalism in recent years has resulted in the lynching of cows and mob lynchings on suspicion of eating beef. Additionally, the forced closure of slaughterhouses, the campaign against love jihad, re-conversion or ghar wapsi (forcing Muslims to convert to Hinduism), etc. reinforce communal tendencies in the society.

Islamic fundamentalism or revivalism pushes for the establishment of an Islamic state based on Sharia law which comes in direct conflict with concepts of a secular and democratic state. In recent years there have been sporadic incidents of Muslim youth being inspired and radicalized by groups like ISIS which is very unfortunate for both India and the world.

Approaches to Overcoming Threats

In a pluralistic society, the best way to nurture secularism is by expanding religious freedom rather than strictly enforcing state neutrality. It is up to us to ensure value education that makes the younger generation understand and appreciate not only their own religious traditions but also other religions of the country.

There is also a need to identify a common framework or shared set of values that allows diverse groups to live together. To implement social reform initiatives like Uniform Civil Code, it is necessary to create a conducive environment and create a sociopolitical consensus.

CHAPTER

6 Art and Aesthetics

LEARNING OBJECTIVES:

In this chapter, we will discuss the following important topics.

- Some important points
- Three approaches to aesthetics
- Gharanas of Hindustani music
- Forms of Hindu temples
- Gender, body, and culture

INTRODUCTION

The sociology of art is a subfield of sociology concerned with the social worlds of art and aesthetics.

Studying the sociology of art throughout history is the study of the social history of art, and how various societies contributed to the appearance of certain artists.

Key scholars in the sociology of art include Pierre Bourdieu, Vera Zolberg, Howard S. Becker, Arnold Hauser, and Harrison White.

SOME IMPORTANT POINTS

- Durkheim established a sociological framework for analyzing the cohesive effects of artistic objects and images on a community.
- The contribution of Du Bois to sociological studies of art was the idea that systemic prejudice limits opportunities for artists of color. Nevertheless, Du Bois made a strong case for artistic autonomy as the most promising path to elevate the status of black artists.
- According to Simmel, art was not merely an object of social scientific study but rather the very basis of a *Lebensphilosophie*, or the philosophy of life that illuminates the modern social condition.
- Marx's ideas about art are developed in different texts over a period of several years. The fine arts, he argued, are a privilege of the ruling classes because they have the money and leisure time to produce and enjoy them. Also influential, particularly in later studies of cultural consumption and status, is Marx's argument that the aesthetic content of art reflects the set of social class relationships from which they arise.
- 'Philosophy of art' is studied and discussed under the branch of philosophy known as 'aesthetics;' one among the normative subjects besides logic and ethics.
- The term 'aesthetics' is essentially derived from the Greek word '*aisthetikos*', meaning 'aesthetic,

sensitive, sentient', which in turn was derived from aisthanomai, meaning "I perceive, feel, sense". The modern usage of the term 'aesthetics' was appropriated and coined with new meaning in the German form aesthetik (modern spelling Ästhetik) by a German philosopher called Alexander Baumgarten in 1735.

- Philosophers use the term 'aesthetics' to refer to a discipline of reasoned discourse such as ethics or epistemology. The subject of aesthetics may be an intuition, feeling, or emotion, but aesthetics itself is part of philosophy and is open to the same demands for evidence and logically controlled reasoning that characterize all philosophy.
- Aesthetics is broadly defined as the philosophical study of the nature of art, beauty, and taste. In the Indian context, aesthetics is the "science and philosophy of the fine arts" covering poetry, music, and architecture.
- Indian scholars from the beginning looked at Aesthetics as philosophy and they have examined the characteristics of art as 'philosophy of fine arts in terms of Aesthetics experience'.
- Shakuka gives the analogy of '*Chitraturganaya*', a picture of the horse as an example to understand the experience of aesthetics. He explains, One who looks at a painting of a horse knows that it is not a real horse, but still thinks it is a horse and at the same time will not doubt whether it is a horse or not. When one looks at a horse painting it creates joy and happiness. This relationship between the creator and the viewer is aesthetic. In Indian aesthetics, it is highly emphasized that it is necessary to have a 'heart' between the creator and the viewer.

THREE APPROACHES TO AESTHETICS

First Approach

The central theoretical term of the first approach is 'beauty'. Edmund Burke attempted to distinguish between the two aesthetic concepts in his famous treatise On the Sublime and the Beautiful.

His distinction between the sublime and the beautiful was extremely influential, reflecting the prevailing style of contemporary criticism. By studying the properties denoted by these concepts, Burke analyzed the various attitudes directed toward them.

According to Burke, the enjoyment of beauty has a relaxing effect on the character of the body, while the sublime, on the contrary, tightens these characters. Thus, by applying the capacity of his imaginative principle, he could distinguish the beautiful and the sublime.

Second Approach

The second approach is concerned with the philosophical study of certain states of mind i.e., responses, attitudes, and feelings believed to be involved in aesthetic experience. In the seminal work of modern aesthetics, The Critique of Judgment (1790), Immanuel Kant enshrined some of the key features of beauty in the faculty of "judgment" by which we take definite positions toward objects, relating them to our scientific interests and our practical concerns. Let's separate.

According to Kant, the key to the aesthetic realm lies in a certain "indifferent" attitude that we can assume towards any object and that can be expressed in opposite ways.

Third Approach

The third approach is based on the philosophical study of the aesthetic object. An aesthetic object is an object or phenomenon that is the focus of aesthetic interest or aesthetic experience.

We can further say that aesthetic objects are objects like paintings, symphonies, dramas, flowers, sunsets, etc. In principle, an aesthetic object can be any sensible object in the world.

This is because any sensible object in the world can be seen or experienced aesthetically. This approach reflects the view that the problems of aesthetics exist primarily because there is a particular class of objects in the world to which we selectively respond and which we describe aesthetically.

GHARANAS OF HINDUSTANI MUSIC

Music gharanas are also called styles. The basis of these schools or gharanas is the traditional mode of musical training and education.

Each household has its own distinct characteristics. The main area of difference between gharanas is the way in which the notes are sung. The concept of guru-shishya leads to the development of gharanas.

Gwalior Gharana

It is the oldest of all *khayal gayaki* (vocal) styles. The distinctive feature of this style of singing has been noted as its clarity and simplicity.

Founder– Ustad Hassu Khan, Ustad Haddu Khan, Ustad Nathu Khan

Exponents– Balkrishna Balchal Karanjikar, Vishnu Digambar Paluskar, Pandit Omkarnath Thakur, Veena Sahasrabuddhe and Malini Rajurkar.

Agra Gharana

The Agra Gharana places great importance on developing strength and depth in the voice so that the swar is powerful and resonant.

Founder– Haji Sujan Khan, Ustad Ghagga Khuda Baksh

Exponents– The prominent singers of this gharana are Fayyaz Khan, Latafat Hussain Khan, and Dinkar Kaikini.

Kirana Gharana

Its name is derived from the birthplace of Abdul Kharim Khan of Kirana near Kurukshetra. In the Kirana style of singing, vocals are used to create an emotional mood through the extension and use of kana-s.

Founder– Abdul Karim Khan and Abdul Wahid Khan

Exponents– Hirabai Barodekar, Begum Akhtar, Bhimsen Joshi, Gangubai Hangal, and Prabha Atre.

Jaipur–Atrauli Gharana

The most distinctive feature of the Jaipur Gharana can be described as its complex and melodic form, which arises from the complex and undulating phrases that comprise the piece.

Founder– Ustad Alladiya Khan

Exponents– Mallikarjun Mansoor, Kesarbai Kerkar, Kishori Amonkar, Shruti Sadolikar, Padma Talwalkar and Ashwini Bhide Deshpande.

Patiala Gharana

The Patiala Gharana is regarded as an offshoot of the Delhi Gharana. The Patiala Gharana is characterized by greater rhythmic playing and layakari with abundant use of bols, especially bol-tans.

Founder– Ustad Fateh Ali Khan and Ustad Ali Baksh

Exponents– Prominent singers of Patiala Gharana are Bade Ghulam Ali Khan, Ajay Chakraborty, Raza Ali Khan, Begum Akhtar, Nirmala Denny, Naina Devi, Parveen Sultana and others.

Delhi Gharana

Delhi Gharana was represented by Tanras Khan and Shabu Khan. Pleasing detail and exquisite compositions are the characteristics of the Delhi Gharana.

Founder– Ustad Mamman Khan

Exponents– Some notable exponents of Delhi Gharana are Chand Khan, Nasir Ahmad Khan, Usman Khan, Iqbal Ahmad Khan, and Krishna Bisht.

Bhindi Bazar Gharana

The most distinctive feature of the Bhindi Bazar Gharana is the presentation of the Khayal, which is an open voice using shapes. Breath control is emphasized and singing long passages in one breath is highly regarded in this gharana.

Founder– Ustad Chhajju Khan

Exponents– Important singers of this gharana are Ustad Aman Ali Khan, Shashikala Koratkar, and Anjanibai Malpekar.

Banaras Gharana

The Banaras Gharana developed as a result of the great exuberant style of khayal singing known by the thumri singers of Banaras and Gaya.

Founder– Pt. Gopal Mishra

Exponents– The main exponents of Banaras Gharana are Rajan Mishra, Sajan Mishra, Girija Devi, etc.

FORMS OF THE HINDU TEMPLE

The basic form of a Hindu temple consists of the following:

1. The sanctum sanctorum (*garbhagriha* literally means 'womb-house'), which was a small chamber with a single entrance, evolved over time into a larger chamber. The sanctum is built to house the main icon which itself is the center of much ritualistic attention;
2. The entrance to the temple which may be a portico or a pillared hall includes space for a large number of worshipers and is known as a *mandapa*;
3. Freestanding temples have a mountain-like shikhara, which may take the shape of a curved shikhara in north India and a pyramidal tower, called a *vimana*, in south India;
4. The *vahana*, i.e., the vehicle of the main deity of the temple or a standard with a pillar or flag is placed axially in front of the sanctum sanctorum.

- Two broad orders of temples are known in the country – Nagara in the north and Dravida in the south. Occasionally, the Vesara style of temples has been referred to by some scholars as an independent style created through a selective mixture of the Nagara and Dravida orders.

GENDER, BODY, AND CULTURE

According to Ann Oakley (1972: 18), Gender is a matter of culture; it refers to the societal classification into Masculine and Feminine. In other words, gender refers to a specific cultural meaning system associated with being male or female.

Jay Mitchell states that the concept of gender was introduced in the early 1970s to distinguish the acquisition of social characteristics from biological ones, for which 'sex' was reserved.

In her view, gender is now an inclusive term that has eventually come to include biology as well. Mitchell believed that there was no history or psychology of gender in which gender came to replace women, as in 'gender studies' versus 'women's studies', precisely at the point where the close relationship between women and reproduction was removed.

She argued that to think of women is to think of women and children; To think of gender is to think of men and women but it is also to think of women and women or men and men.

Differences between Gender and Sex

Barbara F. McManus (1997) also argued that feminist scholars tend to separate sex from gender and see gender as a socially or culturally constructed category. She claims that gender is learned and displayed; This includes the myriad and often normative meanings given to sexual differences by different cultures.

She recognizes that feminists may differ in the importance given to sex, which is a biologically based category, but the idea that gender norms can be changed is central to feminist theory.

Ann Oakley's *Sex, Gender, and Society* (1972) greatly popularized the sex-gender distinction in sociology. For Oakley, sex is a term that refers to the biological difference between man and woman: the visible difference in genitalia, and the corresponding difference in reproductive function.

The term 'sex' and 'gender' can be traced to Robert Stoller, an American Psychiatrist, who used them to deal with cases of individuals whose biological 'sex' did not match their 'gender'.

Simone de Beauvoir (2010: 21) states that male and female are two types of individuals differentiated within a species for purposes of reproduction: they can only be defined correlatively. He said that one is not born, but becomes a woman. Beauvoir explains that gender differences in society make men superior through their role as breadwinners.

At the same time, Aryabandhu (2009) states that gender refers to biological or sexual differences between males and females, which are related to how they behave, relate to, and respond to the needs of family, kinship, caste, community, society. make a substantial difference.

Leela Dube (2001) deals with the intensification of gender in her empirical study of Gond tribal society in southern Chhattisgarh during the 1950s. She pointed out that as an anthropologist an encounter between 'a woman' versus 'society' appears to be a relationship that is determined by gender, flowing from the sensitivity of understanding by the actors involved.

Dube, being a woman anthropologist with rich experience and having the same biological and cultural imperatives of marriage, family, and childbirth that every woman encounters in her life, was able to create a conducive rapport in which she interacted meaningfully with the Gond tribal women and understood about their struggles.

Talcott Parsons, an American sociologist claimed that complementary gender roles between men and women promote the social integration of families and society as a whole. In other words, Parsons opined that gender forms a complementary set of roles that bond women and men into family units for carrying out various important tasks.

Women take primary duty for managing the family and raising children whereas men join the family to the outside world through their participation in the labor force. Parsons argued that distinctive socialization teaches both men and women about their suitable gender identity and skills.

Sherry Ortner (1996) pointed out the intricacies of gender ideology in her work in Nepal among the Sherpas. She opined that in every society, women are viewed as closer to nature, whereas men are identified with culture, a prejudice that she blames for the universal second-class status of women.

She also examined men's obsession with female chastity, and their systematic control of women's social and sexual behavior in traditional societies. She maintains that this ideology was bound up with the emergence of patriarchal extended families, social hierarchies, and the state.

Madhu Kishwar (1996) in her article, *'Who Am I? Living Identities Versus Acquired Ones,'* argued that she became aware of her identity as a woman only on the few occasions when she was confronted with an identity based on her gender. Discrimination was committed, for example, when faced with sexual harassment or favoritism in employment.

Otherwise, her gender identity is only one of her multiple overlapping and crosscutting identities, which peacefully coexist with other identities.

Margaret Mead was one of the first to empirically ground the distinction between the biological and social characteristics of men and women. She did this rather dramatically through her study of the conceptions of masculinity and femininity among the Arapesh, Mundugumor, and Tchambuli, three non-western societies in the New Guinea Islands (Mead 1935).

She found that, among the Arapesh, both males and females displayed a 'feminine' temperament (passive, cooperative, and expressive).

Among the Mundugumor, both males and females displayed a 'masculine'" temperament (active, competitive, and instrumental).

And, among the Chambuli, men and women displayed temperaments that were distinct from each other and contrary to Western patterns. In that society, men were emotional and expressive while women were active and helpful.

Mead's study caused people to rethink the character of femininity and masculinity. It becomes obvious that different gender-related traits, temperaments, roles, and identities could no longer be inextricably tied to biological sex.

CHAPTER

7 Ethics and Morality, Sports and Culture

LEARNING OBJECTIVES:

In this chapter, we will discuss the following important topics.

- Ethics and morality
- Sports and culture

INTRODUCTION

Etymologically, the word "ethics" corresponds to the Greek word "ethos" meaning character, habit, customs, way of behaving, etc. Ethics is also called "moral philosophy". The word "moral" comes from the Latin word "mores" which refers to customs, character, behavior etc. Thus, ethics may be defined as the systematic study of human actions from the point of view of their rightness or wrongness, as a means to the attainment of ultimate happiness. It is the reflective study of what is good or bad in that part of human conduct for which humans have some personal responsibility. In simple words, 'ethics' refers to what is good and how to achieve it, and what is bad and how to avoid it. It refers to what should be done to achieve what is good and what should be done to avoid what is bad.

ETHICS AND MORALITY

In sociology, ethics is a general term describing the collective value orientation of a particular social group that defines 'goodness' according to the particular context.

For example, Max Weber's protestant ethics differs from morality, which requires attribution from individual conscience and proclaims a universal and objective essence

Above all, ethics is defined with a certain extent of relative and descriptive features and morality inevitably entails normative action orientations based on the basic conviction of the doctrines denoting universal goodness.

Morality tends to depict the normative evaluation of a particular intention, process, and consequence of an action, whereas ethics is as a theoretical reflection of morality.

From a sociological perspective, ethics and morality are not confined to any particular social system either an intellectual system with metaphysical thinking or a political system with the primacy of polity—but are abstracted to a more general and synthetic societal level that can overview each operation and consequences in every particular social subsystem.

Ethics and Morality in Modern Society

Weber is one of the first sociologists who studied the modern situation of ethics and morality. According to his rationalization and modernization thesis, the holistic worldview provided by religious belief in

Western societies has become disenchanted, in which ethics and morality that were once supported by religion have now lost their grounds.

This problem can be attributed to historical development. In pre-modern societies, ethical rules were largely regulated in accord with the natural order, myth, or totemic meaning in order to secure group solidarity in terms of conformity. Ethics was intertwined with magic by embodying an inexpressible, mystical, and overwhelming power; no discussion on it is allowed.

As a social institution, ethics and morality were incarnated in religion and law with the function of social sanctions and the motivation of obligatory actions. That is to say, they motivated obligation via the internalization of norms (internal mechanism) and sanctioned through punishment (external mechanism).

The turning point appeared in the age of reason, in which morality had already differentiated from religion insofar as society became more and more complex, and eventually internalized in human agency. Of course, both the internal and external perspectives of morality remained intact in the Enlightenment, but the crucial difference is that human beings are autonomous to choose between moral and immoral actions in modern society.

Therefore, the contingent character of morality that underpins social order became significant, and precisely at this point sociology was established to provide a theoretical reflection on this contingent society. In this regard, moral principles were devised by practical reason—allegedly by the example of the Enlightenment: Immanuel Kant—which characterized the age of reason with the faith that human rationality should couple with morality to foster social progress.

Ethics and Morality in Sociology

In this regard, sociology as a discipline that reflects on society cannot eschew these modem demoralized situations. In its very meaning, sociology was established to comprehend the enormous increase of social complexity, and more importantly, the objective ontic being of the world had been conferred from God and kingship to community and society.

Thus, classical sociologists responded to these questions—how can we conceptualize ethics and morality at the social level and what will they like—seriously by devising moral agendas and descriptions of the moral situation to redeem, if one can, the Enlightenment ideal: the coupling of reason and morality.

Durkheim and Weber: Conception of Ethics and Morality

	Durkheim	Weber
Conceptions of ethics and morality	Objective	Subjective
Functions of ethics and morality	Social integration	Building of personality and group ethos
Diagnosis of ethics and morality in modern society	Division of labour, occupational groups, moral education	Moral relativism, group ethics, ideological apparatus, social conflicts
Methodology	Causal explanation	Causal explanation and sympathetic understanding
The relation between reason and morality	Coupled	Decoupled
The conception of normality	Normal as moral	Normal as immoral

SPORTS AND CULTURE

We cannot deny the role of cultural aspects in sports, but the biological aspect of humans is considerably responsible for performance in any sporting event. The factors like body size, body proportions, physique, and nutrition influence performance in any sporting event. Most of these traits are acquired through heredity but they are also influenced by the environment to a substantial extent.

The study of sports is a specialized sub-discipline in physical anthropology christened as Kinanthropometry. This specialization of physical anthropology assesses the physical structure of an individual in relation to gross motor functions or functioning capacity, taking into account maturation, nutrition, and body composition.

The term Kinanthropometry was coined by Bill Ross in 1972. It was first considered in the Olympic Scientific Congress in Quebec in 1976 prior to the Montreal Olympic Games in 1978.

The goal of Kinanthropometry focuses on selecting the fit genotypes which help individuals attain their fullest potentialities, which means selecting those individuals who possess a genetic constitution which is ideal for a particular sport. It is not just muscular strength that is required for coordinating body movements. But the responsibility of a physical anthropologist lies in selecting the players who have better potential in a particular sport than others.

The sociology of sports, also known as sports sociology, is the study of the relationship between sports and society. It examines how culture and values influence sports, how sports influence culture and values, and the relationship between sports and media, politics, economics, religion, race, gender, youth, etc. It also looks at the relationship between sports and social inequality. and social mobility.

The emergence (though not the name) of the sociology of sport dates back to the late 19th century, with the first social psychological experiments dealing with the group effects of competition and momentum-building.

In addition to cultural anthropology and its interest in sports in human culture, one of the first attempts to think about sports in a more general way was Johan Huizinga's *Homo Ludens* or *Thorstein Veblen's Theory of the Leisure Class*. *Homo Ludens* discusses the importance of the element of play in culture and society. Huizinga suggests that sport, especially sport, is a primary and necessary condition for the formation of culture.

These written works contributed to the rise of the study of the sociology of sport. In the 1970s, sport sociology gained significant attention as an organized, legitimate field of study. The North American Society for the Sociology of Sport was formed in 1978 with the aim of studying the field. Its research outlet, The Sociology of Sport Journal, was established in 1984.

Gender is a major area of study within the sociology of sports, including gender inequality and the role of gender in sports throughout history. For example, in the 1800s, cisgender women's participation in sports was discouraged or banned. It was not until the 1850s that physical education was introduced for cis women in colleges.

Today, gender equality in sports is making progress, although differences still exist. Sports reinforce binary, heterosexual, gender-specific roles starting from a young age. For example, schools do not have programs for cisgender girls in soccer, wrestling, and boxing. And some cisgender men sign up for dance programs. Some studies have found that participation in 'masculine' sports create gender identity conflict for women while participation in 'feminine' sports create gender identity conflict for men.

Sport has always been characterized by racial social relations. The first scientific look at race came in the late 19th century when Count Arthur de Gobineau attempted to prove the physical and intellectual superiority of the white race.

Race is often gendered, with women having fewer opportunities to access and succeed in sports. Once a woman becomes successful, her race is downplayed and her sexuality de-emphasized. In some cultures, especially Muslim ones, women are denied access to sports.

Women's participation in sports is influenced by patriarchal ideologies around the body, as well as ideas of femininity and sexuality. Physical labor inevitably leads to the development of muscles, which are associated with masculinity, which is contrary to the idea of women presented by modern consumer culture. Women who enter sports early are more likely to challenge these stereotypes.

Television networks and corporations focus on showcasing female athletes who are considered attractive, which trivializes the achievements of these female athletes. Women's sports are less covered by the news than men's sports. During sporting events, the camera focuses exclusively on attractive women.

Alan Gutman argues that the erotic component of sport cannot be eradicated, and thus remains one of its major components. Furthermore, attractive male and female athletes will always be in high demand. The erotic component of sport should be researched, not dismissed outright.

Pierre de Coubertin – the 'father' of the modern Olympic Games – believed that sporting events in general and in particular were important tools for the promotion of human rights at the international level. The Games should have a clear function to promote peace, and international understanding activated by mutual respect among people of different origins, ideologies, and creeds.

Popular Games that Originated in Ancient India

Chess was devised in India and was known as *Ashtapada*, meaning 64 squares. Unlike the way the game is played today, it was played on a chessboard with dice but without black and white squares. A few years later, the game came to be called *Chaturanga* (quadruple). It was divided into four parts called *Angas*, which symbolized the four branches of an army. Like the original ancient Indian army, it had pieces called elephants, chariots, horses, and soldiers, and was played to formulate battle strategy. In 600 CE the Persians learned the game and named it *Shatranj*. The word 'checkmate' comes from the Persian word *'shah-mat'* in the game, which means 'the king is dead'.

Carrom. A strike-and-pocket table game popularly played throughout South Asia and some Middle-Eastern countries, carrom is said to have originated in the Indian subcontinent. Although there is no specific evidence, but Indian Maharajas are said to have invented this game centuries ago. You can find an antique glass carrom board in Patiala, Punjab. Carrom gained popularity after World War I and is now played for fun by families or at social gatherings.

Ludo is a board game that was earlier called *Pachisi* in India, and the board was made of cloth or jute. A depiction of Pachisi is found in the Ajanta caves in Maharashtra, indicating that the game was quite popular in the medieval era. In England in 1896, a similar game appeared called Ludo, and thus the name was patented.

Snakes and Ladders, games originated in ancient India. This game originated as a game of morality and has been discovered that this game in ancient India was called variously as *Gyan Chaupar, Mokshapat*, and *Moksha Patamu*. Like *Ludo, Snakes, and Ladders* also became popular around the world after being picked up by the British.

Kho-Kho is considered to be one of the most popular traditional sports in India. However, many historians believe that Kho-Kho was famous in ancient times for its running and chasing, played mainly on 'rathas' or chariots, and was known as Rathera by emperors.

Kabaddi gained recognition as a popular sport after the advent of the Pro Kabaddi League in our country. It is believed that this 4000-year-old sport originated in Tamil Nadu. Moreover, this sport is recognized in five forms in our country — Siranjeevi, Gaminee, Amar, Circle, and Goongi.

Badminton. The modern version of badminton was actually born in India (From the game of battledore and shuttlecock). The British were the first patrons of the modern version of the game. By the 1870's they not only mastered the game but also carried the equipment back home. They were so impressed with the game that it is claimed that the game was introduced in Europe in 1873. Thereafter, many countries adopted the game.

Playing cards. Playing cards is the most common pastime in our country and today we often indulge in games like rummy, bluff, bridge, etc. However, it is very interesting to know that the card game originated in India. They were introduced by the Mughal emperors in the 16th century and the game was called 'Ganjifa'. The game was played with lavish sets of playing cards made of ivory or tortoise shells and decorated with various precious stones.

CHAPTER

8 Pilgrimage and Religious Tourism, Religion and Economy

LEARNING OBJECTIVES:

In this chapter, we will discuss the following important topics.

- Pilgrimage and religious tourism
- Religion and economy

INTRODUCTION

In earlier days pilgrimages were related to 'geopiety'. However, now with more and more commercialization and materialism creeping into our lives, the concept of pilgrimage tourism has also started changing. Today people seek luxury, pleasure and comfort on their pilgrimage trips. All this has changed the very base of pilgrimage tourism to a great extent and has resulted in some unexpected but related developments. Now it requires the development of huge tertiary sector through which all the amenities and facilities can be provided to a tourist. Such development means repairing the existing socio-economic structure of a particular area. This results in the rise of large cities and various crafts. At the same time, it also means disturbing the ecological balance, polluting the environment.

PILGRIMAGE AND RELIGIOUS TOURISM

'Religious tourists' in India are a category of travelers primarily motivated by religious considerations. According to social scientists such as Grabarn (1977), and Jaffrey (1987), although such visits may be considered sacred by the travelers concerned, they differ from the more inclusive concept of tourism as sacred travel. Religious tourism, spiritual tourism, sacred tourism, or faith tourism, is a type of tourism with two main subtypes: pilgrimage, meaning travel for religious or spiritual purposes, and viewing religious monuments and artifacts, a branch of sightseeing.

Pilgrimage is a spiritually or religiously motivated journey, sometimes over long distances, it has been practiced since ancient times and in many religions of the world. The world's largest mass religious gathering takes place at the Kumbh Mela in India, which attracts over 120 million pilgrims. Other major pilgrimages include the annual Hajj to Mecca, which is required once in a Muslim's lifetime.

Historical Perspective of Religious Tourism in India

India is a land of pilgrimage. Travel for religious purposes has been there from the most ancient times. Practically, all religions – Hindu, Buddhism, Jainism, and Sikhism have their major and minor pilgrimage centers in different parts of the country. There are also centers of Sufism, churches, and mosques that are visited by people.

In fact, to a majority of domestic tourists in India pilgrimage has always been the main motivation. In our country, all major temples, shrines, and sacred spots are found scattered all along major riverbanks or in the hills. The confluence of holy rivers called '*Sangam*' 'attracts millions of tourists every year when pilgrims assemble there to take a holy dip in these rivers. For example, on the day of '*Sankranti*' a bath in holy Ganga water is believed to relieve a person of all sins.

Besides rivers, sacred shrines have been visited extensively by domestic tourists all along the period. The twelve Jyotirlingas, five Bhutalingas, and many other temples enshrining 'Lingas' in their sanctorum are the ideal terminal destinations for domestic tourists since the time of great epics.

Thus, religious tourism is a mixture of both ancient and modern cultures, i.e., from the exodus of the past to the present day where religious tourism has become a mainstay of tourism.

Characteristics of Religious Tourism

As in other categories of tourism, there are also wide variations in the practices of religious tourism. For example, within the same religion, there are perceptions related to high or low values related to religious travels.

From this one thing it becomes clear that religious tourism is spiritually purposive. With the objective of attaining one or more of the below-stated purposes of the travel, viz.:

To undertake pilgrimage as an act of worship: It is a widely accepted fact that most religious pilgrimage is an act of worship and salvation, except for Muslims and Jews who make pilgrimages to Mecca (Hajj) and Jerusalem respectively, conditionally imperative. In both religions, it is recognized that all people who are healthy and financially capable of making such a journey should visit the holy shrine at least once in their lifetime.

To express gratitude, to confess, and to make vows: Each of us faces such crises in our life when we are not able to solve our problems through worldly means, most of us turn to divine help. A journey to a holy place dedicated to the deity we believe in, to facilitate communication with the ruling deity of the temple for such help. Here believers acknowledge and express their gratitude as well as announce new resolutions for a more blessed life in the future.

To achieve social and spiritual salvation: Socially, taking religious trips is a mark of piety that carries significance in almost all societies. Most particularly among Hindus, a visit to holy places is one of the means for accumulating religious merits whereas among Buddhists it is considered to be the first step towards enlightenment. Another aspect related to their characteristic is that among all religions it is common to find older members performing pilgrimage as a stage of retiring from social life and as a mark of final departure from this world.

To commemorate and celebrate certain religious events: Every religion has myths and rituals associated with certain events that are regarded as sacred among believers. For example, when Lord Rama returned to Ayodhya, when Lord Krishna was born, when Christ was reborn, and when Prophet Mohammad was born or died all these events are carefully documented in our mythologies or other sacred tenets such events are re-enacted during religious festivities to commemorate these events. Over the years, of course, a new colour has been added to these events.

Religious Tourism and Heritage

Where religious people have created a place of interaction with sacred forces, tourism practice can establish a place that is worth visiting. It cannot be denied that holy places are visited by different people and for very different reasons, ranging from those who are religious and seek transcendental experiences to those who are attracted by factors as diverse as nature or art.

It can be said that the relationship between tourism and religion is becoming increasingly intimate and ideological boundaries are increasingly being diffused. The most visible link between tourism and religion is the thousands of sacred buildings that are of interest to and visited by tourists. It should be added, however, that the basis for this interest must be attributed to their cultural and historical value as heritage elements rather than to their religious purpose.

The best-known classification of religious tourist attractions was published by Nolan and Nolan, who propose a classification of religious tourism resources on the basis of three types that intersect with one another, these being pilgrimage temples, religious tourist attractions, and places where religious festivals are held. The difference between pilgrimage temples and religious tourist attractions is that the former is the object of pilgrimage travel and has little tourist value, while the latter is visited by tourists as well as devotees but is not considered place of pilgrimage.

For Nolan and Nolan, this latter group includes most monasteries and cathedrals, although it is clear that there are also pilgrimage temples that hold a high position as tourist attractions. In fact, it is not uncommon for tourists to outnumber pilgrims at these places, as they are often famous for art, architecture, and/or other features.

The Pilgrimage-Tourism Nexus

Research has been dealing with the complex relationship between pilgrimage and tourism, with all its economic, political, social, psychological, and emotional aspects. While earlier theories focused on different typologies of tourists and pilgrims (Cohen, 1979; 1992; MacCannell, 1973; Smith, 1992; 1989), since the early 1990s, scholars have recognized that the connection between the two phenomena is unclear: consider Eade's 1992 article on the interaction between pilgrims and tourists at Lourdes; Bowman's 1991 study on Jerusalem's role in Christianity; and Rinschede's 1992 description of tourist uses of pilgrimage sites.

Cohen (1992) states that pilgrimage and tourism differ with respect to the direction of travel. 'Pilgrim' and 'pilgrim-tourist' move towards their socio-cultural center, while 'traveler' and 'traveller-tourist' move in the opposite direction. This distinction especially applies to journeys where the destination is a formal pilgrimage. However, a mix of features that characterize both pilgrimage and tourism often mark visits to popular pilgrimage sites.

Stausberg (2011) provided in his book, *'Religion and Tourism'* an overview of the crossover between religion and tourism from a religious studies perspective. It seems that although in its current usage the term 'pilgrimage' connotes the religious journey of a pilgrim - particularly to a shrine or a sacred place - its derivation from the Latin peregrinus allows broader interpretations, including the journey of a foreigner, a wanderer, an exile, or a traveller, as well as that of a newcomer or stranger.

The term 'tourist' also has Latin origins and is derived from T*ornus* – one who makes a circular journey, usually for pleasure, and returns to his or her starting point (Smith, 1992). Smith (1992) argued that the modern usage of the terms, which identifies the 'pilgrim' as a religious traveller and the 'tourist' as a secular vacationer, creates a culturally constructed polarity that blurs travellers' motives.

Pilgrims and Tourists: Theories and Approaches

We can also move from viewing pilgrimage as a general, all-encompassing phenomenon to analyzing it as a personal, specific experience. Until the 1980s, most pilgrimage research was concerned with the location, characteristics, and meaning of sites (Nolan and Nolan, 1989), or the overall sociological characteristics of a community undergoing a marginalization process (Turner and Turner, 1969).

Turner and Turner (1969) introduced several fundamental ideas into the study of pilgrimage. He argued that pilgrimage usually involves a stage of 'marginality' in which the novice finds himself in a transitory state between two established social positions and the 'ritual process'.

To understand the dynamics of the visitor experience, Cohen (1979:180) maintained that the tourist cannot be described as a 'general type' and proposed five main modes of tourist experience based on the place and significance of the given experience in the tourists' total worldview.

Cohen identified these modes as recreational, diversionary, experiential, experimental, and existential, and claimed that tourists travelling in the 'existential mode' are comparable to pilgrims. Both are fully committed to an elective spiritual center, external to the mainstream of their native society and culture because they feel that the only meaningful 'real' life is at the center.

RELIGION AND ECONOMY

The term 'religion' refers to a set of ideas and beliefs about the "supernatural" and its impact on the lives of human beings.

For instance, suffering may be explained by saying that it is "God's way" of testing a man's faith or that it is a punishment for sins committed in past lives. Religious beliefs give meaning to life. They help answer questions about oneself and the world one lives in. They provide certain guidelines of behaviour, and certain codes of conduct that individuals are expected to follow.

According to Émile Durkheim, religion is 'a unified system of beliefs and practices relative to sacred things, that which is separate and forbidden, beliefs and practices which are united in a single moral community, called a church, which all belong to their followers'.

For a society to survive, some basic material needs have to be met. Bread, cloth, and a house are necessary for life. Economy or economic system refers to the arrangements made by society for the production, consumption, and distribution of goods and services.

The Interrelationship Between Religious Ethics and the Economy. This is a brief outline of the meaning of religion and the economy. Superficially, they look different. Religion concerns itself with the beyond, while economics deals with the practical business of working, producing, and consuming.

Max Weber thought so. According to him, it was the ideas, beliefs, values, and worldviews of human societies that directed the way their members acted, even in the economic sphere. As already mentioned, religion lays down certain guidelines for behaviour. It is according to these guidelines that the followers direct or orient their activities. These guidelines are included in the body of religious ethics of each religious system.

According to Max Weber, there were some similarities between the Protestant religious ethic and the economic system known as capitalism. Weber said that these relationships helped capitalism grow in the Western world.

The Protestant Ethic and the Spirit of Capitalism

Weber found a positive correlation between the Protestant ethic and the spirit of capitalism. According to Weber, Western capitalism took its shape because it was supported by a certain belief system, namely the 'Protestant ethic'. Weber argued that the Protestant ethic is closely linked to the spirit of capitalism. To bring out this interrelationship, Weber created ideal types of both the Protestant ethic and the spirit of capitalism.

Spirit of Capitalism

The desire for money or profit is as old as human history. Money has long been considered a symbol of power, status, and prestige. But never before in human history has the desire for money assumed such an organized and disciplined form as it has in modern or rational capitalism. Weber wanted to study this rational capitalism.

According to Weber, capitalists did not desire wealth for enjoyment or luxurious life. They wanted it so that they could use it to create more wealth. The thirst to make money for oneself is the essence of modern capitalism. Capitalism is an economic system aimed at the unlimited accumulation of profit through the rational organization of production.

Capitalism arose in Western countries such as England and Germany, which experienced what we call the 'Industrial Revolution'. The development of the factory system, new techniques of production, and new tools and machines made it possible for capitalists or owners to earn large amounts of money. The production process had to be rationally organized; In other words, efficiency and discipline were essential.

Features Affecting the Development of Capitalism

Protestant sects spread across Europe trying to recapture the lost spirit of the Church. He emphasized on simplicity, austerity, and devotion. Calvinism, founded by the French John Calvin, was one such sect. Calvin's followers in England were called Puritans. He migrated to the continent of North America and was the founder of the American nation. Weber observed that in the West, it was Protestants overall who made the greatest progress in education and employment. He was the top bureaucrat, the most efficient technical staff, and a leading industrialist.

The brand of capitalism that Weber was most interested in was Calvinism.

Main Features of Calvinism

As stated before, to show the link between religion and the economy, or in this particular case between the spirit of capitalism and Calvinism.

Calvin's image of God, Calvin said, was God, all-powerful, transcendent. His divine will was unknowable. It would be foolish of any human being to try to understand the will of God. It cannot be understood simply because it was the will of God!

The doctrine of predestination. At the core of Calvinism is the belief that some individuals are chosen or 'elected' by God to enter heaven, while the rest are damned. The 'chosen' will reach heaven no matter what they do on earth. We cannot bribe God to give us a place in heaven through prayer or sacrifice.

Calvinism and 'this-worldly asceticism' By 'penance' we mean strict self-discipline, control, and victory over desires. In Protestantism, particularly

Calvinism Weber traced this-worldly asceticism. It emphasized rigorous self-discipline to master the environment. Along with hard work, a simple, frugal lifestyle was recommended.

Critical Evaluation of Weber's Studies on Religion and Economy

Weber's work on religion and economics has often been criticized. Some scholars believe that he focused too selectively on certain aspects of religious ethics and interpreted them too narrowly to fit his theory.

For example, in his study on Hindu ethics, Weber looked at only one aspect of Hindu ethics and laid more emphasis on its fatalistic and passive aspects.

According to Milton Singer (1969), if capitalism is to develop in India, it should not be the ape of the West which destroys the traditional way of life. Capitalism in India can rather develop within the given cultural norms and institutions of our society.

CHAPTER

9 Culture and Environmet, New Religious Movements

LEARNING OBJECTIVES:

In this chapter, we will discuss the following important topics.

- Culture and environment
- New religious movements

INTRODUCTION

Culture is a learned behaviour, which includes the life-style, patterns and habits of people that are essential for their survival in a particular environment. Studies show that cultural values, such as collectivism and long-term orientation, influence individuals' environmental attitudes and behaviour. The natural environment can be saved from indiscriminate exploitation of mineral wealth, deforestation, felling of trees, desertification and natural calamities only through culture. The interrelationship between environment and culture is undeniable, from agriculture to arts, industries and businesses that dominate various societies.

CULTURE AND ENVIRONMENT

The terms, society, and culture, have been defined in various ways. The most common way of understanding culture from the point of view of the environment is the definition given by the cultural anthropologist Herskovits. According to him, culture is the man-made part of the environment. It is a complex term that includes what people believe, makes, and believe to be true about the environment or the world.

Keesing (1958), another famous cultural anthropologist, explained culture as 'the totality of socially transmitted behaviour'. A child learns food habits, values, and habits based on his/her culture and they are passed from one generation to another through the process of socialization. Man obtains resources from his environment to meet his needs.

E.B. Tylor, the father of anthropology defined culture as 'that complex whole which includes knowledge, belief, art, law, morals, customs and any other capabilities acquired by man as a member of society'. This complex whole is said to constitute different units of man and his work, thoughts, and behaviours that include both tangible and intangible aspects of culture. Such cultural aspects are passed on from generation to generation through acquired knowledge implying that culture is learned rather than inherited.

The intersection between environment and culture is undeniable, ranging from agriculture to the arts to the industries and businesses that dominate various societies. In places such as Japan or the Caribbean, where fishing is a major livelihood for many people, issues of pollution in the water will be of far greater concern than in landlocked or desert-covered countries. In a region that relies on coal mining such as West Virginia, people may resist much of green energy initiatives and defend their way of life despite an outside narrative that discourages continued use of fossil fuels.

Religion has also had a major impact on the way societies and cultures view and interact with their environment. The Christian Bible teaches that humans are 'stewards' of the earth, which can be interpreted in a number of ways. Some Christians take this as a sign that the natural world is theirs to use as they wish; They are higher than plants and animals and have the right to take any resource they want.

Other Christians see their role as that of a protector; They have a sacred duty to take care of nature and make sure the planet is healthy. However, in many South and East Asian religions, humans are not seen as separate from the rest of the natural world and are instead viewed as a greater spirit or as another component of the cycle of life.

In Hinduism, for example, a person may be reborn as an animal many times until they finally attain nirvana. In Taoism, all energy is part of the Tao: 'the Way' or 'the One', which is sometimes described as the 'flow of the universe' and a manifestation of nature. In both of these traditions, it is essential to show respect for the natural world as followers consider themselves to be inseparable from the all-encompassing 'oneness' of life in the universe.

Culture-Environment Relations: Theoretical Perspectives in Environmental or Ecological Anthropology

Environmental or Ecological Anthropology embraces within its realm, the study of the complex relations between people and their environments.

According to Anderson, in common usage, studies that deal in any way with man-environment relations are labelled 'ecological'. However, as such a broad range is quite ineffective in guiding inquiry; he felt that it is pertinent to start with a workable definition which must begin with what ecology is not.

Environmental Determinism: The theory of environmental determinism claims that environmental features have a direct impact on the features of human behaviour, and thus, on human society. It is based on the belief that the environment (most notably its physical factors such as landforms and/or climate) determines the patterns of human culture and societal development.

Environmental Possibilism: The early work of American anthropologists like that of Goldenweiser was characterized by a stress on historical and cultural descriptions, which focused on the uniqueness of human groups.

According to this view, which has come to be known as historical particularism, the environment was seen as an inert force that narrows human options but which played no dynamic role in the surfacing of observable human traits or institutions.

In The Mind of Primitive Man, Boas noted that the environment furnishes the material out of which people shaped and developed the artifacts of daily life but it was historical forces and diffusion, which primarily explained the particular forms that given artifact took.

Cultural Ecology: During the 1950s, scholars witnessed one of the seminal works regarding the relationship between culture and environment, which remains to this day, a legacy that informs the dominant stream of interactional-analytical thinking on this issue.

This was Steward's basic notion of 'adaptive interaction', which is the basis for his Cultural Ecology. His theory of Cultural Ecology stands intermediate between the deterministic and possibilist position and refers to 'a reciprocal or interactional phrasing of man-environment relations which assumes that neither man nor environment is necessarily dominant'.

Steward developed Cultural Ecology as a framework for a causal explanation of cultural differences and similarities.

Cultural Materialism

Following the above developments in the realm of Environmental or Ecological Anthropology, Marvin Harris attempted to advance the ecological explanation as well as a description of cultures by developing an explicit and systematic scientific research strategy, which he called cultural materialism. Harris and his students applied this research strategy to explain seemingly arbitrary religious beliefs and customs in terms of ecological adaptation.

According to Harris, the granting of sacred status to cattle among the Hindus of India and the consequent prohibition on beef eating was necessary for a high-density population of pre-industrial rural cultivators.

The high caloric and spatial cost of raising livestock for meat consumption could not be sustained and was rejected in favour of more efficient grain consumption. But in this adaptation of grain production and consumption, cattle played an important part, supplying traction for ploughs, manure for fertilizer, and milk and butter for consumption. Holy status protected cattle from consumption as meat and saved them for supporting grain cultivation.

NEW RELIGIOUS MOVEMENTS

The generally accepted term for a new religious movement (NRM), is sometimes called a 'cult'. The term new religious movement has been applied to all new religions that have arisen around the world over the past several centuries.

A new religious movement (NRM) is a religious, ethical, or spiritual group or community with practices of relatively modern origin. NRMs may be novel in origin or they may exist within the confines of a wider religion, in which case they would be distinct from pre-existing sects.

New religious movements are generally seen as syncretic, employing human and material possessions to spread their ideas and worldview, deviating somewhat from the traditional forms or principles of society, especially focused on the self, and having a peripheral relationship that exists in a situation. Tension with established social conventions

NRMs are characterized by several shared traits. These religions are 'new' by definition; They provide innovative religious responses to the conditions of the modern world, despite the fact that most NRMs present themselves as rooted in ancient traditions.

The NRM is also commonly regarded as 'countercultural'; That is, they are regarded (by others and by themselves) as alternatives to the mainstream religions of Western society, particularly Christianity in its idealized forms.

These movements are often highly liberal, pluralistic, and syncretistic; They freely combine principles and practices from diverse sources within their belief systems.

The new movement is usually founded by a charismatic and sometimes highly authoritarian leader who is believed to have extraordinary powers or insight. Many NRMs are tightly organized. In light of their often self-proclaimed 'alternative' or 'outsider' status, these groups often place great demands on the loyalty and commitment of their adherents and sometimes position themselves as alternatives to the family and other traditional social groups.

NRMs arose to meet specific needs that many people cannot satisfy through more traditional religious organizations or modern secularism. They are also products of and reactions to modernity, pluralism, and the scientific worldview.

By the end of the 19th century, the first religious groups imported from India took root in the United States, when Vivekananda attended the World's Parliament of Religions in Chicago in 1893 and then founded the Vedanta Society in New York City.

About 40 years after Vivekananda's trip to the United States, another teacher from India, Paramahansa Yogananda (1893–1952), founded the Self-Realization Fellowship in Los Angeles and introduced Americans to the practice and philosophy of yoga.

The rise of the Arya Samaj and Brahmo Samaj movements in India in the 19th century was a response to the growing British presence in India and the British challenge to Hindu traditions. These movements paved the way for other NRMs, including Ramakrishna's Vedanta movement, which sought to make Vedanta philosophy and practice accessible to Western audiences.

Another such movement was the Transcendental Meditation movement of Maharishi Mahesh Yogi. A third new religion with strong ties to the Bhakti movement of the 12th century was the Hare Krishna movement. Yet another cult was founded by Bhagwan Shree Rajneesh, also known as Acharya Rajneesh and later Osho.

Apocalyptic and Millennial Movements

Some NRMs are characterized by an apocalyptic or millennial dimension – the belief that the end of the world is imminent and that a new heaven or new earth will replace the old. Many world religions have apocalyptic strains, but it is Christian millenarianism – the belief that Jesus Christ will establish a 1,000-year reign of peace on earth before the Last Judgment – which provided the background for the development of many NRMs. West.

William Miller (1782–1849) was the founder of a new religion in the United States. Miller predicted that Christ would return to earth sometime in 1843 or 1844. The failure of Miller's prediction, the so-called "Great Disappointment", did not stop many of his followers, who still believed in the prediction but felt that only Miller's calculations were wrong. defective.

One of Miller's followers, the prophet and visionary Ellen G. White (1827–1915), and the Seventh-day Adventists formed under the leadership of Jehovah's Witnesses (successors of the International Bible Students Association), led by Joseph Franklin Rutherford

(1869–1942) from 1917, the imminent return of Christ and the end of time continue to believe in.

In 1959, Maharishi Mahesh Yogi (1911–2008) founded the Spiritual Regeneration Movement and popularized the technique known as Transcendental Meditation or TM.

Transcendental meditation was also represented as a 'scientific' method for achieving both personal and social peace and harmony; It focused on the repetition and concentration of a personal mantra given to the initiate by the guru.

The Maharishi and his teachings gained great fame and attracted celebrities such as American film star Mia Farrow, American engineer and architect R. Buckminster Fuller, and the English rock group the Beatles.

International Society for Krishna Consciousness (ISKCON)

Another group that emerged from this period of cultural upheaval and change was the International Society for Krishna Consciousness (ISKCON), founded by A.C. Bhaktivedanta (1896–1977) and known as the Hare Krishna movement.

ISKCON is essentially a continuation of a Hindu sect that originated in the pre-colonial period of India, emphasizing ardent devotion to the god Krishna.

Conversion to ISKCON marked not only a change in religious belief and practice but a complete break with Western culture, marked by the adoption of Indian dress and diet and the shaving of the heads of male followers.

ASSESS YOUR LEARNING

PRACTICE QUESTIONS

1. A branch of philosophy that deals with the nature of beauty and taste:
   (a) Aesthetics (b) Epistemology
   (c) Logic (d) Ethics
2. Which of the following pairs of Traditional Gharanas and Musicians is NOT correctly matched?
   (a) Banaras Gharana : Girija Devi
   (b) Gwalior Gharana : Mogubai Kurdikar
   (c) Jaipur Gharana : Kishori Amonkar
   (d) Patiala Gharana : Bade Gulam Ali Khan
3. Who, on the basis of empirical data from Maharashtra and Punjab, has stated that 'ethnicized politics is communalism and not fundamentalism'?
   (a) M. Mohanty
   (b) C P. Bhambri
   (c) T.K. Oommen
   (d) Dipankar Gupta
4. Jallikattu is the traditional sport of which state?
   (a) Tamil Nadu (b) Telangana
   (c) Kerala (d) Karnataka
5. According to Durkheim, the unit of significance in ritual is:
   (a) Role (b) Action
   (c) Feeling (d) Motive
6. While discussing religion who has paid attention to the development of moral ideas?
   (a) R.H. Lowie
   (b) A.R. Radcliffe – Brown
   (c) L.T. Hobhouse
   (d) Max Weber
7. Who made a classic study of 'Rites of Passage'?
   (a) Margaret Mead (b) Arnold Gennep
   (c) Abbe Dubois (d) Caroline Myss
8. The religious organization Prathna Samaj was established by
   (a) V.D Savarkar
   (b) Jyotibha Phule
   (c) Raja Ram Mohan Roy
   (d) Atmaram Panduranga
9. Vallam Kali, which is popularly known as a snake boat race, is a popular sport celebrated in which state/ Union Territory?
   (a) Kerala
   (b) Tamil Nadu
   (c) Karnataka
   (d) Puducherry
10. The Heraka Movement, a religious movement that took place in Nagaland was established by?
    (a) Haipou Jadonang
    (b) Tora Agarwala
    (c) Monica Ingudam
    (d) Waikhom Phajatombi
11. Secularism is added in Indian Constitution by which amendment?
    (a) 42nd (b) 62nd
    (c) 43rd (d) 45th
12. Which of the following does not refer to secularism?
    (a) Equal respect for all religious
    (b) Separation of state from religion
    (c) The state is not theocratic
    (d) Religious leaders can veto any law
13. Who has said that 'Secularism is a sub-process of modernization of Indian Society'?
    (a) A R. Desai
    (b) Yogendra Singh
    (c) T.K. Oommen
    (d) M.N. Srinivas
14. Who among the following founded the Arya Samaj?
    (a) Vir Savarkar
    (b) Keshab Chandra Sen
    (c) Vivekananda
    (d) Dayanand Saraswati
15. Mallakhamba, a traditional Indian sport, is a popular sport in which state?
    (a) Madhya Pradesh
    (b) Karnataka
    (c) Rajasthan
    (d) West Bengal
16. Pehalwani, a traditional form of wrestling is a popular sport played in which state of India?
    (a) Telangana (b) Karnataka
    (c) Gujarat (d) Jharkhand
17. A belief that future births and life situations of a person will be set by actions performed during one's present life.
    (a) Telepathy (b) Karma
    (c) Salvation (d) Reincarnation
18. Which among the following is an example of a revivalist movement in India?
    (a) Brahmo Samaj
    (b) Prarthana Sama
    (c) Arya Samaj
    (d) Aligarh Movement

19. Who is the author of 'Communalism in modern India'?
(a) Bipan Chandra (b) T. N. Madan
(c) Yogendra Singh (d) S. C. Dube

20. The symbol deals with
(a) Transmission of a message
(b) Deviation of a message
(c) Restriction of a message
(d) Dilution of a message

21. Who among the following is not the founder of Gwalior Gharana?
(a) Ustad Hassu Khan
(b) Ustad Haddu Khan
(c) Haji Sujan Khan
(d) Ustad Nathu Khan

22. Who defined culture as 'culture is the man-made part of the environment'?
(a) Herskovits
(b) Claude Kluckhon
(c) Robert Bierstedt
(d) Maciver

23. Who stated Education as a 'Manifestation of perfection already in man'.
(a) Mahatma Gandhi
(b) Indira Gandhi
(c) Swami Vivekananda
(d) Dayananda Saraswati

24. It is an experiential, inner aspect of consciousness. It is the capacity to experience the sacred directly.
(a) Piety
(b) Spirituality
(c) Religious belief
(d) Meditation

25. Who defined 'socialization is the process whereby the helpless infant gradually becomes the self-aware, knowledgeable person, skilled in the ways of the culture into which she or he is born'.
(a) Samir Amin
(b) J C Caldwell
(c) Anthony Giddens
(d) K Davis

26. It refers to the "process of leaving certain social behaviour patterns and roles in order to adopt new ones as part of one's evolution in life"
(a) Re-Socialization
(b) Anticipatory Socialization
(c) Adult Socialization
(d) De socialization

27. Who believes that culture is that total way of life that secures for an individual the satisfaction of his bio-psychic drives and the fulfillment of other wants?
(a) Edward Tylor (b) B Malinowski
(c) Robert Redfield (d) David Bidney

28. Which kind of Magic is based on the principle of 'Like produces like'?
(a) Black Magic
(b) Sympathetic Magic
(c) White Magic
(d) Contagious Magic

29. What is called education acquired without any specific purpose, fixed period, and place?
(a) Direct Education
(b) Non-Formal Education
(c) Informal Education
(d) Formal Education

30. When we do not recognize the labour and the social relationships of work that produced it, nor the social relationship that ties us to its producers when we purchase it. Karl Marx (1818–1883) called this phenomenon as?
(a) Commodity Fetishism
(b) Alienation
(c) Objectification
(d) Commodification

31. Which of the following thinker referred to the function of culture as 'latent pattern maintenance' meaning that the culture the function of maintaining social patterns of behaviour and facilitating orderly pattern change?
(a) R K Merton
(b) Talcott Parsons
(c) A R Radcliffe Brown
(d) B Malinowsky

32. Which one of the following is not a cause of communalism?
(a) Religion is taken as the basis of the nation.
(b) When one religion is discriminated against other.
(c) State has no official religion.
(d) Demands of one religious group are formed in opposition to another.

33. Which of the following perspective understands sexual behaviour as a product of the discourse of sexuality?
(a) Functionalists
(b) Post-structuralists
(c) Conflict theorists
(d) Symbolic interactionists

34. Whose said that 'all art is an uncommitted crime'?
(a) Theodor Adorno
(b) Plato
(c) Martin Heidegger
(d) Immanuel Kant

35. Who is the author of the book '*The Origin of the Work of Art*'?
(a) Theodor Adorno
(b) Plato
(c) Martin Heidegger
(d) Immanuel Kant

36. Who coined the term aesthetics?
(a) Immanuel Kant (b) Aristotle
(c) Hagel (d) Alexander Baumgarten

37. Whose contribution was largely responsible for the foundation of the First Indian Women's University in Bombay?
(a) S S Bangali (b) V M Malabari
(c) D K Karve (d) Dadabhai Naoroji

38. Who among the following is the founder of Jaipur - Atrauli Gharana?
(a) Ustad Hassu Khan
(b) Ustad Haddu Khan
(c) Haji Sujan Khan
(d) Ustad Alladiya Khan

39. Who is the author of the book '*Course in General Linguistics*'?
(a) Martina Low
(b) Bettina Mathes
(c) Karl Schmidt
(d) Ferdinand de Saussure

40. Who defined rituals as non-rational or formalized symbolic beliefs distinct from pragmatic belief?
(a) Evans Pritchard
(b) Bettina Mathes
(c) Sigmund Freud
(d) Ferdinand de Saussure

41. Who has propounded 'Themes of Culture'?
(a) T. Shanin (b) S.C. Dube
(c) Morris Opler (d) Eric Wolf

42. Jataka Tales are related to which religion?
(a) Buddhism (b) Jainism
(c) Sikhism (d) Hinduism

43. Who defined religion as the belief in supernatural beings (animism), such as ghosts, spirits, and gods?
(a) Marett (b) Turner
(c) Pritchard (d) Tylor

44. The Transcendental Meditation movement (TM) are program and organization that promotes the Transcendental Meditation technique were founded by?
(a) Goldenweiser
(b) Maharishi Mahesh Yogi
(c) Rajnish Osho
(d) ParamahansaYogananda

45. Who is the founder of the International Society for Krishna Consciousness (ISKCON) i.e., Hare Krishna Movement?
(a) A.C. Bhaktivedanta
(b) Ellen G. White
(c) Rajnish Osho
(d) William Miller

46. Who is the author of the book '*Ethnic and Tourist Arts: Cultural Expressions from the Fourth World*'?
(a) N.H. Graburn
(b) Graham Ward
(c) Oliver Kelly
(d) Christoph Hermann

47. Which of the following thinker distinguishes between Formal, Real, and Fictitious commodification?
(a) N.H. Graburn (b) Graham Ward
(c) Oliver Kelly (d) Christoph Hermann

48. The study of sports is a specialized sub-discipline called as?
(a) Semiotic (b) Glyptology
(b) Aleoradiology (d) Kinanthropometry

49. Who is called as the father of communal electorates?
(a) Lord Ripon (b) Lord Dufferin
(c) Lord Minto (d) Amartya Sen

50. Ceremonies that mark the transition from one phase of life to another are known as:
(a) Status crystallization
(b) Rites of passage
(c) Role transition
(d) Ideal ceremonies

Answer Key

1. (a)	**9.** (a)	**17.** (b)	**25.** (c)	**33.** (b)	**41.** (c)	**49.** (c)
2. (b)	**10.** (a)	**18.** (c)	**26.** (a)	**34.** (a)	**42.** (a)	**50.** (b)
3. (d)	**11.** (a)	**19.** (a)	**27.** (b)	**35.** (c)	**43.** (d)	
4. (a)	**12.** (d)	**20.** (a)	**28.** (b)	**36.** (d)	**44.** (b)	
5. (b)	**13.** (b)	**21.** (c)	**29.** (c)	**37.** (c)	**45.** (a)	
6. (c)	**14.** (d)	**22.** (a)	**30.** (a)	**38.** (d)	**46.** (a)	
7. (b)	**15.** (a)	**23.** (c)	**31.** (b)	**39.** (d)	**47.** (d)	
8. (d)	**16.** (b)	**24.** (b)	**32.** (c)	**40.** (c)	**48.** (d)	

PREVIOUS YEARS' QUESTIONS

DECEMBER 2023

1. Which among the following is not one of the three main categories of the new religious movement?
   (a) World affirming
   (b) World rejecting
   (c) World conflicting
   (d) World accommodating

2. Who among the following classified mixed types of culture into parochial, subject and participant?
   (a) L. I. Rudolph and S.H. Rudolph
   (b) M.R. Davi and V.A. Lewis
   (c) Robert E. Ward
   (d) G.A. Almond and S. Verba

3. Fundamental types of social process are:
   A. Acculturation
   B. Assimilation
   C. Accommodation
   D. Competition
   E. Differentiation
   Choose the correct answer from the options given below:
   (a) B, C and D only
   (b) A, D and E only
   (c) B, C and E only
   (d) C, E and A only

4. Which among the following are the 'world affirming' new religious movement?
   A. Church of Scientology
   B. Transcendental Meditation
   C. ISKON—International Society for Krishna Consciousness
   D. The Aum Supreme Truth
   Choose the correct answer from the options given below:
   (a) A, B and C only
   (b) B, C and D only
   (c) C and D only
   (d) A and B only

5. Pantheism means:
   A. The belief that there is no God.
   B. The belief that there is one God.
   C. The belief in several Gods.
   D. The belief that the universe is God.
   E. The lack of belief in one way or another.
   Choose the correct answer from the options given below:
   (a) A only
   (b) B only
   (c) D only
   (d) C and E only

JUNE 2023

6. Who among the following is known for sociological studies of body?
   A. B.S. Turner and Sue Scott
   B. David Morgan and B.S. Turner
   C. B.S. Turner and Michel Foucault
   D. Talcott Parsons and Pitrim Sorokin
   E. E.E. Evans-Pritchard and Marc Bloch

   Choose the appropriate answer from the options given below:

   (a) A, B, and C only (b) A, B, and D only
   (c) A, B, and E only (d) A, C, and E only

7. Who propounded the idea of the hidden curriculum?
   (a) Emile Durkheim
   (b) John Dewey
   (c) Ivan Illich
   (d) William Blake

8. Who of the following discussed the relation of advertisement and preservation of capitalist society?
   (a) Durkheim and Mauss
   (b) Popper and Schutz
   (c) Adorno and Marcuse
   (d) Marx and Engels

9. Which sociologist wrote the book *Sociology as an Art Form*?
   (a) Talcott Parsons
   (b) C. Wright Mills
   (c) Alwin Gouldener
   (d) Robert Nisbet

10. Who among the following defines 'culture change' as the process by which the existing order of the society, that is its social, spiritual, and material dimensions is transformed from one type to another?
    (a) C. Levi-Strauss
    (b) T. Parsons
    (c) B. Malinowski
    (d) R. K. Merton

11. Which of the following terms are used to refer to the new religious movement?
    A. Messianic movement
    B. Revitalization movement
    C. Totemic movement
    D. Surrealistic movement

    Choose the appropriate answer from the options given below:

    (a) A and C only
    (b) C and D only
    (c) A and D only
    (d) A and B only

12. The secularization theory explains:
A. Rise of industrial society
B. Modernization of culture
C. Pluralization of life worlds
D. Criminalization of market
E. Marginalization of political groups
Choose the appropriate answer from the options given below:
(a) A, B, and C only
(b) A, B, and D only
(c) A, B, and E only
(d) C, D, and E only

MARCH 2023

13. The 'process through which religion gradually loses its influence over various spheres of social life', is known as
(a) Differentiation (b) Enculturation
(c) Homogenization (d) Secularization

14. Centre for Contemporary Cultural Studies (CCCS), one of the most influential centres to study culture, is attached with
(a) University of Oxford
(b) University of Birmingham
(c) University of Delhi
(d) None of the above

15. The name of the book in which W.F. Ogburn first introduced the hypothesis of 'Cultural Lag' is
(a) *Culture and Society*
(b) *Social Change*
(c) *A Hand Book of Sociology*
(d) None of the above

16. Match List I with List II

List I (Works)	List II (Authors)
A. The Body and Society: Explorations in Social Theory	I. H. Bhabha
B. The Location of Culture	II. B.S. Turner
C. The Coming of Post-industrial Society	III. D. Bell
D. Culture as Praxis	IV. Z. Bauman

Choose the correct answer from the options given below:
(a) A - II, B - IV, C - III, D - I
(b) A - I, B - IV, C - III, D - II
(c) A - IV, B - III, C - I, D - II
(d) A - II, B - I, C - III. D - IV

17. Values, beliefs, and attitudes of a minority group which are in opposition to the mainstream or ascendant culture is known as
(a) Dominant culture
(b) Counterculture
(c) Cultural materialism
(d) None of the above

18. Crypto-religion is defined as
(a) an unconscious religious attitude directed towards an inadequate object.
(b) a conscious understanding of rituals.
(c) a disbelief in supernatural power.
(d) None of the above

19. Who said this, "Civilization is higher stage of cultural development characterized by intellectual, aesthetic technological and spiritual attainment"?
(a) Madver and Page
(b) S.M. Fairchild
(c) Robert Biersted
(d) Gillin and Gillin

20. Who among the following said this statement?
'Education is that part of total socialization through which we learn those roles that are based on derived needs. Thus, we call it as a process of secondary socialization'.
(a) Emile Durkheim
(b) Yogendra Singh
(c) T.K. Oommen
(d) Andre Beteille

DEC 2021 & JUNE 2022

21. Match List-I with List-II

List I (Types of Religious Organisation)	List II (Definition)
A. Sect	I. A small, new and exclusive group whose religious tradition has never been associated with and is often at odds with any established religious experience.
B. Church	II. A religious group that exhibits a general spirit of tolerance and acceptance of other religious bodies.
C. Cult	III. A large group of religiously oriented people that members are usually born in to rather than consciously join.

D. Denomination	IV. A small group of people who see themselves as true believers and who voluntarily join a group, usually broken off from a more established religion to have a personal religious experience.

Choose the **correct answer** from the options given below:
(a) A -I, B - II, C - III, D - IV
(b) A - II, B - IV, C- III, D - I
(c) A - IV, B- III, C - I, D - II
(d) A - IV, B - II, C - III, D - I

22. The book, "Patterns of Culture" is written by:
(a) B. Anderson
(b) Evans-Pritchard
(c) R. Benedict
(d) B. Malinowski

23. Which among the following are relevant and related to the national policy on education?
A. Radha Krishnan Commission
B. Murlidhar Commission
C. Kidwai Commission
D. Kothari Commission
E. Tendulkar Commission
Choose the correct answer from the options given below:
(a) A and B only
(b) A, B and E only
(c) A, B and D only
(d) A, B and C only

24. Who has suggested six dimensions of communalism: assimilationist, welfarist, retreatist, retaliatory, separatist, and secessionist?
(a) Yogendra Singh
(b) A. R. Desai
(c) T. K. Oommen
(d) G. S. Ghurye

25. Cultural phenomena combining inputs and impositions from other cultures with local realities is-
(a) Ethnocentrism
(b) Cultural imperialism
(c) Cultural hybrids
(d) Cultural relativism

26. "Cultural identities are shaped by a complex set of factors, which are associated with the process of evolution of cultural practices and beliefs of a people in course of their historical experiences." Who stated this?
(a) T. K. Oommen
(b) Yogendra Singh
(c) E. B. Tylor
(d) None of the above

JUNE 2021

27. The impact of industry on religion, according to Elton Mayo, is transformation from
(a) A religious to non-religious society
(b) An establishment of normative to open society
(c) A ritualistic to secular society
(d) An established to an adaptive society

28. According to R. Wallis, the three broad categories: World-affirming, World-rejecting and World-accommodating movements are associated with which of the following?
(a) A value-oriented movement
(b) New religious movements
(c) New social movements
(d) New age movements

29. Arrange the Varna Ashrams of the Hindu way of life in the correct sequence
A. Grihastha Ashram
B. Sanyas Ashram
C. Brahmacharya Ashram
D. Vanaprastha Ashram
Choose the correct answer from the options given below
(a) A, B, C, D
(b) D, C, A, B
(c) B, A, D, C
(d) C, A, D, B

30. What is the orientation of bureaucrats in India due to which that bureaucratic structure becomes dysfunctional?
(a) Ethnicity oriented particularism
(b) Class oriented particularism
(c) Caste and Kin oriented particularism
(d) Racial and Class oriented particularism

31. What is assumed about the Indian bureaucracy?
(a) Functional equivalents are operating everywhere
(b) Process of change is occuring everywhere
(c) Dysfunctional pattern
(d) Similarities between the Eastern and Western world

32. In Indian society, dysfunction seems to be related to which one of the following?
(a) Only relative deprivation
(b) Inequality
(c) Structural differentiations
(d) Power and relative deprivation

33. Indian bureaucracy suffers mainly from which one of the following?
(a) External cultural tension
(b) Internal cultural tensions
(c) Role conflict
(d) Normative disorder

34. Which one of the following institutions offers a stable structural foundation and growth of normative order in Indian society?
(a) Political parties (b) Democracy
(c) Bureaucracy (d) Aristocracy

JUNE 2020

35. 'Cultures of Relatedness' by Jannet Carsten is a study of ________
(a) Lankawi Islanders
(b) Coorgs
(c) Nayars
(d) Bhils

JUNE 2019

36. Which of the following terms is used for the study of symbols and signs?
(a) Epimatrix (b) Logocentric
(c) Semiotics (d) Signa matrix

37. Jallikattu is the traditional sport of which state?
(a) Tamil Nadu (b) Telangana
(c) Kerala (d) Karnataka

38. Which ruling party in Cambodia was associated with mass killing in tire 20th century?
(a) National Socialist
(b) Bosnian Nationalist Group
(c) Khmer Rouge
(d) Republican Party

39. Who emphasized that any cultural item can be analyzed through a circuit of culture?
(a) Stuart Hall
(b) David Held
(c) Max Horkheimer
(d) T W Adorno

40. Which of the following pairs of Traditional Gharanas and Musicians is NOT correctly matched?
(a) Banaras Gharana : Girija Devi
(b) Gwalior Gharana : Mogubai Kurdikar
(c) Jaipur Gharana : Kishori Amonkai
(d) Patiala Gharana : Bade Gulam All Khan

41. Who commented on the holocaust and modernity?
(a) Zygmunt Bauman
(b) Norbert Elias
(c) Ernest Gellner
(d) Benjamin Gregg

Answer Key

1. (c)	**7.** (c)	**13.** (d)	**19.** (b)	**25.** (c)	**31.** (a)	**37.** (a)
2. (d)	**8.** (c)	**14.** (b)	**20.** (b)	**26.** (b)	**32.** (d)	**38.** (c)
3. (a)	**9.** (d)	**15.** (b)	**21.** (c)	**27.** (d)	**33.** (b)	**39.** (a)
4. (d)	**10.** (c)	**16.** (d)	**22.** (c)	**28.** (b)	**34.** (c)	**40.** (b)
5. (c)	**11.** (d)	**17.** (b)	**23.** (c)	**29.** (d)	**35.** (a)	**41.** (a)
6. (a)	**12.** (a)	**18.** (a)	**24.** (c)	**30.** (c)	**36.** (c)	

Appendix

Extra Thinkers

Extra Thinkers

C W Mills

IMPORTANT BOOKS

1. The New Men of Power 1948
2. America's Labour Leaders (1948)
3. White Collar (1951)
4. The Power Elite (1956)
5. The Sociological Imagination 1959

IMPORTANT CONCEPTS

The Marxist Influence: Mills was influenced by Marxist ideas. Although he was not a strict Marxist, Mills integrated Marxist ideas into his analysis of power structures and class relations. He was critical of both capitalist and bureaucratic systems and their impact on individual freedom and autonomy.

The Sociological Imagination: He introduced the concept of 'sociological imagination' in his book 'The Sociological Imagination' (1959). The sociological imagination is the ability to connect personal experiences to larger social forces and historical contexts. Mills argued that individuals needed to understand the broader social and historical forces that shaped their lives in order to fully understand their personal troubles.

Public Issues and Private Troubles: Mills argued that individuals often experience personal troubles, but these troubles are not purely personal but are connected to the larger society. He made a distinction between personal problems (private troubles) and broader social problems (public issues). The sociological imagination enables individuals to connect their personal experiences to public problems, thereby realizing social forces.

Power Elite: In his work 'The Power Elite' (1956) Mills examined the distribution and concentration of power in American society. He argued that power in the United States was concentrated in the hands of a few elites, including business, political, and military leaders. According to Mills, this elite made decisions that affected the entire society, thereby determining the direction of the development of the nation.

White Collar: In his work 'White Collar: The American Middle Classes' (1951), Mills analyzed the rise of the white-collar class and its impact on American society. He explored the changing nature of work and the growing importance of bureaucratic organizations. Mills argued that the white-collar class played a key role in shaping modern society, and he examined the challenges and issues associated with this emerging white-collar class.

Mass Society and Mass Communication: According to Mills mass society and mass communication play a vital role in shaping public opinion and individual behaviour. He was concerned about the potential for manipulation and control through mass media and the impact of a conformist society on individual thought and action.

Critique of Abstracted Empiricism: Mills criticized 'extreme empiricism,' which meant an approach that focused only on empirical data. He believed that sociologists should strive for a more comprehensive understanding of social phenomena by implying both empirical research and theoretical frameworks.

Intellectual Craftsmanship: Mills emphasized the importance of 'intellectual craftsmanship' in sociological inquiry. This concept encourages sociologists to pursue their work while focusing on the process with a sense of responsibility and engagement. Mills believed that sociologists should be actively involved in the issues they study, fostering a connection between theory and practice.

The New Men of Power: In his later works, Mills explored the changing nature of power and the emergence of a technocratic elite. He argued that traditional sources of power, such as political and military institutions, were being supplemented by the rise of experts and technocrats who held significant influence in shaping policies and decisions.

Personal Freedom and Alienation: Mills states that a person who does not use reason and passively accepts his or her social status is what Mills calls a 'cheerful robot', in which the individual is completely isolated from the self and society. He explored how the combination of bureaucratic structures, mass communication, and concentration of power could limit personal freedom and autonomy.

DAVID HELD

IMPORTANT BOOKS

1. States and Societies
2. Models of democracy
3. Social theory of modern societies: Anthony Giddens and his critics
4. Modernity and its futures
5. Democracy and the global order: from the modern state to cosmopolitan governance
6. Cosmopolitanism: an agenda for a new world order
7. Globalization/anti-globalization: beyond the great divide

IMPORTANT CONCEPTS

Globalization: Globalization is a multidisciplinary concept that encompasses economic, political, cultural, and social dimensions. Sociologists often study how globalization influences societies and communities. This can involve examining changes in patterns of migration, the spread of global consumer culture, and the impact of transnational corporations on local communities.

Sociologists are interested in how globalization affects social structures, such as the rise of global inequality and the restructuring of labour markets. They may investigate how global networks and communication technologies influence social interactions and identity formation.

Cosmopolitanism: Cosmopolitanism, from a sociological standpoint, can be explored in terms of how individuals and communities identify with global issues. Sociologists study cosmopolitan attitudes and behaviours, looking at factors that shape people's sense of global citizenship, solidarity with distant others, and engagement in transnational social movements.

Held has three main concerns about globalization and how it affects nation-states: Weakened State Control: He believes that as countries become more connected politically, economically, and culturally, their ability to regulate and control things within their own borders is getting weaker.

Cross-Border Effects: Decisions made in one country can have big impacts on others. This means that political and economic changes can happen far away, making it harder for local governments to manage their own affairs.

Changing Identities: Globalization shifts how people see themselves and their political identities. Local and regional groups may start to question how well their central governments represent them, leading to a reevaluation of loyalty and representation.

Global Governance: Sociologists analyze the social dynamics of global governance by studying international organizations, NGOs, and transnational advocacy networks. They explore how these actors influence and interact with national and local institutions and how global policies affect communities.

Research may focus on issues like global health governance, climate change negotiations, or humanitarian interventions, examining the societal impact of these global governance mechanisms.

State Transformation: Sociological research on state transformation involves examining how changes in the nation-state's role impact national identities, citizenship, and social policies. For example, scholars may investigate how states respond to globalization by adjusting immigration policies, welfare systems, and national security measures.

Sociologists explore the social implications of the state's evolving functions, such as how shifts in governance practices affect citizens' perceptions of political authority and their sense of belonging to a nation.

Global Justice: The concept of global justice can be studied from a sociological perspective by investigating the social structures and power relations that underlie global inequalities. Sociologists may explore the root causes of poverty, the distribution of resources, and the impact of globalization on marginalized communities.

Research in global justice often delves into issues such as human rights, labour exploitation, and economic disparities, examining how these phenomena are embedded in social structures and institutions.

Donna Haraway

IMPORTANT WORKS

1. 'Primate Visions: Gender, Race, and Nature in the World of Modern Science' (1989)
2. 'Simians, Cyborgs, and Women: The Reinvention of Nature' (1991)
3. 'When Species Meet' (2008)
4. 'Staying with the Trouble: Making Kin in the Chthulucene' (2016)
5. 'Tentacular Thinking: Anthropocene, Capitalocene, Chthulucene' (2021)

IMPORTANT CONCEPTS

Cyborg Manifesto: In her influential essay 'A Cyborg Manifesto: Science, Technology, and Socialist-Feminism in the Late Twentieth Century' (1985), Haraway introduces the concept of the cyborg as a metaphor for understanding the fluid boundaries between humans and machines. She argues that the traditional boundaries between human and machine, as well as male and female, are becoming increasingly blurred. The cyborg, for her, represents a hybrid, post-gender, and post-human figure.

Situated Knowledge: Haraway advocates for 'situated knowledge,' a concept that emphasizes the importance of acknowledging one's own situated position in knowledge production. She argues that all knowledge is situated and biased by the perspectives and experiences of those who produce it. By recognizing these positions, we can aim for a more inclusive and diverse understanding of knowledge.

The Promises of Monsters: Haraway has explored the idea that monsters can serve as a way to challenge traditional categories and norms. She sees monsters as boundary-crossing figures that disrupt conventional notions of identity, particularly in terms of gender and sexuality. Monsters can offer a new way of thinking about diversity and hybridity.

Companion Species: Haraway has written about the idea of 'companion species' to describe the interconnectedness and co-evolution of humans and animals. She argues that humans and animals have developed interdependent relationships that challenge the traditional hierarchy between the two.

Material Semiotics: Haraway's work often engages with material semiotics, which examines the ways in which meaning is produced through the interaction of material objects and symbols. She emphasizes the importance of understanding how knowledge and power are shaped by these interactions.

Cyberfeminism: Haraway's work has been influential in the development of cyberfeminism, which explores the intersections of feminism and technology. Cyberfeminists often draw on her ideas to critique and challenge the gendered aspects of technology and the internet.

Kinship in the Chthulucene: In her later work, Haraway introduced the concept of the 'Chthulucene' as a way of reimagining the relationships between humans, non-human beings, and the environment. She argues for a more inclusive understanding of kinship that acknowledges the interconnectedness of all life forms.

Dorothy E. Smith

IMPORTANT WORKS

1. 'The Everyday World as Problematic: A Feminist Sociology' (1987)
2. 'Sociology From Women's Experience' (1990)
3. 'Institutional Ethnography: A Sociology for People' (2005)

IMPORTANT CONCEPTS

Standpoint Theory: First-wave standpoint theory emerged in the 1970s and 1980s, was spearheaded by feminist philosophers like Sandra Harding. Smith is best known for developing second-wave standpoint theory, which purports that individuals' social positions and experiences shape their perspectives and understandings of the world. Standpoint theory gives prominence to marginalized groups, such as women as these groups have unique insights about social structures and relationships, which can provide valuable insights into power dynamics and social inequalities.

Feminist Methodology: Smith has made significant contributions to feminist methodology. She introduced the idea of 'institutional ethnography,' a research method aimed at understanding how power operates in various institutional settings and how it affects individuals' lives. This approach focuses on uncovering the everyday experiences of individuals within institutions, with a particular focus on women's experiences.

Women's Work: Much of Smith's work was focused on understanding the work that women do, not just in the paid labour force but also the invisible, unpaid and often undervalued work that women perform in the household and community. Her work has been instrumental in shedding light on how these forms of labour contribute to the functioning of society.

Critique of Traditional Sociology: Smith has critiqued traditional sociological methods and paradigms for their androcentrism, or the approach to view the world from a male perspective. She has argued for a more inclusive and sensitive sociology that recognizes the diverse experiences and perspectives of women and other marginalized groups.

The Unacknowledged Work: Smith's work often explores the concept of 'the unacknowledged work,' meaning the invisible and undervalued work that women perform in the household and community. This work extends beyond paid labour and plays a crucial role in the functioning of society.

Gender Relations: Smith's work extensively examines the complexities of gender relations and explores how these relations intertwine with other aspects of social life, such as class, race, and ethnicity. She is known for her contribution to understanding how gender shapes power dynamics in society.

Androcentrism: Smith criticized traditional sociology for its androcentrism, which is the tendency to view the world from a male perspective. She emphasizes the importance of recognizing diverse experiences and perspectives, particularly the experiences and perspectives of women and marginalized groups.

Ivan Illich

IMPORTANT WORKS

1. "Deschooling Society' (1971)
2. "Tools for Conviviality' (1973)
3. "Medical Nemesis: The Expropriation of Health' (1974)
4. "Gender' (1982)

IMPORTANT CONCEPTS

Deschooling Society (1971): In his book 'Deschooling Society', Illich argued that the formal education system was fundamentally flawed and that it perpetuated social inequalities. He advocated decentralization of education and the promotion of learning outside traditional schools. He believed that individuals should have more control over their education and that society should focus on learning opportunities that are self-directed and learner-centred.

Medical Nemesis (1975): In 'Medical Nemesis,' Illich criticized the medical establishment, arguing that the medicalization of everyday life had led to harmful consequences. He suggested that the overreliance on medical institutions and interventions had resulted in the medicalization of normal human experiences and the erosion of people's autonomy in matters of health. He encouraged a return to more natural and self-reliant forms of healthcare.

Conviviality (1973): Illich's concept of 'conviviality' refers to the idea of creating tools, institutions, and technologies that empower individuals, promoting a more self-reliant and self-sufficient society. He believed that conviviality tools and systems should be designed to enhance human capabilities and promote cooperation rather than reliance on experts and institutions.

Tools for Conviviality (1973): Building on the concept of conviviality, in his book 'Tools for Conviviality', Illich explored the idea of designing technologies and systems that encourage people to take more control of their lives and environments. He criticized the development of large, centralized, and bureaucratic systems, arguing that they hinder individual creativity and freedom.

Energy and Equity (1974): In his work, Illich examined the relationship between transportation and social inequality. He argued that modern transportation systems, such as automobiles and highways, favoured the privileged while disadvantaging those who couldn't afford them. He advocated for the development of more equitable and sustainable transportation solutions.

Shadow work: Illich introduced the concept of 'shadow work,' which refers to the unseen or unappreciated labour and effort required to support and maintain modern industrial society. He believed that the pursuit of more and more services and goods had increased the burden of shadow work and that this contributed to a sense of dissatisfaction and frustration in people's lives.

Karl Popper

IMPORTANT WORKS

1. 'The Logic of Scientific Discovery' (1934)
2. 'The Poverty of Historicism' (1936)
3. 'The Open Society and Its Enemies' (1945)
4. 'All Life is Problem Solving' (1994)
5. 'A World of Propensities' (1990)

IMPORTANT CONCEPTS

Falsifiability: One of Popper's most notable contributions is the principle of falsifiability, which he elaborated on in his 1934 work, *The Logic of Scientific Discovery*. Popper asserted that for a theory to qualify as scientific, it must be falsifiable, meaning that there should be possible observations or experiments that could disprove it. Essentially, a scientific theory should provide specific predictions that can be tested; if these predictions are shown to be false through empirical evidence, it would indicate that the theory is inadequate. He maintained that while a theory cannot be definitively proven true, it can be proven false.

Critical Rationalism: Popper advocated for a critical approach to knowledge acquisition, which he termed 'critical rationalism.' He asserted that knowledge progresses not through verification but through falsification. Scientists should actively seek to test and potentially refute their theories, leading to the elimination of incorrect or inadequate ideas and the advancement of scientific knowledge.

Three Worlds: Popper proposed a tripartite division of reality into three distinct 'worlds.' World 1 consists of physical objects and processes; World 2 comprises subjective experiences and mental states; and World 3 includes the realm of abstract objects such as ideas, theories, and cultural artefacts. Popper suggested that scientific theories primarily belong to World 3, existing independently of individual minds.

The Criterion of Demarcation: Expanding on the idea of falsifiability, Popper introduced the criterion of demarcation. This serves as a framework for differentiating scientific theories from those that are non-scientific. He argued that scientific theories are distinguished by their falsifiability, whereas non-scientific theories, such as metaphysics and pseudoscience, are characterized by their inability to be falsified. This demarcation criterion was aimed at resolving the problem of distinguishing between science and pseudo-science, such as astrology or psychoanalysis, which may appear scientific but lack empirical evidence and falsifiability.

Conjecture and Refutation: Popper's philosophy of science emphasizes the process of conjecture and refutation. According to Popper, scientific knowledge advances through a cycle of conjecture (proposing hypotheses or theories) and refutation (testing these theories against empirical evidence). He argued that scientific progress occurs not by verifying theories through observation, as suggested by the positivist view, but by attempting to falsify them. Thus, science is a dynamic process of continually refining and replacing theories in response to empirical evidence.

The Problem of Induction: Popper criticized the traditional view of induction, which holds that scientific theories are confirmed by accumulating supportive evidence. Instead, he argued that induction is logically flawed because it relies on assuming that past observations can predict future events. Popper proposed a method of 'hypothetico-deductive' reasoning, in which scientists formulate hypotheses and then test them against empirical evidence through deduction. This approach, he believed, avoids the logical problems associated with induction.

The Open Society and Its Enemies: In his exploration of social and political philosophy, particularly in *The Open Society and Its Enemies* (1945), Popper contended that open societies are far superior to closed ones. He critiqued totalitarian ideologies, including Marxism and fascism, viewing them as threats to individual liberty and rational discourse. Popper championed the importance of democratic institutions, freedom of speech, and the critical evaluation of ideas as fundamental elements of an open society.

Louis Pierre Althusser

IMPORTANT BOOKS

1. 'For Marx' (Pour Marx) (1965)
2. 'Lenin and Philosophy and Other Essays' (Lénine et la philosophie) (1971)
3. 'Ideology and Ideological State Apparatuses' (1970, essay)
4. 'On the Reproduction of Capitalism: Ideology and Ideological State Apparatuses' (La reproduction) (1970, co-authored with Étienne Balibar)
5. 'Essays on Ideology' (1973, collection of essays)
6. "The Future Lasts Forever: A Memoir' (1992, originally published posthumously)

IMPORTANT CONCEPTS

For Marx (1965): In this work, Althusser presents a new interpretation of Marxist theory, focusing on its structural and non-humanist elements. He introduces the notion of an 'epistemological break' to describe the transformations in Marx's ideas.

Ideology and Ideological State Apparatuses (ISAs): Althusser posited that society is organized by ideology, which encompasses a set of beliefs and values that help sustain the status quo and reproduce prevailing power relations. He identified ISAs, such as education, religion, and media, as institutions that perpetuate ideology and support the dominant class.

Interpellation: Althusser introduced the idea of interpellation, which describes how individuals are addressed or called into subjectivity by ideological messages. He argued that ideology functions by encouraging individuals to perceive themselves as subjects within the social framework, thereby strengthening their roles in the established power dynamics.

The Reproduction of Capitalism: Althusser claimed that capitalism sustains itself not just through economic practices but also through ideological and cultural processes. He contended that the ruling class utilizes Ideological State Apparatuses (ISAs) to maintain its dominance over society.

Contradiction and Overdetermination: Althusser emphasized the complexity of social structures and the presence of multiple, sometimes contradictory, determining factors in historical events. He rejected a simple, linear view of history and advocated for a more nuanced analysis.

Structural Marxism: Althusser's work contributed to the development of structural Marxism, which focused on analyzing the underlying structures of society and how they shape individuals' thoughts and actions.

Reading Capital: Althusser co-authored *Reading Capital*, which provided a fresh interpretation of Karl Marx's *Capital*, highlighting the significance of understanding the structural elements within Marx's work.

Anti-Humanism: A key aspect of Althusser's philosophy was his critique of humanism in Marxism. He argued that conventional Marxism, which prioritizes the human subject and consciousness, is fundamentally flawed. Instead, he advocated for a more structural and systemic approach to understanding social relations. Althusser posited that the concept of 'humanity' is an unrealistic abstraction that obscures the conflicts between opposing classes; since human rights are abstract, the justice and equality they claim to uphold are also abstract, allowing for significant real-world inequalities.

Contradiction and Overdetermination: Althusser emphasized the complexity of social structures and the presence of multiple determining factors in historical events. His work challenged simplistic and linear views of history by highlighting the intricacies of social contradictions.

Mock Tests

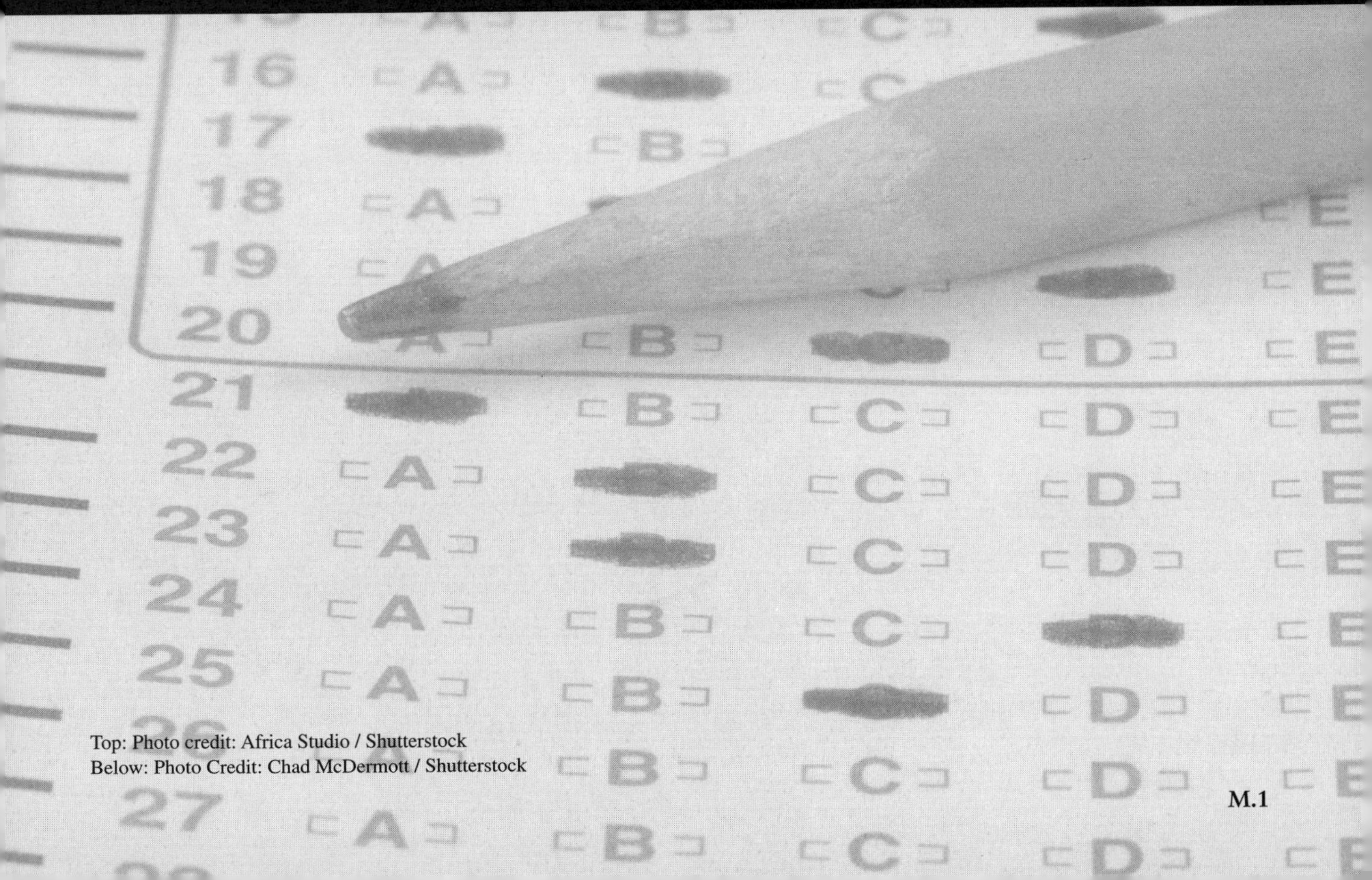

Top: Photo credit: Africa Studio / Shutterstock
Below: Photo Credit: Chad McDermott / Shutterstock

Mock Test 1

1. Identify the correct sequence according to Comte:
   (i) Astrology
   (ii) Mathematics
   (iii) Biology
   (iv) Physics
   (v) Sociology

   (a) (i), (ii), (iii), (v) and (iv)
   (b) (i), (iii), (ii), (iv) and (v)
   (c) (ii), (i), (iii), (iv) and (v)
   (d) (ii), (i), (iv), (iii) and (v)

2. Who of the following is not an evolutionary theorist?
   (a) Lewis H. Morgan
   (b) Emile Durkheim
   (c) Auguste Comte
   (d) R. K. Merton

3. Which of the following are 'sacred' items according to Durkheim?
   (1) A coconut sold in a shop
   (2) A rock with a God sculpture
   (3) A coconut offered at a temple
   (4) An artistic drawing

   Choose the right answer:

   (a) (1) and (2)
   (b) (2) and (3)
   (c) (1) and (3)
   (d) (1) and (4)

4. Which of the following factors is not a hindrance to national integration?
   (a) Casteism
   (b) Communalism
   (c) Regionalism
   (d) Urbanization

5. Statistical data can be divided into:
   (i) Individual
   (ii) Discrete
   (iii) Continuous
   (iv) Qualitative
   (a) (i), (ii) and (iii)
   (b) (ii), (iii) and (iv)
   (c) (i), (iii) and (iv)
   (d) (i), (ii), (iii) and (iv)

6. Which of the following theorist views modernity as an "unfinished project"?
   (a) Jurgen Habermas
   (b) Jeffery Alexander
   (c) James Coleman
   (d) Jean Baudrillard

7. Based on the following statements, which of the codes is correct?
   (i) A statement uninfluenced by our personal bias is said to be objective
   (ii) A statement uninfluenced by our values is said to be objective
   (iii) A statement uninfluenced by our interest is said to be objective

   (a) (i) is true, but (ii) and (iii) are false
   (b) (i) and (ii) are true, but (iii) is false
   (c) (i), (ii) and (iii) are false
   (d) (i), (ii) and (iii) are false

8. Which of the following captures the demographic transition of the population?
   A. High birth rate and high death rate
   B. Low death rate and low birth rate
   C. Declining death rate and high birth rate
   D. Declining birth rate and declining death rate

   The correct order is:

   (A) A – C – D – B
   (B) B – A – D – C
   (C) D – C – A – B
   (D) C – B – D – A

9. The basic idea in social interactionism is that Social Reality is constructed in each human interaction through the use of:
(a) Words (b) Gestures
(c) Symbols (d) Actions

10. Who viewed caste as a system of graded inequality?
(a) M. N. Srinivas
(b) S. C. Dube
(c) David Hardiman
(d) B. R. Ambedkar

11. Match List-I with List-II:

List I	List II
A. Comparative Method	I. Bacon Francis
B. Verstehen	II. J.S. Mill
C. Inductive Method	III. Durkheim
D. Inverse Deductive Method	IV. Max Weber

Code:

(a) (A)–(II),(B)–(IV),(C)–(I),(D)–(III)
(b) (A)–(III),(B)–(IV),(C)–(I),(D)–(II)
(c) (A)–(I),(B)–(III),(C)–(II),(D)–(IV)
(d) (A)–(IV),(B)–(III),(C)–(II),(D)–(I)

12. From the early years of independence, till the early nineties, India's path of development may be characterized as:
(a) Gandhian
(b) Socialist
(c) Capitalist
(d) Mixed

13. Give below are two statements, one labeled as Assertion (A) and the other as Reason (R):

Assertion (A): The Middle Range Theory does not refer to a specific theory, but is rather an approach to theory construction.

Reason (R): Middle Range approach focuses on groups rather an individuals and society

(a) Both (A) and (R) are true and (R) is the correct explanation of (A)
(b) Both (A) and (R) are true and (R) is not the correct explanation of (A)
(c) (A) is true but (R) is false
(d) (A) is false but (R) is true

14. Which of the following are push factors of migration?
A. Poverty
B. War
C. Higher wages
D. Environment pollution
(a) 'A' and 'B'
(b) 'A', 'B', and 'C'
(c) 'A', 'B', and 'D'
(d) 'B', 'C', and 'D'

15. The movement of an individual or group from a lower status to a higher status is known as:
(a) Horizontal mobility
(b) Vertical mobility
(c) Structural mobility
(d) All the above

16. Which factor is responsible for gender discrimination in the world?
(a) Ethnicity
(b) Patriarchy
(c) Race
(d) Education

17. According to Randal Collins the primary basis of conflict is:
(a) Inequality
(b) Coercive force to control others
(c) Authority
(d) Domination

18. Who used the terms 'Simple' and 'Complex' streams to study Indian civilization?
(a) N. K Bose
(b) G. S. Ghurye
(c) Surajit Sinha
(d) Louis Dumont

19. The concept of 'Class in itself' and 'Class for itself' are used by:
(a) Max Weber
(b) Karl Marx
(c) Antonio Gramsci
(d) Kingsley Davis

20. Which of the following energy sources used in houses are environment friendly?
(a) Solar
(b) Coal
(c) Petrol-driven vehicle
(d) Gas

21. Which of the following are the principal types of Social Stratification?
(i) Caste
(ii) Class
(iii) Religion
(iv) Estate
(v) Political Party
(a) (i), (ii) and (iii) are correct
(b) (i), (iii), and (iv) are correct
(c) (i), (ii), and (iv) are correct
(d) (i), (iii), and (v) are correct

22. The second green revolution is based on the introduction of which technology?
(a) Pesticides
(b) Fertilizers
(c) Irrigation
(d) Genetically modified seeds

23. Which of the following 'Tribe in India practice polyandry'?
(a) Nagas (b) Gonds
(c) Baigas (d) Todas

24. Who studied the agricultural system and land relations in South India during British rule?
(a) Henry Maine
(b) Charles Metcalfe
(c) Oscar Lewis
(d) J. H. Hutton

25. Match the thinker with the concepts:

Thinker	Concept
A. Max Weber	I. Logical Action
B. W. I. Thomas	II. Self-fulfilling prophecy
C. B. Malinowski	III. Rational Action
D. V. Pareto	IV. Kula Exchange

Code:
(a) (A)–(III),(B)–(I),(C)–(II),(D)–(IV)
(b) (A)–(II),(B)–(IV),(C)–(I),(D)–(III)
(c) (A)–(III),(B)–(II),(C)–(IV),(D)–(I)
(d) (A)–(II),(B)–(I),(C)–(III),(D)–(IV)

26. Which one of the following forms of the family affect positively in urban industrial society?
(a) Joint family
(b) Nuclear family
(c) Avunculocal
(d) Matrilocal

27. Which one of the following statements is not correct?
(a) Culture is social and learned
(b) Culture is a biological inheritance and it is uniform in all the societies
(c) Culture is continuous and cumulative
(d) Culture is dynamic and adaptive

28. The book '*Sociology*: A *Multiple Paradigm Science*' was written by:
(a) George Ritzer
(b) Anthony Giddens
(c) Herbert Blumer
(d) Thomas Kuhn

29. The Vice-Chancellor of a university is considered as an:
(a) Ascriptive Status
(b) Achieved Status
(c) Ascriptive Power
(d) Both Ascriptive and Achieved Power

30. Indicate the forms of procedure which are recognized and accepted by society and govern the relations between individuals and groups.
(a) Process
(b) Social Action
(c) Institutions
(d) Interaction

31. Match the following:

Theory of Social Change	Social Thinker
A. Unilineal evolution	I. Max Weber
B. Rise and fall	II. Auguste Comte
C. Cyclic theory	III. Tonybee
D. Conflict	IV. Karl Marx

Code:
(a) (A)–(II),(B)–(I),(C)–(III),(D)–(IV)
(b) (A)–(II),(B)–(III),(C)–(I),(D)–(IV)
(c) (A)–(III),(B)–(II),(C)–(I),(D)–(IV)
(d) (A)–(I),(B)–(II),(C)–(III),(D)–(IV)

32. According to Althusser, ideology is:
(a) Submission
(b) Structure
(c) Ritual
(d) Primary obviousness

33. **Assertion (A):** People shape their surroundings
Reason (R): We live in a world in which people and social world are shaped by the structure of language
(a) Both (A) and (R) are correct
(b) (A) is correct and (R) is wrong
(c) (A) is wrong and (R) is correct
(d) Both (A) and (R) are wrong

34. Which unit does not have a membership?
(a) Institution (b) Community
(c) Association (d) Group

35. Giving prizes to competitors is an example of:
(a) Ratio Scale
(b) Interval Scale
(c) Nominal Scale
(d) Ordinal Scale

36. Which matter is important in the 'third' wave of feminism?
(a) Ensure equality with female
(b) Reduce the authority of male
(c) To change the sex ratio
(d) To improve the opportunity for women's development

37. Given below are two statements, which are labeled an Assertion (A) and the other as Reason (R) :
Assertion (A): A positivist approach is based on the physical and natural science model.
Reason (R): It assumes that social phenomena obey the Laws the same way as natural phenomena.
(a) Both (A) and (R) are true and (R) is the correct explanation of (A)
(b) Both (A)and (R) are true and (R) is not the correct explanation of (A)
(c) (A) is true but (R) is false
(d) (A) is false but (R) is true

38. Which one of the following tribals was studied by David G. Mandelbaum?
(a) Kota (b) Garo
(c) Khasi (d) Santhal

39. Based on the following statements, which of the codes is correct?

Statement I: A quartile is a special case of a percentile

Statement II: A quartile is the 25th percentile

(a) I is true but II is false
(b) I is false but II is true
(c) Both I and II are true
(d) Both I and II are false

40. Ashish Bose is well known for his concept of:
(a) Demographic transition
(b) Population explosion
(c) Sustainable development
(d) BIMARU states

41. Which of the following is a probability sampling technique?
(a) Cluster Sampling
(b) Purposive Sampling
(c) Quota Sampling
(d) Snowball Sampling

42. Who amongst the following has studied peasant movements with a historical perspective in the Indian context?
(a) S. C. Dube
(b) David Hardiman
(c) D. N. Dhanagare
(d) A. R. Desai

43. A process in which generalizations are inferred from specific facts is known as?
(a) Deductive method
(b) Inductive method
(c) Retroductive method
(d) Logic

44. Which of the following is not associated with Derrida's contribution?
(a) Cultural capital (b) Logocentrism
(c) Deconstruction (d) Difference

45. Based on the following statements, which of the codes is correct?

Statement I: A tentative statement asserting a relationship between two or more variables is called a Hypothesis.

Statement II: A statement in which we posit no relationship between variables is not a hypothesis.

(a) I is true but II is false
(b) I is false but II is true
(c) Both I and II are true
(d) Both I and II are false

46. Which among the following is categorized as a primitive tribe in Maharashtra?
(a) Dublas
(b) Kathodi
(c) Chaudhari
(d) Gamit

47. Match the following:

List I	List II
A. M.N. Srinivas	I. Shamirpet
B. A. Beteille	II. Rampura
C. S.C. Dube	III. Kishan Garhi
D. M. Marriot	IV. Ram Kheri
	V. Sripuram

Code:
(a) (A)–(II), (B)–(V),(C)–(I),(D)–(III)
(b) (A)–(IV),(B)–(I),(C)–(II),(D)–(III)
(c) (A)–(IV),(B)–(II),(C)–(I),(D)–(III)
(d) (A)–(II),(B)–(V),(C)–(III),(D)–(I)

48. Who has classified social action into logical' and 'non-logical'?
(a) Max Weber
(b) Malinowski
(c) W. Ogburn
(d) V. Pareto

49. Match the thinkers with the concepts they introduced:

Thinker	Concept
A. Homans George	I. In-group and out-group
B. Tonnies, Ferdinand	II. Primary and Secondary Group
C. Cooley, C.H.	III. Gemeinschaft and Gesellschaft
D. Summer, W. G.	IV. Closed and Open groups

Code:
(a) (A)–(IV), (B)–(III), (C)–(II), (D)–(I)
(b) (A)–(IV), (B)–(I), (C)–(II), (D)–(III)
(c) (A)–(III), (B)–(II), (C)–(I), (D)–(IV)
(d) (A)–(IV), (B)–(II), (C)–(III), (D)–(I)

50. A small group of employees in the same work area or doing similar type of work who voluntarily meets regularly for about an hour every week to identify, analyze and resolve work-related problems not only to improve quality, productivity, and the total performance of the organization, but also to enrich the quality of work life of employees. This is known as
(a) Taskforce
(b) Quality circles
(c) Trade Union
(d) Professional Union

51. The perspective which is based on the belief that women are everywhere violently oppressed by patriarchy is:
(a) Radical Feminism
(b) Socialist Feminism
(c) Psychoanalytic Feminism
(d) Liberal Feminism

52. **Assertion A:** In the sense of Durkheimian theory, the Prevention of Domestic Violence Act of India is an example of social fact.

Reason R: Laws are social facts according to Durkheim as they are external to an individual and coercive in nature.

Key:
(a) Both 'A' and 'R' are right and 'R' is the correct explanation of 'A'
(b) Both 'A' and 'R' are correct, but 'R' is not the correct explanation of 'A'
(c) 'A' is correct, but 'R' is not correct
(d) 'A' is wrong but 'R' is correct

53. Who is the author of the book '*The passing of Traditional Society*'?
(a) E.S.N. Eisenstadt
(b) Talcott Parsons
(c) Yogendra Singh
(d) Daniel Lemer

54. According to Robert Merton, function refers to those consequences which are:
(a) not observed but make for the adaptation of a system
(b) observed but latently make for the adjustment of a system
(c) manifest but not recognized for the adaptation of a system
(d) observed and recognized for the adaptation of a system

55. Which of the following sociologists have presented the classification of Agrarian Social Structure in India?
(a) S.C. Dube
(b) Irawati Karve
(c) Daniel Thorner
(d) Robert Redfield

56. Descent traced through both father's kin and mother's kin is known as................. form of descent.
(a) Patrilateral (b) Avuncular
(c) Bilateral (d) Matrilateral

57. Functionalism looks at:
1. a society with different social institutions as disparate from each other
2. a social system as an integrated system
3. each part of the society functioning independently of the other
4. a social system as a system with interrelated parts

Identify the correct code:
(a) (1) and (2)
(b) (2) and (3)
(c) (1) and (4)
(d) (2) and (4)

58. The biological capacity of childbearing in a woman is called:
(a) Birth rate
(b) Pregnancy
(c) Fertility
(d) Fecundity

59. Which of the following features of the action theory of Parsons is mismatched?
(a) Adaptation—economy
(b) Goal attainment—polity
(c) Integration—Law
(d) Latency/pattern maintenance—nature

60. The intermediary position in a Guild System between Guild Master and Apprentice is:
(a) Craftsman
(b) Foreman
(c) Journeyman
(d) Keyman

61. Which of the following is not included in the primary group?
(a) Village community
(b) Neighbour group
(c) Family
(d) Labour union

62. The title of the book authored by Peter Berger and Thomas Luckmann:
(a) The Phenomenology of the Social World
(b) Phenomenology and Social Relation
(c) The Social Construction of Reality
(d) Sociology of Knowledge

63. Which of the following captures Auguste Comte's theory of change?
(a) Theological to metaphysical to positivism
(b) Metaphysical to theological to industrial
(c) Industrial to metaphysical to theological
(d) Positivism to theological to metaphysical

64. Based on the following statements, which of the codes is correct?

Statement I: Caste status is ascribed to the individual by birth, whereas class status is achieved by the individual.

Statement II: Both class and caste are endogamous social units.

(a) I is true but II is false
(b) I is false but II is true
(c) Both I and II are true
(d) Both I and II are false

65. Match Column 1 with Column 2:

List I (Authors)	List II (Books)
A. Judith Butler	I. Vindication of the Rights of Women
B. Simone de Beauvoir	II. Sex, Gender and society
C. Ann Oakley	III. The Second Sex
D. Mary Wollstonecraft	IV. The Other Side of Silence
	V. Gender Trouble

Key:

(a) (A)–(II); (B)–(V); (C)–(IV); (D)–(III)
(b) (A)–(III); (B)–(II); (C)–(I); (D)–(V)
(c) (A)–(V); (B)–(III); (C)–(II); (D)–(I)
(d) (A)–(IV); (B)–(I); (C)–(III); (D)–(II)

66. Emile Durkheim has made a distinction between the following two types of solidarity:
(a) Mechanical Solidarity and Organic Solidarity
(b) Structural Solidarity and Functional Solidarity
(c) Organic Solidarity and Social Solidarity
(d) Social Solidarity and Functional Solidarity

67. **Assertion A:** According to Pareto, the circulation of elites is a change from those having characteristics of lions to foxes and then to lions and so on.

Reason R: For Pareto, the circulation of elites takes place because of changes in economic structure.

Key:

(a) Both 'A' and 'R' are correct and 'R' is the correct explanation of 'A'
(b) Both 'A' and 'R' are right, but 'R' is not the correct explanation of 'A'
(c) 'A' is right, but 'R' is not correct
(d) 'A' is wrong but 'R' is right

68. Match the following:

Author	Book
A. David Harrison	I. End of History and the Last Man
B. Samuel P. Huntington	II. Challenge of World Poverty
C. Francis Fukuyama	III. Sociology of Modernization and Development
D. Gunnar Myrdal	IV. Political Order in Changing Societies

(a) (A)–(III), (B)–(I), (C)–(IV), (D)–(II)
(b) (A)–(IV), (B)–(III), (C)–(II), (D)–(I)
(c) (A)–(II), (B)–(I), (C)–(IV), (D)–(III)
(d) (A)–(III), (B)–(IV), (C)–(I), (D)–(II)

69. Foucault thought that archaeology was a necessary first step towards:
(a) Genealogy of power
(b) Discourse analysis
(c) Clinics and medicine
(d) Deconstruction

70. The Green Revolution was introduced in India during the year:
(a) 1964–65 (b) 1968–70
(c) 1966–67 (d) 1971–72

71. The process by which a person's social values, beliefs, and norms are re-engineered, like in a monastery or mental asylum, is called:
(a) Anticipatory socialization
(b) Socialization
(c) Re-socialization
(d) Adult socialization

72. According to the 2011 Census Report Urban Population in India is:
(a) 27.8% (b) 31.2%
(c) 33.2% (d) 28.5%

73. Who contributed notably to industrial sociology in India?
(a) I. P. Desai (b) N. R. Sheth
(c) A. R. Desai (d) A. M. Shah

74. Which of the following are not related to the measures initiated under Land Reforms in India?
(a) Tenancy Reforms and Ceilings on Agricultural land holdings
(b) Abolition of intermediaries and consolidation of land holdings
(c) Corporate farming and land lease
(d) Reorganization of agriculture and redistribution of land

75. Industrial society tends to be an open society. The assignment of the job as such is according to:
(a) The traditional caste basis
(b) The family status
(c) On the basis of racial preferences
(d) Technical skill

76. Harry Braverman argues that modem capitalism has produced a manufacturing division of labour as a consequence of work is:
(a) Augmented
(b) Curtailed
(c) Deskilled
(d) Skilled

77. Ethnomethodology is known as a(n):
(a) Sociology of everyday life
(b) Critique of phenomenology
(c) Rejection of Herbert Spencer's views
(d) Fusion of Marx and Weber

78. The cornerstone of Functional Theory is:
(a) Parts (b) Interconnection
(c) Consensus (d) Inequality

79. Choose the correct code while using an interview schedule.

A. There is no face-to-face meeting between the interviewer and the respondent
B. There is a face-to-face meeting
C. The questions can be only structured
D. The questions can be structured and unstructured

Key:
(a) (A) and (B) are true
(b) (B) and (C) are true
(c) (A) and (D) are true
(d) (B) and (D) are true

80. Conversation analysis is used in which theoretical approach?
(a) Ethnomethodology
(b) Neofunctionalism
(c) Phenomenology
(d) Positivism

81. In the ______ phase of industrial society, production is organized according to principles of flexible specialization.
(a) Modernism
(b) Fordism
(c) Post Fordism
(d) Post Industrialism

82. Match the column 1 and 2:

Column-I	Column-2
A. Harold Garfinkel	I. The Phenomenology of the Social World
B. Alfred Schultz	II. Studies in Ethnomethodology
C. Peter L. Berger	III. Writing and Difference
D. Erving Goffman	IV. The Presentation of Self in Everyday life
	V. The Social Construction of Reality

Key:
(a) (A)–(II); (B)–(III); (C)–(IV); (D)–(V)
(b) (A)–(III); (B)–(IV); (C)–(V); (D)–(I)
(c) (A)–(V); (B)–(II); (C)–(I); (D)–(III)
(d) (A)–(II); (B)–(I); (C)–(V); (D)–(IV)

83. The French Sociologist who worked on the Trinity of Knowledge, Power, and Truth is:
(a) Auguste Comte
(b) Emile Durkheim
(c) Lyotard
(d) Foucault

84. Under the traditional caste system, which one of the following imposed strict sanctions in the matters of social interactions with the members of other castes?
(a) Varna (b) Caste
(c) Sub-caste (d) Kinship

85. The Death of the subject we find in ______ perspective.
(a) Post Modernist (b) Conflict
(c) Interactionist (d) Structuralist

86. Who has questioned Sociology's commitment to positivism and empiricism?
(a) Historians (b) Modernists
(c) Post-modernists (d) Psychologists

87. Who is the author of the book '*India's urbanization*'?
(a) Asha Bhinde
(b) Tara Kanitkar
(c) Dr. Chandrasekhar
(d) Dr. Ashish Bose

88. Who has studied Indian society with an indological perspective?
(a) M.N. Srinivas (b) S.C. Dube
(c) G.S. Ghurye (d) I.P. Desai

89. The gap that exists between Material Culture and Non-material Culture is called Cultural Lag by:
(a) William Frankhiem
(b) W.I. Thomas
(c) W.F.Ogburn
(d) Karl Manheim

90. Indicate the scholar who used the concept of '*Sacred Complex*' for analysis of the integrative pattern of the culture in India.
(a) T. N. Madan (b) Sacchidananda
(c) S. C. Dube (d) L. P. Vidyarthi

91. Based on the following statements, which of the codes is correct?

Statement I: According to Habermas society is composed of both life world and system.

Statement II: The system in the modem world has come to be controlled by the life world restricting communication.
(a) I is true but II is false
(b) I is false but II is true
(c) Both I and II are true
(d) Both I and II are false

92. Max Weber's research on the rise of capitalism identified .... as the key influences in its development.
(a) Political reforms
(b) Religious ethic
C. The development of technologies
D. Foreign exploration

93. Which of the following is correct regarding Post-Structuralism?

i. they questioned the soundness of ontology and demonstrated the emergence of Truth regimes
ii. they developed new ways of thinking about difference and identity

iii. they are anti-essentialist rather than grounded or fixed a priori.

(a) i only (b) i and ii only
(c) iii only (d) all are right

94. What is ethnomethodology?
(a) The study of sociological research methods
(b) The study of the methods people use to make sense of the world
C. The study of language in everyday conversations
D. The use of experiments in sociological research

95. The typology of Social Action given by Max Weber is:
i. Rational Action in relation to Goal
ii. Rational Action in relation to Value
iii. Traditional Action
iv. Moral Action
(a) i and ii are right
(b) ii and iii are right
(c) i, ii, and iii are right
(d) iii and iv are right

96. Match the following:

List I (Author)	List II (Book)
A. Paul Baran	I. Dependency is Dead: Long Live Dependency and Class Struggle
B. Samir Amin	II. The stages of Economic Growth
C. Rostow	III. Crisis of Nationalism and Socialism
D. Andre Gunder Frank	IV. The Political Economy of Growth

(a) (A)–(II), (B)–(III), (C)–(I), (D)–(IV)
(b) (A)–(III), (B)–(I), (C)–(IV), (D)–(II)
(c) (A)–(IV), (B)–(III), (C)–(II), (D)–(I)
(d) (A)–(III), (B)–(IV), (C)–(I), (D)–(II)

97. Garfinkel's experiments were designed to:
(a) Find out how easy it is to annoy people
(b) Make people be specific about their meaning
(c) Identify unstated assumptions involved in the talk
(d) the study of how social order is produced

98. Which of the following Acts enforces employers to provide maternity benefits to women employees disablement benefits and medical benefits to all employees?
(a) Workmen's Compensation Act, 1923
(b) The Employees Provident Fund and Miscellaneous Provisions Act, 1952
(c) The Payment of Gratuity Act, 1952
(d) The Employees State Insurance Act, 1948

99. Yogendra Singh's contribution to 'Modernization of Indian Tradition' is based on which perspective?
(a) Marxian
(b) Ethnomethodological
(c) Structural-functional
(d) Evolutionary

100. It is an organized association of workers in a trade or profession, formed to further their rights and interests.
(a) Taskforce (b) Quality circles
(c) Trade Union (d) Professional Union

Answer Key

1. (d)	**16.** (b)	**31.** (b)	**46.** (b)	**61.** (d)	**76.** (d)	**91.** (a)
2. (d)	**17.** (a)	**32.** (b)	**47.** (a)	**62.** (c)	**77.** (a)	**92.** (b)
3. (b)	**18.** (c)	**33.** (a)	**48.** (d)	**63.** (a)	**78.** (b)	**93.** (d)
4. (d)	**19.** (b)	**34.** (a)	**49.** (a)	**64.** (a)	**79.** (d)	**94.** (b)
5. (b)	**20.** (a)	**35.** (d)	**50.** (b)	**65.** (c)	**80.** (a)	**95.** (c)
6. (a)	**21.** (c)	**36.** (a)	**51.** (a)	**66.** (a)	**81.** (b)	**96.** (d)
7. (b)	**22.** (d)	**37.** (a)	**52.** (a)	**67.** (c)	**82.** (d)	**97.** (d)
8. (a)	**23.** (d)	**38.** (a)	**53.** (d)	**68.** (d)	**83.** (d)	**98.** (d)
9. (c)	**24.** (a)	**39.** (c)	**54.** (d)	**69.** (a)	**84.** (c)	**99.** (c)
10. (d)	**25.** (c)	**40.** (d)	**55.** (c)	**70.** (a)	**85.** (a)	**100.** (c)
11. (b)	**26.** (b)	**41.** (d)	**56.** (c)	**71.** (c)	**86.** (c)	
12. (b)	**27.** (b)	**42.** (b)	**57.** (d)	**72.** (b)	**87.** (d)	
13. (c)	**28.** (a)	**43.** (b)	**58.** (d)	**73.** (b)	**88.** (c)	
14. (c)	**29.** (b)	**44.** (a)	**59.** (d)	**74.** (c)	**89.** (c)	
15. (b)	**30.** (c)	**45.** (a)	**60.** (a)	**75.** (d)	**90.** (d)	

Mock Test 2

1. Which of the following are associated with the Social Contract Theory?
   (i) Jean Jaques Rousseau
   (ii) Herbert Spencer
   (iii) John Locke
   (iv) Voltaire
   (v) Thomas Hobbes
   (a) (i), (iii) and (iv)
   (b) (ii), (iii) and (v)
   (c) (i), (iii) and (v)
   (d) (i), (ii) and (iii)

2. The consequence of a cultural item that lessens the adaptation and adjustment of a system is:
   (a) Function
   (b) Eufunction
   (c) Manifest Function
   (d) Dysfunction

3. The idea of 'Risk Society' was explored by:
   (a) U. Beck
   (b) J. Habermas
   (c) A. Schultz
   (d) H. Blumer

4. Statistical data can be divided into:
   (i) Individual
   (ii) Discrete
   (iii) Continuous
   (iv) Qualitative
   (a) (i), (ii) and (iii)
   (b) (ii), (iii) and (iv)
   (c) (i), (iii) and (iv)
   (d) (i), (ii), (iii) and (iv)

5. Who believe that meaning, mind, and the social world are shaped by the structure of language?
   (a) Functionalists
   (b) Interactonists
   (c) Anthropologists
   (d) Structural Linguists

6. A tribal chief enjoys which form of authority?
   (a) Rational-legal
   (b) Charismatic
   (c) Traditional
   (d) Magical

7. The series of changes in Indian Society as a result of 150 years of British rule in Indiais referred to as:
   (a) Modernization (b) Westernization
   (c) Globalization (d) Anglicanization

8. Anthony Giddens, in his structuration theory, makes a distinction between two forms of consciousness. They are:
   (a) False consciousness and rational consciousness
   (b) Discursive consciousness and practical consciousness
   (c) Conscious and unconscious mind
   (d) Individual self and social self

9. A Socio-psychological condition of the individual that involves his estrangement from some aspects of his social existence is called:
   (a) Retreatism
   (b) Alienation
   (c) Rebellion
   (d) Ritualism

10. Louis Dumont is known for which study?
    (a) Marriage as Sanskara
    (b) Family organization
    (c) Caste-system
    (d) Kinship types

11. Based on the following statements, which of the codes is correct?

    Statement I: Spearman introduced the concept of Rank correlation.

    Statement II: He based his concept on the correlation between qualitative variables.

(a) I is true but II is false
(b) I is false but II is true
(c) Both I and II are true
(d) Both I and II are false

12. Which article provides for the employer to give maternity benefits to his employees?
(a) Article 42 (b) Article 40
(c) Article15 (d) Article 20

13. Match List-I with List-II:

List I	List II
A. Economy	I. Adaptation
B. Polity	II. Latency
C. Family	III. Goal Attainment
D. Religion	IV. Integration

Code :
(a) (A)–(I), (B)–(III), (C)–(II), (D)–(IV)
(b) (A)–(III), (B)–(IV), (C)–(II), (D)–(I)
(c) (A)–(III), (B)–(I), (C)–(II), (D)–(IV)
(d) (A)–(I), (B)–(II), (C)–(IV), (D)–(III)

14. Which two terms are often used interchangeably?
(a) Post-modernism and modernism
(b) Post-modernism and critical theory
(c) Marxism and post-modernism
(d) Post-modernism and post-structuralism

15. Based on the following statements, which of the codes is correct?

Statement I: The mean of a population is known as a parameter.

Statement II: The mean of a population can be computed from a sample of the population.

(a) I is true but II is false
(b) I is true but II is true
(c) Both I and II are true
(d) Both I and II are false

16. Which of the following is not seen in slums?
(a) Inadequate water supply
(b) High density of population
(c) Poverty
(d) White-collar crimes

17. Which of the following concept is associated with C.W. Mills?
(a) Empiricism
(b) Functional Imperatives
(c) Sociological Imagination
(d) Symbolic Interactionism

18. The white revolution is associated with bringing changes inthe production of which commodity in India?
(a) Wheat (b) Wool
(c) Cotton (d) Milk

19. Which of the following is not a characteristic of the Caste System?
(a) Endogamy
(b) Social Hierarchy
(c) Hereditary Occupation
(d) Achieved Status

20. After the 73rd amendment, which unit of the Panchayati Raj institution is not constituted for a particular period?
(a) Panchayat Samiti
(b) Sarpanch
(c) Gram Sabha
(d) District Panchayat President

21. Students saying good morning to a teacher can be regarded as an example of:
(i) Folkways
(ii) Mores
(iii) Laws
(iv) Morals
(v) Customs

(a) (i) and (v)
(b) (iv) and (v)
(c) (ii) and (v)
(d) (i), (iv), and (v)

22. The death of women during pregnancy or childbirth is captured by which measure?
(a) Infant mortality rate
(b) Crude death rate
(c) Maternal mortality rate
(d) Fertility rate

23. Which of the following are elements of a complex organization?
(i) Identified goals
(ii) Ascribed roles
(iii) Membership by birth
(iv) Voluntary membership
(v) Authority structure
(vi) A set of clear-cut rules

(a) (i), (ii), (iv), (v), and (vi)
(b) (i), (iii), (iv), (v), and (vi)
(c) (ii), (iii), (iv), (v), and (vi)
(d) (i), (iv), (v), and (vi)

24. According to demographers, what fertility rate in a country ensures a stable population?
(a) 3.5
(b) 3.1
(c) 2.5
(d) 2.1

25. Identify the chronological order in which the works of Durkheim appeared?
(i) Rules of the Sociological Method
(ii) Suicide
(iii) Elementary forms of Religious Life
(iv) Division of Labour in Society

(a) (i), (iii), (iv) and (ii)
(b) (iv), (i), (iii) and (ii)
(c) (i), (iii), (ii) and (iv)
(d) (iv), (i), (ii) and (iii)

26. Who has studied sociologically the Jajmani system in the Indian village?
(a) Oscar Lewis
(b) A. C. Mayer
(c) Robert Redfield
(d) Owen Lynch

27. Given below are two statements, one labeled as Assertion (A) and the other as Reason (R):

Assertion (A): The state is different from Government

Reason (R): The state is one of the organs of the Government

(a) Both (A) and (R) are true and (R) is the correct explanation of (A)
(b) Both (A) and (R) are true and (R) is not the correct explanation of (A)
(c) (A) is true but (R) is false
(d) is false but (R) is true

28. Complete the following phrase: Neo-Functionalism was originally intended as:
(a) A grand theory of integration
(b) A response to the failures of intergovernmentalism
(c) A theory of integration for Latin America
(d) A practical theory of integration

29. Given below are two statements, one labeled as Assertion (A) and the other as Reason (R):

Assertion (A): There is a relationship between the concepts of Sanskritization and Reference Group behaviour.

Reason (R): Sanskritization can be considered as ease of Reference Group behaviour.

(a) Both (A) and (R) are true and (R) is the correct explanation of (A)
(b) Both (A) and (R) are true and (R) is not the correct explanation of (A)
(c) (A) is true but (R) is false
(d) (A) is false but (R) is true

30. According to post-modernists, which ideas of modernity are considered as 'dead'?
(a) Reason, rationality, and progress
(b) Rationality, progress, and objectivity
(c) Legality, progress. and objectivity
(d) Reason, legality, and rationality

31. Which one of the following is an example of community?
(a) Hindu Religion
(b) Caste
(c) Race
(d) Village

32. Which one of the following statements is true from a conflict perspective?
(a) Stability requires a consensus and the support of a society's members
(b) Cultural traits all work toward stabilizing society
(c) A common culture serves to maintain the privileges of certain groups
(d) Practices such as prostitution continue to survive because they contribute to the overall social stability

33. Kerala achieved a high sex ratio (1084 females per 1000 males in 2011) because of :
(a) respect for women
(b) higher literary among men
(c) higher literary among women
(d) better maternal healthcare

34. Which is the concept linked to Geographical Area?
(a) Institution
(b) Association
(c) Society
(d) Community

35. Which of the following statements is not correct?
(a) Sociology is a pure science and not an applied science
(b) Sociology is a concrete science
(c) Sociology is a categorical and not a normative discipline
(d) Sociology is a rational and an empirical science

36. According to Radhakamal Mukherjee, value means culturally determined.....
(a) Norms (b) Desires and goals
(c) Religion (d) Law

37. Robert Merton believed the following are not essential postulates for functional analysis:
(i) Postulate of functional unity
(ii) Postulate of functional differentiation
(iii) Postulate of functional universality
(iv) Postulate of functional adaptation
(v) Postulate of functional indispensability

(a) (i), (ii), (iii) are correct
(b) (i), (iii), (v) are correct
(c) (ii), (iii), (iv) are correct
(d) (ii), (iv), (v) are correct

38. The spread of 'invention and discovery from one area to another' identified by William Ogburn is referred to as:
(a) Evolution (b) Diffusion
(c) Revolution (d) Functionalism

39. Given below are two statements, one labeled as Assertion (A) and the other as Reason (R).

Assertion (A): Most sociologists believed that social progress is inevitable.

Reason (R): Social change is due to socioeconomic, political, and technological factors.

(a) Both (A) and (R) are true and(R) is the correct explanation of (A)
(b) Both (A) and (R) are true and (R) is not the correct explanation of (A)
(c) (A) is true but (R) is false
(d) (A) is false but (R) is true

40. Who said that a sociologist who wants to understand the caste system must free himself from the hold of the Varna model?
(a) J. H. Hutton
(b) McKim Marriot
(c) M. N. Srinivas
(d) S. C. Roy

41. The Standard Deviation for the following data is:
10, 10, 10, 10, 10, 10, 10, 10, 10, 10, 10
(a) 1 (b) 10
(c) 100 (d) 0

42. Who coined the term 'ethnocentrism'?
(a) W. G. Sumner (b) W. Ogbum
(c) Max Weber (d) T. Adorno

43. According to which scholar, most often action is routine and relatively unreflexive?
(a) Harold Garfinkel
(b) Erwing Goffman
(c) Alfred Schultz
(d) Max Weber

44. Indicate the true statement, postmodernism:
(a) advocates methods of science
(b) is a reaction to grand theorization
(c) attempts a functional analysis
(d) is eventually a political discourse

45. **Assertion 'A':** Low child-sex ratio in India is mainly due to female foeticide.
Reason 'B': Son preference is quite strong in India owing to the patriarchal system.
Codes:
(a) Both 'A' and 'R' are true and 'R' is the correct explanation of 'A'
(b) Both 'A' and 'R' are true, but 'R' is not the correct explanation of 'A'
(c) 'A' is true, but 'R' is false
(d) 'A' is false, but 'R' is true

46. According to Max Weber, values have an important role while attempting which aspect of sociological research?
(a) selecting a research problem
(b) collecting data
(c) analyzing data
(d) theorizing about research

47. Which of the following technique of data collection is more suitable for historical research and cross-cultural studies?
(a) Interview Schedule
(b) Case Study
(c) Content Analysis
(d) Projective techniques

48. **Assertion 'A':** There is a growing need for the indigenization of sociology in developing societies.
Reason 'R': The major sociological theories were based on the experiences of developed countries in the west.
Codes:
(a) Both 'A' and 'R' are correct, and 'R' is the correct explanation of 'A'
(b) Both 'A' and 'R' are true, but 'R' is not the correct explanation of 'A'.
(c) 'A' is true, but 'R' is false
(d) 'A' is false, but 'R' is true

49. Plan that directs the research design, which does not require a working hypothesis to conduct a research study:
(a) Exploratory Research Design
(b) Descriptive Research Design
(c) Experimental Research Design
(d) Quasi-Experimental Research Design

50. D. P. Mukerjee observes that in order to be an Indian sociologist, one must be an Indian first in the sense that:
(a) Must be born in India
(b) One must be an uncritical admirer of Indian society and culture
(c) One must be a Sanskritist scholar
(d) One must be acquainted with Indian tradition and culture

51. Based on the following statements, which of the codes is correct?
Statement I: When the calculated value of Chi-square is lower than the critical value, the null hypothesis is rejected.
Statement II: When the null hypothesis is rejected, we can say that there is no relationship between the variables in question.
(a) I is true but II is false
(b) I is false but II is true
(c) Both I and II are true
(d) Both I and II are false

52. The ability to control others in spite of resistance is called by Max Weber as:
(a) Power (b) Authority
(c) Class (d) Charisma

53. Identify the measures of variability among the following:
(i) Mean
(ii) Range
(iii) Mean Deviation
(iv) Median
(v) Standard Deviation

(a) (i), (ii), and (v)
(b) (ii), (iii), and (v)
(c) (i), (iii), and (v)
(d) (iii), (iv), and (v)

54. The observation which occurs most frequently in a sample is, called:
(a) Median
(b) Mean deviation
(c) Standard deviation
(d) Mode

55. Match the following:

List I	List II
A. Test of Variance	I. F-test
B. Test of Association	II. Correlation
C. Test of Difference	III. T-test
D. Test of interdependency	IV. T-test
	V. Regression

Code:
(a) (A)–(III),(B)–(I),(C)–(IV),(D)–(II)
(b) (A)–(I),(B)–(II),(C)–(IV),(D)–(III)
(c) (A)–(I),(B)–(III),(C)–(III),(D)–(IV)
(d) (A)–(III),(B)–(I),(C)–(II),(D)–(IV)

56. Who is the author of the book *'The Holy Family'*?
(a) Marx
(b) Weber
(c) Durkheim
(d) Comte

57. Which of the following are the characteristics of a Modern society?
(i) Familialism
(ii) Liberalism
(iii) Dogmatism
(iv) Market economy
(v) Secularism

(a) i, ii and v
(b) ii, iv and v
(c) ii, iii, and iv
(d) i, iv and v

58. Which scholar studied social life as a series of dramatic performances, similar to those performed on a stage?
(a) Peter Berger
(b) Erving Goffman
(c) Alfred Schutz
(d) Garfinkel

59. The clan is an:
(a) Endogamous kinship group
(b) Exogamous kinship group
(c) Both endogamous and exogamous kinship group
(d) None of the above

60. An alternate hypothesis is also called:
(a) Null Hypothesis
(b) Statistical Hypothesis
(c) Simple Hypothesis
(d) Research Hypothesis

61. Displacements of human beings are caused by:
1. Construction of Irrigation Projects
2. Laying of four lanes, six lanes roads
3. Construction of Special Economic Zones
4. Housing Schemes

(a) 1 and 2 are correct
(b) 1, 3, and 4 are correct
(c) 1, 2, and 3 alone are correct
(d) 2, 3, and 4 are correct

62. The term 'core' in the theories of modernization refers to the societies based on:
(a) free-market economy
(b) mixed economy
(c) agricultural activities
(d) developing societies

63. Ethnomethodologists use ____________ experiments.
(a) Breaching (b) Listening
(c) Etcetera (d) Langeter

64. In Weber's theory of action, which of the following forms of action characterizes bureaucracy?
(a) Traditional (b) Affective
(c) Utilitarian (d) Rational

65. Michel Foucault used the concept of bio-power, which includes:
(a) Knowledge, Power, and Pleasure
(b) Discipline and Punishment
(c) Discourse and Discontent
(d) Content and Discontent

66. Which one of the following is useful for a qualitative study?
(a) Survey method
(b) Case study
(c) Census
(d) Sample

67. The Bhopal Industrial disaster took place affecting 5,21,000 people through death or gas related illness in the year________:
(a) 1974
(b) 1984
(c) 1994
(d) 2004

68. Which of the following matching the author and book is not correct?
(a) Louis Dumont – *Homo Hierarchicus*
(b) T. K. Oommen – *Functional theory of stratification*
(c) Bernard Barber – *Social stratification*
(d) B. R. Ambedkar – *Castes in India: Their Mechanism, Genesis, and Development*

69. When a caste consolidates horizontally and asks for special policies for its development, it acts like a:
(a) Political Party
(b) Pressure Group
(c) Dominant Caste
(d) Class for itself

70. When a couple, after marriage, set up residence in a new place, it is called which form of residence?
(a) Patrilocal
(b) Matrilocal
(c) Neolocal
(d) Avunculocal

71. Match the following:

List I	List II
A. Kaka Kalelkar	I. Investigate the Death of Subhas Chandra Bose
B. Kothari	II. Backward Class Commission
C. Kapur	III. Investigate the Death of Mahatma Gandhi
D. Khosla	IV. Patten of Education in India

Code:
(a) (A)–(II), (B)–(III), (C)–(IV), (D)–(I)
(b) (A)–(I), (B)–(IV), (C)–(III), (D)–(II)
(c) (A)–(II), (B)–(IV), (C)–(III), (D)–(I)
(d) (A)–(I), (B)–(III), (C)–(II), (D)–(IV)

72. What is the term used when one places a priority on understanding other cultures, rather than dismissing them as 'strange' or 'exotic'?
(a) Ethnocentrism
(b) Culture shock
(c) Cultural relativism
(d) Xenocentrism

73. ______ is an unconscious self that determines the activity of a person.
(a) Id
(b) Ego
(c) Reflexivity
(d) Supergo

74. Who explained the difference between positivism and interpretative sociology?
(a) Auguste Comte
(b) C. Wright Mills
(c) Anthony Giddens
(d) Alvin W. Gouldner

75. 'Protestant Ethic and the Spirit of Capitalism› was the classic work of:
(a) Emile Durkheim
(b) Max Weber
(c) Talcott Parsons
(d) Karl Marx

76. Who defined a sample as a smaller representation of a larger whole?
(a) Walker and Lev
(b) Mueller and Schuessler
(c) Goode and Hatt
(d) Wilson Gee

77. Giddens defines modernity in terms of:
1. Capitalism
2. Control of means of violence
3. Industrialism
4. Globalization
5. Surveillance capacities
(a) 1, 2, 3, and 5
(b) 1, 2, 3, and 4
(c) 2, 3, 4, and 5
(d) 1, 3, 4, and 5

78. Who first gave the concept of multiple statuses?
(a) R.K. Merton
(b) Ralph Linton
(c) Kingsley Davis
(d) Michel Foucault

79. Which of the following Sociologist is not concerned with the concepts of Little Traditions and Great Traditions?
(a) D.N. Majumdar
(b) Robert Redfield
(c) Melton Suiges
(d) Mckim Marriot

80. Math the author in the column -I with their work in column-2.

Column I	Column II
A. S.C. Dube	I. Social Tensions in India
B. N.K Bose	II.Indian Village
C. G.S. Ghurye	III. People of India
D. K.S. Singh	IV. The Structure of Hindu Society

Key:
(a) (A)–(I); (B)–(III); (C)–(IV); (D)–(II)
(b) (A)–(III); (B)–(I); (C)–(II); (D)–(IV)
(c) (A)–(II); (B)–(IV); (C)–(I); (D)–(III)
(d) (A)–(IV); (B)–(II); (C)–(III); (D)–(I)

81. The Concentric Zone Theory related to the patterns of Urban Growth was propounded by:
(a) Hoyt
(b) E.J.Miller
(c) M. Carstairs
(d) Burgess

82. According to Max Weber, an ideal type is a:
(a) Common situation in a given society
(b) Model society aspired for
(c) Conceptual tool to understand social phenomena
(d) Statistical findings of a social researcher

83. Scientific Management was propounded by:
(a) Harry Braverman
(b) F.W. Taylor
(c) E.B. Tylor
(d) Pennock

84. Which one of the following is not a measure of correlation?
(a) Chi-square
(b) Student's t-test
(c) Mean dispersion
(d) Product movement coefficient

85. Which of the following are the methods of Settlement of Industrial Disputes?
1. Conciliation
2. Cooperation
3. Arbitration
4. Adjudication
5. Participation

(a) 1, 3, and 4 alone are right
(b) 1, 2, and 4 are right
(c) 1, 3, 4, and 5 are right
(d) All are right

86. In the participant observation technique :
(a) the respondent knows the benefits of the research to him/ her
(b) the researcher participates in a social situation
(c) the respondent does not know the purpose of the research
(d) the researcher tries to influence the course of the situation

87. Match the following concept/notion with the thinker in the context of modernity:

Notion	Thinker
A. Unfinished Project	I. Anthony Giddens
B. Runway	II. Zygmund Bauman
C. Holocaust	III. Ulrich Beck
D. Risk Society	IV. Habermas

(a) (A)–(III),(B)–(II),(C)–(IV),(D)–(I)
(b) (A)–(I),(B)–(II),(C)–(IV),(D)–(III)
(c) (A)–(I),(B)–(II),(C)–(III),(D)–(IV)
(d) (A)–(IV),(B)–(I),(C)–(II),(D)–(III)

88. Which of the following theory states that individuals learn deviant behaviour from those close to them who provide models of and opportunities for deviance?
(a) Labelling theory
(b) Differential association theory
(c) Cultural deviance theory
(d) Social disorganization theory

89. The colonized societies are also referred to as:
(a) Third World (b) Feudal Societies
(c) Second World (d) First World

90. Match the following:

Theoretical Perspective	Social Thinker
A. Structural-Functional Perspective	I. David Hardiman
B. Marxian Perspective	II. N.K. Bose
C. Civilizational Perspective	III. M.N. Srinivas
D. Subaltern Perspective	IV. D.P. Mukherjee

(a) (A)–(III),(B)–(IV),(C)–(II),(D)–(I)
(b) (A)–(IV),(B)–(III),(C)–(I),(D)–(II)
(c) (A)–(II),(B)–(III),(C)–(IV),(D)–(I)
(d) (A)–(III),(B)–(I),(C)–(IV),(D)–(II)

91. Symbolic Interactionism is severely criticized because it gives too much emphasis on the interaction of the self and ignores the:
(a) Culture (b) Social structure
(c) Social change (d) Language

92. Modern society is not a single social system with related parts but several systems with some commonly recognized institutions:
(a) Geoffrey Alexander
(b) Niklas Luhman
(c) George Ritzer
(d) Talcott Parsons

93. The roots of critical theory in sociology are based on the thinking of the scholars who promoted it.
(a) Subjective understanding of Max Weber
(b) Idealism of Karl Marx
(c) Ethnomethodological perspective
(d) Phenomenological understanding

94. The ________ of lower castes of the ways of higher castes, which M.N. Srinivas calls Sanskritization.
(a) Social Conflict
(b) Imitative Behaviour
(c) Anticipatory Socialization
(d) Social Change

95. Who is known for using participant observation while doing fieldwork among the tribals?
(a) D.N. Majumdar (b) T.B. Naik
(c) Verrier Elwin (d) Indra Dev

96. The classification of Action into Logical and Non-logical Action was given by:
(a) Max Weber
(b) Vilfredo Pareto
(c) Talcott Parsons
(d) R.K.Merton

97. Who is the author of the book, '*The Presentation of Self in Everyday Life*'?
(a) Garfinkel
(b) Goffman
(c) G. H. Mead
(d) C.H.Cooley

98. Who stressed that the primitive people also had a rational view and discovered the principle of reciprocity?
(a) Radcliffe-Brown
(b) Bronislaw Malinowski
(c) Golden Weiser
(d) C. Kluckhohn

99. Who have separately made a contribution to the study of social movements in India?
(a) Rudolph and Rudolph
(b) A.R. Desai and Pillai
(c) M.S.A. Rao and T.K. Oomen
(d) S.C. Dube and Leela Dube

100. Based on the following statements, which of the codes is correct?

Statement I: The number of female babies born is always higher than male babies

Statement II: Starting from conception, the death rate of females is higher than that of males
(a) I is true but II is false
(b) I is false but II is true
(c) Both I and II are true
(d) Both I and II are false

Answer Key

1. (c)	**16.** (d)	**31.** (d)	**46.** (a)	**61.** (c)	**76.** (c)	**91.** (b)
2. (d)	**17.** (c)	**32.** (c)	**47.** (b)	**62.** (a)	**77.** (a)	**92.** (b)
3. (a)	**18.** (d)	**33.** (d)	**48.** (a)	**63.** (a)	**78.** (b)	**93.** (b)
4. (b)	**19.** (d)	**34.** (d)	**49.** (b)	**64.** (d)	**79.** (b)	**94.** (b)
5. (b)	**20.** (c)	**35.** (d)	**50.** (d)	**65.** (b)	**80.** (c)	**95.** (c)
6. (c)	**21.** (a)	**36.** (b)	**51.** (a)	**66.** (b)	**81.** (d)	**96.** (b)
7. (b)	**22.** (c)	**37.** (b)	**52.** (a)	**67.** (b)	**82.** (c)	**97.** (b)
8. (b)	**23.** (d)	**38.** (b)	**53.** (a)	**68.** (b)	**83.** (b)	**98.** (b)
9. (b)	**24.** (d)	**39.** (d)	**54.** (d)	**69.** (b)	**84.** (c)	**99.** (c)
10. (c)	**25.** (d)	**40.** (c)	**55.** (b)	**70.** (c)	**85.** (d)	**100.** (a)
11. (a)	**26.** (a)	**41.** (d)	**56.** (a)	**71.** (c)	**86.** (b)	
12. (a)	**27.** (c)	**42.** (a)	**57.** (b)	**72.** (d)	**87.** (d)	
13. (a)	**28.** (a)	**43.** (c)	**58.** (b)	**73.** (a)	**88.** (b)	
14. (b)	**29.** (b)	**44.** (b)	**59.** (a)	**74.** (c)	**89.** (a)	
15. (a)	**30.** (a)	**45.** (a)	**60.** (d)	**75.** (b)	**90.** (a)	

Mock Test 3

1. According to Comte, ________ will be the Supreme Commandment in the religion of humanity.
(a) Sociocracy
(b) Live for others
(c) Egoism
(d) Positivism

2. From a Marxian perspective, the source of power in society lies in the
(a) Exploitation
(b) Poverty
(c) Coercion
(d) Legitimacy

3. In the military society, individuals exist for the benefit of the:
(a) Society
(b) State
(c) Groups
(d) Civilians

4. Who has written the book *'The origin of Family, Private Property, and State'*?
(a) Hobhouse
(b) Hobbes
(c) Fredrich Engels
(d) Pavne

5. Mechanical Solidarity is solidarity of:
(a) Resemblance
(b) Difference
(c) Repressive
(d) Punitive

6. Neo-Marxism believes in at least Semi Autonomy of
(a) The religious sphere
(b) The political sphere
(c) The production sphere
(d) The social sphere

7. 'Remember, that time is money.' Who made this statement?
(a) Marx
(b) Weber
(c) Merton
(d) Spencer

8. What are the four distinguishing transformations that took place in 'Modernity' according to Lee and Newby?
(a) Industrialization, Capitalism, Urbanism, and Liberal Democracy
(b) Industrialization, Capitalism, Colonialism, and Liberal Democracy
(c) Urbanism, Capitalism, Colonialism and Industrialization
(d) Colonialism, Capitalism, Urbanism and Liberalism

9. Logical actions are motivated by reasoning while non-logical actions are by ________.
(a) Legal
(b) Sentiments
(c) Objective realities
(d) Localized behaviour

10. The concept of a 'Symmetrical family' was propounded by
(a) Young and Willmott
(b) Talcott Parsons
(c) Robin Fox
(d) David and Moore

11. At the height of the class conflict the petty bourgeoisie and the lumpenproletariat became drawn into the rank of ________.
(a) Bourgeoisie
(b) Petty Bourgeoisie
(c) Proletariat
(d) Capitalist

12. Who among the following advocated a separation between 'an account of what happened and of what the researcher thought about the event'?
(a) Lofland
(b) Howard Becker
(c) P. Atkinson
(d) C. Geertz

13. Which of the following logic of Hegel was rejected by Marx?
(a) Idealistic trammel
(b) Dialectics
(c) Idealism
(d) Materialism

14. Identify the process by which the quality of earth is worsened and its valuable natural elements are stripped away through overuse, drought or inadequate fertilization.
(a) Desertification
(b) Deforestation
(c) Soil Degradation
(d) Landfill

15. Who among the following explained Sociology as a humanistic discipline?
(a) Thomas Luckman
(b) Derrida
(c) Peter Berger
(d) Althusser

16. According to Karl Marx the notion of 'Alienation' of labour first comes in
(a) Class struggle
(b) Production of objects for exchange in the market
(c) Highly developed division of labour
(d) Surplus value

17. Which of the following names is associated with the concept of 'Network Society'?
(a) Bill Deval
(b) Manuel Castell
(c) Daniel Bell
(d) Ulrich Beck

18. In which of the following reports published by the United Nations the concept of '*Sustainable Development*' was introduced?
(a) Our Common Future
(b) Human Rights Development
(c) Millennium Development Goals
(d) World Summit Report on sustainable development.

19. Who criticized the functional unity of society?
(a) Bronislaw Malinowski
(b) Coser
(c) Parsons
(d) Robert K Merton

20. While describing the importance of meaning in human action, who developed a premise that human beings act towards things on the basis of the meanings that the things have for them.
(a) George Herbert Spencer
(b) George Simmel
(c) Talcott Parsons
(d) Herbert Blumer

21. Malinowski's functional analysis is largely based on ________.
(a) Needs
(b) Tribes
(c) Culture
(d) Values

22. In terms of the classification of social groups, match the thinkers in List – I with, their concepts in List – II and choose the correct answer from the codes given below.

List I (Thinkers)	List II (Concepts)
A. F. H. Giddings	I. In-groups and out-groups
B. G. Simmel	II. Genetic and congregate groups
C. P. A. Sorokin	III. Reference group
D. Muzaffer Sheriff	IV. Small groups and Large groups
E. W. G. Sumner	V. Primary and Secondary group
	VI. Vertical and Horizontal group

Codes:
(a) A–III, B–IV, C–VI, D–I, E–V
(b) A–II, B–V, C–VI,D–III, E–I
(c) A–II, B–IV, C–VI, D–III, E–I
(d) A–IV, B–VI, C–V, D–II, E–III

23. Who among the following has said 'Households are factories which produce human personalities'?
(a) Talcott Parsons
(b) William Goode
(c) Philip N. Cohen
(d) George Murdock

24. The mental picture of oneself is called ________.
(a) Mind
(b) Vision
(c) Looking glass self
(d) Feelings

25. Who among the following expounded the theory of 'Socio-cultural change'?
(a) Robert Redfield
(b) Pitirim Sorokin
(c) Charles H. Cooley
(d) Edward B. Taylor

26. Who among the following introduced phenomenology to American Sociology?
(a) Peter Berger (b) Thomas Luckman
(c) Alfred Schutz (d) Humans

27. Match the thinkers in List – I with their concepts in List – II and choose the correct answer from the codes given below.

List I (Thinkers)	List II (Concepts)
A. Oscar Lewis	I. Relative deprivation
B. Kate Millet	II. Trained Incapacity
C. Diana Pearce	III. Culture of poverty
D. Samuel Stouffer	IV. Feminization of poverty
E. Thorstein Veblen	V. Sexual politics
	VI. Strangers to Ourselves

Codes:
(a) A–III, B–IV, C–VI, D–I, E–II
(b) A–III, B–V, C–IV, D–I, E–II
(c) A–II, B–V, C–IV, D–III, E–I
(d) A–IV, B–VI, C–V, D–II, E–I

28. ________ is a political action beyond the rules of the established political system.
(a) Ethnic conflict
(b) Sub nationalism
(c) Corruption
(d) Terrorism

29. With regards to the forms of social control, match the thinkers in List – I with the forms of social control in List – II and choose the correct answer from the codes given below.

List I (Thinkers)	List II (Control form)
A. Karl Manheim	I. By sanction and by socialization
B. C. H. Cooley	II. Positive and Negative
C. Kimbal Young	III. Physical force and human symbol
D. Hayes	IV. Direct and Indirect
E. Lumby	V. Formal and Informal
	VI. Conscious and unconscious

Codes:
(a) A–IV, B–VI, CII–, D–I, E–III
(b) A–IV, B–V, C–II, D–III, E–I
(c) A–II, B–IV, C–VI, D–I, E–III
(d) A–IV, B–VI, C–V, D–II, E–III

30. Power is not simply repressive or coercive but can be productive. Who proposed this view?
(a) Derrida (b) Bourdieu
(c) Foucault (d) Althusser

31. Match List – I with List – II and indicate the correct answer using the codes given below.

List I	List II
A. 'Elites and Society'	I. T.B. Bottomore
B. 'Voting behaviour in an Indian village'	II. S.V. Kogekar
C. 'Reports on the Indian general election'	III. W.H. Morris Jones
D. 'Parliament in India'	IV. A.H. Somjee

Codes:
(a) A–I, B–II, C–IV, D–III
(b) A–III, B–IV, C–II, D–I
(c) A–I, B–IV, C–II, D–III
(d) A–III, B–II, C–IV, D–I

32. Time-space Distanciation refers to the fact that:
(a) Relationships are tied to locals
(b) Relationships are no longer tied to specific locals
(c) Relationships are unlimited
(d) More relations are dangerous

33. Which one of the following is not one of the four elements of alienation in industrial societies according to Robert Blauner?
(a) Powerlessness
(b) Insulation
(c) Meaninglessness
(d) Isolation

34. According to Habermas, distorted communication is the equivalent of Marx's ________.
(a) Class Consciousness
(b) False Consciousness
(c) Rationality
(d) None of these

35. Given below are two statements, one labelled as Assertion (A) and the other as Reason (R). examine the statements and indicate the correct answer by choosing the codes below.

Assertion (A): Female literacy in India is still not satisfactory.

Reason (R): Women's employment may improve girl education.

Codes:
(a) Both 'A' and 'R' are individually true and 'R' is the correct explanation of 'A'
(b) Both 'A' and 'R' are individually true but 'R' is not the correct explanation of 'A'
(c) 'A' is true but 'R' is false
(d) 'A' is false but 'R' is true

36. Match the following:

List I	List II
A. Protection of certain rights regarding freedom of speech	I. Article 334
B. Equality of Opportunity in public employment	II. Article 16
C. Reservation of seats in legislative bodies for SCs & STs	III. Article 338
D. National Commission for SCs & STs	IV. Article 19

(a) A–IV, B–III, C–I, D–II
(b) A–II, B–IV, C–III, D–I
(c) A–III, B–II, C–IV, D–I
(d) A–IV, B–II, C–I, D–III

37. Which one of the following is central to the phenomenological method?
(a) First-person point of view
(b) Second-person point of view
(c) Third-person point of view
(d) Social point of view

38. Which of the following statement is correct?
(a) Hypothesis must be specific
(b) Hypothesis must be consistent with laws of nature
(c) Hypothesis should be related to a body of theory
(d) Hypothesis should always be correct

39. Which one of the following is not a feature of caste?
(a) Mobility
(b) Hierarchy
(c) Occupation
(d) Heredity

40. Measurement of variables can be performed at four levels. They are nominal, ordinal, interval and ______.
(a) Ratio
(b) Numerical
(c) Quantitative
(d) Explanatory

41. Given below are two statements, one labelled as Assertion (A) and the other are Reason(R). examine the statements and indicate the correct answer by choosing the codes below.

Assertion (A): Better prospects among Dalit students depend on the attainment of higher education.

Reason (R): The reservation policy provides opportunities for higher education for Dalit students.

Codes:

(a) Both 'A' and 'B' are individually true and 'R' is the correct explanation of 'A'
(b) Both 'A' and 'R' are individually true but 'R' is not the correct explanation of 'A'
(c) 'A' is true but 'R' is false
(d) 'A' is false but 'R' is true

42. Lottery method is an example of ______.
(a) Non-Probability
(b) Convenient sampling
(c) Probability
(d) Quota sampling

43. "Post-Fordist" systems of production are described as
(a) More Productive
(b) More homogenous
(c) More efficient
(d) More flexible

44. Research design provides us with a ______.
(a) Theory
(b) Sample
(c) Experimental method
(d) Blueprint

45. Given below are two statements, one labelled as Assertion (A) and the other are Reason (R). examine the statements and indicate the correct answer by choosing the codes below.

Assertion (A): City dwellers satisfy their needs through secondary groups.

Reason (R): Urban problems cannot be solved by primary groups.

Codes:

(a) Both 'A' and 'R' are individually true and 'R' is the correct explanation of 'A'
(b) Both 'A' and 'R' are individually true but 'R' is not the correct explanation of 'A'
(c) 'A' is true but 'R' is false
(d) 'A' is false but 'R' is true

46. One of the limitations of the questionnaire is:
(a) Low cost
(b) Time saving
(c) Greater anonymity
(d) Only for educated people

47. Families meet the needs of society to socialize children and reproduce new members. This statement most closely reflects
(a) Marxism
(b) Feminism
(c) Functionalism
(d) Interactionism

48. Which among the following is not a purpose of the Case study?
(a) To probe the phenomenon deeply
(b) To get anecdotal evidence
(c) To refute a universal generalization
(d) To analyze the context

49. According to phenomenologists, phenomena can only be studied
(a) Subjectively (b) Objectively
(c) Imaginatively (d) Insightfully

50. Correlation between tests and criterion are called ________.
(a) Validity Coefficient
(b) Reliability
(c) Operational validity
(d) Pragmatic validity

51. According to Peter Berger and Thomas Luckmann the disintegration of socially constructed knowledge systems lead to
(a) Anomic
(b) Alienation
(c) Disorientation
(d) Adaptation

52. ________ is a firm belief that man is a reasonable animal able to think out of difficulty and to serenity.
(a) Anthropocentrism
(b) Rationalism
(c) Idealism
(d) Humanism

53. George Ritzer refers to the adoption of characteristics of Fordism in food industries as
(a) Food colonialism
(b) Food-Fordism
(c) McDonaldism
(d) Burgerism

54. A way of writing for change and of relating to the world through policy initiative, activism, and social movements is called ________.
(a) Public Sociology
(b) Engaged Sociology
(c) Reflexive Sociology
(d) Political Sociology

55. Neo-functionalism is an attempt to overcome which of the following shortcomings of structural functionalism?
(a) Empiricism and systematism
(b) Over-determinism and reductionism
(c) Anti-individualism and conservatism
(d) Idealism and dynamism

56. IPCC is associated with ________.
(a) Global warming
(b) Climate change
(c) Waste disposal
(d) Rural Community care

57. The process through which the general concepts are translated into specific measurable variables is known as
(a) Operationalization of concepts
(b) Conceptualization of variables
(c) Translation of concepts
(d) Conceptualization of facts

58. Who among the following proposed Intermediate technology for development?
(a) Wallerstein (b) Rostow
(c) M.K. Gandhi (d) Schumacher

59. Knowledge as the basis of stratification is found in
(a) Industrial Societies
(b) Pre-industrial societies
(c) Post-industrial societies
(d) Pre-modern societies

60. Champaran Agitation in Bihar was led by:
(a) Gandhiji
(b) Naxals
(c) Zagoria
(d) Communist party

61. The concept 'Out-group' was first coined by
(a) Charles Cooley
(b) Ferdinand Tonnies
(c) Emile Durkheim
(d) William Sumner

62. According to G.S Ghurye, which among the following is not a foundation of culture?
(a) Toleration
(b) Religious Consciousness
(c) Justice
(d) Civilization

63. If a 'reference group' is viewed from the point of 'Shared World-perspective' providing meaning to the 'Self' which of the following sociological perspectives encompasses that view
(a) System perspective
(b) Structuralist perspective
(c) Functionalist perspective
(d) Symbolic Interactionist Perspective

64. Match the following:

List I	List II
A. Sociology	I. Ferdinand Tonnies
B. Sociography	II. E O Wilson
C. Sociobiology	III. J L Moreno
D. Sociometry	IV. Auguste Comte

(a) A–II, B–I, C–IV, D–III
(b) A–II, B–IV, C–III, D–I
(c) A–IV, B–I, C–II, D–III
(d) A–IV, B–II, C–I, D–III

65. Which of the following names is associated with 'Social Epidemiology'?
(a) Margaret S. Archer
(b) Graham Scambler
(c) Richard G. Wilkinson
(d) Mike Bury

66. Who among the following conducted a Village study at 'Shamirpet'?
(a) N.K. Bose
(b) Yogendra Singh
(c) S.C. Dube
(d) Ranjit Guha

67. Which of the following research designs is employed in phenomenological research?
(a) Experimental and analytical
(b) Diagnostic and interpretative
(c) Experimental and descriptive
(d) Descriptive and interpretive

68. The 'gender role' refers to
(a) The biological fact that we are male and female
(b) The role that is given to us by a teacher
(c) The role that is given to us in play
(d) The role that is given to us by society

69. The Indian sociologist who applied the Marxist perspective to the study of Indian social culture:
(a) M.N. Srinivas
(b) A.R. Desai
(c) D.D. Kosambi
(d) Radhakamal Mukherjee

70. Who of the following is known for his contributions to 'World System Theory'?
(a) Shamir Amin
(b) Immanuel Wallerstein
(c) Max Weber
(d) Talcott Parsons

71. Which of the following stage is not discussed by Karl Marx?
(a) Primitive Communism
(b) Ancient Society
(c) Feudal society
(d) Complex Society

72. Who classified societies into 'simple, compound, doubly compound, trebly compound?
(a) Marx
(b) Comte
(c) Herbert Spencer
(d) Sorokin

73. The Indian sociologist who considered that property relations are crucial because they shape and control the objectives underlying production:
(a) Dhanagare
(b) Andre Beteillie
(c) A.R. Desai
(d) T.K. Oommen

74. The name of the family among Khasis is
(a) Loga
(b) Ling
(c) Masai
(d) Guna

75. Facial expression is an example of ____ communication.
(a) Paralanguage
(b) Paralinguistics
(c) Verbal
(d) Non-verbal

76. The book '*Peasant struggle in India*' is written by
(a) B.C. Biswas
(b) A.R. Desai
(c) Kathleen Gough
(d) Bela Bhatia

77. ISO 14000 is a series of International Standards for ____________.
(a) Environmental Management
(b) Environmental pollution
(c) Environmental efficiency
(d) Environmental degradation

78. Who wrote '*Social Origins of Dictatorship and Democracy*'?
(a) Barrington Moore
(b) A.M. Khusro
(c) L.P. Vidhyarthi
(d) Radhakamal Mukherjee

79. Kyoto Protocol is a legally binding international agreement to reduce ____________.
(a) Air pollution
(b) Water pollution
(c) Soil pollution
(d) Greenhouse gas emission

80. Who distinguished between 'Status Society' and 'Class Society'?
(a) Robert Merton
(b) Talcott Parsons
(c) Max Weber
(d) Emile Durkheim

81. The United Nations Conference on Human Environment held in Stockholm was implemented by the Government of India by creating the:
(a) Environment Protection Act
(b) Water Pollution Act
(c) Air Pollution Act
(d) Wildlife Protection Act

82. Which of the following is not a measure of Central tendency?
(a) Arithmetic Mean
(b) Median
(c) Mode
(d) Standard Deviation

83. The process of entering one country from another to take a permanent or semi-permanent residence is called ____________.
(a) Migration (b) Immigration
(c) Net migration (d) Out migration

84. Which of the following is true about Arithmetic mean?
(a) It is known and most frequently used average
(b) It is not affected by the value of every case in the series
(c) It is inferior to either median or mode
(d) It is less reliable than the median

85. One of the causes of the failure of Gram Sabhas:
(a) Lack of people's participation
(b) Lack of programmes
(c) Lack of audit
(d) Lack of Funds

86. Who among the following is a proponent of a dialectical approach to the study of Indian Society?
(a) M.N. Srinivas
(b) D.P. Mukherji
(c) Andre Beteille
(d) Y.B. Damle

87. ____________ refers to electronic media that work on digital codes.
(a) Digital arts
(b) Digital media
(c) Digital Convergence
(d) Digital technology

88. A satisfactory average should be
(a) Complex in nature
(b) Abstract in form
(c) Definite and rigorously defined
(d) Smaller in size

89. ____________ refers to electronic media that work on digital codes.
(a) Digital arts
(b) Digital media
(c) Digital Convergence
(d) Digital technology

90. ____________ are being established online and transcend geographical boundaries, eliminating social restrictions.
(a) Internet
(b) Virtual Communities
(c) Facebook
(d) Globalization of news

91. Who stresses, 'The Primacy of Power and the consequent inevitability of the conflict'?
(a) Karl Marx
(b) Ralf Dahrendorf
(c) Michel Foucault
(d) Anthony Giddens

92. ____________ is an area of social living marked by some degree of social cohesion.
(a) Society
(b) Association
(c) Committee
(d) Community

93. Caste system is believed to have a divine origin, while class is:
(a) Conservative
(b) Closed
(c) Secular
(d) Ascribed status

94. Panchayati Raj system is based on the principle of
(a) Rule of Law through Panchayats
(b) Democratic decentralization of administration
(c) Administration through government officials
(d) Effective central administration for the improvement of Villages

95. Hindu marriage is a ____________
(a) Sanction (b) Contract
(c) Agreement (d) Sacrament

96. Feminization of poverty means
(a) The critical deconstruction of poverty by feminist theorists
(b) Women's increased chances of being in poverty due to low pay and greater welfare dependency
(c) The way in which managing a budget and avoiding poverty tends to be a women's responsibility within the home
(d) The disproportionate number of female sociologists who do research on poverty

97. Who among the following had said that 'Knowledge is Power'?
(a) Francis Bacon
(b) Ivan Illich
(c) Wilbert. E Moore
(d) Kingsley Davis

Carefully read the following passage and answer questions 98, 99 and 100.

Social movements come in all shapes and sizes. Some are very small, numbering no more than a few dozen members; others may include thousands or even millions of people. While some social movements carry on their activities within the laws of the society in which they exist, others operate as illegal or underground groups. Social movements often arise; with the aim of bringing about change on a public issue, such as expanding civil rights for a segment of the population.

In response to social movements, counter-movements sometimes arise in defense of the status quo. The campaign for women's right to abortion, for example, has been vociferously challenged by anti-abortion (pro-life) activists, who argue that abortion should be illegal.

We can view new social movements in terms of a 'paradox of democracy'. While faith in traditional politics seems to be waning, the growth of NSMs is evidence that citizens in late modern societies are not apathetic or uninterested in politics, as is sometimes claimed. Rather there is a belief that direct action and participation are more useful than reliance on politicians and political systems.

More than ever before, people are supporting social movements as a way of highlighting complex moral issues and putting them at the centre of social life.

98. As per the text, social movements emerge with the intention of
(a) Bringing about change in the personal sphere
(b) Bringing about change on a public issue
(c) Bringing improvement in profit rates of industries
(d) Encouraging a person to change his/her lifestyle

99. As per the text, countermovements sometimes emerge
(a) in defense of the status quo
(b) in support of changing the lifestyles of groups
(c) in support of bringing equality among social groups
(d) in defense of democracy

100. As per the text, the following is the meaning of the 'paradox of democracy'
(a) The citizens in the late modern societies an uninterested in politics
(b) The citizens in the late modern society have full faith in traditional political systems
(c) With the declining faith in the traditional polities, people believe in direct action and participation
(d) The citizens in the late modern societies try to over through political systems.

Answer Key

1. (b)
2. (c)
3. (b)
4. (c)
5. (a)
6. (a)
7. (b)
8. (d)
9. (b)
10. (a)
11. (c)
12. (a)
13. (a)
14. (c)
15. (c)
16. (b)
17. (b)
18. (a)
19. (d)
20. (d)
21. (c)
22. (c)
23. (a)
24. (c)
25. (b)
26. (c)
27. (b)
28. (d)
29. (a)
30. (c)
31. (c)
32. (b)
33. (b)
34. (b)
35. (a)
36. (d)
37. (a)
38. (d)
39. (a)
40. (a)
41. (a)
42. (c)
43. (d)
44. (d)
45. (c)
46. (d)
47. (c)
48. (d)
49. (a)
50. (a)
51. (b)
52. (c)
53. (c)
54. (a)
55. (c)
56. (b)
57. (a)
58. (d)
59. (c)
60. (a)
61. (d)
62. (d)
63. (d)
64. (c)
65. (c)
66. (c)
67. (d)
68. (d)
69. (b)
70. (b)
71. (d)
72. (c)
73. (c)
74. (b)
75. (d)
76. (b)
77. (a)
78. (a)
79. (d)
80. (c)
81. (a)
82. (d)
83. (b)
84. (a)
85. (a)
86. (b)
87. (b)
88. (c)
89. (b)
90. (b)
91. (b)
92. (d)
93. (c)
94. (b)
95. (d)
96. (b)
97. (a)
98. (b)
99. (a)
100. (c)

Mock Test 4

1. Theoretical Saturation' as a concept refers to:
   (a) a state where no additional data are being found to develop properties of the category
   (b) a criterion for judging when to increase the sample size
   (c) a state where the researcher feels confident about redrawing the sample size
   (d) a state researcher finds his sampling as biased

2. Wife's brother's son is an example of ________ kin.
   (a) Primary kin
   (b) Secondary kin
   (c) Tertiary kin
   (d) Supplementary kin

3. The relative deprivation approach attempts to
   (a) Measure the poverty of those below the poverty line
   (b) Determine the privileges of the rich
   (c) Assess the minimum food requirements
   (d) Assess the deprivation of a section of the population as compared to the others

4. According to Spencer, which among the following is not a basic law of evolution?
   (a) Law of persistence of Force
   (b) Law of distractibility of matter
   (c) Law of continuity of motion
   (d) Law of evolution of religion

5. 'Secrecy' and 'taking a role' in a group setting are seen in
   (a) Participant observation
   (b) Non-participant observation
   (c) Interview
   (d) Group discussion

6. In primitive societies, the common conscience ________ individual differences.
   (a) Blankets (b) Overcome
   (c) Unveil (d) Expose

7. 'Sub-nuclear family' consists of
   (a) a husband only
   (b) a wife only
   (c) husband and wife only
   (d) husband, wife, and son only

8. ________ is an analytical construct that serves as a measuring rod to ascertain similarities as well as deviations.
   (a) Protestantism
   (b) Bureaucracy
   (c) Ideal type
   (d) Organic Solidarity

9. Who authored a sociological classic '*Street Corner Society: The Social Structure of Italian Slum*'?
   (a) Pauline v. Young
   (b) William J. Goode
   (c) William F. Whyte
   (d) Herbert G. Blumer

10. Pareto's scientific procedure is known as ________.
    (a) Treatise
    (a) Equilibrium
    (c) Residues
    (d) Logico Experimental method

11. Who among the following made a combined analysis of class, status, and power?
    (a) Ralf Dahrendorf
    (b) Weber
    (c) Parsons
    (d) Andre Beteille

12. The economic system of production and distribution is considered as the ________ of society, according to Marx.
    (a) Basic structure
    (b) Superstructure
    (c) Dialectical process
    (d) Conflict

13. Who among the following is associated with the concept of 'Total Institutions'?
(a) Emile Durkheim
(b) J. H. Goldthorpe
(c) Erving Goffman
(d) Ralf Dahrendorf

14. Marx identified four stages of human history on the basis of the mode of production. They are primitive Communism, ________, feudalism, and Capitalism.
(a) Ancient Slave production
(b) Semi-feudalism
(c) Pre-capitalism
(d) None of these

15. The major credit for introducing the 'case study method' in social research goes to
(a) William Goode
(b) Emory Bogardus
(c) Fredrick Le play
(d) Paul Lazarsfeld

16. Protestant Ethic insists that work is a virtue in itself since it contributes to the ________.
(a) Salvation
(b) Development of capitalism
(c) Asceticism
(d) Glory of God

17. Who authored the book '*Our Final Century: will the human race survive the twenty-first century*'?
(a) Ulrich Beck
(b) Martin Rees
(c) Bauman Zygmunt
(d) Denis McQuail

18. Adaptation, goal attainment, integration and ________ are the functional prerequisites according to Parsons.
(a) Social change
(b) Equilibrium
(c) Socialisation
(d) Pattern maintenance

19. According to Karl Marx which of the following has 'Use Value' and 'exchange value'?
(a) Capital (b) Commodity
(c) Labour Power (d) Market

20. "Function refers to partial activity made to the total activity of which it is part". Who defined?
(a) Radcliff Brown
(b) Malinowski
(c) Levi Strauss
(d) Frans Boas

21. Who distinguished conflict as External Conflict and Internal conflict?
(a) Karl Marx (b) Ralf Dahrendorf
(c) Lewis Coser (d) Anthony Giddens

22. Authority Structure according to Dahrendorf involves relations of ________ and ________.
(a) Superordination, Subordination
(b) Exploitation, Exploited
(c) Function, non-function
(d) Legal, non-legal principles

23. In understanding sociology, match the nature of sociology in List – I with the proponents in List – II and choose the correct answer from the codes given below.

List I (Nature)	List II (Proponents)
A. Public sociology	I. Albion small
B. Clinical sociology	II. Bindeshwar Pathak
C. Qualitative sociology	III. Herbert Gans
D. Positive sociology	IV. Dv
E. Action sociology	V. Herbert Spencer
	VI. Auguste Comte

Codes:

(a) A-III, B-IV, C-I, D-IV, E-II
(b) A-II, B-IV, C-VI, D-V, E-I
(c) A-II, B-IV, C-VI, D-III, E-I
(d) A-I, B-IV, C-V, D-II, E-III

24. Match the following:

List I	List II
A. Homo Hierarchicus	I. Peter Berger
B. Invitation to Sociology	II. Louis Dumont
C. Development as Freedom	III. Mead
D. Philosophy of the Present	IV. Amartya Sen

Chose the correct answer from the codes given below:

(a) A–IV, B–III, C–I, D–II
(b) A–II, B–I, C–IV, D–III
(c) A–III, B–II, C–IV, D–I
(d) A–I, B–III, C–II, D–IV

25. Match the Sociologists in List – I with their nationality in List – II and choose the correct answer from the codes given below.

List I (Sociologists)	List II (Nationality)
A. Jeffrey Alexander	I. Indian
B. Pierre Bourdieu	II. German
C. George Simmel	III. Italian
D. Andre Beteille	IV. British
E. Morris Ginsberg	V. French
	VI. American

Codes:

(a) A–III, B–IV, C–VI, D–I, E–V
(b) A–III, B–V, C–VI, D–IV, E–I
(c) A–II, B–IV, C–VI, D–III, E–I
(d) A–VI, B–V, C–II, D–I, E–IV

26. The study of folk or common sense methods employed by people to make sense of every day activities by constructing and maintaining social reality is called ______________.
(a) Phenomenology
(b) Ethnomethodology
(c) Dramaturgy
(d) Epistemology

27. George Simmel's classification of groups as 'monad', 'dyad', and 'triad' is based on
(a) Physical proximity
(b) Nature of Membership
(c) Social relations
(d) Size

28. The means by which a ruling/dominant group wins over a subordinated group through ideas. Such a process according to Gramsci is called:
(a) Hegemony
(b) Segregation
(c) Restoration
(d) Social Cohesion

29. The term 'intergenerational mobility' is
(a) Movement into a different occupational category over a person's lifetime
(b) Movement into different occupational categories between generations
(c) Movement into a higher occupational category
(d) Movement into an occupation that generates a lower income

30. In Foucault's discourse, he developed four strategies of knowledge and power which is collectively called ______________.
(a) Disciplinary society
(b) Discontinuities
(c) Proactive behaviour
(d) Biopower

31. Given below are two statements, one labelled as Assertion (A) and the other as Reason (R). examine the statements and indicate the correct answer by choosing the codes below.

Assertion (A): Violence against women is on the increase in Indian families.

Reason (R): Economic dependence of women on their husbands may be reduced by women's empowerment.

Codes:

(a) Both 'A' and 'R' are individually true and 'R' is the correct explanation of 'A'
(b) Both 'A' and 'R' are individually true but 'R' is not the correct explanation of 'A'
(c) 'A' is true but 'R' is false
(d) 'A' is false but 'R' is true

32. 'Recursivity' according to Giddens's theory of Structuration refers to ______________.
(a) Feedback
(b) Agency
(c) Structure
(d) Reflexivity

33. Who among the following expressed the view that demographic density is a major determinant of societal evolution?
(a) Georg Simmel
(b) Emile Durkheim
(c) Talcott Parsons
(d) Lewis Coser

34. 'Human nature is freedom'. Who explained this?
(a) Althusser
(b) Gramsci
(c) Habermas
(d) Homans

35. The process in which a culture merges itself with the dominant is known as
(a) Cultural adaptation
(b) Cultural adoption
(c) Cultural assimilation
(d) Cultural absorption

36. Public Sociology is associated with:
(a) American Sociological Association
(b) Indian Sociology
(c) British Sociology
(d) Marxian Sociology

37. Given below are two statements, one labelled Assertion (A) and the other Reason(R). Examine the statements and indicate the correct answer by choosing the codes below.

Assertion (A): The teaching method today required student-friendly relations.

Reason (R): Trained teachers find difficult to handle the students.

Codes:

(a) Both 'A' and 'R' are individually true and 'R' is the correct explanation of 'A'
(b) Both 'A' and 'R' are individually true but 'R' is not the correct explanation of 'A'
(c) 'A' is true but 'R' is false
(d) 'A' is false but 'R' is true

38. The role of concept is to establish some kind of ----
(a) Link with the social world
(b) Link with theory
(c) Link with the hypothesis
(d) Link with the null hypothesis

39. Which one of the concepts given below refers to material culture changing faster than non-material culture?
(a) Cultural relativity
(b) Cultural dynamism
(c) Cultural imbalance
(d) Cultural lag

40. The sum total of all units that conform to some designated set of specification is called ___________.
(a) Sample
(b) Element
(c) Universe
(d) Parameters

41. Considering the books on caste, match the titles of books in List – I with the author in List – II and choose the correct answer from the codes given below.

List I (Title)	List II (Author)
A. Castes and Tribes of Southern India	I. Andre Beteille
B. Interrogating caste	II. Sujatha Gidla
C. Caste, class, and power	III. G.S. Ghurye
D. Ants among Elephants	IV. Surinder S. Jodhka
E. Caste in contemporary India	V. Dipankar Gupta
	VI. Edgar Thurston

Codes:
(a) A–III, B–IV, C–I, D–II, E–V
(b) A–II, B–V, C–I, D–III, E–IV
(c) A–II, B–IV, C–VI, D–III, E–V
(d) A–VI, B–V, C–I, D–II, E–IV

42. ___________ is a small-scale replica and a rehearsal of the main study.
(a) Pre test
(b) Pilot study
(c) Action study
(d) Situation study

43. Which of the following is not a 'Probability sample'?
(a) Simple random sample
(b) Systematic sample
(c) Cluster sample
(d) Quota sample

44. Likert scale is used to determine the ___________ of different items or statements.
(a) Indicators
(b) Responses
(c) Dimensions
(d) Relative intensity

45. What kind of suicide results when society fails to maintain order?
(a) Altruistic (b) Anomic
(c) Egoistic (d) Religious

46. Focused Interview is one which is focused on a specific ___________.
(a) Group
(b) Topic
(c) Area
(d) Interest

47. he 'managerial revolution' of John Scott refers to
(a) Owners becoming managers
(b) Separation of ownership from management
(c) Revolution by management
(d) Managers becoming the owners

48. ___________ is the most frequent value or score in the distribution.
(a) Mean (b) Median
(c) Mode (d) Dispersion

49. The process by which any body of knowledge comes to be socially accepted as reality is known as
(a) Social construction of reality
(b) Social recognition of knowledge
(c) Social discovery of reality
(d) Social explanation of knowledge

50. Summated Rating scale is associated with ___________.
(a) Guttman
(b) Bogardus
(c) Likert
(d) Thurston

51. According to Goffman, the process wherein the audience overlooks the flows in a performance to help the performer is known as
(a) Studied non-observance
(b) Stage blindness
(c) Face-saving behaviour
(d) Defence mechanism

52. ___________ is a belief that through the use of science, the reality could be understood and human life could be made better.
(a) Empiricism
(b) Intellectualism
(c) Humanitarianism
(d) Scientism

53. The important feature of a 'good sample' is its
(a) Small size
(b) Large size
(c) Representativeness
(d) Enough number

54. Given below are two statements, one labelled Assertion (A) and the other Reason(R). Examine the statements and indicate the correct answer by choosing the codes below.

Assertion (A): In plural society minority groups often develop a mistrust of the majority.

Reason (R): Minority groups are frequent targets of prejudice and discrimination.

(a) Both (A) and (R) are true and (R) is the correct explanation of (A).
(b) Both (A) and (R) are true and (R) is not the correct explanation of (A).
(c) (A) is true, but (R) is false
(d) (A) is false, but (R) is true

55. Neo-Marxists believed that ruling class domination is more effective if it is not involved in
(a) Religion
(b) Politics
(c) Militia
(d) Civics

56. Who among the following considers that class struggle is the engine of social change and development?
(a) Max Weber
(a) Marxian thinkers
(a) Andre Gundar Frank
(a) Samir Amin

57. The concept of 'Culture industry' pertains to which one of the following?
(a) Development of culture as an industry
(b) Culture of industrial society
(c) Cultural products being bought and sold for profit
(d) Industry becoming a part of the culture

58. Socialist conception of development proposes ------.
(a) Structural flexibility
(b) Wellbeing
(c) Social security
(d) Education of all

59. The process by which working-class people assume lifestyle and individualistic values of the so-called middle classes is known as
(a) Embourgeoisement
(b) Emancipation
(c) Empowerment
(d) Amelioration

60. Tebhaga movement was organized by -------.
(a) Kisan Sabha
(b) Cultivators
(c) Tenants
(d) Kisan unions

61. Who made a classic study of 'Rites of Passage'?
(a) Margaret Mead
(b) Arnold Gennep
(c) Abbe Dubois
(d) Caroline Myss

62. Who among the following gave great importance to the role of language in the process of nation-building in India?
(a) S.C Dube
(b) Ambedkar
(c) Kosambi
(d) G.S Ghurye

63. According to the 2011 census of India report, which type of stream of migration is still dominant?
(a) Rural to Urban
(b) Urban to Rural
(c) Rural to Rural
(d) Urban to Urban

64. M.N Srinivas described the concept of ________ by explaining the interaction in the ritual context of different castes in Coorgs.
(a) Functional unity
(b) Values
(c) Varnas
(d) Purities

65. Who among the following conceptualized the history of western society as a transition from 'status' to 'contract'?
(a) Max Weber
(b) Sir Henry Maine
(c) Ralph Linton
(d) Robert Merton

66. What are the two ideas that are the core of Foucault's methodology?
i. a historical perspective
ii. an interpretative perspective
iii. a discursive methodology
iv. comparison method

Chose the correct answer from the codes given below:
(a) i and ii
(b) ii and iii
(c) i and iii
(d) i and iv

67. Jajmani system indicates a set of
(a) Political affiliation
(b) Caste dominance
(c) Economic relations
(d) Social obligation

68. The Indian sociologist who preferred to call him a "Marxologist":
(a) D P Mukherji
(b) Romila Thapar
(c) Louis Dumont
(d) Yogendra Singh

69. The Book '*The Death of the Family*' is written by
(a) Oscar Lewis
(b) David Cooper
(c) Robert Redfield
(d) Talcott Parsons

70. Who among the following argued that Dalits should come forward, educate, organize, and agitate?
(a) Sree Narayana Guru
(b) Ayyankali
(c) Ambedkar
(d) Gandhiji

71. Herbert Spencer has classified societies into four types. Which of the following is an example of Doubly compound societies?
(a) The Eskimos or the Guinea tribes.
(b) The Homeric Greeks and the New Zealanders
(c) The 13th Century France and the 11th Century England.
(d) The Assyrian Empire, modern Great Britain, France, Germany, Italy

72. In its simplest form, the content analysis method consists of
(a) Words (b) Events
(c) Actions (d) Codes

73. A population pyramid is used to show
(a) Rapid population growth
(b) Dependency ratio of a population
(c) Net migration of a population
(d) A population's age and sex

74. The book _________ is a milestone marking the birth of Environmental movements.
(a) Threatened Forest
(b) Silent Spring
(c) Species Diversity
(d) Ecological Sanitation

75. Who among the following has authored the work "The interpretation of cultures"?
(a) B. Malinowski
(b) Clifford Geertz
(c) S. F. Nadel
(d) Evans Pritchard

76. Considering the Kerala society, who among the following emphasizes that peasant solidarity is a necessary condition for political action?
(a) K.C Alexander
(b) T.K Oommen
(c) Barrington Moore
(d) William Logan

77. Who described culture as 'an organized body of conventional understandings manifest in art and artifact, which, persisting through tradition, characterizes a human group'?
(a) S.C. Dube (b) Irawati Karve
(c) Daniel Thorner (d) Robert Redfield

78. Which perspective is based on the assumption that Indian Society is unique and the Indian Social institutions can be better studied through the text?
(a) Subaltern (b) Indological
(c) Civilizational (d) Structural functional

79. Agrarian relation refers to the relation between:
(a) Landowners and landless
(b) Workers and non-workers
(c) Landlords and tenants
(d) Those people engaged in the process of production

80. The patterns of settlement and dispersal of a population are called:
(a) Population Explosion
(b) Population Change
(c) Population distribution
(d) Population density

81. Who studied the structural, functional unity of joint family in 'Mahua'?
(a) K. M. Kapadia
(b) Neera Desai
(c) I. P. Desai
(d) A. M. Shah

82. Who is the author of the book 'Woman in Modern India'?
(a) K. M. Kapadia
(b) Neera Desai
(c) I. P. Desai
(d) A. M. Shah

83. The committee emphasized the principles of the three-tier structure of local governing bodies:
(a) Sarkaria
(b) Ashok Mehta
(c) Balwant Rai
(d) L.M Singhvi

84. '*Feeding the Baniya: Peasants and Usurers in Western India*' is written by
(a) A. R. Desai
(b) David Hardiman
(c) B. R. Ambedkar
(d) G. S. Ghurye

85. The S.N.D.P Yogam is a social service organization that has been representing the Ezhava community founded by?
(a) Sree Narayana Guru
(b) Ayyankali
(c) T.K Madhavan
(d) K. Kelappan

86. Pearsonian correlation ranges in value from
(a) Positive one (+1.0) down through zero (0.0) to negative one (–1.0)
(b) Zero (0.0) to negative one (–1.0)
(c) Negative one (–1.0) to zero (0.0)
(d) One (+1.0) to zero only (0.0)

87. Who has written the book '*Urbanization and Family Change*'?
(a) Iravati Karve
(b) M. S. Gore
(c) Leela Dube
(d) I. P. Desai

88. D P Mukherji asserted three principles of change that are recognized in Indian tradition. They are Sruthi, Smriti, and ______________.
(a) Beliefs (b) Dharma
(c) Karma (d) Anubhava

89. Who among the following developed the 'Circular Cumulative Causation' theory?
(a) A. G. Frank
(b) Gunnar Myrdal
(c) A. Escobar
(d) Samir Amin

90. ______________ is an evolving business practice that incorporates sustainable development into a company's business model.
(a) Corporate Social responsibility
(b) Targeted marketing
(c) Sustainable business
(d) Conscious capitalism

91. The book '*India's Path of Development*' is authored by
(a) A. R. Desai
(b) Yogendra Singh
(c) M. N. Srinivas
(d) K. M. Kapadia

92. The Rotary Club is an example of ______________.
(a) Institution
(b) Association
(c) Committee
(d) Social group

93. An organization deliberately formed for the collective pursuit of some interest or a set of interests, which its members share is called as?
(a) Society
(b) Association
(c) Committee
(d) Community

94. ______________ is a condition of competition.
(a) Scarcity (b) Values
(c) Conflict (d) Morality

95. In whose writings, African-American Women's Self-definition is central?
(a) Patricia Hill Collins
(b) G. H. Mead
(c) Max Weber
(d) E. Goffman

96. The feeling that one's own culture is better than the other is called ______________.
(a) Acculturation
(b) Ethnocentrism
(c) Diffusion
(d) Cultural relativism

97. The idea of 'theoretical sampling' is associated with
(a) Barney G. Glaser and Anselm L. Strauss
(b) Claude Levi Strauss
(c) John Lofland
(d) Earl Babbie

98. ______________ is a grouping of classes that are related by traditions of common descent.
(a) Moieties (b) Phratry
(c) Avoidance (d) Amitate

99. Who among the following has used the term 'Juggernaut' to describe the modern world?
(a) Fredric Jameson
(b) Jean Baudrillard
(c) P. Bourdieu
(d) A. Giddens

100. The major role of the educational system according to Bourdieu is ______________.
(a) Elimination
(b) Power position
(c) Accumulation of knowledge
(d) Inequality

Answer Key

1. (a)	**16.** (b)	**31.** (b)	**46.** (b	**61.** (b)	**76.** (c)	**91.** (a)
2. (c)	**17.** (b)	**32.** (a)	**47.** (b)	**62.** (d)	**77.** (d)	**92.** (b)
3. (d)	**18.** (d)	**33.** (b)	**48.** (c)	**63.** (c)	**78.** (b)	**93.** (b)
4. (d)	**19.** (b)	**34.** (a)	**49.** (a)	**64.** (a)	**79.** (d)	**94.** (a)
5. (a)	**20.** (a)	**35.** (c)	**50.** (c)	**65.** (b)	**80.** (c)	**95.** (a)
6. (a)	**21.** (c)	**36.** (a)	**51.** (a)	**66.** (c)	**81.** (c)	**96.** (b)
7. (c)	**22.** (a)	**37.** (c)	**52.** (d)	**67.** (c)	**82.** (b)	**97.** (a)
8. (c)	**23.** (d)	**38.** (a)	**53.** (c)	**68.** (a)	**83.** (c)	**98.** (b)
9. (c)	**24.** (b)	**39.** (d)	**54.** (a)	**69.** (b)	**84.** (b)	**99.** (d)
10. (d)	**25.** (d)	**40.** (c)	**55.** (a)	**70.** (c)	**85.** (a)	**100.** (a)
11. (b)	**26.** (b)	**41.** (d)	**56.** (b)	**71.** (c)	**86.** (a)	
12. (a)	**27.** (d)	**42.** (b)	**57.** (c)	**72.** (a)	**87.** (b)	
13. (c)	**28.** (a)	**43.** (d)	**58.** (a)	**73.** (d)	**88.** (d)	
14. (a)	**29.** (b)	**44.** (d)	**59.** (a)	**74.** (b)	**89.** (b)	
15. (c)	**30.** (d)	**45.** (b)	**60.** (a)	**75.** (b)	**90.** (a)	

Mock Test 5

1. The process whereby an individual internalizes the norms of the group is called ____________.
   (a) Self (b) Culture
   (c) Socialisation (d) Learning
2. ____________ is called the Learned way of behaviour.
   (a) Subculture (b) Culture
   (c) Norms (d) Personality
3. Who among the following used the term 'Dominant Castes'?
   (a) M.N Srinivas
   (b) G.S Ghurye
   (c) S.C Dube
   (d) Senart
4. The practice of several brothers sharing the same wife is called:
   (a) Polyandry
   (b) Non-fraternal
   (c) Wife lending
   (d) Fraternal Polyandry
5. Emotional base is a fundamental characteristic of ____________.
   (a) Caste
   (b) Family
   (c) Class
   (d) Kinship
6. Caste and class are the two aspects of ____________.
   (a) Dialectics
   (b) Social system
   (c) Stratification
   (d) Social processes
7. Who among the following enlarged Durkheim's concept of anomie into a general theory of deviant behaviour?
   (a) R.K Merton
   (b) Parsons
   (c) Malinowski
   (d) Pareto
8. Indian democracy is an example of ____________.
   (a) Direct democracy
   (b) Indirect democracy
   (c) Simple democracy
   (d) Pure democracy
9. For Durkheim which sub-discipline studies the territorial basis of the life of people and also the problems of the population such as volume and density, local distribution, etc.?
   (a) Social morphology,
   (b) Social physiology
   (c) General sociology
   (d) Social Processes
10. ____________ is one of the factors that has contributed to the degradation of Indian politics.
    (a) Corruption (b) Religion
    (c) Terrorism (d) Regionalism
11. ____________ is often referred to as a Parallel economy.
    (a) Corporates (b) Multinationals
    (c) Bribe (d) Black money
12. ____________ poverty refers to whether or not individuals or groups feel they are poor.
    (a) Subjective poverty
    (b) Relative poverty
    (c) Absolute poverty
    (d) Visual poverty
13. Who wrote the famous book '*Sociological Imagination*'?
    (a) Max Weber (b) C. Wright Mills
    (c) Giddens (d) John Stewart Mills
14. ____________ is the belief that ethnic or cultural groups can peacefully co-exist in society and show respect for one another's cultures.
    (a) Globalisation
    (b) Multiculturalism
    (c) Cultural racism
    (d) Racialism

15. ____________ refers to the culture of ordinary people, particularly those living in pre-industrial societies.
(a) Mass culture
(b) Subculture
(c) Folk culture
(d) Popular culture

16. Who among the following examined the institution of family as a Universal social institution?
(a) George Peter Murdock
(b) Edmund Leach
(c) William J. Goode
(d) Robin Fox

17. One of the functional prerequisites according to Parsons is:
(a) Socialisation (b) Equilibrium
(c) Institutions (d) Adaptation

18. Language is the ________________ of culture.
(a) Supportive (b) Vehicle
(c) Dimension (d) Foundation

19. ________________ is a rule of marriage in which an individual has to marry outside his own group.
(a) Endogamy
(b) Gotra Exogamy
(c) Exogamy
(d) Village Exogamy

20. Static is tantamount to ________________ according to Comte.
(a) Structure (b) Dynamics
(c) Change (d) Function

21. Given below are two statements, one labelled as Assertion (A) and the other as Reason (R). examine the statements and indicate the correct answer by choosing the codes below.

Assertion (A): Life history research can help to raise people's consciousness and awareness of their exploitation.

Reason (R): Life history research encourages people to reflect upon the factors that have shaped their life experiences.

(a) Both (A) and (R) are true and (R) is the correct explanation of (A).
(b) Both (A) and (R) are true and (R) is not the correct explanation of (A).
(c) (A) is true, but (R) is false
(d) (A) is false, but (R) is true

22. Which one of the following movements of people cannot be termed as migration?
(a) Primitive migration of people
(b) People move from their country of origin to a country of destination for performing specific assignments for three months
(c) Refugee movement
(d) Periodic migration of people

23. Which of the following is not a data-collection method?
(a) Research question
(b) Unstructured interview
(c) Postal survey questionnaire
(d) Participant observation

24. How is a modern society governed?
(a) Through conventions
(b) By rule of law
(c) By divine law
(d) Through a physical force

25. The source of power, in the Marxian perspective, lies in the concept of?
(a) Legitimacy (b) Exploitation
(c) Alienation (d) Coercion

26. The National Commission for Scheduled Castes was established under which article?
(a) Article 338 (b) Article 219
(c) Article 164 (d) Article 250

27. Sir Syed Ahmad Khan is associated with which movement?
(a) Khilafat (b) Aligarh
(c) Wahabi (d) Faraizi

28. Which among the following is NOT a feature of the sect?
(a) They have significantly smaller memberships than churches
(b) Membership is ascribed at birth
(c) They demand a high level of commitment from their members
(d) Sects have a charismatic leader

29. Raja Ram Mohan Roy was the founder of:
(a) Arya Samaj
(b) Prarthana Samaj
(c) Ramakrishna Mission
(d) Brahmo Samaj

30. Who described symbols as vehicles of culture?
(a) Clifford Geertz
(b) G. H. Mead
(c) Erving Goffman
(d) E B Taylor

31. Who is the author of the book '*Primitive Culture*'?
(a) Claude Levi Strauss
(b) Clifford Geertz
(c) A.R Radcliffe Brown
(d) Edward B. Tylor

32. ____________ form of barter in which goods are exchanged without any direct contact between the traders. It is also known as dumb barter.
(a) Kula Exchange
(b) Jajmani System
(c) Silent Trade
(d) Potlatch

33. "Monopoly" is a market structure classified on the basis of?
(a) Place
(b) Function
(c) Time
(d) Competition

34. Who among the following is a leading proponent of "Alternative Development"?
(a) David Korten
(b) Amartya Sen
(c) Adam Smith
(d) None of the above

35. Agenda 21, which was held in 1992 under the UN seeked to promote?
(a) Sustainable Development
(b) Manufacturing and iron production
(c) Economic Development
(d) Global Warming

36. Under whose tenure, the 'Project Tiger' 1973 was initiated?
(a) Indira Gandhi
(b) Manmohan Singh
(c) Rajiv Gandhi
(d) Atal Bihari Vajpayee

37. An example of community is:
(a) A Trade Union
(b) Varna
(c) A political party
(d) Tribal group

38. The book 'Social Structure of Values' was written by ________.
(a) M.N. Srinivasan
(b) Radhakamal Mukherjee
(c) S.C. Dube
(d) Yogendra Singh

39. Where did Andre Beteille conduct his fieldwork for his study of 'caste, class and power'?
(a) Rampura
(b) Sripuram
(c) Khalapur
(d) Kisangarhi

40. Urban sprawl refers to:
(a) A city that emphasizes self-sustaining resilient structure and function of the natural ecosystem.
(b) A very large city, typically with a population of more than 10 million people.
(c) The unrestricted growth in many urban areas of housing, commercial development, and roads over large expanses of land.
(d) A small community that has no major industries and that is lived in by people who go to another town or city to work.

41. The committee that recommended a three-tier Panchayati Raj system in India:
(a) Balwant Rai Mehta Committee
(b) Singhvi Committee
(c) Ashok Mehta Committee
(d) Hanumantha Rao Committee

42. Which of the following section of the Indian Penal Code deals with homosexuality?
(a) Section 243
(b) Section 301
(c) Section 377
(d) Section 375

43. The National Panchayati Raj Day is celebrated on:
(a) 11 January
(b) 28 March
(c) 24 April
(d) 16 July

44. The reason behind the failure of the attempt to integrate communities:
(a) Ethnic groups living in proximity
(b) Attempt to develop a degree of homogeneity doomed to failure
(c) To have desirable consequences from ethnic groups there should have some friendly attempt to reduce the gap between them
(d) Derecognition of minority ethnic cultures.

45. Who authored '*Citizenship and Social Class*'?
(a) T. H. Marshall
(b) Stuart Hall
(c) Friedrich Engels
(d) Antonio Gramsci

46. Who introduced the phrase "invisible hand"?
(a) John Locke (b) David Hume
(c) Adam Smith (d) Immanuel Kant

47. Esping-Andersen identified three types of welfare state regimes. Which among the following is not one of them?
(a) Liberal
(b) Authoritarian
(c) Social democratic
(d) Conservative

48. 'The theory of Communism may be summed up in a single sentence: Abolition of private property.' This statement belongs to:
(a) David Ricardo
(b) Anthony Giddens
(c) Adam Smith
(d) Karl Marx

49. Who wrote '*Capitalism and the Production of Poverty*'?
(a) Hamza Alavi
(b) Utsa Patnaik
(c) Uma Chakravarti
(d) Amartya Sen

50. It is a gift-giving ceremony practiced among indigenous groups of the Pacific Northwest Coast of Canada and the United States.
(a) Potlatch (b) Sundance
(c) Burbung (d) Jajmani

51. Which among the following is incorrectly matched?
(a) Culture of poverty: Oscar Lewis
(b) Dependency theory: Andre Gunder Frank
(c) Knowledge-gap hypothesis: Jurgen Habermas
(d) Embeddedness: Karl Polanyi

52. Which of the following is not a part of World System Theory?
(a) Core
(b) Periphery
(c) Semi-periphery
(d) Concentric zone

53. ______________ is a phenomenon whereby an individual or group is in a state of poverty over an extended period of time.
(a) Near poverty
(b) Relative poverty
(c) Chronic poverty
(d) Situational poverty

54. In the following question, two statements are given. One is assertion (A) and the other is reason (R). Examine the statement carefully and mark the correct answer according to the instruction given below

Assertion (A): It is extremely important to bridge the gender digital divide.

Reason (R): The gender digital divide is a major roadblock to women's economic empowerment.
(a) Both (A) and (R) are true and (R) is the correct explanation of (A)
(b) Both (A) and (R) are true but (R) is not the correct explanation of (A)
(c) (A) is false but (R) is true
(d) (A) is true but (R) is false

55. The Head of the Joint Hindu Family Firm is known as:
(a) Karta (b) Director
(c) Rakshak (d) Heritor

56. A. R. Desai has identified the following major trends of rural social change:
(1) Rapid transformation of agrarian society from a subsistence economy to the market economy.
(2) Rapid transformation followed by the introduction of modern technology.
(3) Moderate level of transformation resulted from the gradual induction of Indian technology.
(4) Abolition of intermediaries such as zamindar & biswedar.
(5) Emergence of various associations and institutions having non-linkages with urban and national organizations.

Find the correct combination from the following:
(a) (1), (2) & (3) are false, and (4) & (5) are true.
(b) (1), (3) & (4) are false, and (2) & (5) are true.
(c) (2), (3) & (4) are false, and (1) & (5) are true.
(d) (1), (2) & (3) are true, and (4) & (5) are false.

57. Which one of the following is not a correct variation of tenants available in Colonial India?
(a) Croppers & Crop-share tenants
(b) Landowners' sponsored tenants
(c) Cash & share-cash tenants
(d) Other & unspecified tenants

58. The share of urban population to the total population, according to the 2011 census, is close to
(a) 30%
(b) 31%
(c) 32%
(d) 33%

59. Subaltern refers to that category of people
(i) who has access to the hegemonic power of society.
(ii) who can raise their voice about the different problems of society.
(iii) who socially, politically, and culturally or in any other way exists outside the power structure.
(iv) who finds special mention in the conventional historiography of the society.

Choose the right combination from the below:
(a) (iv) is true, (iii) is false.
(b) (ii) is true, (i) is false.
(c) (ii) is false, (i) is true.
(d) (iv) is false, (iii) is true.

60. Sanskritization promotes:
(a) Structural mobility
(b) Functional mobility
(c) Downward mobility
(d) Inter-religious mobility

61. Which one of the following Scheduled Caste groups has the highest representation of the total Scheduled Caste population of West Bengal?
(a) Namasudra
(b) Rajbanshi
(c) Pod
(d) Bagdi

62. Ethnocentrism in a multicultural society results in:
(a) Cultural harmony
(b) Cultural conflict
(c) Cultural reciprocity
(d) Cultural lag

63. The piece, *Annihilation of Caste*, was written by
(a) G. S. Ghurye
(b) David Hardiman
(c) B. R. Ambedkar
(d) M. N. Srinivas

64. The notion of the 'Hindu Method of Tribal Absorption' was advanced by
(a) M. K. Gandhi (b) D. P. Mukherjee
(c) G. S. Ghurye (d) N. K. Bose

65. The Indian sociologist who did not sympathize with the Marxian perspective was
(a) A. R. Desai
(b) Ramkrishna Mukherjee
(c) M. N. Srinivas
(d) D. N. Dhanagare

66. In the Protestant Ethic and the Spirit of Capitalism Max Weber has pointed out the elective affinity between the attributes of capitalism and
(a) Catholic religion (b) Judaism
(c) Calvinism (d) Hinduism

67. The substitution of Malinowski's cultural functionalism by structural functionalism to better explain the nature of social relationships was made first by:
(a) Talcott Parsons
(b) Claude Levi-Strauss
(c) R. K. Merton
(d) A. R. Radcliffe-Brown

68. Which one of the following is an essential feature of historical materialism?
(a) Society takes birth, grows, and matures like an organism.
(b) Society is inherently mutable in which changes are produced by internal contradiction.
(c) Society starts as a small aggregate and with the passage of time grows in size.
(d) Society develops with the development of scientific personnel.

69. The relation between the rain-mating ceremony of a community and the gathering together of persons performing it is, according to Merton, an example of
(a) Manifest function
(b) Manifest dysfunction
(c) Latent dysfunction
(d) Latent function

70. Tick the pair which does not find a room in the inventory of 'pattern variables' suggested by Talcott Parsons:
(a) Quietism vs. Aggressive action
(b) Self-orientation vs. Collective orientation
(c) Affectivity vs. Affective neutrality
(d) Universalism vs. Particularism

71. Ghotul is an example of a youth dormitory traditionally found among them:
(a) Santal of Bihar
(b) Angami Naga of Nagaland
(c) Muria of Chattisgarh
(d) Jarwa of Andaman

72. Which one of the following is a matrilineal community?
(a) Muria of Chattisgarh
(b) Khasis of Meghalaya
(c) Bhills of Madhya Pradesh
(d) Oraon of West Bengal

73. The belief in the spiritual existence of animals, plants, and inanimate objects on the earth is described as
(a) Animism
(b) Positivism
(c) Spiritualism
(d) Holism

74. When a person marries his wife's sister it is termed as the practice of:
(a) Sororal Polyandry
(b) Fraternal Polyandry
(c) Fraternal Polygyny
(d) Sororal Polygyny

75. Who among the following elaborated the notion of gender regime?
(a) Margaret Mead
(b) Bob Connell
(c) Alva Mirdal
(d) Ester Boserup

76. Select the correct statement:
(a) Deducting reasoning works from general to specific while inducting reasoning works from specific to general.
(b) Deductive reasoning works from specific to general while inductive reasoning works from general to specific.
(c) Both the deducting and inducting reasonings work from general to specific in the industrial society.
(d) Both the deducting and inducting reasonings work from general to specific in all societies.

77. Match List-I with List-II:

List I	List II
A. Max Weber	I. Habitus
B. Karl Marx	II. Binary Opposition
C. Emile Durkheim	III. Primitive Accumulation
D. Claude Levi Strauss	IV. Social Fact
E. Pierre Bourdien	V. Social Action

Select the correct answer:

Code:

	A	B	C	D	E
(a)	(I)	(IV)	(III)	(V)	(II)
(b)	(IV)	(I)	(III)	(V)	(II)
(c)	(V)	(III)	(IV)	(II)	(I)
(d)	(IV)	(V)	(III)	(II)	(I)

78. The term 'Global Village' is coined by:
(a) Talcott Parsons
(b) Marshall McLuhan
(c) Adam Smith
(d) Ulrich Beck

79. Who among the following coined the term 'Virtual Community' to describe communities engaged in social discussions on the internet?
(a) Howard Rheingold
(b) Bob Connell
(c) Manual Castells
(d) Peter Drucker

80. The notion of 'time-space compression' is used by sociologists in the context of:
(a) Pre-agrarian society
(b) Agrarian society
(c) Industrial society
(d) Information/Knowledge society

81. Among the following, who did not establish a positive relationship between population growth and social change?
(a) Karl Marx (b) Max Weber
(c) Talcott Parsons (d) Auguste Comte

82. Who considered that 'most often action is routine and relatively unreflexive'?
(a) M. Garfinkel
(b) Alfred Schutz
(c) Max Weber
(d) E. Scheller

83. Who among the following used the method of Concomitant Variation?
(a) Karl Marx
(b) Talcott Parsons
(c) Max Weber
(d) E. Durkheim

84. The deductive approach as an alternative methodology in both natural science and sociology is supported by whom?
(a) Thomas Kuhn (b) Max Weber
(c) Karl Popper (d) Fayerabend

85. Who defines Praxis as practical reflective activity in critical social research?
(a) Lee Harvey
(b) Max Weber
(c) Thomas Kuhn
(d) Douglas

86. The basic principles of symbolic interactionism include:
(i) human capacity for thought process.
(ii) social institutions and social interactions.
(iii) mind and Social Consciousness,
(iv) meanings and symbols that facilitate action and interaction.

Select the appropriate code from the following:
(a) (i) and (ii)
(b) (ii) and (iii)
(c) (iii) and (iv)
(d) (i) and (iv)

87. Who among the following elaborated the concept of 'functional imperative'?
(a) Talcott Parsons
(b) B. Malinowski
(c) A. R. Radcliffe-Brown
(d) Robert K. Merton

88. Who differentiated between 'we relations' and 'they-relations' within the social world?
(a) C. H. Gooley
(b) Alfred Schutz
(c) E. Husserl
(d) H. Garfinkel

89. Who among the following is the author of the work '*When a Great Tradition Modernises*'?
(a) M. N. Srinivas
(b) Milton Singer
(c) M. Marriot
(d) Kathleen Gough

90. '*The Unquiet Woods: Ecological Change and Peasant Resistance in the Himalayas*' is written by
(a) Chandi Prasad Bhatt
(b) Sunderlal Bahuguna
(c) Ramchandra Guha
(d) D. N. Majumder

Directions (91–95): Read the following passage carefully

In pursuance of the Constitution of India and constitutional provisions, various programs have sought to abolish the caste system and improve the social and economic conditions of the weaker castes. e.g., Reservation of seats for Other Backward Classes (OBCs) in educational institutions and the public sector is the latest step taken for the welfare of the depressed classes. The influence of the caste system is gradually diminishing, yet the change must be in the attitude of the people and in the mortality rate.

One still has to depend on one's caste to a great extent for help at important times of one's life, such as marriage and death. Elections in India are fought a lot on the basis of casteism. We find casteism perpetuated in government services. e.g., Seats are reserved for backward and scheduled castes in the government. services as well as in the legislatures. The special scholarship is given for education. Institutions have been given legal freedom to maintain their separate identity in the name of minority caste. Thus, we see that Indian democracy in practice has encouraged rather than discouraged the caste system.

Attitudes of exclusivity and distrust exist between castes. The Supreme Court judgment in the Mandal case has given a new lease of life to the cancer of casteism for an uncertain future. There is doubt that our political leaders who thrive on casteism will ever give up their caste character. With the spread of education, political reforms, and change in economic status it is hoped that the Indian people will rise to this problem and do away with the caste system.

Answer the following questions based on the facts/information described in the above passage:

91. What is the aim of the reservation of seats for Other Backward Classes (OBCs) in educational institutions and the public sector?
(a) to rectify the past and historical injustice
(b) to ensure that equal representation
(c) to provide an equal platform for everyone
(d) the welfare of the depressed classes

92. The influence of the caste system is
(a) Gradually increasing
(b) Neither increasing nor decreasing
(c) Gradually diminishing
(d) None of the above

93. Elections in India are fought a lot on the basis of
(a) Secularism
(b) Communalism
(c) Casteism
(d) Election commission

94. Indian democracy in practice has encouraged rather than
(a) discouraged the federalism
(b) discouraged the communalism
(c) discouraged the secularism
(d) discouraged the caste system

95. The Constitution of India and its constitutional provisions have sought to abolish
(a) The poverty
(b) The zamindari System
(c) The disharmonic system
(d) The caste system

Directions (96–100): Read the following passage carefully

The Indological view provided some concepts, theories, and frameworks that the scholars claimed to have emerged from their study of Indian civilization. They primarily adopted a historical and comparative approach. Their understanding of Indian society and its structure is largely based on their study of classical Sanskritic and Persian texts and literature.

It is only that the Indologists of the 18th century and onwards gave a more systematic account. We must also note that while an account of these earlier writings helps us to know how the political, economic, and social systems differed from the later era and what the similarities are, i.e. the broad categories by which we understand India today, all of them cannot strictly be categorized as an Indological perspective from the methodological point of view. Thus, the ideological construction of India can be found in the accounts of travellers like Megasthenes (mentioned above), historians like Al-Biruni, and later Abul Fazl Allami, the early Colonialists. Megathenes, because of his inability to understand native languages makes no reference to Varna theory. Instead, his understanding is that of a class-based society divided more around occupations.

On the other hand, Al Biruni and Abul Fazl through their familiarity with Sanskritic sources arrive at the Varna theory of the caste system and even recognised the internal divisions of caste. The very fact that there is a reference to caste groups as kin-based social categories reflects that both the textual understanding of the Varna system co-existed with the practical operational understanding of the caste groups. Moreover, while the European accounts show fascination about the matrilineal and polyandrous groups, the significance of untouchability and commensality taboos, etc., most of them tend to focus on Mughal courts and on political and commercial matters rather than on Indian society, the people and culture. Dutch accounts of Hinduism were published in 1670 and that of a French merchant and traveller Jean Baptiste Tavernier between 1631-1667, with a brief reference to the caste system. It is not until much later, in the late eighteenth and early nineteenth century that we find more comprehensive narratives about society and culture.

Answer the following questions based on the facts/information described in the above passage:

96. The Indological view adopted a
(a) historical and comparative approach
(b) experimental approach
(c) observation method
(d) explorative approach

97. Indologists understanding of Indian society and its structure is largely based on their study of:
(a) European texts and literature
(b) Sanskritic and Persian texts and literature
(c) Hindu text and literature
(d) Indian arts and culture

98. Most of the European accounts tend to focus on
(a) The Indian Society
(b) The Mughal courts
(c) The Sikh culture
(d) Indus Valley Civilization

99. Megathenes in his account makes no reference to:
(a) Caste system
(b) internal divisions of caste
(c) Varna theory
(d) Indian Sculptures

100. The ideological construction of India can be found in the accounts of travellers like
(a) Megasthenes
(b) Al-Biruni
(c) Abul Fazl Allami
(d) All of the above

Answer Key

1. (c)	**16.** (a)	**31.** (d)	**46.** (c)	**61.** (b)	**76.** (a)	**91.** (d)
2. (b)	**17.** (d)	**32.** (c)	**47.** (b)	**62.** (b)	**77.** (c)	**92.** (c)
3. (a)	**18.** (b)	**33.** (d)	**48.** (d)	**63.** (c)	**78.** (b)	**93.** (c)
4. (d)	**19.** (c)	**34.** (a)	**49.** (b)	**64.** (d)	**79.** (a)	**94.** (d)
5. (b)	**20.** (a)	**35.** (a)	**50.** (a)	**65.** (c)	**80.** (d)	**95.** (d)
6. (c)	**21.** (a)	**36.** (a)	**51.** (c)	**66.** (c)	**81.** (a)	**96.** (a)
7. (a)	**22.** (b)	**37.** (d)	**52.** (d)	**67.** (d)	**82.** (b)	**97.** (b)
8. (b)	**23.** (a)	**38.** (b)	**53.** (c)	**68.** (b)	**83.** (d)	**98.** (b)
9. (a)	**24.** (b)	**39.** (b)	**54.** (a)	**69.** (d)	**84.** (c)	**99.** (c)
10. (a)	**25.** (d)	**40.** (c)	**55.** (a)	**70.** (a)	**85.** (a)	**100.** (d)
11. (d)	**26.** (a)	**41.** (a)	**56.** (d)	**71.** (c)	**86.** (c)	
12. (a)	**27.** (b)	**42.** (c)	**57.** (b)	**72.** (b)	**87.** (d)	
13. (b)	**28.** (b)	**43.** (c)	**58.** (b)	**73.** (a)	**88.** (b)	
14. (b)	**29.** (d)	**44.** (c)	**59.** (d)	**74.** (d)	**89.** (b)	
15. (c)	**30.** (a)	**45.** (a)	**60.** (b)	**75.** (b)	**90.** (c)	

Further Readings

1. Berger, P. *Invitation to Sociology* A *Humanistic Perspective*, Anchor Books Double Day & Company, Inc., New York, 1963
2. Bottomore, T.B. *Sociology A Guide to Problems and Literature*, George Allen & Unwin Ltd., London, 1962
3. Inkeles, A. *What is Sociology*? Prentice-Hall: New Delhi, 1975,
4. Bailey, F.G. *Tribe and Caste in India. Contributions to Indian Sociology*, 1961
5. Ghurye. G.S. *The Scheduled Tribes*. Bombay: Popular Prakashan, 1963
6. Ritzer, George, *Sociological Theory* Us. Mc Graw-Hill, 1996
7. Haralambos, M., Holborn, M. and Heald, R. *Sociology: Themes and Perspectives*. New Delhi: Oxford University Press, 1980
8. Majumdar, D.N. and Madan, T.N. *An Introduction to Social Anthropology*. Bombay: Asia Publishing House, 1957
9. Sharma, K.L., *Essays in Social Stratification*, Rawat Publication, 1980
10. Ram Ahuja, *Indian Social System*, Rawat Publication, New Delhi, 1966
11. Dube, S. C. *Indian Society*. New Delhi: National Book Trust, 1990
12. Horton, Paul B. and Hunt, Chester L. *Sociology*. New York: Tata McGrawHill, 2004
13. Saravanavel P. *Research Methodology*, Kitab Mahal, Allahabad, 2011
14. Morgan, John H. and Abraham, *Francis Sociological Thought: From Comte to Sorokin*, Bristol, U.S.A. : Wyndham Hall Press, 1989